The American Aviati

The American Aviation Experience
A History

Edited by Tim Brady

Southern Illinois University Press

Carbondale and Edwardsville

Library of Congress Cataloging-in-Publication Data
The American aviation experience : a history / edited by Tim Brady.
p.   cm.
Includes bibliographical references and index.
1. Aeronautics — United States — History. I. Brady, Tim, 1939–
TL521 A7183 2000
629.13'0973 — dc21
ISBN 0-8093-2325-7 (cloth : alk. paper)
ISBN 0-8093-2371-0 (paper : alk. paper)   99-088092

Printed in the United States of America

Contents

Preface

THE ORGANIZATION of this textbook is primarily chronological from chapter 1, "The Ancients," through chapter 12, "Military Airpower Developments after World War II." Subject matter in these chapters is dealt with in the period in which it occurred, as each of the chapter titles suggests. Beginning with chapter 13, "Government and Aviation," and continuing through chapter 17, "Space History," the organization of the material is chronological within each chapter, from the beginning to the current day.

The book is suited to courses with titles such as "Aviation History," "The Development of Aviation," "Aviation in America," and similar titles. It can also be used to teach or supplement courses such as "Women in Aviation," "The Government in Aviation," "African Americans in Aviation," "The Development of the U.S. Space Program," "Lighter-than-Air Development," and other courses that would focus on chapters 13 through 17 and use selected chapters as supplementary or background information.

Our intention in writing this book is to offer the learner certain events, developments, and activities that help describe aviation history primarily (but not exclusively) from an American perspective. By no means do we intend this book to be an "encyclopedia" of aviation history. Each fact, event, individual, airplane, or situation is a book within itself, and it was not our goal to describe all of the events. Our hope is that the learner will find something of interest that will propel him or her to look more deeply into that subject matter.

One final note: The authors have collectively decided that whatever proceeds from the sale of the book that would normally be paid to the authors will instead be used for college scholarships for aviation students.

Acknowledgments

A WORK SUCH AS THIS results from the efforts of many who have contributed to its success. Prime among those were two graduate assistants at Central Missouri State University, Stephanie Wessells and Kristine Powell. Stephanie toiled with the editing and organization of the book for more than a year. Her duties included writing letters to authors, reminding everyone of deadlines, gaining the necessary permissions for the use of photographs and other artifacts in the book, and just being an uncommonly delightful colleague. When she left to find a teaching job in Iowa, we were concerned that her work would suffer in the transition. But that was not to be. Kristine stepped in and did a magnificent job. The authors of the book and the students who will benefit from their labors can celebrate the fact that each of these wonderful women, Stephanie and Kristine, has earned herself a place in aviation history.

We owe a special thanks to Stan Hardison, who created the cartoon character "Fleagle" and who also has a nationally syndicated cartoon called "Neighbors" that appears in many newspapers around the country. Fleagle is the zany bird whose antics grace the beginning of each of our chapters. Stan created each of these cartoons based on the subject matter of the chapter. He then donated them to us.

Fleagle himself is a unique part of aviation history. For the last thirty or so years, Fleagle has delivered the safety message to thousands of United States Air Force pilots and crews in his tongue-in-cheek fashion. In the 1960s, 1970s, and 1980s, while Tactical Air Command existed, Stan's Fleagle appeared each month on the back cover of the command's safety periodical, *Tac Attack*. Today the publication is called *The Combat Edge,* and Fleagle is still there promoting aviation safety.

Finally, we would like to express our appreciation to Central Missouri State University and Embry-Riddle Aeronautical University for their assistance in terms of labor and funding. Without the help of these two great institutions, this book would not have been possible.

The American Aviation Experience

1

The Ancients

Tim Brady

THE DESIRE TO FLY has been a part of the human condition for perhaps as long as our species has existed. Throughout our history, we have looked to the sky and to the creatures, primarily birds, who use the air as a transportation medium. We have wished for that same kind of freedom, mobility, speed, and imagined exhilaration.

In most societies that have left written or pictorial records of themselves, one can find evidence of the desire to fly. This compelling desire has been manifested in various cultures throughout all recorded time. We have seen this desire in legends, gods, theories, scientific thought, accidents of nature, and some actual experiments.

Legends

If one attempts to sort out the plausible human condition the implausible embellishments in ancient legends, what often emerges is surprising. For example, let's look at the Greek legend of Daedalus and Icarus (see fig. 1.1).

Greece. Daedalus supposedly lived about 1,700 years before the birth of Christ.

The English poet Saxe begins our story:

There lived and flourished long ago, in famous Athens town,
One Daedalus, a carpenter of genius and renown;
('Twas he who with an augur taught mechanics how to bore,
An art which the philosophers monopolized before.)

Fig. 1.1. *Daedalus and Icarus* by Joseph-Marie Vien. Courtesy of the USAF Museum.

As the legend is traditionally told, Daedalus, a carpenter from Athens, was hired by King Minos of Crete to build a Labyrinth. The purpose was to contain a horrible monster, the Minotaur, which was half man and half bull. Somehow Daedalus and his son, Icarus, became trapped in the Labyrinth and discovered that their only way out was to go over the cliffs. Daedalus fashioned two pairs of wings.

> Now Daedalus, the carpenter, had made a pair of wings,
> Contrived of wood and feathers and a cunning set of
>   springs,
> By means of which the wearer could ascend to any height,
> And sail about among the clouds as easy as a kite.

Daedalus and his son launched themselves out over the sea. Daedalus had warned his son not to fly too close to the water or the sun, as told in this poem by the Greek poet Ovid (Elton's translation).

> "My Icarus!" he says; "I warn thee fly
> Along the middle track: nor low nor high;
> If low, thy plumes may flag with ocean's spray;
> If high, the sun may dart his fiery ray."[1]

Icarus ignored his father's warnings. He flew too close to the water, then zoomed up too close to the sun. The wax in his wings melted, and the wings came apart. Icarus plunged to his death in the waters that now bear his name, the Icarian Sea (see fig. 1.2).

The story is usually told to emphasize the point that sons should heed the wisdom of their fathers' advice lest they permanently and prematurely hang up their flight suits. Nevertheless, to put such a narrow spin on the story is to miss some important ingredients. For example, what happened to Daedalus?

What happened? He made it! Daedalus flew! This often neglected artifact of the legend is thunderously important to aviation professionals. If we examine the legend more closely, we will find that he flew either (1) to Sicily, or (2) to Cumae and from there went to Camicus on the island of Sicily, or (3) to Italy.[2] Consistent in most of the writings about Daedalus is that he flew from Crete to some location and he eventually made his way to Sicily (see fig. 1.3).

Daedalus was an Athenian, so why was he in Crete at all? Daedalus had established himself in Athens as "a carpenter of renown." The term *carpenter* in this context is more closely related to the term *engineer* in today's in-

Fig. 1.2. Sculpture of Daedalus and Icarus. Courtesy of the USAF Museum.

terpretation of the kinds of things Daedalus accomplished. For example, Daedalus is credited with having invented the sail, the axe, and the saw. He was also a gifted artist, sculptor, and architect.

Daedalus came to Crete from Athens apparently seeking political asylum after having been expelled from (or having escaped from) Athens for the murder of his nephew Talus. He accomplished this nasty deed by pushing Talus off a roof because he was jealous of Talus's blossoming abilities and could not stand a rival. As the legend goes, Minerva, a Greek goddess, changed Talus into a bird, the partridge, which bears his name.

Daedalus found favor with King Minos and was employed by him as the court architect. Daedalus also found favor with Pasiphae, King Minos's wife. One of the Greek gods gave Minos the gift of a beautiful white bull, which Minos was to use as a sacrifice. Minos could not bear to sacrifice such a beautiful animal and turned the bull loose. This so angered the god that he caused Pasiphae to fall madly in love with the bull. Pasiphae had Daedalus construct a wooden cow, which she used to disguise herself. Pasiphae had a sexual union with the bull during which she was impregnated. (This disgust-

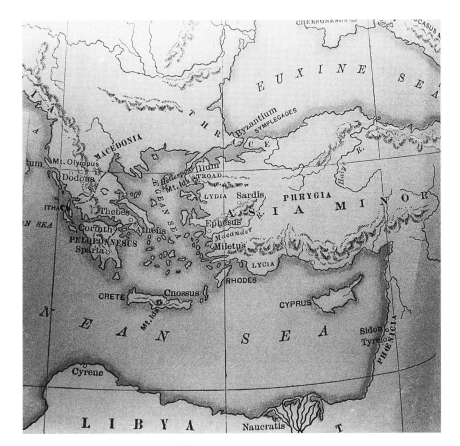

Fig. 1.3. Map of the area of ancient Greece. Helene A. Guerber, *Myths of Greece and Rome*, 1893.

Fig. 1.4. Ancient coin with King Minos on one side and the Labyrinth on the other side. Arthur Fairbanks, *The Mythology of Greece and Rome*, 1907.

ing thought is a testament to the notion that the Greeks were not at all dainty in describing real or concocted behaviors.) One can imagine the scene when the pregnant Pasiphae goes to her husband and says, "Listen, Honey, I have this little problem."

The offspring of this affair was a creature with the body of a bull and the head and torso of a man. This creature was called a Minotaur (Minos's bull). Minos called upon Daedalus to build a prison for the Minotaur, a castle with so many twists and turns that, once imprisoned inside, one was not likely to escape. This structure was called the Labyrinth (see fig. 1.4).

When, for some unexplained reason, Daedalus evoked the king's disfavor, he and his son were imprisoned in the Labyrinth. Pasiphae supplied them with food, information, and other essentials. They escaped from the Labyrinth by using the wings that Daedalus built.

Daedalus then made his way to Sicily, where he again entered the sphere of Greek royalty. He became the court architect to King Cocalus. Daedalus designed and built many buildings on Sicily and on the Italian peninsula. He also helped found a colony on the island of Sardinia. King Cocalus was so impressed by Daedalus that he had a temple built to the god Apollo. In the temple, the wings of Daedalus's flight were dedicated and displayed. King Cocalus's daughters were also fond of Daedalus, and one fell in love with him. This was most useful to Daedalus because his enemy, King Minos, was still looking for him and was murderously angry.

When Minos discovered that Daedalus was in Sicily, he mounted a naval force to kill him. Minos was welcomed by King Cocalus, who was in league with Daedalus, now in hiding. While Minos was bathing, Cocalus's daughters killed Minos by scalding him with boiling water. Minos's followers, now leaderless, wandered off and established the town of Minoa in Sicily and another community in southern Italy. Daedalus presumably lived happily ever after.

Now let us examine the legend and extract what we can loosely term the facts. First, was Daedalus a real man? I think we can reasonably establish that all of the people (not necessarily the gods) mentioned in the legend existed: Daedalus, Icarus, Talus, Minos, Pasiphae, Cocalus, and his daughters.

Second, was Daedalus a genius? His reputation as an engineering genius, artist, and architect can probably be proven. If he did invent the sail, he probably had some applied knowledge of aerodynamics—certainly not in those terms and not in the sense of mathematical equations, but more in the realm of an artist's "feel" for the forces involved.

Third, why did Daedalus kill his nephew, particularly by pushing him off a roof? Was he so heartless? If so, why didn't he use his other invention, the axe, to achieve the same purpose? Perhaps Daedalus had been experimenting with human flight and had persuaded Talus to strap on a pair of his wings and jump off a high building to test the invention. It was one of those "Oh well, back to the drawing board" situations that so often occur in a trial-and-error methodology.

Fourth, why did Daedalus fall into disfavor with King Minos and get thrown into the Labyrinth? It can probably be established that Daedalus had a fondness for women of royalty, using his later relationship with Cocalus's daughters to bolster this notion. Perhaps Daedalus and Pasiphae were so fond of one another that she became pregnant by Daedalus. This might cause Minos to imprison Daedalus and invent some far-fetched story involving the gods, a bull, and a Minotaur to cover up the palace scandal.

Fifth, did Daedalus fly? Here we have to consider his condition. He was imprisoned on Crete high on the cliffs overlooking the sea, a place where the eagles nested. He and his son probably killed some of the birds for food. Daedalus had an opportunity to study the birds' anatomy, the relationship of body weight to wingspan, the shape, curvature, width to length relationships, placement of feathers, and so on. With this information, Daedalus could have used feathers, twigs from the eagles' nests, and his carpentry tools, making it reasonable to believe that he was capable of building something

with the performance characteristics of a modern-day hang glider.

One could even speculate that if he had used his nephew as a willing test pilot, he also used his own son to test the second version of his wings. Daedalus profited by the mistakes he observed in his son's fatal flight. Later, he covered it up with the story about flying too close to the sun. The tale was easily accepted by people who knew so much less than he did about natural phenomena and who were so eager to accept any story citing the follies of the young.

Did he fly from Crete to Sicily, a distance of five hundred miles? Probably not. This is far beyond any reasonable range for a device such as a hang glider. More than likely, he flew to another location on Crete and from there boarded a ship to Sicily, or he timed his flight to land in the water near a passing ship, hoping they would pick him up. Whatever the route of his flight, Daedalus and his wings eventually made it to Sicily.

Before we leave the fascinating story of Daedalus, let us examine one intriguing line from Saxe's poem relating to the construction of Daedalus's wings: "Contrived of wood and feathers and a cunning set of springs." Did the springs exist, or were they a fabrication of Saxe, a word to rhyme with *wings?* If they did exist, for what purposes were they used?

What must be kept in mind is that the events surrounding Daedalus's flight occurred almost four thousand years ago. In writing about these events in the nineteenth century, Saxe either stumbled upon an important artifact (the existence of springs) or embellished the existing information with artistic license.

If the springs did exist, perhaps they were used to move some component such as a motive power to flap the wings. If so, this gives rise to a fascinating conclusion built on a stack of unproven hypotheses that not only did flight occur almost four thousand years ago but it was a *powered* flight. With that idea planted, let us now move from the ancient Greeks to other regions of the world and other times.

The idea of manned flight has occurred to most civilizations and on all continents. Cited are but a few examples.

Persia. In about 1500 B.C., King Kai Ka'us had a rectangular mechanism built upon which rested a throne and at each corner poles were erected. Large pieces of meat were tied to the end of each pole. He then had four hungry eagles tethered to the mechanism, and as the poor starving eagles flapped in vain to reach the meat, they lifted the mechanism. The eagles flew all the way to China, where they pooped out and crash-landed in a forest. King Ka'us apparently survived the ordeal, but he abandoned any further notion of flight. He instead turned his efforts and skills to erect what we know as the Tower of Babylon.

Egypt. In about 1000 B.C., Egyptians worshiped a god called Khensu who had the body of a man and had wings on his upper back (see fig. 1.5).

Rome. Mercury, a minor god to both the Romans and Greeks, was swift as the wind, a messenger of the gods, and the patron of Roman commerce. Mercury achieved flight with his winged helmet and sandals (see fig. 1.6).

Assyria. Assyrian architecture from about 700 B.C. shows a creature with a human head and the body of a bull with wings (see fig. 1.7). Another Assyrian winged god was Asshur.

Fig. 1.6. Bronze sculpture of Mercury (c. 1564–80), messenger of the gods, by Giovanni da Bologna. Courtesy of the USAF Museum.

Fig. 1.5. Khensu, an Egyptian god. Courtesy of the USAF Museum.

Fig. 1.7. An Assyrian winged bull with a man's head. Courtesy of the USAF Museum.

Africa. Kibaga, a legendary chieftain of an African tribe, was said to be able to make himself invisible by donning a cloak. He would then fly over his enemies and cast down spears, arrows, rocks, etc. Much to his chagrin, an enemy tribe set up an ambush for him. They sent out a volunteer group of decoys and watched as the weapons of war rained down upon them. Kibaga was hiding in the branches above. Then, triangulating on the apex of the onslaught, the enemy loosed a volley of arrows at Kibaga's invisible location and brought him down.

In seeking to separate the truth from the fiction, Kibaga was most likely a master of camouflage, a stealth warrior, and so equipped could hide unseen among the branches of the trees. Once hidden, he could inflict serious injury on those enemies passing underneath or within the range of his weapons. So it was then; so it is now with the F-117 fighter aircraft (fig. 1.8) and the B-2 bomber aircraft: same philosophy of warfare (stealth) but different weapons-systems delivery methodologies.

The Americas. Several examples of the desire to fly exist in the cultures of pre-Columbian America. For example, in Chile, archaeologists discovered the grave of a seventh-century Moche Indian princess. She was wearing golden earrings about the size of an American half-dollar. Each earring was inlaid with carved semi-precious stones, such as turquoise, in the shape of a winged warrior (see fig. 1.9).

The Incas, also of ancient South America, had a deity called Ayar Utso. As the legend would have it, Ayar Utso, in his finest hour, grew a set of wings and flew off into the sun.

Theories, Scientific Thought, and Experiments

The Tower Jumpers

The common characteristic of those who can be accorded the title "tower jumper" was that little if any scientific thought was given to the concepts of flight. Instead, each felt that they had the personal power (or magic) to fly. Each of them learned, with their last experiment, that personal power was no match for gravity. Representatives of this group included the following:

Simon the Magician. Simon, who lived in Nero's time (about A.D. 60), assembled a crowd in the Roman Forum. He climbed to the top of a tower constructed solely for his demonstration. With robes flowing majestically in the wind, he jumped gracefully from the tower. Death soon followed.

Fig. 1.8. F-117 fighter, a modern "Kibaga." Courtesy of the USAF Museum.

Fig. 1.9. Stained glass of winged Moche runner, by Tim Brady.

Bladud, King of Britain. In A.D. 863, Bladud, the father of Shakespeare's King Lear, affixed a set of wings to his arms and launched himself from a tall structure in London flapping his wings in vain as the crowd watched below. According to Geoffrey of Monmouth, he "came down on the top of the Temple of Apollo in the town of Trinovantum and was dashed into countless fragments." Alas, poor Bladud, we knew him well.

The Monk of Malmsbury. In 1010, the monk Elmer, who later became known as Oliver the Monk of Malmsbury, attached wings to both his arms and legs. He leaped from the tall tower of the Malmsbury Abbey and achieved a glide of about two hundred yards before thudding into the ground. Permanently crippled, he remained steadfast in his belief that man would one day fly. If ever in England, stop and toast his memory at the Flying Monk Inn.

Saracen. In approximately A.D. 1100, a Saracen attempted to fly around the hippodrome of Constantinople in the presence of Emperor Comenius. His robes were stiffened and stretched out behind him in a wide arc. Similar to Simon's earlier attempt, his brief flight was spectacular but short with an abrupt and fatal landing.

John Damien. In 1507, John Damien, near Stirling, Scotland, attempted to fly with a set of wings made of chicken feathers. After breaking several bones in the attempt, he blamed his lack of success on the chicken. He concluded that he made his wings out of the wrong kind of feathers, because chickens, as we all know, do not fly.

Marquis de Bacqueville. In 1742, the marquis de Bacqueville attached a set of wings to his arms and legs and soared from the top of a building in Paris out over the Seine. He had intended to fly about 500 yards to the other side, but wound up 250 yards short, landing painfully on a washerwoman's barge. He survived, surprisingly with minor injuries, but vowed never again to attempt to fly.

Emperor Shun. Turning to China, there are two artifacts that deserve mentioning. The first is the story of the Emperor Shun, which has more of the quality of legend about it than of experiment or theory. Shun, as the story goes, was a prince and direct heir to the throne occupied by his father. Shun was a small child about ten years old who weighed about forty pounds. The ruling emperor learned that one of his lieutenants was planning to have him killed, upon which his son Shun would assume the throne. The lieutenant would then be in control of the empire through his close relationship with the boy.

When the emperor learned of this plot, he ordered that a tall tower be built and that his son be placed atop the tower. Brush would be stacked around the base of the tower and set fire, killing the prince. All was in order, and the prince was dressed in his fineries, which included two large ceremonial coolie hats. The prince was placed at the top of the crow's-nest structure. (The coolie hat resembles a sombrero, with a pointed crown and a base large enough to shade the worker as he or she toils in the fields.)

When the tiny prince felt hot air rising from the great fire below, he decided that a quick death was preferable to being consumed by the flames. Shun grabbed his two hats and jumped over the side. Much to the amazement of all in attendance, the boy floated to the surface and gently landed, having escaped the event unscathed.

It would be a fitting end to this story, perhaps, if the young prince in a burst of instant wisdom shouted, "Eureka, I have invented the hot air balloon and the parachute." However, no such words were uttered to anyone's knowledge.

Chinese Kitesmen. The second event that occurred in China's history, of which Marco Polo wrote upon his return to Venice (about 1300), was the use of man-carrying kites. As reported in the *Chronicle of Aviation:*

> Chinese businessmen are reluctant to board merchant ships until it has been ascertained whether or not the journey will be prosperous. To do this, a drunkard or fool is seized by the ship's crew and tied to a huge kite made of cloth and wood, attached by eight ropes to the main tethering rope, held by the crew.
>
> When set opposite the wind, the kite rises into the sky, often with the frightened passenger screaming for pity. If the kite leans, the men on the ground pull the rope. This sets it upright once more, and by letting out more rope it rises higher. Once it is seen to fly well, the businessmen rush to the ship to sign aboard. If the kite does not fly well the merchants believe they must look for another ship, and the vessel remains in port for that year.[3]

Nothing further is said about the fate of those drunkards and fools who were strapped to the kites.

Scientists

Roger Bacon. Bacon was a Franciscan monk and a leading scientific thinker in 1280. He theorized about flight and came to the following conclusion: "It is not necessarily impossible for human beings to fly, but it so happens that God did not give them the knowledge of how to do it. It follows therefore that anyone who claims that he can fly must have sought the aid of the Devil. To attempt to fly is therefore sinful."

With this as the prevailing religious and scientific attitude about flight in medieval Europe and also a burning at the stake for anyone convicted of being in league with the devil, there is little wonder that any potential student of flight would quickly change his or her curriculum.

St. Joseph of Cupertino. An event that is said to be inscribed in the tomes of the Vatican was made in the presence of Pope Urban VIII by Joseph of Cupertino in the late sixteenth century. He is said to have flown by the power of his mind alone, by levitation, witnessed by many in the Vatican at the time. The Roman Catholic Church believes that this event occurred. After having studied the issue for one hundred years, the Church canonized Joseph.

Leonardo da Vinci. The idea of flight had its strongest proponent in Leonardo da Vinci (1452–1519). At the time that Columbus was busy discovering America, Leonardo was developing a body of work in the study of the mechanics of birds and flight. He was abstracting these into designs for vehicles that would allow manned flight. His work was so insightful that we can properly accord him the title "the Prophet of Flight" (fig. 1.10)

Leonardo is perhaps best known in history for his artistic achievements, including his painting of the Last Supper of Christ and the portrait popularly known as the *Mona Lisa.* His artistic duels with his fellow artistic genius Michelangelo, who was his creative peer in the world of art, became legendary. The duels gave rise to such modern-day novels as *The Agony and the Ecstasy.* This competition also fueled the creative drive of each man. However, in the area of mechanical sciences, Leonardo had no peer. He said, "Mechanical science is most noble and useful above all others, for by the

Fig. 1.10. Self-portrait of Leonardo da Vinci. Courtesy of the USAF Museum.

means of it all animated bodies in motion perform their operations."

Leonardo's genius in the mechanical sciences covered a variety of applications. He was an architect of military fortifications, a designer of ordnance such as the catapult, a military strategist, a student of the mechanics of the human body, a geologist, and an engineer. Leonardo filled many notebooks with his sketches, engineering and scientific diagrams, and drawings with detailed explanations of mechanical devices for all manner of applications. His genius seemed boundless in the mechanical sciences area.[4] Princes, military commanders, nobles, and heads of state constantly sought out his services. At this time in European history, the city-states of what had been the Roman Empire were constantly at war with one another. Leonardo's talents were sought by many of the princes of these city-states in their efforts to improve their defensive or offensive military positions.

In one of Leonardo's paintings, a woman sits with a child on her lap. The child is holding a small toy pro-

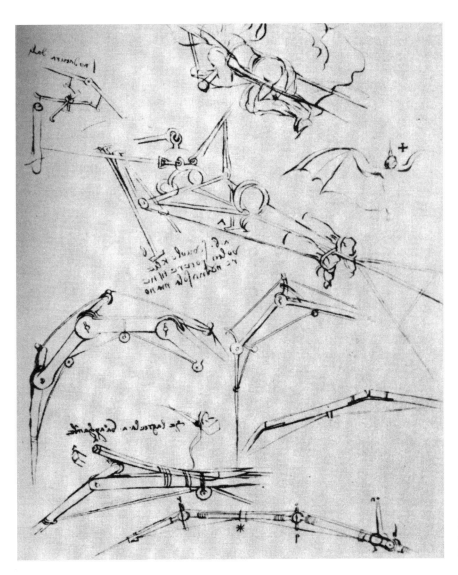

Fig. 1.11. Leonardo da Vinci's winged device. Courtesy of the USAF Museum.

peller with a string attached. We know that this toy dates to a much earlier period in China. It was likely that Marco Polo brought a similar toy back from his journeys to the Far East around 1300. Leonardo used the idea of the propeller to create a steam turbine. To achieve this, he used a restricted-opening pot filled with water and heated until steam was produced above which a crude propeller was placed. As the steam pressure came into contact with the blades of the propeller, the propeller turned, moving gears that were linked to a long arm. The long arm was a spit on which meat was placed to turn, unattended over a fire.

He also invented the parachute and the helicopter (or helix, as he referred to it), which was powered by a set of springs. As the springs released their energy, they turned the propeller, which looked like a large spiral screw. His theory was that by using air as the medium, this device would screw itself upwards into the air as the spiral turned.

Of most interest to the students of aviation, however, were his studies of the mechanics of winged flight. On the idea of the airplane Leonardo said, "The great bird will take its first flight filling the whole world with amazement and all records with its fame, and it will bring eternal glory to the nest where it was born."

There exist almost five hundred sketches and diagrams and more than 35,000 words of his dealing with the subject of flight. Some of his drawings have been built in modern times and found to be airworthy.

Much of his work centers around the mechanics of the bird and the mechanics of the human anatomy. Of the bird he said, "A bird is an instrument working according to mathematical law, which instrument is within the capacity of man to reproduce in all its movements." Curiously, Leonardo concentrated his studies to the ornithopter or flapping wings concept for propulsion. In his studies of both the bird and human anatomy, Leonardo knew that it was not possible for people to fly simply by fastening wings to their arms and flapping. His winged devices attempted to use the strength of not only the arms but also the thighs and legs to produce the motive power, as one will note in figure 1.11, a diagram by Leonardo.

Taking a momentary sidestep and comparing the physiological features of both bird and human seems

Table 1.1 Physiological Comparison of Selected Birds to Humans

Animal	Size of Heart (weight)	Size of Heart (% of body weight)	Heartbeat Rate (beats per minute)
Man	.5 pounds	.05%	70
Golden eagle	8 pounds	8%	200
Hummingbird	22 pounds	22%	1,200

useful. In table 1.1, for the sake of comparison, we will assume that each creature, including man, weighs exactly a hundred pounds. Of course, none of us would care to encounter a hundred-pound hummingbird; nevertheless, the assumption of a common weight makes for a useful comparison.

Clearly, the human metabolism is ill suited for flight unaided by some mechanism offering mechanical advantage. Leonardo addressed this issue by concluding that a bird's great strength gives it a reserve of power that allows it to fly fast or high. People do not possess such a great reserve of power. He also concluded than people do possess more than double the strength necessary to lift their own weight through some flight mechanism.[5]

Of course, we know that in today's times, muscle-powered vehicles using some form of mechanical advantage have, indeed, flown. The current record of 71.52 miles in 3 hours and 54 minutes was set in 1988 in the *Daedalus,* a muscle-powered aircraft built at the Massachusetts Institute of Technology.

In 1860, another Italian scientist, Giovanni Borelli, concluded that humans were too weak to fly. He used the laws of dynamics and statics to analyze the musculature of birds as compared with those of humans.

Despite his genius, Leonardo clung to the ornithopter idea, never conceptually separating the device that produces lift (the wings) from a device that produces propulsion such as a powered propeller. This development was not to occur for another three hundred years, until the advent of Sir George Cayley in the late 1700s. Interestingly enough, however, Leonardo's airscrew vehicle, a device whose twirling wing resembled a large screw, conceptually produced both lift and power, the power provided by a set of wound springs. Given an appropriate amount of power, this device may have been capable of flight.

There is also strong evidence that Leonardo built at least two flying devices under contract to various warlords. It is not known whether manned flight was attempted in these devices. Furthermore, Leonardo wrote of the theory of why flight occurs on a wing (the term *lift* lay in the future) by capturing the idea of the compressibility of air under the moving wing. He said that air beneath the movable substance (structure) is condensed while the air above it is rarefied.[6] An ardent understudy, had there been one, could perhaps have taken this idea and literally flown with it.

With the works of Leonardo da Vinci as a scientific foundation, we should have flown much earlier than we did. However, two major factors impeded the development of heavier-than-air flight.

First, with the Italian city-states at war, Leonardo's drawings and notebooks were scattered among the many Italian princes or other heads of state in Europe. Some notebooks were not discovered until after we had achieved powered flight. For example, two of Leonardo's notebooks, Codex Madrid I and II, were placed in the library of King Philip V of Spain, where they remained until 1830. They were then transferred to a national library and incorrectly cataloged. The notebooks disappeared into the depths of the library until being rediscovered more than a century later in 1965.

The second major factor that impeded the development of heavier-than-air flight was the emergence of lighter-than-air flight, which seemed to capture the fancy of anyone interested in flight. The balloon in both hot air and enclosed bag varieties led potential thinkers away from heavier-than-air experimentation for almost a hundred years. (The development of lighter-than-air flight is a fascinating study. This subject is covered in its entirety in chap. 14.)

A final thought before leaving Leonardo da Vinci. One can describe the intellect of both Daedalus and Leonardo with the same descriptors: engineer, scientist, architect, artist, inventor, genius, disciple of flight, and designer of vehicles, whose purpose was to achieve manned flight. One can also place them geographically and regionally on the Italian peninsula. What separates them is approximately 3,200 years (1700 B.C. to A.D. 1500).

An idea that evolves from this abstraction is the notion (perhaps a hypothesis) that Leonardo da Vinci might be on a branch of the Daedalus family tree.

Daniel Bernoulli. Before we leave our ancestors of flight, we need to mention the achievements of an individual who probably had no thought or notion of flight. However, Daniel Bernoulli's work made our understanding of the physical nature of flight possible.

Bernoulli was born in 1700 to a family of Swiss mathematicians and scientists. His studies centered around the properties of pressure and velocity in water, a medium with characteristics very similar to that of air. He studied the flow of water in pipes and in 1738 described his findings in his book *Hydrodynamica*.

From his work, he derived the formula for how lift occurs. The formula can be expressed in a variety of ways, including

$$\text{Static pressure} \times \text{Dynamic pressure (velocity)} = \text{Constant}$$

So if the static pressure is five units and the dynamic pressure is four units, the constant is twenty units. If one induces a change in the flow, such as inserting an airfoil, then the static pressure will drop. Let us drop to four units, and the velocity will increase to five units while the constant remains at twenty units. The lower static pressure on top of the airfoil relative to the undisturbed pressure on the bottom of the airfoil will cause the airfoil to rise.

Of course, Bernoulli knew nothing of airfoils and was dead some sixty years before Cayley (discussed in chap. 2) began his scientific exploration of flight dynamics. Nevertheless, his work led to the scientific explanation of the property described as lift.

Notes

1. The poems of Saxe and Ovid are found in Guerber, *Myths of Greece and Rome*, 253–55.

2. Various interpretations of the myth can be found in Guerber's *Myths of Greece and Rome*, Fairbanks's *Mythology of Greece and Rome*, Pinsent's *Greek Mythology*, Guirand's *Greek Mythology*, and Tatlock's *Greek and Roman Mythology*.

3. Gunston, *Chronicle of Aviation*, 13.

4. For a more complete description of Leonardo da Vinci's work in the mechanical sciences, see Heydenreich, Dibner, and Reti, *Leonardo the Inventor*.

5. McCurdy, "Leonardo da Vinci and the Science of Flight," 135.

6. For an excellent discussion of Leonardo's contributions to flight theory, see McCurdy. This powerful article reveals more of Leonardo's genius than contemporary resources provide. A complete copy of this article is included as an appendix to the present volume.

References

Bartell, Edward E., Jr. *Gods and Goddesses of Ancient Greece.* Coral Gables: University of Miami Press, 1971.

Brown, Carl A. *A History of Aviation.* Daytona Beach: Embry-Riddle Aeronautical University, 1980.

Cooper, Margaret. *The Inventions of Leonardo da Vinci.* New York: Macmillan, 1965.

Cosgrove, C. Burton. *Fantasy in Flight.* Albuquerque: Cosgrove, 1974.

Fairbanks, Arthur. *Mythology of Greece and Rome.* New York: D. Appleton Century, 1907.

Gayley, Charles M. *Classical Myths.* Boston: Ginn, 1893.

Guerber, Helene A. *Myths of Greece and Rome.* New York: American Book, 1893.

Guirand, Felix. *Greek Mythology.* London: Paul Hamlyn, 1963.

Gunston, Bill, ed. *Chronicle of Aviation.* Paris: Jacques Legrand, 1992.

Heydenreich, Ludwig H., Bern Dibner, and Ladislao Reti. *Leonardo the Inventor.* New York: McGraw-Hill, 1980.

Howe, George, and G. A. Harrer. *Handbook of Classical Mythology.* New York: F. S. Crofts, 1929.

Kane, Robert M., and Allan D. Vose. *Air Transportation.* 8th ed. Dubuque: Kendall/Hunt, 1999.

McCurdy, Edward. "Leonardo da Vinci and the Science of Flight." *19th Century* 68 (July 1910): 126–42.

McDonald, William A. *Progress into the Past.* New York: Macmillan, 1967.

Pinsent, John. *Greek Mythology.* New York: Peter Bedrich Books, 1969.

Smith, H. C. *The Illustrated Guide to Aerodynamics.* 2d ed. Blue Ridge Summit, Pa.: Tab Books, 1992.

Solberg, Carl. *Conquest of the Skies.* Boston: Little, Brown, 1979.

Tatlock, Jessie M. *Greek and Roman Mythology.* New York: D. Appleton Century, 1917.

Developments Before the Wright Brothers

Charles Rodriguez

As DEMONSTRATED throughout chapter 1, creating a successful flying machine proved to be no easy feat. What were the secrets known to flying creatures that allowed them to fly through the air? To further complicate matters, what form should a flying machine take? Should it flap its wings like a bird, or should the wings remain stationary and should a separate means of propulsion be used? Maybe there should be a lifting screw capable of sustaining the aircraft, as suggested by Leonardo da Vinci? What form of power would keep such a machine in the air? How would the operator control the direction of flight? These issues were only a sample of the hurdles faced by early investigators.

This chapter summarizes the progress made in aviation between 1790 and 1910. Numerous investigations and trials were conducted to solve the mystery of mechanical flight. From this effort emerged the science of aeronautics.

Forerunners of the Practical Airplane

Sir George Cayley. A true visionary and progenitor to mechanical flight was Sir George Cayley (see fig. 2.1). Born 27 December 1773 in Scarborough, England, Cayley became interested in human flight in 1783, when the hot air balloon was invented. His preoccupation with flight continued until his death in 1857. He established many

Fig. 2.1. Sir George Cayley. By permission of the National Air and Space Museum, Smithsonian Institution, ©1999 Smithsonian Institution.

aeronautical principles, including basic aerodynamics and the general form of an airplane. His contributions to the problem of heavier-than-air flight has earned him acclaim as the rightful inventor of the airplane and corresponding title "Father of Aerial Navigation."[1]

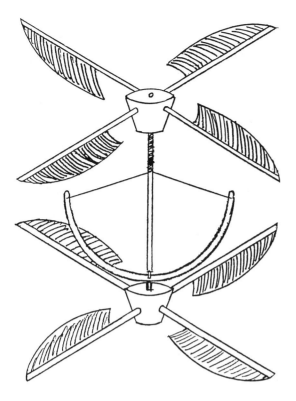

Fig. 2.2. Cayley's model helicopter. Courtesy of the USAF Museum.

Early model helicopter. As a young man, Cayley developed a model helicopter based on the work of Launoy and Bienvenu.[2] As shown in figure 2.2, this model employed two four-bladed rotors attached to opposite ends of a shaft. It was powered by a flexible bow and string. The rotors were wound until the bow was adequately stressed. Upon release, the straightening action of the bow imparted a whirling motion to the rotors, resulting in flight.

1799 silver disc. Although his early research involved a helicopterlike device, Cayley shifted his investigations to fixed-wing designs. His intuition concerning the forces acting on a wing and the basic shape of an airplane were preserved by etchings made on a silver disc in 1799. Figure 2.3 shows the side of the disc illustrating the aerodynamic forces of lift and drag as applied to a flat plane placed at a moderate angle of attack. The flip side illustrates in specific detail the basic configuration of an airplane. This sketch, shown in figure 2.4, clearly depicts the following items: (a) a fixed, cambered wing, (b) a tail

structure with vertical and horizontal surfaces, (c) a pair of aerial oars for the production of thrust, and (d) a fuselage to carry the operator.

The aerial oars, although ineffective, demonstrated Cayley's foresight in terms of separating lift from thrust. Many inventors attempted to combine lift and thrust through the use of wing-flapping mechanisms. Such devices were unsuccessful. When considering the attributes of the aircraft shown in figure 2.4, there is little question that Cayley was pursuing the proper form of an airplane. This historic silver disc is enshrined in the Science Museum in London.

Whirling arm device. In 1804, Cayley conducted a series of experiments using a whirling arm device as shown in figure 2.5. He attached sample airfoils or other articles to the extremity of a rotating arm. As the arm revolved around its vertical axis, the object swept through the air in a circular course. Reactions of the airfoil were evaluated to determine its aerodynamic characteristics.

By using this instrument, Cayley collected data relevant to the response of airfoils at varying angles of attack. Benjamin Robins in 1746 originally used the

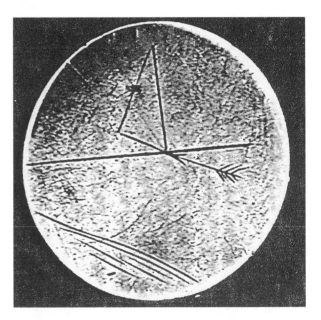

Fig. 2.3. One side of a silver disc on which Cayley illustrated the aerodynamic forces acting on an inclined plane. By permission of the National Air and Space Museum, Smithsonian Institution, ©1999 Smithsonian Institution.

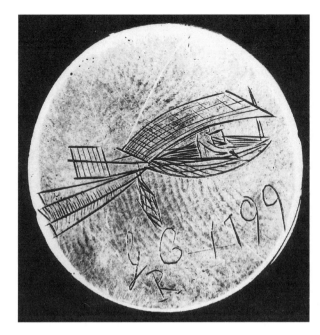

Fig. 2.4. The other side of Cayley's silver disc on which he engraved his concept for a fixed-wing aircraft in 1799. The disc is presently in the Science Museum in London. By permission of the National Air and Space Museum, Smithsonian Institution, ©1999 Smithsonian Institution.

whirling arm for ballistic tests; Cayley's adaptation of this apparatus for aeronautical research demonstrates his brilliance. The results of his whirling arm tests were subsequently applied to his model glider.[3]

Model glider. Cayley's 1804 model glider, shown in figure 2.6, was described by the eminent aviation historian Charles H. Gibbs-Smith as the first modern airplane. Through this model, Cayley gave form to theory. The glider employed a 154-square-inch wing secured to the fuselage at a six degree angle of incidence. A movable weight on the underside of the fuselage provided a means for setting the center of gravity. An adjustable cruciform tail was attached to the craft via a universal joint and used to control its flight path.

Cayley operated this model by launching it from a hilltop. Watching his glider sail downhill precipitated his notion that a large-scale machine could be used to transport humans and goods down steep inclines better than "the surefooted mule."[4]

Calorific engine. Recognizing that a major obstacle to sustained flight in heavier-than-air flying machines involved the application of power, Cayley undertook the development of a calorific, or hot air, engine. Aware that steam engines were cursed with low power-to-weight ratios, he explored alternate forms of motive force. His 1807 experiments involved a gunpowder engine.

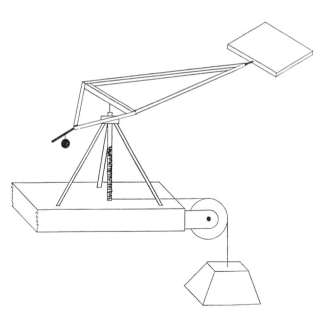

Fig. 2.5. Cayley's whirling arm. Courtesy of the USAF Museum.

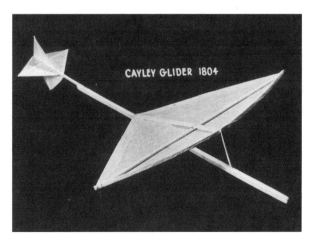

Fig. 2.6. Model of the 1804 Cayley glider made by Paul K. Guillow of Wakefield, Massachusetts. By permission of the National Air and Space Museum, Smithsonian Institution, ©1999 Smithsonian Institution.

This power plant employed two superposed cylinders. The lower cylinder was akin to a combustion chamber in that it received expanding gases from the combustion process. Directly above the pressure chamber was a cylinder containing a piston. During combustion, expanding gases from the pressure chamber acted on the piston in the upper cylinder. As a result, the piston and associated components traveled upwards. This, in turn, caused the cords attached to the cross member of the piston rod to bend the stout bow affixed to the underside of the base. A wire connected to the cross member opened and closed valves that controlled the next powder charge and pressure chamber vent. The pressure chamber vent opened at the top of the stroke. The straightening action of the bow then returned the piston to the bottom of its cylinder. When the gunpowder control valve opened, the next charge traveled down a special pipe that was heated by a lamp. As this charge ignited, the expanding gases were once again directed to the pressure chamber, and the next cycle was under way.[5]

Although his gunpowder engine showed a high level of ingenuity, Cayley was unable to produce a lightweight, successful internal combustion engine. One must wonder how the availability of a suitable power plant would have affected his progress in aeronautics.

1808 ornithopter. Cayley conducted experiments with a flapping model using two umbrella-shaped wings around 1808. Octave Chanute, an early aviation scholar and investigator, revealed that these wings were composed of two ribs arranged in a perpendicular fashion and bent to form a concave-shaped structure. Tightly stretched fabric was applied to this framework to provide an umbrella effect. The device had a surface area of 54 square feet, and it weighed 11 pounds. Without divulging the source of power or the rapidity of the flapping action, Cayley claimed the device could lift 9 stone (126 pounds) when set into motion.[6]

The flapping machine described by Chanute was not the only ornithopter designed by Cayley. As demonstrated in his notebook of 1799–1826, Sir George Cayley conceived a number of ornithopters.

1809 advancements in aeronautics. Through continued investigations into the problem of heavier-than-air flight, Cayley made a number of discoveries concerning aerodynamics. By 1809, he became aware of the effects of camber on lift production as he determined that an area of low pressure was generated above the wing. He also found that the center of pressure of a wing was not stationary. Cayley further came to appreciate the value of streamlining.

Cayley conducted experiments to solve problems associated with longitudinal and lateral stability. As an outcome, he discovered dihedral enhanced lateral stability. Other aeronautical advancements developed by Cayley included the use of bamboo in the construction of aircraft and a lightweight, tension-spoked wheel.

1809 glider. As in 1804, Cayley constructed an aircraft based on his research. The 1809 machine was a full-scale glider weighing 56 pounds and employing 300 square feet of wing surface. This aircraft was flown primarily as a pilotless machine carrying some 84 pounds of ballast. There were instances when the glider became airborne with the individual performing the launch. Such events occurred when he was running downhill with the machine during takeoff. These gliders flew only a few yards.

Dirigibles. In 1816, Cayley contemplated a number of improvements regarding aerostatic flight. He suggested streamlining for enhancing the performance of lighter-than-air vessels. One of his proposed dirigibles was a Montgolfière (hot air aerostat) 300 feet in length, 90 feet wide, and 45 feet tall. Cayley also recommended dividing large airship envelopes into smaller gas bags. The intent of separating the envelope into smaller units was to prevent catastrophic loss of ascension gas in case of a tear. To further advance aerostatic flight, he suggested using a rigid structure for maintaining the streamlined shape of an airship. For propulsion, Cayley recommended propellers.

Cayley proposed a second airship in 1837. Unlike the previous model, this ship was to be a Charlière or hydrogen balloon. The 432-foot-long vessel was to be propelled by a steam engine and a pair of five-bladed propellers. Cayley ambitiously declared the machine could carry 500 men for an hour or 50 men for two days with a range of 960 miles.

1843 convertiplane. In 1843 Cayley conceived a new craft that was a cross between a helicopter and an airplane. The convertiplane employed two pairs of superposed rotors to produce lift for takeoff and a pair of propellers

Fig. 2.7. Cayley's 1843 converti-plane. By permission of the National Air and Space Museum, Smithsonian Institution, ©1999 Smithsonian Institution.

for thrust (see fig. 2.7). The rotors transformed into wings when in forward flight.[7] The features of this machine demonstrate Cayley's awareness regarding the need to take off and land in confined areas.

1849 boy carrier. As a result of his investigations of aircraft structures, Cayley believed it was better to use multiple small wings to increase wing area rather than to use a single large wing. This theory was tested in 1849 on a full-scale triplane shown in fig. 2.8. The craft exhibited many familiar Cayley features, including wings with dihedral, a cruciform tail, a fuselage, landing gear, and a propulsion system.

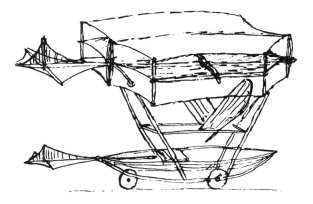

Fig. 2.8. Cayley's boy carrier. By permission of the National Air and Space Museum, Smithsonian Institution, ©1999 Smithsonian Institution.

Concerning the system of propulsion, one must question why he decided to include a form of aerial oars for this machine. Previously, Cayley had envisioned using the propellers for his dirigibles. A possible explanation may be power plant related. A lighter-than-air vessel could carry a heavy power plant by simply augmenting the volume of the envelope and ascension gas. In contrast, overcoming the burden of lifting a heavy engine was far more complex in a fixed-wing design. Without question, his aerial oars, although ineffective, were much lighter than other forms of propulsion available at the time.

The 1849 triplane machine flew successfully as a glider. It was flown in ballast and with a small boy.[8] Consequently, it became known as "Cayley's boy carrier."

1852 man carrier. A craft, initially labeled a "governable parachute" on the 25 September 1852 cover of *Mechanics' Magazine*, later became known as the "man-carrying glider" (see fig. 2.9). It was originally designed to be released from a balloon during flight and to glide safely back to earth. This aircraft featured a single wing with eight degrees of dihedral. The wing was attached to the fuselage using a forward and aft strut along with support lines. The upper cruciform apparatus affixed to the rear of the machine was an adjustable stabilizer. Cords connected to the upper and lower sides of this control caused it to pivot about a hinge. This action provided an

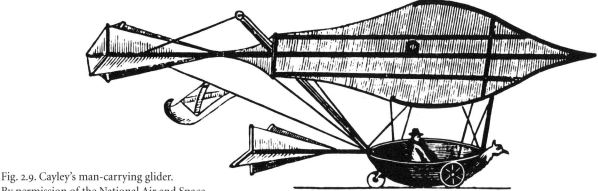

Fig. 2.9. Cayley's man-carrying glider.
By permission of the National Air and Space
Museum, Smithsonian Institution, ©1999 Smithsonian Institution.

adjustable trim system for longitudinal stability.[9] The lower cruciform control provided a means through which the operator could steer the craft during flight. Cayley thoughtfully included a wheeled landing gear. It is likely the wheels not only served landing purposes but also allowed for rapid acceleration of the craft during downhill takeoffs.

Whereas this machine made many flights with ballast, there were also instances when human flights occurred. On two occasions, a ten-year-old boy flew for a few yards. This machine, however, gained fame for its flight across a small valley near Brompton Hall with Cayley's coachman aboard. The coachman, who may have sustained injuries as a result of the landing, was reported to have said, "Please, Sir George, I wish to give notice. I was hired to drive, not fly."[10]

Spreading the word. One aspect of Cayley's work that should be considered paramount to the advancement of aviation was his dissemination of aeronautical knowledge. It was one thing to advance the science of aeronautics, but to do so in isolation would have had little impact on the work of others. There is no accurate way to determine the total effect that Cayley's work had on others or how long the solution to powered, heavier-than-air flight would have been delayed if he had not revealed his findings to the world. By sharing his knowledge and expertise, Cayley accelerated the progress of others by providing a proven starting point. His work also provided guidance as to the direction investigators should pursue in their quest to invent a powered, heavier-than-air flying machine.

Accounts of Cayley's ten years of research into the problem of mechanical flight, from 1799 to 1809, were published as "On Aerial Navigation." This series of three articles appeared in the November 1809, February 1810, and March 1810 issues of *Nicholson's Journal of Natural Philosophy, Chemistry, and Arts.*

In 1816, he published two monographs on lighter-than-air vessels in *Tilloch's Philosophical Magazine.* He fully expected powered flight to first be attained by dirigible craft. The following year, *Tilloch's Philosophical Magazine* printed "On Aerial Navigation." After a hiatus of twenty years, he published "Practical Remarks on Aerial Navigation" in *Mechanics' Magazine* (1837). In 1843, "Retrospect of the Progress of Aerial Navigation" and "On the Principles of Aerial Navigation" appeared in *Mechanics' Magazine.* This periodical also published "Aerostation—Mr. Luntley's Pamphlet" in 1851 and "Sir George Cayley's Governable Parachutes" in 1852. A French journal, *Bulletin of the Société Aerostatique et Météorologique de France* (no. 4), printed his article "Mémoire sur le Vol Artificiel" in 1853.

Henson and Stringfellow

Two Englishmen, William Samuel Henson and John Stringfellow, were profoundly inspired by Cayley's work. They not only followed Cayley's published works but they also sought his advice and financial support for their aeronautical endeavors.

William Samuel Henson. It may never be known with certainty when Henson first became interested in mechanical flight. However, his desire to create a heavier-than-air flying machine may be traced to 1840 when he began building small-scale gliders. Realizing the limitations of gliding machines, Henson later worked on a solution to powered flight. He began by mounting small steam engines on models. These efforts were futile, as the low power-to-weight ratios of the available engines in combination with underdeveloped aerodynamic designs proved no match for gravity.

Undaunted by the lack of success of his powered models, Henson turned to the creation of a large-scale aircraft. He conceived his famous "Aerial Steam Carriage" in 1842.[11] The design of this craft became the basis for Patent 9,478, provisionally issued to Henson in 1842 and completed in 1843. Technically, this patent was not for an airplane but for "certain improvements in locomotive apparatus and machinery for conveying letters, goods and passengers from place to place through the air."[12]

The Aerial Steam Carriage, as described by Henson, was a machine having 4,500 square feet of wing surface to support a gross weight of 3,000 pounds (see fig. 2.10). It was designed with a delta-shaped 1,500-square-foot horizontal tail surface along with a vertical rudder. The propulsion system included a 25–30-horsepower steam engine and pair of propellers. There was also a cabin section with a wheeled undercarriage. Although never built, this machine served as a prototype airliner.

Unable to solicit adequate financial support for his hypothetical aircraft, Henson constructed "working" models of the Aerial Steam Carriage in 1843. Miniature versions of this aircraft were powered by clockwork mechanisms or steam engines. Displays and demonstrations of these models took place at Adelaide Gallery in the Strand at London. To Henson's misfortune, failures of these models to fly misfired in terms of stirring financial support. The models also generated criticism concerning the soundness of his proposed Aerial Steam Carriage. Having exhausted his funds and wishing to recruit a partner with mechanical aptitude and insight, Henson joined forces with Stringfellow late in 1843.

John Stringfellow. While working in the production of lace, John Stringfellow (1799–1883) developed exceptional mechanical abilities. With the lace industry becoming mechanized, Stringfellow was exposed to a multiplicity of intricate mechanical devices used to make lace. He later gained notoriety as a skilled artisan in the trade. His competence in designing and constructing state-of-the-art steam engines was also well established.

Stringfellow's association with Henson, in terms of aeronautics, began with modeling. His son, Frederick, recalled that Stringfellow first made a small model powered by a spring. Frederick was uncertain as to the precise details, but this unit may have been an ornithopter.

A second model was a scaled unit based on the patented specifications of the Aerial Steam Carriage. This machine had a wingspan of 20 feet and a chord of some 3.5 feet. A steam engine powered a pair of four-bladed propellers measuring 3 feet in diameter. The con-

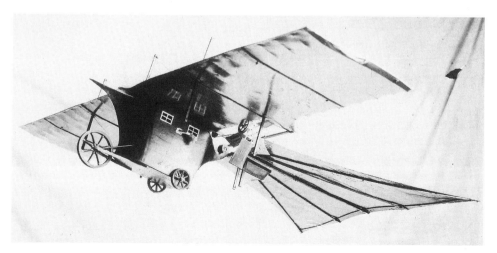

Fig. 2.10. William Samuel Henson's Aerial Steam Carriage. By permission of the National Air and Space Museum, Smithsonian Institution, ©1999 Smithsonian Institution.

Fig. 2.11. John Stringfellow's steam-powered monoplane. By permission of the National Air and Space Museum, Smithsonian Institution, ©1999 Smithsonian Institution.

struction and development of this model involved many months of work and numerous modifications. It was tested in 1845 in a secluded area known as Bala Down near Chard. Weeks of testing and modifications failed to make this machine fly.

Henson abandoned his pursuit of building the Aerial Steam Carriage. He married and left England around 1848, reportedly traveling to Peru, Mexico, and the United States.

Stringfellow continued his investigations in mechanical flight. His next machine emerged in 1848 as a steam-powered monoplane. As shown in figure 2.11, this model bears a striking resemblance to the Aerial Steam Carriage. It had a 10-foot wingspan and a twin propeller system. The curved wings and omission of a vertical tail surface, however, were obvious deviations from the proposed Aerial Steam Carriage.

Stringfellow tested the model indoors to eliminate the likelihood of encountering unstable wind conditions. The launch mechanism for this craft was ingenious. The model was suspended beneath a tandem-wheeled hangar that allowed it to travel along a guide line. This line, which was inclined for rapid acceleration, had a stop-block that caused the launch mechanism to disengage itself from the model at a predetermined position. At this point, the liberated machine was in free flight.

Accounts concerning the success of this model vary widely. According to Frederick, the machine flew after being launched at Chard and Cremorne Gardens in 1848. If such was the case, this model may have been the first powered, heavier-than-air machine to fly. However, examination of the machine by aeronautical engineers revealed the 1848 model had only a slight chance of sustaining itself in the air.[13]

For whatever reason, Stringfellow slackened the intensity of his aeronautical research. Evidence of his work later appeared in the form of a bat-wing model and a triplane. Stringfellow entered his triplane in a contest sponsored by the Aeronautical Society of Great Britain in 1868. Although the machine failed to win, Stringfellow received a prize for the production of a lightweight steam engine.

Félix Du Temple de la Croix

Born in 1823, Félix Du Temple, a French naval officer, began experimenting in aeronautics during the 1850s. His first notable achievement involved a flyable model developed in 1857–58. The model was originally powered by a clockwork mechanism. It was subsequently changed to steam power. This craft was credited with being the first airplane, although a model, to take off using its own power, sustain itself in flight, and land safely.

There are a couple of differences between the models by Stringfellow and Du Temple that are worth noting. If Stringfellow's 1848 machine actually flew after being released from its launch mechanism, it may be the first powered, heavier-than-air craft to fly. Its success, however, depended on an accelerated, not to mention elevated, takeoff using the inclined guide wire and release apparatus. By contrast, the Du Temple machine took off, flew, and landed without an assisted takeoff procedure.

Sensing he was on the right track, Du Temple patented in 1857 a full-scale airplane based on his findings. As shown in figure 2.12, the machine was a tractor monoplane with forward swept wings. The tail included controllable horizontal and vertical surfaces. The fuselage, which closely resembled the hull of a small boat, had three retractable landing gear legs.

Du Temple built the machine described in his patent. Following its construction, he and his brother, Louis, conducted trials. Chanute suggested that a variety of power plants were employed while they were attempting to fly the machine. Forms of motive power included steam, hot air, and electricity.

Historians generally credit this craft as being the first powered, heavier-than-air machine to carry a human. This accolade is based on a flight that occurred in 1874 at Brest, France. The operator of the craft was not Du Temple but a young mariner.[14] It is imperative to note that the machine was launched into the air following an accelerated takeoff down a ramp. In reality, the machine experienced more of a brief "powered hop" than an actual sustained flight.

Alexander Feodorovich Mozhaiski

A captain of the Imperial Russian Navy, Alexander F. Mozhaiski, exhibited his interest in heavier-than-air flight through modeling. Mozhaiski flew models publicly in St. Petersburg in 1876. It is likely such modeling was conducted as a means of testing a design for an airplane he conceived in 1875. A patent for this flying machine was issued in 1881, and the craft was built in 1883.

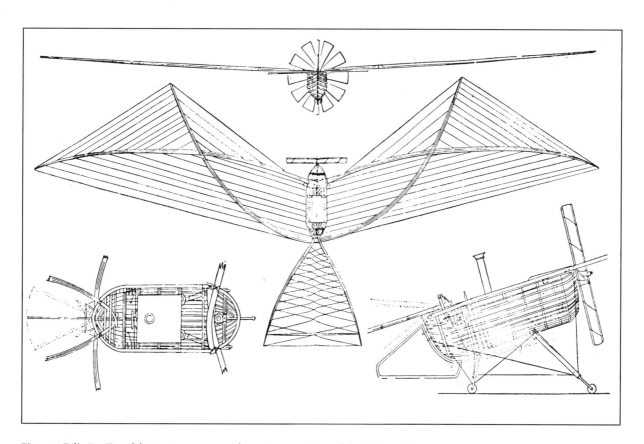

Fig. 2.12. Félix Du Temple's 1857 tractor monoplane. By permission of the National Air and Space Museum, Smithsonian Institution, ©1999 Smithsonian Institution.

Fig. 2.13. Alexander F. Mozhaiski's machine. By permission of the National Air and Space Museum, Smithsonian Institution, ©1999 Smithsonian Institution.

The airplane was powered by a steam engine of 20–30 horsepower (see fig. 2.13). One tractor and two pusher propellers provided thrust. To a degree, the wing resembled Henson's Aerial Steam Carriage wing with its rectilinear shape. In terms of dimensions, the wing was rather large with a span of 69 feet and a chord of 46 feet. A movable cruciform tail was used for flight control. The tail also provided a measure of stability.

Mozhaiski's machine was readied for takeoff and flown in July 1884. The location of this "flight" was at Krasnoye Selo in the St. Petersburg area. At the controls was I. N. Golubev. As this machine was launched using a ski-jump-type ramp, historians classify this occurrence as a "powered hop." As with Du Temple, the reason behind such a classification is warranted because the craft was unable to sustain itself in the air for more than a few seconds. It was reported that the machine crashed on this occasion and damaged a wing.[15]

Francis Herbert Wenham

Francis Wenham (1824–1908), a naval architect by trade, became a significant aeronautical figure during the latter half of the nineteenth century. Wenham, who was active in the Aeronautical Society of Great Britain, established various theories concerning mechanical flight and built and tested multiplane designs (for which he made a patent application in 1866). He also became one of the first to employ wind tunnels in the study of aeronautics.

In 1866, Wenham experimented with a series of multiplane craft. He first constructed a model using six high-aspect ratio wings with 3-foot spans and 3-inch chords. The performance of this model encouraged him to continue his investigations with full-scale aircraft. Two such machines were built. Neither flew with any degree of success.

Despite the disappointment, Wenham continued his work in aerodynamics. In 1871, he and his assistant, John Browning, began wind tunnel experiments for the Aeronautical Society of Great Britain. The purpose of this work was to determine the relationship between airspeed and air pressure exerted on airfoils.

Wind tunnel investigations ultimately became a popular and effective form of testing airfoils and other aerodynamic principles. The list of experimenters using wind tunnels during this pioneering period includes Horatio Phillips, Hiram Maxim, Charles Renard, Albert Zahm, and the Wrights.

Alphonse Pénaud

Born in 1850, Alphonse Pénaud was destined to follow in his father's footsteps and join the French navy. However, a debilitating medical problem with his hips prevented this. It is likely he worked as a marine engineer. By the age of twenty, Alphonse had begun displaying his aeronautical abilities. From 1870 to 1880, he experimented extensively with various forms of models, established longitudinal stability, and developed a plan for a full-scale aircraft. His work influenced the direction taken by other aeronautical investigators.

PÉNAUD MODELS

Helicopter. One of Pénaud's first aeronautical accomplishments involved the design and construction of a model helicopter in 1870. This device was a coaxial, counter-rotating craft employing a pair of rotors (see fig. 2.14). It was powered by twisted rubber bands. Pénaud originally intended to extract power from tightly stretched elastic bands. But the beefier structure required to withstand the force of the rubber bands in tension led him to designs in which rubber bands were twisted. To this day, twisted rubber bands are used to power model aircraft.

Somewhat resembling the helicopter built by Cayley, this machine flew exceptionally well. Chanute indicated the model could soar 50 feet and remain aloft for some 26 seconds. Although the performance of this machine was impressive, it did not lead to a full-scale aircraft capable of carrying humans. As a note of interest, Milton Wright, father of Wilbur and Orville, gave the boys a toy helicopter built à la Pénaud. Fred C. Kelly reported the brothers performed a number of experiments and modifications to the original design.

Planophore. The following year, 1871, Pénaud advanced the science of fixed-wing designs with his "Planophore." The 20-inch model had a wingspan of 18 inches and an approximate chord of 4 inches (see fig. 2.15). The wings were turned up near the tips to enhance lateral stability, and a horizontal tail surface was engineered to provide longitudinal stability. A rubber band powered the two-bladed pusher propeller.

This monoplane flew successfully and served as a test bed for developing stability. The Planophore achieved longitudinal stability through the critical arrangement of its center of gravity, center of pressure, and alignment of its horizontal tail. Pénaud positioned the wing so the center of pressure was aft of the center of gravity. This arrangement generated a nose-down attitude. To counter this nose-low moment, the tail was mounted with an angle of incidence eight degrees below that of the wing. This produced a nose-up attitude. The result was an inherent equilibrium that caused the machine to maintain a level flight path. It had the tendency to return to a level attitude following disturbances while airborne. This method of maintaining longitudinal stability was a notable breakthrough in the science of aeronautics. A vertical surface was added to provide directional control.

Ornithopter. Having successfully created fixed- and rotary-winged models, Pénaud turned his investigations to ornithopters. From this work emerged a wing-flapping model in 1872. This craft used a twisted rubber band to power the beating motion of its wings. A tail surface was

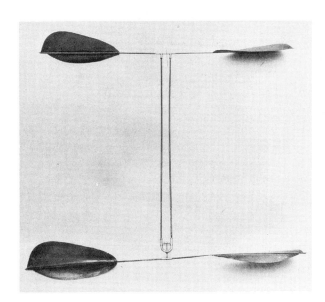

Fig. 2.14. Side view of a miniature helicopter designed by Alphonse Pénaud in 1870. By permission of the National Air and Space Museum, Smithsonian Institution, ©1999 Smithsonian Institution.

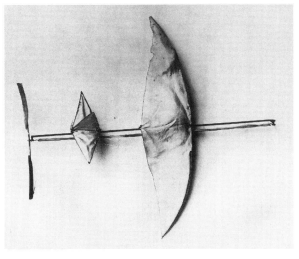

Fig. 2.15. Top view of a National Air Museum reconstruction of a Pénaud Planophore, a flying model designed by Alphonse Pénaud and first demonstrated to the public 18 August 1871 in the garden of the Tuileries, Paris. By permission of the National Air and Space Museum, Smithsonian Institution, ©1999 Smithsonian Institution.

included for stability. Chanute reported the machine was incapable of achieving flight unless hand launched. However, once airborne, the mechanical bird flew until the force of its rubber band was depleted.

Proposed airplane. Pénaud's next design phase involved a full-scale airplane. Beginning in 1876, Pénaud and his partner, Paul Gauchot, worked on a two-place monoplane. The machine was to be an amphibious unit employing two counter-rotating, tractor propellers (see fig. 2.16). The elliptical wings had floats at their tips for water operations. The elevator and rudder were to be operated by a control stick. The proposed landing gear was retractable, and a glass canopy was included to protect the crew. This machine was patented in 1876 but was never built. Pénaud ended his life in 1880 at the age of thirty.

Clément Ader

Born 2 April 1841, Clément Ader gained fame for his expertise in electronics and work in aeronautics. An electrical engineer who prospered in the emerging telephone industry, Ader became interested in the problem of mechanical flight. Throughout his search for a solution to heavier-than-air flight, he pursued an unconventional design format despite advances made in aviation prior to his investigations. In spite of his uncanny approaches, Ader is credited with achieving the first unassisted takeoff in a powered, heavier-than-air machine in 1890.

Early work. As with many pioneer investigators, Ader studied the actions and characteristics of flying creatures. He focused primarily on eagles, bats, and vultures.

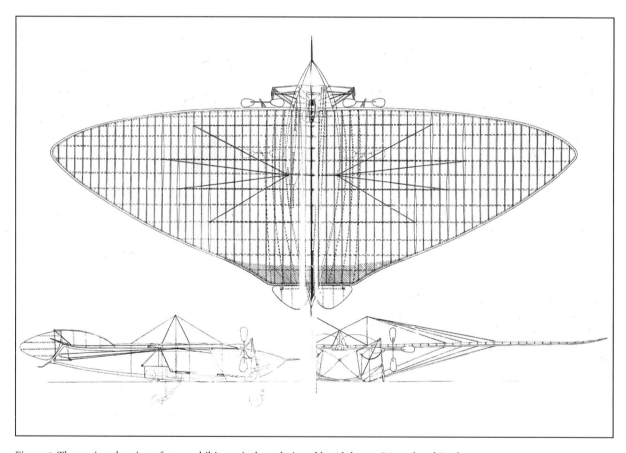

Fig. 2.16. Three-view drawing of an amphibious airplane designed by Alphonse Pénaud and Paul Gauchot. The drawing is described as "L'Aeroplane Amphibie de Pénaud et Gauchot, d'apres les Dessins du Brevet de 1876" (after the 1876 patent drawings). By permission of the National Air and Space Museum, Smithsonian Institution, ©1999 Smithsonian Institution.

Fig. 2.17. Engraving showing Clément Ader's Éole in flight. Courtesy of the USAF Museum.

This experience led him to build a large artificial bird in 1872–73 that was able to lift a person when strong winds were present.

Éole. His next major experiment involved the construction of a full-scale machine. This project began in 1882 and was completed by 1890. From this work emerged his famous Éole (god of the winds). This machine received Patent 205,155 in August 1890. The Éole is credited with performing the first takeoff solely under its own power (see fig. 2.17).

In contrast to Du Temple's and Mozhaiski's machines, which became airborne following assisted takeoff procedures, the Éole lifted from the surface and traveled some 50 meters (164 feet) through the air on 9 October 1890. This achievement, however, is viewed not as a controlled flight but as a powered hop because the machine was incapable of sustaining or controlling itself in the air.

Avion III. The next significant endeavor by Ader involved the manufacture of an airplane for the French Ministry of War. Government funding for the project exceeded 650,000 francs. From 1892 to 1897, Ader undertook this challenge. Building on the success of the Éole, he began, but abandoned, construction of his second airplane. His third machine, Avion III, was completed in 1897 (see fig. 2.18).

Testing of the Avion III occurred on 12 and 14 October 1897 before official witnesses appointed by the French government. During the first day of testing, Ader developed a feel for the machine. He taxied the Avion III around a circular runway specially constructed at Satory, near Versailles. Gauging the depth of the marks

Fig. 2.18. Ader's Avion III. By permission of the National Air and Space Museum, Smithsonian Institution, ©1999 Smithsonian Institution.

made by the wheels in the soil, the observers noted that when the taxi speed of the machine was increased, the wheel marks became less pronounced. Thus it was concluded that the wings must have supported a portion of the Avion III's weight. This revelation was encouraging, as only a third of the available power was used during this test.

On the second day of testing, disaster struck. As revealed in an official account written after the 14 October trial,[16] the Avion III experienced a steering problem while on the ground. The difficulty was due to the lifting of the tail wheel from the runway. During its ground run, the machine suddenly left the track and crashed alongside the runway. It sustained a fair amount of damage to its propellers, left landing gear, and left wingtip. Ader and the observers attributed the accident to wind gusts and the inability to control the machine on the ground after its steerable tail wheel lost contact with the surface. Although the Avion III may have lifted off the surface before crashing, this incident did not constitute a flight of any kind. Following the accident, the project was discontinued.

This episode did not end with the cancellation of the project. Reacting to the successful flights by Alberto Santos-Dumont in 1906, Ader publicly claimed he had flown the Avion III for a distance of 300 meters (984 feet) on 14 October 1897. This assertion falsely altered aviation history for a number of years, as many believed the Avion III actually flew. In time, aviation historians revealed the truth about the 1897 tests of the Avion III.

Otto Lilienthal

An individual who made important contributions to the fledgling science of aeronautics was Otto Lilienthal. Born in 1848 near Anklam, Germany, Lilienthal developed an interest in aviation during his youth. Along with his younger brother, Gustav, Otto studied bird flight and aspired to invent flying machines. By the time he was fourteen, Otto and his brother had fashioned a pair of wings measuring 2 meters (6.56 feet) by 1 meter (3.28 feet). After attaching these wings to their arms, the boys attempted to achieve flight by running downhill and flapping their wings. As with other aeronautical experimenters who discovered that the muscular might of one's arm was no match for gravity, the brothers resorted to designing machines using leg power.

Ornithopters. In 1867, Otto and Gustav began experimenting with ornithopters. Their fascination for wing-flapping machines continued throughout their lives. In fact, Gustav was working on a large ornithopter at the time of his death in 1933 at age eighty-three.

Their 1867 machine was a composite structure of wood and goose feathers. The design allowed the feathers to open on the upstroke (to reduce drag) and close on the downstroke. To test the machine, the brothers suspended the unit and applied the flapping action. The ornithopter did not perform to their expectations.

The following year, Otto and Gustav built a larger machine. Their testing procedure was somewhat more elaborate. They suspended the machine for its trial and measured lift via a system of pulleys and counterweights, as shown in figure 2.19. Using a similar technique in which the slats opened on the upstroke and closed on the downstroke, they found that six wings could support approximately half the combined weight of the machine and operator when vigorously pumped.

After serving in the Franco-Prussian War, Otto resumed his experiments with ornithopters. He manufactured at least three wing-flapping models. Two were spring-operated units, and a compound steam engine

Fig. 2.19. Otto Lilienthal's measurement of lift. By permission of the National Air and Space Museum, Smithsonian Institution, ©1999 Smithsonian Institution.

powered the third. One of the spring-powered models achieved some degree of flight.

Gliders. After establishing himself as a distinguished engineer, Otto Lilienthal resumed his study of aeronautics. He initiated an in-depth study of aerodynamics and bird flight, which he published in a book, *Der Vogelflug als Grundlage der Fliegekunst* (Bird flight as the basis of aviation) in 1889.

Lilienthal's book was considered a crucial reference source filled with valuable engineering data. It included data concerning wing shape and sizes, lift production, air pressure, and other important aerodynamic elements. It was translated into many languages and proved beneficial to other pioneer experimenters. The Wrights, however, concluded that the tables were not entirely accurate and decided to conduct their own investigations (see chap. 3).

Lilienthal decided to test his theories through gliding experiments. From 1889 through 1896, he designed and built sixteen model gliders and two ornithopters. His first glider, the Model Möwe, had a wingspan of 11 meters (36 feet) and no tail. The second model had a wingspan of 10 meters (32.8 feet) and a horizontal tail. Neither were considered successful machines.

The third glider, manufactured in 1891, was his first successful flying machine. This craft had a wingspan of 7.5 meters (24.6 feet) and a horizontal and vertical tail.

The next seven machines had various wing sizes, tail configurations, and other novel features such as wings that could be folded for easy storage.

The eleventh glider, Normal Segelapparat, became his standard machine. It was one of the earliest production model aircraft. With eight copies produced and distributed around the world, this machine made its appearance in many countries outside Germany. In the United States, William Randolph Hearst, a newspaper magnate from New York City, purchased one of these machines in 1896. On a gloomier note, the Normal Segelapparat was the machine involved in the 9 August 1896 crash that claimed Lilienthal's life. Before dying the following day in a Berlin clinic, he remarked, "Sacrifices must be made."[17]

In 1895, Lilienthal built four gliders. One used an auxiliary system of flight controls involving leading edge ailerons and vertical surfaces near the wingtips. It was reported that Lilienthal had little success with his experiments involving movable flight controls.[18] The other three machines were biplane gliders. Lilienthal recognized the value of a multiplane design for increasing wing surface area while minimizing wingspan.

After achieving success with gliders, Lilienthal's desire to create an ornithopter resurfaced. He constructed two such machines between 1893 and 1896. The first ornithopter was closely related to his gliders with the exception that a carbonic acid engine powered a series of

Fig. 2.20. Lilienthal's ornithopter was designed to use a compressed carbonic acid motor. The craft was tested in flight without its engine. When tested with the engine, the wings (at least on one occasion) failed. By permission of the National Air and Space Museum, Smithsonian Institution, ©1999 Smithsonian Institution.

flappers at the wingtips (see fig. 2.20). Lilienthal opted to experiment with this type of power plant, as it had marked advantages over conventional steam engines. It did not require a firebox, boiler, or steam chest. Instead, it used a cylinder with control valves and a small reservoir for liquid acid.[19] This power plant functioned in a manner similar to a steam engine without the aforementioned components. There were a number of inherent difficulties with this design. As the carbon dioxide (CO_2) flowed through the system, it experienced a rapid expansion. This sometimes resulted in acidic clumps. In addition, ice often formed in the valves and plumbing.[20] Lilienthal was pleased with the power output of the engine. He was disappointed, however, when the wings of his machine failed during an experimental run.[21] The second model was a large wing flapper completed in 1896, which Lilienthal did not have a chance to test. His final machine was a glider.

The soundness of Lilienthal's theories and designs were proven through some two thousand flights. As these machines were unpowered, Lilienthal launched his glider from specially built hills and elevated structures (see fig. 2.21).

Aside from the aeronautical data emerging from these trials, the flights served to heighten the level of airmindedness. Many people had considered mechanical flight to be nothing more than a fantasy. Lilienthal's aerial accomplishments also influenced scores of inventors. His progress was reported in newspapers throughout the world, which often printed photographs of the inventor flying one of his machines.

A major weakness of Lilienthal's work was in the area of flight control. Except for a few isolated experiments with movable control surfaces, Lilienthal manipulated the flight path of his gliders by shifting body weight. This method required him to suspend the lower torso of his body beneath the wing(s) of the glider. He would then shift his body and legs in the desired direction. As an example, study the position of Lilienthal's legs in figure 2.22. Despite certain limitations associated with this form of flight control, Lilienthal was able to advance the science of aviation and the art of flying.

Fig. 2.21. Lilienthal's conical hill. By permission of the National Air and Space Museum, Smithsonian Institution, ©1999 Smithsonian Institution.

Fig. 2.22. Otto Lilienthal aloft in glider. By permission of the National Air and Space Museum, Smithsonian Institution, ©1999 Smithsonian Institution.

Fig. 2.23. View of the modified Bat, a glider designed by Percy Sinclair Pilcher. By permission of the National Air and Space Museum, Smithsonian Institution, ©1999 Smithsonian Institution.

Percy Sinclair Pilcher

An individual inspired by the achievements of Lilienthal was Percy Sinclair Pilcher (1867–99). Pilcher's sister, Ella, was his supporter and companion throughout his aeronautical experiments. She revealed that the idea of flight had fascinated him since boyhood. Later in life, the allure of flight led Pilcher to a series of investigations that paralleled the gliding work of Lilienthal. Upon completing his course of studies at the Naval College, Pilcher served on a variety of ships. After leaving the navy in 1887, he became an apprentice in an engineering department at a shipbuilding yard and worked as a drafter. He experienced several career changes before becoming an assistant lecturer of naval architecture and marine engineering at Glasgow University in 1891. Following Pilcher's departure from the university in the spring of 1896, he worked for Hiram Maxim. He later joined forces with Walter Wilson to form Wilson and Pilcher Limited in 1897. This firm specialized in the design, manufacture, repair, and modification of engines. This line of work allowed Pilcher to pursue the production of powerful, lightweight engines for aeronautical purposes.

Bat. While working at the university, Pilcher's passive interest in aviation was rekindled by reports of the flights by Lilienthal. Inspired by Lilienthal's success, Pilcher constructed his own machine, the Bat, in 1895. As shown in figure 2.23, the Bat was a monoplane design with a pronounced dihedral angle and vertical fin. Originally there was no horizontal tail. Before flying the Bat, Pilcher made arrangements to visit Lilienthal in Germany in April 1895 and observe his flights. This experience paid off, as Lilienthal offered sound advice to the aspiring aviator.

Upon returning from Germany, Pilcher attempted to fly the Bat. Unwilling to initially heed the warning from Lilienthal regarding the need for a horizontal tail surface, Pilcher made a number of failed attempts at flight.

Fig. 2.24. Testing the modified Bat. By permission of the National Air and Space Museum, Smithsonian Institution, ©1999 Smithsonian Institution.

A modified version of the Bat, which included a horizontal tail, proved successful. After a short period of abandonment, the Bat was reconfigured with wings having a more moderate degree of dihedral (fig. 2.24).

Beetle. The second machine Pilcher manufactured during the summer of 1895 was the Beetle. It was designed to be a powered craft. Pilcher intended to first fly the machine as a glider and later add an engine and other components necessary for powered flight.

The Beetle was a monoplane having no perceptible dihedral. Its beefy structure was made to withstand the additional loads that an engine and propeller system would impose. The tail included both vertical and horizontal members. Test flights of the Beetle as a glider were a disappointment. After retiring this aircraft, Pilcher resumed his experiments with the modified Bat.

Gull. Pilcher manufactured a third glider, the Gull, during the fall of 1895. As with the Beetle, Pilcher intended to add a power plant and propeller system to the Gull after he became proficient at flying it as a glider. It is interesting that Pilcher considered using airscrews as opposed to following Lilienthal's ornithopter approach. One possible suggestion that may explain Pilcher's choice of propulsion was his experience with maritime vessels. Certainly marine propellers of his time were vastly superior to oars. Even if the latter were powered,

they would still be inferior to a well-designed marine propeller. It is likely he recognized the advantages offer by propellers over flapping devices.

The Gull was a large machine with 300 square feet of wing area. This was double the area of the Bat and much larger than the 170-square-foot Beetle. His intentions regarding the type of power plant wavered. He indicated that a carbonic-acid engine was to be used, but he later specified a petrol (gasoline) engine. It appears that Pilcher lost interest in pursuing powered versions of the Gull after it crashed on several occasions when flown as a glider.

Hawk. Pilcher's fourth design, known as the Hawk, was to be a powered machine (fig. 2.25). As with the Beetle and Gull, Pilcher intended to build and test the machine as a glider and then convert it to a powered aircraft. A proposed motorized version of this craft was patented. The Hawk was his most successful model, even though a structural failure of the tail on 30 September resulted in a crash that killed Pilcher on 2 October 1899.

The Hawk, as described by Jarrett, was a monoplane with 170 square feet of surface area. For some unknown reason, Pilcher originally decided to omit the vertical stabilizer and use only a horizontal tail. Later versions of the Hawk included both vertical and horizontal tail surfaces. The tail unit was hinged near the trailing edge of the main wing. This feature prevented damage to the tail

Fig. 2.25. Pilcher's Hawk in flight. His glider is constructed of soft, lightweight muslin (nainsook) stretched over a wooden frame and braced with piano wire; the design includes a rudder, ca. 1896, probably at Cardross, Dumbartonshire, England. By permission of the National Air and Space Museum, Smithsonian Institution, ©1999 Smithsonian Institution.

during landings and other ground-related incidents. The Hawk was equipped with a shock-absorbing wheeled undercarriage. Pilcher may have been thinking ahead to the day when he would add a power plant and propeller(s) to the machine. The weight of a powered Hawk would certainly limit the ability of the operator to support it safely during takeoff and landing. In addition, the wheels facilitated ground handling.

The Hawk became the basis for Patent 9,144 granted 6 March 1897. Pilcher applied for his patent on "Improvements in Flying and Soaring Machines" on 30 April 1896.[22] In the narrative of this document, he continued to demonstrate his indecision concerning a choice of motive force. Pilcher stated that the machine had an engine fueled by oil, spirits, or some other means. He was also indecisive about the propeller configuration, as he allowed for either one or two screws.

Multiplane machines. The next two designs demonstrated a reversal of Pilcher's initial opinion concerning multiwing aircraft. After his second visit with Lilienthal in 1896, Pilcher indicated he was not in favor of multiplane designs that placed one wing considerably above the operator. Although he flew one of Lilienthal's biplane gliders during this visit, Pilcher was not convinced of the soundness of a multiplane design. However, his interactions with Chanute, and perhaps Hargrave,[23] persuaded him to reverse his opinion and build a triplane. He also contemplated a quadruplane.

Pilcher had just completed, or nearly finished, the triplane before his death in 1899. His quadruplane was basically the triplane with an additional wing.

One question that remains unanswered concerning the work of Pilcher is whether he would have succeeded in making a powered aircraft. Although there were a number of issues to be resolved in the transition from a glider to a powered machine, we have to consider the talent shown by Pilcher. His intention to employ propellers rather than experimenting with powered ornithopters placed him ahead of his mentor Lilienthal. His untimely death in 1899 has left us wondering whether he would have prevailed where others failed.

Hiram Maxim

A gifted inventor, Sir Hiram Maxim (1840–1916) was an expatriate American who resettled in England (see fig. 2.26). Known primarily as a maker of machine guns,

Fig. 2.26. Sir Hiram Maxim. *Scientific American,* 2 October 1909.

Maxim applied his mechanical talents to the problem of heavier-than-air flight through a systematic investigation of aeronautics. Beginning with models and experiments using a wind tunnel and a large whirling arm, Maxim studied numerous design aspects of powered flight. His whirling arm investigations laid the foundation for a series of experiments involving an enormous test machine.[24]

1894 machine. Although large and ungainly, the 7,000-pound machine (see fig. 2.27) created by Maxim was in reality a test bed for aeronautical research. It was designed to run safely along a special track (as opposed to free flight). Maxim used it to test power plant and propeller performance, lift production, and control. His guide track provided a smooth ground path and incorporated a specially devised safety railing to prevent the machine from gaining much altitude.

Fig. 2.27. Maxim's flying machine. By permission of the National Air and Space Museum, Smithsonian Institution, ©1999 Smithsonian Institution.

Thrust research was perhaps the least complicated test performed. To measure thrust, Maxim simply attached the machine to a scale, stoked the boiler, pressurized the steam engines, and motored the two large pusher propellers. Keeping in proportion with the rest of the machine, these propellers measured 17 feet 10 inches in diameter. This testing technique enabled Maxim to evaluate modifications made to the engines and propellers.

Maxim employed a creative technique for measuring the quantity of lift produced by his enormous wing. He devised special loadmeters, called dynagraphs, that measured the weight of the machine applied to its front and rear wheels. This clever approach for determining lift worked by comparing the amount of weight remaining on the wheels during its test run with the total weight of the craft. The dynagraphs recorded the weight applied to their respective wheel on paper drums that made one revolution for each 1,800 feet of travel along the track. One drum was specially equipped to record the speed of the craft. This method of measuring lift helped Maxim determine lift production at various speeds and angles of attack. He was able to ascertain that

his 7,000-pound craft could become airborne. This fact was verified when the machine flew off its track and crashed.

Maxim's concept of flight control was as cumbersome as the machine itself. He intended to use differential thrust for directional control.[25] The addition of a steerable rudder was an option to be employed if varying thrust between propellers proved ineffective. There was no provision for roll control. Instead, Maxim decided to use auxiliary surfaces with considerable dihedral to ensure stability. This technique was commonly employed before the Wrights developed the three-axis control network. Pitch control was accomplished by movable control surfaces. Initial plans called for using only a rear elevator. A forward control surface was to be added if the aft control proved ineffective.

Fearing the pilot would be unable to safely control the aircraft during flight, Maxim devised a mechanism to automatically maintain pitch. The proposed system, termed Gyrostat, used a gyroscope to sense changes in pitch. It was to be connected to the elevators and function in a manner similar to an autopilot in terms of pitch control. Although never fully developed, this technique for maintaining an aircraft's attitude in relation to the horizon demonstrates the inventiveness of Maxim.

Maxim was unable to complete his investigation concerning the problem of control. His machine was severely damaged in 1894 when it lifted from the guide track and became entangled with the safety railing. Further investigations were canceled due to the extensive damage to the machine and the fact Maxim had already spent £20,000 on this project.

Other work by Maxim. Hiram Maxim wrote a number of articles addressing his experiences in aviation. After the crash of his large machine in 1894, he curiously abandoned the study of aviation. In 1908, he published a book, *Artificial and Natural Flight,* in which he alleged that successful airplanes that arose following his work from 1891 to 1894 were built along the lines of his large machine.

In 1910, Maxim designed and manufactured a biplane. This machine had a front and rear elevator, wing warping, and three pusher propellers. Despite the experience of this talented inventor and aeronautical knowledge that existed at the time, he was unable to coax the machine into the air.

Samuel Pierpont Langley

Born 22 August 1834, Samuel Pierpont Langley received his elementary and secondary education in Boston. Following graduation from Boston High School in 1851, Samuel moved to Chicago and St. Louis, where he worked as a civil engineer and architectural drafter.

In 1864, he returned to Boston and pursued his interest in astronomy. Langley spent a year abroad visiting observatories where he learned all he could about the latest developments in astronomy. Upon his return home in 1865, Langley was hired as an assistant at the Harvard Observatory. He later accepted a position as an assistant professor at the U.S. Naval Academy, where he became director of the observatory. In 1866, Langley joined the staff at Western University in Pennsylvania as a professor of physics and director of the Allegheny Observatory. He remained at that institution for two decades.

While at the Allegheny Observatory, Langley established himself as a top-notch scientist. His sterling reputation as an observer and experimenter earned him a preeminent standing in the scientific community. He received many honorary degrees and medals. In November 1887, Langley became the third secretary of the Smithsonian Institution, where he conducted experiments involving aircraft known as "aerodromes."

Whirling table. As with many other aeronautical pioneers, Langley's interest in aviation dated back to his childhood. He recalled that as a lad he would gaze at hawks with amazement as they effortlessly sustained flight on outstretched wings without making a single flap. This interest was rekindled by Israel Lancaster's 1886 presentation to the American Association for the Advancement of Science at Buffalo, New York. The topic of this inspiring presentation pertained to soaring birds and human flight.

In an attempt to understand why the problem of mechanical flight had not been solved, Langley wondered whether the approaches taken to uncover its secret were misguided. He was of the opinion that instead of trying to unravel the mystery of flight by building flying machines based on some unfounded theory, the laws of nature controlling the principles of flight should first be discovered. Once these principles were known, the design of a flying machine could be tailored to fulfill nature's requirements. Based on this conviction, Langley began his study of aviation through aerodynamic research.

Up to this point, there existed a common belief that a great deal of power was required to advance objects through the air. Further to compound the problem, the relationship between the speed of an object traveling through the air and its power requirement was that the amount of power increased significantly as speed increased. Langley did not accept this theoretical power-speed relationship because he remembered the ease with which hawks soared.

He explored the relationship between speed and power through the use of a whirling table (what Cayley, Lilienthal, and Maxim called a whirling arm). Langley's whirling table approach was not unique, but his machine, like Maxim's, was unusually large. This apparatus had a 30-foot boom. It was powered by a steam engine. Langley's whirling table was capable of reaching speeds of 70 mph. This seems slow by today's standards, but it was more than adequate for the flying machines of the late nineteenth century.

Following three years of research with the whirling table, Langley formed a conclusion that countered the relationship between speed and power previously held to be true. For some reason, he decided that it took less power to make an object travel faster through the air. This finding became the basis for "Langley's Law." As expected, other investigators discredited this law.

Up to this point, Langley gathered a vast quantity of aerodynamic data crucial to the design of a flying machine. He continued his study of mechanical flight using a series of models.

Aerodrome models. Langley began his experiments with models where Alphonse Pénaud had left off. Impressed by what the Frenchman was able to accomplish before his death in 1880, Langley built between thirty and forty rubber band–powered models. Note in figure 2.28 the similarities between No. 11 (upper left corner) and Pénaud's Planophore, presented in figure 2.15. Although Langley could get many of his models to fly, he was unable to match Pénaud's achievements.

The next series of models, begun in 1891, were powered by steam and carbonic-acid engines. Langley called these models "aërodromes." As evident from his 1891 article, "The Possibility of Mechanical Flight," he mistakenly thought this name meant "air-runner." Actually, the term *aerodrome* signifies a location where machines fly, not the actual flying machine. In any event, Langley and

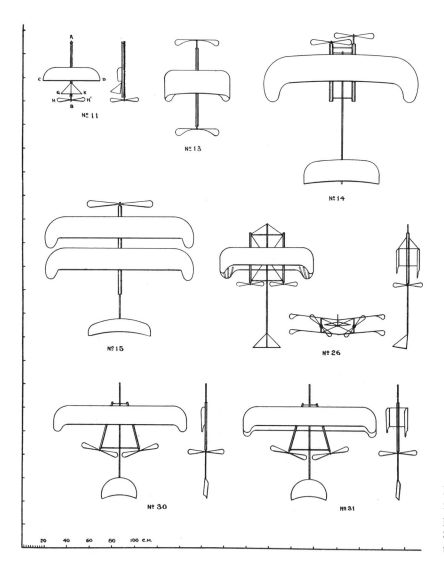

Fig. 2.28. Samuel Pierpont Langley's rubber band–powered models. By permission of the National Air and Space Museum, Smithsonian Institution, ©1999 Smithsonian Institution.

Fig. 2.29. Langley aerodrome no. 5 in flight, 6 May 1896. By permission of the National Air and Space Museum, Smithsonian Institution, ©1999 Smithsonian Institution.

his crew used this name for a series of large-scale models and full-scale machines.

Langley constructed his first steam-powered aerodrome, designated No. 0, in November 1891. This proved to be a formidable challenge because no one on his crew was exactly sure how to construct an aircraft. Aside from applying common sense in making the craft strong, lightweight, and powerful, they knew little else. After completing No. 0, Langley abandoned it without a test flight. The same fate befell the second and third aerodromes. Both No. 1 and No. 2 were underpowered. Aerodrome No. 2 was fitted with a carbonic-acid engine. No. 3 was an improved version of the previous models but also underpowered.

Aerodrome No. 4 was flight tested. To minimize breakage of these flimsy models, Langley opted to launch them over water. His hope was that in case of failure, serious damage might be averted by having the machine enter the water as opposed to crashing on dry land. On 8 January 1894, this concept was tested. No. 4 was set into operation and released above the Potomac

River. It instantly fell into the water. The lack of airspeed at the point of release emphasized the need for providing a running start for the aerodromes. This need was met via a catapult arrangement set atop a houseboat.

By 7 October 1894, Langley and his team were prepared to test the rebuilt and modified No. 4 and a new aerodrome, No. 5. No. 4 experienced a distortion of its wing during takeoff and crashed into the water. No. 5 assumed a nose-up attitude after launch and stalled shortly thereafter. It too suffered from an undesirable twisting of the wing. Although No. 5 did not perform well, the crew was encouraged.

They spent the winter of 1894 and the spring of 1895 mending the perceived weaknesses of No. 4 and No. 5. No. 4 was modified so extensively that it was redesignated No. 6. Trials resumed on 9 May 1895, when No. 5 managed to fly for some 6 seconds.

After nearly a year of work and modifications, the aerodromes were again ready for flight testing on 6 May 1896. On this historic day, No. 6 was damaged during launch. However, No. 5 stunned those present with an outstanding flight of about 1.5 minutes in which it covered an estimated half mile. The launch was photographed by Alexander Graham Bell (fig. 2.29). In its second flight, No. 5 repeated its earlier performance. This day marked the first time in history that a heavier-than-air flying machine remained aloft for so long and flew so far.

Aerodrome No. 6 was tested again on 27–28 November 1896. Although the machine had some success the first day, a flight on 28 November was truly remarkable. This time No. 6 remained airborne for nearly three-quarters of a mile. Unlike the circling flight path taken by No. 5, this machine flew a gentle 270 degree curve. The performance of aerodrome No. 6 added credence to the methods employed by Langley in his quest for mechanical flight. With the success of No. 5 and No. 6, there was little doubt he had achieved his objective in creating a machine capable of mechanical flight.[26]

Great Aerodrome project. Having proven to the world that aerial transportation was within reach, the aging Langley was content with his achievements. He had advanced the science of aviation to this point. It would be up to others to build machines capable of human flight.

Langley's resignation from aeronautics was short-lived. Following the successful flights of No. 5 and No. 6, the military became acutely interested in flying machines as implements of war. This heightened interest may have been precipitated by the impending Spanish-American War.

After a period of deliberations, the U.S. Army Board of Ordnance and Fortification granted Langley $50,000 for the construction of an aerodrome capable of carrying a pilot. The money was doled out in two installments. Half was issued by the end of 1898 with the balance paid the following year.

An interesting set of conditions was stipulated by Langley concerning the acceptance of this project. First, he demanded absolute control over all aspects of this undertaking. Perhaps fearful that Army involvement might disrupt his work, Langley maintained he needed assurance that his pursuit of producing a piloted craft would not be impaired by others. Next, he wanted complete control over financial matters. Aware of the complications associated with government accounts, Langley asserted he needed free rein in terms of purchasing and other financial dealings involved with this venture. Fi-

nally, Langley insisted on working in complete secrecy. This stipulation was more than likely his desire to avoid the press and other media people. To Langley's consternation, news of this secret project somehow leaked to the press and was divulged in the *Washington Post* before work on the Great Aerodrome even started.

Langley employed a team of workers to help him with this project. He was able to retain experienced members from his earlier crew. However, he wanted to add an assistant to the group. He hired Charles Manly, a student near graduation from Cornell's Sibley School of Mechanical Engineering. Manly not only proved his mechanical aptitude in solving complex problems but also served as test pilot.

As with many experimenters who began their investigations using models, Langley considered the best approach for creating a piloted airplane was to simply scale up one of his successful models. After all, if a design worked on a large aerodrome model, it should function as a full-scale machine. The major differences between the two entailed the inclusion of a cabin for the operator and a control system to provide a means for steering the craft. The operator's compartment was a simple matter to design, but the control system was a new obstacle Langley would have to surmount.

After contemplating a number of complex designs, including the use of gyroscopes and pendulums for stability, he developed a control system. For lateral stability, he used a considerable amount of wing dihedral. He controlled pitch by altering the position of the cruciform tail. He used a separate rudder to control yaw. Aside from managing the engine, the operator had two control wheels to manipulate, one for pitch and the other for yaw.

Langley probably thought that this machine would fly inherently straight and level as his models were able to do. As a consequence, pitch and directional controls were more for making fine adjustments during flight. The control network incorporated in the Great Aerodrome can be likened to a modern-day trim system used on airplanes.

Another design element that had to be considered was the need for an improved power source. Unlike his aerodrome models, which had only a couple minutes of fuel and water, a piloted machine would have to lift the weight of its occupant(s) and carry a substantial quantity of fuel to have a useful range. To meet these additional requirements, Langley opted to use a powerful internal combustion power plant. He sought an engine manufacturer to supply his needs and finally contracted with the Balzer Company in New York to deliver a 100-pound, 12-horsepower gasoline engine.

In the end, Balzer was unable to deliver the proposed engine. After long delays, cost overruns, and a search for an alternate engine, Balzer was instructed to deliver the unfinished engine to Langley. At this point, Manly became involved in modifying the power plant for use in the Great Aerodrome. The final product surpassed original expectations as the Balzer-Manly engine produced 52.4 horsepower at a total weight of 207.5 pounds.

With the basic design of the Great Aerodrome established, a system of controls decided upon, and a suitable power plant in the works, Langley and his crew proceeded with the project. During the construction process, Langley adopted a technique for lightening wooden members employed by Clément Ader. This procedure involved the removal of "unnecessary material" by routing and hollowing. It was used primarily during the construction of the wings.[27] One must won-der whether overuse of this technique compromised the structural integrity of the wings.

A series of tests were undertaken during the manufacturing process along with the construction of a larger catapult system. During the course of the project, aerodrome models No. 5 and No. 6 were modified and flown as test machines along with an unpowered eighth-scale model of the Great Aerodrome. A quarter-scale version of the Great Aerodrome, as shown in figure 2.30, was also manufactured and tested. This machine was powered by a 1.5-horsepower Balzer engine. Its primary purpose was to test the proposed design on a craft more closely resembling the full-scale aerodrome. The quarter-scale model flew four times on 19 June 1901. These flights were moderately successful hops between 100 and 350 feet. The inability of the machine to remain aloft was power plant related.

The quarter-scale machine was flown again on August 8, 1903, just before the attempted flights of the Great Aerodrome. Manly was not pleased with the model, however, as it flew for just 27 seconds and 1,000 feet. This performance did not match the flights of aerodromes

Fig. 2.30. Quarter-scale aerodrome in flight. By permission of the National Air and Space Museum, Smithsonian Institution, ©1999 Smithsonian Institution.

Fig. 2.31. View showing Langley's Great Aerodrome in place on catapult on houseboat. The photograph was taken prior to the flight trial on 7 October 1903. By permission of the National Air and Space Museum, Smithsonian Institution, ©1999 Smithsonian Institution.

No. 5 and No. 6 in 1896. On an encouraging note, the quarter-scale model did demonstrate a fair amount of stability and balance. No additional test flights were conducted after the decision was made to try the full-scale machine.

First flight attempt. After years of preparation and translating theory into form, the Great Aerodrome was ready for its attempt at flight on 7 October 1903. This was to be no ordinary flight attempt. The Great Aerodrome was making its bid to become the world's first airplane. Manly, who had no prior experience in controlling a machine in the air, was to have the distinction of becoming the first person to fly an airplane if everything went according to plans. Such an accomplishment would forever be a monumental event in the annals of history.

Aside from the possible kudos and sweet smell of success, there was a great deal at stake. Langley had spent $50,000 of the government's money, not to mention many thousands more from the Smithsonian. Failure of the project would have serious repercussions. It must be remembered that despite the previous success of the aerodrome models, public opinion concerning human flight was far from positive. A botched attempt would only reinforce the belief that if the Creator had intended for us to fly, we would have been born with wings.

Regardless of the pluses and minuses of success and failure, the decisive moment had arrived. Prepared for its first launch, as pictured in figure 2.31, the Great Aerodrome was no longer concealed. It was ready to go public. With its engine operating at full speed, Manly gave the order to release the machine. The Great Aerodrome

Fig. 2.32. The aerodrome diving toward the Potomac. By permission of the National Air and Space Museum, Smithsonian Institution, ©1999 Smithsonian Institution.

sped along its track atop the houseboat and plunged into the Potomac. The attempt was a complete failure. The photo presented in figure 2.32 was taken as the machine departed the launching track. Note the distortion to the forward set of wings.

Public criticism resulted. One newspaper reported, "When it [the Great Aerodrome] reached the end of the support car [catapult mechanism] it simply slid into the water like a handful of mortar."[28] This was truly a gloomy day for Langley and his crew.

The Great Aerodrome was recovered from the river and closely inspected. Langley concluded that the catapult mechanism had fouled the launch. The machine was repaired, and a second attempt was scheduled.

Final flight attempt. On 8 December 1903, the Great Aerodrome made another bid to become the first airplane. Again with Manly at the controls, the signal was given to launch the machine.

The Great Aerodrome traveled down its track and into the air. This time the nose pitched straight up, and the Great Aerodrome slid into the icy Potomac. As evident in figure 2.33, the rear wings of the aircraft crumpled as "the after part [tail] of the ship [Great Aerodrome] fell upon the deck of the houseboat."[29] Manly went down with the disintegrating Great Aerodrome but emerged unharmed.

Following 8 December 1903. As might be predicted, the barrage of public condemnation from the press and political figures following the second failed attempt of the Great Aerodrome was ruthless. Langley's reputation was ruined. His previous victories were forgotten. The courage he demonstrated in undertaking such a formidable task was never considered. He died in 1906, dejected and scorned.

Remains of the Great Aerodrome were stored at the Smithsonian. It was reassembled in 1914 by Glenn Curtiss and others and flown after a series of modifications. The resurrected Great Aerodrome was used in a conspiracy to discredit the accomplishments of the Wrights (see chap. 4).

Fig. 2.33. The second failed flight attempt of the Great Aerodrome. Note the distorted right forward wing, crumpled rear wings, and missing tail. By permission of the National Air and Space Museum, Smithsonian Institution, ©1999 Smithsonian Institution.

Octave Chanute

One of the leading figures to emerge during this period of aeronautics was Octave Chanute. Born in 1832 in Paris, he migrated to the United States with his father, Joseph Chanut, at the age of six. Living with his father in New Orleans, Octave grew up in an unusually restrictive environment. He was educated at home and not allowed to mix with other children. In 1844, Octave and his father moved to New York, where he entered school. After settling in New York, Octave added the letter *e* to his surname Chanut to extract a more correct pronunciation by his American schoolmates. This discouraged them from nicknaming him "naked cat" as translated from the French *chat nu*.[30]

In 1849, Octave began his railroad career. Although no positions were available at the time, he applied with the Hudson River Railroad volunteering to work for free. This spunky attitude opened the door to his distinguished career as a civil engineer in the emerging railroad industry. Following his retirement, Chanute moved to Chicago, where he established a wood preservative business for telegraph poles, railroad ties, and telephone poles.

Fig. 2.34. Octave Chanute's glider. By permission of the National Air and Space Museum, Smithsonian Institution, ©1999 Smithsonian Institution.

Scholarly and advisory work. The study of aeronautics was another activity taken up by Chanute following his retirement. His involvement in aviation was instrumental on two fronts. First, he realized one reason advances in aviation were progressing at a snail's pace was that investigators were unable to benefit from the work of others. There existed no formal lines of communications between those conducting experiments. In an attempt to shed some light on the progress reached by investigators, Chanute gathered and published an extensive summary of the work performed in the realm of mechanical flight. Second, he became involved in designing, constructing, and testing a variety of gliders (see fig. 2.34).

By amassing and documenting data regarding accomplishments in aeronautics, Chanute emerged as a premier aviation scholar and adviser. His extensive studies led to the 1894 publication of *Progress in Flying Machines*. This book was a compilation of articles written by Chanute for *The American Engineer and Railroad Journal* beginning in 1891. There is little question this book heavily influenced the work of others, including the Wrights.

Chanute's association with the Wrights was not limited to this single book. His direct correspondence with the brothers beginning in 1900 involved several hundred letters over ten years. He also visited the Wrights occasionally and served as their sounding board.

Beyond his writings, Chanute became involved in promoting aviation by bringing together scientists, engineers, and enthusiasts. He was a principal organizer of aviation seminars held during meetings of the American Association for the Advancement of Science. One such gathering took place at Buffalo, New York, in 1886, and another was held at Toronto in 1889. Samuel Langley claimed that Israel Lancaster's 1886 presentation on soaring birds revived an idle interest he had in flight. A third major aeronautical symposium, the International Conference on Aerial Navigation, was held during the 1893 World's Columbian Exposition in Chicago. In addition to organizing professional meetings, Chanute made a number of influential presentations to members of the aeronautical community.

Not only did Chanute encourage the pursuit of mechanical flight through these scholarly activities but he also sponsored experiments undertaken by others in the field. One man who received support from Chanute was Louis Mouillard. After the latter had fallen on hard times, Chanute gave him 2,500 francs to build a glider. Unfortunately, this glider would not fly.

Gliding experiments. Having perhaps the most comprehensive database of aeronautical information, Chanute initiated a series of gliding experiments. He followed the approach taken by Lilienthal and others who felt the best way to develop a powered machine was to first perfect a glider, then add a system of propulsion. However, the aging Chanute, who was sixty-four by the time of his 1896 glider trials, sought the involvement of younger men in this endeavor. He was assisted in 1896 by Augustus Herring, William Avery, and William Paul Butusov.

The first series of tests were conducted on two gliders. One was patterned after a Lilienthal machine, and the other was an original Chanute design. The Lilienthal, a standard monoplane replica built by Herring, was flown with some success. By contrast, Chanute's creation was somewhat unique. It had twelve wings arranged in six pairs. These pairs of wings were superposed. This machine, which became affectionately known as the "Katydid," had an unusual design that allowed its wings to pivot. Chanute employed the pivoting feature of the wings to test his theory involving equilibrium and automatic stability. After failing to fly as expected, the Katydid underwent many reconfigurations. Despite various modifications and Chanute's enthusiasm for this design, the machine was never a huge success. The group departed their campsite near Miller, Indiana, on 4 July.

Before the end of the summer, Chanute and his team set out with three machines for a second series of trials on 20 August 1896. Gliders to be tested at a new site near Dune Park, Indiana, included a completely reworked Katydid, a new triplane, and a craft designed by Butusov called the Albatross.

The most promising results from this second period of testing were from the new triplane glider following its conversion to a biplane. Unlike the Katydid, the wings of the new machine were not allowed to pivot. Instead, they were rigidly braced using a system known as Pratt

Fig. 2.35. Two-surface machine. By permission of the National Air and Space Museum, Smithsonian Institution, ©1999 Smithsonian Institution.

trussing. This technique was later employed by the Wrights in the construction of their machines. The cruciform tail was provided with a measure of automatic stability by virtue of a universal ball joint and elastic mechanism. The *Chicago Tribune* called this device the "Herring Regulator."[31] Following the removal of its lower wing, the two-surface glider (shown in fig. 2.35) performed superbly. It had little trouble generating glides of more than 200 feet. One flight by Herring reportedly covered 359 feet in 14 seconds.

Following the 1896 trials, Chanute continued to conduct experiments in aeronautics. However, subsequent gliding ventures were less successful. In 1901, he employed Edward Huffaker to build a glider from paper tubing. This machine was a flat failure when tested at the Wright brothers' camp at Kitty Hawk. Charles Lamson built an oscillating-wing machine for Chanute in 1902. Seeking to develop a system of automatic stability, the latest machine devised by Chanute was closely related to the Katydid. It had three sets of superposed wings "mounted so that they could rock, or oscillate, about a transverse horizontal axis as the center of pressure moved back and forth."[32] Similar to the Katydid, this machine performed poorly.

In the end, Chanute continued to believe in the need for automatic stability. His persistence in pursuing such a design prevented him from following a more fruitful line of experimentation. Aside from his inflexibility in finding a solution for automatic stability, Octave Chanute merits an enormous amount of credit for his contributions to the study and perpetuation of aeronautics during this era.

Alberto Santos-Dumont

Alberto Santos-Dumont was born on 20 July 1873 to a wealthy Brazilian coffee planter. While growing up in Brazil, young Alberto had visions of flying machines. However, it was not until he moved to Paris at the age of eighteen that he was able to pursue his dreams of flight.

His first adventure in aeronautics involved aerostatics or lighter-than-air flight. Santos-Dumont began with spherical balloons and quickly progressed to dirigibles. He designed, built, and flew a number of airships, but he is best known for his prize-winning flight around the Eiffel Tower on 19 October 1901 in dirigible no. 6. He was subsequently awarded the Deutsch Prize of 100,000 francs for this accomplishment. The magnanimous Brazilian donated half his prize to the poor. The remainder was distributed between his assistant and his crew. The former received 30,000 francs, and the latter shared the balance.

Always in search of a challenge, the adventurous Brazilian undertook the study of heavier-than-air flight. Decidedly influenced by the glider flights conducted by Gabriel Voisin,[33] Santos-Dumont began work on his first airplane, no. 14 bis. The plane was named after dirigible no. 14, which was used during the testing phase of this airplane. No. 14 bis was unveiled during the spring of 1906; its design incorporated the box-kite principle. The wings, which were at rear of the craft, were six box-kite cells set at a high dihedral angle. The plane was initially controlled solely by the forward-mounted cell. It moved up and down for pitch and pivoted left and right to control yaw. A later version of the craft included octagonally shaped ailerons located in each outer wing cell. Originally operated with a 24-horsepower Antoinette engine, no. 14 bis was later equipped with a 50-horsepower Antoinette.

Although an unconventional design, No. 14 bis has the distinction of being the first European heavier-than-air craft to fly. In this capacity, no. 14 bis won two awards: the Archdeacon Prize of 3,000 francs for flying a minimum of 25 meters (82 feet) and the Aéro Club of France Award of 1,500 francs for flying 100 meters (328 feet). The former was won on 23 October while the latter on 12 November 1906. This marginally successful machine was retired following its flights of April 1907.

Santos-Dumont built airplanes of various configurations between 1907 and 1909. These machines were largely unsuccessful except for no. 20, the Demoiselle. No. 20 was the third version of the Demoiselle following no. 19 and no. 19 bis. Santos-Dumont sold copies of this machine through 1910. He also built two additional versions of the Demoiselle, nos. 21 and 22. These machines used different engines and were slightly modified. They were the last models designed by the Brazilian.

Later in life, Santos-Dumont returned to Brazil. Depression got the better of him, and he committed suicide on 23 July 1932. Reflecting on the aeronautical work by Santos-Dumont, his major contributions were in elevating interest, enthusiasm, and confidence in aviation. His celebrated flight around the Eiffel Tower and his noteworthy flights with no. 14 bis were instrumental in heightening the interest and acceptance of aviation around the world.

Aeronautical Advances

By the end of the era defined from Cayley to Santos-Dumont, a solution to the problem of mechanical flight emerged in the form of no. 14 bis. As demonstrated by the limited performance of this machine, the road to success was not easy. Before anyone could break the bonds of gravity with a heavier-than-air flying machine, the requisite knowledge and technology had to be developed and properly implemented.

Aerodynamics

The quest for human flight began with the study of the atmosphere. What secrets did the air hold? How did birds and other flying creatures exploit the properties of air to achieve flight?

In search of answers to such questions, early scientists observed birds in flight and conducted in-depth investigations of their anatomy. This rudimentary work led ultimately to basic airfoil shapes, particularly the concept of cambered wings.

Next, early pioneers performed experiments concerning characteristics of the air itself. What happens as objects travel through the atmosphere? Discoveries revealing resistance, or drag, and pressure changes were made. Cayley was perhaps the first to gather useful data on the characteristics of air through whirling arm experiments and modeling. His work laid the foundation for others pursuing the challenge of aviation including Wenham, Lilienthal, Maxim, Langley, and the Wrights, to name a few. As knowledge in aerodynamics evolved, crude but functional wings emerged.

Structures

Once the general shape of a wing was known, the next issue involved construction details. Major attention was given to building strong, lightweight structures. This was a major challenge as overbuilt structures might keep the machine earthbound, while underbuilding could result in structural failures.

As with the problem of aerodynamics, construction techniques for aircraft were refined. Beginning with Cayley, who suggested the use of bamboo and invented a special wheel for aircraft, lightweight structures emerged. Except for Langley's Great Aerodrome, which failed during launch, structures developed during the pre-Wright period were generally proven through actual trial. In particular, the work by Chanute and his 1896 gliding team on the two-surface machine paved the way for future structures during the early period of practical aviation.

Power Plants

The obstacle involving power was a major hurdle faced by early aviators. In an attempt to mimic the birds, many of the earliest flying machines were powered by human muscle. This form of motive force proved inadequate as human might was required to lift not only its own weight but also the weight of the machine.

Realizing the inability of humans to propel themselves through the atmosphere, investigators turned to developing alternate forms of power. As previously discussed, Sir George Cayley attempted to develop a lightweight power plant suitable for aeronautics. Although steam engines were at Cayley's disposal, he was aware of their low power-to-weight ratios. To overcome this problem, Cayley searched for a more efficient means of converting heat and expanding air into power. From this effort emerged the calorific engine. One engine was designed to use gunpowder as fuel. This power plant contained no boiler, condenser, or other bulky components required by steam engines. Its lightweight construction was ideal for aeronautical use. Unfortunately, Cayley was unable to fully refine a calorific engine.

Although advanced steam engines were developed and used by a number of early pioneers (e.g., Stringfellow, Du Temple, Mozhaiski, Ader, Maxim, Langley), the low power-to-weight problem was a limiting factor. Advancing the development of a calorific engine, Etienne Lenoir designed and patented an internal combustion power plant in 1860. Built on the principle of a double-action steam engine, this power plant alternately burned a mixture of gas and air in each end of its cylinder. The output from this engine was somewhat weak as the mixture was not adequately compressed before combustion.

A major advancement in the design of aeronautical power plants came in 1885. Gottlieb Daimler built an engine based on the four-stroke Otto cycle. Although his product was used originally on airships, Daimler ultimately produced a number of excellent power plants for airplanes.

Fortunately for aircraft designers, the piston engine evolved quickly in terms of performance and reliability. Its role in the fledgling automotive industry accelerated its development. In due time, aircraft designers sought the services and expertise of automobile engine manufacturers. They wanted power plants that were lightweight, powerful, and reliable.

Points of Stagnation

Technological advancements in aerodynamics, structures, and power plants from the late 1700s to the early 1900s were crucial to the development of the airplane. Despite the technological breakthroughs made during this period, the airplane was incomplete without a suitable control system and propeller. The development of flight controls was no easy task, as differing viewpoints over how to steer an airplane through the air resulted in a variety of control systems and philosophies. The painstaking attention given to devising a system of control was laborious as investigators generated all sorts of control networks. By contrast, propellers received little consideration and were, for the most part, primitive until the Wrights undertook the challenge of creating efficient propellers.

Control Systems

Control systems were one of the most baffling design element of the airplane. Flight controls ranged from simple weight-shifting techniques to complex systems employing mechanisms for ensuring "automatic stability." One reason the development of a functional control system was so elusive was that the examples provided by Nature were not easy to duplicate. In other words, birds and other flying creatures had innate abilities that allowed them to control their direction of flight and maintain aerial balance. To devise some means for accomplishing what birds did instinctively was a major challenge.

Drawing from examples of maritime vessels and applying a little common sense, it was an easy matter to recognize the need for a rudder and elevator. After all, ships were steered via a rudder, and naturally an air-

plane needed some means of ascending and descending. The problem lay not with pitch and yaw but with recognizing the need for a three-axis control system involving roll.

Lacking the foresight to develop a three-axis control network, early pioneers devised all sorts of ineffective alternatives. Most of these efforts focused on inventing some means of "automatic stability" designed to keep the craft flying straight and level when a wind gust or other meteorological phenomenon disturbed its flight path. The assumption underlying the need for automatic stability was that humans would be unable to maintain the aerial balance of the machine. Therefore, it was deemed necessary to manufacture aircraft with built-in features that would maintain this balance. Such a system would have required the pilot to simply direct the craft up and down and steer it left and right. Gibbs-Smith classified individuals following this design philosophy as "chauffeurs" rather than "airmen." The distinction between the two is that chauffeurs wanted to navigate their stable craft through simple control movements as if they were steering an automobile or a boat in the air. By contrast, airmen preferred to establish complete control over the machine.[34] In the end, the Wrights demonstrated the ability of humans to maintain aerial balance using a three-axis flight control system. Their success in this matter is more fully covered in chapter 3.

Propellers

Where ornithopters developed both lift and thrust from the flapping action of their wings, those designing a fixed-wing aircraft faced a new challenge. They would somehow have to convert the power output of the engine into enough thrust to sustain the minimum flying speed of the aircraft. This conversion, although solved by propellers, proved difficult.

As drawings, photographs, and other documents clearly demonstrate, early aircraft designers used airscrews that were little more than motorized windmills. Propellers were often made by stretching cloth across a simple framework to form propeller blades. Others manufactured crude propellers from wood or metal, but the basic shape of the blades lacked efficient aerodynamic properties. Out of necessity, early designers resorted to using large, inefficient propellers to meet the thrust requirements of their flying machines. This, in turn, triggered an engineering chain reaction requiring more powerful engines, heavier structures, and additional wing surface. These unwelcomed additions further served to compromise any prospect of flight.

Aside from the work of Maxim, who conducted an extensive series of thrust tests involving some fifty experimental propellers, little attention was given to the problem of converting power into thrust. The question of propulsion focused on the creation of powerful engines and not efficient propellers. Ultimately, measures taken by the Wrights to design efficient propellers proved invaluable to the solution of heavier-than-air flight. Refer to chapter 3 for more information concerning the development of the Wright propeller.

The Total Airplane

In the preceding paragraphs, the various elements of an airplane were discussed in isolation. It should be noted, however, that a successful airplane is a complex amalgamation of its aerodynamic design, structure, control network, and propulsion system. For centuries, investigators were unable to correctly blend a proper aerodynamic form with a lightweight structure, three-axis control system, and an abundant amount of thrust.

Advancements made in aeronautics from 1790 to the early 1900s were paramount to the invention of the airplane. Investigators learned about aerodynamics, structures, and power plants. Some progress was also made in the areas of flight control and propeller design. Unfortunately, despite all the knowledge acquired, the secret for sustained heavier-than-air flight remained unsolved as the best "flights" were little more than powered hops. Although the efforts discussed in this chapter failed to generate a practical airplane, the information gained during this era laid the foundation for future success.

Notes

1. See Pritchard, *Sir George Cayley: The Inventor of the Aeroplane*, 189–90, for a copy of a letter written to Cayley by William Henson on 28 September 1846 in which he refers to Cayley as the "Father of Aerial Navigation." The use of this term may have been prompted by Henson's desire to solicit money from Cayley for aerial experimentation purposes.

2. Launoy and Bienvenu demonstrated their counter-rotating helicopter model before the French Academy of Sciences in 1784. They intended to build a full-scale aircraft. See Chanute, *Progress in Flying Machines*, 49–50.

3. See Newcomen Society, *Aeronautical and Miscellaneous Note-Book*, 22–25.

4. Newcomen Society, 27.

5. Newcomen Society, 42–44.

6. Chanute, 17.

7. Gibbs-Smith, *Sir George Cayley (1773–1857)*, 15.

8. Gibbs-Smith, *The Invention of the Aeroplane*, 12.

9. Gibbs-Smith, *The Aeroplane: An Historical Survey*, corrigenda.

10. Pritchard, 206.

11. In his book, *An Ancient Air*, Penrose indicated that this machine was called the "Aerial Steam Carriage."

12. Penrose, 46.

13. Gibbs-Smith, *The Aeroplane: An Historical Survey*, 14.

14. Gibbs-Smith, *The Aeroplane: An Historical Survey*, 314.

15. Villard, *Contact!* 217.

16. Gibbs-Smith, *Clément Ader*, 19–25.

17. Gibbs-Smith, *The Invention of the Aeroplane*, 25.

18. Gibbs-Smith, *The Invention of the Aeroplane*, 25.

19. Vernon, "The Flying Man."

20. Crouch, *A Dream of Wings*, 135.

21. Vernon.

22. Jarrett, *Another Icarus*, 160–65.

23. Laurence Hargrave was an aeronautical pioneer who conducted a series of flight experiments during this period. In particular, he was known for his box-kite designs. For more information, see Chanute, 218–33.

24. See Maxim, "Aërial Navigation: The Power Required," in which he summarized his experiments using a large whirling arm measuring 31 feet, 9.9 inches. A unique feature of this whirling arm was that the propulsive force generating its rotation originated from powered propellers mounted at the extremity of the arm. In contrast, most other whirling arms applied a motive force to a vertical axle at the center of rotation. This design gave Maxim the ability to not only experiment with airfoils and such, but to investigate propeller designs and efficiency.

25. A similar technique was used by Ader with his Avion III. To some degree, the use of differential thrust paralleled steering procedures used by maritime vehicles employing multiple screws.

26. Both No. 5 and No. 6 were tandem wing designs. Langley, however, was not the originator of this wing configuration. Gibbs-Smith traced the tandem wing format to Sir George Cayley in 1815. Because Cayley did not publish this design, credit is often given to Thomas Walker. The Walker machine of 1831 inspired the tandem wing glider of D. S. Brown, an Englander. Brown's 1874 model subsequently influenced

Langley. See Gibbs-Smith, *The Invention of the Aeroplane,*
10–11, 16.

27. Crouch, *A Dream of Wings,* 268.

28. "Buzzard a Wreck."

29. "Airship Breaks in Two."

30. Crouch, *A Dream of Wings,* 22.

31. "Go Coasting in the Air."

32. Howard, *Wilbur and Orville,* 90–92.

33. Gabriel Voisin and his brother Charles became interested in flight when they were young. The brothers experimented with box kites. Later in life, Gabriel was inspired by one of Ader's machines, probably the Avion III, while it was on display. He formally entered the field of aeronautics by test flying a biplane glider for Ernest Archdeacon. Following this experience, Voisin began manufacturing aircraft. He teamed up with Charles to form a successful aircraft manufacturing firm. See Harris, *The First to Fly,* 61, 65–66, 68–70.

34. Gibbs-Smith, *The Invention of the Aeroplane,* 3–4.

References

"Airship Breaks in Two." *New York Times,* 9 December 1903, 1.

"Airship Total Wreck." *Washington Post,* 9 December 1903, 2.

"Buzzard a Wreck." *Washington Post,* 8 October 1903, 1–2.

Chanute, Octave. *Progress in Flying Machines.* Long Beach, Calif.: Lorenz and Herweg, 1972.

Crouch, Tom D. *The Bishop's Boys: A Life of Wilbur and Orville Wright.* New York: W. W. Norton, 1989.

———. *A Dream of Wings: Americans and the Airplane, 1875–1905.* Washington, D.C.: Smithsonian Institution Press, 1989.

Gibbs-Smith, Charles H. *The Aeroplane: An Historical Survey of Its Origins and Development.* London: Her Majesty's Stationery Office, 1960.

———. *Clément Ader: His Flight-Claims and His Place in History.* London: Her Majesty's Stationery Office, 1968.

———. *The Invention of the Aeroplane, 1799–1909.* London: Her Majesty's Stationery Office, 1966.

———. *Sir George Cayley (1773–1857).* London: Her Majesty's Stationery Office, 1968.

"Go Coasting in the Air." *Chicago Tribune,* 8 September 1896, 1.

Harris, Sherwood. *The First to Fly: Aviation's Pioneer Days.* Blue Ridge Summit, Pa.: Tab Aero, 1991.

Hetherington, Norris S. "Langley's Aerodrome." *W.W.I Aero: The Journal of the Early Aeroplane,* no. 131 (February 1991): 3–23.

Howard, Fred. *Wilbur and Orville: A Biography of the Wright Brothers.* New York: Ballantine Books, 1987.

Jakab, Peter L. *Visions of a Flying Machine: The Wright Brothers and the Process of Invention.* Washington, D.C.: Smithsonian Institution Press, 1990.

Jarrett, Philip. *Another Icarus: Percy Pilcher and the Quest for Flight.* Washington, D.C.: Smithsonian Institute Press, 1987.

Kelly, Fred C. *The Wright Brothers: A Biography Authorized by Orville Wright.* New York: Bantam Books, 1983.

Langley, Samuel P. The "Flying-Machine." *McClure's,* June 1897, 646–60.

———. "The Possibility of Mechanical Flight." *Century,* September 1891, 783–85.

Lyle, Eugene P., Jr. "Santos-Dumont Circling the Eiffel Tower in an Air Ship." *Smithsonian Institution Report 1901,* 574–92.

Magoun, F. A., and E. Hodgins. *A History of Aircraft.* New York: McGraw-Hill, 1972.

Maxim, Hiram S. "Aërial Navigation: The Power Required." *Century,* October 1891, 829–36.

———. "The Aeroplane." *Cosmopolitan,* June 1892, 202–8.

McFarland, Marvin W. *The Papers of Wilbur and Orville Wright: Including the Chanute-Wright Letters and Other Papers of Octave Chanute,* vol. 1, 1899–1905; vol. 2, 1906–1948. New York: McGraw-Hill, 1953.

"Men Fly in Midair." *Chicago Tribune,* 24 June 1896, 1.

Meyer, Robert B., Jr. *Langley's Aero Engine of 1903.* Washington, D.C.: Smithsonian Institution Press, 1971.

Newcomen Society. *Aeronautical and Miscellaneous Note-Book (ca. 1799–1826) of Sir George Cayley: With an Appendix Comprising a List of the Cayley Papers.* Cambridge: W. Heffer and Sons, 1933.

"100: Lilienthal." *W.W.I Aero: The Journal of the Early Aeroplane,* no. 132 (May 1991): 3–7.

Penrose, Harald. *An Ancient Air: A Biography of John Stringfellow of Chard, the Victorian Aeronautical Pioneer.* Washington, D.C.: Smithsonian Institution Press, 1989.

Pritchard, John L. *Sir George Cayley: The Inventor of the Aeroplane.* New York: Horizon Press, 1962.

Rolt, L. T. C. *The Aeronauts: A History of Ballooning, 1783–1903.* New York: Walker, 1966.

Smith, Herschel H. *Aircraft Piston Engines: From the Manly Balzer to the Continental Tiara.* Manhattan, Kans.: Sunflower University Press, 1986.

Vernon. "The Flying Man: Otto Lilienthal's Flying Machine." *McClure's,* September 1894, 323–31.

Villard, Henry S. *Contact! The Story of the Early Birds.* Washington, D.C.: Smithsonian, 1987.

"Wait for the Flying Machine." *Washington Post,* 14 November 1898, 6.

Wolko, Howard S. *The Wright Flyer: An Engineering Perspective.* Washington, D.C.: Smithsonian Institution Press, 1987.

Wykeham, Peter. *Santos-Dumont: A Study in Obsession.* New York: Harcourt, Brace and World, 1962.

Orville and Wilbur Wright

Paul A. Whelan

The Early Years

TODAY IT IS almost impossible to imagine a world without airplanes streaking across the sky leaving their telltale trails of white vapor. How commonplace now, yet as the twentieth century began, piloted powered flight was still just a dream. This chapter traces the discovery by Wilbur and Orville Wright of the secret that unlocked the magnificent gift of flight.

As the century began, people had already seen the world shrink more in their lifetime than in all of recorded history. Advances in transportation and communication technology convinced them they had greater control over their lives than ever before. Automobiles, trains, urban trolleys, and "safety bicycles," which greatly interested the Wright brothers, made travel between cities commonplace. It was even possible to travel halfway around the world in less than two weeks on modern ships that were truly floating palaces.[1]

To be sure, there were experimenters who tampered with flight, but still the general public adopted the saying "You might as well try to fly" when they wanted to express that something was impossible to do. James Henry Gatling, the brother of Richard Gatling, who invented the Gatling gun, was one such inventor. He designed and built a prototype of a flying machine that he felt imitated a bird's wings. However, his prototype was far off the mark from a scientific point of view.[2] In the

1880s, two engineers, Octave Chanute and Samuel Langley, undertook studies that would seriously challenge the current skepticism about manned flight.

Born in Paris, Chanute lived in New Orleans and then in New York City. He read everything he could about our attempts to fly. Chanute developed a network of scholars and inventors interested in flying throughout Europe and the United States. He brought his studies and research together in his classic book *Progress in Flying Machines.*[3] Chanute, like Langley, was very sensitive about his fascination with flight. To avoid ridicule, he shared his ideas with only a few close friends.

As noted in chapter 2, Langley directed his scientific experiments toward how much power would be required to sustain a wing in flight. Paul Garber, a later head of the Smithsonian, watched one of Langley's attempted manned launches on 8 December 1903.[4] He recalled standing on the banks of the Potomac with a large group of spectators, waiting for the Langley machine to attempt a second takeoff. (The first attempt had failed.) The machine was launched from the deck of a houseboat in the middle of the river. When the aircraft engine was cranked, its pulsating rhythm could be heard on shore. After a little delay, the craft was launched. It reached the end of the platform and fell ignominiously into the water (see fig. 3.1). The crowd gasped, then waited to see whether the pilot, Charles Manly, was all right. As soon as he surfaced, he signaled he was unin-

Fig. 3.1. Towing the wreck of the Langley aerodrome. *Scientific American,* 2 October 1909.

jured. This was Langley's last attempt to fly. On 17 December, two unknown bicycle mechanics from Dayton, Ohio, changed the world.

Chanute, for his part, understood enough from his own sponsored glider flights to realize that no one was anywhere close to developing a powered craft. Early experiments were inconclusive, leaving the Wright brothers with little to guide them.[5] Considering the fact that they had almost nothing on which to base their own experiments, it is truly amazing what the Wright brothers accomplished in the next few years.

Looking back to the beginning of the twentieth century, we can now understand some of the strange circumstances that led to the Wright brothers' discovery of the secret that the best scientific minds of the time had not been able to unlock. In the span of four and a half years, the Wright brothers struggled against almost insurmountable odds to reveal the mysteries of flight. They had survived many dangerous encounters with physical laws. However, when they flew, their accomplishments remained unheralded. This was partly their own fault and partly due to a series of circumstances

that completely disenchanted them. They became obsessed with the idea that everyone around them was trying to steal or otherwise exploit their discoveries.[6]

From their earliest recorded experiences, Orville and Wilbur acted as though they were a single person. As children, they played, worked, and thought together.[7] They owned the same toys, and as they grew, they shared all their thoughts and aspirations. Nearly everything they did was the result of "conversations, suggestions, and discussions between us."[8] The brothers were good athletes, fun-loving, and curious, and each had a keen sense of humor. They were honest, direct, and humble men of middle-class background with a rich family heritage, which accounted for their dedication and strong family loyalty.

Wilbur, the older, came across as unsmiling and humorless, which hid the sensitivity deep within him. His determination to succeed enabled him to overcome frustration and keep him focused on his goals.

Orville displayed a practiced impassivity until he trusted an individual. However, when Orville would open up, he was much more expressive, and he rarely hid the volatility and puckishness of his curious mind, which leapt from one idea to the next.[9]

The brothers' maternal grandfather, John G. Koerner, emigrated to the United States from Germany to escape military conscription and settled in Virginia. He married Catherine Troy, an American girl of mixed German and Swiss heritage, and Susan Catherine was born in 1831. Their great-great-grandmother on their father's side, Catherine Benham Van Cleve, moved westward in 1790 with her husband, John. After Indians killed John in the area now known as Cincinnati, Ohio, Catherine remarried and moved north to Dayton in 1796. Her daughter, Catherine, married Dan Wright, a descendent of early New England settlers, in 1818. Their son, Milton, was born in Indiana in 1828. Milton graduated from Huntsville College in Indiana and then received a license to preach from the Church of the United Brethren of Christ in 1853. He became an itinerant minister and headed west by way of railroad to Panama, then by steamer to San Francisco, and finally overland to the Willamette Valley in Oregon. After several years of roaming, he returned to Huntsville, where he married his childhood sweetheart, Susan Catherine Koerner, on 24 November 1859.

The couple had five children: Reuchlin (1861), Lorin (1863), Wilbur (1867), Orville (1871), and Katharine (1874). Milton Wright's clerical duties required frequent traveling. While the family was living in Cedar Rapids, Iowa, Milton brought home a toy, the Pénaud "helicoptere." This balsa, cork, and paper model was powered by tightly wound rubber bands, and it so fascinated Wilbur (13) and Orville (9) that they built several models of their own by copying the toy. Conjecture is that this early toy sparked their interest in flying.

After living in Richmond, Indiana, the family reestablished residence in Dayton at 7 Hawthorne Street, where Orville and Katharine had been born. Wilbur had just finished high school. Orville, showing great promise in mathematics, completed his studies in Dayton. Both boys were avid readers, and encouraged by their father (now a bishop), they became well versed in the classics. Orville was high-spirited, a bit impish, and prone to anger when slowed down or harnessed in any way. Perhaps he was even a bit hyperactive, but he was a skilled craftsman able to make almost anything.

Nurturing and Training

Wilbur entered Yale University Divinity School in 1885, anxious to follow in his father's footsteps.[10] Just as their father passed on his love for reading and research, their mother passed on an innate knowledge of the principles of physics and a fascination with the mechanical world. Both boys had an intense curiosity and tenacity for learning that complemented their athletic ability. In 1885, eighteen-year-old Wilbur was badly injured and facially disfigured while playing a stick ball game like hockey. Suffering terrible physical and emotional pain, he dropped out of Yale and remained at home in seclusion for more than four years.

While Wilbur wrapped himself in morose depression, Orville developed an interest in printing that became a serious business. Pursuing his interest in improving all his printing equipment, Orville was continually innovating and experimenting with new gadgets that he pieced together from scrap parts he had scrounged. Whenever he lacked knowledge, he dug into library reference books and encyclopedias, reading everything he could on the subject. This was characteristic of the way he approached anything that interested him.

Meanwhile, Susan Wright had been caring for Wilbur, and it was taking its toll. She began to decline physically. Soon, barely able to walk and reduced by consumption to a frail shadow of her former self, she was forced to depend on others for all of her needs. It was not long before she was completely bedridden.

Stirred from his lethargy, Wilbur turned his attention to his mother, returning the loving care she had devoted to him for so long. For two years, he dedicated himself to nursing her, but in spite of his efforts, Susan Wright died in 1889. Bishop Wright was busy with his church work, so Katharine assumed the role of family caregiver. Except for the two years she attended Oberlin College to get her teaching credentials, she remained the nucleus of this tight-knit family. Katharine showed the love, compassion, and support needed to weld the unique abilities of Wilbur and Orville into the single talent they were to become.

As he helped his teenage brother Orville in inventing a press and expanding the business, Wilbur slowly emerged from his isolation. As new interests drew their attention, the mental harmony exhibited in their printing business became increasingly important. In 1892, the brothers discovered the new "safety bicycle," which had wheels of equal size. Their overriding interest became their ability to fix them. Orville soon took up racing the bicycle. Orville became so completely absorbed in the "Columbia" bicycle, with its inflatable rubber tires, that it was not long before he abandoned the printing business. Wilbur also left the printing business behind and started to accompany Orville to bicycle meets. Although Orville entered the races with abandon, Wilbur was still in too much pain to compete. Both of the brothers were excellent mechanics, and their talents were in such demand that they opened a bicycle shop on West Third Street in Dayton.

Business was excellent, and their shop rapidly expanded to meet the ever-increasing need for servicing and repair. Discovering the weaknesses of the products they serviced, the brothers began to design and sell their own "improved" products. The Wright Cycle Company quickly became a success.

As the business expanded, the relationship between Wilbur and Orville also matured. They did virtually nothing unless they did it together, functioning so closely as an intellectual and business team that it never occurred to them to do anything separately. Even after they opened a joint financial account, neither one ever bothered to explain to the other any transactions he had made. Throughout their lives, this was the way they ran business. Although the brothers performed as a single entity much of the time, Wilbur was still shackled by his illness and often seemed somewhat aimless. The one thing that sparked his excitement and a desire in life was the challenge their business stimulated. It was here that his suppressed brilliance began to emerge. As Wilbur's health improved, he even thought of returning to school, not to continue his studies in theology but perhaps to become a teacher. Even so, he seemed content with the bicycle business. Both he and Orville constantly looked for new challenges and jumped from one interest to another as it piqued their curiosity.

The Restless Years

In September 1894, Wilbur read an article in *McClure's* magazine about Otto Lilienthal (shown in fig. 3.2) and his manned glider flights from the cliffs in Germany. The idea of glider flight intrigued Wilbur, and he began to ponder the mysterious forces that governed flight. His studies began in a small wilderness near Dayton known as the Pinnacles, where Wilbur studied vast numbers of birds that gathered, moving in great waves among the air currents as they maneuvered from surface to sky. Their instinctive and effortless use of the air caused Wilbur to wonder about the physical principles that guided their flight. Finally, his brilliant mind was tackling a fascinating challenge, and he began to emerge from his self-imposed isolation. During the next few years, he would take this fascination with the flight of birds to new horizons.

In August 1896, Lilienthal was killed in a glider crash. At that time, Orville had typhoid fever and Wilbur had been tending to him. After the fever broke and Orville began to recover, he found himself with ample time to argue with Wilbur about the probable causes of Lilienthal's mishap. Their lively discussions often involved switching sides in the argument. One thing the brothers

Fig. 3.2. Otto Lilienthal. *Scientific American,* 2 October 1909.

did agree on was that mechanical objects had to behave according to laws or principles. If the object did not seem to obey a law or principle, it was not because the knowledge of the principle did not exist—the real principle had not been discovered yet!

Lilienthal had been a crack investigative scientist. His designs confirmed that a wing with a "gentle parabolic curve" like a bird's could produce lifting power. However, he did not know why this subtle bulge produced lift. It seemed to Wilbur that the scientists had been pursuing a wrong idea. Lilienthal's death had been the direct result of his lack of understanding of the principle of lift. This became evident by the errors they soon discovered in his mathematical findings.

Finally, the brothers realized Lilienthal's fatal error. It was not the curvature of the wing that produced lift, nor was it a flapping motion. The directional control produced by shift in body weight also did not produce lift. The amount of lift produced depended directly upon the amount of forward speed the glider attained. Lilienthal's death had resulted when his glider stalled because of insufficient lift to keep it flying.

As the brothers plunged deeper into the mysteries of flight, their intellectual bond grew ever stronger. Their contrasting temperaments and talents formed a complementary working union. The brothers' loyalty and affection for one another was to remain the hallmark of their accomplishments.[11] Although bachelors themselves, the Wright brothers had a very exciting and full family life. Nieces and nephews all lived close by, and they all adored their uncles, who regaled them with marvelous stories.

The late nineteenth century was a time of great advances in the application of technology. The telegraph, automobiles, trains, and great steamships had became part of everyday life. On 30 May 1899, Wilbur wrote to the Smithsonian, boldly stating that manned flight was possible and requesting that they send him everything they had on the subject of flight. Quick to point out that he was no crank, Wilbur emphasized that he was just an enthusiast, anxious to carry out research on the topic.[12] Ironically, by this time the brothers' investigation had been so thorough that the Smithsonian could offer them nothing new.

In the course of their pursuit of all the world's knowledge of flight, Orville and Wilbur made several interesting discoveries. One of them involved Percy Pilcher, a Scottish engineer who had experimented with towing a glider aloft rather than launching it from a cliff. Even though he had used the principle involving increased speed equaling increased lift, he had not realized it. The Wrights' research led them to one conclusion: much had been written about the possibilities of manned flight, but no one had managed to do it. On the other hand, no one had proved it could not be done. Could they be the ones to do it?

Preparation and Discovery

At this juncture, there was no accurate accepted scientific body of knowledge about manned flight. It was left to the Wrights to identify, define, and outline the problem of attaining what people had long sought—to fly like birds under their own power. They proposed six problems that needed to be addressed:

1. For people to fly, they must first comprehend the physical principles involved. Only then could they mechanically reproduce bird's flight.

2. The issue of lift and equilibrium needed to be solved.

3. A three-dimensional control system was needed.

4. The vehicle needed to be strong enough to support a person.

5. The power-to-weight ratio needed to be correct.

6. The pilot needed sufficient training and skill to fly the machine and not destroy it.[13]

The brothers were quick to differentiate the problem of lift and equilibrium from that of control, and they addressed the two separately. Early in their investigations, the issue of control became the subject of endless deliberation and arguments. Wilbur was first to come up with the solution that came to be known as "wing warping." The term *wing warping* grew as the Wrights developed the concept of controllable flight. Originally, they used the term *twisting* or *helical twisting* to describe the changing of a wing's angle of incidence at its tip to achieve lateral control. Octave Chanute seemed to have first used the term, and the Wrights soon picked it up.[14] The wings on either side of the body could be twisted and warped so their surfaces reached different angles of incidence. This created unequal lift on either side, giving the pilot the ability to control turns in either direction.

Wilbur then designed a system that let him warp the

wings in flight. Using a system of cables and pulleys, he built an impressive flyable model with a five-foot wingspan.[15] Wilbur flew his model many times, taking copious notes on its performance. Both brothers were pleased with the amount of the lateral control, but they were puzzled by the tendency of the model to plunge downward from time to time. Later, they discovered the inherent danger in the wing warping (arc of parabola). For now, however, wing warping worked.

Throughout the next year, the brothers discussed glider control with Octave Chanute. He respected what the Wrights were doing and became an enthusiastic supporter. Although the Wrights did not always trust his motives, Chanute's collection of flight data was enormous and he had done important work with wing gliders. His association with the Wrights was both controversial and helpful. Chanute acted as critic and advocate of their ideas. The brothers used his concepts in their airplane design and incorporated his biplane idea into their machines. Wilbur even asked Chanute to recommend a place to test their machine that would provide some seclusion and could ensure sustained average winds of 15 mph with reasonably good weather.

Orville and Wilbur Wright diligently sifted through ideas as they studied anew the progress of Langley, Lilienthal, and Chanute. By August 1899, Wilbur had researched all the available literature. As typical of his analytical approach, he followed an exacting process of isolating a problem, defining it precisely, and making detailed notes by cutting through to the central issue. Wilbur incessantly asked, What does a machine require in order to fly? He identified three things: wings that would lift it into the air, a power plant to move it forward with sufficient speed so that the air flowing over its wings would generate that lift, and a means of controlling the machine in the air.[16] Before he could consider a power plant, Wilbur would have to know how much power would be required to guarantee balance and control. To do this correctly required a machine that would support a person to manage the machine by operating the controls. Traditional modes of thinking would have to be abandoned in providing control in three axes.

The airplane was the first vehicle that would require control in three axes of motion. These axes can best be understood as imaginary lines around which a machine in the air is free to rotate: Pitch (a horizontal line running from wing tip to wing tip); roll (a horizontal line running through the center of the craft from nose to tail); and yaw (a vertical line running directly through the center of the aircraft).[17]

The genius of Wilbur Wright was that he had an uncanny ability to comprehend an essential principle involved in a mechanical situation. He could apply this knowledge to solve a series of problems that were seemingly unrelated.[18] It was this genius that enabled him to solve the power/control problem.

Through the process of elimination, the Wrights decided that Kitty Hawk on the Outer Banks of North Carolina was the best place to test their theories. This spot was especially inviting, since their inquiries had produced a positive response from William Tate, the postmaster and commissioner of the area.

In September 1900, Wilbur left Dayton for Kitty Hawk. After a harrowing trip across Kitty Hawk Bay, he met Tate, who helped him establish a camp. Once camp was set up, Wilbur constructed the glider he had designed and began his series of experiments (see fig. 3.3). Orville arrived at Tate's house on 28 September 1900. He and Wilbur completed the glider within six days, and by 14 October they had flown it three times. In four more days, the glider had flown three times at 400 feet for 15 seconds.

A savage storm forced the Wrights to postpone their return to Dayton. This gave them an opportunity to carry out a series of low skimming "semiglides" to see what would happen to the machine with a man onboard in a prone position. The wind was about 12 mph, providing just the right speed to test the sensitivity of the controls. Each glide provided the opportunity to adjust the control movement to correct any imbalance in fore and aft control. The glides were disappointingly brief, each lasting only a few seconds. The ambitious plans for flying many hours had totaled less than 3 minutes in the air. The 1900 glider had not performed as expected; however, it had given sufficient evidence for them to confirm that the principles of control that they developed were far superior to those of Pilcher and Lilienthal. On 23 October, they left for home already planning their next steps.

Guesswork was out of the question for Orville and Wilbur. They simply had to question the engineers and physicists who had been wrong concerning the problems of lift, drag, coefficient of air pressure, and control. There was nothing to do but develop their own

Fig. 3.3. Early glider being flown here as a kite. Courtesy of the USAF Museum.

data by experiment and testing. The brothers designed a device that consisted of an airfoil test rig mounted on the handlebars of a bicycle. Using Lilienthal's airfoil figures, they proved that there was an error somewhere in his calculations.

The Wrights then constructed their first wind tunnel to check the results of their bicycle-wheel experiment and quickly confirmed their findings. There was nothing left to do but make a small model of Lilienthal's wing and test it at every angle of attack and calculate the coefficients themselves. They went further and tested a wide range of shapes and sizes to find the most efficient lifting surface. This meant the need for a better wind tunnel, one that would produce a smooth flow of air at a steady 27 mph. To produce this flow, they developed a small gasoline engine to drive a fan that would produce the correct airflow. The tunnel and necessary balance devices designed to calculate lift and drag coefficients were completed in late November. The brothers' testing produced dramatic results. They were on the verge of answering questions that had been asked for ages, and they knew it. Old assumptions were dashed, replaced by the facts and figures that they had carefully gathered and recorded. Wilbur and Orville returned to the Outer

Banks again in 1901 and continued to verify their data with more successful flights.

Through extensive communication with Chanute and others who were exploring the possibility of flight, it became increasingly clear to the brothers that they had no serious rivals. Knowing this, they became somewhat more open to Chanute's plea that they share their research with other serious aviation enthusiasts and that they entertain releasing at least some moderate publicity about their work. Wilbur even promised Chanute he would publish the results of the wind tunnel tests.

Armed with the results of their Glider testing data, the brothers were back at their Kitty Hawk camp in 1902. An improved glider performed as expected except that the fixed double rudders were found to be inadequate. The double rudders were replaced with a single rudder that worked in conjunction with wing warping and improved directional control to the desired degree (see figs. 3.4–3.6). This modification would go through several changes before finally being incorporated in the new model.

That year, they were joined at Kitty Hawk by several other enthusiasts who brought Chanute's gliders to test their own theories. The camp became crowded, and the

Fig. 3.4. First version of the 1902 glider; fixed double rudders were inadequate. Courtesy of the USAF Museum.

Fig. 3.5. Glider modified with a single rudder. Courtesy of the USAF Museum.

Fig. 3.6. Orville Wright is the pilot of the 1902 glider. Wilbur Wright is holding onto the right wing, and Dan Tate is holding onto the left wing. Courtesy of the USAF Museum.

brothers were not pleased at all. Their intensity of concentration and desire for perfection in their work made the situation very uncomfortable for everyone. In addition, they constantly feared that their design would be stolen and that others would capitalize on their hard work. However, they felt they were very close to success and did not wish to compromise the momentum of their effort.

Things progressed very quickly. The elevator and new rudder were added. Wilbur noted in a letter to Chanute that by 21 September 1902 they had completed fifty gliding flights in the new machine.

Wilbur, who had done all the flying to this point, now shared the time aloft with Orville, who had learned to fly. On 23 September, with Orville at the controls and Wilbur shouting instructions from the ground, a glider was successfully launched, then it nosed up, stalled, and fell backwards onto the sand. Fortunately, Orville emerged from the rubble without injury, averting a near disaster.[19]

A week later after extensive repair to the glider, they were back in the air again. By October, they were making as many as twenty-five glides a day for distances of up to 500 feet. The 1902 glider performed well beyond their expectations, and Wilbur and Orville could not have been more pleased. However, it was evident that the fixed rudder was part of their control problem. On the evening of 3 October, while lying in bed in the rafters above the workshop, Orville came up with the idea of hinging the rudder. This provided additional control so that the pilot could compensate for the increased drag on the upward wing in a turn. The idea was further refined by linking the rudder directly to the wing-warping cradle operated by the hips. The rudder would work automatically to counter the drag. A single vane was introduced, replacing the double surface of the fixed rudder.

When Chanute arrived in a heavy rain with Augustus Herring (his glider builder and engineer friend), things became very confused at the camp. Two more people squeezed into the shed made sleeping almost impossible. During their stay, there were numerous attempts to launch differently designed gliders. Every craft failed except the Wright glider. It was clear to all that the Wrights had the technically superior machine. After Chanute left the Outer Banks, he visited Langley and shared with him the Wrights' outstanding progress, suggesting he go see for himself what they had accomplished.

After the departure of all the visiting flying enthusiasts, testing progressed rapidly. Although this was disappointing to Chanute, it was not in his nature to express anything but praise for the brothers' progress. The Wrights completed glides of more than 550 feet regularly.[20] On 23 October, Wilbur set a new record of 622.5 feet in flight. Wilbur and Orville had achieved their goal. With the 1902 glider, they had solved the basic problems of flight (see fig. 3.7). They now were ready to construct a powered airplane. Before they broke camp for the season, they calculated the wing size and the weight of the craft and pilot. These calculations would determine the size of engine they needed to achieve flight. The calculations were clear. They would need 520 square feet of wing surface to lift a total weight of 625 pounds, including the engine and pilot. Everything else was a design problem and could be completed back in Dayton.

The Dream of Flight and Reality

In 1903, it was time to begin to add power to the flying machine. However, one essential invention was needed: the propeller. In the operation of a propeller and engine in a flying machine, there were so many simultaneous reactions to consider that it was almost impossible to know where to begin. Characteristically, Orville and Wilbur fell into their unique way of thinking with one mind to solve a problem. Both had volatile tempers, and each would try to outshout the other. They bickered incessantly to hammer home a point. Then, abruptly, they would switch sides and just as vigorously argue the opposite position, all the while listening intently to the other's position. When such a session started, and it could be anywhere and at any time, the two brothers became oblivious to anyone around them.

The design of the propeller was a result of just this kind of intense interchange. They spent hours admiring all sorts of ideas and concepts, and slowly their theory began to jell. By the early spring of 1903, the concept of the propeller was complete and ready to be tested. It was not the result of a blinding flash of insight but a tightly measured, logical progression.

Until now, propeller design had been viewed as a screw such as that used on a ship, boring through the air instead of water. The Wrights viewed a propeller as the same thing as a wing but on a different axis.

To their amazement, they could not find any data on propellers. There was nothing for them to do but create their own data. Until they undertook the task, no one in the world had designed an aeronautical propeller.

They reasoned that because the propeller is an airfoil, it needed to resemble a section of a wing. It functioned the same way, producing a difference in pressure with more on the back of the blade than on the front. This difference in pressure produced the tendency to move toward the axis of less pressure. They calculated the angle at which various parts of the propeller struck the air and worked out the formula for the thrust reaction that resulted.

Fig. 3.7. Version of the Wright glider parked in front of the Wrights' living quarters and hangar at Kill Devil Hill. Courtesy of the USAF Museum.

There was still a major problem because there was no way to calculate thrust when it was constantly changing due to the compressibility of the air. As the machine moved and accelerated, a decreasing grip on the air by the propeller resulted thereby decreasing the thrust. Wilbur and Orville needed to know exactly what this loss would be. If there was not enough thrust to maintain the flying speed of the aircraft, power-controlled flight would be impossible.[21]

The brothers reviewed the wind tunnel experiments they had conducted using variously shaped airfoils. They settled on a design that provided the best "gliding angle" and that yielded the greatest efficiency at varying speeds and changing angles of attack. This at least partially seemed to answer the thrust problem. However, the solution created a new problem.

The width of the propeller relative to length was addressed using the data collected and stored in their collection of notebooks. They concluded that the best power and least performance loss would be developed using two propellers 8.5 feet in length. Their calculations, though complex in nature, accurately established the correct ratios for the propeller design. It was a startling breakthrough.

In early February 1903, they carved a piece of wood with a helicoidal twist and tested it in a shed behind the bicycle shop. The next month, they modified their calculations and built two propellers 8.5 feet long. "They used three laminations of spruce and covered the tips with a thin layer of light duck canvas, glued on tightly to keep the wood from splitting. Each propeller was then coated with aluminum paint."[22]

Next the Wright brothers addressed the problem of engine design in their usual manner. They were assisted by Charlie Taylor, their storekeeper, who had joined them in 1901. Although Katharine Wright never liked Taylor, he was a valuable asset in running the bicycle business. Taylor had some knowledge of engines, although he had never constructed one. Neither Wilbur nor Orville had more than minimal knowledge of engine building, so even Taylor's limited experience was a big help. The brothers had a rough idea of what they thought was needed. They sketched out a rough drawing and began putting an engine together using materials they had on hand and a drill press and lathe in the bicycle repair shop.

Fig. 3.8. The Wright-Taylor engine. Courtesy of the USAF Museum.

To save weight, the engine block was made of aluminum. Taylor molded the block and crafted the pistons. A radiator was mounted separately from the engine and attached to the forward upright of the airplane to ensure aerodynamic balance. The engine's four cylinders produced 8–9 horsepower, which they calculated was sufficient (see fig. 3.8). The gas tank held four-tenths of a gallon.

To the Wrights, the key to success lay in matching propeller design and engine size to achieve the optimum power needed. After much calculation, they determined that two slowly rotating propellers, mounted behind the wings, would obtain the optimum lift and thrust. The two propellers were installed to rotate in opposite directions to eliminate the torque effect (shown in fig. 3.9). Their bicycle experiences gave them the idea of a chain-drive connection between the propellers and the engine drive shaft.

The engine and propeller match was testimony to the genius of the Wrights and Charlie Taylor. They had constructed from scratch a propulsion system that successfully performed its designed function for a total of 101 seconds. When tested on the Outer Banks the following fall, the system delivered the calculated thrust within 1 percent.

The brothers remained in constant contact with Octave Chanute, keeping him up to date on their progress with engine and propeller designs. He in turn followed

Fig. 3.9. The propeller, engine, and chain-drive combination. Courtesy of the USAF Museum.

their work closely. Chanute felt that the calculations were cut too tightly. He calculated there could be a power loss of 25–30 percent between the engine and propellers. The Wrights had allowed for only a 10–15 percent loss. If Chanute was correct, powered flight would be impossible. The brothers calculated an engine efficiency of 12 horsepower. They rightly disputed Chanute's conclusions. Later they went on to prove on the Outer Banks that power loss would be only 5–10 percent, they knew they had calculated correctly, and they would achieve powered flight.[23]

The time came to return to the Outer Banks to put their theories and machine to the real test. The brothers realized they were on the brink of success. Their excitement mounted as they embarked on the journey through Elizabeth City, Roanoke Island, and on to Kitty Hawk and their camp.

The camp had suffered badly from the ravages of a gale that had struck the area earlier. Strong winds and heavy rain further complicated the task of renovation and new construction. However, in spite of poor working conditions, a new hangar big enough to house the

new machine was completed within several weeks. Orville and Wilbur planned to start powered flight trials by late October. Meanwhile, research would be continued using the 1902 machine. When the winds were favorable, glides would be conducted, and when the winds were calm, more work would be done on the powered machine.

By 28 September, it was estimated the Wrights had made almost a hundred gliding flights that averaged over 20 seconds each. On 3 October, Wilbur's flight lasted 43 seconds over a distance of 450 feet. Each flight was carefully recorded, and the results of each variation were noted. Careful and detailed documentation continued to be the hallmark of the brothers' research. These complete records would become invaluable later, proving beyond question the validity of the Wright brothers' accomplishment.

The airplane parts arrived on 8 October 1903, the day after Samuel Langley experienced the first failure in his attempt at powered flight. It was ironic that he had almost limitless external financial resources and maximum publicity supporting his efforts. In contrast, the

Wrights' accomplishments were done in obscurity and solely with their own funds. Although Octave Chanute was aware of the progress of both Langley and the Wrights, he respected the brothers' request that he not publicize their plans and accomplishments.

Meanwhile, their airplane parts were carefully unpacked. When a severe storm struck with winds of over 50 mph, it hampered glider flights. However, it provided time for them to sort out and begin assembling the newly arrived parts. Even as the storm raged, construction went well. The upper wing assembly was soon completed, with the addition of hinges and fabric covering rapidly following. Things came together very well. By the next month, the lower wing construction had begun. It was designed to accommodate the pilot and engine, requiring the right wings to be a few inches longer than the left. This provided additional lift to compensate for the heavier engine mounted slightly right of center and for the pilot who lay to the left of the centerline (see fig. 3.10).

All the other component parts, tail surfaces, shafts, braces, wires and pulleys, elevator, and vertical stabilizers were added and fully integrated into the wing-warping system. By early November, it was time to assemble, mount, and test the engine.

Problems began to develop on 5 November, when the propeller shaft was damaged during engine run up. It had to be returned to Dayton so that Charlie Taylor could repair it. Things around camp ground to a halt. Octave Chanute visited, but there was not much for him to see. The new machine was inoperable, and the glider was all but useless. Orville had begun studying German and French to pass the time. Provisions were low. It was not a happy time (fig. 3.11).

The shaft finally arrived back in camp on 20 November, but it was so bone chilling cold that little was done beyond testing the engine and reinstalling the propeller shaft. When the engine was finally tested, severe engine vibration resulted. After some quick adjustments, the engine was ready. Still another problem was discovered on 28 November. This time a propeller shaft had cracked. Orville rushed back to Dayton to help Charlie Taylor fabricate another one out of better steel.

Orville returned on 11 December. While on the trip, he read that Samuel Langley had again failed, marking the end of his efforts to fly. It had just proved to be too

Fig. 3.10. The pilot lay prone to the left of center with the engine mounted to the right of center. Courtesy of the USAF Museum.

Fig. 3.11. One of the Wright brothers in the kitchen of their living quarters/hangar passing the time by cleaning a gun. Courtesy of the USAF Museum.

expensive. Now the Wright brothers were the only contenders in the manned powered flight arena. Quickly, the new shafts were installed, and again the brothers excitedly planned to fly, but to no avail. The winds were too light. Then, when they practiced starting the engine on the "junction railroad" track used for launching the machine, the tail frame broke. Once it was repaired, they prepared to fly again. On 14 December, they hung the signal flag to alert the Kill Devil Hills life station crew so they could witness the event.[24]

With the helpers in place, the Wrights prepared for the launch. A toss of a coin determined Wilbur should go first. The plane moved down the launch track before Orville was ready. He reached up to grab a wing, but was quickly passed by the plane. Wilbur overcontrolled the airplane, and the result was a stall from about 15 feet in altitude approximately 60 feet out. The left wing hit, and then a skid dug into the sand. Braces and elevators broke on impact. The craft had flown 105 feet in 3.5 seconds. By the Wrights' standards of measurement, this was not considered a successful flight. Nonetheless, it did confirm they were on the verge of success. In fact, they were confident enough that in writing home they urged the family to keep it quiet. The family all agreed and waited

in excited anticipation for news of the successful flight so they could tell the world.

The broken parts were repaired by noon on 16 December. They set up for launch from level ground, this time to comply with requirements of their test criteria that the powered flight needed to be unassisted. The landing point had to be as high as the takeoff point to ensure the validity of the flight. Unfortunately, the winds dwindled to a calm. The men waited several hours and then dejectedly returned the machine, now known as the *Flyer,* back into the hangar for the night.

The morning of 17 December 1903 was cold, and the wind was as high as 25 mph, but the Wrights were determined to fly. They posted the signal to alert the lifesavers of their intention. Their photographer, John Daniels, one of the lifesaver spectators, tells what happened next:

The *Flyer* was mounted on the track about a hundred feet west of camp heading south to north. The Wrights each cranked a propeller and let the motor run. Wilbur and Orville walked off from us and stood close together on the beach, talking low to each other for some time. . . . After a while they shook hands, and we couldn't help notice how they held onto each other's hand, sort of like they hated to let go; like two folks parting who weren't sure they'd ever see each other again. It was an uncharacteristic bit of drama for the Wrights.[25]

It was Orville's turn to fly. He got aboard and checked all the special instruments they depended upon to collect their carefully recorded data.

Daniels was in place and prepared to take what was to become his famous picture that forever captured the critical moment. This was probably one of the most carefully studied photographs in history, and in the end it provided irrefutable evidence that the Wrights had achieved successful powered flight.

At 10:35, Orville headed down the tracks. The *Flyer* lifted off in 45 feet. There were control problems, but Orville continued the flight. When he landed, he had traveled 120 feet in 12 seconds (see fig. 3.12). "It was the first time in history that a heavier-than-air craft had taken off from level ground, moved forward under its own power, and landed at a point as high as that from which it began."[26]

A skid broken in the first flight was quickly repaired, and two more successful flights were completed. At noon, Wilbur flew the *Flyer* 852 feet for 59 seconds. Victory was theirs. All the years of painstaking effort had proved the Wrights' genius. Happy beyond belief, they carried the *Flyer* back to camp and immediately began making plans for longer flights. Suddenly, a strong gust of wind caught the *Flyer* and began flipping it. Orville grabbed a brace. So did John Daniel, but to no avail. The *Flyer* tumbled over the dune and ended up a total wreck. Its job was over.

Under the circumstances, no more flights would be possible before Christmas. The parts were all boxed up and shipped back to Dayton. But first it was time to call home and let the world know of their success. Orville and Wilbur set off to walk the four miles to the weather bureau office and telegraph the good news.

Flush with success, the brothers put into motion their carefully developed plan to notify the world. Their news release was to be based on a telegram to the family at home, but from the start, everything went wrong. The stories that appeared in newspapers were false, containing exaggerated happenings and untruths. This infuriated both Wilbur and Orville. The way the newspapers reported their activities became a problem that would plague them for years. As the brothers became more contemptuous of the press, the reporters became less interested in accuracy as far as the whole flight business

Fig. 3.12. The first powered flight. Courtesy of the USAF Museum.

was concerned. This led to utter frustration and a mutual news blackout. Their work was "being ignored, misunderstood or misinterpreted."[27]

In spite of the bad relations with the press, the brothers knew there was still much work to do before flight could become commonplace. So far they had solved the mystery of flight; they knew the proper power-to-weight ratio; and they had built an engine that successfully transferred power through their propeller, which developed the proper thrust. The control system managed the aircraft effectively. The wing curve was correct. The lift-to-weight formula was accurate. However, even with all these accomplishments, they realized that the airplane was still marginal in design. It was a good beginning, but only that.

In 1904, they tackled the control problems and aircraft design improvements. It had become evident that they were losing a lot of time going back to the Outer Banks each year, so they began to search for a location near home that would be suitable for test flights. Since they continued to reject any offer of outside financial support, they were somewhat limited in what they could afford.

Then Terrance Huffman, a Dayton banker, offered to let the brothers use a nine hundred–acre plot he owned. Huffman Prairie was ideal because it was on a rail line but relatively isolated. (Wright-Patterson Air Force Base is now partly situated at this location.) Huffman thought the Wrights were fools for trying to fly in their machines, but he let them go ahead. The field was cleaned, and the cows and horses were fenced so as not to endanger them during the flight trials. In mid-April, a shed was built, and work began on the 1904 *Wright Flyer II*.

Since much of the original *Flyer* had been abandoned at Kill Devil Hill, the new machine, patterned after the original, had some major modifications. The wing was now cambered to 1-in-25 from 1-in-20 and the engine produced about 16 horsepower. The pilot was still prone, and the wing warp and rudder controls were still linked. The launching track was lengthened to 160 feet.

The first flight, on 23 May, attracted about forty people, including a dozen reporters. The engine was started, and the craft labored down the track. The aircraft went straight off the end and never got airborne. With this failure, the reporters lost all interest in the flights at Huffman Prairie.

The early 1904 flights never exceeded 300 feet. The difference in temperature, humidity, and the 815-foot increase in altitude on Huffman Prairie had a definite impact on flight performance. This effect came to be known as "density altitude." A high density altitude would adversely affect an aircraft's ability to perform in many ways. The engine never developed full horsepower, and the wing did not produce as much lift as the Kitty Hawk flights. The combination of forces simply did not allow for sufficient thrust to overcome weight and drag to allow the aircraft to fly. Although they did not understand these principles yet, the brothers knew that if they were going to fly they needed some additional thrust.

Fig. 3.13. The catapult-launch system. *Scientific American,* 29 August 1908.

The brothers then constructed a catapult that included a tower erected behind the *Flyer* (as shown in fig. 3.13). Using a system of pulleys, they hoisted an 800-pound weight (later increased to 1,600 pounds). A group of people pulled this weight to the top of the tower with a long rope where it cocked the catapult. The rope extended under the track and connected to an automatic decoupling device. When the start was signaled, a cord was pulled, releasing the weight and whipping the *Flyer* forward.

The mechanism was first used on 7 September 1904, and it gave sufficient acceleration for the aircraft to take off. As the autumn days cooled, the density altitude decreased, increasing the *Flyer*'s performance and allowing their flights to became a series of record breakers.

On 20 September, Amos I. Root wrote the first eyewitness account of a powered airplane flight and published it in his magazine, *Gleenings in Bee Culture.* There were 105 flights in 1904, with the longest taking place on 1 December. Orville circled the *Flyer* over Huffman Prairie two and a quarter times. He remained in flight for 5 minutes and 8 seconds and covered a distance of three miles.[28] All told, the brothers flew for 45 minutes. The Wrights were confident enough in their progress to first offer their machine to the U.S. government. They did this through a letter to Robert Lenin on 18 January 1905. They were rejected.

Throughout 1905, the machine was improved in almost every way. From what seemed an inauspicious beginning with only short flights during the first half of the year, the brothers painstakingly tested, reused, fixed, and improved the *Flyer,* increasing its performance dramatically. By the end of August, the brothers were approaching their top performance of the previous year. Finally on 6 September 1905, Orville matched the best flights of 1904. He circled the field four times in about 5 minutes for a distance of approximately three miles. Then on 26 September, Wilbur remained aloft 18 minutes.

So it went into October when, after days of increasingly successful flights, Orville flew for more than 39 minutes at an average of 38 mph, making twenty-nine complete circuits of the field.

The Legacy

As spectacular as these events were, the engineering marvel the Wright brothers had achieved went unnoticed. Their genius had developed an entirely new concept. As their flying experience increased, the Wrights further improved their machine by separating the joint wing-warp rudder control system. This gave them fully independent control over pitch, roll, and yaw and marked the first time a fully controlled airplane had been built and flown. The importance of this achievement would also escape notice for several years, partly because of media disinterest and partly because of a decision the brothers made the next day.

Exasperated with press coverage, the Wrights promised a flight for the press to witness. Wilbur was scheduled to make the flight, but the stormy November weather thwarted it. The press was not kind. By the end of 1905, the Wrights, having had enough of the way their activities were reported and disgusted by the government's rejection, simply withdrew into isolation. They believed that flight belonged to them and that the world was out to exploit them. From that day until May 1908, the Wright Brothers did not fly again. This proved to be a near catastrophic decision.

> The next two and a half years were grueling for the Wright brothers. It is a dreary picture that we have of these two proud and sensitive men of great integrity and innovative capacity, but with stubborn minds and undemonstrative characters, rejected by their government, wandering part of the time around Europe and being exposed to political intrigue, graft, doubts, misrepresentation—all that the international financial world offers up.[29]

It is almost unbelievable that so many people in the Dayton area had not believed what had actually happened there. In spite of the evidence, the *Dayton Daily News* was not impressed enough to make even casual mention of the brothers' accomplishments. Perhaps it was because people were still not able to distinguish between Santos-Dumont circling the Eiffel Tower in Paris in a gas balloon with rudimentary controls and a heavier-than-air machine actually flying under the complete control of a pilot.

The Wright brothers freed humankind from the bonds of gravity. The world was forever changed in those 12 seconds on 17 December 1903 at Kill Devil Hill on the Outer Banks of North Carolina.

In spite of their stunning achievement, a number of heartbreaking years would pass before Orville and Wilbur Wright would be given the credit they deserved.

Notes

1. Combs, *Kill Devil Hill,* 48.
2. Kirk, *First in Flight,* 8.
3. Chanute, *Progress in Flying Machines.*
4. Interview with Paul Garber, 1983.
5. Kirk, 15.
6. Combs, 13.
7. Wilbur's letter cited in Combs, 24.
8. Wilbur's letter cited in Combs, 24.
9. Combs, 25 ff.
10. Crouch, *The Bishop's Boys,* 75.
11. Combs, 44.
12. Combs, 50.
13. Combs, 63–64.
14. Combs, 70.
15. Crouch, 183.
16. Wilbur Wright, "Some Aeronautical Experiments," 5.
17. Crouch, 167.
18. Crouch, 170.
19. Crouch, 237.
20. Crouch, 241.
21. Combs, 180.
22. Combs, 186.
23. Kirk, 23.
24. For a full story of the helpful note these men played, see Kirk, 137–50.
25. Kirk, 179.
26. Kirk, 181.
27. Kirk, 154. Detailed coverage of the problems the Wrights had with the press is further expanded in Combs, 226–35; Crouch, 270–72; and Kirk, 185–94.
28. Combs, 241.
29. Combs, 253.

References

Abbot, C. G. *The Relations Between the Smithsonian Institution and the Wright Brothers.* Washington, D.C.: Smithsonian Institution Press, 1928.

Brown, Aycock. *The Birth of Aviation, Kitty Hawk, N.C.* Winston-Salem, N.C.: Collins, 1953.

Chanute, Octave. *Progress in Flying Machines.* New York: Forney, 1894. Reprint, Long Beach, Calif.: Lorenz and Herweg, 1976.

———. "Wright Brothers' Flights." *Independent* 64, no. 4 (June 1908): 1287–88.

Charnley, Mitchell V. *The Boys' Life of the Wright Brothers.* New York: Harper and Brothers, 1928.

Combs, Harry, with Martin Caidin. *Kill Devil Hill: Discovering the Secret of the Wright Brothers.* Boston: Houghton Mifflin, 1979.

Courtney, W. B. "Twelve Seconds That Shrank the Earth." *Collier's,* 25 December 1948.

Crouch, Tom. *The Bishop's Boys: A Life of Wilbur and Orville Wright.* New York: W. W. Norton, 1989.

———. "December: Diamond Anniversary of Man's Propulsion Skyward." *Smithsonian,* December 1978.

Crowther, J. G. *Six Great Inventors.* London: Hamish Hamilton, 1954.

Drinkwater, Alpheus W. "I Knew Those Wright Brothers Were Crazy." *Reader's Digest,* November 1956, 188–89, 192, 194.

East, Omega G. *The Wright Brothers.* Washington, D.C.: Government Printing Office, 1961.

Gibbs-Smith, Charles H. "The Wright Brothers: The Family Background of the American Pioneers in Aviation." *History Today* (London), February 1974.

Glines, Carroll V. *The Wright Brothers—Pioneers of Power Flight.* New York: Franklin Watts, 1968.

Hallion, Richard P., ed. *The Wright Brothers: Heirs of Prometheus.* Washington, D.C.: National Air and Space Museum, Smithsonian Institution, 1978.

Harris, Sherwood. *The First to Fly: Aviation's Pioneer Days.* New York: Simon and Schuster, 1970.

Harrison, Michael. *Airborne at Kitty Hawk.* London: Cassell, 1953.

Hooven, Frederick J. "The Wright Brothers' Control System." *Scientific American,* November 1978.

Howard, Fred C. *Wilbur and Orville: A Biography of the Wright Brothers.* New York: Alfred A. Knopf, 1987.

Kelly, Fred C. "They Wouldn't Believe the Wrights Had Flown: A Study in Human Incredulity." *Harper's,* August 1955, 286–300.

———. *The Wright Brothers: A Biography Authorized by Orville Wright.* New York: Harcourt, Brace, 1943.

Kirk, Stephen. *First in Flight: The Wright Brothers in North Carolina.* Winston-Salem, N.C.: John F. Blair, 1995.

McFarland, Marvin W., ed. *The Papers of Wilbur and Orville Wright.* 2 vols. New York: McGraw-Hill, 1953.

McMahon, John R. *The Wright Brothers: Fathers of Flight.* Boston: Little, Brown, 1930.

Nolan, Patrick A., and John Zamonski. *The Wright Brothers Collection: A Guide to the Technical, Business and Legal,*

Genealogical, Photographic, and Other Archives at Wright State University. New York: Garland, 1977.

Parramore, Thomas C. *Triumph at Kitty Hawk: The Wright Brothers and Powered Flight.* Raleigh: Division of Archives and History, North Carolina Department of Cultural Resources, 1993.

Renstrom, Arthur G. *Wilbur and Orville Wright: A Bibliography.* Washington, D.C.: Library of Congress, 1968.

———. *Wilbur and Orville Wright: A Chronology Commemorating the Hundredth Anniversary of the Birth of Orville Wright, August 19, 1871.* Washington, D.C.: Library of Congress, 1975.

———. *Wilbur and Orville Wright: Pictorial Materials, a Documentary Guide.* Washington, D.C.: Library of Congress, 1982.

Ritchie, Malcolm L. *The Research and Development Methods of Wilbur and Orville Wright.* Dayton, Ohio: Wright State University, 1976.

Tate, William. "I Was Host to the Wright Brothers at Kitty Hawk." *U.S. Air Services,* December 1943, 29–30.

U.S. Congress. *Twenty-Fifth Anniversary of the First Airplane Flight.* 70th Cong., 2d sess., 1929. H. Doc. 520.

Walsh, John Evangelist. *One Day at Kitty Hawk: The Untold Story of the Wright Brothers and the Airplane.* New York: Thomas Y. Crowell, 1975.

West, Rupert E. "When the Wrights Gave Wings to the World." *U.S. Air Services* 12 (December 1927): 19–23.

Wright, Orville. "Diary of the First Flight." *Collier's,* 25 December 1948.

———. *How We Invented the Airplane.* Edited with commentary by Fred C. Kelly. New York: McKay, 1953.

———. "How We Made the First Flight." *Flying,* December 1913.

Wright, Wilbur. "Some Aeronautical Experiments." Presented to the Western Society of Engineers, 18 September 1901, reprinted in the 1902 Smithsonian Institution annual report.

Wright, Wilbur, and Orville Wright. *Miracle at Kitty Hawk: The Letters of Wilbur and Orville Wright.* Edited by Fred C. Kelly. New York: Farrar, Straus, and Young, 1951.

———. *The Papers of Wilbur and Orville Wright: Including the Chanute-Wright Letters and Other Papers of Octave Chanute.* Edited by Marvin W. McFarland. 1953. Reprint, Salem, N.H.: Ayer, 1990.

———. "The Wright Brothers' Aeroplane." *Century,* September 1908.

4

Advancements in Powered Flight Before World War I

Tim Brady

The Wrights' Marketing Attempts

THE FIRST FEW YEARS after the Wrights' brilliant achievement were bitter ones for the two brothers. Funding for their experiments had come from their own pockets and from the generosity of their sister, Katharine. The sale of a farm in Iowa, left to them by their father, also contributed to the fund.[1] Convinced of the military usefulness of the airplane, in 1905 the Wrights made several attempts to interest the U.S. Army in their invention, but they were unsuccessful. They made the same forays with the military in England and in France, where some interest was shown. Finally in May 1907, through a New York bank and investment firm, the Wright brothers were invited on an all-expenses-paid trip to France to demonstrate their invention. They disassembled and crated up one of their airplanes, and Wilbur Wright sailed for France. His brother and Charlie Taylor soon joined him.

Unfortunately, their negotiations with the French government stalled, and the brothers and Taylor returned home not having flown a minute. In fact, the aircraft had not been removed from its shipping crate. They did, however, hold out some hope that the roadblocks with the French government would someday be removed, so they decided to leave the aircraft in France, still crated.

On the return trip to the States, Wilbur contacted the U.S. War Department and found that a shift to more airminded personnel had occurred. The Army was set to announce bids for an airplane competition. Shortly afterwards, a French syndicate offered the Wrights a substantial business agreement for the rights to manufacture Wright aircraft in Europe. However, the Wrights had to demonstrate to the French the success of their machine by making two flights of 50 kilometers in an hour or less. At that time, flight distance success in Europe was being measured in meters rather than kilometers.[2] As a result of the French offer and the U.S. Army opportunities occurring simultaneously, the brothers decided that Wilbur would return to France and Orville would handle the Army trials scheduled in Fort Myer, Virginia.

Wilbur in France

Wilbur arrived in France and selected a site near a race track at Le Mans. After taking delivery on the still-crated airplane dubbed the "White Flyer" and discovering the condition of the delicate craft inside, Wilbur was furious. He accusingly and angrily wrote to his brother: "I am sure that with a scoop shovel I could have put things in within two or three minutes and made fully as good a job of it."[3] Actually, Orville had taken some care in packing the aircraft, but French customs officials had trashed the contents of the crate during their inspections. Wilbur worked day and night for two months to restore the aircraft to flying shape.

This added further fuel to the fire of French criticism that had surrounded the Wrights' claims. There was much skepticism, created in part by the Wrights themselves. In wishing to protect their investment, the Wrights had not shared with Octave Chanute the full aeronautical details of their invention. When Chanute wrote and lectured in Europe about the Wrights' discoveries, French aviators attempted to duplicate the Wright designs and found that they would not fly very well. The French then became convinced that the Wrights were frauds. Every day that Wilbur delayed the demonstration flights solidified the suspicion, but it also heightened anticipation. As luck would have it, when he was ready to conduct the demonstration flights, a hose came loose from the running engine, sprayed him with scalding water that seriously injured his hand, and caused more delays. Now even the English papers were calling him a fake.

Finally, on 8 August 1908, all was ready. Then a brisk wind came up. The wind velocity was such that it would have grounded any European aircraft. The skeptics were amazed that Wilbur Wright would even attempt a flight. Wilbur took off, made a circular flight with beautifully coordinated turns, and landed softly. The crowd went wild. Cheers erupted, and hats were thrown into the air.

Many famous French aviators such as the Voisins, Alberto Santos-Dumont, Roland Garros, and Louis Bleriot knew they had just witnessed a flight by the master in a machine that was far superior to anything in Europe. Delagrange, a great French flyer, said, "We are beaten: we do not exist."[4] Bleriot said, "It is marvelous" and "A new era of mechanical flight has commenced."[5] Ernest Archdeacon, a French aviator and an extremely vocal critic of the Wrights, admitted, "For too long a time the Wright brothers have been accused in Europe of bluff. . . . They are today hallowed in France" (fig. 4.1).[6]

Over the next six months, Wilbur made more than a hundred flights. Along the way, he won the 20,000 franc Michelin trophy by staying aloft for almost two and a half hours. He signed agreements with France and with businesses in England.

Orville at Fort Myer, Virginia

The U.S. Army had listed several specifications for the type of aircraft desired: (1) The machine must be able to carry two people with a seat arrangement to permit a maximum field of observation, (2) the operator must be able to control the machine from either seat, (3) the machine must carry enough fuel for 125 miles, (4) it must be able to travel at least 10 miles cross-country, and (5) it must maintain a speed of at least 40 mph (fig. 4.2). Several respondents expressed an interest, but only the Wright brothers would bring a machine to Fort Myer.

The Army requirements meant that the Wright brothers needed to build an entirely new airplane with two seats rather than the previous designs that had the operator lying prone. The Army bid proposal offered the suc-

Fig. 4.1. Members of a French parliamentary commission inspect the launching rail of a Wright Type A airplane at Pau, France, February 1909. The Wright airplane can be seen in the background. By permission of the National Air and Space Museum, Smithsonian Institution, ©1999 Smithsonian Institution.

SIGNAL CORPS SPECIFICATION, NO. 486.

ADVERTISEMENT AND SPECIFICATION FOR A HEAVIER-THAN-AIR FLYING MACHINE.

TO THE PUBLIC:

Sealed proposals, in duplicate, will be received at this office until 12 o'clock noon on February 1, 1908, on behalf of the Board of Ordnance and Fortification for furnishing the Signal Corps with a heavier-than-air flying machine. All proposals received will be turned over to the Board of Ordnance and Fortification at its first meeting after February 1 for its official action.

Persons wishing to submit proposals under this specification can obtain the necessary forms and envelopes by application to the Chief Signal Officer, United States Army, War Department, Washington, D. C. The United States reserves the right to reject any and all proposals.

Unless the bidders are also the manufacturers of the flying machine they must state the name and place of the maker.

Preliminary.—This specification covers the construction of a flying machine supported entirely by the dynamic reaction of the atmosphere and having no gas bag.

Acceptance.—The flying machine will be accepted only after a successful trial flight, during which it will comply with all requirements of this specification. No payments on account will be made until after the trial flight and acceptance.

Inspection.—The Government reserves the right to inspect any and all processes of manufacture.

GENERAL REQUIREMENTS.

The general dimensions of the flying machine will be determined by the manufacturer, subject to the following conditions:

1. Bidders must submit with their proposals the following:
   (a) Drawings to scale showing the general dimensions and shape of the flying machine which they propose to build under this specification.
   (b) Statement of the speed for which it is designed.
   (c) Statement of the total surface area of the supporting planes.
   (d) Statement of the total weight.
   (e) Description of the engine which will be used for motive power.
   (f) The material of which the frame, planes, and propellers will be constructed. Plans received will not be shown to other bidders.

2. It is desirable that the flying machine should be designed so that it may be quickly and easily assembled and taken apart and packed for transportation in army wagons. It should be capable of being assembled and put in operating condition in about one hour.

3. The flying machine must be designed to carry two persons having a combined weight of about 350 pounds, also sufficient fuel for a flight of 125 miles.

4. The flying machine should be designed to have a speed of at least forty miles per hour in still air, but bidders must submit quotations in their proposals for cost depending upon the speed attained during the trial flight, according to the following scale:

   40 miles per hour, 100 per cent.
   39 miles per hour, 90 per cent.
   38 miles per hour, 80 per cent.
   37 miles per hour, 70 per cent.
   36 miles per hour, 60 per cent.
   Less than 36 miles per hour rejected.
   41 miles per hour, 110 per cent.
   42 miles per hour, 120 per cent.
   43 miles per hour, 130 per cent.
   44 miles per hour, 140 per cent.

5. The speed accomplished during the trial flight will be determined by taking an average of the time over a measured course of more than five miles, against and with the wind. The time will be taken by a flying start, passing the starting point at full speed at both ends of the course. This test subject to such additional details as the Chief Signal Officer of the Army may prescribe at the time.

6. Before acceptance a trial endurance flight will be required of at least one hour during which time the flying machine must remain continuously in the air without landing. It shall return to the starting point and land without any damage that would prevent it immediately starting upon another flight. During this trial flight of one hour it must be steered in all directions without difficulty and at all times under perfect control and equilibrium.

7. Three trials will be allowed for speed as provided for in paragraphs 4 and 5. Three trials for endurance as provided for in paragraph 6, and both tests must be completed within a period of thirty days from the date of delivery. The expense of the tests to be borne by the manufacturer. The place of delivery to the Government and trial flights will be at Fort Myer, Virginia.

8. It should be so designed as to ascend in any country which may be encountered in field service. The starting device must be simple and transportable. It should also land in a field without requiring a specially prepared spot and without damaging its structure.

9. It should be provided with some device to permit of a safe descent in case of an accident to the propelling machinery.

10. It should be sufficiently simple in its construction and operation to permit an intelligent man to become proficient in its use within a reasonable length of time.

11. Bidders must furnish evidence that the Government of the United States has the lawful right to use all patented devices or appurtenances which may be a part of the flying machine, and that the manufacturers of the flying machine are authorized to convey the same to the Government. This refers to the unrestricted right to use the flying machine sold to the Government, but does not contemplate the exclusive purchase of patent rights for duplicating the flying machine.

12. Bidders will be required to furnish with their proposal a certified check amounting to ten per cent of the price stated for the 40-mile speed. Upon making the award for this flying machine these certified checks will be returned to the bidders, and the successful bidder will be required to furnish a bond, according to Army Regulations, of the amount equal to the price stated for the 40-mile speed.

13. The price quoted in proposals must be understood to include the instruction of two men in the handling and operation of this flying machine. No extra charge for this service will be allowed.

14. Bidders must state the time which will be required for delivery after receipt of order.

JAMES ALLEN,
Brigadier General, Chief Signal Officer of the Army.

SIGNAL OFFICE,
WASHINGTON, D. C., *December 23, 1907.*

Fig. 4.2. Specifications for the U.S. Army's first airplane. Courtesy of the USAF Museum.

cessful candidate $25,000 for the machine plus a bonus of $2,500 for each mile per hour faster than 40.

On 9 September 1908, Orville conducted the first flight demonstration at Fort Myer in a previously untested aircraft with some ten thousand unbelievers present (fig. 4.3). The aircraft was launched by "dropping of some heavy weights that were suspended from the tower and connected by rope to a two-wheeled starting car" upon which the aircraft rested.[7] The first flight lasted for one minute and ten seconds. He conducted twelve more flights, of varying durations, some lasting an hour or more with several passengers. On the thirteenth flight, Orville decided to install larger propellers on the aircraft to try to gain a modicum of improved performance; after all, every mile per hour of increased speed over 40 meant an additional $2,500.

For this flight on 17 September, Orville invited as a passenger Lt. Thomas E. Selfridge (fig. 4.4). The Army had asked Selfridge to act as one of the judges of the flight demonstrations. Selfridge was a very air-minded officer who had been participating with Alexander Graham Bell's Aerial Experiment Association in attempting to develop a flyable aircraft.

They took off and made three flawless circles around the field. Things were going even better than previous flights, but as they pointed the aircraft toward Arlington Cemetery for the fourth lap, something happened (figs. 4.5 and 4.6). Orville told Wilbur:

I heard (or felt) a light tapping in the rear of the machine. A hurried glance behind revealed nothing

Fig. 4.4. Lt. Thomas E. Selfridge. *Scientific American,* 2 October 1909.

Fig. 4.3. Orville Wright in flight at Fort Myer, Virginia, in 1908. Courtesy of the USAF Museum.

Fig. 4.5. Orville Wright and Lt. Thomas E. Selfridge just before Selfridge's fatal flight at Fort Myer. Courtesy of the USAF Museum.

Fig. 4.6. The wreckage of the Wright Flyer at Fort Myer. Courtesy of the USAF Museum.

wrong, but I decided to shut off the power and descend as soon as the machine could be faced in a direction where a landing could be made. This decision was hardly reached, in fact, I suppose it was not over two or three seconds from the time the first taps were heard, till two big thumps, which gave the machine a terrible shaking, showed that something had broken. . . . The machine then turned to the right and I immediately shut off the power. I then discovered that the machine would not respond to the steering and lateral balancing levers, which produced a most peculiar feeling of helplessness. Yet I continued to push the levers, when the machine suddenly turned to the left (the right wing was rising high in the air) till it faced directly up the field. I reversed the levers to stop the turning and to bring the wings on a level. Quick as a flash, the machine

turned down in front and started straight for the ground. Our course for 50 feet was within a very few degrees of the perpendicular. Lieutenant Selfridge up to this time had not uttered a word, though he took a hasty glance behind when the propeller broke, and turned once or twice to look into my face to see what I thought of the situation. But when the machine turned headfirst for the ground, he exclaimed Oh! Oh! in an almost inaudible voice.

I pulled the front lever to its limit, but there was no response in the course of the machine. Thinking that, maybe, something was caught and that the rudder was not completely turned, I released the lever a little and gave another pull, but there was no change. I then looked to the rudder and saw that it was bent to its limit downward, and that the pressure of air on the under side was bulging cloth up between the ribs. The first 50 ft. of that plunge seemed like half a minute, though I can hardly believe that it was over a second at most. The front rudder in that distance had not changed more than five or ten degrees. Suddenly just before reaching the ground, probably 25 feet, something changed—the machine began to right itself rapidly. A few feet more and we would have landed safely.[8]

Selfridge was thrown clear of the wreckage, but his head struck something on the ground. He died a few hours later, becoming the first person to lose his life as the result of a powered (heavier-than-air) aircraft accident. Orville sustained four broken ribs, a broken leg, and several fractures of the hip.

When Orville had recovered enough to function, he conducted his own accident analysis by asking that parts of the airplane be brought into his hospital room. From his examination, Orville concluded that one of the blades of the wooden propeller on the right had split,

setting up a strong vibration. The vibration loosened its housing and caused it to shift a few inches. This caused the propeller to come into contact and cut the main wire stay that braced the tail control surfaces. The plane then plunged out of control.

Orville and Wilbur rebuilt their aircraft and returned to Fort Myer in July 1909 to continue the Army evaluation flights. The aircraft performed beautifully and met all of the Army's requirements. On 30 July 1909, the final flight was conducted. The aircraft had to be flown cross-country to Arlington and back over some rugged terrain to meet the Army's 10-mile cross-country requirement.[9] Army Lt. Benjamin Foulois was Orville's passenger. The aircraft was clocked at an average speed of 42.58 mph. For the extra 2 mph, the Wrights earned a bonus of $5,000 (fig. 4.7).

Recognition for the Wrights was a long time in coming, but at last the U.S. government had recognized their achievements, and the press began to praise their efforts

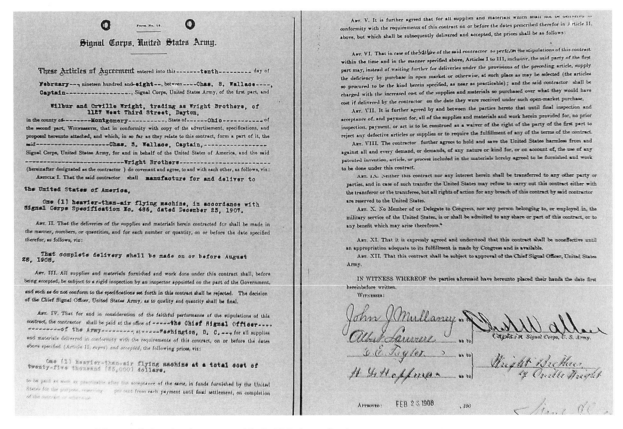

Fig. 4.7. A copy of the Wright brothers' contract with the U.S. Army for the first American military airplane. Courtesy of the USAF Museum.

as explained by the following quotation from a 1909 article:

> What electricity, what the automobile, what steam has done, is nothing—so say the wise ones—to what the art of flying will do. Aeroplaning is but a part of this art. But it is a big part, and it is good to have seen its beginnings; good to have seen some of its dangers and accidents, and good, indeed, to have seen pluck and nerve win out in the end, and to know that the premier machine of the world is an American machine, and the premier aviators of the world American men.[10]

Alexander Graham Bell's Aerial Experiment Association

Alexander Graham Bell had long been a follower of advances in flight. He had done some experiments himself and was both an admirer of and a contributor to Langley's attempts to build a man-carrying flying machine. Bell had been a witness to some of Langley's earlier experiments in which Langley had built and flown a steam-powered model. Nevertheless, Bell and most of the American scientific community were slow to recognize the Wright brothers' achievements and knew little of the aerodynamic principles the Wrights had discovered. For example, Bell was not convinced that the current line of pursuit in heavier-than-air machines was the correct course to follow. He began to experiment with large tetrahedron gliders. He believed that lighter craft emphasizing the qualities of the kite would be preferable to heavier crafts. Apparently, Bell did not have a clear picture of the forces involved in aerodynamics. For example, when speaking of a motorized aircraft that experiences an engine stoppage, Bell said that "should an accident happen to the propelling machinery . . . the aviator could cast anchor and the machine would continue flying as a kite."[11]

In October 1907, Bell created an organization chartered as the Aerial Experiment Association (AEA). Its goal was to build a successful man-carrying flying machine, starting practically from scratch. This was unmindful of the Wrights' achievements four years previously. Even as the AEA began, Wilbur Wright was in France preparing for a series of flights that would stun Europe.

Among those in the AEA were Glenn Curtiss, recruited by Bell because of his expertise in engine building, and Lt. Thomas Selfridge. The AEA tried in vain to fly Bell's tetrahedron. The other members of the AEA persuaded Bell to abandon the tetrahedron idea and to begin a more conventional heavier-than-air craft with Selfridge appointed as the project director. At Bell's urging, Selfridge contacted the Wright brothers "to obtain information to enable the association's aircraft to make successful flights. The Wrights, having great respect for Dr. Bell, gave Selfridge the information with the provision that it would never be used to manufacture aircraft for sale."[12]

The AEA's first effort was an aircraft known as the Red Wing, so named because of the fabric used to cover the wings. The fabric was some of Bell's leftover red silk that he had used to cover kites in earlier experiments. The aircraft, which was powered by a Curtiss 40-horsepower, air-cooled V-8 engine, made a partially successful flight on 12 March 1908. The aircraft had a glaring deficiency, however; there was no way to control the lateral movement of the aircraft. On a subsequent flight attempt, a gust of wind caught the machine and flipped it on its side, causing major damage.

The second aircraft, the White Wing (Bell's supply of red silk fabric having been exhausted, a white cotton material was used), was moderately successful (figs. 4.8 and 4.9). The aircraft had the same engine as the first, but it had movable control surfaces at the tips of the wings for lateral control. These devices were suggested by Bell, who "believed for some time that he was the inventor of these devices."[13] In actuality, these were an extrapolation of the Wright's wing-warping method of lateral control and had been applied by French aviator Robert Esnault-Pelterie to his 1904 glider. The term *aileron* to describe such devices was invented by the French aviator Henry Farman.[14]

Until it crashed, the White Wing was moderately successful, making one flight of more than 1,000 feet (horizontal). The next aircraft constructed by the AEA was the June Bug, which was a modified and improved White Wing using the same engine. The aircraft was so successful that the AEA decided to enter a competition. *Scientific American* offered a trophy for the first aircraft to fly at least one kilometer (at 3,281 feet this was less than a mile). This was a curious prize considering the

Fig. 4.8. Front view of the Aerial Experiment Association's White Wing. *Scientific American*, 30 May 1908.

Fig. 4.9. The White Wing in flight. *Scientific American*, 30 May 1908.

fact that Wilbur Wright was conducting flight exhibitions in France measured in hours, not minutes, and tens of kilometers (or miles), not kilometers (less than a mile). "*Scientific American* was in an awkward position. Then, as now, one of the country's leading scientific journals, it had been slow to recognize the work of the Wright brothers. As of late January 1906, *Scientific American* had been skeptical about the Wrights' long flights in 1905, its editorial board feeling that if the reports were true, then certainly the enterprising American press would have given them great attention."[15] Finally, on 7 April 1906, the magazine stated that "in all the history of invention, there is probably no parallel to the unostentatious manner in which the Wright brothers of Dayton, Ohio, ushered into the world their epoch-making invention of the first successful aeroplane flying-machine."

Nevertheless, the June Bug won the *Scientific American* trophy. In all fairness to *Scientific American*, however, they did contact Orville Wright and offer him the opportunity to compete for the trophy. Orville declined, stating that to compete he would have to equip his air-

craft with wheels to meet the self-launching requirement for the trophy. He was also too busy readying the aircraft for the Army trials at Fort Myer to take the time to modify the aircraft.

The AEA was disbanded following Selfridge's death in September 1908. Perhaps the AEA's greatest contribution was not in advancing the science of aeronautics but in stirring the interest of Glenn Curtiss in a life's work in aviation. The advancing of aeronautics had been achieved by the Wright brothers as well as several European aviators at least two years previously.

S. F. Cody

The first man to make a controlled, powered flight in England was an American, Samuel Franklin Cody (not to be confused with "Buffalo Bill" Cody, although there were some career similarities). Cody had been stranded in England when his Wild West show ran out of steam. His long-standing interest in aviation led him to design and build man-carrying kites for the British army. When

Fig. 4.10. Right side view of the S. F. Cody biplane. By permission of the National Air and Space Museum, Smithsonian Institution, ©1999 Smithsonian Institution.

Wilbur Wright brought his airplane to France, Cody traveled there to see him fly. Cody then returned to England and built an aircraft of his own design but similar to the Wright airplane (shown in fig. 4.10). Cody made a successful, controlled, powered flight on 16 October 1908 at Farnborough, England. The aircraft, powered by a 50-horsepower Antoinette engine driving two propellers, was built under contract by Cody for the British War Office.

A. V. Roe

Alliott Verdon Roe is given credit as the first English-born citizen to design and fly an "all-English" airplane. This event occurred on 5 June 1909. The airplane, the Avroplane, was of a three-wing (triplane) design pow-

ered by a 9-horsepower JAP air-cooled motorcycle engine coupled to a propeller installed in a tractor (puller) arrangement. With its lightweight construction, the aircraft, pilot, and all other on-board items weighed only 399 pounds. Roe had been experimenting with airplanes for several years and realized that the tail of the airplane should be raised while accelerating for takeoff speed. In his earlier experiments, Roe had so many failures resulting in so many crashes that he was hailed as a public menace. The authorities went so far as to create an ordinance forbidding the use of public commons and parks around London by pilots who were attempting to fly experimental aircraft.[16] However, the persistent Roe began to build some very effective airplanes and founded a highly successful company, AVRO, which became important to England's early aviation achievements (fig. 4.11).

Fig. 4.11. A. V. Roe's persistence paid off. This is an AVRO 504 Trainer used during World War I. Courtesy of the USAF Museum.

The First Flight Across the English Channel

One of the most important events in the early development of aircraft was the crossing of the English Channel by air in a heavier-than-air machine. Its significance, foretold almost a year before the event itself, is quoted from this excerpt from an article written in September 1908 by a military correspondent for the *Times* of London:

> The old cry that England, being an island, is only secure from attack by the upkeep of a powerful Navy is fully recognized by all grades of society and all denominations of politicians; but it is not yet realized that England's safety as an island will vanish if not insured against aerial attack . . . aeroplanes are undoubtedly going to prove enormously powerful factors in any warfare of the future."[17]

In 1908, to stimulate competition and growth of aviation in England, the *London Mail* offered £500 to the first aviator who could fly across the English Channel in a heavier-than-air machine. There being no takers, the newspaper raised the prize to £1,000 in 1909. Three competitors were poised to try for the prize: Hubert Latham (fig. 4.12), Count Charles de Lambert, and Louis Bleriot (fig. 4.13).

Latham was a Frenchman with English blood who had the impressive financial backing of Leon Levavasseur, the builder of the graceful Antoinette aircraft. It was Latham who would make the first attempt on 19 July 1909. After a few days of blustery weather and rain, the weather cleared sufficiently to permit the fragile Antoinette monoplane to fly. Just after dawn, Latham was airborne and out over the French coast, heading for the cliffs of Dover. As he flew into a cloud, the torpedo boat *Harpon* lost sight of him. A few seconds later, the Antoinette's normally trustworthy engine began to show signs of breaking down. Despite Latham's best efforts, the engine quit and Latham began a 900-foot glide to the surface of the water. He spotted the *Harpon* about a

Fig. 4.12. Informal portrait of Hubert Latham. By permission of the National Air and Space Museum, Smithsonian Institution, ©1999 Smithsonian Institution.

Fig. 4.13. Louis Bleriot. By permission of the National Air and Space Museum, Smithsonian Institution, ©1999 Smithsonian Institution.

Fig. 4.14. Latham in the Antoinette IV, having ditched in the English Channel, 19 July 1909. By permission of the National Air and Space Museum, Smithsonian Institution, ©1999 Smithsonian Institution.

mile away. The aircraft settled gently into the water at 45 mph and floated majestically (fig. 4.14). Latham had scarcely gotten wet, and when picked up about five minutes later, he was sitting with his feet up casually smoking a cigarette. His aircraft was towed back to France but was in no condition to fly again any time soon. Latham immediately ordered another Antoinette be sent to the field at Calais, where the aviators had gathered. Meanwhile Bleriot, on crutches and suffering from a recent burn from his engine catching fire in flight, arrived with his Bleriot XI aircraft. The aircraft was a monoplane powered by a 3-cylinder Anzani engine of about 30 horsepower.

Bleriot's successes as an aircraft designer and aviator were punctuated by many crashes during his trial-and-error approach to achieving reliable flight. Bleriot had been present when Wilbur Wright conducted his marvelous flight exhibitions at Le Mans in 1908. He invited Wright to his field. Wright had been very helpful and worked out a series of business arrangements allowing Bleriot to use the Wright patent to cover his aircraft. As a result of Wright's influence, Bleriot had abandoned his rotating wingtip ailerons for a wing-warp mechanism. He also created a new flight control system for his number XI aircraft described as follows:

A fully developed stick-and-rudder system of controls in the pilot's cockpit made its appearance for the first time in No. XI. The stick controlled the wing warping and the up-and-down motion of the elevators. To make the airplane go up, the stick was pulled back and to nose over it was pushed forward. Sideways motion of the stick banked the airplane gently (and not always very effectively) in the direction in which the stick was moved. There were two rudder pedals—one for each foot. Pressing on the left pedal tended to move the plane's nose toward the left and kicking the right slewed the nose to the right. There was a little wheel rigidly fixed to the top of the stick to make the control column easy to grasp with either hand."[18]

Fig. 4.15. Right side view of the Louis Bleriot Model XI on the ground with Louis Bleriot in cockpit. This was the first airplane to fly across the English Channel, on 25 July 1909. By permission of the National Air and Space Museum, Smithsonian Institution, ©1999 Smithsonian Institution.

Fig. 4.16. Count Charles de Lambert in his Wright biplane. By permission of the National Air and Space Museum, Smithsonian Institution, ©1999 Smithsonian Institution.

This control system became the standard method of controlling the three axes of an aircraft and is still in use today.

Bleriot brought his Model XI aircraft to the Calais vicinity at a small town, Les Baraques, to try for the English Channel prize (fig. 4.15). By the time that Bleriot was prepared to fly, Latham's new Antoinette had arrived at his location in the nearby village of Sangatte, and he, too, was ready. It was turning into a horse race. The third contender, Count de Lambert, who had arrived with two Wright biplanes, had pulled out of the race because one of his aircraft had been damaged in an earlier flight (fig. 4.16).

Both Latham and Bleriot were ready to fly on 24 July, but the weather and high winds kept them on the ground. It seemed unlikely that the winds would die down enough for an attempt the next day. Both Bleriot and Latham retired for the evening. A business friend of Bleriot was having a sleepless night, and he was awake early the next morning when the weather seemed to change and the winds were calming. He woke up Bleriot, and together they drove to the field at Les Baraques.

Bleriot cast aside his crutches and was helped into his airplane at 4 A.M. He took off and made a 15-minute flight around Calais. He then landed at the jumping-off point to await sunrise. One condition of the prize was that the flight had to be conducted between the hours of sunrise and sunset. At 4:30 A.M., Bleriot could see sunlight all around, the winds were calm enough to permit a takeoff, and the sky was clear. At 4:35 A.M., Bleriot took off.

I am in the air, my engine making 1,200 revolutions —almost its highest speed—in order that I may get quickly over the telegraph wires along the edge of the cliff. As soon as I am over the cliff I reduce my speed. There is now no need to force my engine.

I begin my flight, steady and sure, towards the coast of England. I have no apprehensions, no sensations. . . . The Escopette [a French Navy destroyer] has seen me. She is driving ahead at full speed. She makes perhaps 42 kilometers [about 26 miles an hour]. What matters? I am making at least 68 kilometers [42 miles per hour].

Rapidly I overtake her, traveling at a height of 80 meters [about 260 feet]. . . . Ten minutes have gone. I have passed the destroyer, and I turn my head to see whether I am proceeding in the right direction. I am amazed. There is nothing to be seen, neither the torpedo-destroyer, nor France nor England. I am alone. . . . For ten minutes I am lost. It is a strange position, to be alone, unguided, without compass, in the air over the middle of the Channel.

I touch nothing. My hands and feet rest lightly on the levers. . . . For ten minutes I continue, neither rising nor falling, nor turning. And then twenty minutes after I have left the French coast, I see the green cliffs of Dover.[19]

Bleriot continued his flight and, despite some tricky winds at his landing site, managed to get the airplane down with only minor damage to the machine upon landing. He had flown 20 miles in 37 minutes.

Meanwhile, Levavasseur awoke at 4:30 A.M. and spotted Bleriot flying toward the coast. He woke up Latham, who scrambled out to his aircraft. Unfortunately, the winds had freshened enough so that Latham could not fly. Four days later, Latham gave it a second try with similar results as his first. He ditched the aircraft in the Channel, this time much closer, about 7 miles from the coast of England.

Bleriot was an immediate hero in both England and France, and he enjoyed his fame well into World War I. However, for England, the world had changed forever. The Channel, England's protective moat, heretofore defensible with a strong navy, was now a mere stream, and the navy would become almost meaningless as a defensive barrier.

The First Air Meet

The first air meet of a slightly international flavor was held in the champagne region of France at Rheims in August 1909. Scarcely three years had passed since the first powered heavier-than-air flight had occurred in Europe. This, of course, had been accomplished by Brazilian Alberto Santos-Dumont on 23 October 1906.

During the summer of 1908, Wilbur Wright had flown exhibition flights in LeMans, and the "secret" of how the Wright brothers controlled their flying machines was well known. The secret had already shown up in several European-designed aircraft. Around the time of the Rheims air meet, Orville and Wilbur Wright were both busy. Orville was in Germany, and Wilbur was at Fort Myer, Virginia, putting their aircraft through its final paces to gain the U.S. Army contract. They had rebuilt the aircraft following Orville's recovery from the crash that had killed Thomas Selfridge. Neither of the great American pioneers attended this first air meet. The only American entrant was Glenn Curtiss.

Most of the other great names in aviation were there, including Latham, Farman, and Bleriot from France and George Cockburn, England's sole representative. In addition, there were several dignitaries in attendance, such as Winston Churchill, then England's president of the Board of Trade, and Lloyd George, Britain's chancellor of the exchequer.

Thirty-eight entrants brought aircraft of the following types to the meet: seven Voisins, six Wrights (built under contract in Europe), five Bleriots, four Farmans, four REPs, three Antoinettes, two Curtisses (one new aircraft flown by Curtiss), one Santos-Dumont, one Breguet, one Sanchis, and four types that were nameless.

French aircraft designs dominated the field. Thirty were designed and built in France, and the remaining eight were American designs. There were no airplanes of British design in the competition.[20] At this point, Britain lagged far behind both France and the United States in aviation technology. Perhaps this was due to Lloyd George's foolish misappraisal of the value of the airplane to the security of England. He stated, "As to the use of the aeroplane in warfare it appears too frail and flimsy to be taken seriously and I apprehend no danger of any airship invasion."[21]

The Rheims air meet carried with it all of the excitement of a Superbowl or an international soccer championship (fig. 4.17). At stake was some 200,000 francs, including a trophy race for speed created by the American newspaper tycoon Gordon Bennett. This prize alone, scheduled for the last event, was worth 25,000 francs.

Fig. 4.17. View from the grandstand of the first air meet, held in 1909 in Rheims, France. By permission of the National Air and Space Museum, Smithsonian Institution, ©1999 Smithsonian Institution.

Fig. 4.18. The race is on at the air meet in Rheims. By permission of the National Air and Space Museum, Smithsonian Institution, ©1999 Smithsonian Institution.

There were some 200,000 paid spectators from all over Europe and the United States along with about 100,000 unpaid watchers scattered around the surrounding hills. Most of the "fans" arrived in horse-drawn carriages, and a few came in motorcars, themselves a novelty in the day-to-day living of the local French citizens. The event was well publicized as the Prix de la Champagne to honor the champagne industry. Several competitive events were scheduled, including those for distance over a closed circuit (in the language of the day, the one who could fly farthest without alighting), altitude, and most exciting of all, speed (fig. 4.18).

Henry Farman, flying one of his own airplanes powered by a new Gnome Rotary engine, won the 50,000 francs Grand Prix for distance (fig. 4.19). Farman won for completing a flight of 112 miles (nonstop) in less than 3 hours and 5 minutes. Hubert Latham took second place (25,000 francs) with a 96-mile flight, and he won first in the altitude contest (FF25,000) for achieving an altitude of 490 feet in his Antoinette.

The most exciting event was the Gordon Bennett trophy race for speed, which became a contest between two aggressive competitors, Bleriot and Curtiss. Curtiss had

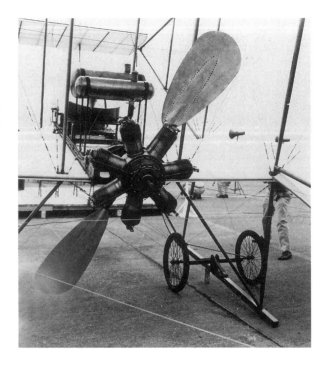

Fig. 4.19. Henry Farman aircraft shown with a Gnome Rotary engine used at Rheims. Courtesy of the USAF Museum.

Fig. 4.20. View of Curtiss-Herring No. 1 "Rheims Racer" on the ground in 1910. By permission of the National Air and Space Museum, Smithsonian Institution, ©1999 Smithsonian Institution.

built a biplane powered by a newly designed engine, a 50-horsepower V-8. The engine had never been installed in the airplane, and the airplane had never been flown (fig. 4.20). Since Curtiss had brought only this one aircraft and engine, the Bennett race would be the only event in which he would participate.

Bleriot was flying one of his monoplanes, a Bleriot XII, powered by a souped-up 8-cylinder, 80-horsepower, water-cooled engine (fig. 4.21).

On the morning of 28 August, the weather was acceptable. Curtiss started his engine and flew a trial run. Despite some turbulence, he felt that it was time to make his run at the prize. He notified the judges and took off. He climbed to 500 feet and began his 20-kilometer circuit with full throttle and in a continuing descent. He crossed the finish line 15 minutes and 50 seconds later. Many of his fellow countrymen rushed over to congratulate him, thinking he would be the winner, but Bleriot had yet to fly.

For most of the day Bleriot had fine-tuned his airplane, changing propellers, tinkering with the engine, checking the rigging, until he was satisfied. Curtiss's heart sank when Bleriot's first lap was completed in less time than Curtiss had turned in. However, the race was not over, and in the second circuit Bleriot's time had been slower. Curtiss had won the race with 5.8 seconds to spare.

Curtiss and Bleriot squared off again the next day for a three-lap prize. Bleriot crashed his aircraft, but escaped with only burns on his face and hands. Curtiss claimed the prize. To Bleriot's credit, he did win the speed contest for one circuit of the 10-kilometer course. This is a summary of the events and the winners:[22]

Longest flight	Farman—111.78 miles
One-lap speed (10 kilometers)	Bleriot—7 min. 47.8 sec.
Two-lap speed (Bennett Cup)	Curtiss—15 min. 50.6 sec.
Three-lap speed	Curtiss—23 min. 20.2 sec.
Passenger-carrying contest (Two passengers; one lap)	Farman—10 min. 39 sec.
Height flight	Latham—490 feet

The First Long-Distance Race

In 1906, the *Daily Mail* posted £10,000 for the first person who could fly from London to Manchester, a distance of about 185 miles, in 24 hours or less. Since no one in Europe had yet flown even 5 miles, this seemed

Fig. 4.21. The Bleriot team. *Scientific American,* 4 September 1909.

like a preposterous proposal. In their typical sarcastic jibes, a competing London newspaper said it would pay the same sum for the first person to journey to the center of the earth and return in a fortnight or travel to Mars and back in a week. The *Daily Mail* was, of course, trying to stimulate interest to develop English aviation, which was lagging behind that of France and America. Nevertheless, the prize went untried for three years.

The first to try for the prize was the very likable Claude Grahame-White. Through his exploits in flight, he had charmed his way into the hearts of his fellow countrymen (and women). Grahame-White had considered flying his Bleriot XI for the attempt, but decided instead to purchase a Farman biplane equipped with a Gnome Rotary engine of 50 horsepower arranged in a pusher-type (propeller aft) arrangement. He felt that the Farman was strong, reliable, and easier to fly than the Bleriot.

On the morning of 23 April 1910, Grahame-White took off from a field near London to the cheers of several thousand well-wishers. After a flight of about 85 miles, he landed at the town of Rugby. He refueled and took off again heading for Crewe (figs. 4.22 and 4.23). However, because of a rough-running engine and turbulence that had developed because of winds, Grahame-White put down safely at Lichfield, about 117 miles north of London. A short time later, the winds increased, flipping the Farman over and causing substantial damage. Grahame-White disassembled his machine and had it transported back to London to be repaired for another attempt. He and some helpers worked feverishly, without rest, to restore the aircraft to flyable condition. When it was done, he took a well-deserved nap.

Meanwhile, Louis Paulhan, who was the other contestant, arrived with an identical Farman and immediately began to assemble the craft. Just before 3:00 P.M. on 27 April, Paulhan completed the task. Since the winds were light, he decided to begin, without so much as a test flight. At 5:30 P.M. Paulhan was off. Following a train arranged as a guide, Paulhan headed toward Manchester. He flew on until it grew dark and, spotting the lights of Lichfield, decided to land in a meadow. Paulhan tells what happened next:

> Suddenly my motor stopped, every drop of petrol exhausted, and my machine swooped downwards almost like a stone dropping. What should I do? Beneath me was the brewery and a certain smash; behind me was a narrow field which was almost a

Fig. 4.22. Claude Grahame-White in flight in his Farman aircraft. Courtesy of the USAF Museum.

Fig. 4.23. Grahame-White at Rugby, England, 23 April 1910. By permission of the National Air and Space Museum, Smithsonian Institution, ©1999 Smithsonian Institution.

spider's web with a mesh of telegraph wires. I had an imperceptible fraction of a second in which to make up my mind, and I decided to risk the telegraph wires. As I sank I made a sharp twist right back on the line of my course, and was lucky enough to lift myself over the wires."[23]

Paulhan landed safely, and a short time later he went to bed, ready to rise early the next morning to make the final leg of the journey in daylight. Meanwhile, Grahame-White had been notified that Paulhan was on his way. He hurried out to the field and at 6:30 P.M. quickly took off for Manchester despite a strong breeze. At 7:55 with the light failing, he landed his aircraft at Roade, some 57 miles behind Paulhan. It was there that Grahame-White made a historic decision. He decided to attempt a night flight to catch and pass his competitor. "To ascend in the darkness had never yet been attempted by any airman. Mr. White carried no map—it had been left behind in the rush of departure—and in any case would have been useless."[24] He was counting on the moon to help illuminate his way once he was airborne. To make sure he had enough light to see his takeoff area, he ral-

lied automobile and motorcycle drivers to line up on either side of the field and to turn on their lights. He took off and headed for the lights of the railway station. "I could see absolutely nothing of the ground below me. It was all a black smudge. I went right over the railway station lights and then—fortunately for only a second or two—my engine missed fire. I began to sink towards the inky darkness below me. . . . And then to my joy, my engine picked up again and I rose once more."[25] The engine problem, according to one account, was caused when his coat sleeve had "snagged the ignition switch and turned it off."[26] The engine responded immediately when the switch was returned to the appropriate position.

Grahame-White flew aided by trains and through a prearranged agreement with a friend who situated his automobile to shine its lights on the side of a pub. Grahame-White had no trouble recognizing this signal. However, as daylight approached, the turbulence increased and he was forced to land in a field near Polesworth just after 4:00 A.M. He remarked, "My struggle was not with the darkness, but with the wind. It was

Fig. 4.24. Louis Paulhan in flight in his Farman aircraft during the first long-distance race. By permission of the National Air and Space Museum, Smithsonian Institution, ©1999 Smithsonian Institution.

fierce gusts which eventually brought me down."[27] Grahame-White had reached a point just 10 miles short of where Paulhan was readying his aircraft for flight. About three minutes later, Paulhan took off and finished the flight to Manchester without further mishap. He neatly collected the £10,000.[28] Paulhan, it seems, was the more experienced aviator in combating the wind (fig. 4.24).

The significance of this event to aviation history is not so much that it was the first "long-distance" air race but that it tested the psychological, and in some cases physiological, barriers to flight posed by the onset of darkness. These were cast into that pit where all other debunked myths sleep. The flight of Grahame-White demonstrated that an aircraft could take off, navigate, and land in darkness given the pilot's ability to see and to ascertain the attitude of the aircraft relative to the ground. It would be another twenty years before reliable attitude instruments would make their way into airplane cockpits, but it started here, on the perilous night flight from London to Manchester.

Air Shows and Air Races

The first American air show was held at Dominguez Fields south of Los Angeles in January 1910. Although not as big as the Rheims air show, it attracted 175,000 spectators and was important to the advancement of aviation in the United States (fig. 4.25). The competitors included Glenn Curtiss, Louis Paulhan, and Eugene Ely.

The Schneider Cup was important to the development of sea planes. It was first offered by a wealthy French arms maker, Jacques Schneider, in 1913 at Monaco (fig. 4.26). The rules stated that each contestant must taxi on the water for half of the first lap, then take off and fly the remaining 28 laps totaling some 173 miles. The contestants were American Charles Weymann in a Nieuport, Frenchmen Roland Garros in a Morane-Saulnier, Gabriel Espanet in a Nieuport, and Maurice Prevost in a Deperdussin. Garros had engine problems, Weymann had to quit on lap 24, Espanet retired with engine problems, and Prevost landed on his final lap short of the finish line and taxied over it. This was not

Fig. 4.25. Los Angeles Airshow, 1910. By permission of the National Air and Space Museum, Smithsonian Institution, ©1999 Smithsonian Institution.

Fig. 4.26. First Schneider Cup race, Monaco, 1913. *Above left,* a Farman; *right,* a Nieuport; *below left,* Roland Garros in a Morane-Saulnier; *right,* a Breguet. By permission of the National Air and Space Museum, Smithsonian Institution, ©1999 Smithsonian Institution.

allowed, so Prevost had to return to the air and complete the final lap. Of course, by that time he was the sole remaining competitor, so he won the first Schneider Cup.

Pioneering Naval Operations

Shipboard Operations

Glenn Curtiss, in attempting to duplicate the Wrights' success in doing business with the U.S. Army, approached the U.S. Navy with a number of ideas. One was to explore the use of aircraft aboard naval vessels. He had earlier gotten the Navy's attention on 30 June 1910 by bombarding a warship-shaped target with eighteen out of twenty "bombs" (pieces of lead pipe) dropped on separate passes from one of his airplanes.[29]

Two ideas that Curtiss wished to pursue were the launching of an aircraft from the deck of a warship and the landing and subsequent takeoff from the deck of a warship. Spurred on by the two unsuccessful attempts to launch an airplane from the deck of a Hamburg American ocean liner 50 miles at sea for the purpose of delivering mail, the naval authorities warmed to Curtiss's ideas. They had a wooden platform that measured 25 by 85 feet, constructed on the forward deck of the scout cruiser USS *Birmingham*. The platform extended over the bow of the vessel and had a slight downward slope toward the bow.

On 18 November 1910, a Curtiss Pusher was hoisted to the deck of the *Birmingham* (fig. 4.27). Eugene Ely, a test pilot for Glenn Curtiss, had been selected to fly the biplane. The ship steamed out some 30 miles into Chesapeake Bay at 11:30 A.M. Light rain was falling as the ship anchored; an hour later the weather had cleared sufficiently so that Ely could attempt the flight. Shortly before 3:00 P.M., Ely started his engine and began his takeoff. As he reached the end of the platform, the aircraft nosed over and was lost from sight of those on the ship. The aircraft descended the 30 feet from the bow of the ship and the wheels hit the water, dousing Ely (fig. 4.28). The aircraft bounced back into the air, and Ely was able to climb to 150 feet. He then flew to a beach near the Hampton Roads Yacht Club, a point about 2.5 miles from the *Birmingham*. His intended destination had been the navy yard at Norfolk, about 30 miles from where the *Birmingham* was anchored. Ely inspected his aircraft and found the propeller damaged, but otherwise the aircraft was in fine shape. Ely attributed his 30-foot plunge to his faulty movement of the control wheel.[30]

Fig. 4.27. Eugene Ely in a Curtiss Pusher, 1910. The aircraft is being loaded aboard the USS *Birmingham*. By permission of the National Air and Space Museum, Smithsonian Institution, ©1999 Smithsonian Institution.

Fig. 4.28. Eugene Ely in a Curtiss Pusher just off the deck of the USS *Birmingham*, 18 November 1910, "heading for a bounce off the water." By permission of the National Air and Space Museum, Smithsonian Institution, ©1999 Smithsonian Institution.

On 18 January 1911, the experiment was carried further, this time with the USS *Pennsylvania,* an armored cruiser anchored in San Francisco harbor and specially equipped for the experiment. A wooden platform measuring 32 by 127 feet was constructed on the aft deck of the ship. Curtiss wrote,

> The platform was like that built on the *Birmingham,* but in case of a flight to, instead of from, a ship the serious problem is to land the aeroplane on the deck and stop it quickly before it runs into the masts of the ship or other obstructions. The platform was built across the quarterdeck . . . with the slope toward the stern of some twelve feet. Across this runway we stretched ropes every few feet so they could catch in grap-hooks which we placed under the main centerpiece of the aeroplane, so that catching in the ropes the heavy sand bags attached would drag until they brought the machine to a stop.[31]

Eugene Ely was again the pilot selected for this duty. He took off from Selfridge Field near San Francisco in the modified Curtiss biplane, climbed to 2,000 feet, and flew over the San Bruno Mountains. He began a descent passing over the *West Virginia* and other smaller ships. He lined up on the *Pennsylvania,* and at just the right moment, he shut off his engine and glided down to the platform, landing successfully.[32] This was both a dramatic event and a significant feat of airmanship. Ely landed on the deck of a warship scarcely wider than the wingspan of his aircraft (fig. 4.29). After a reception on the ship that lasted about an hour, Ely returned to his aircraft and took off from the deck of the ship smoothly and without a repetition of his previous "near calamity" of his takeoff from the *Birmingham.* He flew for thirteen minutes and landed at the point from which he had started. These early experiments were the beginning of naval aviation.

Float Plane Achievements

The Navy was also interested in having an aircraft that could take off from and land on the water. The aircraft would then be hoisted onto the deck of a ship. When this was expressed to Glenn Curtiss, he immediately began designing floats for his aircraft. He had begun this work earlier, in 1908, with a float-modified June Bug, which he renamed the Loon. He had achieved a small amount of success but was not able to get the aircraft into the air.

In France on 28 March 1910, Henri Fabre, a hydrodynamics engineer, flew a float aircraft off the surface of Lake Berre. In 1906 and 1907, he had built and tested

Fig. 4.29. Eugene Ely at the moment of landing on the deck of the USS *Pennsylvania,* 18 January 1911. By permission of the National Air and Space Museum, Smithsonian Institution, ©1999 Smithsonian Institution.

several float designs. His first aircraft was a monoplane equipped with three floats and three engines; he felt additional power was needed because of his notion that it took more power to fly off the water than off the land. The aircraft performed well on the water but would not fly.

On the aircraft that he actually flew, the floats were designed to be flat on the bottom and curved on the top. The floats were a part of the control system; their angle of attack could be adjusted both on the water and in the air and would act as additional airfoils once in the air. The aircraft, in which Fabre flew, was powered by a single Gnome Rotary engine arranged in pusher fashion. Having achieved a short flight on 28 March, he invited several local citizens to witness a trial on 29 March. Although he had never flown before, this twenty-eight-year-old engineer took off from the surface of the lake and flew 4 miles at a height of 150 feet and landed on the water successfully (fig. 4.30).

Fabre continued improving his float design and in October 1910 took his aircraft to the Paris Aeronautical Exhibition. There Curtiss approached Fabre and inquired about his float design. Fabre, a wealthy man, had no need to earn income from his work; therefore, he openly shared information with Curtiss. Whereas Fabre

eventually lost interest in aviation, Curtiss designed what became very successful float planes.[33] It is to Fabre, however, that the title "Father of the Float Plane" seems most appropriately awarded.

The First Flight Across North America

Calbraith P. "Cal" Rodgers is credited with having made the first flight across North America, coast to coast. The plane left Sheepshead Bay race track near Coney Island, New York, on 17 September 1911 and landed in Pasadena, California, some forty-nine days later. Rodgers was attempting to win a $50,000 prize offered by newspaperman tycoon William Randolph Hearst to the first person who could fly coast to coast in thirty days or less. He did not win that prize. However, his sponsor, the Armour Meat Packing Company, was promoting a grape-flavored soft drink product, Vin Fiz (also the name of his aircraft), and Armour paid Rodgers $5 per mile for each of the 4,321 miles he flew.

Rodgers flew a Wright biplane and crashed nineteen times en route (fig. 4.31). Spare parts were carried in a train that followed the aircraft. He consumed enough spare parts to build four other Wright aircraft. The only original parts to complete the journey were the rudder

Fig. 4.30. Henri Fabre's flight at Lake Berre, 1910. *Scientific American,* 5 August 1911.

Fig. 4.31. Wright EX "Vin Fiz" on a horse track. By permission of the National Air and Space Museum, Smithsonian Institution, ©1999 Smithsonian Institution.

and two wing struts. Most crashes were caused by engine failures and weather, and Rodgers twice hit fences during takeoff. Rodgers blamed one of the fence crashes on engine failure that caused him to make a forced landing. On the next takeoff, after his engine had been repaired, he hit a fence and crashed. His reasoning was that if his engine had not failed, causing him to land, he would not have found himself in that predicament in the first place. Therefore, the cause of the crash was listed as "engine failure." In another incident while on takeoff, he "fouled" a tree, smashing his machine.[34]

To avoid flying over the Rockies, Rodgers traveled by way of Chicago, Kansas City, Dallas, San Antonio, El Paso, Phoenix, and Long Beach. His total flight time was 82 hours and 4 minutes at an average speed of about 52 mph.

The Greatest Flight Ever Made

Lincoln Beachey was the best-known American "stunt pilot" of the era. He had been taught to fly by Glenn Curtiss and those pilots who worked with Curtiss. Beachey was not an easy student. During his training, he dinged so many airplanes that the Curtiss camp hated to see him coming. Nevertheless, his persistence paid off and he became a very accomplished pilot who performed around the country. Orville Wright described him as the greatest aviator of them all.

Beachey attempted stunts that today would get his license suspended—and rightfully so (fig. 4.32). But in those early days, people such as Beachey, Curtiss, Grahame-White, Bleriot, and Farman were, in a sense, unpaid test pilots pushing the state of the art as far as it could go. They tested airframes and engines up to and beyond their endurance. This would pay off in future airplane and engine design, as budding engineers gathered anecdotal and hard data about aircraft structures, loads, airfoil design, structural integrity, human endurance, and a host of other parameters that led aviation to where it is today. Nevertheless, these pioneers weren't called "experimental test pilots." They were called "stunt pilots."

The stunt that Cal Rodgers called "the greatest flight ever made" occurred on 11 June 1911, when Beachey took off from Buffalo, New York, and flew to Niagara Falls. He had heard of people going over the falls in a barrel, and

Fig. 4.32. Lincoln Beachey flying a stunt. By permission of the National Air and Space Museum, Smithsonian Institution, ©1999 Smithsonian Institution.

he wanted to try it in an airplane. Once there he circled the falls a couple of times, then nosed the airplane over the falls in a vertical dive to the gorge below. He emerged from the mist below dripping wet but intact. He continued the flight under the bridge, a space that measured 168 feet high and 100 feet wide. Somehow he made it through that tiny space with his Curtiss biplane and then pointed it upward to the Canadian cliffs that lay beyond. He managed to clear them by a few feet, then plunked the airplane down on the level ground beyond.

Beachey left the stunt pilot business after Eugene Ely's wife accused Beachey of murdering her husband by encouraging him to fly dangerously. Beachey went on the vaudeville circuit until he learned that a Frenchman, Adolphe Pegoud, had flown the world's first loop, an outside loop. Pegoud pushed the nose of the airplane over, winding up at the bottom of the loop inverted. He continued to push the nose of the airplane over, flying up the backside of the loop, arriving in the position from which he started.

That did it for Beachey; he ordered a new airplane from Curtiss. When all was ready, he took off in the airplane, gained altitude, and pushed the nose over as Pegoud had done. However, instead of continuing to push, Beachey pulled back on the controls and made an inside loop, winding up at the top of the loop upside down, rather than at the bottom of the loop as would be the case in an "outside" loop. Later, Beachey adapted both the outside and the inside loop in what he termed a "Vertical S" maneuver. The top half of the maneuver was the first half of an outside loop, and the bottom half was half of an inside loop (what we refer today as the "Split S"). This maneuver would eventually claim his life. For many of his flights, Beachey used a specially built biplane he named the Little Looper (fig. 4.33).

Beachey ordered a sleek little monoplane from designer/builder Warren Eaton. This aircraft embraced, perhaps, the most modern aeronautical concepts in the United States at the time (fig. 4.33). On an exhibition with the aircraft on 21 February 1915 over the San Francisco Bay, Beachey completed the first half of a Vertical S

maneuver without difficulty. However, as he attempted to pull out of the 250–300 mph dive on the second half, he overstressed the aircraft and its wings failed; the left one separated first, followed shortly by the right one.[35]

Beachey's fate was similar to many that we have discussed in this chapter. Theirs was a gift and a legacy that made the twentieth century the most exciting, challenging, and moving century, perhaps, of all time.

Aircraft Engine Development

This chapter began just after the Wright brothers made the first powered heavier-than-air flight and came to a close with World War I, a time that witnessed dramatic improvements on all sides of aircraft development.

Fig. 4.33. A replica of Beachey's Little Looper. By permission of the National Air and Space Museum, Smithsonian Institution, ©1999 Smithsonian Institution.

When the Wright-Taylor engine flew, it was not the best "aviation" engine in existence. Most likely, that distinction belongs to the Langley-Balzer-Manly engine installed on the Langley "Aerodrome" aircraft. The Langley engine was a technologically advanced liquid-cooled radial engine that developed 52.4 horsepower and weighed 207.5 pounds. The Wright-Taylor engine, on the other hand, developed 13 horsepower and weighed 150 pounds. The Langley engine was superior to the Wright engine in every parameter except the one that counts the most: the Wright engine flew, whereas the Langley engine did not.

From the first Wright flight until the beginning of World War I, there were many achievements in engine design. Most of the designs can be described as evolutionary, derivatives of previously designed engine types. But there was an engine that can be properly described as revolutionary, an engine that the Seguin brothers, Laurent and Lewis, designed in France. The Gnome Rotary engine became one of the stars of the Rheims air meet in France in 1909 (fig. 4.19).

In this lightweight, air-cooled engine, the crankshaft was bolted to the airframe, and the cylinders were arranged in a circle that turned along with the propeller around the crankshaft. This engine, produced in versions from 50 to 230 horsepower, was the cause of the "rapid development of practical aviation" during the period.[36] The engine development was so important that virtually every English airplane that was deployed to France at the beginning of the World War I was equipped with the French Gnome Rotary engine.

The Wright Lawsuit

When Alexander Graham Bell formed the Aerial Experiment Association, he had in mind to advance the science of flight. But compared with the Wright brothers' depth of knowledge of aerodynamics, his was rudimentary. He openly acknowledged the achievements of the Wright brothers, but he was convinced that theirs was not the only solution to the problem of flight.[37] He invited Lt. Thomas Selfridge to join the association because of his background in aviation. He also invited Glenn Curtiss to join because of his outstanding accomplishments in reciprocating engines.

Bell insisted that the AEA's goals were to get his tetrahedron kites into the air and then to design and man- ufacture airplanes for scientific purposes. The AEA attempted to fly Bell's giant tetrahedron kite pulled behind a boat, and the kite became airborne with Selfridge as its pilot, but a short time later the kite came to rest on the water in an unexpected landing, drenching Selfridge and destroying the kite.[38] The other AEA members then turned their attention to designing and building their first aircraft. It became obvious to Selfridge, who was the designer of the first aircraft, the Red Wing, that they would need information that the Wrights had already discovered if the AEA was to succeed. Selfridge wrote the Wright brothers asking for aerodynamic information and construction to be used for experimental purposes by the AEA. The Wrights released some information to Selfridge and referred him to the information contained in their 1906 patent, which covered the aerodynamic points in question. The use of this information, according to the Wrights, allowed the AEA to produce several flying machines, the most successful of which was the June Bug. It is doubtful whether information in the letter alone helped the AEA achieve its goals, but the information contained in the patent most likely was used without the Wrights' approval.[39]

The Wrights—particularly Wilbur, who was more the businessman of the two—had been careful to record their accomplishments with photographic and other evidence and had applied for a patent in 1906. They invented the workable flying machine, and understandably they wanted to profit from it.

After Selfridge was killed during the Wright Army aircraft trials at Fort Myer and the AEA began to dissolve, Bell invited Curtiss to join with him to take advantage of the AEA's achievements and establish a company to manufacture aircraft for commercial purposes. Curtiss considered the idea, but he had been approached by Augustus M. Herring to accomplish the same purpose. Herring, who was something of a "snake oil salesman," was described by some as "the inventor of unseen aircraft and maker of unobserved flights."[40] He had been dabbling in aviation for some time and had applied for patents (so he said) for some of his mystical inventions. Herring had also offered the Wright brothers a similar proposition, but they had turned him down. Herring visited Curtiss in Hammondsport, New York, and told him that the time to make money in airplanes was now, "before the Wrights took to the courts with their patent and tried to monopolize the business."[41] After giving the idea some thought, Curtiss accepted, and together they formed the Curtiss-Herring Company in March 1909 to manufacture aircraft for sale. In June 1909, Curtiss delivered the first commercial aircraft manufactured and sold in the United States to the Aeronautical Society of New York.[42] On 18 August 1909, the Wrights brought a lawsuit charging the company of Curtiss-Herring and Curtiss individually with patent infringement. The case centered on the wing-warping mechanism and its derivatives, which the Wrights maintained was exclusively a Wright discovery. The case centered on the question of whether or not the use of ailerons constituted an infringement of the Wrights' wing-warping claim. The case was tried in the U.S. Circuit Court in Buffalo, New York, on 14 and 15 December 1909. Judge John R. Hazel decided in favor of the Wrights and applied a broad interpretation to the Wrights' claim. He ruled that ailerons were the equivalent of wing-warping and that dissimilarities in structure had no bearing on the case.[43] The lawsuit was appealed, but as a result of the finding, the Curtiss-Herring Company disbanded. By this time, Herring's nefarious ways of doing business had shown up, and the directors of the Curtiss-Herring Company were in the process of ousting him. He sued the company that was to follow. Curtiss created his own company and began to manufacture commercial airplanes. A new lawsuit was initiated by the Wrights against the new Curtiss Company.

Somewhat earlier (November 1909), with financial backing from wealthy bankers and others, the Wrights had formed their own company. Wilbur was made president. He died in 1912 of typhoid, and Orville became president as the patent wars raged on, not only against Curtiss but also against foreigners such as Paulhan from France and Grahame-White from England. Each had been stopped from giving exhibitions in this country because of Wright patent infringement. In 1915, Orville sold the Wright Company to a group of financiers and bankers. The new owners continued to press the suit against the Curtiss Company.

Curtiss had tried several methods to avoid the Wright patent. One method was to place the ailerons between the wings of his biplanes. The idea was moderately successful from an aerodynamic perspective, but it did not circumvent the patent. All manner of approaches were attempted, including an attempt to demonstrate that the Wright brothers were not the first to build a control-lable, powered, heavier-than-air machine. Encouraged to continue the lawsuit battle by Henry Ford, who was concerned that the Wright patent was having a negative effect on the U.S. aircraft manufacturing industry, Curtiss persuaded one of his former employees and a stockholder in the Curtiss Company, Lincoln Beachey, to ask Albert Zahm, director of the Langley Aerodynamical Laboratory of the Smithsonian Museum, for permission to conduct experiments with Langley's aircraft, the Aerodrome. Zahm, who had previously testified for Curtiss in court, took the matter to the Smithsonian's board, of which Bell was a member. Not only did the Smithsonian give permission to use the Aerodrome but they also provided $2,000 to help fund the project. The stated goals of Curtiss's efforts were high-sounding scientific efforts, but in a letter to Beachey, Curtiss revealed his true purpose. He stated that if he could rebuild the machine and make it fly, "it would go a long way toward showing that the Wrights did not invent the flying machine as a whole."[44] In essence, the Curtiss camp felt that they could prove that the Wrights' discoveries rightfully belonged to Langley and consequently were in the public domain.

In preparing the Aerodrome for flight, Curtiss abandoned the idea of attempting to launch the machine from the top of a houseboat; instead, he decided to put the machine on floats and fly it from the surface of a lake. Curtiss had great success in designing float airplanes using float information obtained from French inventor Henri Fabre. In attaching the floats to the Aerodrome, Curtiss strengthened the lateral structure of the airframe, which had been one of its prime weaknesses. He also changed thirty or so other design items on the Aerodrome, including changing the airfoil shape of the tandem wings, eventually removing the Manly engine when the machine achieved only a 150-foot hop off of the water and installing one of Curtiss design, changing the position of the pilot, strengthening the wing carry-through, and changing the tail operating mechanism from a Langley design to one of his own. But Curtiss did nothing to give the machine a means of lateral control, which was the essence of the Wright patent. The highly modified Aerodrome achieved flights of 25–65 seconds in duration. Despite all of Curtiss's modifications, on its last flight the rear wings of the Aerodrome folded upwards and the machine fell into the lake, never to make another attempt at flight. The machine was restored and returned to the Smithsonian, where it hung with a sign underneath that proclaimed: "The first man-carrying aeroplane in the history of the world capable of sustained free flight. Invented, built, and tested over the Potomac River by Samuel Pierpont Langley in 1903. Successfully flown at Hammondsport, N.Y., June 2, 1914."[45] It was a lie, pure and simple. To Orville Wright, it was more than a lie or an annoyance; it was the culmination of Curtiss's efforts to devalue all that the Wright brothers had accomplished. He became so incensed that he sent the Kitty Hawk flyer to England, where it remained until the end of World War II.

The patent wars continued until they were settled at the beginning of World War I largely because of the efforts of the Manufacturers of Aircraft Association.[46] While the Wrights may have eventually won the patent wars, the victory belongs more to Curtiss. By 1916, the company that he had created was the largest manufacturer of airplanes in this country.[47]

Notes

1. Hodgins and Magoun, *Sky High*, 189.
2. Harris, *The First to Fly*, 105.
3. Harris, 106.
4. Brown, *A History of Aviation*, 30.
5. "World Rivalry in Flying Machines," 243.
6. Gunston, *Chronicle of Aviation*, 63.
7. "First Flight of the Wright Aeroplane," 169.
8. Harris, 136–37.
9. "Completion of the Government Contract," 111.
10. Claudy, "With the Wright Brothers at Fort Myer," 936.
11. Bell, "History of Aerial Locomotion and the Aerodrome," 263–64.
12. Brown, 36.
13. Harris, 130.
14. Gunston, 1908.
15. Harris, 132.
16. Brett, *History of British Aviation*, 28.
17. "World Rivalry in Flying Machines," 239.
18. Harris, 116–17.
19. Hodgins and Magoun, 216–17; Harris, 121–23.
20. Brett, 32–33.
21. Harris, 144.
22. "Flying Wonders at Rheims," 12,102.
23. "The Flight from London to Manchester," 397.
24. Williams, *Conquering the Air*, 114.
25. "The Flight from London to Manchester," 398.
26. Harris, 193.
27. "The Flight from London to Manchester," 398.

28. Brett, 44.
29. Gunston, 82.
30. "Launching an Aeroplane from a Warship," 418.
31. Harris, 230–31.
32. "First Flight from Shore to Ship," 108.
33. Brown, 38.
34. "The First Trans-Continental Aeroplane Flight," 449.
35. Harris's treatment of the Lincoln Beachey story in *The First to Fly*, 280–96, is exceedingly well done.
36. Brett, facing p. 26.
37. Howard, *Wilbur and Orville*, 210.
38. Howard, 21.
39. Howard, 235.
40. Howard, 231.
41. Howard, 309.
42. Brown, 36.
43. Howard, 331–34.
44. Howard, 395.
45. Howard, 401.
46. This short essay on the Wright lawsuit does not do justice to the many intricate issues and side issues that were involved in the whole of its importance to the development of aviation in this country. The student is invited to more deeply pursue this subject. A good place to start is to read Howard's *Wilbur and Orville*.
47. Howard, 405.

References

"Aerial Exhibits at Rheims." *Scientific American,* 4 September 1909, 159.

"Aeroplane Development: Great Britain." *Scientific American,* suppl. 1725, 23 January 1909, 53–54.

"Amazing Progress in Aviation." *Scientific American,* 5 August 1911, 114.

Bayles, J. C. "Floating and Flying Navies." *Cassier's Magazine,* December 1908, 263–74.

Bell, Alexander G. "History of Aerial Locomotion and the Aerodrome." *Scientific American,* suppl. 1638–40, 25 May–8 June 1907.

Black, Archibald. *The Story of Flying.* New York: McGraw-Hill, 1940.

Brett, R. Dallas. *History of British Aviation, 1908–1914.* Surrey: Air Research, 1933.

Brown, Carl A. *A History of Aviation.* 2d ed. Daytona Beach: Embry-Riddle Aeronautical University, 1980.

Bryan, G. H. "London to Manchester." *Nature* 83 (5 May 1910): 273–79.

———. "Progress in Aviation." *Nature* 78 (29 October 1908): 668–72.

"Capt. Cody's British Army Airplane." *Scientific American,* 18 September 1909, 198.

Chanute, Octave. "Aerial Navigation." *Scientific American,* 26 March 1904, 23598–600.

Claudy, C. H. "With the Wright Brothers at Fort Myer." *World Today* 17 (September 1909): 929–36.

"Completion of the Government Contract by Orville Wright at Fort Myer," *Scientific American,* 14 August 1909, 111–12.

"Curtiss' Great Flight." *World's Work* 20 (June 1910): 13,110–12.

"Decision in the Wright Aeroplane Patent Case." *Scientific American,* 22 May 1913, 273.

Dientsebach, C. "Did Professor S. P. Langley Invent the First Practical Flying Machine?" *Scientific American,* 25 July 1914, 59.

"First Flight Exhibit and Tournament." *Scientific American,* 10 June 1909, 29.

"First Flight from Shore to Ship." *Scientific American,* 4 February 1911, 108.

"First Flight of the Aerial Experiment Association's Second Aeroplane." *Scientific American,* 30 May 1908, 392.

"First Flight of the Wright Aeroplane at Fort Meyer." *Scientific American,* 12 September 1908, 169.

"First Successful Cross-Channel Flight." *Scientific American,* 7 August 1909, 88.

"First Trans-Continental Aeroplane Flight." *Scientific American,* 18 November 1911, 449.

"Flight from London to Manchester: The Aviators' Own Accounts." *Scientific American,* 14 May 1910, 397–98.

"Flying Wonders at Rheims." *World's Work* 18 (October 1909): 12,099–12,103.

"Glenn Curtiss Wins the Scientific American Trophy." *Scientific American,* 14 January 1911, 29.

Grahame-White, Claude, and Harry Harper. "Air: Our Future Highway." *Living Age* 278 (26 July 1913): 195–201.

Gunston, Bill, ed. *Chronicle of Aviation.* Paris: Jacques Legrand, 1992.

Harris, Sherwood. *The First to Fly: Aviation's Pioneer Days.* New York: Simon and Schuster, 1970.

Hodgins, Eric, and F. Alexander Magoun. *Sky High—The Story of Aviation.* Boston: Little, Brown, 1929.

Howard, Fred. *Wilbur and Orville: A Biography of the Wright Brothers.* New York: Alfred A. Knopf, 1987.

Howland, Harold J. "Sons of Daedalus." *Outlook* 90 (26 September 1908): 153–69.

Hudson, James J. *Hostile Skies.* Syracuse: Syracuse University Press, 1968.

"June Bug Aeroplane." *Scientific American,* 4 July 1908, 13.

Karup, Marius C. "The Coroner's Inquest: Why Men Are Killed in Aeroplanes." *Scientific American,* 13 May 1911, 464–65.

"Langley's Folly Flies." *Outlook* 107 (3 June 1914): 326.

"Launching an Aeroplane from a Warship: Ely's Flight from the Cruise Ship *Birmingham.*" *Scientific American,* 26 November 1910, 418.

Loening, Grover C. "New Development in Aeroplane Construction: European Types." *Scientific American,* 11 November 1911, 428–29.

"Long-Distance Flights of Farman and Bleriot." *Scientific American Supplement* 66 (12 December 1908): 381–82.

McFarland, Marvin W., ed. *The Papers of Wilbur and Orville Wright.* New York: McGraw-Hill, 1953.

Melklejohn, R. "Conquest of the Air." *World's Work* 13 (December 1906): 3283–96.

"Men Who Flew at Rheims." *Outing* 55 (November 1909): 142–47.

Post, A. "Aeronautics in America." *Independent* 62 (21 February 1907): 437–44.

Rivet, M. Banet. "Early Experiments in Air Flight." *Popular Science,* March 1900, 603–7.

Squirer, O. "Recent Progress in Aeronautics." *Science* 29 (19 February 1909): 281–89.

"Talk with Wilbur Wright." *Scientific American,* 23 October 1909, 290.

"Testing the Langley Aeroplane at the Curtiss Aerodrome." *Country Life,* June 1910, 212.

White, C. H. "With the Spectators at Rheims." *Harper's Weekly,* 18 September 1909, 30.

Williams, Archibald. *Conquering the Air.* New York: Thomas Nelson and Sons, 1926.

Wood, G. F. Campbell. "Aerial Exhibits at Rheims." *Independent* 67 (16 September 1909): 625–32.

Woodhouse, Henry. "Year of Aviation 1910." *Independent* 70 (16 February 1911): 346–49.

"World Rivalry in Flying Machines and Motor Boats," *Current Literature* 45 (September 1908): 239–44.

"Wright Aeroplane Infringement Suit." *Scientific American,* 28 August 1909, 138.

"Wright Brothers Aeroplane in France and the U.S." *Scientific American,* 29 August 1908, 140–41.

"Wright Injunction." *Scientific American Supplement,* 19–26 February 1910, 122–23, 135.

"Wright vs. Paulhan." *Scientific American,* 19–26 March 1910, 182–83.

5

World War I

Tim Brady

Aircraft did not, however, play the leading role in that conflict. Armies and navies settled that issue.

—Gen. Henry H. Arnold

WITHIN A FEW WEEKS after Archduke Franz Ferdinand, heir to the Austrian-Hungarian throne, was assassinated at Sarajevo on 28 June 1914, Europe was embroiled in a conflict that was to spread far beyond the continent. This conflagration was to become known as the Great War. Twenty-five years later, when war again erupted in Europe, the Great War acquired the title of World War I.

The assassination did not cause the war; however, it acted as the hand that pulled the lanyard on a cannon. The nations of Europe had been slowly priming the cannon for over half a century. The war had no single cause. It was the result of a complex set of social, nationalistic, and political elements that became unbalanced. The mixture included Germany's desire for commercial outlets, which was manifested as a vision of world power, Britain's movement away from isolationism, the confusing racial problems of the Hapsburg vestige, Austria-Hungary, the fear of the Russian bear's quest for territory, and France's preoccupation with the Alsace-Lorraine territory that Germany had annexed during a previous conflict. Without doubt these are gross generalizations, but they serve as a filmy backdrop for the war.[1]

Austria declared war on Serbia on 28 July 1914. Fearing a German mobilization, Russia was the first great power to mobilize. Russia's fears were well grounded: Germany mobilized next. Following an ultimatum by Germany, France then mobilized. England had an alliance with France; however, England did not mobilize immediately. Instead, London sent a diplomatic message to Germany, stating that if Germany would not attack France, Britain would remain neutral. A later message indicated, however, that Britain was not promising neutrality. While the British Parliament was wavering, Germany invaded neutral Belgium. This was enough to convince Parliament to mobilize, and the race was on. America entered the war three years later and was unprepared.

This chapter will look at World War I, 1914–18, to judge the influence of aviation on the conflict and perhaps, more important, to assess the influence of the conflict on aviation. From a military standpoint, this chapter will explore the development of the aircraft as a vehicle of combat.

Early Air Combat

The reports of the numbers of aircraft possessed by each side at the beginning of the war differ widely. For example, one source claimed that when the war began, Germany had about 1,000 airplanes, France about 300, and England about 250. Another source stated that Germany had a strength of 294 airplanes, France had 136, and England had 270. Yet another source declared that Germany went to war with well over 600 airplanes, France had between 500 and 600, and Britain had 82 serviceable airplanes.[2]

Whatever the number, the airplanes were not armed. The airplane was little more than a toy, and in some cases it was seen as an unwanted contraption that frightened the horses. Wars were fought with artillery, infantry, cavalry. Each side played some massive chess game, moving troops about to gain advantage and surprise. For centuries, the battlefields had been confined to the land and the sea. The nineteenth-century military theories of Carl von Clausewitz dominated military thinking.

Using the sky as a battlefield was beyond traditional thought. By 1918, this tradition would fall, but the road to 1918 was to be agonizingly long. It was now 1914, and airplanes were gossamer things.

To gain a notion of how flimsy airplanes were at the beginning of the war, we can look to the British deployment to France. In August 1914, an English expeditionary force of thirty-seven assorted aircraft assembled at Dover for the perilous flight across the Channel to France. The Channel had been crossed for the first time by Louis Bleriot only five years earlier. It had been a hazardous flight, and no technological leap in aircraft design had occurred since then. Many pilots were grimly apprehensive. The airplanes were heavily laden with rations, extra fuel, and spare parts.

Each pilot and observer had been given a revolver, field glasses, a pair of goggles, a small stove, a tin of biscuits, some cold meat, a piece of chocolate, soup cubes, and orders that nothing else be carried in their planes. In violation of these orders some of the more skittish pilots wrapped inner tubes around their waists as make-shift water wings.[3]

The pilots were also given rather disconcerting orders to ram any Zeppelins they encountered.[4] This deployment was considered the first mass movement of airplanes in history, and it was done at an unfortunate cost. Five men died, and ten airplanes were lost.

After arriving in France, the surviving airplanes were pressed into service as reconnaissance vehicles. Their worth was not immediately recognized, however. The aircrews were attempting to provide reconnaissance over an area for which there were no maps and with which they were initially unfamiliar. The quality of the reconnaissance information naturally suffered. On occasion, British and French alike would see German aircraft accomplishing the same role. Since the aircraft were not armed, the crews at times waved at one another in a friendly fashion; however, this did not last long.

As the quality of the reconnaissance began to improve and affect the outcome of the battles below, it became important to deny the enemy the advantage of aerial reconnaissance. In addition, each side had begun to use aircraft as airborne artillery spotters to a most effective degree. It became necessary to attempt to deny the air to the enemy; pilots would try to shoot down the opponent, if possible. The Allies began to arm their airplanes. Crews had been armed for some time and had taken pot shots at one another, but this proved ineffective.

The first attempt to use the machine gun on an aircraft in combat was made by Lt. Louis Strange, one of the original group of aviators deployed to France from England. Strange devised a machine gun mount for his Farman pusher biplane and attached a Lewis machine gun (see fig. 5.1). A German Taube aircraft (shown in fig. 5.2) appeared overhead on its daily reconnaissance flight. Strange took off to intercept and shoot it down. Unfortunately, Strange had not accounted for the extra weight of the machine gun. He began to struggle, not being able to coax the Farman higher than about 3,000 feet while the Taube sauntered off at a comfortable 5,000 feet or so. When he landed, his commander told Strange to take the machine gun off his airplane. "Machine guns are for use on the ground," the commander said.

Experiments with machine guns mounted on aircraft had been attempted much earlier. For example, on 7 June 1912, during experiments conducted for the U.S.

Fig. 5.1. Early Farman biplane pusher. Courtesy of the USAF Museum.

Fig. 5.2. German Taube. Courtesy of the USAF Museum.

Fig. 5.3. Vickers pusher with forward-firing machine guns. Courtesy of the USAF Museum.

Signal Corps, Capt. Charles Chandler fired a Lewis machine gun mounted on a Wright Model B aircraft at a bedsheet spread on the ground. This experiment demonstrated the military feasibility of firing at ground targets with a machine gun mounted on an airplane. Nevertheless, shooting at airplanes was another matter entirely.

The airplane operates in three dimensions, and each of the two potential combatants are moving in each of those three dimensions at different rates, times, and directions. An analogous situation is to bag a duck while standing on the bow of a boat floating in a choppy lake. One's chances are much improved if one has a rapid fire repeating shotgun. By the same token, one's chances of shooting down an airplane are much improved if one uses a machine gun rather than a rifle, pistol, or shotgun.

Very early in the war, aircraft began to appear in the skies armed with machine guns. These aircraft came in two basic designs. One was a pusher aircraft in which the observer rode in the front cockpit, which was equipped with a machine gun that acted in a mobile arc. The range of fire of the gun was forward, somewhat to the sides and down. Typical of this model was the British Vickers Gun Bus (see fig. 5.3).

The other aircraft model was a tractor (propeller in front) in which the engine was up front and the observer sat in a cockpit behind the pilot. The observer station was equipped with a machine gun (see fig. 5.4). The range of fire was somewhat to the sides, rear, and down.

Combat between these two types of aircraft while certainly possible was difficult. Closing on the pusher type was not difficult for the faster tractor type aircraft; however, the tractor could not fire forward. The pusher could fire forward, but it was not as fast as the tractor. Favorable tactical firing positions could be achieved through maneuver and using the advantage of altitude, but to achieve any advantage was difficult at best.

Fig. 5.4. A typical tractor with rearward-firing machine guns. *Everybody's Magazine,* January 1918.

Roland Garros

One French officer, Roland Garros (shown in fig. 5.5), discovered that he could negate many of those factors by pointing the airplane at the target aircraft and keeping the nose of the aircraft on line with the other machine. He practiced this many times and felt that if he had a gun that could fire forward, through the propeller arc, he could hit the enemy aircraft.

Garros had been a famous French stunt pilot before the war began. On the day that war was declared, Garros was in Berlin giving a flying demonstration in his Morane-Saulnier single-wing aircraft (see fig. 5.6). Fearing correctly that the Germans were not going to let him leave, Garros pretended to overindulge in wine at a dinner party that evening. He staggered into the restroom, much to the amusement of his German officer dinner host, and crawled out the window. Arriving at the airfield about midnight, he bribed the guards to let him go to his airplane, which he had fueled before tying it down for the day. Garros pointed the airplane into the wind and started the rotary engine, which roared to life at full power. Normally, it took several men to hold down the airplane while the engine was started. The rotary had only two speeds: full speed and stop.

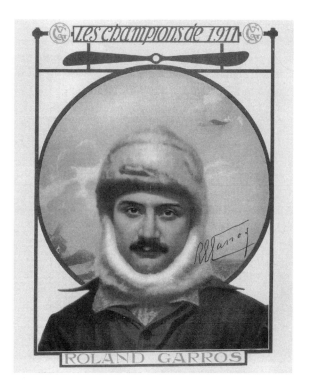

Fig. 5.5. Roland Garros. By permission of the National Air and Space Museum, Smithsonian Institution, ©1999 Smithsonian Institution.

Fig. 5.6. Morane-Saulnier monoplane. Courtesy of the USAF Museum.

As the engine roared to life, the airplane jumped forward and the wing caught Garros at midchest. He had propped the engine to life and managed to jump to one side, missing the propeller. Incredibly, he hung onto the wires and struts of the wing, pulling himself up over the leading edge of the wing. This all happened while the airplane bounced and bumped its way across the field. Garros then struggled into the cockpit and completed the takeoff in the dead of night, which was enough of a hazard.

Garros made it back to Paris and immediately joined the French forces, becoming a flight officer after first completing cavalry school, old military traditions being hard to break. Over the next few months, Garros considered the problem of firing through the arc of the propeller.

Raymond Saulnier, a French aircraft designer and manufacturer, had also been studying the problem. He had experimented with a device to synchronize the fire of a machine gun through the arc of the propeller, but he could not develop a workable system. He discarded the idea of a synchronizer and instead devised pointed triangular steel plates that could be mounted on the back of the propeller. The devices were designed to deflect the bullets away from the pilot. When Garros heard about Saulnier's experiments, he went to the factory and observed a Morane-Saulnier Bullet aircraft. The aircraft

was fitted with a propeller unit affixed with steel plates and equipped with a Hotchkiss machine gun (see fig. 5.7). Impressed, he took the airplane back to his escadrille (squadron). His squadron mates were skeptical and feared the bullets striking the prop would cause it to splinter and break.

On 1 April 1915, Garros showed just how deadly efficient his machine was. Thinking they had nothing to fear from the approaching tiny Morane-Saulnier tractor aircraft, the German aviators must have been shocked to realize that the tiny French single-wing machine was firing through the propeller with deadly precision. Garros killed both men, and the airplane fell to the ground.

Fig. 5.7. View of a Roland Garros propeller from a Morane-Saulnier monoplane, ca. 1915. The steel deflector plate can be seen at the shank of the propeller; this was intended to deflect machine gun bullets as they were fired through the arc of the propeller. By permission of the National Air and Space Museum, Smithsonian Institution, ©1999 Smithsonian Institution.

Garros claimed his first victory. Ten days later, he shot down two more planes, and before the end of the month he had shot down five. He was a hero and the toast of Paris. They proclaimed him an ace, meaning outstanding. From that moment on, the term *ace* defined an aviator who had achieved five aerial victories.

Unfortunately for Garros, on 19 April he was forced to land behind German lines following an engine failure on his Morane-Saulnier. Before he could burn the airplane, he was captured and his aircraft was confiscated.

Anthony Fokker

Garros was quite a catch; he was almost as famous in Germany as he was in France. His tactics had thrown a scare into the ranks of German airmen, who felt defenseless against an aircraft that could fire through the propeller. The German general staff was understandably anxious to duplicate Garros's machine. They immediately contacted Anthony Fokker (shown in fig. 5.8), whose aircraft manufacturing plant was some 220 miles to the north of Berlin. Fokker examined Garros's airplane and was given the propeller and a parabellum machine gun. He was told to copy the method and equip as many Fokker E-1 Eindekker (one-wing) aircraft as he had at his plant within 48 hours. Fokker, a Dutchman, came to this point in his life through a curious route.

Fig. 5.8. Anthony Fokker in his airplane. Permission by The New York Times/NYT Pictures.

Fokker was born in Java, the son of a Dutch planter, and came to Holland as a small boy. By the time he was sixteen, he had built his first airplane. At the age of twenty, he had built one of the fastest, most stable airplanes in the world. Yet he was unable to peddle it to his own Dutch countrymen, the Russians, or even the English. No one, it seemed, wanted to buy an airplane from a smooth-cheeked youngster who did not have a college degree and who was unknown in the aviation world. Finally, the Germans placed an order for a dozen airplanes in 1913, and a steady stream of aircraft orders followed. It was understandable that the general staff had summoned Fokker to Berlin to study Garros's machine gun.

Fokker looked at the propeller with its triangular wedges on the back of the propeller blades. He discarded the idea, feeling that the constant pounding of bullets on the metal plate would eventually shatter the propeller. Having never seen a parabellum machine gun, while on the train back to his factory, he disassembled the gun to familiarize himself with how it worked. He remembered how as a boy he had tossed stones through the slowly revolving blades of a Dutch windmill. Fokker seldom hit one of the blades.

As he saw it, the problem was how to shoot between the blades of a propeller connected to an engine that was turning the propeller at 1,200 times a minute (1,200 rpm). Because it was a two-bladed propeller, this meant a blade was passing in front of the machine-gun barrel 2,400 times a minute. Once he stated the problem to himself in those terms, the solution came to him in a flash. As Fokker stated, "The obvious thing to do was to make the propeller shoot the gun, instead of trying to shoot the bullets through the propeller." The mechanics of the system developed quickly from the idea. He soon mounted the machine gun on the nose of an Eindekker Scout and experimented with the gun (see fig. 5.9). After a few initial adjustments, the mechanism worked perfectly. He hooked the airplane on the back of his touring car and drove to Berlin to demonstrate it for the general staff. Even after successful firings at ground targets from the air, the skeptics were still unconvinced. They wanted Fokker to shoot down an enemy airplane. Fokker reluctantly agreed. To avoid being shot as a spy if captured (his homeland, Holland, was neutral), Fokker was fitted out in the uniform of a German flying officer. He was given an identification card that signified he was Lt. Anthony Herman Gerard Fokker of the German Air Force.

Fig. 5.9. Fokker E-1 Eindekker. By permission of the National Air and Space Museum, Smithsonian Institution, ©1999 Smithsonian Institution.

A few days later while flying over the front, Fokker had the opportunity to prove his invention. A Farman two-seat pusher biplane appeared below. Fokker dived his Eindekker. The Farman was now in his sights, and his finger tightened on the trigger. Fokker tells what happened next.

My imagination could vision my shots puncturing the gasoline tanks in front of the engine. The tank would catch fire. Even if my bullets failed to kill the pilot and observer, the ship would fall down in flames. I had my finger on the trigger. What I imagined recalled my own narrow escapes; the time the gasoline tank burst; the breaking of the wing at Johannisthal when my passenger was killed. I had no personal animosity toward the French. I was flying merely to prove that a certain mechanism I had invented would work. By this time I was near enough to open fire, and the French pilots were watching me curiously, wondering why I was flying up behind them. In another instant it would be all over for them.

Suddenly, I decided that the whole job could go to hell. It was too much like "cold meat" to suit me. I had no stomach for the whole business, nor any wish to kill Frenchmen for Germans. Let them do their own killing.[5]

Nevertheless, the Germans began to employ Fokker's invention. Oswald Boelche took up Fokker's special Eindekker and brought down the enemy. Air combat was now fully born. From that moment, the nature of air combat changed drastically.

Making the airplane an offensive weapon was now possible. With airplanes designed for that purpose, it was possible to stalk and shoot down enemy planes and to protect airplanes designed for bombing or reconnaissance. Now it was time for men with names like Richthofen, Boelche, Fonck, Guynemer, Mannock, Bishop, Rickenbacker, and Luke to forever brand into the pages of history the role of the airplane as air combat.

American Perceptions

When the United States entered World War I on 6 April 1917, they were woefully underprepared to conduct any kind of aerial combat. There are several reasons for the lack of preparation.

At the beginning of the war in Europe, America was a country of mixed loyalties toward the combatants and had a misunderstanding of European politics. In the summer of 1914, if the European war trigger had been rated at ten pounds of pull, the assassination of Austrian archduke Ferdinand provided the next to last ounce of pressure. The last ounce came when the government of Austria-Hungary presented the Serbian government with an ultimatum. Americans viewed both events as simply another of the crises that had dominated European politics for a decade. However, immediately following the ultimatum, the great powers of Europe declared war on one another. To the American mind, it was as if all of Europe had suddenly gone mad.

In the opening moments of the war, at first, America was paralyzed by what was occurring, then indignant at the thought that civilized nations would behave in such a manner. America immediately proclaimed its neutrality because its friendships ran deep on both sides of the conflict. Sympathies were equally divided between the English and the Germans. If anything, there may have been a slight shift in Germany's favor due to the lingering distrust and suspiciousness of England passed down since the American Revolution. Public opinion changed after the British media circulated stories of German atrocities in neutral Belgium.[6]

While divided in sympathies toward England and Germany, there was almost unanimous U.S. sympathy for the French. France was fondly remembered as the nation that had helped America win its independence from the British. When the French turned back the German invasion with a victory at the Marne in September 1914, most Americans were overjoyed.

The fondness for the French tended to move American sympathies toward the Allies, but it was not enough to sway neutrality. The turning point came with the German folly in sinking the *Lusitania* on 7 May 1915. "The *Lusitania* massacre is one of the great landmarks in history, not alone in American history but in human history."[7] It was the single event that ensured German defeat in World War I by rocketing American public opinion solidly into the Allied camp. From that moment on, America was gradually drawn toward the conflict, and the world would not be the same again.

Aircraft Manufacturing

The United States entered the war in the spring of 1917 with a fledgling aircraft industry. A few companies had received orders from the Army, Navy, and Allied nations. In addition, the U.S. government had placed orders amounting to 334 aircraft with sixteen manufacturers for the Army and the Navy. Six of these manufacturers had never built more than ten aircraft each. In fact, when the United States entered the war, there was no aviation manufacturing industry of any magnitude, and the number of men trained as aeronautical engineers was pitifully small.[8]

To further complicate the problem, there were bitter rivalries within the industry concerning patents stemming from the bitter court struggles between the Wright and Curtiss camps. In total, some 130 patents were issued with others pending that were so basic to aircraft design that no aircraft could be built without them. Each patent was a potential lawsuit, and when a builder turned out an airplane, the company was invariably threatened with court action.

Months before the United States declared war, the secretary of the Navy, Josephus Daniels, called upon the National Advisory Committee for Aeronautics (NACA), the forerunner of today's NASA, for help in solving the patent problem. NACA called a meeting of aircraft manufacturers. They met in several sessions, but many manufacturers were not on speaking terms, and negotiations were painfully attempted.[9]

On 12 May 1917, Congress appropriated $10.8 million for aeronautics, and on 15 June 1917, they appropriated another $43.45 million. On 24 July, another $640 million was passed into law, making it the largest appropriation ever made by Congress for a single purpose.[10]

English, French, and Italian missions soon arrived in the United States and began to state their aircraft requirements. Before their arrival, War Department strategists had determined that 2,500 aircraft were needed. This assumed that there would be one aircraft needed for every thousand ground troops. Aircraft manufacturers felt that they could handle that number without further expansion. However, when the French, English, and Italian missions arrived, they scoffed at the paltry number and stated that at least 25,000 airplanes would be needed.

Reacting to a telegram from Premier Ribot of France, who underscored these needs, the Joint Army and Navy Technical Board recommended a manufacturing program that called for 22,000 airplanes. Ten thousand airplanes were to be used for training purposes and 12,000 for the front in France. All of this was to be completed by 1 July 1918. This recommendation led to the large congressional appropriations of June and July 1917.

For the aircraft manufacturing industry, it was now a brand-new ball game. A tenfold expansion would obviously be necessary if the nation was going to meet its goals. The large companies that made up the aircraft manufacturing industry were largely under the control of automotive companies. Hudson Motor Car Company controlled Dayton-Wright, Willys-Overland Car Company controlled Curtiss, and Simplex Auto Company controlled Wright-Martin. Suddenly, old rivalries, jealousies, and distrust began to wither under the heat of the dollar fanned by the fires of patriotism. The manufacturers agreed to set up a cross patent agreement whereby any manufacturer could use the patents by paying a fee to an organization set up by the patent holders. This organization would then apportion the fees to the various patent holders. The Manufacturers' Aircraft Association was thus created to collect and apportion fees and to speak for the industry.[11]

With the patent problems now behind them, the aircraft manufacturing industry executives returned to their factories ready to produce airplanes and engines. However, what airplanes and engines would be manufactured?

The government obviously needed a centralized form of manufacturing control. The small Signal Corps, which exercised control over Army aviation, was grossly understaffed to produce aircraft. They called for help. The government set up an independent Aircraft Production Board. Howard Coffin, an official of the Dayton-Wright Company and an automobile manufacturer (one of the founders of Hudson Motor Car Company), was made chairman. Coffin had been involved with aircraft development. Edward Deeds, also of Dayton Wright, was appointed to the board. He then accepted a commission to colonel and was made chief of the equipment division of the Signal Corps. The duties included both the engineering and production of all of the equipment requirements of the Signal Corps, including aviation.

Deeds was a successful engineer and manufacturer. He had a long-standing interest in aviation and was a protege of Orville Wright. In an attempt to bring order to the manufacturing task, Deeds sought assistance from successful manufacturers using production line methods. To fill the various positions, he brought aboard Sidney Walton of Packard Motor Car Company as assistant chief, R. L. Montgomery, a banker, as chief of finance, George Mixner of Deere and Company as chief of inspection, Harry Shepler of Willys-Overland Motor Car Company as chief of airplane production, and others from the manufacturing industry. Most admitted they had little experience with aircraft engineering or construction.

With a target production of 22,500 airplanes, the Aircraft Production Board broke the problem down into several components:

1. There was no compelling knowledge of which models of airplanes should be built.

2. A need existed to create a training structure for pilots, mechanics, and aircraft manufacturing technicians.

3. There was a need to dramatically expand a small aircraft manufacturing industry by at least eightfold.

4. A large technical and engineering force would have to be established.

5. It would be necessary to create the logistics to support such a manufacturing effort: procuring the needed materials, securing the necessary raw materials, and the Aircraft Production Board discovering the means of shipping the finished product.

The Bolling Mission

It seemed there was no end to the parade of "experts" and would-be manufacturers who volunteered to advise the government on what airplanes and engines it should build. Confusion was rampant, but a philosophy emerged that was to dominate the American aircraft manufacturing effort. We viewed ourselves as a member of the Allied team and assumed that their views of the uses of airpower were those that we should adopt. The Allies were the air combat experts with firsthand experience. This proved to be both a blessing and a curse.

To make sense out of the chaotic information coming from our Allies and our own "experts," the Army appointed Maj. Raynal C. Bolling (shown in fig. 5.10) to head a commission to go to Europe and find out exactly what kind of airplanes were needed. Bolling had only recently been commissioned, but his background in business and aviation qualified him to lead the commission.

Bolling had five goals:

1. To secure manufacturing rights to various European aircraft and components,

2. To select and send back home various aircraft and components,

3. To pave the way for purchasing aircraft in Europe,

4. To prepare for the training of Americans in Europe, and

5. To assist the Allies in the allocation of raw materials.

The Bolling Commission made several major recommendations that determined the nature of the American aircraft manufacturing effort. First, they recommended that pursuit or fighter-type aircraft should be bought from the Allies and manufactured in Europe. Originally, they had recommended that the United States build

Fig. 5.10. Col. Raynal Cawthorne Bolling, for whom Bolling Air Force Base, Washington, D.C., is named. By permission of the National Air and Space Museum, Smithsonian Institution, ©1999 Smithsonian Institution.

the French Spad and the English Bristol pursuit aircraft. However, before any significant effort to produce these airplanes could get under way, the commissioners changed their recommendation. The reason was that the technology and science of air combat was changing so rapidly at the front. By the time an aircraft could be produced in the United States and transported by ship to Europe and then ferried to the front, it would be obsolete.

Second, the commissioners recommended that observation and bomber aircraft should be manufactured in the United States and shipped to Europe. The missions for these types of aircraft were less sensitive to rapid changes in technology than the fighter aircraft. The aircraft could also be manufactured in the United States without fear of becoming obsolete in transit. The aircraft chosen for this role was the English De Havilland DH-4, a single-engine aircraft to be powered by the newly developed American Liberty engine.

Third, the commissioners recommended that training airplanes and engines to power those airplanes should be designed and manufactured in the United States.

The suggestions of the Bolling Commission were accepted, and an eager industry undertook the tasks that it had set for itself in response to the needs expressed by the Aircraft Production Board.

Deceptions, Allegations, and Investigations

One great strength the United States had to offer the Allies was its genius in quantity production. The production-line concept was an American invention. The cornerstone of the ability to make the production-line concept function was the idea of standardization. Designs, blueprints, production machines, and the training of the people centered on this highly disciplined method of production. Machine operator A operating machine A who produced Widget XYZ in Detroit would produce the same part as machine operator B using machine B to produce Widget XYZ in Seattle. The parts must be identical, otherwise they would not fit properly into the structure as it was being produced. Without precise standardization, no two parts would be the same, and mass production would be impossible to achieve.

Unfortunately, Europeans did not follow mass production techniques, and each of their airplanes was handmade; the technician compensated for the sloppy blueprint or drawing by adapting the part or component to solve the problem. This was true for airframe components and engines.

The clash of these two concepts proved to be villainous in the efforts of the United States to first realize that no two European airplanes of the same species were alike. Second, it was necessary to create an accurate set of drawings converting metric to American standards

Fig. 5.11. American-manufactured DH-4 during combat in France, 1918. A French Nieuport 24 is in the background. Courtesy of the USAF Museum.

from which a standardized product eventually could be mass produced.

This led to delays in the production of the DH-4. Americans, who had been led to believe that the aviation industry would "blacken the skies of Europe," were thoroughly disappointed.

As 1917 began, the production capacity had been rated by the Aircraft Production Board at 7,200 airplanes per year. By January 1918, production had reached 700 engines and 800 airplanes, 700 of which were trainers (mostly JN-4s). Late in February, it was announced that the first American combat airplanes were en route to France. Actually, only one DH-4 was en route, and it was flying from Dayton to Hoboken. By the time the war ended, however, 3,431 of the American DH-4s had been delivered to the Army (see fig. 5.11). Of those, only 196 reached the front. Had the war continued, there is little doubt that the original production figures could have been realized.

Unfortunately, other problems plagued the DH-4. Since the airplane design already had an operational flight history in Europe, the American-produced DH-4s were not given any extensive flight testing before being dispatched to the front. The aircraft did not perform well, and a lot of dissatisfaction was expressed. This led to a flight test program for the aircraft in which one of the most skilled pilots in the United States, Col. Henry Damm, was killed when the aircraft entered an unrecoverable spin. Further, most combat pilots believed that the airplane was not suited for either bombing or reconnaissance missions. They believed the aircraft was vulnerable to enemy fighter aircraft because of the location and design of fuel tanks. The preponderance of blind spots that the enemy could use to approach the aircraft was also a problem.

Dismayed by the poor production effort, President Wilson appointed jurist Charles Evans Hughes to investigate. Hughes reported that "the aircraft production program was largely placed in control of great automobile and other manufacturers who were ignorant of aeronautical problems."

Despite allegations and innuendo, none of the principals involved in aircraft production (namely, Coffin and Deeds) were ever convicted of any wrongdoing. Their "crime" was in underestimating the time it would take to spin up an entire industry from scratch.

As a result of the Hughes investigation, Army aviation was moved up a link on the military chain of command and designated an air service. This allowed it to be heard with a louder and stronger voice in War Department and other government circles.

In addition, John D. Ryan, former head of Anaconda Copper Company, was made head of the Aircraft Production Board (now called the Aircraft Board). Three months later, in August 1918, Wilson appointed Ryan to head the newly created Air Service. With this streamlined organizational structure, production began to accelerate, and there is little doubt that had the war continued, the original production numbers could have been realized (see figs. 5.12 and 5.13). As the war ended, the United States was outproducing all of the Allies combined in aircraft and aircraft engine production.

The total U.S. manufacturing effort was as follows:

5,229   aircraft were bought from the Allies
7,095   engines were bought from the Allies
13,894   aircraft were built in the United States
41,953   engines were built in the United States

Another important point to consider is the Navy aircraft production effort. They had a different philosophy. Aircraft production was in the hands of a few small companies who produced airplanes of American design. Of the Navy production effort, 570 aircraft reached the front before armistice. Many Navy airplanes used the American-designed Liberty engine, which was the other success story of manufacturing during the World War I.

The Liberty Engine

An outstanding American technical and manufacturing achievement, which was a source of pride for the country, was the design and production of the Liberty engine, an excellent power plant of high horsepower. As one story goes, engineers E. J. Hall of the Hall-Scott Company and J. E. Vincent of the Packard Motor Company secluded themselves in a suite in the Willard Hotel in Washington, D.C., and within 48 hours had designed the Liberty engine. This story is partially true.

Failure and achievement are two sides of the same coin. If Colonel Deeds shares in the failure of the aircraft industry to meet production estimates, he must also be given credit for providing the leadership that produced the Liberty engine. With the authority, Deeds made the decision to design and manufacture the Liberty engine. Deeds brought Vincent and Hall together in that Washington hotel and told them facetiously that they would be shut up in the room until they produced an acceptable design. The design would have to meet the following characteristics: (1) it must be lightweight in proportion

Fig. 5.12. DH-4s in production at Fisher Bodyworks in Detroit. Courtesy of the USAF Museum.

Fig. 5.13. DH-4 number 1000 ready to leave for the front. Courtesy of the USAF Museum.

to power output, (2) it must embody no new theory but use existing knowledge and practices, (3) it must be adaptable to mass production, and (4) it must develop greater power than any other proven engine then operating. Colonel Deeds also demonstrated his power of persuasion when he ensnared a drafter by the name of J. M. Schoonmaker who was on his honeymoon. Deeds persuaded him to postpone his honeymoon and become a part of the team.

Vincent and Hall proved to be a perfect blend of engineering talents. Vincent was the "theoretical" engineer and Hall the "hands-on" engineer, the scholar-engineer and the mechanic-engineer. Deeds also made assets available to the team of outside advisers from any of the large producers such as Cadillac, Hudson, and Packard. Within five days, they had produced a design that was ready for the refining touches of the drafters. The engine was produced in two models, the V-8 and the V-12.

The first Liberty engine, a V-8, was produced in late June 1917, about a month after Vincent and Hall first began to think about the engine. Such production speed was achieved by farming out the production of various components to twelve manufacturers. The first 8-cylinder engine was tested on 4 July and the first 12-cylinder engine on 14 August. The 12-cylinder version turned out to be an outstanding engine. Contracts to produce 22,000 engines were issued immediately to Packard, Lincoln, Ford, Nordyke and Marman, and General Motors (Buick and Cadillac). By the time the war ended in November 1918, less than a year later, these companies had produced 13,574 Liberty engines.

Manufacturing Analysis

Theodore Knappen's statement sums up the manufacturing situation completely: "In striving for peace it [the United States] had failed to prepare for war." The aircraft manufacturing industry was less than an embryo, the air forces were laughable, the infrastructure support to build up any kind of massive aircraft manufacturing effort was nonexistent, and the knowledge of combat technology relative to our European friends was rudimentary. But what was lacking in all of these things was made up for in enthusiasm, patriotism, and the willingness to tackle the tasks that needed to be done.

It is no wonder, then, that production efforts failed. Coffin and Deeds were not at fault; indeed, they were probably great patriots. It simply takes time to spin up an entire aircraft industry. The United States learned this lesson in World War I then repeated it again in World War II.[12]

Also, the United States was operating from an inappropriate premise: that aircraft and engines of European design should be built. This suggests a lack of either strong leadership or of national self-confidence. The United States encountered successes when it had confidence in its own abilities and proceeded accordingly such as in the development of the Liberty engine and in the Navy aircraft production program.

It seems to this historian that the United States could have achieved better results if someone had shown the engineers the operating parameters of, say, a Sopwith Camel and had told them to design and build 10,000 similar aircraft—only make them stronger, faster, and more maneuverable. As it was, the United States tried to copy something that was imperfect, the DH-4, and in the process adapt a machine manufactured in Europe using a production process entirely different from American mass production methods.

The Shifting Fortunes of War in the Air

Anthony Fokker's invention of the interrupter gear had a dramatic impact on the war in the air. As more of the Fokker Eindekkers equipped with parabellum machine guns were added to the inventory, the number of enemy kills rose. In the summer of 1915, the parabellum machine gun–equipped Fokker E-1 began to establish a name for itself (fig. 5.14). The Germans began to mount some impressively lopsided victories and managed to keep the synchronized gun a secret for four or five months.

An early test for the value of airpower came at Verdun, France, early in 1916. The Germans viewed the upcoming conflict as a decisive battle that would capture Paris and end the war. The Germans sought to destroy the Allies' reconnaissance ability by employing Fokker E-1s to eliminate the ability of reconnaissance aircraft to detect the gathering of German troops and supplies intended for the surprise offensive. French losses in the air were heavy, but their aviators did succeed in detecting the German buildup. However, the aviators were singularly unsuccessful in convincing the French general staff that a battle was brewing. The French staff predicted that no army would attack in February during the dead of winter. They were wrong.

With artillery followed by ground troops, the Germans successfully attacked Fort Douaumont, an "impregnable" stronghold that constituted the outer defenses of Verdun. The Allied air forces did not challenge German air over Verdun, but instead harassed troops in the rear areas. This eroded the confidence of the German infantrymen,

Fig. 5.14. The Fokker E-1. Courtesy of the USAF Museum.

who were shaken by the pounding from the attacking French and English airplanes. The German infantry demanded protection, as their oath illustrates: "God damn England, France, and Uncle Willy's Air Force." (Uncle Willie was Kaiser Wilhelm.)

The Allied air strategy worked; it drew the German air forces away from Verdun. This action and the cost of the lives of half a million French and English soldiers on the ground saved Verdun; it held.

Although the Germans had dominated the skies with their E-1 monoplanes and accounted for many Allied aircraft losses, victory was not to be theirs. Fighting initially with equipment inferior to the Germans, Allied airmen kept bringing the war to the enemy in spite of losses. The Allies developed make-do kinds of aircraft equipped with machine guns such as the French "Baby

Fig. 5.15. Flying scale model of a Nieuport 11. By permission of the National Air and Space Museum, Smithsonian Institution, ©1999 Smithsonian Institution.

Nieuport" (shown in fig. 5.15). This aircraft had the machine gun mounted on the top wing to fire forward over the arc of the propeller. The French Spad designed by the Societi pour la Production des Appareils Deperdussin (Spad) was first introduced to the front in 1916. The early models were troublesome; nevertheless, they gave the Allies some offensive (but mostly defensive) firepower.

Then one night, a German aviator became lost in the fog and landed his machine gun–equipped Eindekker on a French airport. The secret of Fokker's interrupter gear was out. With the arrival on the front of machine gun–equipped Nieuport 17s and De Havilland DH-2s in the spring and early summer of 1916, the Allies could check the Fokker menace, and the airpower edge went to the Allies.

The Germans were quick to counter in the fall of 1916 with newer technology: the Albatross D-2 and the even better D-3. With these aircraft, they were able to regain air superiority. They were able to maintain that superiority until the late spring of 1917. In April 1917, Baron Manfred von Richthofen added twenty-one British aircraft to his mounting count. Before his death in April 1918, Richthofen was credited with downing eighty British aircraft.

April 1917 was known as Bloody April by the British because of their heavy losses in air combat. Between 31 March and 11 May, the British lost 151 airplanes against losses of only 30 by the Germans. However, the fortunes were to switch once again.

In late spring 1917, a new British fighter airplane appeared that outclassed anything the Germans had in their inventory. This was the Sopwith Triplane, called by some the Tripe Hound (shown in fig. 5.16). It was the first three-wing fighter aircraft to enter combat, and it was equipped with the new Constantinesco-Colley (CC) interrupter gear. Richthofen praised this aircraft in a report to the German general staff. By July, a British naval squadron known as Black Flight was to account for eighty-seven downed German aircraft.

On the heels of the Sopwith Triplane, the British introduced the Sopwith Camel, a biplane that was deadly efficient (see fig. 5.17). The Sopwith Camel ran up a string of victories whose total numbers exceeded that of any other airplane in the war.

As the Allies gained air superiority in late spring 1917, designers of German aircraft, who had been resting on

Fig. 5.16. Sopwith Triplane. Courtesy of the USAF Museum.

Fig. 5.17. Sopwith Camels in France. Courtesy of the USAF Museum.

Fig. 5.18. Fokker DR-1 triplane. Courtesy of the USAF Museum.

their laurels, rushed back to their drawing boards with a new vigor. From Fokker came the DR-1, a three-winged aircraft (Dreidekker) similar to the Sopwith Triplane (see fig. 5.18). The second DR-1 off the production line went to Manfred von Richthofen in September. As he had done with his previous aircraft, Richthofen had the airplane painted red.

The DR-1 was highly maneuverable and enjoyed short success at the front. However, by October, two German flyers had been killed when each of their aircraft experienced structural failure. The DR-1s were removed from service, strengthened, and reissued in December, but they never recovered from their initial setback. Soon afterwards, Fokker produced the DR-7, which was an outstanding airplane. With this aircraft, a semblance of parity was reached in terms of air superiority with advantages shifting from one side to the other reflecting momentary events or battles.

In the early spring of 1918, the Germans felt the overwhelming weight of having fought the great Allied powers alone for four years. The tide of control in the air shifted to the Allies, where it remained until the end of the war. But shifts in air superiority aside, a question still lingers: Which fighter aircraft was the best?

Because of the record of the Sopwith Camel, some historians regard this aircraft as the best. This point has been controversial since 1918, flavored by those who had personal experience with other aircraft such as the French Spad and the Fokker D-7. Gibbs-Smith, a British aviation historian, considers the Fokker D-7 the finest all-around fighter of the war with such a combination of desirable qualities as its rate of climb and superb maneuverability.

The Use of Aircraft as Bombers

Heavier-than-air and lighter-than-air aircraft were both used in World War I. The lighter-than-air Zeppelins did not add much to the effort, except perhaps in frightening those below who knew Zeppelins were loaded with bombs.

The Germans were probably the first to use strategic bombing in the war. At one time, the Germans had designed and built a Zeppelin to make a strategic bombing mission to New York. Fortunately, the war ended before the plan could be put into effect. By war's end, Germany had dropped some 275 tons of bombs on the Allies, mostly from heavier-than-air craft. For example, on London alone, Germany dropped 53 tons of bombs from Zeppelins, mostly at night, and 63 tons from heavier-than-air craft, mostly on day missions. The English, on the other hand, dropped about 5,000 tons of bombs on Germany in 1918. Interestingly enough, not one ocean vessel was sunk by aircraft bombing during the war. This was quite amazing in light of the British success in converting several cruisers and ocean liners to crude aircraft carriers. Catapult-launched airplanes were carried on most English battleships by the end of the war.[13]

Pilot Training

The engine is the heart of an airplane, but the pilot is its soul.

—Walter Raleigh

To find the elements of the pilot training system used in the United States, we need to look to its roots in Europe.

At the beginning of the war, training was similar in most European countries on both sides of the conflict. Overall there was little organized curriculum, and various training aircraft and methodologies were used. No thought was given to training military pilots to do anything other than fly the aircraft for the purpose of reconnaissance. In some models of aircraft, the student sat above and behind the instructor. The instructor's cockpit had no stick, no wheel, and no pedals. The instructor could communicate only by leaning over the side of the cockpit, cutting the engine, and shouting at the student. Students often soloed with only 1.5 hours of flying time.

The English Method

Before the war, military student pilots received instruction on how to fly at the Central Flying School (CFS) of the Royal Flying Corps (RFC). However, little mention was made of military subjects such as aerial photography, bomb-dropping, or the use of the "wireless."

Students began their training in Farmans with a period of dual instruction. After soloing the aircraft and flying a few cross-countries, students moved to a more advanced aircraft such as the AVRO or BE-2 in which they received dual instruction and then flew solo for a few flights. Their final test was a cross-country flight at about 3,000 feet followed by a dead-stick (failed engine) spiral approach and successful landing.

At the beginning of the war, most of the aviation

resources were sent to the front, including those at the CFS. It was mostly stripped of both airplanes and instructors to bolster the units at the front. This decision began to take its toll as the number of pilots produced did not meet the levels of attrition. To resolve this problem, England set up many reserve squadrons based in England that would provide initial training in the Farman aircraft. Then the student would move either to the CFS or to a service squadron to receive advanced training. After some experimentation, the system that evolved was one in which the casualties were replaced out of resources produced at the CFS. The reserve squadrons acted as units where complete squadrons could be built up, trained, and then broken off as complete units and sent to the front. Further training would take place in the mission aircraft at the front. This system served their needs at first, but as experience with the military uses of aircraft grew, so did the need for advanced training. Eventually, more training was needed in such areas as maneuvers, formation flying, and other flight skills unique to combat.

Next, a three-phase system was put into place using the reserve squadron and CFS structure. The student first received training in a primary aircraft in which basic skills were taught. The next phase was in an advanced squadron where an advanced aircraft was used and the student was taught more flight maneuvers. More knowledge about the military uses of the airplane and its systems were discussed in this phase. From there students moved to the third tier, the operational squadron, where they learned combat procedures and tactics, many times while in combat.

This system worked reasonably well but had some serious shortcomings, such as (1) there was no standardized method of conducting the training at any level; the instructor was on his own and taught what he felt was necessary by means of the method that he thought was appropriate to the subject, (2) there was no system to the instruction, and (3) communication between the instructor and student was woefully inadequate, consisting mostly of shouting above the wind and engine noise. Clearly, something had to be done.

The Gosport system. The RFC set up an experimental group near the village of Gosport, England, to study and improve pilot training. The outcome of this study was a system that had two defining characteristics: standardized training and effective communication.

Standardized training. The three-stage system was retained, but the first two stages were taught at schools in England under a standardized flight training curriculum. In each of the first two stages, a student was assigned to an instructor with whom he remained for the duration of the training in that stage. Flight checks were given by other instructors. The flight checks by other instructors were done not only to assess the proficiency of the student but also to ensure that the standards were being met by their instructors. The goals of the first two stages of training were to teach the students how to fly and also to teach them procedures and tactics common to all of the combat aircraft they would eventually fly.

In the third stage, the training was conducted in the operational unit and by different instructors. Here it was felt that the more exposure to the various techniques of combat veterans in a rapidly changing environment, the better the quality of the training.

Communication. The Gosport system also introduced an excellent form of one-way communication. Two cups were sewn into the students' helmets, one over each ear. Hollow rubber tubes were inserted into the cups, joined as one tube and snaked between the cockpits. At the other end of the device, the tube was connected to a funnel device into which the instructor spoke. Students could hear the instructor perfectly; however, they could not respond verbally.

The Gosport system was very effective in reaching its goals. In 1917, Brig. Gen. W. S. Brachner, who was the RFC officer in charge of flight training for the RFC during most of the war, describes the training this way:

> [The student] first has to join the service as a cadet and go through a course in the Cadet's School, at which military subjects, pure and simple, are taught. He gets a grounding of drill and discipline, care of arms, interior of economy, military law and the use of the machine gun; this course lasts about two months. From this the Cadet is sent to a Flying Corps training school, where he begins his technical training on the ground. He goes through a course in the care of engines and rigging. He is given some ideas on the theory of flight. He is taught wireless signaling and receiving. He gets instruction in the care of machine guns, in the use of the camera, in map reading, in the observation of artillery fire with models, and in his spare moments he gets a certain amount of drill. This course lasts another two

months, and if he gets through this successfully, he is given a commission. . . . He then joins a preliminary training squadron as a pupil, and starts his instruction usually on a Maurice Farman, his training on military and technical subjects going on concurrently. After reaching a certain standard of efficiency and having completed a certain number of hours in the air, he is sent on to an advanced training squadron or service squadron, where he learns to fly service types of machines for military purposes and eventually qualifies for his wings. He is then gazetted as a Flying Officer of the R.F.C. and posted to a service squadron. . . . During the period of advanced training he goes through a course of aerial gunnery. . . . The total time in the air usually required to reach the qualification stage is about thirty hours solo. . . . Flying up to a certain standard is extraordinarily easy, but the standard of military qualifications is getting higher and higher, and more difficult to attain, and at the same time the quality of our flying demanded is growing greater every day.[14]

The French System

The French used a similar system to that of the British to train their bomber and reconnaissance pilots. However, for their chasse pilots (in today's vernacular, fighter pilots), it was an entirely different story.

The underlying training philosophy for chasse pilots seemed to be that since these men were to fly alone in single-seat aircraft, they would train alone in the aircraft. The chasse pilot had no dual instruction in his training. It worked like this: The student reported to his first training squadron, received ground instruction in numerous aviation and aircraft related subjects, and was assigned to a flight instructor. The flight instructor prepared the student to operate an aircraft with no wings. Obviously the machine would not fly, thereby its name was the Penguin. The goal of this phase of training was to prepare the student to operate the aircraft on the ground, which was no small feat. These wingless aircraft were equipped with rotary engines that had very limited control of engine speed. The cockpit had a throttle and air mixture control that was largely ineffective. In essence, the engine was running either at full tilt or at idle.

The only other engine speed control that the pilot had at his command was a group of "blip" buttons. When pressed, the buttons would ground the magnetos, which would deny a electrical spark to the selected engine

cylinders and the cylinders would quit running. Controlling the blip buttons was a critical skill to learn. If one held the blip buttons in too long, the affected cylinders would load up and would not restart once the buttons were released.[15] To make matters more difficult for the fledgling pilot, the characteristic of the rotary engine was that the crankshaft of the engine was fixed while the cylinders and propeller rotated around the crankshaft. This terrific mass moving at high speed induced a turning moment that made controlling the aircraft extremely difficult whether on the ground or in the air.

In addition, the aircraft had a tail skid instead of a tail wheel. To turn the aircraft, the student had to give the engine a burst of power that would lift the tail, then kick the rudder in the direction of the turn while the tail was up. Turning to the right was relatively easy, since the mass of the rotating engine was aiding the turn. Compared with a right turn, turning to the left was a maneuver from hell, since the moment produced by the whirling engine mass had to be overcome to accomplish the maneuver.

During this early phase of training, there were many accidents as the pilots were turned loose on an open field with instructions to accomplish a variety of ground maneuvers. When the students were able to control the airplane without killing anyone or tearing up the airplane, they were graduated to the next phase of flight.

In the second stage of training, the students trained on aircraft similar to those in the first stage except the aircraft had short "clipped" wings. The wings provided enough of a lifting surface for the students to get ten or fifteen feet in the air with a good run into a crisp head wind. Often, the instructor would stand on one of the stubby wings and shout encouragement to his student. The purpose of this phase of training was to enable the student to gain skills in both takeoff and landing. Once the student mastered this stage of training, he was sent to yet another field for continued training.

The third stage of training was conducted in a combat aircraft. The assigned instructor carefully briefed the student on various flight procedures and techniques and peculiarities of the airplane. The student then took off, made one circuit of the field and landed, all within view of the instructor. Next came a series of tasks of increasing complexity to include flight maneuvers, navigation, aerobatics, formation flying, air-to-air engagement tactics, and ground attack techniques and procedures.

Upon completion of this training, the pilot was posted to a line unit for duty as a combat chasse pilot.

The German System

The Germans used a pilot training system similar to that of the British. The system was effective in producing well-trained pilots when it was used properly. However, when times were rough at the front, the Germans would send their skilled instructors to combat, which slowed pilot production dramatically. The time it took to train other instructors cost them dearly in their push to keep up with battlefield attrition.

The American System

When the United States entered the war, there were very few skilled pilots (sixty-five), a skimpy number of training fields (three), and very few training aircraft. The training fields were located at Mineola, New York (Long Island); Essington, Pennsylvania; and San Diego, California. The total air arm of the Signal Corps including pilots, mechanics, cooks, and clerks amounted to only 1,200 people counting both officers and enlisted. It was clear from the start that the United States was going to have to conduct a large part of the training. The facilities in Europe were not capable of handling the numbers of American aviators that needed to be trained.

The United States adopted elements of the English Gosport system in that three phases of training were conducted: ground, primary, and advanced. For the ground phase, the Army turned to the Universities of California, Illinois, and Texas plus Ohio State University, Massachusetts Institute of Technology, Princeton University, Georgia Institute of Technology, and Cornell University. Each established a school of military aeronautics.

While spending eight to twelve weeks at one of the universities, the cadet received instruction in theory and principles of flight, use of the machine gun, operation and care of aircraft engines, assembling and care of aircraft airframes and components, theory and operation of radios (wireless telegraphy), using code, principles of aerial tactics, map reading and cross-country navigation, principles of photography, meteorology, astronomy, and a collection of military courses including military law, discipline, and military customs and courtesies (see figs. 5.19–5.21). The cadet was to be an Army officer and soldier, albeit a flying one, and he received a

Fig. 5.19. U.S. Army cadets training in Jennies. Courtesy of the USAF Museum.

substantial amount of military training in classical areas such as drills, calisthenics, and behaviors expected of an Army officer.

Once the cadet completed the ground phase of training, he was posted to a flying field where he would receive flight training. In the summer of 1917, there were not enough flying fields to meet the demand, so training fields in Canada were used. Through its various contractors, the Signal Corps was building training facilities at a vigorous rate. By December, fifteen training sites were open for business. These included many facilities that are still open today in some form or another such as

Fig. 5.20. Cadets learning to read maps. *Everybody's Magazine*, January 1918.

Fig. 5.21. A French instructor teaching U.S. Army cadets. *Everybody's Magazine,* January 1918.

Kelly Field and Brooks Field in San Antonio; Love Field at Dallas; Ellington Field at Houston; Scott Field at Belleville, Illinois; Chanute Field at Rantoul, Illinois; Selfridge Field at Mt. Clemens, Michigan; Wright Field at Dayton, Ohio; Langley Field at Hampton, Virginia; Mather Field in Sacramento; and Post Field at Ft. Sill, Oklahoma.

The cadet typically spent six to eight weeks at the primary training site, where he received training in the American-built JN-4 Jenny. Initially, the training was not standardized, but as the lessons of the Gosport system were implemented, standardized training followed. The cadet received between 40 and 50 hours of flight training composed of both dual and solo flight training events. He was given a flight exam at the end of training, called the RMA (Reserve Military Aviator) test. If successful, he received both his pilot's wings and an Army commission as a second lieutenant. From primary training, the trainee was usually sent to some training facility in Europe (England, France, or Italy) for advanced training. Of the 15,000 cadets who entered pilot training, approximately 8,700 were graduated, making the "washout rate" about 42 percent. Another 1,000 cadets received their primary training in Europe (approximately 500 in England and 444 in France). Some of these had experiences that tested their morale and resolve. For example, several hundred cadets were posted to a primary flight training school in Issoudun, France, a facility that was still under construction and was not yet equipped with primary training aircraft. They found themselves doing construction work and other unexpected and menial tasks. Delay after delay forced their start training dates forward, and many of them entered training just as their counterparts who were trained in the United States were arriving in Europe sporting their wings and commissions. In an effort to correct the inequity, the Army commissioned these "European cadets" at a time corresponding to the time they would have been commissioned had they trained in the United States.

The advanced flying course in France took from two to three weeks to complete (see fig. 5.22). The pilot received both dual and solo training in five aircraft. Each aircraft was faster and more difficult to fly, and the maneuvers were more difficult to accomplish as the aviator moved up the scale. As the pilot trainee progressed from airplane to airplane, the wings on the biplanes got shorter and the engines grew larger. The first aircraft had a wing spread of 28 meters and was equipped with an 80-horsepower engine. The next machine had a wingspan of 23 meters followed by one with 18 meters and a 110-horsepower engine. The fourth and fifth in the series were single-seat aircraft; the fourth had a wingspan of 15 meters, and the final aircraft had a wingspan of 13 meters with a 125-horsepower engine.[16]

After becoming proficient in the fifth aircraft, the pilot practiced the finishing touches, as told by Henry Woodhouse, a famous aviation expert of the day:

A week of aerobatic flying follows, during which the now full-fledged aviator practices banking at an angle of ninety degrees, "cork screwing" down with the machine descending faster than in a vertical

Fig. 5.22. French training facility. *Everybody's Magazine,* January 1918.

dive; side-slipping, nose-diving, and flying in squadron formation.

Then comes the period of transformation, during which the pilots practice the use of machine guns on different types of aeroplanes, shooting at toy balloons, and flying from four to ten hours each day, while waiting to be called to join a squadron at the front.[17]

And then the newly trained pilots were given the final test: they were posted to a line squadron at the front.

Engine Development

Before the war in Europe, aircraft engines of all varieties were available to power aircraft. These included in-line engines of four, six, and eight cylinders, rotary engines, and V-type engines of varying numbers of cylinders. The most notable of the V-type engines was the French Antoinette V-8 adapted from a marine engine in 1905. This engine had fuel injection, evaporative cooling, and a sculpturelike quality. The water jackets surrounding each cylinder were finished with electrolytically deposited copper, which gave the engine a lovely golden-red cast full of artistry and beauty. However, the dominant engine, at least for the Allies at the start of the war, was the rotary engine.

The French rotary engines powered most of the aircraft that were then flying, even the English aircraft. The rotary engine was characterized by its round shape with the cylinders arranged in a circle. This type of engine had been pioneered by an American, F. D. Farwell, in 1896 and a version of the Farwell rotary flew in 1909.[18] However, it was the French Seguin brothers whose genius made the rotary engine a success. Some features that made this a desirable engine design were its smoothness and lack of vibration; these were necessary in a aircraft that was fragile and intolerant of engines with poor balance and bad vibration habits. The rotary engine was also very reliable when viewed in the framework of other existing engines. However, the rotary type of engine was not without faults.

The rotary was an air-cooled engine in which the crankshaft was held stationary while the cylinders and propeller rotated around the crankshaft. This terrific amount of rotating mass created difficult torque and gyroscopic forces that the pilot had to overcome using

the aircraft's flight controls. Typical of this design were Gnome and Le Rhone rotaries.

Another fault of the rotary engine was the lubricant, which it flung around with abandon. Mineral oils with the high operating temperature qualities used today in aviation and automobile engines were not available until near the end of the war. The lubricant that was then used was an agricultural product made from the castor bean, called castor oil. Pilots flying the rotary-powered aircraft had to endure breathing a mixture of burnt and unburnt castor oil, often with undignified side effects. "Sitting in an open cockpit and steadily inhaling the stuff for an hour or two often produced in pilots those purgative symptoms for which oleum ricini was pharmaceutically notorious."[19]

This side effect notwithstanding, the rotary engines were widely built in France, Italy, Britain, and the United States. The Germans also had rotary engines as well as some excellent in-line engines that were water-cooled.

The cylinders of the in-line engine were arranged in a row, one behind the other, which aided in streamlining the design of the aircraft. Some in-line engines were mounted upside down. This not only allowed for a streamlined design but also gave the pilot an added range of visibility over the nose of the aircraft compared with a rotary or an upright mounted in-line engine. Most of the German aircraft were powered by some form of the in-line engine built by familiar companies such as Mercedes, Daimler, and BMW.[20]

As the war progressed, the British produced some excellent engines. Initially, Henry Royce of Rolls-Royce was reluctant to build aeronautical engines because his partner and friend, C. S. Rolls, had been killed in 1910 while piloting an aircraft. The Rolls-Royce Company produced excellent engines for their automobiles, and Royce was persuaded to manufacture airplane engines, the first of which was a derivative of the in-line six cylinders, overhead valve auto engine. Later, the engine was doubled to a V-12 and was a very successful engine, eventually producing about 360 horsepower.

The Spanish also produced some highly successful engines. Such engines as the Hispano-Suisa were used in a variety of aircraft including the French Spad and the British SE-5. The "Hisso" engine was produced under contract in both Britain and in the United States.

Reliability was (and is) a necessary feature in all aviation engines. The rotary engine would run about 15 hours before it needed to be overhauled. Compared with the piston engines of today that have TBOs (Time Between Overhaul) of 2,000 hours and more, at 15 hours, the TBO of the rotary was dismal, but in its time, a 15-hour TBO was highly respectable.[21] Toward the end of the war, as engine quality and reliability improved in such engines as the Rolls-Royce in-line and V engines and the Mercedes in-line engines, TBOs moved upward to the 500-hour range.

The American Airman at War

The first American airmen joined the war effort before the United States entered the war, some flying for Canada, others for England, and yet others for France. One of the most famous units was a French unit staffed almost entirely from American volunteers. This unit was called the Lafayette Escadrille named after a French general who aided America in its war for independence. The Lafayette Escadrille actually began as the Escadrille Americanne.

The all-American French Flying Squadron was the product of the work of Norman Prince, an American who had joined the French Air Service in 1915. Prince and his cohorts were successful in convincing the French government of the value of an American volunteer fighter (chasse) squadron. On 21 March 1916, the Escadrille Americanne was born. The unit was equipped with French Nieuports, and soon its fame spread to the point that the unit could not accommodate the large number of U.S. volunteers. This led to the formation of a larger group called the Lafayette Flying Corps, under which selection of volunteers was conducted and selectees joined either the Escadrille Americanne or other French reconnaissance, pursuit, or bomber units.

In the fall of 1916, the German ambassador complained to the U.S. government that Americans were fighting with the French against the Germans. To top it off, the aircraft were painted with the head of a Sioux Indian in full war paint. Since the United States was still neutral, the U.S. government capitulated and the squadron became known as the Lafayette Escadrille. When the United States entered the war, the Lafayette Escadrille joined the U.S. air effort as the 103d Aero Squadron (see fig. 5.23).[22]

Some American squadrons (the Seventeenth and the 148th) were trained for combat by the British and assigned to the British sector. They flew British equip-

Fig. 5.23. SPAD XIII of the 103d Aero Squadron. Courtesy of the USAF Museum.

ment, primarily the Sopwith Camel powered by a 140-horsepower Clerget Rotary engine. Others were trained by the French and were equipped with French equipment. Entire American aviation units did not join the effort until the war was almost over. America's air combat time was about seven months. Yet American pilots flying English, French, and Italian airplanes destroyed 776 enemy planes and 72 balloons. This was accomplished against a loss of 290 planes and 37 balloons. In addition, American squadrons conducted 150 air raids and dropped 270,000 pounds of bombs.

In the early spring of 1918, two American fighter squadrons were assigned to the relatively quiet Toul sector (see figs. 5.24 and 5.25). The Ninety-fifth and the Ninety-fourth Pursuit Squadrons arrived in the combat area in February and March. Each of these squadrons had been trained in French combat squadrons and were equipped with French aircraft.

The assignment to the Toul sector was done to give the U.S. pilots and other aircrew men time to gain combat experience without sacrificing them to the more ex-

Fig. 5.24. The "Hat in the Ring" insignia of the Ninety-fourth from Eddie Rickenbacker's SPAD XIII. Courtesy of the USAF Museum.

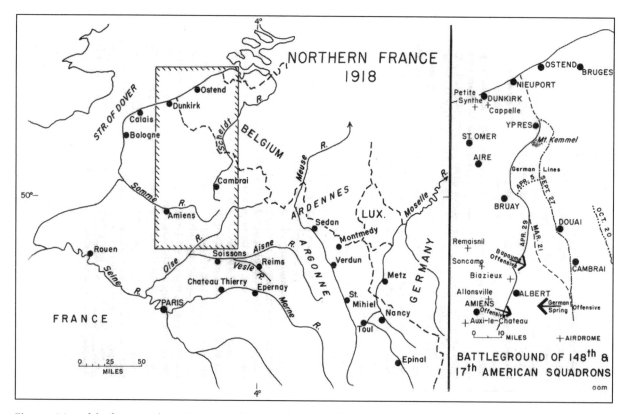

Fig. 5.25. Map of the front, northern France, 1918. James Hudson, *Hostile Skies*, 1968. Courtesy of Syracuse University Press.

perienced enemy in "hotter" sectors of the war. In mid-March, the units began to receive French Nieuports powered by 160-horsepower Gnome rotary engines. By mid-April, the Ninety-fourth, the "Hat-in-the-Ring" squadron, had claimed its first victory. Eddie Rickenbacker and Raoul Lufbery flew for the Ninety-fourth. In May 1918, two more American fighter squadrons, the Twenty-seventh and the 147th Aero Squadrons, joined the group.

A month earlier, an American reconnaissance squadron, the First Aero Squadron, arrived in the sector. After having received their initial training in the states, these pilots had received only three weeks of advanced training in Bleriots, Penguins, and Nieuports before being assigned to combat. Once there they were given airplanes that were practically obsolete: Renault-powered French Avion Renault (AR) aircraft and a few underpowered two-seat Spad XIs. The flyers called the ARs "Antique Rattletraps." This unit was destined to get the American-manufactured DH-4s, still months in the future. It was good fortune indeed that this unit was assigned to a "quiet" sector. Otherwise, these slow and clumsy aircraft would have been easy prey for a German Albatross or Fokker.

The first American bombardment squadron to arrive at the front was the Ninety-sixth. This unit was equipped with worn-out French Breget 14-B2 aircraft powered by 300-horsepower Renault engines. Trying to keep these aircraft airworthy was nearly impossible because parts were scarce. Had it not been for the crash of an aircraft that became a spare parts bin, the squadron's aircraft would have been impossible to maintain. As it was, operations came to a virtual standstill in late June. The work of the bombardment squadrons waxed and waned with the arrival or losses of aircraft. The long-awaited American-built De Havilland DH-4 aircraft powered by a 400-horsepower Liberty engine arrived at the front in the summer of 1918. The aircraft had its supporters and detractors, some describing it as "best on the front," and others calling it "two wings on a hearse" or the "flaming coffin." An example of the latter was reported by Eddie Rickenbacker, then the squadron commander of the Ninety-fourth Pursuit Squadron equipped with French Spad aircraft.

From every side Fokkers were diving on the clumsy Liberty machines which, with their criminally con-structed fuel systems, offered so easy a target to the incendiary bullets of the enemy that their unfortunate pilots called this boasted achievement of our Aviation Department "flaming coffins." During that one brief flight over Grand Pre, I saw three of these crude machines go down in flames, an American pilot and an American gunner in each "flaming coffin" dying this frightful and needless death.[23]

Most of the criticism was aimed at the airframe and its attendant problems of pilot visibility, seat locations, and gasoline tank location. What was universally liked about the airplane by the men who flew it was the Liberty engine.[24]

There was also some consternation and criticism from American combat pilots about the lack of life-saving equipment such as the parachute, already in use by the enemy. Late in the war Rickenbacker saw a German pilot leap from his burning Fokker and descend gently under the canopy of a parachute. Of this incident he said,

I was sorry that I had no time to watch his spectacular descent. I truly wished him all the luck in the world. It is not a pleasure to see a burning airplane descending to earth bearing with it a human being. Not unmixed with my relief in witnessing his safe jump was the wonder as to why the Huns had all these humane contrivances and why our own country could not at least copy them to save American pilots from being burned to a crisp.[25]

Naval Aviation

In his 1909 book *l'Aviation Militaire*, the French inventor and visionary Clement Ader said, "An aircraft-carrying ship becomes indispensable. These vessels will be constructed on plans very different from those now in use. Firstly, the deck will be clear of all obstacles: flat, as wide as possible, . . . it will have the aspect of a landing field."[26]

The "flat-top" flights of Eugene Ely in November 1910 and January 1911 were the beginning of naval aircraft carrier operations. However, it was the British navy that initially took the most advantage of Ely's pioneering work under the leadership of Charles R. Samson, then a lieutenant. Samson repeated Ely's flights launching from a modified battleship, the *Africa*, in January 1912. Later that year, the light cruiser *Hermes* was outfitted as a launch vessel for seaplanes. In the early part of the war, land-based British navy aircraft were used to fly reconnaissance missions and bombing missions against the Zeppelin sheds.

The first sinking of a surface ship by an air-launched torpedo occurred in August 1914 in the Aegean Sea. Flight Comdr. C. H. Edmonds, flying his Short 184 seaplane from the seaplane carrier *Ben-My-Chree,* sank a 5,000-ton Turkish supply ship. A few days later, another torpedo-plane pilot from the same carrier experienced engine trouble and had to land in the sea. Undaunted, he taxied his aircraft into a position with the nose of the seaplane pointed toward a Turkish barge. He then released his torpedo, which scored a direct hit.

The first "true" aircraft carrier was a English vessel that carried Sopwith Pups, wheeled aircraft that could be launched from the ship. Unfortunately, the aircraft could not then be landed on the ship's platform. Aircraft launched from the ship would either land at a land base or be ditched alongside the ship. The *Manxman* was the first of such vessels. The wheeled aircraft were far superior to seaplanes in their ability to defend the fleet and in their ability to attack other airborne machines, such as Zeppelins. The first aircraft carrier that could both launch and recover wheeled aircraft was the *Furious.* However, there were many more attempts than successful landings aboard the ship. Attempting to land aboard the vessel was a supreme challenge with the hot gases pouring from the centerline funnel destabilizing the air mass in the landing area. A form of an arresting gear was tried but was largely unsuccessful. The only landing aid the British navy aviator had was a strong headwind. Nevertheless, the navy used ship-borne aircraft very successfully in the World War I and arrayed the problems of aircraft carrier operations that led to successful aircraft carrier designs in later years.

The American Impact on the Aerial War Effort

The United States participation had little impact on the outcome of the air war except the notion of what could have happened had the war persisted. We must also recognize that the potential weight of the U.S. industrial machine perhaps made the Axis powers seek a speedier end to the conflict than would have otherwise been effected.

Nevertheless, if the U.S. presence had little impact on the war, the war had a tremendous impact on the thinking of a few men of vision in the use of the airplane as a weapon of war, men such as Billy Mitchell who gained a vision of the airplane as a strategic bomber. Mitchell formed, or perhaps solidified, his view of the value of the airplane and the role of strategic airpower from Maj. Gen. Hugh M. Trenchard, commander of the Royal Flying Corps. Mitchell had visited Trenchard in May 1917 at the British front. Under Trenchard's tutelage, Mitchell accepted Trenchard's dictums that the airplane is an offensive, not a defensive, weapon, that the airplane should be used to bomb deep behind the lines, and that airpower should be employed under a unified command rather than portioned out to various field commanders. These were the views that would eventually lead the United States to develop a separate air service and a strategic bombing force.

Interestingly, however, Trenchard was convinced that bombers could be equipped with enough defensive firepower to fight their way to a combat target and back without accompanying escort by fighter aircraft. Eddie Rickenbacker noted this in World War I:

> Some of these British bombing squadrons . . . flew De Havilland 9-A two seaters with the Liberty motor and each machine carried almost a ton of bombs. About twenty of these bombing squadrons were under command of General Hugh Trenchard, the greatest authority on war aviation in the world, in my opinion, and they were designated as the Independent Air Force because they were not subject to any army orders. Their one function was to drop bombs on German cities. . . . No fighting machines ever accompanied these bombers. They relied solely on their close flying formation to beat off all attackers.[27]

It was this philosophy that underscored the development of the B-17 "Superfortress" bomber in World War II and led to the loss of many B-17 aircraft to German fighters before the theory was proven incorrect and fighter escorts were employed to protect the bomber formations.

Notes

1. Simonds, *History of the World War,* 11–37.

2. Brown, *A History of Aviation,* 47.

3. See Reynolds, *They Fought for the Sky.*

4. The use of Zeppelins by the German military had a significant impact on the war. See chapter 14 for complete information.

5. Norman, *The Great Air War,* 82.

6. Simonds, 11.

7. Simonds, 11.

8. Mixner and Emmons, *U.S. Army Aircraft Production Facts,* 6–7.

9. Mingos, *The Birth of an Industry,* 12–15.

10. Mixner and Emmons, 7.

11. Berry, *Aircraft in War and Commerce,* 12.

12. Nearly a century ago, George Santayana observed, "Those who cannot remember the past are condemned to repeat it," but the opposite of that statement is not necessarily true; people can have a knowledge of the past and still make the same mistakes. The former is understandable; the latter is unacceptable.

13. Hodgins and Magoun, *Sky High,* 246–47.

14. Brachner, "Training in Military Aviation," 242–43.

15. A vivid illustration of this point is provided by Captain Bishop, the famous Canadian Balloon Buster, as told by Woodhouse in "Training Our Army 'Eagles,'" 9–16:

> I . . . spotted my balloon, now on the ground. I dived again, absolutely vertical. At 500 feet, I commenced to fire flaming bullets at it. At 200 feet it burst into flames. . . . Then horror of horrors, my engine would not pick up. I glided over the country and prepared to land my machine and burn it. . . . I worked frantically with the throttle and adjustments, and with a roar she picked up and I raced twenty-five feet up.

16. Woodhouse, 9–16.

17. Woodhouse, 9–16.

18. Setright, *The Power to Fly,* 25.

19. Setright, 27.

20. Setright, 17–33.

21. Setright, 49.

22. Hudson, *Hostile Skies,* 233–37.

23. Rickenbacker, *Fighting the Flying Circus,* 267.

24. Hudson, 134–35.

25. Rickenbacker, 252.

26. Wragg, *Wings over the Sea,* 1.

27. Rickenbacker, 82.

References

"Aircraft Production." *Congressional Record,* 56, 65th Cong., 2d sess., report no. 555, 22 August 1918.

"Aircraft Production Board." *Academy of Political Science Proceedings* 7 (February 1918): 104–14.

Arnold, Henry H. "History of the Aviation Section (Signal Corps) and Division of Military Aeronautics, April 1917 to October 1918." Unpublished. Washington, D.C.: Library of Congress, 1918.

Berry, W. H. *Aircraft in War and Commerce.* New York: George H. Doran, 1918.

Brachner, W. S. "Training in Military Aviation, the Methods of the British Schools." *Scientific American,* 21 April 1917, 242–43.

Brett, R. Dallas. *History of British Aviation, 1908–1914.* Surrey: Air Research, 1933.

Brown, Carl A. *A History of Aviation.* Daytona Beach: Embry-Riddle Aeronautical University, 1980.

Chapman, Victor E. *Victor Chapman's Letters from France.* New York: Macmillan, 1917.

Cooke, David. *The Planes They Flew in World War I.* New York: Dodd, Mead, 1969.

Faulkner, G. L. "Britain's Bid for the Control of the Air: Training the British Airman for Army and Naval Service." *Scientific American,* 28 April 1917, 422–23.

Fokker, Anthony H. G., and Bruce Gould. *Flying Dutchman.* New York: Holt, 1931.

Gibbs-Smith, C. H. *Flight Through the Ages.* New York: Thomas Y. Crowell, 1974.

Hodgins, Eric, and F. Alexander Magoun. *Sky High.* Boston: Little, Brown, 1929.

"How the Hispano-Suisa Engine Came to the Forefront of Aviation." *Scientific American,* 6 July 1918, 7.

Hudson, James J. *Hostile Skies.* Syracuse: Syracuse University Press, 1968.

Jones, Ira. *King of the Air Fighters.* London: Greenhill Books, 1934.

Knappen, Theodore M. *Wings of War.* New York: G. P. Putnam, 1923.

Kroes, Michael J., Thomas W. Wild, Ralph Bent, and James L. McKinley. *Aircraft Maintenance and Repair.* New York: Macmillan/McGraw-Hill, 1992.

"Liberty Aero Oil Which Meets the Requirements of Aviation." *Scientific American,* 7 September 1918, 200.

McConnell, James R. *Flying for France.* New York: Doubleday, Page, 1917.

Mingos, Howard. *The Birth of an Industry.* New York: W. B. Conkey, 1930.

Mixner, G. W., and H. H. Emmons. *U.S. Army Aircraft Production Facts.* Washington, D.C.: Government Printing Office, 1919.

Norman, Aaron. *The Great Air War.* New York: Macmillan, 1968.

Page, Victor W. "Development of Aviation Engines." *Scientific American,* 6 October 1917, 247, 258–59.

Patrick, Mason M. *The United States in the Air.* Garden City, N.Y.: Doubleday, 1928.

Person, Henry G. *A Business Man in Uniform: Raynal Cawthorne Bolling.* New York: Duffield, 1923.

Rae, John B. *Climb to Greatness: The American Aircraft Industry, 1920–1960.* Cambridge: MIT Press, 1961.

Reynolds, Quentin. *They Fought for the Sky.* New York: Rinehart, 1957.

Rickenbacker, Eddie V. *Fighting the Flying Circus.* Garden City, N.Y.: Doubleday, 1965.

Saunders, Hilary St. George. *Per Ardua: The Rise of British Air Power, 1911–1939.* London: Oxford University Press, 1945.

Setright, L. J. K. *The Power to Fly: The Development of the Piston Engine in Aviation.* London: George Allen and Unwin, 1971.

Simonds, Frank H. *History of the World War.* 4 vols. Boston: Houghton Mifflin, 1922.

Simonson, G. R., ed. *The History of the American Aircraft Industry.* Cambridge: MIT Press, 1968.

Smith, Daniel M. *American Intervention, 1917: Sentiment, Self-Interest, or Ideals?* Boston: Houghton Mifflin, 1966.

"Tricks and Acrobatics of the Air Fighter: What the Pilot Is Taught at the French Finishing School." *Scientific American,* 17 September 1918, 188.

Walcott, Stuart. *Above the French Lines.* Princeton: Princeton University Press, 1918.

Williams, Archibald. *Conquering the Air.* New York: Thomas Nelson, 1926.

Williams, Bertram W. "The Classification of Military Aeroplanes." *Scientific American,* 5 October 1918, 248–51.

———. "Recent Enemy Aircraft." *Scientific American,* 5 October 1918, 274.

Woodhouse, Henry. "Training Our Army 'Eagles.'" *Everybody's Magazine* 38 (January 1918): 9–16.

Wortley, Rothesay S. *Letters from a Flying Officer.* London: Oxford University Press, 1928.

Wragg, David. *Wings over the Sea: A History of Naval Aviation.* New York: Arco, 1979.

6

U.S. Airlines Before 1930

Tim Brady

HARDISON

THE HISTORY of the great U.S. airlines of today is inseparably linked to the beginnings of airmail service in the United States. To try and pry the two apart would be as foolish as trying to separate the development of the gasoline engine from the development of the aeronautics embodied in that brilliant machine that flew at Kitty Hawk in 1903. The beginnings of airmail and the history of the airlines are rich with human passion and courage. They reflect the excitement of the birth of something new, something dynamic, and something great.

Early Airmail Experiments

A few people of insight recognized the utility of the airplane from the moment it became a practical reality. One such person was Morris Sheppard, a congressman from Texas. In 1910, Sheppard introduced a bill in Congress to "experiment and report . . . in order that it may be definitely determined whether aerial navigation may be used for the safe and rapid transmission of the mails." A number of experiments followed which, in truth, were little more than stunts. The most notable experiment was when pilot Earle Ovington flew an exhibition sponsored by the Nassau Aviation Corporation on 23 September 1911. Ovington carried about fifteen pounds of airmail in his Bleriot monoplane from Sheepshead Bay, Long Island, New York, to Mineola, a distance of about six miles, and air-dropped it to those waiting below (see fig. 6.1).

Thirty-one "experimental" flights were conducted. Most of them were part of the organized activities for county or state fairs and were done in barnstorming fashion.

When war erupted in Europe in 1914, interest in Rep. Sheppard's bill waned and almost disappeared. Then, in 1916, Sheppard, now a senator, pushed another bill through Congress that created an airmail appropriation of $100,000. So strong was the war fever by this time that few were aware that such a sum had been appropriated for airmail flights. They were also not aware of the proviso that if the money were not used by July 1918, it would flow back into the federal coffers. A gentleman by the name of Benjamin B. Lipsner knew of the appropriation and of its time limits.

Capt. Benjamin Lipsner

A few years before the beginning of World War I, Benjamin Lipsner developed an interest in the idea of using the airplane as an instrument of mail service. Trained as a mechanical engineer, Lipsner was understandably attracted to the airplane. After college, he began to frequent Checkerboard Field in Chicago as something of

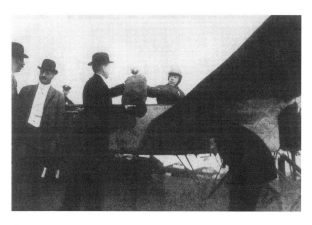

Fig. 6.1. Earle L. Ovington, in the cockpit of a Bleriot-type monoplane, receiving a bag of mail from Postmaster General Frank H. Hitchcock before the first U.S. airmail service from Nassau Boulevard to Mineola, Long Island, New York, 23 September 1911. By permission of the National Air and Space Museum, Smithsonian Institution, ©1999 Smithsonian Institution.

an "airport bum." He helped keep the facility clean and occasionally worked on Farman and other airplanes. He assisted in tearing down and rebuilding Gnome engines and learned how to taxi the airplanes around the field. Although he did not learn to fly, he developed a kindred relationship with pilots Earle Ovington and Claude Grahame-White. When Ovington made that first airmail flight to Mineola, Lipsner was there to witness it. From this background, the notion of an airmail service began to take shape in his mind. But then his career took an oblique turn away from aviation.

His education as a mechanical engineer led him to several positions with large trucking firms. He surveyed various maintenance activities and developed efficient maintenance schedules and repair cycles. When America entered World War I, Lipsner was working for the Texas Company (Texaco) as a lubricant researcher. When his boss at Texaco threw his hat into the ring, Lipsner followed suit along with a fellow worker, O. J. May. At the time, the Army was seeking a lubricant that was as efficient but much more plentiful than the scarce and expensive castor oil. This oil, with its odor so unique that anyone who had been exposed to its vapors would not soon forget, had the high-temperature qualities needed in aviation engines. General Pershing had determined that he needed some 5 million gallons of castor oil for his airplanes. This quantity represented the entire pro-

duction capability of the United States for a three-year period. It was clearly a serious problem that needed a quick solution.

Primarily through the efforts of May with Lipsner's assistance, Liberty Aero Oil was developed.[1] The lubricating quality of Liberty Oil, a petroleum product, was plentiful and superior to castor oil. It became the general engine lubricant for the services.

By the time the project was completed, it was early 1918 and the war was still being fought. Nevertheless, Lipsner was temporarily left with no specific task to accomplish or assignment to consider. With such freedom to ponder the future, he began to wonder whatever had happened to the $100,000 airmail appropriation. He visited the postmaster general's office and discussed the issue with a clerk. By this time, Lipsner had thought the problem completely through and felt that he had devised a workable plan to put an airmail service into operation. The clerk was so impressed with the plan that he contacted his boss, Otto Praeger, the second assistant postmaster general. Praeger listened very carefully to Lipsner's plan. "Captain," he said, "this has been an interesting two hours. Where can I reach you when I want to go further into this?"[2]

Lipsner did not expect to hear from Praeger soon, but the very next day he was told that the post office wanted to borrow him from the Army for a few weeks to create an airmail system. The next few months were ones of feverish activity for Lipsner. He arranged to borrow pilots, airplanes, and mechanics from the Army. The four pilots were Torrey Webb, George Boyle, James Edgerton, and Harry Culver, all Army lieutenants. The aircraft provided by the Army were four Curtiss JN-4H Jenny training aircraft built for the Army's cadet training program. Each airplane was powered by a 150-horsepower, water-cooled Hispano-Suisa engine. The front cockpit of each airplane had been modified with canvas straps to hold the mail pouches. Mail capacity with a full fuel load and pilot was about 160 pounds.

The route planned was a rather simple one that included three cities: New York, Philadelphia, and Washington. Mail would be loaded on airplanes at Washington and New York that would take off in time to rendezvous at Philadelphia. There, two pilots would be waiting with their planes ready to go. Mail would be transferred to the appropriate airplane, which would take off and fly to its respective New York or Washington destination. Lieutenant Webb was chosen to fly the inaugural route from New York to Philadelphia, and Lieutenant Boyle was chosen to fly from Washington to Philadelphia. Waiting at Philadelphia would be Lieutenant Edgerton to receive Webb's mail from New York and fly it to Washington, and Culver would take Boyle's mail to New York.

The occasion was to be a grand one. Truly, the inauguration of the first airmail service in the United States was a somber and historic moment. The date for the event was set for 15 May 1918. Otto Praeger and Benjamin Lipsner had invited a number of dignitaries, including President Woodrow Wilson. The day before the flight, Lipsner was restless. He kept trying to think of what calamity could occur to upset the whole show. In his mind's eye, for example, he could see the Jenny aircraft smashing into the trees on takeoff from the Polo Grounds. The Polo Grounds had not been designed as an airfield, and towering trees stood at the end. The Polo Grounds had been used successfully many times by JN-4s; nevertheless, it was a nagging worry.

An hour before the scheduled event on 15 May, the Jenny, which Boyle was to fly to Philadelphia, was flown into the Polo Grounds by Maj. Ruben Fleet. The help that Fleet provided Lipsner was invaluable. He acted as a technical adviser and an organizer for the project. Fleet gave Boyle a map and explained the route to him. Fleet, incidentally, would eventually become head of the Consolidated Aircraft Corporation.

Twenty minutes before Boyle was to take off, a line of cars paraded onto the field. The presidential party had arrived: President and Mrs. Wilson, Postmaster General Albert S. Burleson, Second Assistant Postmaster General Otto Praeger, and Assistant Secretary of the Navy Franklin Delano Roosevelt.

By now, a large crowd had gathered, including news reporters, aviation enthusiasts, and other well-wishers. A siren sounded, and the crowd parted to let the mail truck, escorted by motorcycles, enter the field. The mail was taken off the truck and ceremoniously strapped into the front cockpit of the Jenny while Boyle strapped himself into the rear cockpit. The mechanics who had worked on the airplane formed a five-man chain to pull the prop through and start the engine.

"Switch off!" the chief mechanic shouted.

"Switch off!" Boyle echoed. In perfect unison the mechanics pulled the prop through two revolutions.

"Contact!" yelled the chief mechanic.

"Contact!" repeated Boyle as he reached down and turned the switch on.

Again, the mechanics pulled the prop through, but this time they attempted to start the engine. The engine coughed, caught for a brief instant, then stopped dead. Several times the cycle was repeated but to no avail. The pesky Hispano would not cooperate. President Wilson began to get a little edgy. He had recently become disenchanted with mechanical things. Several weeks earlier, he had been burned during an Army demonstration when he placed his hand on the hot exhaust pipe of a tank during an Army demonstration. His hand was still heavily bandaged.

With the prop standing tall, there was a great deal of confusion, embarrassment, head scratching, and milling around. Lipsner asked the chief mechanic if he had filled the gas tank after the plane landed. The mechanic's mumbled response told Lipsner the problem. He said that the gauge read full, so he did not add any gas. The gauge on the Jenny was designed to read correctly in level flight. On the ground, with the nose pointed skyward at a good angle, the gauge could read full with an empty tank. Boyle's tank was, in fact, empty.

Lipsner pushed his way through the crowd, siphoned twenty-one gallons of gas from a dismantled plane and an automobile, and filled the Jenny's tank. This time when the mechanics propped the engine it caught and started smoothly. Things seemed to be looking up. Boyle taxied to the end of the field, turned into the wind, and "gave 'er the gun." Moments later he was airborne, and a heart-stopping moment later he was over the tall trees. Lipsner breathed a sigh of relief. Boyle turned the airplane to gain altitude, then headed south. Lipsner's

Fig. 6.2. A letter carried aboard George Boyle's aircraft. *Scientific American*, 1918.

stomach knotted: Philadelphia was to the north. Soon Boyle disappeared from view and Lipsner knew that the dreaded calamity had happened. Boyle later made a forced landing near Waldorf, Maryland, exactly opposite from his intended route (see fig. 6.2).

The day was not lost, however. Torrey Webb took off from New York and arrived in Philadelphia on schedule (see fig. 6.3). Edgerton received Webb's mail and flew it to Washington, D.C., completing the circuit. Boyle's mail was picked up by car and then placed on a train for New York.

Lieutenant Boyle was obviously not a "seasoned" pilot. Why then was he chosen for such an important mission when many other pilots were more qualified? The answer is, perhaps, a familiar one. Boyle was related to a well-placed member of government who had sought to secure this moment in history for young Boyle. Indeed, the moment is secure.

Despite its jerky start, the airmail service using Army pilots, planes, and mechanics was a success. It was never intended that the Army would fly the mail indefinitely. It was used as a mechanism to get the idea of an airmail service moving. On 10 August 1918, the Army pilots flew their last airmail routes. In three months they had flown 254 trips, logged 29,500 miles, and made sixteen forced landings.

While Lipsner was busily running the Army-supported airmail service, he was also building a cadre of civilian pilots to fly the mails when the Army tenure expired. Additionally, Congress appropriated $100,000 for the purchase of specially designed airmail planes. Lipsner advertised for bids and discussed the requirements with several airplane manufacturers. He chose the Standard Aircraft Corporation of Elizabeth, New Jersey.

By 12 August 1918, Lipsner had hired a full staff, including pilots, mechanics, riggers, and office workers, and he had taken delivery on six custom-built airmail planes. In Lipsner's view, prior to this time commercial aviation had been only a theory. However, on 12 August, when that first civilian pilot flew that first commercial airplane on an airmail route, commercial aviation had been born.

Released from the Army, Lipsner remained as superintendent of the aerial mail service until December 1918. For months, the airmail service operated efficiently and was largely ignored by politicians. However, with the arrival of Armistice in November, thousands of veterans, many of them pilots, and a few of them with strong relatives in government, began coming home to search for scarce jobs. Thus far, Lipsner had been able to operate autonomously. He had been able to handpick his pilots, mechanics, and staff. Suddenly, his authority was usurped. Applicants whom he had turned down were hired; Otto Praeger abruptly discharged two of Lipsner's most respected pilots for failing to fly in ground fog that had cut visibility to 25 feet. Further, decisions were made on new routes without Lipsner's knowledge. When Lipsner confronted Praeger with each of these issues, Praeger responded that the plans would be carried out regardless of what Lipsner said or did. Lipsner promptly resigned, a casualty of peace more than of the war. Although Otto Praeger would eventually become known as the "Father of Airmail," it was Benjamin Lipsner whose ideas, efforts, zeal, creativity, and heart had given commercial aviation its first breath of life.[3]

Expansion

That first year of airmail service yielded some fairly impressive operational figures. Of the 1,263 flights scheduled, 55 were canceled, 37 were not completed because of engine problems, and 55 were forced down because of bad weather. This amounted to a respectable 89 percent success rate.

The end of the war brought a plethora of pilots, mechanics, and other aviation specialists into the market. The war also made available an abundance of aircraft to be had for the asking. About a hundred American-built De Havilland DH-4s came into the post office's inventory before the year was out. The DH-4, named the Flaming Coffin during the war because of its fuel system design and its propensity for burning during a crackup, was the culprit in many accidents in December and January. As a result, the DH-4 was taken out of airmail service in January 1919 to solve the problems with the airplane.

Several modifications were made to the airplane to make it acceptable to the post office. Before modification, the pilot flew the airplane from the front cockpit with the mail placed in the rear cockpit. This sandwiched the pilot between the gas tank and the mail, with a hot engine up front waiting to ignite the gas during a crash landing. Once modified, the airplane was flown from the rear cockpit, which gave the pilot a "shock absorber" up front where the mail was carried. Other modifications included steel landing gear struts and a steerable tail skid. The airplane was put back into service as the DH-4B (shown in fig. 6.4). It remained the line aircraft and workhorse of the post office until 1926.

With the addition of these new airplanes, Praeger began to expand the airmail route structure, aiming toward a transcontinental route system. By July 1919, a New York–Chicago route had been established, and by May 1920, routes were added that stretched westward from Chicago to Iowa City and Omaha. The final linkup was made in September 1920 to complete the transcontinental route to San Francisco. The route extended from

Fig. 6.4. DH-4B mailplane. Kansas Aviation Museum Collection.

Omaha to North Platte, Nebraska; then to Cheyenne, Rawlins, and Rock Springs, Wyoming; on to Salt Lake City, Utah, Elko, and Reno, Nevada; and finally to San Francisco.

It was principally a daylight operation. At night, the mail traveled by train. Weather was also a continuous problem. In these early days of flying, there were no reliable instruments to determine aircraft flight attitude except the God-given senses of the pilot: eyes, ears, and the seat of the pants. If the eyes were subtracted from the equation—for instance, if the pilot had flown into a cloud—then the pilot relied on his other senses to make a decision. The decision is the difference between maintaining control of the airplane and losing control or, perhaps, crashing.

On the ground, the fluid flowing in the semicircular canals in the inner ear performs beautifully as a mechanism to maintain balance. However, the fluid flow can easily be fooled by the motion of the airplane without the eyes to correct the wrong impressions. In flight sans eyes, these balance devices were worse than worthless. They lied.

The ears were useful in discriminating sounds. The sound of the wind rushing past the airplane was one of the most reliable "instruments" of the day. In straight and level flight at certain speeds, the sounds of the wind flowing against the wires and turnbuckles are different from the sounds of the wind flowing against those same wires in a climbing right turn with airspeed decreasing. The pilots' ability to refine this sense of sound and interpret its meaning with regard to aircraft attitude often represented the difference between life and death.

Worse, it seemed that the person in charge of the airmail service, Otto Praeger, knew little about aviation or the hazards of attempting to fly with low visibility. He did not know the difference between a monoplane and a biplane. Pilots said that he made decisions for mail flights operating out of New York by looking out his office window in Washington. If he could see the Capitol Dome, he assumed the weather was good enough to fly in New York. On a particular morning at Belmont Park, New York, a thick fog covered the field. Airmail pilots Lee and Smith were scheduled to fly, but they wanted to wait until the fog lifted before making an attempt. When the station manager reported this decision to Washington, Praeger fired back a telegram that stated, "Fly by

compass. Visibility not necessary." When Lee and Smith still refused to take off in the zero visibility condition, Praeger wired back, "Discharge both pilots, Lee and Smith." This action caused the pilots to go on strike. After a few days without mail moved by air, a settlement was reached whereby the station manager made the decision on whether or not the planes would fly. While this decision did not completely satisfy the pilots, it was enough of a compromise to get the mail back into the air again.

Weather was not the only problem; the power plant on the DH-4 also caused its share of grief. The engine was an American-designed Liberty engine that had the annoying characteristic of just quitting. At one moment the engine would be roaring perfectly, and the next moment there would be a horrible silence. This usually occurred because the timing chain in the engine had snapped. No amount of knob twisting and throttle manipulation could coax the engine back to life once the timing chain broke. The only thing to do was to look for a place to land. In such an incident, Dean Smith lost his engine (see fig. 6.5). He tells what happened next.

> To my left was a cup-like basin with a small clearing. One thing I could not know: the clearing was choked with brush and weeds, hiding a three-foot ledge of rock directly in front of my landing spot. The ledge slammed into the undercarriage as I hit. The plane

Fig. 6.5. Dean Smith's landing. Cartoon by Stan Hardison.

snapped like popper on the end of a bull whip. I was catapulted into a long headfirst dive, like a man shot from a cannon. Fortunately I landed in the brush and rolled to a stop in a sitting position. The padded leather ring that rimmed the cockpit hung from my neck like a lei. I was still holding the rubber grip pulled loose from the control stick. My seat belt lay across my lap. I felt around to determine that I had no broken bones. The wreckage was piled in a heap, like crumpled paper.[4]

Bad weather and engine failures combined to make the forced landing a way of life for the airmail pilot. In 1920 and 1921, for example, there were some eighty-nine crashes in which nineteen pilots lost their lives. In 1921, the average airmail pilot made a forced landing every eight hundred miles. On any given round-trip between two route points, a pilot would likely make one forced landing. For this they received the princely sum of $250 per month with one stipulation: no fly, no pay.

Jack "Skinny" Knight

In 1921, the airmail service operated on a transcontinental route in the same way as the pony express had operated the western mail service some sixty years earlier. In a relay system that contained fifteen points, airplanes would take off from New York and San Francisco and in a series of relatively short flights. The flights would cover the coast-to-coast distance in about twenty-two hours less than a similar letter traveling the entire distance by train. Considering the speed differential between train and plane, the time saved was not spectacular. The time that was saved by air in the day was lost at night when the mail traveled by train. Airplanes did not fly at night. Instead, the mail was loaded on trains for the nighttime portion of the journey.

Undoubtedly, flying the mail by night as well as by day would have been the next step in the evolution of airmail. However, a revolution was called for, not evolution. President Wilson, a strong supporter of the airmail service, was the outgoing chief executive, and the incoming economy-minded Harding administration was looking at the airmail service as a target for budget cuts. To further fuel the fire, the railroad industry was not reacting kindly to a government service, the post office, intruding into the private sector. The post office was

becoming directly competitive with what the railroad people viewed as "their" business. It was clearly time for an aggressive event that would endear the airmail service to the hearts of Americans. Otto Praeger decided to demonstrate the capability of the airmail service by flying the airmail both day and night. He asked for volunteers, and ten pilots accepted the challenge.

The plan was to launch two DH-4s each from New York and San Francisco, westbound and eastbound, respectively, proceeding in a relay fashion. The relay method changed pilots and airplanes at designated points flying day and night until the mail from San Francisco reached New York and vice versa.

The airplanes were not equipped for either night flying or flying in bad weather. The instruments on the DH-4 were crude. The compass was often incorrect, particularly on an easterly heading. The airspeed indicating system, which gathered air through a small pipe called a Pitot tube, located on the leading edge of the bottom wing, worked all right except when it became plugged; unfortunately, this occurred often because of the proximity of the Pitot tube to the surface of the field and the proliferation of mud on sod or grass fields. The altimeter, which measures height, read 1,000 feet for each half-inch of scale around the face of the circular instrument. With such a small scale value representing such a large chunk of altitude, reading any altitude below 1,000 feet was difficult, and of course, those last 1,000 feet are the most important. The instrument group also included a tachometer, which told engine rpms reliably, and an engine water temperature gauge. That was it. None of the modern instruments such as gyro-stabilized artificial horizon or even a simple turn and bank indicator existed. To complicate matters more, the instruments that were installed in the cockpit of the DH-4 were not lighted. Lights were not installed on the airplane for landing. The airfields being used were not lighted except by some last-minute gasoline drums placed along the runway for this event. Lighted airways, ground beacons to guide the pilots, and radio navigation were things of the distant future.

Praeger was guided more by the political reality of the situation than by any knowledge of seasonal meteorological trends. Praeger picked the worst time of the year to conduct such a bold demonstration. He chose Washington's birthday, 22 February 1921, for the attempt.

With scud rolling low over New York, two pilots, E. J. Leonhardt and Ernest M. Allison, took off that morning into the heavy air. Less than an hour later, Leonhardt was forced to land in a potato field near DuBois, Pennsylvania, because his 12-cylinder Liberty had failed to deliver full power.

Because of the low weather ceiling, Allison was never able to climb higher than 800 feet before running into a wall of snow. He tried to spiral closer to the ground in order to keep it in sight but to no avail; he could not even see as far as the propeller.

> The wind whistled through the steel wires, and with his ears tuned to the pitch, he unconsciously made minor corrections to keep the plane level. He chewed a big wad of chewing gum, for this made him swallow, and that, in turn, kept his ears open. A shrill whine told him that the plane was diving. A tiny vibration in the wires warned him that the speed was too low. A sudden gust of wind on the side of his face told him that the DH turned in a skid. Sound, feel, pressure on the seat of his pants—these were Allison's instruments.[5]

Fighting the clouds, the cold, and the terrain, Allison made it to Cleveland with his 350 pounds of mail. From there, Wesley L. Smith took the mail and, struggling with similar problems, made it into Chicago, but there the westbound flights ended. The rotten weather had forced cancellation.

On the other side of the nation in the predawn darkness of California, William Lewis and Farr Nutter took off in their DH-4s from San Francisco for the first leg eastward to Reno, Nevada. The pilots had to climb their DH-4s to 12,000 feet in order to clear the mountains. Any altitude in an open cockpit in the dead of winter is bad, but at 12,000 feet in the primitive, unheated cockpits of the DH-4s, the cold was intense. Pilots would line their clothing with newspapers to keep out the cold. They would alternate hands on the control stick so they could sit on the unused hand to warm it up and get the blood flowing.

As Nutter was landing at Reno, he spotted Lewis behind him descending for landing. Lewis rolled into a turn and then lost control. The crash destroyed the airplane and killed Lewis. In stunned silence, Nutter and the ground crew transferred his mail pouches to Jack Eaton's waiting airplane. With both westbound flights

down and one eastbound flight down, the mission rested on the remaining flight. If the mail was to get through, it would be up to the relay pilots of this last flight.

Eaton made it to Salt Lake City without any unusual difficulty, and the mail was transferred to Jimmy Murray's airplane. Murray's flight to Cheyenne was uneventful, and Frank Yeager was waiting to take the mail on to North Platte, a flight that would be made in the darkness. Yeager had no particular difficulty and touched down at North Platte in darkness. Jack "Skinny" Knight was waiting, and they discussed the discouraging weather reports for the stations ahead. Knight's airplane was undergoing repairs for a damaged tailskid. Knight had often flown with damaged tailskids, but this mission was so important that the postal authorities insisted that the tailskid be fixed. It turned out to be a fortuitous decision, despite the fact that it caused a three-hour delay.

Knight had very carefully studied his route from North Platte to Omaha. He had flown the route many times during the day, but never at night. He made comprehensive notes on landmarks; he drove the route by automobile and talked to townspeople and farmers along the way, giving them his anticipated arrival time in their area. He requested that they light bonfires to serve as navigational checkpoints.

Finally, with his airplane fixed at 10:45 P.M. on the night of 22 February 1921, Skinny Knight pulled the heavy DH-4 into the air. As he approached Lexington at 2,000 feet above the ground, he did not expect to see a bonfire because he was so late, but there it was. The good citizens of Lexington had braved the winter cold and, although it was after midnight, had waited for the mailplane. Knight signaled his appreciation by throttling back, then pushing forward on the throttle to cause a backfire. Below, his unseen friends cheered. The further he flew, the lower the worsening weather forced him to descend, staying under the clouds. But the bonfires kept him on his course. As he approached Omaha, he was flying in snow that had been steadily increasing in intensity. He spotted the airfield by the lighted gasoline drums that marked the runway. He landed and was greeted by a reception committee. Wearily, he asked the station manager, Bill Votah, where the next pilot was. Votah told him that his relief had washed out in Chicago because of the weather. By now, the weather had developed into a blizzard, and the fate of the transcontinental mission rested with one man: Jack Knight. He turned to Votah and said, "I'm going to take the flight on."

Knight had never flown the Omaha to Des Moines to Iowa City route. He went to an all-night lunch counter, pulled out an old Rand McNally road map, and began studying the route from Omaha to Des Moines. Meanwhile, the oil and water were drained from his airplane and warmed. Otherwise, the fluids would freeze or congeal and Knight would not be able to get the engine started. After a short time, the blizzard abated somewhat. Knight trudged through the snow to his airplane and told the mechanics to pour the fluids back into his engine. Even with warm fluids, he could only try two or three times to start the engine before it was necessary to remove the fluids and reheat them. Luckily, the engine started on the first attempt, and Knight was off into the black snowstorm.

He climbed to 600 feet and headed for Des Moines. Unfortunately, a more northerly wind component than he expected shifted him south of his course. Knight knew that he was lost. He spotted a landmark and then, using a flashlight he had picked up in Omaha, attempted to identify the landmark on the Rand McNally road map. In the process, he momentarily blinded himself and lost control of the airplane. He recovered the airplane just in time to keep from slamming into the trees and climbed back to 600 feet. Then, using a more careful technique of flicking the flashlight on and off, he was able to identify his position. As he approached Des Moines, he spotted his landing field but found it covered with snow. He had no choice; he had to go to the alternate field in Iowa City. En route, his engine sputtered, draining the last of the gas out of the main tank. He switched to the gravity tank, which would give him a few more minutes of flight. Twenty minutes later, Knight's worst fears were realized: his gas gauge read empty and he had not a clue as to the location of the field at Iowa City. As he prepared to turn his airplane away from the populated area for a forced landing, he spotted a single light on the ground, a flare. He figured that it must be the airfield, since nobody else would be outside this time of night in this kind of weather. He aimed the DH-4 at the light and landed right on top of it just as he ran out of gas. A man ran up to the airplane and said, "Start up the engine. I help you taxi back to the shack." Knight responded, "I can't start the engine. There's no gas left."

When Knight asked about his replacement pilot, he was told, "There be no other pilots, boy. With the weather acting this way, everybody thinks the flying be over for the night. I be the watchman—the only one here. I hear your engine and decide you be needing some help, so I run out and light a fusee."

Knight asked for gasoline for the Chicago leg. The watchman replied, "Chicago, boy? Be you crazy? In this snow and all?"

"I guess I am a little crazy," Knight said, "but damn if I can see quitting now."

So Jack Knight, weary, cold, and determined, was off again, this time for Chicago. His navigation would be easier this leg, he reasoned. He would head the airplane northeasterly until he hit the shore of Lake Michigan, then follow the shoreline south to Chicago. The snow abated and the cloud cover decreased, but then a new problem crept in: fog began to obscure the ground. At daybreak, however, the fog began to dissipate rapidly, and Knight made it to Chicago.

To his surprise, he was greeted on landing by a large group of people in formal attire. Women were in long evening dresses and men in tuxedos. When he had left Omaha, news had flashed throughout the clubs across the nation about his daring attempt. The welcoming party decided to stay up and wait for him. Naturally, a party followed, but not before the mail was transferred to Jack Webster's airplane. Knight watched Webster take off and climb toward Cleveland. Again because of the weather, Webster was forced to fly the entire route at a maximum altitude of 300 feet above the ground. In Cleveland, waiting for him was Allison, who would experience a similar flight. Allison landed in a snowstorm at Hazelhurst Field in Long Island at 4:50 P.M. on 23 February 1921. The entire coast-to-coast flight covered a distance of 2,629 miles and took 25 hours and 16 minutes of actual flying time. Total time from takeoff at San Francisco to touchdown in New York was 33 hours and 21 minutes. Otto Praeger had his public relations event. Jack Knight and the other courageous men of the Aerial Mail Service had saved the service from budget-cutting politicians. Congress was quick to appropriate $1,250,000 for the expansion of the airmail system. This appropriation included funds to create a route system lighted by navigational beacons.[6]

Prelude to Private Ownership

Experiments were soon conducted using night-lighted airways. When the experiments proved the validity of the concept, airway beacon lights and airfield lights were erected. By 1923, a lighted system extended eastward from Chicago to Cleveland and westward from Chicago to Rock Springs, Wyoming. Eventually, the system stretched from New York to Salt Lake City, a distance of 2,045 miles.

The reputation of the airmail system grew as did the demand for its services. The steady increase in mail loads created the demand for an airplane capable of carrying greater loads. Several aircraft builders were invited to compete, and Douglas Aircraft Company was selected as the winner with deliveries to start in May 1926. A water-cooled engine powered the Douglas M-2 and could carry twice the load of a DH-4 at a faster speed. The post office bought fifty-one airplanes. By placing these airplanes on the transcontinental route, it eliminated several fuel stops. On the western portion, the stops at Iowa City, North Platte, and Rock Springs were deleted. On the eastern portion of the transcontinental route, stops at Bellefonte, Bryan, and Rawlins were deleted. The Douglas M2 was the last airplane purchased by the post office.

By 21 December 1927, responsibility for delivering the mails was turned over to private companies but not before the service achieved an enviable record. For example, the Air Mail Service received the Collier Trophy in 1922 and 1923. In 1927, an airmail pilot received the Harmon Trophy. Undoubtedly, the pilots in the Air Mail Service were the best in the world. Most had over 2,000 hours of flying time to their credit with much of it at night. However, it is a sad commentary of the times that from 1919 to 1926, thirty-one of the first forty pilots hired by the post office died while flying the mail. Even so, the number of fatal aircraft accidents decreased dramatically over the seven-year period. In 1919, one pilot was killed for every 115,324 miles flown; by 1926, that rate had improved to one fatality for every 2,583,056 miles flown.

The entire government expenditure, from the conception of the Air Mail Service in 1918 to the last flight operation, amounted to approximately $17 million. During the same period, about $5 million in airmail postage was collected. On paper, the figures add up to a net loss, but the experience gained and the thrust given to commercial aviation from the expenditures made the entire enterprise a genuine bargain.

The Private Companies

While airmail and airlines are almost inseparable entities in terms of their common wellsprings, a few companies began by carrying passengers without the support of airmail funds. For example, Aero Limited began operations before 1919 by shuttling passengers between New York City and the steamy fleshpots of Atlantic City.

West Indies Airways, which began by flying fishermen and vacationers from Key West, Florida, to Havana, was purchased by Inglis M. Uppercu, a Manhattan Cadillac dealer. During World War I, Uppercu formed the Aeromarine Plane and Motor Company to manufacture twin-engine flying boats for the Navy. When the war ended, Uppercu had a few of the flying boats left. He purchased a few more from the Navy, and with seven airplanes he established a thriving business. In his first year of operation, he flew 95,000 miles and carried almost 7,000 passengers between Key West and Havana. During the summer, he moved the operation to the Great Lakes and carried passengers between Detroit and Cleveland.

In his second year of operation, Uppercu expanded his fleet to fifteen aircraft and was conducting brisk business when, in the winter, tragedy struck. One of his airplanes had an engine failure over the Gulf of Mexico and was forced to land on the water quite heavily. The five passengers and pilot floated for several days atop the airplane. Many ships passed in sight of the stranded passengers, but none on the ships spotted the stricken seaplane. One by one the water-starved, parched, weak passengers slipped into the shark-infested water. Soon only the pilot remained. Finally, a passing ship saw and rescued the pilot, who was burned, salt caked, shriveled, but alive. The resulting horror stories in the newspapers did nothing to promote aviation or West Indies Airways. In 1923, this bankrupt airline faded into history.

The Beginning of Boeing

The first private operator to receive an airmail contract was Eddie Hubbard, a protégé of William E. Boeing. Flying a Boeing B-1 Flying Boat, Hubbard flew the mail run from Seattle to Victoria, British Columbia, from 1920 until 1927 without a mishap. These efforts elevated the prestige of Boeing products and helped launch the company to a premier position within the industry.

William Boeing of Seattle had become rich by 1914 through a generous inheritance and through some timely purchases of timberlands in the Pacific Northwest. On 4 July 1914, Boeing and a friend, Conrad Westervelt, watched a pilot fly a Curtiss hydroplane. Westervelt was a Navy pilot stationed at the Puget Sound Navy Yard. He and Boeing had become acquainted through their mutual attraction to fast powerboats. This was a natural affinity, since both had been trained as engineers, Boeing at Yale and Westervelt at the U.S. Naval Academy at Annapolis.

Boeing and Westervelt took a ride in the Curtiss hydroplane to see the Puget Sound Navy Yard. After this flight, Boeing became very interested in the potential financial rewards represented by the airplane. He contacted Glenn Martin, who had a small manufacturing facility in San Diego, to buy one of Martin's seaplanes. Included in the deal were flying lessons for Boeing with Martin as the instructor.

Earlier, Boeing had bought a small boatworks in Seattle where he and Westervelt became convinced that they could build a better floatplane than the Curtiss hydroplane. Together they began to build an airplane that they intended to call the B & W, for Boeing and Westervelt. By the time the first airplane was completed, Westervelt had been reassigned to Washington, D.C. In June 1916, Boeing flew the test flight himself. About a month later, Boeing put up $100,000 of his own money and formed a manufacturing company. His second airplane, an improvement over the first, was called the Model-C. Boeing completed it just before the United States entered the war. Westervelt, who now held an important position in military procurement, urged Boeing to apply for a government contract. He did. By the time the war ended, Boeing had manufactured fifty trainers for the Navy.

At the end of the war, Boeing scrounged what orders he could from the Army and Navy; however, the company was held together with his own funds. One day, a man from Vancouver approached him to find out if Boeing thought that one of his flying machines was capable of carrying mail between Vancouver and Seattle. To demonstrate his confidence that it could be done, Boeing selected one of the company pilots, Eddie Hubbard, to fly a Boeing Model-C floatplane. Hubbard and Boeing flew to Vancouver on 3 March 1919, picked up a

Fig. 6.6. Boeing CL-4S (formerly C-700) floatplane nosed up onto a seaplane ramp; men posed in front with mail bag are probably William Boeing and Edward Hubbard, who, on 3 March 1919, made a demonstration international airmail flight from Vancouver to Seattle. Boeing Company Historical Archives.

small packet of sixty letters, and flew them to Seattle. This was hailed as the first international airmail run (see fig. 6.6).

Hubbard became engrossed with the idea of flying the mail from Seattle to Vancouver and back. He approached the post office with the idea and received a contract. Also, he ordered an airplane from Boeing to conduct the business. This was the first commercial order placed for a Boeing airplane, and the design that resulted was a graceful model created by Boeing engineer Clair Egtvedt. It was a single-engine pusher biplane with an open cockpit built on a boatlike hull and designated the Boeing B-1. This airplane's consistently good performance established Boeing's stature in the commercial aviation manufacturing industry.[7]

The Kelly Act

When Benjamin Lipsner and Otto Praeger discussed the idea of an airmail service in 1918, they agreed that government operation would be a temporary measure to provide the impetus for private growth. The post office accomplished its goals; when the aviation industry was struggling merely to stay alive, the post office kept aviation at the forefront of American thought, thus paving the way to the future.

The Airmail Act of 1925, called the Kelly Act after its sponsor, Rep. Clyde Kelly, chairperson of the House Post Office Committee, opened the door for private airmail contractors. The title of his bill clearly defined its purpose: "An act to encourage commercial aviation and to authorize the Postmaster General to contract for the mail service." Almost immediately, Postmaster General Harry S. New began placing newspaper advertisements calling for bids on airmail routes.

In the early stages of transition for post office control to contractor control, it was felt that the transcontinental route, now called the Columbia route, would be retained by the post office. Private contractors had to demonstrate their dependability by flying the feeder routes that connected communities to the transcontinental route. Before bids would be offered for the route, the post office made it clear in its advertisements that it would only award contracts to those responsible businesses that owned adequate equipment. One airplane barnstorming operation was dismissed without serious consideration.

By September 1925, bids had been received on eight feeder routes. Five contracts were awarded in October, and by January 1926, contracts were awarded for all twelve feeder routes (see figs. 6.7–6.11). These contract airmail routes (CAM) were

CAM-1 New York to Boston—
    Awarded to Colonial Air Lines, which began operations on 18 June 1926.

CAM-2 Chicago to St. Louis—
    Awarded to Robertson Aircraft Corporation, which began operations on 15 April 1926.

CAM-3 Chicago to Dallas–Ft. Worth—
    Awarded to National Air Transport, which began on 12 May 1926.

CAM-4 Los Angeles to Salt Lake City—
    Awarded to Western Air Express, which began operations on 17 April 1926.

CAM-5 Elko, Nevada to Pasco, Washington—
    Awarded to Varney Speed Lines, which began operations on 6 April 1926.

CAM-6 Detroit to Cleveland—
    Awarded to Ford Air Transport, which began flying the mail on 15 February 1926.

CAM-7 Detroit to Chicago—
    Awarded to Ford Air Transport, which began flying the mail in February 1926.

CAM-8 Los Angeles to Seattle—
    Awarded to Pacific Air Transport, which began operations on 15 September 1926.

CAM-9 Chicago to Minneapolis–St. Paul—
    Awarded to Charles Dickenson, who began flying on 7 June 1926.

CAM-10 Atlanta to Jacksonville and Miami—
    Awarded to Florida Airways Corporation, which began flying the mail on 1 September 1926.

CAM-11 Cleveland to Pittsburgh—
    Awarded to Clifford Ball, who began operations on 21 April 1927.

CAM-12 Pueblo, Colorado to Cheyenne—
    Awarded to Western Air Express, which began flying in December 1926.

Colonial Air Lines, awarded CAM-1, New York to Boston, was a highly respected business whose presi-

Fig. 6.7. Robertson airmail aircraft. Kansas Aviation Museum Collection.

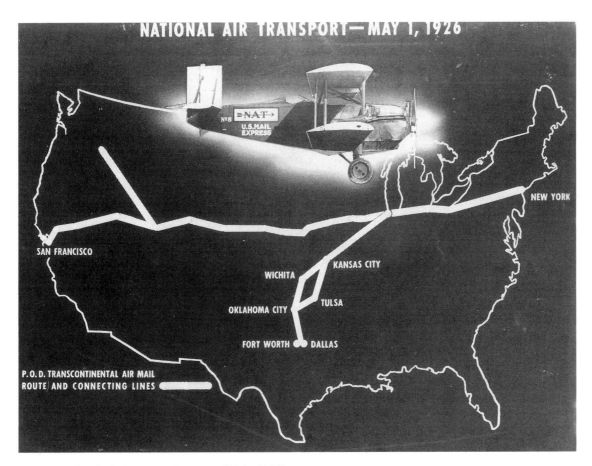

Fig. 6.8. National Air Transport. Courtesy of United Airlines.

Fig. 6.9. Boeing B-40 flown by Western Air Express. Courtesy of TWA.

Fig. 6.10. Swallow flown by Varney Speed Lines. Courtesy of United Airlines.

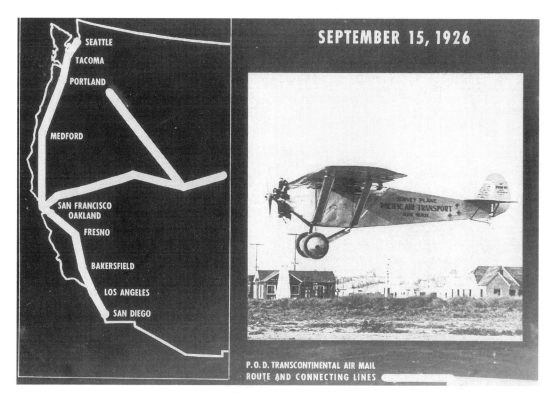

P.O.D. TRANSCONTINENTAL AIR MAIL
ROUTE AND CONNECTING LINES

Fig. 6.11. Pacific Air Transport. Courtesy of United Airlines.

dent, General O'Ryan, was well known in aviation. The vice president for operations was Juan Trippe, of whom much more will be said later in connection with Pan American Airlines. Trippe had formed a group of financially impressive backers, who had been flying club members at Yale. This group established a company called Eastern Air Transport. Fearing that the company would lose in an airmail bid to the better organized and financed Colonial Air Lines, Trippe proposed a merger between the two. The merger was accepted, and Trippe became Colonial's chief operating officer.

Robertson Aircraft Corporation of St. Louis was awarded CAM-2, Chicago to St. Louis. The Robertson brothers, William B. and Frank, were war pilots who had established a business in St. Louis centered around repairing and rebuilding government-surplus aircraft. They also conducted training and offered "joy" rides. When they received the CAM contract, they hired as chief pilot Charles A. Lindbergh. On 15 April 1926, Lindbergh flew the inaugural flight from Chicago to St. Louis.

National Air Transport, awarded CAM-3, Chicago to Dallas–Ft. Worth, had an impressive list of officers, directors, and backers. It formed the nucleus of what was to become the aviation empire of financier Clement M. Keys, of which more will be said later. The general manager of this airline was a former second assistant postmaster general, Paul Henderson. Henderson had guided the Air Mail Service through the years when the transcontinental route was developed for night flying. His work earned him the distinction of being referred to as the "Father of the Night Mail." Other powerful figures involved with the airline included Howard Coffin, vice president of the Hudson Motor Co., and Charles Lawrance, president of the Wright Aeronautical Corporation. National Air Transport began operations in May 1926, flying Curtiss Carrier Pigeons, biplanes powered by war-surplus Liberty engines.

Western Air Express was awarded CAM-4, Los Angeles to Salt Lake City, and CAM-12, Pueblo, Colorado, to Cheyenne, Wyoming. Harry Chandler, a newspaper publisher in Los Angeles, and William M. Garland, a real estate dealer, were upset that San Francisco had been chosen instead of Los Angeles as the terminus point on the transcontinental route. To bring Los Angeles into the proper limelight, they formed Pacific Air Transport (PAT). Their intention was to bid on any route that began or ended in Los Angeles. Harris M. "Pop" Hanshue, the chief operations officer for Western Air Express (shown in fig. 6.12), decided not to compete with PAT in its bid on the Los Angeles to Seattle route. He bid instead on the Los Angeles to Salt Lake City route. He based his decision primarily on terrain considerations, fearing the Siskipu Mountain Range along the spine of California.

Western Air Express began operating on 17 April 1926, with Douglas M-2 biplanes, the kind that the post office had purchased to replace their vintage DH-4s. Western began earning a profit almost immediately and was one of the first airlines to begin carrying paying passengers.

Varney Speed Lines was awarded CAM-5, Elko, Nevada, to Pasco, Washington. Walter T. Varney, a flyer in World War I, opened a flying school after the war and offered an air service between San Francisco, Stockton, and Modesto in California. Varney bid on the route from Elko to Pasco via Boise. Since many viewed the route as a flight from nowhere to nowhere, he bet he would be the only bidder. He was right.

Varney's company began flying the mountain routes with 90-horsepower Swallows. However, they found that the engine did not have enough courage to lift the plane, pilot, and mail over the mountains. He requested and received from the post office a ninety-day grace period to put new engines in his Swallows or to reequip the company with an airplane capable of flying the routes. Vern Gorst of Pacific Air Transport came to his aid by promising Varney the first three Ryan M-1 monoplanes originally destined for PAT.[8] The monoplanes put Varney back into the air. During the down time, he received permission to change the terminus point on his route from Elko to Salt Lake City. This gave him a linkup with Pop Hanshue's Western Air Express and a much more lucrative connection with the Columbia route. Varney later bought several big 575-horsepower Stearman aircraft and modified his anemic Swallows by replacing the 90-horsepower OX-5 engines with 200-horsepower Wright engines.

Ford Air Transport was awarded both CAM-6, Detroit to Cleveland, and CAM-7, Detroit to Chicago.

Fig. 6.12. Harris M. "Pop" Hanshue. Courtesy of TWA.

Henry Ford had created this company to move employees to key spots. Initially, he used an airplane created by William B. Stout that was based on a design by German designer Hugo Junkers. The wing on the Stout monoplane was internally braced, which eliminated the need for wire bracing and struts. The first Stout design was a single-engine airplane powered by a Liberty 400-horsepower engine. This airplane was called the Flying Washboard because of the corrugated metal used on its wings and fuselage. Henry Ford was so impressed with the airplane that he bought the entire company. Later, when the Wright Whirlwind engine became available, the airplane was enlarged to take three engines, and the famous Tin Goose, the Ford Trimotor, was born.

When the contracts for the airmail routes from Detroit to Cleveland and Chicago were advertised, the Ford Company, which was already flying to those points routinely, submitted a bid. When the contracts were awarded by the post office to Ford for the two routes, it became a simple matter of carrying the mail. With its Stout monoplanes, Ford became the first airline to begin domestic airmail service.

Pacific Air Transport was awarded CAM-8, Los Angeles to Seattle. Like William Boeing, Vern Gorst was an aviation pioneer. Gorst owned several bus lines in Oregon and California, and like Boeing, he had bought a Martin seaplane and learned to fly it. He was seriously injured in a crash and spent many months convalescing. During this time, he studied flying and airplanes intensely. He developed the notion that an airplane could become a passenger-carrying vehicle capable of competing with surface transportation modes.

After his recovery, he became aware that airmail contracts were being offered. He persuaded his colleagues in the bus business to form a company to bid on the Los Angeles to Seattle route. He had surveyed the route in a fairly primitive 90-horsepower Swallow airplane and was convinced that the route could be flown profitably. As the other aviation forces began to gather in southern California, Gorst's marginally financed operation looked like it might fall to the much better financed Western Air Express. However, at the last minute, WAE decided against bidding on the Los Angeles to Seattle route, and Gorst boldly submitted his bid. The post office looked suspiciously at Gorst's precarious financial picture but awarded the route to him after he promised to raise his capitalization to $500,000. Gorst sold the route to PAT for half the stock and thus became PAT's principal owner. Gorst hired pilots and bought two Travel Air airplanes for the price of getting them out of hock with lien holders. Next, he approached Claude Ryan of San Diego. When Ryan demonstrated his M-1 monoplane to Gorst, he immediately contracted the first ten planes off the line (see fig. 6.13).

The company did not fare well during the first winter of operation. Even though Gorst bought old ship searchlights and installed them in the hills around San Francisco, the California weather was overpowering. In that first winter, three of the first ten pilots he hired were killed. His financial position became so precarious that he had to pay his pilots in stock. The airmail contract that had seemed so lucrative initially was not sufficient to pay the bills. Gorst approached W. A. Patterson of the Wells Fargo Bank of San Francisco for a loan. Despite advice from other bankers, Patterson granted the loan and began to help Gorst run the airline. Even with this help, the airline struggled for years, never really achieving any spectacular success despite its potentially lucrative route system.

Charles Dickerson, awarded CAM-9, Chicago to the Twin Cities. Dickerson had been one of the early airmail pilots, and he won his contract because he owned five airplanes of varying vintage and quality. Within four months, Dickerson lost four of his five airplanes. One pilot died, and the other pilots quit. Dickerson withdrew from the contract, and Northwest Airways was awarded the route. Among the stockholders of this new airline was William Stout of Ford Trimotor fame. The airline became quite successful and is known today as Northwest Airlines.

Florida Airways Corporation was awarded CAM-10, Atlanta to Jacksonville and Miami, and it began operation with one Liberty-engined Stout, two Travel Airs, a Curtiss Lark, and a Stinson Detroiter. The route did not connect with any terminus on the Columbia route or with any northbound or westbound routes out of Atlanta. Despite its healthy posture on paper, the airline soon lost its airmail contract because of financial insolvency. Although

Fig. 6.13. Ryan M-1 mailplane flown by Pacific Air Transport. Courtesy of United Airlines.

refinancing was attempted, Harold Pitcairn submitted a lower bid for the route and was awarded it. Florida Airways remained intact in a legal sense. Juan Trippe's syndicate later absorbed the company.

Pitcairn's story is somewhat unusual. On a whim he bid on a route from New York to Atlanta. In a comedy of errors, he also received the contract for the route vacated by the financial demise of Florida Airways: CAM-10, Atlanta to Jacksonville and Miami. Pitcairn was primarily an airplane manufacturer who, in a shop outside Philadelphia, built a stubby-winged biplane powered by a Wright Whirlwind engine. The name came naturally: the Pitcairn Mailwing. After being awarded the airmail contracts, Pitcairn put his plant on a three-shift operation to supply enough planes for his routes.

Somewhere in the midst of the confusion, he changed the name of his airline to Eastern Air Lines and began flying the mail in April 1928. Four months before the stock market crashed, Pitcairn sold the airline to North American Aviation Inc. for $2.5 million. The North American Aviation Inc. was a holding company for Clement M. Keys's rapidly expanding aviation empire.

Clifford Ball was awarded CAM-11, Cleveland to Pittsburgh. Ball had been a barnstormer, who flew OX-5 powered Wacos from McKeesport flying field near Pittsburgh. He was an automobile dealer, and through some real estate transactions he had come into possession of an airfield. Several of the pilots who kept their airplanes at Ball's field came into financial hardships and would not render payment on their parking and storage fees. Ball foreclosed on several airplanes. By the time the CAM contracts were announced, Ball had accumulated a small fleet. Seeing another business opportunity, he bid on the CAM route.

Ball named the route between Cleveland and Pittsburgh the "Path of the Eagle." His first fare-paying passenger was a vaudeville performer from Oklahoma, Will Rogers, who rode on top of the mail sacks. After the Lindbergh success, Ball replaced his Wacos with five-place Ryan Broughams and began charging passengers twenty dollars each way on the route. By 1930, the airline had been absorbed by another corporation, Pennsylvania Airlines.

The Columbia Route

When the post office announced that it would give up control of the Columbia route to commercial air carriers, Eddie Hubbard rushed into William Boeing's office with the news that the Chicago to San Francisco portion of the route would be offered first. Boeing had been watching the performance of the feeders and knew that flying the CAM routes was a risky business. Regardless, he felt that with proper management and the right airplane, it could succeed.

Hubbard suggested that they build their own airplane. Clair Egtvedt, Boeing's premier engineer, was taken aback. Hubbard began to produce facts and figures that he had been gathering. Although Boeing had been building military airplanes almost exclusively, a Model 40 airplane designed to carry mail for the post office was in the works. Hubbard complained that the Model 40 was based on the World War I–vintage Liberty engine and was bound to be inefficient. Egtvedt, who had been designing Navy fighters that used the powerful and newly developed Pratt and Whitney Wasp engine, said, "How would you like to have an air-cooled engine?"

With the air-cooled Wasp, which was 200 pounds lighter than the Liberty engine, and the new B-40 airframe, mail could be carried much cheaper than any of the other potential competitors. Pouring over the figures repeatedly, Boeing and Company submitted a bid for the western half of the Columbia route (Chicago to San Francisco). This low bid shocked the rest of the industry.

Boeing had offered to fly the mail from Chicago to San Francisco for the same price that other contractors were charging to fly it from New York to Boston. At $1.50 per pound for the first 1,000 miles and fifteen cents per pound for each additional 100 miles, Boeing's bid was far below that of the next closest bidder. The closest bid was Pop Hanshue of Western Air Express, who bid $2.24. Hanshue and the others who had been outbid protested based on the belief that Boeing was using the assets of his manufacturing company to underwrite the obvious losses he was going to experience flying the mail.

But Boeing's ace in the hole was his friendship with Fred Rentschler of Pratt and Whitney and the well-paid lobby he had in place in Washington, D.C. With these connections, he convinced the Navy to allow Pratt and Whitney to ship five Wasps a month from the original

Fig. 6.14. The Columbia route in 1927. Courtesy of United Airlines.

Navy production schedule to the Boeing plant in Washington. Egtvedt redesigned the B-40 to accommodate the Wasp engine and, at Boeing's insistence, added two seats in an enclosed area between the wings forward of the pilot, who sat in an open cockpit. These seats were planned to be used to ferry pilots and mechanics.

By 1 July, Boeing was ready to fly. To maintain the airplanes, Eddie Hubbard hired the post office pilots and mechanics who were temporarily out of work. They were a trained, eager, and willing group.

The airline made money from the start, much to the amazement of the other airline professionals. Boeing explained that rather than flying radiators, plumbing, and cooling fluids over the mountains, he was carrying the mail. With his Wasp-powered B-40, Boeing jumped into a full year lead over his competitors. (An example of the B-40 is shown in fig. 6.9.)

The eastern portion of the Columbia route, Chicago to New York, was won by National Air Transport (NAT), an airline under the control of Clement M. Keys. The airline was already operating successfully on the Chicago to Dallas–Fort Worth (CAM-3) route. NAT began flying the Chicago to New York route on 1 September 1927 (see fig. 6.14).

In the early days of the Kelly Act, airlines could not turn an attractive profit flying the mail. The airmail rate was ten cents per half ounce, which placed it in the luxury service category. Additionally, airlines were paid only a percentage of the mail revenues collected. The accounting procedure was extremely complicated and time-consuming. On many routes, the average load of mail did not produce enough revenue to meet expenses. If the airmail system and commercial aviation were to grow, something had to be done.

Rep. Kelly came to the rescue again by sponsoring amendments to his original bill. As a result of these amendments, in May 1928, the postage rate was set at five cents per ounce. This change caused a large upswing in the volume of mail carried. Also, as a result of the amendments, the airlines were now paid on a pound-per-mile basis. The net effect of these changes was to double the income of the airlines with CAM routes without appreciably changing their overhead expenses. The post office realized a net loss in revenues, but Postmaster General New refused to reduce the rate paid to the airlines. In substance, this amounted to a subsidy that benefited the struggling airmail carriers. However, airlines were being paid more for carrying the mail than the post office was receiving on a per pound basis. It became quite profitable for the airlines to mail themselves hefty loads of telephone books, bricks, and other bulky items. This was not an unusual occurrence.

The Air Commerce Act of 1926

It had become apparent to most that a standardized nationwide system of airspace control and allocation and a system for registering aircraft and aircrew was essential. However, confusion and uncertainty of the legal issues involved hampered legislation. Certain groups feared the heavy hand of government would impact on one's "right to flight." Other groups had chosen to skirt the constitutional questions by proposing a constitutional amendment. Several legislative measures were proposed, but they failed at some point in the legislative process. For example, the Civil Aeronautics Bill of 1923, which sought to regulate airspace and establish federal licensing standards, failed in the committee. Some states passed regulating legislation before Congress could work out a solution to all of the problems.

Finally, compromises were made, and a new federal law established the relationship between the federal government and the development of commercial aviation: the Air Commerce Act of 1926. Rather than being a heavy-handed regulatory mechanism, this act sought to help commercial aviation develop. These were the six major provisions of the act:

1. Licensing of aircraft.
2. Licensing of airmen.
3. Marking of aircraft, both licensed and unlicensed.
4. Requirements in the operation of aircraft.
5. Air traffic rules.
6. Rating of air navigation facilities, which includes airports and airways.[9]

Through the Air Commerce Act of 1926, which brought order to the commercial aviation industry, and the Kelly Act, which opened the airmail route structure to private contractors, the stage was set. The air transportation industry was poised to reap the rewards of the Lindbergh miracle.[10]

The Lindbergh Influence

In just over 33 hours in May 1927, Charles Augustus Lindbergh Jr. became the greatest hero of the twentieth century.[11] Suddenly, everyone wanted to fly. To be accused of not being air-minded was tantamount to being accused of being un-American. Investors rushed forward with their dollars. Established aircraft builders ex-

panded their factories four- and fivefold, and scores of other aircraft manufacturers began to pop up. Barns became factories, and hardly a day went by without the public announcement of some new aviation company. In January 1929, 232 companies were engaged in aircraft manufacturing. To get a feel for the magnitude of the expansion, one can compare it with the American automobile industry during its days of rapid expansion. But at its height, the automobile industry involved no more than about ninety-five manufacturers.

An aircraft manufacturing industry that had produced 302 airplanes in 1921 produced 5,000 in 1928 and 7,000 in 1929. The expansion was so rapid that Fred Rentschler, president of both the Aeronautical Chamber of Commerce and United Aircraft and Transport Company, warned, "Sound engineering development is what the aeronautical industry needs most at the present time, not capital."[12] The industry realized that firm markets for their airplanes had not been established.

Nevertheless, it was a time of mergers, acquisitions, and empire building. Massive aviation combines were created, such as the Keys group under the holding company North American Aviation, the Boeing group under the holding company United Aircraft and Transport, and the Aviation Corporation (AVCO), a group supported by eastern financiers. The genesis of each of these giants is worth developing further.

United Aircraft and Transport Corporation

The successful marriage of the Pratt and Whitney Wasp engine to the Boeing B-40 airframe produced more than just a highly successful mailplane. It also produced an idea.

William Boeing and Fred Rentschler had been friends for years. They joined forces after persuading the Navy to transfer twenty-five engines from the Pratt and Whitney production run to Boeing. In early 1929, they formed a holding company, United Aircraft and Transport Co., that absorbed the stock of Boeing Aircraft and Transport Co. and the stock of Pratt and Whitney Aircraft. Also joining the merger were Hamilton Aero Manufacturing, which made propellers; Sikorsky, Northrop, and Stearman, all airplane manufacturers; Standard Steel Propeller; and Stout Airlines.

Before these mergers, Boeing had added some stunning jewels to its aviation crown. In late 1928, Vern Gorst of Pacific Air Transport had come to Boeing to see about purchasing some B-40s to fly his routes along the California coast. At $25,000 per copy, the B-40 was too expensive for Gorst. Unable to raise money for the airplanes, Gorst's financial difficulties worsened. Hanshue of Western Air Express offered to buy Gorst's stock for $250 per share. This would have given WAE control of the Los Angeles to Seattle CAM route plus control of PAT. Boeing made a similar offer to Gorst, except Boeing agreed to retain all of PAT's employees. The loan officer of the Wells Fargo Bank in San Francisco, W. A. Patterson, advised Gorst to take the Boeing offer. Gorst did. Impressed by the manner in which Patterson had handled himself, Boeing brought him to Seattle. Patterson would later guide United Airlines through its greatest period.

Boeing also acquired Varney Speed Lines. Walter Varney had fashioned a successful operation, but he was something of a high flyer himself. His lavishness often exceeded his airline's capacity to support it. As a result, he kept running out of money. Some of the backing for Varney Speed Lines had come from the Keys group. The

moves that were being made by Varney, supported financially by Keys, convinced Boeing that their "territory" was coming under attack. For example, Varney had approached Boeing to buy some B-40Bs that were equipped to carry two passengers. Varney's intent was to move into the Pacific Northwest with a passenger-carrying capability. These actions led Boeing to buy up Varney Speed Lines, merge them with Boeing, and effectively take them out of competition (see fig. 6.15).

The headline in a 23 April 1930 issue of *Business Week* magazine stated: "Powerful Groups in Battle for Air Route Supremacy." The property was National Air Transport. The two combatants were United Aircraft and Transport represented by Fred Rentschler and North American Aviation represented by Clement M. Keys.

Some years earlier, NAT had bid and won the eastern half of the Columbia route at about the same time Boeing had captured the western half. In serving the San Francisco to Chicago route, Boeing had grown significantly and had begun to carry passengers. The introduction of the Boeing B-80 (shown in fig. 6.16), a three-engine aircraft, could carry eighteen passengers.

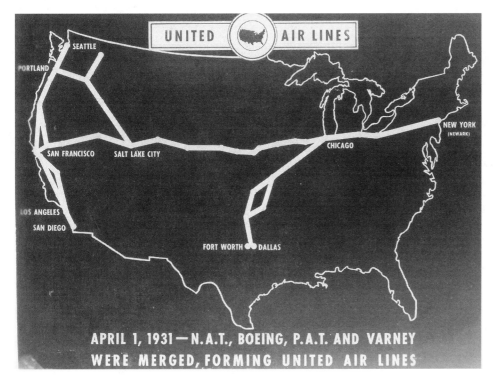

UNITED AIR LINES

APRIL 1, 1931 — N.A.T., BOEING, P.A.T. AND VARNEY WERE MERGED, FORMING UNITED AIR LINES

Fig. 6.15. The formation of United Air Lines. Courtesy of United Airlines.

However, the passengers could only fly as far as Chicago. National Air Transport did not follow the same passenger philosophy and had not expanded into the passenger market as fast as Boeing. Passengers could fly from the West Coast to Chicago, but they would have to take a train from there to most points east. Boeing wanted the entire transcontinental route. So, typical of its past actions, Boeing proposed a merger with NAT. Keys refused the merger, and the lines were drawn. When the battle was joined, Keys had spread himself so thin with stock that Rentschler was able to buy up enough stock to pry NAT loose from the Keys group. This gave United sole control of the only transcontinental route in the United States.

The Keys Group

As an editor for the *Wall Street Journal,* Clement M. Keys developed a group of extremely powerful friends in financial circles. It had been his dream to establish a business empire that spanned the entire depth and breadth of aviation, from manufacturing engines and airplanes, to flying mail and passengers, to insurance and airports and aviation training. Although he was not a man of great personal wealth, Keys was most skillful in raising capital. He kept those who supported his ventures far enough apart so as not to represent a threat through a combined stock effort (see fig. 6.17). Some of the companies that Keys had managed to acquire were Curtiss

Fig. 6.16. Boeing B-80. Courtesy of United Airlines.

Fig. 6.17. Maddux Air Lines—one of those in the Keys Group. Courtesy of TWA.

Aeroplane and Motor Co., Sperry Gyroscope Co., North American Aviation, Transcontinental Air Transport, and National Air Transport.

Transcontinental Air Transport had been formed to take advantage of the Lindbergh success. This airline was a combination of air and train travel. Passengers would travel by train at night through the rugged Alleghenies from New York to Columbus, Ohio. Then they would board one of TAT's Ford Trimotors for Waynoka, Oklahoma, where they would board another train for Clovis, New Mexico. At Clovis, they would again board TAT Trimotors for the flight to Los Angeles. The total time for the journey was 48 hours (see fig. 6.18).

Keys had persuaded Lindbergh to throw his very heavy aeronautic weight behind the TAT venture. It became widely advertised as the "Lindbergh Line." Pilots jokingly referred to TAT as "Take A Train." In eighteen months of operation, this combined air and rail system lost money steadily, totaling $2.7 million. This loss, along with the loss of NAT to United, started the unraveling of the Keys empire.

The Aviation Corporation (AVCO)

Reeling with the sudden opportunities produced by the Lindbergh flight, the financial community reacted quickly. Averill Harriman and Robert Lehman, both investment bankers, raised $30 million and formed AVCO. They began to buy all manner of aviation properties, including Fairchild Aviation Corporation, Robertson Aircraft Corporation, Colonial Airways Corporation, Northern Air Lines, Embry-Riddle Co., Southern Air Transport, and Roosevelt and Curtiss Fields in New York (see fig. 6.19).

They were so eager to buy anything connected with aviation that they bought a company called Airline Route, which turned out to be a bus company. All totaled, AVCO controlled about eighty companies. In 1930, all of the airlines in the AVCO group were pulled together and renamed American Airways.

The three large combines—AVCO, the Keys group, and United—were the most powerful entities in the airline industry. However, there were many other airlines

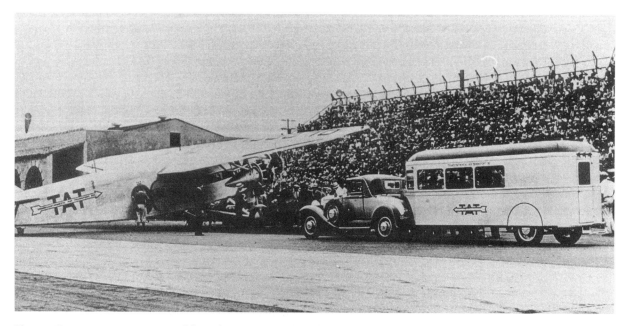

Fig. 6.18. Passengers were transported from the train terminal via "aerocar" to board one of TAT's Ford Trimotors. Courtesy of TWA.

Fig. 6.19. As noted on the tail, this aircraft was owned by the Embry-Riddle Co., one of those acquired by AVCO. Kansas Aviation Museum Collection.

flying mail, passengers, or both. In 1930, eighty-nine domestic airlines and twenty-seven American-operated foreign airlines were on the books. The number of passengers carried domestically between 1926 and 1930 are reflected below. Notice the 500 percent jump between 1927 and 1928, a vivid indication of the Lindbergh influence.[13]

Year	Passengers Carried
1926	5,782
1927	8,679
1928	48,312
1929	161,933
1930	384,506

Pan American

Another airline played an important part in the growth of the air carrier industry in the United States, particularly in the international arena. The airline was Pan American (Pan Am), led by a Yale graduate, Juan Trippe, "a man with a contagious energy and reckless love of success."[14]

Born in 1899 to a wealthy family of stockbrokers, Trippe had learned to fly at a Curtiss school. He had logged about 500 minutes of flight by the time he volunteered for naval aviation duty in World War I. In that conflict, he flew bombers. After the war, he continued his education at Yale, where he formed a flying club "with some of his wartime flyboy friends, among them John Hambleton, son of a Baltimore banker, Cornelius Vanderbilt, 'Sonny' Whitney, and William H. Vanderbilt. . . . He knew something about aviation, and he had some quite wealthy buddies willing to back him up."[15]

Entering his father's Wall Street firm, Trippe did not care for the life of a stockbroker. He resigned and bought some war-surplus aircraft to start a flying business. It soon failed. When the Kelly Act was passed in Congress, Trippe was leading an airline called Eastern Air Transport (not the Eastern associated with Pitcairn). He learned that Colonial Airways intended to bid on a route from New York to Boston. Colonial was a well-financed airline. Feeling that he could not best them in a bid war, Trippe approached the leadership of Colonial and offered to merge with the airline to avoid the inevitable competition. Seeing Eastern's impressive list of backers, Colonial accepted the offer, and Juan Trippe was

made vice president and general manager. This union worked until Trippe displayed another of his characteristics: act first, then ask for permission. He ordered several Fokker airplanes without first seeking approval. This displeased the Colonial leaders, who were not shy in so informing Trippe. The net result was that Trippe and his friends left the company. They struck out on their own, forming a company called Aviation Corporation of America.

Soon afterwards, Trippe learned that the post office was going to advertise for bids on a route from Key West to Havana. Two other carriers were also interested: Eddie Rickenbacker's Florida Airways and Pan American Airways. Trippe approached both groups and proposed a merger. This proposal was not accepted, and Trippe had little to offer such an alliance. However, he was the consummate entrepreneur. He and a friend made a quick trip to Havana and convinced the Cuban president to issue exclusive landing rights to Trippe's airline. With this leverage, the other two carriers quickly agreed to the merger. Aviation Corporation of the Americas became the holding company with Pan American Airways as a subsidiary. Trippe headed Pan Am, which made its first flight to Havana on 19 October 1927.[16]

Pan Am would become respected around the world. This carrier, like others, fell victim to the effects of the Airline Deregulation Act of 1978. The airline lacked the inability to adjust to a free market system.

Notes

1. "The Liberty Aero Oil," 200.

2. Lipsner, *The Airmail.*

3. For a more detailed account of this period, consult Lipsner.

4. Smith, *By the Seat of My Pants.*

5. Solberg, *Conquest of the Skies.*

6. For an excellent discussion of additional elements of this period, see Komons, *Bonfires to Beacons.*

7. A highly readable history of the Boeing Company is in Serling, *Legend and Legacy.*

8. A modified version of this airplane and number 16 in the M-1 series achieved fame as the *Spirit of St. Louis.*

9. For additional discussion of the birth of this law, see Komons.

10. A deeper coverage of this period can be found in Davies, *Airlines of the United States since 1914.*

11. The influence of Charles Lindbergh's epic flight is

reported here. A full account of Lindbergh's life and experiences is reported in chapter 7.

12. Rentschler, "Is Aviation Over Extended?"
13. *FAA Statistical Handbook of Aviation.*
14. Van Doren, "Pan Am's Legacy."
15. Levering, *The Clipper Heritage,* 16.
16. Brown, *A History of Aviation,* 105–6.

References

"Aerial Mail Service." *Literary Digest,* 17 July 1915, 108.

"American Air Travel Quadrupled." *Literary Digest,* 20 December 1930, 16.

"Aviation—Retrospect of the Year 1914." *Scientific American,* 2 January 1915, 7.

"Aviation—Retrospect of the Year 1915." *Scientific American,* 1 January 1916, 7.

"Aviation—Retrospect of the Year 1916." *Scientific American,* 6 January 1917, 7.

"Aviation—Retrospect of the Year 1917." *Scientific American,* 5 January 1918, 7.

Bender, Marylin, and Selig Altschul. *The Chosen Instrument: Pan Am, Juan Trippe, the Rise and Fall of an American Entrepreneur.* New York: Simon and Schuster, 1982.

Black, Archibald. "American Air Transport." *Annals of the American Academy of Political and Social Science* 131 (May 1927): 68–70.

Brown, Carl A. *A History of Aviation.* 2d ed. Daytona Beach: Embry-Riddle Aeronautical University, 1980.

Bryan, Leslie A. *Aerial Transportation.* Winfield: Anderson Press, 1925.

"Congress Hits the Air Mail." *Literary Digest,* 11 February 1922, 14.

Davies, R. E. G. *Airlines of the United States since 1914.* London: G. P. Putnam, 1972.

Davis, W. Jefferson. "Clearing the Air for Commerce." *Annals of the American Academy of Political and Social Science,* 131 (May 1927): 141–50.

Douglas, D. W. "The Airplane as a Commercial Possibility." *Scientific American,* April 1920, 339–43.

Ernst and Ernst. "Groupings in the Aviation Industry." *Scientific American,* July 1929, 58.

Frederick, John H. *Commercial Air Transportation.* 5th ed. Homewood, Ill.: Richard D. Irwin, 1961.

Glover, Irving W. "The Air Mail." *Annals of the American Academy of Political and Social Science* 131 (May 1927): 43–48.

Klemin, Alexander. "American Passenger Air Transport." *Scientific American,* October 1929, 324–29, 404–7, 514–17.

Komons, Nick A. *Bonfires to Beacons.* Washington: Smithsonian Institution Press, 1989.

Levering, Robert. *The Clipper Heritage.* Inter-Collegiate Press, 1984.

"Liberty Aero Oil Which Meets the Requirements of Aviation." *Scientific American,* 7 September 1918, 200.

Lipsner, Benjamin B. *The Airmail, Jennies to Jets.* Chicago: Wilcox and Follett, 1951.

MacCracken, William P., Jr. "Air Regulations." *Annals of the American Academy of Political and Social Science* 131 (May 1927): 118–23.

"Our Civil Aviation Now Leading the World." *Literary Digest,* 13 November 1926, 23–24.

"Our Winged Postmen Completing Our Postal Progress with First Aerial Mail Route Between Washington and New York." *Scientific American,* 25 May 1918, 476–77.

"Postmaster-General New on Air Transport Problems." *Literary Digest,* 28 August 1926, 48–49.

"Powerful Groups in Battle for Air Route Supremacy." *Business Week,* 23 April 1930, 14.

Rentschler, Frederick B. "Is Aviation Over Extended?" *Magazine of Business* 56 (July 1929): 31–38.

Serling, Robert J. *Legend and Legacy: The Story of Boeing and Its People.* New York: St. Martin's Press, 1992.

Shamburger, Page. *Tracks Across the Sky: The Story of the Pioneers of the U.S. Air Mail.* Philadelphia: J. B. Lippincott, 1964.

Smith, Dean C. *By the Seat of My Pants.* Boston: Little, Brown, 1961.

Solberg, Carl. *Conquest of the Skies.* Boston: Little, Brown, 1979.

"Sporting Instinct vs. Air Traffic Laws." *Literary Digest,* 9 October 1920, 82–84.

Van Doren, Carolyn S. "Pan Am's Legacy to World Tourism." *Journal of Travel Research* (summer 1993): 3–12.

Walton, Francis D. "Where Is Aviation?" *Harper's* 161 (1930): 108–15.

Warner, Edward P. "Development of Transportation by Air." *Scientific Monthly* 18 (April 1924): 383–93.

Whitehouse, Arch. *The Sky's the Limit.* New York: Macmillan, 1971.

7

Developments
Between the Wars

James E. Crehan and Tim Brady

AND THEN IT WAS OVER. The war to end all wars ended on 11 November 1918, and an aircraft manufacturing industry that had been spun up to produce 21,000 aircraft annually to "blacken the skies of Europe" had lived up to its promise. The industry that had grown from 5,000 employees to more than 175,000[1] was brought to an abrupt halt within three days[2] after Armistice (see fig. 7.1).

Barnstormers

Some periods in aviation history, although short, seem longer and are filled with adventure, excitement, and romance. Representative of this is the history of the barnstormers or, as they were originally called, the Flying Gypsies. This period began in the spring of 1919, and by the mid-1920s it had faded.

Barnstorming began with a unique set of circumstances: cheap airplanes, an abundance of pilots and aircraft mechanics, and few other commercial flying jobs.

Cheap airplanes. At the end of World War I, the government found itself with an abundance of airplanes that far exceeded the needs of the radically reduced military forces. Those that were least desirable were put up for sale at a fraction of the cost to manufacture them. Most of these airplanes were JN-4 Jennys, a tandem cockpit two-place trainer. These had cost $5,000 to build but were sold for a few hundred dollars.[3] Some went for as little as $150 (see figs. 7.2 and 7.3). A slightly higher price would bring a spare 90-horsepower OX-5 engine. At such prices, however, many of these airplanes were "ob-

solete planes that were considered unsafe for the Army and Navy, with only a mild warning that they be overhauled before being flown."[4]

Many pilots and few jobs. When the demobilized pilots who had trained for combat returned home, they found a nation that had not yet become air-minded. The airmail service had not yet expanded, and there were virtually no other commercial flying jobs available. Wanting to pursue the career of aviation with which they had fallen in love, many of these pilots bought the war-surplus Jennys and began demonstrating their craft around the country to whomever would pay. They gave exhibitions, did stunt flying, staged dogfights, wing-walked, dangled from the landing gear, dropped parachutists, and switched airplanes in midair.

This last trick they did "by using rope ladders or by interlocking wings" to change from one aircraft to another. In addition, they gave rides to passengers for about a dollar a minute. This fee dropped to less than

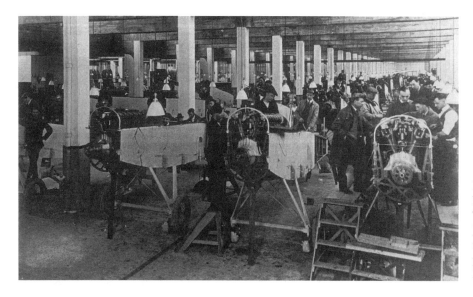

Fig. 7.1. Then the economic boom in aviation was over. These builders of the JN-4 Jenny at the Dayton-Wright factory were soon to be unemployed. Courtesy of the USAF Museum.

half that as accidents increased, causing public interest to fade. Most barnstormers lived hand-to-mouth, but others were paid handsomely. Bigger Johnson, for example, who was one of the better known barnstormers, grossed $70,000 in six months.[5]

A boon or a bane to aviation? The barnstormers were a colorful group of flyers who brought aviation to the rural United States and undoubtedly increased the air-mindedness of the American people. However, there were many accidents partially because pilots lacked spare parts or the logistic ability to get a part to the location. The pilots, "lacking facilities for repair and maintenance . . . usually overlooked such details. Without

landing fields they made emergency landings in hay fields and pastures. They repaired their machines with whatever materials they found convenient."[6] The crashes made the news and created a group of "picturesque figures, but the sensational stunts and attendant fatalities created a misunderstanding and fear of aviation that took years to erase."[7]

We must give the barnstormers their historic due, however. Many of these flyers and mechanics went on to

Fig. 7.2. Jennies were plentiful. Courtesy of the USAF Museum.

Fig. 7.3. Typical of the barnstorming acts of the 1920s, the Marie Meyer Flying Circus put on a big show at Lambert Field, St. Louis. Shown here is the "Standard" aircraft, similar to a Jenny. Courtesy of the Fred Roos Collection.

establish the first fixed base operators (FBOs). They built and maintained airfields and hangars, operated aircraft maintenance facilities, sold fuel and airplanes, and in general promoted aviation. Perhaps the most famous of all was one who gained fame not as a barnstormer but as a "lone eagle."

Lindbergh

On 20 May 1927 at 7:34 A.M., Charles Augustus Lindbergh Jr. took off from Roosevelt Field in New York. It was to be a grueling 33 hours and 30 minutes to Le Bourget Field in Paris, a flight that would stimulate the growth of aviation throughout the world.

Lindbergh's early childhood did not hint at the great achievement that was to be his. His mother was a chemistry teacher from Detroit who met Charles Lindbergh Sr. soon after moving to Little Falls, Minnesota. Lindbergh and Evangeline Land were married on 27 March 1901, and their son was born in Detroit on 4 February 1902.[8]

The marriage did not work well at all, and by 1907 the Lindberghs had decided to live apart but remain married to keep up appearances. Lindbergh was preparing to enter politics, and a divorce would have disturbed many of his Roman Catholic constituents. In 1907, the Sixth District in Minnesota elected him to Congress. Charles and his mother spent most of their time on a farm in Little Falls. Charles had a pleasant childhood, spending much of his time outdoors. On his occasional visits, his father taught him to hunt and fish. In 1913, Lindbergh brought a Ford Model T to the farm and gave it to his wife. He was not a mechanical whiz. He often drove into ditches or fences when he mistook reverse for first on the manual gear box. But for Charles the car was the start of a relationship with mechanical things that would shape his destiny.[9]

Charles's mother had a sharp tongue, shunned any social activity, and criticized her son when he attempted to play with other boys. In summer 1915, his father was commissioned to explore the headwaters of the Mississippi arising out of Lake Itasca. Charles accompanied his father on this grueling trip, spent a good deal of time with the Chippewa Indians, and was made an honorary Indian himself. This became a defining time in Charles's childhood. The following year, his father left his House seat after five terms to run for the Senate, but he lost, having been branded a communist sympathizer. Evangeline now had no need to "keep up appearances," and she severed the relationship with her husband but did not divorce him.[10]

Charles had not been a good student in school, and he was secretly planning to leave school and join the Army to become a pilot. However, the war ended before he had a chance to carry out his wish. At his mother's insistence, he enrolled at the University of Wisconsin in Madison, but he dropped out during his sophomore year and announced to his mother that he was thinking of becoming a pilot. She urged his father to attempt to persuade him otherwise, but Charles had already written to the Nebraska Aircraft Company in Lincoln, Nebraska, to inquire about flying lessons. The year was 1922. In early spring he climbed on his Excelsior motorcycle and headed for a flight career.[11]

The Nebraska Aircraft Company was going bankrupt, but not before it fleeced Lindbergh of $500 for which he received about eight hours of flight time; unfortunately, he was not allowed to solo. Almost broke, he teamed up with a barnstormer, Erold Bahl, and began to perform around the Midwest. Lindbergh acted as mechanic, ticket taker, wingwalker, and parachutist. That winter, Lindbergh went home and persuaded his father to co-sign a $900 note at the bank so that he could buy an airplane. He bought a dilapidated Jenny (JN-4) powered by a 90-horsepower OX-5 engine that was in much better shape than the airframe. With this airplane, he began his own barnstorming act. When he learned of an airshow to be held at Lambert Field in St. Louis, he decided to fly down. There he met Marvin Northrop, a St. Louis airplane builder, who convinced him to sign up with the Army as an air cadet. Soon Lindbergh was at Brooks Field, Texas, learning to fly the Army way.[12]

Just after Lindbergh entered training, his father, who was attempting one last try at a Senate seat, died of a brain tumor. Lindbergh was given a compassionate leave by the Army so that he could attend the funeral.

He did well in pilot training. Of the 104 cadets who began the course, only 18 finished. His training was not without mishap, however. He had chosen to become a pursuit (fighter) pilot, and he completed his training at Kelly Field, Texas. On 6 March 1925, while flying solo in a training formation of nine Bristol SE-5s, maneuvering to intercept and engage a formation of DH-4 aircraft (also trainers), he collided with another SE-5 in the formation. Lindbergh and the other pilot parachuted to safety. Within the month, Lindbergh was graduated and given a reserve commission. He bought a one-way ticket to St. Louis determined to find some kind of a flying job.[13]

In St. Louis, he was offered a job by the Robertson brothers from Lambert Field, who had recently bid on a contract airmail (CAM) route between St. Louis and Chicago. Lindbergh was only twenty-three at the time, but he had an excellent reputation as a pilot and he had flown the DH-4. He agreed to the "if and when" offer but meanwhile found a job as a barnstormer and test pilot. It was as a test pilot in a new commercial airplane, the OXX-6 Plywood Special that Lindbergh was presented with a second opportunity to hit the silk. The aircraft entered an unrecoverable spin and Lindbergh had to bail out.[14] In January 1926, the Robertsons won the contract and Lindbergh began to set up the airmail business. He hired two other pilots, and on 15 April 1926 he made the inaugural flight from St. Louis to Chicago.

Things progressed smoothly until September 1926, when he loitered trying to find a break in the fog over Chicago. He then headed south to find another field where he could land and wait out the weather. He thought he had enough fuel to fly for another hour. But suddenly his engine died, starved of gas. Without Lindbergh's knowledge, a mechanic had switched out the 110-gallon tank for one that held only 85 gallons to repair the larger tank. That hour's worth of gas was never there. He changed to the reserve tank, but it held only twenty minutes of extra fuel. The engine soon quit again. With all of his options gone and the ground shrouded by fog, Lindbergh bailed out. As his parachute opened, the aircraft nosed over. The small amount of fuel left surged forward, and the engine restarted. In his haste, Lindbergh had left the switches on. The DH-4 was in a turn headed for Lindbergh as he descended in his parachute. His experience as a parachutist enabled him to slip the parachute out of the plane's flight path. The DH-4 continued to spiral as it and Lindbergh entered the fog bank. Lindbergh landed in a cornfield and eventually made his way in the fog to the farmhouse. He and the farmer retraced his steps to the wreckage. Lindbergh removed the mail bags and took them to the local post office in time to catch the 3:30 train to Chicago.

In November 1926, Lindbergh found himself in a similar situation, but this time it was a Chicago snowstorm that prevented him from landing. Once again as the last drop of gas was exhausted from his tanks, and with no other course of action available, Lindbergh went over the side. This time he landed on a barbed wire fence. The *New York Times* carried the story, spelling his name incorrectly. Nevertheless, he went into the record books as the "first pilot in the United States ever to have made four emergency parachute jumps from a plane."[15]

As flying the mail became more routine, Lindbergh found himself with a lot of time to think about the future of aviation. He avidly followed its developments. One evening he attended a movie. In those days, a newsreel usually preceded the feature movie. From the newsreel Lindbergh learned that Raymond Orteig was offering $25,000 to the first flyer or group of flyers "who shall cross in a land or water aircraft (heavier than air) from Paris or the shores of France to New York, or from New York to Paris or the shores of France, without stop."[16] The newsreel had pointed out that the Sikorsky Company had manufactured a three-engined aircraft in which the famous French war ace Paul-Rene Fonck and three other crewmen were going to try for the prize. Lindbergh decided that a far better (and cheaper) effort could be made with one man flying one aircraft designed for such a flight. He feeling was reinforced when, on 20 September 1926, Fonck's Sikorsky aircraft crashed on takeoff from Roosevelt Field. Fonck and his copilot survived, but the other two crewmembers were killed.

Lindbergh became convinced that with the right kind of airplane, he could make the flight. Although he was normally shy and reticent, he began to talk to St. Louis businessmen about his plans. He received financial backing from Maj. Albert Lambert, a World War I veteran after whom the St. Louis airport was named, the Robertson brothers, Harry Knight, a St. Louis newspaper man, and Harold Bixby, a local bank president. Soon Lindbergh had $15,000, enough to buy an aircraft. Initially, he tried to follow through with the idea while continuing to fly the mails, but he found that there was precious little time to do both because there were other competitors out there, including Adm. Richard E. Byrd, who had gained fame at the North Pole. Lt. Comdr. Noel Davis was refurbishing an Army bomber, and Paul-Rene Fonck was gearing up to make another attempt in a Sikorsky. At the urging of his backers, Lindbergh took a leave of absence from his job and began to work on the project full-time.

Earlier, Lindbergh had sent letters to the Travel Air Manufacturing Company, Bellanca, and Ryan Airlines (a manufacturer) with the general specifications for the airplane. Travel Air would not accept the order. Ryan had said they could build the machine for $6,000 less engine. Adding the Wright Whirlwind engine would bring the price to about $10,000, well within budget. As Lindbergh was preparing for a trip to California to check out the little-known Ryan Airlines, he received a telegram from Bellanca stating that the company could build an airplane to his specifications and inviting him to New York to discuss the idea. Lindbergh accepted Bellanca's invitation. After discussing the project with Bellanca officials and agreeing to approach his partners on the $15,000 price tag, Lindbergh returned to St. Louis in high spirits. Bixby and the other partners agreed, and with a $15,000 check in hand, Lindbergh returned to New York. As he handed the check over to Bellanca, he was informed that the price was contingent upon Bellanca selecting the crew who would fly the aircraft. Lindbergh was incensed; he refused the offer and after much discussion in which neither side budged, Lindbergh returned to St. Louis with a $15,000 check but no airplane. He was so despondent that he was ready to abandon the project. Bixby and Knight took him to dinner and convinced him to stick with the project.[17] Within the next few days he left for California to what he felt was his last hope for a try at the Orteig prize: the Ryan offer.

His first impression of the Ryan factory was not positive. The factory was in an "old dilapidated building near the waterfront. . . . There's no flying field, no hangar, no sound of engines warming up; and the unmistakable smell of dead fish from a nearby cannery mixes with the banana odor of dope from drying wings."[18] However, after Lindbergh had a chance to discuss the project with the engineers and builders, he was convinced that the company was capable of creating the aircraft he needed for the flight. They agreed to build the machine within sixty days; the date was 24 February 1927.

Lindbergh remained in California, planning the flight. He had never flown long distances over land or water. He discussed the navigational problem with Navy personnel and bought charts to plot his overwater routes. Having learned in his Army navigation training classes that on a globe the shortest distance between two points is a circle called a great circle, which if extended to the center of the earth would slice the earth into two equal halves, he first plotted his course from New York to Paris on a Gnomic projection chart in which a great circle route is a straight line; he then broke the route into 100-mile segments, reasoning that his airplane would travel about 100 air miles each hour. Next, he transferred the 100-mile segments to a Mercator projection chart in which a great circle is a curved line. On each line he marked the distance from New York and the magnetic course to the beginning of the next 100-mile route segment. He had calculated the distance from New York to Paris at 3,610 miles.[19]

Navy pilots read about what was being done at the factory and dropped by to see for themselves. They invited Lindbergh to the base to give a presentation on long-range navigation, which he accepted. The presentation was highly effective, and the naval officers showed a great deal of interest in the flight. Lindbergh found their company enjoyable.

Meanwhile, the world was not standing still. Other competitors were racing the clock. On 9 April, Noel Davis took his Keystone bomber on its maiden flight and pronounced it fit; Clarence Chamberlain and Bert Acosta set an endurance record of more than 51 hours in their Bellanca on 14 April in a dress rehearsal for their attempt at the prize; and Byrd and others were injured while testing a Fokker aircraft. Lindbergh's aircraft, the *Spirit of St. Louis,* made its maiden flight on 28 April 1927 (see fig. 7.4).

By 4 May, Lindbergh had completed the final speed and load tests, but he needed to conduct more weight tests by adding 50 gallons of fuel to each test until he had tested the aircraft to its full 400-gallon capacity. Then on 8 May, the newspapers reported that the team of Nungesser and Coli, famous French pilots from the war, had left Paris for their attempt. Lindbergh was convinced that his efforts had all been in vain. But Nungesser and Coli disappeared. Lindbergh took off on 10 May from San Diego for St. Louis at 3:55 P.M. (see fig. 7.5). There had not been enough time to test the airplane to its greatest weight with full fuel tanks. As the sky darkened over the inhospitable Rocky Mountains, the engine on the *Spirit of St. Louis* began to sputter and miss. At one point because of a loss of altitude, Lindbergh thought he would have to attempt a forced landing. But after he experimented with mixture adjustments and throttle settings, the Whirlwind J-5 engine perked back up, and Lindbergh returned to a safe altitude. He arrived in St.

Fig. 7.4. *Spirit of St. Louis* (Ryan N-Y-P, NX-211) in flight. Courtesy of the Fred Roos Collection.

Fig. 7.5. *Spirit of St. Louis* on the ground at San Diego shortly before Lindbergh left for St. Louis and New York. Courtesy of the Fred Roos Collection.

Louis, having broken the record for a nonstop flight from the West Coast. On 20 May, after a short stopover in St. Louis, he flew to New York.

Once there, he discovered that both Byrd in the Fokker and Chamberlin in the Bellanca were set to take off. All were waiting for a break in the weather. Lindbergh's crew took advantage of the bad weather to repair some aircraft discrepancies (broken spinner) and to equip the Whirlwind engine with a carburetor air heater to prevent carburetor ice. Lindbergh and his mechanics had determined that carburetor ice was the likely culprit in the near engine-failure episode over the Rockies.

On the evening of 19 May, the Lindbergh team learned that the weather might permit a takeoff the next morning. They rushed to the field to begin final preparations. On arrival they noticed no activity at either the Chamberlin or the Byrd hangars. Around midnight, Lindbergh went to his room to sleep until his wake-up call at 2:15 A.M. Just as he was dropping off, there was a loud knock at the door. The person Lindbergh had positioned outside the door to keep others out of his room opened the door and said, "Slim, what am I going to do when you're gone?"[20] Lindbergh was now fully awake.

Early the next morning, 20 May 1927, Lindbergh positioned the aircraft at the end of the runway at Roosevelt

Field. He ran the engine and found that it was producing thirty revolutions too low because of the muggy conditions. There were other complications. The field was soggy from days of rain, and the wheels of the plane were buried in the mud. After the aircraft was towed into position and the last drop of gasoline was added to the tanks, the wind switched around to a tailwind, meaning that the takeoff would require more distance than with a headwind. Otherwise, the airplane would have to be defueled to move it to the other end of the field and then refueled. By that time, Chamberlin and Byrd might beat them to the opportunity. He would have to clear telephone wires at the end of the airfield. The airplane had never been flown with a full fuel load. Lindbergh pondered each of these problems as he started the engine in preparation for the flight; he looked at the runway stretched out in front; it seemed so short (see fig. 7.6). In Lindbergh's words,

> The mechanics, the engineers, the blue uniformed police officers standing there behind the wing, everyone has done his part. Now, it's up to me. Their eyes are intently on mine. . . . Wind, weather. Power, load—gradually these elements stop churning in my mind. . . . Sitting in the cockpit, in seconds, minutes long, the conviction surges through me that the wheels will leave the ground, that the wings will rise above the wires, that it is time to start the flight. . . . I buckle my safety belt, pull goggles down over my eyes, turn to the men at the blocks and nod. Frozen figures leap to action. . . . The *Spirit of St. Louis* feels more like an overloaded truck than an airplane. . . . A takeoff seems hopeless; but I may as well go on for another hundred feet before giving up. . . . Gradually the speed increases. . . . The stick wobbles loosely from side to side, and the slipstream puts hardly any pressure against the rudder. Nothing about my plane has the magic quality of flight. But men begin stumbling off from the wing struts. We're going faster. A hundred yards of runway passes. The last man drops off the struts. . . . Pace quickens. . . . The halfway mark streaks past. . . . I pull the stick back firmly and—The wheels leave the ground. . . . The wheels touch again. The next hop's longer—I could probably stay in the air but I let the wheels touch once more—lightly. . . . The *Spirit of St. Louis* takes herself off the next time.[21]

Thirty-three and a half hours later, Lindbergh touched down at Le Bourget Airport in Paris.[22]

Fig. 7.6. Shortly after takeoff from Roosevelt Field on his epic flight to Paris, Lindbergh is spotted by another aircraft. Courtesy of the Fred Roos Collection.

General Aviation

Barnstormers created an industry that was to become as important to this country as the airlines. By the mid-1960s, the number of general aviation aircraft would grow to forty-five times that of the airlines.[23] For that alone, we owe the barnstormer pioneers our sincerest gratitude.

At first, general aviation was called private aviation, and it included such things as private (or recreational) flying, air photography, business flying, training, air taxi, agricultural applications (crop dusting), and other activities not considered either military or commercial.

Clyde Cessna. One of the first to recognize the possibilities of general aviation was Clyde Cessna, a garage me-

Fig. 7.7. Clyde Cessna's prewar exhibition advertisement. He used an airplane that he had built himself. Robert J. Pickett Collection, Kansas Aviation Museum.

chanic from Enid, Oklahoma, who actually began building his airplanes before World War I (see figs. 7.7 and 7.8).[24] His machines were heavily influenced by the French Bleriot monoplanes.[25]

After the war (in 1924), Cessna joined forces with Walter Beech and Lloyd Stearman to form the Travel Air Manufacturing Company. Together they produced a series of moderately successful Travel Air aircraft (see fig. 7.9). The design features of their aircraft included a high wing and an enclosed cabin. Captivated by the clean look of the cantilever wing, Cessna left Travel Air in 1927 to form his own company. He built the Cessna A model until the Great Depression forced him to close down between 1931 and 1934. He did manage to keep his hand in the business, however, by building custom-designed racing planes. The company was revitalized when Cessna's nephew, Dwane Wallace, fresh from Wichita University with an aeronautical engineering degree, convinced his uncle and enough stockholders to reopen the Cessna plant. A product of this was the Cessna C-34 Airmaster, which had a high cantilevered wing and a cowled radial engine; it was one of the first light airplanes to employ wing flaps. This C-34 aircraft held great appeal to the business flyer and was hailed as the "world's most efficient plane" (shown in fig. 7.10). With an engine in the range of 145 to 165 horsepower, the Airmaster cruised at 150 mph+, had a range of about 600 miles, and carried four passengers. At a price of $4,995 in 1936, the Airmaster made business flying economically feasible.[26]

This airplane put the Cessna Aircraft Company on the map, as it proved to be a highly successful design. The success continued as the company designed and produced its first twin-engine design, the Model T-50 (see fig. 7.11). This model was used to train military pilots during World War II.[27]

Clyde Cessna retired in 1936. His successful company continued under the leadership of Dwane Wallace.

Walter Beech. Following a stint in the military as an instructor pilot, Walter Beech flew his war-surplus Curtiss Jenny biplane in the barnstorming tours that were so popular after World War I. This led him to Wichita, Kansas, in 1921, where he worked for Laird Aircraft Company as a test pilot. He demonstrated the Laird Swallow, a tandem open cockpit biplane (shown in fig. 7.12), in air shows around the United States. Laird reorganized in 1923 as the Swallow Airplane Manufacturing Company and put Beech in charge of all fieldwork. He

Fig. 7.8. The site of the old Burton Car Works in Wichita where boxcars had been manufactured. It became Cessna's first factory. Some of the early Cessnas are shown behind the groups of people. Robert J. Pickett Collection, Kansas Aviation Museum.

Fig. 7.9. Travel Air Model 6000. Kansas Aviation Museum Collection.

Fig. 7.10. Cessna Airmaster C-34. Robert J. Pickett Collection, Kansas Aviation Museum.

Fig. 7.11. Cessna T-50 owned by Parks College of Saint Louis University at Parks Airport. The aircraft was part of the student-run Parks Air College Airline. Courtesy of the Fred Roos Collection.

Fig. 7.12. Laird Swallow. Courtesy of United Airlines.

Fig. 7.13. Travel Air Model E-4000. Kansas Aviation Museum Collection.

quickly rose to the position of general manager, but then had a falling out with the owner over a decision to use wood or metal for a new airplane design. Beech left to form Travel Air with Clyde Cessna and Lloyd Stearman. When Cessna left Travel Air, Beech remained as president. Under his leadership the company produced several models of the Travel Air (see fig. 7.13). In 1929, their share of the marketplace was about 10 percent. By 1930, the total number of commercial airplanes produced had dropped almost 70 percent (from 5,357 to 1,582). Beech sold Travel Air to the Curtiss-Wright Company.[28]

But his retirement from the business was not to last long. In 1932, he and his wife, Olive Ann (his former secretary at Travel Air), formed the Beech Aircraft Corporation. Beech's goal was to build a high-speed (200 mph) aircraft that had a range close to 1,000 miles and a cabin large enough to carry four passengers in the comfort they had become accustomed to in a high-priced automobile.[29] The aircraft also needed to possess amiable flying characteristics and land at about 60 mph. What emerged from these thoughts was the incomparable Model 17, perhaps better known as the Staggerwing Beech because of the negative stagger of its upper and lower wings (shown in fig. 7.14). (The lower wing was positioned forward of the upper wing.) Even though

this was the first aircraft series produced by Beech, it carried the model number "17." This was because the last series that Walter Beech had been working on at Travel Air was the model "16." He simply continued the numbering system into the new company.[30]

This aircraft was produced with a variety of cowled radial engines ranging in horsepower from 225 to more than 400. It was produced until 1948 and used for a variety of missions in World War II. This aircraft toppled existing aircraft records, proving to be one of the most versatile designs of the day.

In 1935, Beech designed the Model 18 Twin Beech, a twin-engine monoplane. More than eighteen hundred were sold during its production run. The success of the Beech Model 17 and Model 18 aircraft was crucial to the early success of the United States entering World War II. Beech stopped all commercial production to meet the demands of the military, building the Model 18 as a bombing and gunnery trainer and the Model 17 as a personnel transport.

Other Manufacturers

William B. Stout. Stout, a noted inventor and pioneer builder of all-metal airplanes, saw the market for further

Fig. 7.14. The beautiful Beech Model 17, also known as the Staggerwing Beech. Kansas Aviation Museum Collection.

development of the aircraft for commercial purposes. He formed Stout's Metal Airplane Company and, following a strong marketing program, convinced Edsel Ford to manufacture aircraft. Henry Ford purchased Stout's company in 1924 and built an airport in Detroit and a factory for aeronautical projects.

After seeing a Fokker trimotor aircraft on a tour in the United States, Henry Ford decided that the three-motor concept was viable and the Ford should build one. He put a team on the project, and the Ford Trimotor aircraft, the "Tin Goose," was introduced in 1926; it became the mainstay of the air transport industry for years. Not all of Ford's designs were successful, however. Ford moved out of the airplane business in the mid-1930s.[31]

Donald W. Douglas. Just before the end of World War I, the Glenn Martin Company hired a young engineer, Donald W. Douglas. He had designed a twin-engine airplane as a bomber. This airplane had exceeded even Douglas's expectations, and its design carried the Martin Company through the hard years immediately following the war, when most airplane manufacturers went out of business. The Army was selling surplus planes, which negatively impacted the ability of manufactories to sell new planes. Even though Douglas had a good job with Martin, he resigned in March 1920 to form his own company in Los Angeles.[32]

Douglas made a vow that as he designed aircraft, each model would be a seed plane for models to follow.[33] This concept was not the norm at that time in the evolution of the airplane, and it would prove to be a fortuitous decision, positively affecting the future of Douglas airplanes. The Davis-Douglas Airplane Company began work on its first airplane, the C-1C Cloudster, which was built specifically for a 2,800-mile flight from California to Long Island (shown in fig. 7.15).[34] The airplane was to be flown at a speed of 85 mph for 33 hours to get to Long Island.

The pilot, Eric Springer, launched the aircraft on 27 June 1921 and was en route to Long Island when the engine suddenly stopped over Texas. Springer was forced to land at Ft. Bliss near El Paso. During the three weeks it took to repair the aircraft, Army Lt. Oakley Kelly and Lt. John Macready flew nonstop from New York to San Diego in a Fokker T-2.[35]

Douglas used the Cloudster design to submit to the Navy a design for a torpedo plane, the DT-1. The Navy was impressed with the design and ordered three aircraft. This began a long and fruitful relationship between the U.S. military and the newly named Douglas Aircraft Company.

Fig. 7.15. Douglas C-1C Cloudster. By permission of the National Air and Space Museum, Smithsonian Institution, ©1999 Smithsonian Institution.

Fig. 7.16. Lockheed Vega. Courtesy of the Fred Roos Collection.

Douglas established a company that was equally adept at producing aircraft for either the military or civilian market, such as the venerable DC-3. Douglas's concept was one of using proven designs as a basis for future designs. This concept stood his company in good stead in the highly competitive industry.

John Knudson Northrop. Jack Northrop studied drafting in high school, then got a job with fledgling airplane builders Allen and Malcolm Loughead. He was put to work on a ten-passenger flying boat that the Lougheads were building. With little training, Northrop designed and stressed the 71-foot wings of the F-1 flying boat, at that time the world's largest seaplane. He was soon promoted to project engineer. He designed a primitive wind tunnel, consisting of hanging shapes to be tested in a glass tube, with a man smoking a cigar and puffing the smoke into the tube so Northrop could see how the smoke flowed around the shape. Northrop worked for the Loughead (later changed to Lockheed) brothers until times were lean, then went to work for Donald Douglas, where he designed both military and civilian airplanes. When Douglas missed out on a critical mili-

tary contract and was forced to lay off engineers, Northrop was the only one he kept.[36]

Northrop moonlighted for other manufacturers, including some design work on the Ryan M-1 monoplane, the predecessor to the *Spirit of St. Louis.* Like so many other designers, Northrop wanted to build his own plane. So in 1926 he took his design for a large wooden monocoque fuselage with a single cantilevered wing, capable of carrying a pilot and four passengers, to the Lockheeds. The Lockheeds, Tony Stadlman, and Northrop formed the new Lockheed Aircraft Company, which immediately began to build Northrop's "dream ship," called the Lockheed Vega (shown in fig. 7.16). The Vega made its maiden flight on 4 July 1927 and proved to be the first of a long line of successful aircraft using that design.[37]

Northrop is most famous, however, for designing the Avion Experimental No. 1, dubbed the "flying wing." Northrop had begun building this airplane using innovative procedures, to include covering the aircraft with a newly developed Alclad reinforced aluminum skin, adding strength and a better covering.

One day, William E. Boeing visited the Avion Corporation. He was so impressed by what he saw that he urged United Aircraft to buy out Avion, and he formed a new company, Northrop Aviation Corporation. This company proceeded to build a long string of aircraft for civilian and military use.

William T. Piper. Piper was in the oil business in Pennsylvania in 1928 when he bought a few shares of stock in Taylor Brothers Aircraft, which was producing the tandem-seated two-place E-2 called the Cub. When Taylor Brothers went broke in 1931, Piper left the oil fields, purchased the Taylor assets, and created the Piper Aircraft Company.

In 1935, Piper gave a recent Rutgers graduate, William Jamouneau, the opportunity to redesign the E-2. Jamouneau rounded off the squarish tail surfaces, and the airplane was given a new designation, the J-3 Cub, after its (re)designer (see fig. 7.17). The aircraft was equipped with a 50-horsepower Continental 4-cylinder (opposed) engine and was painted a bright yellow with a black speed stripe down the side of the fuselage.

Piper hung on during the Depression and kept the price of the J-3 at $995. Buyers received eight hours of free flying lessons. By 1940, according to *Fortune* magazine, Piper was building more than any other manufacturer in the world.[38] The J-3 Cub stayed in production until 1947. More than 14,000 J-3 Cubs were produced.

The Guggenheim Foundation

After World War I, the U.S. government was not inclined to provide funding for aviation enterprises. This stands to reason, as the government was attempting to find buyers for the aircraft it already had in stock. Government officials saw no need for improving the tools of war, especially in the environment of world peace now in force. So it fell to the budding aviation industry to find funding for further development. It was at this time that one family, with the vision and wisdom to foresee the value and need for aircraft, decided to bankroll the development of aviation.

The Guggenheims of Philadelphia had made their fortune in copper, gold, tin, nitrate, and rubber. During

Fig. 7.17. Piper J-3 Cub. By permission of the National Air and Space Museum, Smithsonian Institution, ©1999 Smithsonian Institution.

the war, Harry Guggenheim flew as a combat observer in torpedo bombers. He gained an immediate respect for aviation and a vision for an expanded use of the airplane after the war. Realizing that there was no pool of qualified aeronautical engineers to assist in development, his father, Daniel Guggenheim, created the Guggenheim Foundation for the Promotion of Aeronautics in 1926. He made available $2.5 million for the endowment of university programs in aeronautical engineering. The Guggenheim Foundation had four goals: to promote aeronautical education, to support aeronautical research, to aid in the development of commercial aircraft, and to foster the use of aircraft in business and industry.[39]

The Guggenheims awarded medals for exceptional individual contributions to the world of aviation; the first went to Orville Wright in 1930. The foundation also provided cash awards for safe, effective designs of airplanes.

James H. Doolittle. Daniel Guggenheim wished to foster the development of technology to allow pilots to "blind fly" aircraft under marginal weather conditions. The Army assigned a test pilot, James H. Doolittle, to develop procedures for flying without external visual cues, aided only by instruments in the cockpit. Doolittle held a doctorate in aeronautical engineering from the Massachusetts Institute of Technology. The Guggenheim Foundation provided $85,000 for a flight laboratory on Long Island, where Doolittle, Elmer Sperry Jr., and Paul Kollsman developed a gyrocompass, an artificial horizon, and a precision altimeter.

Doolittle developed a system of using aural signal differentials from ground-based beacons to provide information to an instrument aboard the aircraft. With this system, he could tell his direction from a beamed signal using the amplitude of vibrations received on a headset, and he could also tell when he was flying directly over the signal source.[40]

After several aborted attempts, Doolittle completed the first successful blind flight to great fanfare on 24 September 1929, using the newly designed instruments and the radio navigation techniques developed during his experimental flights at Mitchel Field, Long Island. This capability, to fly despite poor visibility and low ceilings, is thought by many to be Doolittle's crowning achievement as an aviator.

Aircraft Engine Development

The bulk of the story of engine development during this period can be told in its shortened version by mentioning the names of two companies: Curtiss-Wright and Pratt and Whitney. At the apex of both of those companies was an engine designer by the name of Charles L. Lawrance.

Charles L. Lawrance. Lawrance began experimenting in 1916, when he designed a 2-cylinder opposed reciprocating engine. Three years later, he built a 3-cylinder radial engine based on the 3-cylinder rotary but one in which the engine cylinders were stationary and the crankshaft rotated. He displayed this engine in Washington, where it caught the attention of the Navy, which was interested in finding an air-cooled radial engine to replace the liquid-cooled engines used in some of its aircraft. If such engines could be found, the Navy could shorten the length of its airplanes, which meant that it could fit more aircraft onto an aircraft carrier without, it hoped, sacrificing any engine efficiency. In addition, such an engine would be more likely to survive in a combat situation. One bullet into the cooling system could disable a liquid-cooled engine. A radial engine, they surmised, could take hits in the cylinders without necessarily jeopardizing the engine.

The Navy's Bureau of Aeronautics provided a grant to Lawrance, who then designed a 9-cylinder air-cooled radial engine in 1921. Chance Vought described it as "the prototype for the modern American radial engine."[41] The 200-horsepower engine had cast aluminum cylinders with steel liners and a cast aluminum crankcase. The Navy ordered two hundred engines, which was far more than Lawrance could produce out of his little loft shop. Lawrance and the Navy's Bureau of Aeronautics approached the Wright Company and the Curtiss Company to produce the engine, but neither was interested. The Wright Company was quite comfortable producing the 200-horsepower, water-cooled Hispano-Suisa (Hisso) engine under contract, and the Curtiss Company was getting fat with its 400-horsepower, water-cooled in-line D-12 engine. Neither saw any reason to change. Then the Navy threatened to cancel the Wright Company's contract for Hisso engines. The Wright Company saw the error of its ways and, characteristically, bought out

Lawrance, making him a vice president.[42] The engine was an immediate hit not only with the military but with commercial developers who were starved for a reliable engine to give them an alternative to the less efficient engines that dominated the field. For example, the engine that it became, the Wright Whirlwind, was the engine that powered the *Spirit of St. Louis* over the Atlantic.

The president of the Wright Company was Frederick B. Rentschler, a Princeton graduate, who had been a lieutenant in the Signal Corps working as an engine inspector at the Wright-Martin Company. He stayed on after the war, eventually becoming president of the reorganized company. In 1924, Rentschler broke with the Wright Company because they refused to allocate enough funds to research a larger engine.

Pratt and Whitney. Rentschler and a group of Wright engineers founded a new company to build a larger air-cooled radial engine. Rentschler was convinced that a military market existed for such an engine, and he was anxious to begin. The venture was funded by Niles Tool, whose president was none other than Edward Deeds of World War I aircraft production fame. Niles Tool offered an idle machine shop, the Pratt and Whitney machine tool plant in Hartford, Connecticut, as a production facility. Rentschler accepted the facility and kept the name because the company had an excellent reputation for making precision equipment. Adm. William Moffett was exceptionally interested in Pratt and Whitney's engine, which existed only on paper, and found $90,000 that was available for experiments to buy six experimental engines. This covered about half of the development costs; the rest of it was put up by the financial backers. The engine, to be called the Wasp, was ready in just six months after the founding of the company. It met the Navy's requirement of a weight of 650 pounds or less and delivered 425 horsepower. The Navy immediately ordered two hundred Wasps.[43]

With merger mania being the name of the aviation game with an eye toward vertical integration, United Aircraft and Transport acquired the Pratt and Whitney Company, and the Keys group, North American Aviation (and later General Motors), acquired what had become, ironically, the Curtiss-Wright Company. Boom times were ahead.

While the rest of America agonized in the fires of the Depression, the aviation industry was booming thanks to the subsidy for the airmail carriers and the military contracts for engines and airplanes. But the days of reckoning were ahead. When the voters threw out the Hoover Republicans, blaming them for the Depression, and elected Democrat Franklin Delano Roosevelt as president, it was time for a "New Deal." Senator Black investigated the airmail subsidy, and he was particularly intrigued by the incredible profit resulting from government outlays. Charles W. Deeds, the son of Edward Deeds, was one of the original stockholders in Pratt and Whitney and an employee of United Aircraft and Transport. He bought two hundred shares of Pratt and Whitney stock, which was issued privately, at 20 cents a share. In November 1928, stock dividends transformed the 200 shares into 16,000 shares. In January 1929, the stock had split again and now amounted to 34,720 shares. By May, the stock was worth $160 a share, or $5,555,200.[44] This was not bad for a $40 investment by Charles Deeds at the ripe old age of twenty-six.

The Development of the Jet Engine

The development of the jet engine is, broadly, the story of three men: Henri Coanda, Sir Frank Whittle, and Pabst von O'Hain.

Henri Coanda. Coanda, a Romanian, displayed an aircraft in Paris in October 1910 that was powered by what he called the Turbo-Propulsor (shown in fig. 7.18). The engine was a combination reciprocating engine and compressor. The reciprocating engine turned the compressor, which was mounted in front of the reciprocating engine. The compressor pulled air through a tubular opening built around the compressor and reciprocating engine. Fuel was injected into the vent and ignited. On a trial run when Coanda ignited the fuel, the aircraft rapidly gained speed, lifted off the ground, and flew for about a thousand feet before crashing into a wall. Coanda was not injured, but he gave up further development of the power plant.[45]

Sir Frank Whittle. Whittle was born in 1907 in England, the son of a machinist. As a child he followed his father around the machine shop, learning about tools and the secrets of the art. He won a scholarship to a secondary school and developed an interest in both astronomy and flight. In 1922, he attempted to enter the Royal Air Force Academy, but he was rejected because he was too short.

Fig. 7.18. Coanda's Turbo-Propulsor. By permission of the National Air and Space Museum, Smithsonian Institution, ©1999 Smithsonian Institution.

He tried again a year later and was accepted. After spending three years as an apprentice at Cranwell, he applied to become an aviation cadet but finished seventh in a six-man race; fortunately for him, the sixth man flunked the eyesight test and Whittle was in. In his final term at Cranwell, he wrote a thesis entitled "Future Developments in Aircraft Design" in which he recognized the shortcomings of the reciprocating engine and the propeller and outlined how an airplane might be powered by a jet engine. In the RAF college journal of 1928, he published a short article entitled "Speculation" in which he described the basic thermodynamic equations necessary for a jet propulsion system that could propel an aircraft at the unheard-of altitude of 115,000 feet.

Upon graduation, Pilot Officer Whittle was assigned to the Central Flying School. There, his commanding officer was so excited by his jet-propulsion ideas that he arranged an interview with the Air Ministry, where Whittle was received with polite indifference. Whittle also approached several industrial firms, but they rejected his proposals because, in their view, there were no metals available that could stand the internal operating temperatures of the engine that Whittle was proposing. Nevertheless, in 1930 he took out a patent.

Five years later, Whittle formed Power Jet Limited, a company established with financial backing from four other parties. The goal was to build a single-stage turbine engine with a single-stage centrifugal-flow compressor. The engine was designed to produce 17,750 rpms. To do this, Whittle needed to find a company that could produce a metal for the combustion chamber that could tolerate high temperatures. The only company to respond to the challenge was the Scottish firm of Laidlaw, Drew and Company. Through a series of successes, failures, designs, and redesigns, Whittle produced an operational engine in 1937. Further refinements were made,

Fig. 7.19. Gloster E 28/39. By permission of the National Air and Space Museum, Smithsonian Institution, ©1999 Smithsonian Institution.

Fig. 7.20. View of a model of the Heinkel HE 178 turbojet aircraft. This was the first turbojet aircraft to fly, on 27 August 1939. By permission of the National Air and Space Museum, Smithsonian Institution, ©1999 Smithsonian Institution.

and finally the firm received a contract from the Air Ministry.

The first English plane to be powered by one of Whittle's engines was the Gloster E 28/39 (shown in fig. 7.19), which conducted its maiden flight on 15 May 1941. The aircraft had a wingspan of 29 feet, a length of 25 feet, a gross weight of 3,700 pounds, and a maximum speed of 338 mph.[46]

As dramatic as the achievement was, it was not the first jet engine to propel an aircraft. That distinction belongs to Germany.

Pabst von O'Hain. One of Germany's premier aircraft designers, Ernst Heinkel, hired Pabst von O'Hain to design an airplane free from the restrictions imposed by both the reciprocating engine and the propeller. O'Hain had been working on jet propulsion since the early 1930s. In 1937, he produced a turbojet engine that ran on hydrogen. On 27 August 1939, O'Hain and Heinkel's HE 178 made the world's first jet flight. Powered by a thrust turbojet engine weighing 838 pounds, the HE 178 had a wingspan of 23 feet, a length of 24 feet, a gross weight of 4,405 pounds, and a maximum speed of 435 mph (see fig. 7.20).[47]

Notes

1. Rae, *Climb to Greatness,* 2.
2. President Wilson's administration allowed some contracts to continue for a short time to ease the pain of transition. For example, as Herschel Smith points out in *A History of Aircraft Piston Engines,* 81, some 2,543 Liberty engines were manufactured after the Armistice.
3. Bilstein, *Flight in America,* 60–61.
4. Fruedenthal, *The Aviation Business,* 67.
5. Taylor and Munson, *History of Aviation,* 180.
6. Simonson, *The History of the American Aircraft Industry,* 49–50.
7. Bilstein, 61.
8. Mosley, *Lindbergh,* 8–9.
9. Mosley, 11–12.
10. Mosley, 24–25.
11. Mosley, 26–33.
12. Mosley, 35–55.
13. Mosley, 59.
14. Berg, *Lindbergh,* 88.
15. Mosley, 69.
16. Mosley, 73.
17. Lindbergh, *The Spirit of St. Louis,* 64–78.
18. Lindbergh, 79.

19. Lindbergh, 89–101.
20. Lindbergh, 175.
21. Lindbergh, 182–87.
22. To appreciate the full force of the Lindbergh flight, the author recommends that the student read the full text of the flight in Charles Lindbergh's book, *The Spirit of St. Louis.*
23. Bernardo, *Aviation and Space in the Modern World,* 57.
24. Rae, 16.
25. Gunston, *Chronicle of Aviation,* 103.
26. Bilstein, 112.
27. Phillips, "Clyde Cessna," 41–47.
28. Phillips, 43–44.
29. For more background on the history of the Guggenheim and the actions leading up to the formation of the Guggenheim Fund, see Hallion, "Daniel and Harry Guggenheim and the Philanthropy of Flight."
30. Robert T. Smith, *Staggerwing,* 15.
31. Leary, *Aviation's Golden Age,* 3–17.
32. Morrison, *Donald W. Douglas,* describes in great detail the life of Donald Douglas and provides a true understanding of the impact that Douglas had on the aircraft manufacturing industry.
33. Morrison, 17.
34. Morrison, 24.
35. Morrison, 25.
36. Allen, *The Northrop Story,* 3–5.
37. Allen, 7.
38. Bilstein, 110.
39. Hallion, 19, 23.
40. For a detailed description of the system used for aerial navigation during Doolittle's experiments, see Glines, "Doolittle's Instrument First."
41. Rae, 27.
42. Rae, 28–29.
43. Rae, 29–31.
44. Fruedenthal, 95–96.
45. Brown, *A History of Aviation,* 140.
46. Generally, two sources were used to write this section, Brown, 140–41, and Taylor and Munson, 332–35.
47. Taylor and Munson, 339.

References

Allen, Richard S. *The Northrop Story, 1929–1939.* New York: Orion Books, 1990.
Bauer, Eugene E. *Boeing in Peace and War.* Enumclaw, Wash.: TAB, 1990.
Berg, A. Scott. *Lindbergh.* New York: G. P. Putnam, 1998.
Bernardo, James V. *Aviation and Space in the Modern World.* New York: E. P. Dutton, 1968.
Bilstein, Roger E. *Flight in America, 1900–1983.* Baltimore: Johns Hopkins University Press, 1984.

Brown, Carl A. *A History of Aviation.* Daytona Beach: Embry-Riddle Aeronautical University, 1980.

Fruedenthal, Elsbeth E. *The Aviation Business.* New York: Vanguard Press, 1940.

Gammack, Thomas H. "The Aircraft Industry Soars." *Outlook* 152 (10 July 1929): 429.

Gibbs-Smith, Charles H. *Aviation: An Historical Survey from Its Origins to the End of World War II.* London: Her Majesty's Stationery Office, 1970.

Glines, C. V. "Doolittle's Instrument First." Reprinted in *TAC Attack,* November 1971, 20–23.

Gunston, Bill, ed. *Chronicle of Aviation.* Paris: Jacques Legrand, 1992.

Hallion, Richard P. "Daniel and Harry Guggenheim and the Philanthropy of Flight." In *Aviation's Golden Age,* ed. William M. Leary, 18–34. Iowa City: University of Iowa Press, 1989.

Klemin, Alexander. "Learning to Use Our Wings." *Scientific American,* May 1930, 388–91.

Leary, William L., ed. *Aviation's Golden Age: Portraits from the 1920s and 1930s.* Iowa City: University of Iowa Press, 1989.

Ley, Willy. *Rockets Missiles and Space Travel.* New York: Viking Press, 1957.

Lindbergh, Charles A. *The Spirit of St. Louis.* New York: Charles Scribner's Sons, 1954.

McCurdy, E. "Leonardo da Vinci and the Science of Flight." *19th Century* 68 (July 1910): 126–42.

Merritt, D. "America in the Air: An Interview with Charles Lanier Lawrance." *Outlook* 147 (19 October 1927): 207–8.

Morris, Lloyd, and Kendall Smith. *Ceiling Unlimited: The Story of American Aviation from Kitty Hawk to Supersonics.* New York: Macmillan, 1953.

Morrison, Wilbur H. *Donald Douglas: A Heart with Wings.* Ames: Iowa State University Press, 1991.

Mosley, Leonard. *Lindbergh, a Biography.* New York: Doubleday, 1976.

Nevin, David. *The Pathfinders.* Alexandria, Va.: Time-Life Books, 1980.

Payne, L. G. S. *Air Dates.* New York: Frederick A. Praeger, 1957.

Phillips, Edward H. "Clyde Cessna and the Birth of a Legend." *Aviation History,* January 1996, 41–47.

Pownall, C. A. "Better Engines for Navy Planes." *Scientific American,* December 1931, 376–78.

Rae, John B. *Climb to Greatness.* Cambridge: MIT Press, 1968.

Roseberry, C. R. *Glenn Curtiss: Pioneer of Flight.* Syracuse: Syracuse University Press, 1991.

Scamehorn, Howard L. *Balloons to Jets.* Chicago: Henry Regnery, 1957.

Simonson, G. R., ed. *The History of the American Aircraft Industry.* Cambridge: MIT Press, 1968.

Smith, Herschel. *A History of Aircraft Piston Engines.* Manhattan, Kans.: Sunflower University Press, 1981.

Smith, Robert T. *Staggerwing.* Media, Pa.: Private Press of Robert Maney, 1967.

Taylor, John W. Ransom, and Kenneth Munson. *History of Aviation.* New York: Crown, 1972.

Viemeister, Peter. *A History of Aviation: They Were There.* Bedford, Va.: Hamilton's, 1990.

8

U.S. Airlines from 1930 to World War II

Tim Brady

In 1930, the Great Depression was under way. The stock market had crashed in October 1929, seemingly without warning. The United States was poised at the brink of utopia when it plunged almost overnight into an economic tailspin. However, while the economy was skidding, the airlines were building. The "big four" airline power groups in January 1930 were Aviation Corporation (AVCO), the Keys group, United Air Lines, and Eastern Air Transport. This chapter will describe the events that led to the continuing formation of the giants in the domestic airline industry.

President Herbert Hoover, Aviation's Friend

Many Americans attributed the Great Depression to Herbert Hoover (shown in fig. 8.1), who was elected president in 1928. His name was synonymous with misery, joblessness, lost fortunes, soup lines, businessmen leaping to their death from buildings, and other economic horrors. The Depression had such a profound effect on Americans that its aftermath still affects voting patterns today. The memories of the Depression are so fresh among many who witnessed it that, although their political beliefs are those espoused by the Republican Party, they would not vote for the party of Hoover. Nevertheless, to the developing aviation industry, Herbert Hoover was a friend.

Fig. 8.1. President Herbert Hoover. By permission of the National Air and Space Museum, Smithsonian Institution, ©1999 Smithsonian Institution.

Hoover's election was a quantum leap from his previous government position, that of secretary of commerce under Calvin Coolidge. Largely through Hoover's leadership and his pressure on President Coolidge, the Air Commerce Act of 1926 was passed, an act described as a cornerstone of civil aviation. Functionally it was more of an act designed to promote civil aviation rather than to regulate it. This act has been described as perhaps the only significant legislative achievement of the Coolidge administration. Still, the development of the act sensitized Hoover to the needs of the civil aviation industry. The act helped him form a vision that was to govern the development of the airline industry in a lasting way. Hoover knew that civil airlines lived or died by virtue of airmail contracts, and his conviction was that if airlines were to grow into genuine passenger-carrying entities, they would do so through some form of government encouragement. Hoover saw the lack of a vigorous air transportation system designed to carry passengers as a piece of unfinished business left over from his stint as secretary of commerce. To continue his ideas, he appointed Walter Folger Brown to the task of postmaster general. Brown was a Harvard-educated Toledo attorney, a friend, and one who had helped guide Hoover's election campaign to its successful conclusion.

Walter Folger Brown

Walter Brown had served as assistant secretary of commerce under Hoover, and he was keenly aware of the political machinery through which Washington operated. He also shared Hoover's vision for the development of air transportation. On the dark side, Brown could be single-minded, arrogant, and sometimes ruthless in the pursuit of his convictions.

Brown's first self-appointed task was to gather data and to analyze the airline industry before taking any action. After about a year, he had digested all of the facts and found these conditions:

1. The post office paid airlines for mail carriage on the basis of a weight-mileage formula. According to the Airmail Act of 1925, the airmail carriers were expected to stand alone. This meant that the revenues paid to the air carriers for mail would not exceed the revenues that the government collected. This funding formula was apparently not sufficient to keep the struggling air carriers

afloat. Through a series of amendments to the original Kelly Bill, the airlines were paid more than the government collected in what amounted to a subsidy. The airlines fared quite well under this arrangement. However, it did not take a rocket scientist to figure out that on the weight-mileage formula, the airlines could make money by sending mail to themselves. For example, at 5 cents per ounce, a pound of mail or freight would cost 80 cents to ship 1,000 miles or less. The carrier was paid up to $3 for this. Therefore, a carrier could send its own mail by air to itself and pocket $2.20 per pound, less operating costs.[1] It was not long before the airmail carriers were mailing themselves bricks, aircraft engines, and heavy telephone books. These items would round out a load in those situations where the aircraft was not fully loaded.

2. Few airmail contract holders were interested in carrying passengers. The airlines were making a good profit carrying the mail; carrying passengers did not produce the same profits.[2] For example, to carry a passenger in a space in which mail could be carried did not provide as much of a profit. For those few who carried passengers, a typical flight from New York to San Francisco would cost the passenger around $300. Assuming a mail load weighing the same as the passenger (approximately 200 pounds), the money collected for the mail carriage would amount to about $1,800, six times as much money. So why carry passengers? Special facilities had to be developed to meet the physiological needs of the passengers; they were either too cold or too hot and they had to get someplace on time. Not so the mail: it never complained, it did not get too hot or cold, and it did not care if it arrived someplace a few hours late. In addition, the air carriers were in the business to make a buck, and passengers were not profitable.

Of course, this was the prevailing attitude but not the all-encompassing one. United and Western Air Express were notable exceptions. They had begun carrying passengers to supplement their airmail income. Western Express was doing quite well carrying passengers between Los Angeles and San Francisco because of its slow, ambling, rambling railway service. In addition, a few independents were trying to make a living by carrying passengers alone, but they were vested in a mantle of economic failure; carrying passengers in 1930 as a sole source of revenue was hardly enough to keep any airline solvent.

3. Relay of passengers from airline to airline and from route to route was uncoordinated and often resulted in long delays for the passengers or abandonment altogether.

4. Most routes were short. There were fifty-three established routes. Forty-three were less than 500 miles in length, and eight covered distances between 500 and 1,000 miles. Only one airline ran coast to coast: United Air Transport with its two segments of the Columbia route. As to passenger support, whole sections of the country were unserved. For example, until August 1930, there was no air passenger service available south of Washington, D.C., along the eastern seaboard and into Florida.

5. Passengers and flight crews alike feared flying at night. (Ever wonder where the phrase "It is a fly-by-night outfit" came from?) In the late 1920s, night beacons illuminated the major airways. Advances had been made in aircraft instruments that could be used for night flying; however, most air carriers were not willing to dip into their profits to equip their airplanes with these expensive "gadgets." Two-way aircraft radios used for both communication and navigation had been developed, but they also were too expensive. One airline, Transcontinental Air Transport (TAT), was created as an air-rail transportation medium. Passengers would fly by day in Ford Trimotors and travel by train at night on a coast-to-coast voyage. The trip took 48 hours. TAT was jokingly referred to by line pilots of other airlines as "Take a Train." Although TAT had a very influential list of backers, including Clement Keys, Charles Lindbergh, and Amelia Earhart, it never proved to be economically viable.

6. Airlines were not interested in using the most modern equipment available, aircraft included. They were making a profit using their equipment. Much of the equipment was holdover technology from World War I, such as the DH-4 and other Liberty engine–powered equipment. So why risk the investment and perhaps lose profits?

7. Instrument flying and sophisticated equipment were available, such as the gyro stabilized compass, aircraft attitude indicator, and artificial horizon. Radio aids were also available for both navigation and communication, but few aircraft were equipped with such devices, and even fewer pilots were trained in their use. The

equipment cost money, and airline officials could forecast little payback to justify the investment. As a result, flying in the weather on existing rudimentary aircraft instruments (blind flying) was unpopular (as well as deadly).

8. Perhaps the most important of Brown's findings was that the system lacked order. It was a tangled, hodgepodge system of this and that, some air carriers going in one philosophical direction and other carriers going in the opposite direction. Except for the airmail contracts, no common glue bound together all of the airlines.

Because of these factors, the current air carriers were not interested in larger aircraft equipped with more than one engine or aircraft designed for more speed or equipped with devices that enhanced safety. Well enough was good enough.

To Hoover's ordered engineer's mind, and Brown's loathing of chaos, the current state of the industry was unthinkably unacceptable if the industry was to move forward into its conceived destiny: a true passenger-carrying air transportation industry. Out of Brown's analysis and the commitment of each man came what has been termed the Hoover-Brown Philosophy of Air Transportation.

The Hoover-Brown Philosophy

Several factors dominated the Hoover-Brown philosophy:

1. Both men disliked open competition. Brown said,

If we throw these matters open to competitive bidding you will find promoters coming in and wanting to bid off the contract, having no knowledge of the costs . . . of the factors of obsolescence . . . of bad luck . . . [or the] usual losses that are not directly incident to the operations. They will come in and bid a price that will be lower than the experienced man who has had his fingers burned . . . and we will be doing the most unbusinesslike thing of throwing away an invaluable industry.[3]

Rather than unbridled competition, Brown and Hoover favored a regulated competition: based on performance instead of promises, capital instead of investment potential, and airplanes instead of air heads.

2. They disliked a monopoly, and one was looming in the north. Since United Air Transport had acquired con-

trolling interest in National Air Transport, United now controlled the only coast-to-coast route, the Columbia route. The Columbia route stretched from New York to San Francisco by way of Chicago. To Brown, United must have looked like a shark that was poised to eat the minnows such as Western Air Express, American Airways, and the fifty or so others.

3. They wanted three things: stability, efficiency, and growth. Brown wanted to avoid the government's mistakes made earlier with the railroad industry, the problems associated with the short-line railroads that were small lines that began nowhere and ended nowhere.[4] These smaller rail lines with their bonded indebtedness, frequent change of ownership, and failure rates had sucked millions of dollars from American taxpayers. America's investment in air transportation thus far seemed inconsequential by comparison. Brown felt that the airline industry was beginning to move into these dangerous patterns. American Airways, for example, had such a chaotic route system that it was already being described as an air carrier that went from nowhere to nowhere. This was the antithesis that Brown was seeking to avoid. He wanted an articulated system of air carriers that could swiftly achieve the goals of stability, efficiency, and growth. He wanted to see strong airline companies but with regulated competition.

The Airmail Act of 1930

Brown had formed his conclusions and had a definite plan in mind. He decided there should be three transcontinental route structures plus an Atlantic and a Pacific north-south coastal system.[5] He also wanted each of those systems flown by a single carrier. Mail subsidies could provide dependable service over long, continuous routes. To achieve his objectives, Brown thought it was necessary to change the law regarding airmail and payments. What resulted was the Airmail Act of 1930, called the McNary-Watres Act. (Technically, the legislation was the Third Amendment to the Air Mail Act of 1925.) The main provisions of the act were as follows:

1. The bill gave the postmaster general almost dictatorial powers over airmail contracts and routes. In fact, the original language did provide those powers by dispensing with competitive bidding altogether. This left the selection entirely to the discretion of the postmaster

general. However, Brown made a mistake: he failed to consult with Rep. Clyde Kelly, who was known as the congressional father of airmail. Kelly took his revenge and insisted that competitive bidding language be restored to the bill. Brown backed off. The wording of the bill instead contained the phrase "the lowest *responsible* bidder, who has owned and operated an air transportation service on a fixed daily schedule over a distance of not less than two hundred and fifty miles and for a period of not less than six months prior to the advertisement of the bids."[6] This was not the wording that Kelly intended, and the potential power in the new wording slipped past him. On balance, Brown had his victory. The amended wording was all the power that Brown needed to accomplish his goals; it effectively cut out the little guy and almost closed the door to pioneer carriers.

Another provision of the bill gave the postmaster general the authority to extend or curtail routes. This judgment was made to benefit the public.

Both provisions together gave the postmaster general economic control over the airlines. One attribute of a free-market system of economics is to allow a business to make the most basic of business decisions: where to sell the product. However, in the case of fledgling airlines, this decision was to be made for them by the postmaster general. The economic regulation of the airlines begun in 1925 was intensified by the McNary-Watres Act in 1930. It was modified several times over the next five decades, and it endured until 1978, when the epochal Airline Deregulation Bill was passed into law, throwing the unprepared air carriers into a brand-new economic world, that of a free-market economy. And what a ride it was to be. However, now it was 1930, and Brown was struggling to get a handle on the industry.

2. The McNary-Watres Act also changed the method of payment from a weight-mileage basis to a payment of space made available. The maximum rate would be $1.25 per mile, to be paid whether or not the space was filled. This encouraged the use of larger airplanes and the carriage of passengers; any passenger carried to fill the space unfilled by mail would be pure gravy.

3. The act also gave the post office the authority to pay extra for multiengine aircraft and air carriers using the latest technology in aircraft instrumentation and navigational aids.

The sum of these provisions was to encourage air carriers to buy larger, safer aircraft capable of carrying passengers. As was Brown's plan, these provisions also favored the larger companies.

The So-Called Spoils Conferences

Herbert Hoover signed the McNary-Watres Act into law in April 1930. Brown wasted no time in putting his plan into action. He called for a meeting in Washington on 19 May 1930. In attendance were representatives from sixteen airlines or holding companies, including United Air Transport, Transcontinental Air Transport, Western Air Express, American Airways, Northwest Airways, and Eastern Air Transport. These meetings were not held in secret, but invitations to attend were given to an elite few who represented large corporations. Naturally, these invitations did not say, "You are cordially invited to attend Postmaster General Brown's spoils conferences." That unfortunate moniker was to be attached later by a different group of political leaders. Brown's goal in the conferences was to create three intercontinental routes. The first was to be the northern route running from New York to San Francisco via Chicago. This route was already in existence, operated by a single carrier, the United conglomerate.

The second route was to be the central route from New York to Los Angeles via Pittsburgh and St. Louis. To achieve his goals on this route, Brown suggested a merger between Transcontinental Air Transport and Western Air Express. Harris M. "Pop" Hanshue, president of Western Air Express, did not warm to the idea of a merger and did not hesitate to express his views. However, Brown made it abundantly clear to Hanshue that he could either endorse the merger or be squeezed out of the airmail picture entirely. Hanshue grudgingly capitulated, and Transcontinental and Western Air (TWA) was born—a shotgun marriage to be sure, but a marriage nevertheless. TWA was awarded the central route (see fig. 8.2).

The third route, the southern route, did not proceed quite so smoothly. Brown had wanted to award the southern route to the newly formed American Airways, but American did not meet the requirements of the McNary-Watres Act. The act required that the carrier have at least six months experience flying a route of at least 250 miles. Another problem was the wording that Brown had inserted in the bid specifications requiring that potential bidders must have had at least six months experience flying at night. Clearly, this requirement was an attempt by Brown to shoulder out the smaller carriers. He inserted this requirement as part of his interpretation of the grant of authority under the McNary-Watres Act. Brown concluded that he had the authority to create such regulations as necessary to carry out the provision

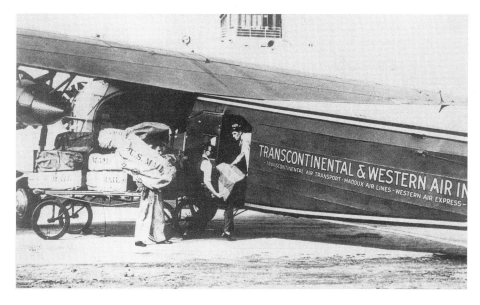

Fig. 8.2. A Transcontinental and Western Air (TWA) Ford trimotor loading mail. Courtesy of TWA.

of the act that required him to determine those "responsible" bidders.

Yet another problem that plagued Brown in bringing the southern route under control was Oklahoma oil man Erle Haliburton. Haliburton was operating an airline radiating from Tulsa to Kansas City, St. Louis, Dallas and Fort Worth. This airline was called Southwest Air Fast Express (SAFE) and popularly known as SAFEway. Using a fleet of Ford Trimotors, Haliburton was carrying many satisfied passengers, but he was not turning a profit. To make a profit, Haliburton felt he needed a small airmail contract. He bid on a transcontinental route from New York to Los Angeles via Salt Lake City at a rate that represented about one-third of the cheapest rate currently being paid. Brown was horrified; this was precisely what he did not want. Brown turned Haliburton down because he did not meet the night provision of the bid requirement. However, Haliburton was not one to roll over and die. He thoroughly researched the McNary-Watres Act and could find no provision requiring night flying. Several important people supported Haliburton's view, including Representative Kelly, who felt that Brown's action was violating the law. Nevertheless, Brown persisted. He suggested to United that they buy out Haliburton, but they refused. One of Brown's representatives then holed up in a Washington hotel room and worked out a deal whereby American would buy out Haliburton for $1.4 million. The actual worth of SAFEway was about $800,000.[7]

The deal also involved TWA, which at this point in the negotiations had not yet been awarded the central route. American was going to get the money from TWA to pay off Haliburton under the assumption that each got the route they wanted. TWA agreed to pay American $284,500 for an interest in a hangar and some property in Tulsa, plus an additional $1,115,000 for 20,000 shares of Western Air Express stock held by American. The total was $1.4 million. There were other pieces to the puzzle as well.

American Airways bought out Standard Airlines from Western Air Express after Brown had extended Standard's route system as far east as Dallas. Brown ac-

Fig. 8.3. Stinson Trimotor, operated by American Airways. By permission of the National Air and Space Museum, Smithsonian Institution, ©1999 Smithsonian Institution.

complished this under his authority to "extend routes." American also bought out Delta, which had the Atlanta to Dallas route. Brown had boldly thrown all of the puzzle pieces into the air, and they had fallen to the table in precisely the right places. American was granted its coveted southern transcontinental route on 16 September 1930, and Brown had what he wanted: three transcontinental routes operated by large, well-financed air carriers, each completely independent of the other (see fig. 8.3).

Brown achieved his and Hoover's visions. In 1929, U.S. domestic airlines carried 160,000 passengers. By 1932, the number had zoomed to 474,000. Growth was strong, aircraft were becoming more reliable, and aircraft manufacturers were on the verge of producing some remarkable aircraft such as the Boeing 247 and the Douglas DC-3. Brown continued to manage the empire to make sure that competition was controlled and that monopolistic tendencies were thwarted. For example, United attempted to take over Eastern Air Transport in the same way that it had gained control of National Air Transport. United did this by carefully buying up the stock to gain a controlling interest. When Brown caught wind of it, he put his foot down and forced United to withdraw from its foray.

The Hoover administration was proud of what it had done to create an effective airmail and airline passenger service. However, Brown was not well liked. He had made many enemies, and the price he paid to create the air carrier system was to be realized. However, Brown must be given his due:

Walter F. Brown . . . changed the airline map from a sporadic collection of mainly unconnected networks into a set of routes which "went from somewhere to somewhere." The fact that he achieved this by somewhat dubious means does not detract from the immensity of the task or the comprehensiveness of the result. . . . Postmaster General Brown, in effect, created the necessary environment to stimulate the development of a new breed of aircraft. He went into office with a dream of an airline network to surpass the world. When he left office, this had been achieved, handsomely. More than this, the airlines were about to be equipped with aircraft which outflew the rest of the world's best; and the United States manufacturing industry has never faltered or looked back since.[8]

Roosevelt Elected

In the national elections of 1932, the Hoover administration and many Republicans in Congress, unable to find even a patchwork solution to stop the hemorrhaging American economy, were swept from office in a Democratic landslide. The Depression showed no signs of lessening. Already, the gross national product had dropped 45 percent (from $103 billion to $58 billion), the unemployment rate went from 3.2 percent in 1929 to 23.6 percent in 1932, and for those who were employed, the average annual wage went from $1,356 in 1929 to $754 in 1932. Other than the unemployment rate, about the only things that were climbing were the suicide rates and, interestingly enough, airline growth.

The airline industry seemed Depression-proof. Passenger miles flown went from approximately 43,000,000 in 1929 to 85,125,000 in 1930 and 127,433,000 in 1932. Compared with 1929, the number of passengers carried in 1932 had tripled, airmail had doubled, and the number of employees hired by the air carriers had increased by more than 250 percent.

Much of the profitability of the air carriers came from airmail revenues, about $56 million between 1931 and 1933. Against expenses of about $22 million, the airlines made a profit of about $34 million on airmail subsidies alone. The post office paid out $56 million and brought in revenues amounting to about $18 million and had expenses of about $8 million. This means that the post office paid subsidies of $46 million above its revenue minus expenses. Where did the money come from? It came from the pockets of the Depression-ridden taxpayers, of course.[9]

To the man on the street, air transportation was viewed as a luxury, reserved for what was left of the affluent but financed by the working class. The situation was ripe for scandal, and it was not long in coming.

Luddington, Lewis, and Scandal

The Hoover administration had convened several panels to investigate the Machiavellian maneuvering of Brown, but nothing of a recriminating nature was revealed. A particular episode, however, came to the attention of a young newspaper reporter for the Hearst newspaper chain, Fulton Lewis. He learned that the Luddington Line, an aggressive passenger air carrier out of Philadelphia with routes linking New York, Philadelphia, and Washington, D.C., had bid 25 cents per mile to carry the mail on this route. With an innovative shuttle that left New York every hour for Philadelphia and Washington, Luddington was attracting many passengers. Brown, however, awarded the mail contract to Eastern Air Transport for 89 cents per mile. The award of this contract allowed the larger Eastern eventually to squeeze Luddington out of the market and to buy the airline.

Smelling a rat, Lewis dug into post office records and found a long list of similar transgressions. Lewis completed his investigation and sent his report to William Randolph Hearst, who sat on it. Chagrined over Hearst's reluctance to publish the report, Lewis turned the information over to an influential someone on Capitol Hill. As a result, Sen. Hugo L. Black was appointed to head an investigation of the airmail situation.

Despite their prosperity, many in the air carrier industry were not fond of Brown and his tactics. Roosevelt and the New Deal Democrats were welcomed by the industry. Paul Henderson of United, for example, was so furious with Brown for extending Northwest's routes into those being flown by United that he volunteered to give Black all that he knew about Brown's actions.

With the Black investigation under way, Roosevelt called for his own investigation conducted by his postmaster general, James A. Farley. Brown, it was discovered, had taken many files with him when he left office, but when contacted, he voluntarily turned the files over to Farley.[10] Farley appointed Karl Crowley, the post office solicitor, to research the files. Crowley worked seven days a week, night and day, to get to the bottom of the situation. Meanwhile, during a lunch meeting with President Roosevelt on 26 January 1934, Senator Black strongly suggested that Roosevelt cancel all airmail contracts.[11] On 7 February, Crowley finished his investigation and briefed Farley on his findings, which were contained in a 100-page report. Crowley concluded that Brown had granted airmail contract route extensions that were probably illegal under the McNary-Watres Act. Airmail carriers had acted in collusion to restrict competitive bidding. Postmaster General Farley then picked up the telephone, called Roosevelt, and made an appointment to brief him the following day.

For the next 48 hours, the Roosevelt administration grappled with the airmail problem. Crowley's report was persuasive, particularly in light of what Black had recommended about a week earlier.[12] Everyone, it seemed, was for immediate contract cancellation. However, the problem was, what then were they to do? Someone suggested that the Army could fly the mail. Roosevelt liked the idea and called in Maj. Gen. Benjamin G. Foulois, head of the Army Air Corps. Roosevelt wanted to get assurances from Foulois that the Air Corps was up to the task.

Foulois was not prepared for the meeting; he thought that Roosevelt had called him in to get his opinion on the developing airmail crisis. Like a thunderbolt from the sky, Roosevelt asked Foulois if the Army could carry the mail if he canceled the airmail contracts. Foulois, knowing that he needed to thrust the needs of the punily equipped Air Corps before the public eye to gain support for more funding, said he could do it. When asked how long it would take to get ready, Foulois estimated a week to ten days.

That was all the assurance that Roosevelt needed. He immediately signed the executive order canceling all airmail contracts. The order affected forty route certificates held by nine carriers. Cancellation went into effect at midnight on 19 February 1934.[13]

When Foulois returned to his office, Gen. Douglas MacArthur, the Army chief of staff, angry that Foulois had not consulted with him, jumped down his throat and told him that he was on his own.

The Army Flies the Mail

The Army was pitifully equipped to fly the airmail and did not have time to prepare for the arduous tasks. Also, that winter was one of the worst in memory. Whereas the air carriers had highly experienced pilots, most of whom had many thousands of flight hours and experience in instrument flying, the average Army pilot had been an active pilot for less than two years and had only a few hundred hours with little or no flight time using electronic navigational equipment and aircraft flight instruments. Despite this fact, Foulois announced that the Air Corps pilots had a great deal of experience in flying at night, in fog, in bad weather, and under other difficult conditions.

When the Air Corps studied the problem more deeply, it found that its open cockpit airplanes could only carry one-sixth of the average airmail load. The Army was attempting to cover 27,000 route miles with some 200 officers and 324 enlisted men, a task that had kept some 7,000 air carrier pilots and technicians busy. To do this, it had 148 combat aircraft, mostly open cockpit biplanes and a few Martin B-10 bomber aircraft. All were crudely equipped by airline standards. The Army would have to scale back its efforts to cover only twelve routes (16,000 route miles), flying only those routes that linked cities that had Federal Reserve Banks (see fig. 8.4).

In the ten days during which the Air Corps scrambled to set up routes, way stations, and other logistical activities, three pilots were killed while practicing for airmail routes. Within a week, two more crashes claimed two lives. The next day an aircraft ferrying a group of Army airmail pilots crashed, killing one of the pilots. The Roosevelt administration, already criticized soundly for its decision to cancel the airmail contracts, now was criticized even more heavily. Statements were appearing in the national press such as "legalized murder," "the cancellation of the airmail contracts is being written in the blood of young army aviators," and "stop the slaughter."[14]

The Roosevelt administration was blasted for the deaths of the Army flyers and was stung in the press. Roosevelt called Generals MacArthur and Foulois into the White House and gave them ten minutes of the severest tongue lashing on record. Roosevelt began by asking Foulois, "General, when are these airmail killings going to stop?"[15] The one-way conversation went downhill from there. Foulois returned to his headquarters and ordered a ten-day stand-down during which time the Army downscaled its efforts.

The Airmail Act of 1934

Roosevelt was working on a permanent solution to the problem, which included two conditions: (1) Companies having any affiliation with aircraft or aircraft part manufacturers, or other air carrier companies flying competitive routes were barred from bidding on airmail contracts, and (2) no contract would be made with any companies whose officers were party to obtaining former contracts under circumstances that were clearly contrary to good faith and public policy, which is to say, all spoils conference participants were to be banned from bidding.[16] This second provision was clearly punitive. As Congress was debating this bill, another Army pilot was killed on an airmail flight. This brought the total to twelve. Roosevelt realized that he had made a significant error in judgment by canceling the airmail contracts so quickly. Now he could not wait for congressional action. He called Farley into his office to work on an interim solution.

Fig. 8.4. A Martin B-10 bomber flies the mail. Most of the U.S. Army's aircraft put into service were far cruder than the Martin B-10. Courtesy of the Fred Roos Collection.

Late in March 1934, the post office advertised for bids on ninety-day contracts. However, none of the companies whose contracts had been canceled for fraud or collusion could bid. The air carriers found a clever way around this obstacle. They simply changed their corporate names. American Airways became American Airlines, United Airlines became United Airlines, Inc., Eastern Air Transport became Eastern Air Lines, and Northwest Airways became Northwest Airlines.[17] Like an amoeba, TWA split into two brand-new airlines, TWA, Inc. and WAE, Inc., and bid separately for the routes it had flown previously. Later, the old TWA and the new TWA merged and reincorporated under its old name, Transcontinental and Western Air.[18]

Later in 1934 when the Black-McKellar Act was passed, the temporary airmail contracts were made permanent, or in the actual language used, they were "continued in effect for an indefinite period." The act also followed Roosevelt's two recommendations with some minor alterations. This forced the breakup of the large conglomerates like United. United Airlines Inc. was forced to separate itself from Boeing and Pratt and Whitney (aircraft manufacturer and engine manufacturer, respectively).

Careers were crushed under the Roosevelt New Deal. Foulois, having taken a calculated risk and lost, came under such heavy criticism from the press, Congress, and others that he resigned in 1935. William Boeing, so humiliated from his drubbing at the foot of Hugo Black, took early retirement.[19] Paul Henderson of United was let go because he had attended the spoils conference. A score of other important airline officials were also released as a result of the so-called collusion relating to the spoils conferences and the lack of competitive bidding. With Postmaster General Farley there to take the hit, Roosevelt dodged the golden BB and emerged mostly unscathed.

Although Foulois lost personally, he did achieve his goal of bringing the Air Corps to the public's attention in the hope of gaining funding for more and better equipment. Congress became much more attentive and responsive to Air Corps needs and more generous with the budget dollar.

Also, putting the Air Corps losses in perspective is important. During a fifteen-week period while carrying the mail in 1934, the Air Corps lost twelve pilots. By comparison, during a ten-week period in 1933, the Air Corps lost sixteen pilots during routine combat training. Neither statistic is a deed for which this country can demonstrate pride, for it shows how little we cared for either the safety or the preparedness of service airmen in those somewhat early days of our military aviation history.

The Boeing 247 and the DC-1

In February 1933, Boeing flew its first B-247, hailed as the first modern airliner (shown in fig. 8.5). The aircraft was an all-metal, twin-engine aircraft powered by 525-horsepower Wasp engines, and it had retractable landing gear. The aircraft was based on its military predecessor, the B-9, which had lost in competition for a military bomber. The aircraft was of rugged construction and could carry ten passengers in relative comfort. Passengers could stand upright in the cabin of the aircraft. One feature that was annoying to passengers was the wing carry-through spar, which created a hump in the aisle floor that the passengers had to step (or more likely trip) over. By the end of June, United had placed these aircraft in service and had quickly broken the coast-to-coast speed record by 7 hours held by TWA in their Ford Trimotors. By the fall, United was operating ten daily coast-to-coast trips, whereas American and TWA were operating only one each. United ordered sixty of the aircraft, which effectively tied up Boeing's production effort. Jack Frye of TWA (shown in fig. 8.6) would have liked to order some 247s; however, the corporate relationship between United and Boeing was such that a competing airline like TWA did not stand a chance of getting the airplane.

Undaunted, Frye drafted a letter listing the specifications for a new airliner and cast it to the potential builders. His specifications called for a three-engine, all-metal aircraft capable of carrying twelve passengers in relative comfort, and a cruise speed of 146 mph. It also had to have a range of more than 1,000 miles and have a cruise ceiling of at least 21,000 feet.

Donald Douglas and his team of engineers decided to enter the competition. They headed for New York for a meeting with Frye and other TWA officials, including adviser Charles Lindbergh. Douglas was convinced that he could build a two-engine aircraft that would meet all of Frye's specifications. Lindbergh then added some requirements: the aircraft had to be able to take off fully loaded on one engine from any of TWA's operating loca-

Fig. 8.5. A Boeing 247 operated by United Airlines at Chicago's
Midway Airport. Courtesy of United Airlines.

Fig. 8.6. TWA president Jack Frye. Courtesy of TWA.

Fig. 8.7. The Douglas DC-1 built to TWA specifications. Courtesy of TWA.

tions, and it had to be able to maintain level flight on one engine over the highest mountains along any of TWA's routes. Douglas accepted the challenge and received the order. Eleven months later on 1 July 1933, the DC-1 made its maiden flight (see fig. 8.7). The airplane met all of Frye's expectations.

The DC-1 was powered by two Pratt and Whitney engines with very clean aerodynamics. Like the B-247, it was a low-wing aircraft with retractable landing gear. However, the fuselage sat on top of the wing so that the cabin did not have that annoying B-247 hump. TWA promptly ordered twenty-five DC-2 aircraft, a stretched version of the DC-1 that increased the passenger-carrying capacity from twelve to fourteen.

On the eve of the airmail contract route cancellations following the spoils investigations, Frye made a defiant gesture; on the night of 18 February 1934, he and Eddie Rickenbacker flew the DC-1 from Los Angeles to Newark in the record-breaking time of 13 hours and 4 minutes.

Other airlines such as Eastern and American began to order the DC-2 aircraft, and soon Douglas was awash in orders. These aircraft were superior to the B-247, even the modified version. Then American Airlines changed the formula.

In late 1934, American approached Douglas with the idea of expanding the DC-2 to make it into a "sleeper"

aircraft. Douglas was reluctant at first, fearing that the market for the DST (Douglas Sleeper Transport) was slim and too risky to commit much of the company's money. Responding to influence from American, Douglas stretched the DC-2 to accommodate fourteen berths. In so doing, Douglas created an aircraft that used the same cabin area not for berths but for seats, seven more than the DC-2, a total of twenty-one; the aircraft was the DC-3 (see fig. 8.8).

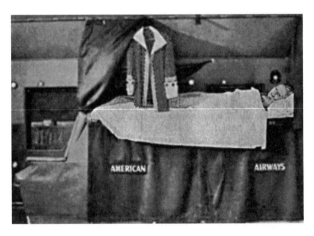

Fig. 8.8. Typical berth in the Douglas Sleeper Transport (DST), which became the DC-3. *Scientific American,* August 1934.

Fig. 8.9. DC-3s of United Airlines. Courtesy of United Airlines.

The DC-3 was an incredible leap in operating efficiency over the DC-2. For only a 10 percent increase in cost, the DC-3 increased the payload by 50 percent over the DC-2. Now it was possible for air carriers to make a profit carrying passengers without the need for an airmail contract. Soon most airlines were flying the DC-3. Even United abandoned its B-247 for the more efficient DC-3 early in 1937. It is interesting that at the beginning of World War II, 80 percent of the aircraft operated by domestic airlines were DC-3s (see fig. 8.9).

This adds an interesting twist to the validity of the Brown approach to reshaping the airline industry. Before the development of the DC1-2-3 and principally the DC-3, the large air carriers tended to buy those aircraft that were a part of the aviation conglomerate. United purchased Boeings, TWA bought Fokkers, and Eastern and American bought Curtiss aircraft. Brown had not discouraged this kind of activity.

Douglas was an independent aircraft manufacturer with no previous attachment to any air carrier. It was through competition that the DC-3 emerged. If Brown's philosophy had endured, would the world have seen the DC-3 at all, or would his philosophy have at least slowed down such development?

This by no means discredits Brown for all of the good things that happened because of his and Hoover's actions, which led to the development of larger, safer multiengine aircraft, such as the Boeing 247 and the DC-3. But what it does call into question is his and Hoover's unwillingness to let the forces of a free economy shape the air carrier industry after government incentives had been provided.

Notes

1. Komons, *Bonfires to Beacons*, 192–94.
2. Frederick, *Commercial Air Transportation*, 72.
3. Komons, 200–203.
4. Cleveland, "Airmail," 290–91.
5. Cleveland, 291.
6. Komons, 201.
7. Howard, "Pie in the Sky," 234.
8. Davies, *Airlines of the United States since 1914*, 138–45.
9. Elmer Davis, "A Blow at the Foundations," 634, 635.
10. "Air-Mail Subsidies under Fire," 6.
11. Davies, 143.
12. Davies, 145.
13. "Air-Mail Subsidies under Fire," 6.
14. "Air-Mail Subsidies under Fire," 7.
15. Davies, 145.

16. Komons, 201–3; Davies, 143–45.
17. Davies, 145.
18. Serling, *Howard Hughes Airline*, 46.
19. Davies, 141.

References

"Air-Mail in Politics." *Literary Digest,* 10 March 1934, 7.

"Air-Mail Subsidies under Fire." *Literary Digest,* 17 February 1934, 6–7.

"American Air Travel Quadrupled." *Literary Digest,* 20 December 1930, 16.

"The Army Carries the Air-Mail." *Literary Digest,* 24 February 1934, 117–18.

"Boeing Testifies at Senate Air Mail Investigation." *New York Times,* 7 February 1934.

Brown, Carl A. *A History of Aviation.* 2d ed. Daytona Beach: Embry-Riddle Aeronautical University Press, 1980.

Cleveland, R. M. "Airmail." *Scientific American,* June 1934, 290–91.

Davies, R. E. G. *Airlines of the United States since 1914.* London: G. P. Putnam, 1972.

Davis, Elmer. "A Blow at the Foundations: Roosevelt and His Air Mail Policy." *Harper's Monthly,* May 1934, 633–40.

Davis, Sidney F. *Delta Airlines.* Atlanta: Peachtree, 1988.

Davis, W. Jefferson. "Clearing the Air for Commerce." *Annals of the American Academy of Political and Social Science* 131 (May 1927): 141–50.

Ernst and Ernst. "Groupings in the Aviation Industry." *Scientific American,* July 1929, 58.

Frederick, John H. *Commercial Air Transportation.* Homewood, Ill.: Richard D. Irwin, 1961.

Glover, Irving W. "The Air Mail." *Annals of the American Academy of Political and Social Science* 131 (May 1927): 43–48.

Gunston, Bill, ed. *Chronicle of Aviation.* Paris: Jacques Legrand, 1992.

Howard, K. "Pie in the Sky: The Air Mail Controversy Down to Date." *New Republic,* 11 April 1934, 232–35.

Kane, Robert M., and Allan D. Vose. *Air Transportation.* Dubuque: Kendall/Hunt, 1982.

Klemin, Alexander. "American Passenger Air Transport." *Scientific American,* October 1929, 514–17.

Komons, Nick A. *Bonfires to Beacons.* Washington: Smithsonian Institution Press, 1989.

Lewis, W. David, and William Trimble. *The Airway to Everywhere.* Pittsburgh: University of Pittsburgh Press, 1988.

Lipsner, Benjamin B. *The Airmail, Jennies to Jets.* Chicago: Wilcox and Follett, 1951.

MacCracken, William P., Jr. "Air Regulations." *Annals of the American Academy of Political and Social Science* 131 (May 1927): 118–23.

"Powerful Groups in Battle for Air Route Supremacy." *Business Week,* 23 April 1930, 14.

"Praise from Sir Hubert (Hugo Black)." *New Republic,* 25 April 1934, 311.

Rentschler, Frederick B. "Is Aviation Over Extended?" *Magazine of Business* 56 (July 1929): 31–38.

"Roosevelt and the Power Problem." *New Republic,* 11 April 1934, 235–37.

Serling, Robert J. *Howard Hughes Airline.* New York: St. Martin's/Marek, 1983.

———. *Legend and Legacy.* New York: St. Martin's Press, 1992.

Shamburger, Page. *Tracks Across the Sky: The Story of the Pioneers of the U.S. Air Mail.* Philadelphia: J. B. Lippincott, 1964.

Smith, Dean C. *By the Seat of My Pants.* Boston: Little, Brown, 1961.

Solberg, Carl. *Conquest of the Skies.* Boston: Little, Brown, 1979.

"The Week (Airmail)." *New Republic,* 7 March 1934, 85.

Whitehouse, Arch. *The Sky's the Limit.* New York: Macmillan, 1971.

"William Edward Boeing." *Scientific American,* August 1934, 95.

World War II

Thomas J. Connolly

BEFORE WORLD WAR II, a number of long-range military visionaries began to think of building large aircraft for the purpose of implementing a new theory of strategic bombing. Their vision stimulated the investment and creative technology necessary for the development of transport category aircraft after World War II. These men included Sir Hugh Trenchard of Great Britain; Giulio Douhet of Italy; and William "Bull" Halsey, Chester Nimitz, and Billy Mitchell of the United States.[1]

Giulio Douhet was the first to develop the idea. As early as 1909, even though he had seen only three airplanes and had never actually flown himself, he had written two books on the subject of strategic bombing.

> To us who have until now been inexorably bound to the surface of the earth, it must seem strange that the sky, too, is to become another battlefield no less important than the battlefields on land and sea.
>
> Today we are fully aware of the importance of having command of the seas; soon command of the air will be equally important. . . . The army and navy must recognize in the air force the birth of a third brother—younger but nonetheless important in the great military family.[2]

In 1911, Italy became the first nation to effectively use the airplane as a weapon of war in an invasion of Tripoli (now Libya). Douhet had already initiated plans to build a three-engine, 300-horsepower bomber. In 1921, he published his book, *Command of the Air*, in which he developed the theme that airpower would change warfare and the world.

In 1912, Maj. Hugh Montague Trenchard (fig. 9.1) was thirty-nine years old and in what was reported to be a dead-end career in the British army. Like Douhet, he had never been in an airplane, but he could see the future, and he volunteered for flight training at the newly established Sopwith Flying School near London. There he logged a total of 64 minutes before receiving Pilot Certificate no. 270, and although he apparently was not a particularly good pilot, he was an experienced army officer and was consequently appointed as the adjutant for the new Central Flying School. As adjutant he was responsible for awarding wings to those who successfully completed the program, and so, soon after taking command, he declared himself qualified and proceeded to pin on his wings as an army aviator. In 1920, while serving as the Royal Flying Corps chief of staff, he had an opportunity to prove his theory on the effectiveness of airpower and ordered a dozen aircraft to attack the supporters of Mohammed Abdullah Hasan, the mullah of Somaliland. The British had been fighting Hasan's supporters for over twenty years without success, and Trenchard was able to end the conflict in three weeks. He had demonstrated to one and all that airpower was the way of the future.[3]

Without a doubt, the one person who, more than anyone else, saw the full potential of the airplane was Brig. Gen. Billy Mitchell (fig. 9.2). During World War I, control of the U.S. Army's planes was given to the Signal Corps, Mitchell's branch of the service. He became fascinated with the heavier-than-air vehicles and their

Fig. 9.1. Hugh M. "Boom" Trenchard, known as the Father of the Royal Air Force. By permission of the National Air and Space Museum, Smithsonian Institution, ©1999 Smithsonian Institution.

Fig. 9.2. Billy Mitchell. By permission of the National Air and Space Museum, Smithsonian Institution, ©1999 Smithsonian Institution.

military possibilities. He learned to fly in 1916 and was sent to Europe as an observer before the United States declared war in April 1917. While in Europe, he took the initiative and began to organize an American expeditionary air force. When General Pershing came to Paris in 1917 to take command of the American forces, Mitchell joined his staff.

Mitchell steadily rose through the ranks as the war progressed, finally commanding the air units of the First Army Group.

In September 1918, Mitchell launched an attack with 1,481 French and American planes during the Battle of the St. Mihiel salient, the greatest air assault of the war. He was planning strategic bombardment of Germany and large-scale use of paratroopers—extremely radical concepts for the day—but the Armistice was declared before he could try out his theories.

He was one of the first to talk about all-metal bombers, transport category aircraft for moving large numbers of soldiers, and government support for private aviation to provide a pool of qualified pilots in case of war. He was also convinced that the strategic bombing capability of the airplane would prove to be the decisive element in future military conflicts, and he never missed an opportunity to make his argument. In 1919, he organized a coast-to-coast air race to demonstrate the potential of long-distance flight, which led to the founding of a national system of airways and airports. To further prove his point, in 1921 he conducted an aerial bombing demonstration and sank the German battleship *Ostfriesland* (fig. 9.3).

The *Ostfriesland* was captured from the Germans during World War I and was considered by everyone to be one of the greatest warships afloat. At that time, the battleship was the first line of defense and was considered to be invulnerable to anything but another battleship. To demonstrate the potential of the aircraft as a military weapon capable of sinking a battleship, Mitchell's pilots

Fig. 9.3. Mitchell's Army bombing trials, 1921. The captured German warship, the *Ostfriesland,* rolls over after being bombed by Mitchell's planes. By permission of the National Air and Space Museum, Smithsonian Institution, ©1999 Smithsonian Institution.

Fig. 9.4. A Martin MB-2. Courtesy of the Fred Roos Collection.

flew the MB-2, a twin-engine aircraft built by the Martin Aircraft Company and equipped with a specially developed new gyro stabilized artificial horizon developed by the Sperry Aircraft Company (fig. 9.4). Mitchell's pilots bombed and sank the *Ostfriesland*. This sinking using airpower, which everyone said could not be done, took 21 minutes in front of observers from around the world, including those from Italy and Japan. Many in the United States, however, were not willing to listen to Mitchell's predictions. In 1925, he ignored a direct order to quit his forceful lobbying for the aircraft as a weapon of war and was court-martialed for insubordination and forced to resign. The reports of his demonstrations of airpower along with his many predictions were studied around the world. His contributions were officially recognized at the conclusion of World War II, and he was posthumously awarded the Medal of Honor in 1946.[4]

The theory of superior airpower spread, and in the 1930s technology finally caught up with the idea. The application of the theory was only waiting for a time and a place. Nowhere was the growth of airpower more rapid than in Japan, and the Japanese set out to prove the concept against the Russians and later the Chinese.

While the Japanese were applying the concept of strategic bombing in China, the Italians were developing their concept of air-to-ground tactics in Ethiopia. The Italian military took advantage of weak military resistance to perfect their tactics and to train their pilots. In 1936, the Italians were able to apply what they had learned when they joined up with Germany to fight with Gen. Francisco Franco in the Spanish civil war. The Germans used the Junkers JU-52 transport to airlift thousands of rebels and materiel, including artillery and heavy machine guns, into Spain in an exercise known as Operation Magic Fire (fig. 9.5). They then provided the Heinkel HE-51 and the Fiat CR-32 fighters, which gave the rebels the edge until the Russians came to the aid of the government with their Politkarpov I-15 and the I-16 Mukha (Fly), which proved to be the superior fighters in the early stages of the war (see figs. 9.6–9.8).[5]

Probably the most devastating demonstration of airpower at that time was carried out against the rebels in 1938 at the Battle of Guadalajara. Franco brought together a force of over 30,000 troops to march on the city of Guadalajara, which would have opened the way to Madrid. When the attack became stalled in bad weather, the Soviet air force caught them strung out on the highway in a battle that served to convince both sides that airpower was best employed for tactical support of ground operations. American pilot Eugene Finick was flying with the Russians in that attack, and he wrote the following description of the battle:

Fig. 9.5. A Bristol Blenheim bomber flies over the burned remains of a Junkers JU-52/3m transport. By permission of the National Air and Space Museum, Smithsonian Institution, ©1999 Smithsonian Institution.

Fig. 9.6. View of a Heinkel HE-51A on the ground. Although the aircraft is military, a civil code D-IQEE is on the fuselage. By permission of the National Air and Space Museum, Smithsonian Institution, ©1999 Smithsonian Institution.

Fig. 9.7. Left side view of a Fiat CR-32 on the ground. By permission of the National Air and Space Museum, Smithsonian Institution, ©1999 Smithsonian Institution.

Fig. 9.8. Politkarpov I-15. By permission of the National Air and Space Museum, Smithsonian Institution, ©1999 Smithsonian Institution.

We tore the rolling, mechanized offensive into ribbons. You looked down on that dark, endless column and it seemed as if they'd keep going from sheer physical weight. We came over, squadrons of fifteen in close formation. We dumped every bomb we had on the tanks in front and the road—tons of explosives. We dropped them flying low, so there was no mistake about where they'd hit. In two minutes time the tanks and the road were a shambles. The tanks were blown up, overturned, piled up in knots.[6]

The Mukha resembled the U.S. Boeing P-26 (fig. 9.9) and was the most advanced of the Russian fighters. The German Luftwaffe (air force) introduced its new Messerschmitt ME-109C in 1937 and the ME-109D, immediate forerunner of the ME-109E, and would all but rule the Spanish skies from that point on (figs. 9.10–9.12).

From their experience in the Spanish civil war, the Germans perfected the Stuka dive-bomber for daylight unescorted bombing raids, and the pilots were able to perfect their skills and tactics (see fig. 9.13). These lessons led to the Luftwaffe's devastating support for ground operations against Poland and the Netherlands in the early days of World War II. The concept of aerial

Fig. 9.9. Boeing P-26 Peashooter. Courtesy of the Fred Roos Collection.

Fig. 9.10. ME-109C (Bf-109C). By permission of the National Air and Space Museum, Smithsonian Institution, ©1999 Smithsonian Institution.

Fig. 9.11. View of a Messerschmitt ME-109D in flight. By permission of the National Air and Space Museum, Smithsonian Institution, ©1999 Smithsonian Institution.

Fig. 9.12. ME-109E escorting a Stuka. By permission of the National Air and Space Museum, Smithsonian Institution, ©1999 Smithsonian Institution.

Fig. 9.13. JU-87 Stuka. By permission of the National Air and Space Museum, Smithsonian Institution, ©1999 Smithsonian Institution.

the sun." By 1939, the Luftwaffe comprised more than 4,000 modern combat aircraft, making it the most formidable force in the world.[7]

Although the United States was not involved in the many conflicts before World War II, Billy Mitchell's ideas prevailed, and the nation was producing the hardware that would lead the way for the rest of the world. Douglas Aircraft Company was building the DC-3 airliner, and the Martin Company had the B-10, an all-metal monoplane with twin engines, enclosed cockpits, and machine-gun turrets. The B-10 would fly at 212 mph with a useful load of 2,260 pounds. When the government called for a bomber with a range of 2,000 miles at a speed of 250 mph, Boeing created a four-engine airplane, the B-17 Flying Fortress (shown in fig. 9.14). The B-17 would become probably the best bomber of its day and, without a doubt, one of those aircraft that would change the future of aviation.

ground support was proved in the Spanish civil war and was further developed with the use of armor-piercing projectiles for attacking tanks and ships. Adolf Hitler learned the lesson well and announced a massive program of rearmament, called the Reichsluftwaffe, that would put a "steel roof over Germany" and "black out

The War Begins

The German leaders were determined to regain territory that they had lost as a result of the Treaty of Versailles at the conclusion of World War I. The one element of the treaty that caused them the most irritation was the one

Fig. 9.14. Boeing B-17 Flying Fortress. Courtesy of the USAF Museum.

giving Poland a 50-mile-wide corridor to the Baltic Sea. This part of the treaty served to isolate Germany's province of East Prussia and put the German seaport of Danzig (today's Gdansk) under League of Nations' supervision and Polish economic control.[8]

World War II began on 1 September 1939, when German forces crossed the Polish border without warning. The attack was led by 1st Lt. Bruno Dilley flying the Junkers JU-87 dive-bomber, called the Stuka, and was followed by formation after formation as the Germans pushed deeper into Poland. Within 24 hours, the Polish air force had been eliminated as a fighting force and Germany had control of the skies. Poland ceased to exist as an independent state by the end of the month.

The Luftwaffe's other primary aircraft at that time were the Dornier 17 and the Heinkel 111, which were twin-engine aircraft with medium-range bomb-carrying capacity (see figs. 9.15 and 9.16). Other primary aircraft were the Messerschmitt 109 and 110, which performed the job of fighter planes (see fig. 9.17). The speed of the conquest of Poland astounded the world. A new form of "lightning war," the Blitzkrieg, had been unveiled and was successful only because of the close support rendered to the German ground troops by the pilots of the Stukas and the Heinkels. The key to the German success, in the words of British military historian J. F. C. Fuller, was "the velocity of aircraft and armored forces operating as one integrated force." Hitler had used the threat of his Luftwaffe to gain his demands, and now the other countries looked to their own air forces, remembered China, Ethiopia, and Spain, and pondered the predictions of Douhet, Trenchard, and Mitchell.[9]

Based on the lessons of the Spanish civil war, the Luftwaffe was built with three specific goals in mind: to maintain aerial supremacy, to disrupt the enemy supply lines, and to provide ground support for its own troops. The Luftwaffe accomplished all three goals, and without a doubt the ground support mission proved to be its most important contribution.[10]

Two days after Germany attacked Poland, France and Great Britain declared war against Germany. What followed was afterwards called "The Phony War" because for seven months German troops faced French and British troops on the western front along the French-built Maginot Line. The Maginot Line was a continuous set of massive fortifications that stretched along the German border north to the Ardennes Forest, which the French believed to be impenetrable. Little happened, and Hitler declared that the responsibility for opening hostilities should rest with England and France.[11]

Building on their success in Poland, on 9 April 1940, the Germans unleashed the Blitzkrieg against Denmark

Fig. 9.15. Dornier DO-17 3/4, left front view on ground from above. By permission of the National Air and Space Museum, Smithsonian Institution, ©1999 Smithsonian Institution.

Fig. 9.16. Heinkel HE-111H bomber in flight. The photo has been heavily retouched; there are no unit codes visible, and the national markings are irregular and disproportionate. By permission of the National Air and Space Museum, Smithsonian Institution, ©1999 Smithsonian Institution.

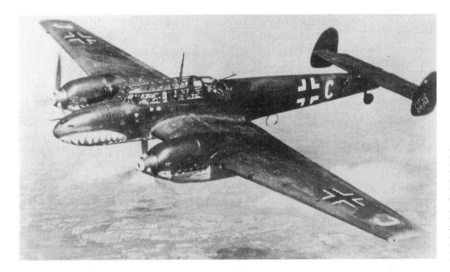

Fig. 9.17. View of a Messerschmitt Bf-110 "Eismeer." The aircraft is painted with a shark-mouth design on the front fuselage. By permission of the National Air and Space Museum, Smithsonian Institution, ©1999 Smithsonian Institution.

and Norway in an effort to protect their northern flank before beginning the conquest of the Low Countries and France. Most experts agree that the conquest of Denmark and Norway and the march across Western Europe were made possible by the new application of aircraft as a military weapon and "were among the most brilliant military operations of modern times."[12]

On 10 May 1940, as Winston Churchill was succeeding Neville Chamberlain as the British prime minister, Hitler's Stukas led the invasion of Holland and Luxembourg and inaugurated the Battle of France. Due largely to the Luftwaffe's awesome performance, within five days all was over with the Low Countries, and after two weeks of intensive action, the British and French armies had been pushed to Dunkirk on the English Channel.

The events that happened next became the Luftwaffe's first setback. More than 400,000 French and British troops had their backs to the sea, and Field Marshal Hermann Goering was preparing to use the Luftwaffe alone to "destroy the enemy," potentially another demonstration of air superiority. For the first time, the British committed to the battle their newest and best fighter, the Spitfire (shown in fig. 9.18), and operating from their home bases in southern England they were able to face the Luftwaffe on somewhat equal terms. The British fighters formed an aerial umbrella over the beaches and challenged the German Luftwaffe so effectively that by 4 June the Allied force had been totally evacuated to England. Close to 340,000 British and French troops had escaped, and yet only ten days later, on 20 June 1940, France fell to the Germans.[13]

The Battle of Britain

The Germans needed to gain control of the air and weaken England's defenses before activating Operation Sea Lion, the code name for the invasion of England. During the summer of 1940, the Luftwaffe used a large force of medium-range bombers, Stuka dive-bombers, and Messerschmitt 109 and 110 fighters against a total British force of less than 1,000 Hurricanes and Spitfires (see fig. 9.19). The British suffered heavily under the continuous bombing, but even with their small numbers they were able to inflict significant damage on the Luftwaffe, both in planes and pilots.[14]

What the Germans did not know and did not learn until late in the summer was that the British had developed a new defense consisting of a chain of radar stations strung along the southern and eastern coasts. With radar in place, the German bombers paid a heavy price in their attack against the Royal Air Force fighters. The RAF was able to punish the Luftwaffe and buy British industry the time it needed to gear up fighter production. Germany made a serious mistake in underestimating England's industrial capacity, and during this critical time Germany was outproduced in aircraft production.[15]

On the night of 24 August 1940, what turned out to be another serious error occurred when a Nazi Heinkel 111 dropped its bombs over central London. Churchill be-

Fig. 9.18. RAF's Spitfire. Courtesy of the USAF Museum.

Fig. 9.19. Hawker Hurricane. By permission of the National Air and Space Museum, Smithsonian Institution, ©1999 Smithsonian Institution.

lieved it was a deliberate act and ordered the RAF to conduct reprisal raids on Berlin on the following night. Many historians believe that this was the beginning of the end. Goering had boasted that enemy bombs would never fall on Berlin, and the German people believed him. This attack represented a serious blow to German morale and opened a whole new phase to the war that Germany was not equipped to conduct. The German planners had focused on bombers capable of ground-support missions and professed that long-range strategic bombers were unnecessary.

Hitler now felt he had to respond with massive bombings of London. The assault on London, to the neglect of the RAF bases, continued day after day, allowing the RAF fighter pilots to take control of the air. Churchill would later say, "Never in the course of human events has so much been owed by so many to so few."

By the end of the spring of 1941, it was obvious to everyone that the RAF had won the Battle of Britain. There would be no invasion of England, and in the end the Germans had suffered the loss of over two thousand aircraft to an RAF total of one thousand.[16]

Western Europe, 1942–1943

In 1942, the British began to take the offensive, and the balance of the air war over northwest Europe swung in their direction. The British were now busy developing strategic air operations designed to inflict decisive damage on Germany's war-making capabilities, and tactical air operations intended to inflict attritional losses on the Luftwaffe and raise the level of Allied air superiority.

Within this overall scheme, the goal came to be the destruction of important targets in German-occupied northwest Europe as well as in Germany proper. The Vickers Wellington medium bomber was the single most important bomber in the RAF's inventory, and it was directed mainly against targets in Germany. A mixture of lighter bombers was used for tactical bombing and for escorted daylight raids on targets in German-occupied northwest Europe. By the summer of 1942, the British Bomber Command began to acquire newer four-engine heavy bombers like the Avro Lancaster and the Handley Page Halifax, and it focused on the night bombing offensive against targets in Germany. During this period, however, navigational and therefore bombing accuracies were poor, and the force frequently had to rely as much on obsolescent twin-engine medium bombers as on the modern four-engine heavy bombers with their heavier bombloads, greater range, and superior operational survivability.[17]

America Prepares

In 1922, America's airpower numbered 952 pilots and other officers and about 9,000 enlisted personnel. Even as late as 1938, the U.S. Army Air Corps was "practically nonexistent," according to Gen. Henry H. "Hap" Arnold. As a combat arm, it had effectively been demobilized. The 1938 Air Corps could boast only some 19,000 men. Every plane being flown by the new active squadrons was obsolete, with the sole exception of the B-17 (see fig. 9.20). But the Air Corps possessed only thirteen of these

appropriately named Flying Fortresses from the Boeing Company, with another twenty-nine on order.[18] As the war in Europe continued to expand, America realized the importance of airpower and how far behind it was. In January 1939, President Roosevelt asked for and received $300 million for the Air Corps to build 5,500 planes a year and to train 20,000 men. The next year $896 million was appropriated by Congress to build 50,000 airplanes. The Air Corps training system, which was turning out some 300 pilots annually in 1939, was to be expanded to train 50,000 pilots each year by mid-1942.[19]

The situation with naval aviation was somewhat better than that of the Air Corps. The U.S. Navy had learned the lesson of the *Ostfriesland* and was in a better political position to obtain the necessary funding at a time when the Air Corps was still working to gain support in Congress. The Navy's first aircraft carrier, the

Fig. 9.20. The Boeing B-17 in mass production. Courtesy of the USAF Museum.

Langley, was converted from the coal ship *Jupiter* in 1922. Her wooden flight deck superstructure, supported by an exposed framework of webs, beams, and girders, led her to be affectionately known as the "Covered Wagon," but her official designation was CV-1 (Cruiser, Heavier-than-Air, Craft No. 1). The only carrier in service until the introduction of the Lexington Class in 1927, *Langley* provided a valuable testing ground for carrier operations and training of pilots.[20]

Langley's former coal holds were used to store aviation fuel, elevator machinery, and disassembled aircraft, which could be lifted by crane to the "hangar" deck (formerly the upper deck). Aircraft were assembled, loaded onto the elevator, and hoisted to the flight deck. *Langley* also had two cranes to lift seaplanes from the water into the hangar deck. Initially, seaplanes were launched from two pneumatic catapults set in the flight deck, but these were removed in 1928 due to infrequent use.

Langley's initial configuration included both longitudinal (fore-and-aft) and transverse (cross-deck) wires, but the fore-and-aft wires failed to improve landing safety and were removed. Although speed was never satisfactory, this experimental carrier's main problem was smoke disposal, which was finally solved with a pair of hinged funnels, which could be lowered during flight deck operations.[21]

As a result of the 1922 Washington Naval Disarmament Treaty, the *Lexington* and her sister ship, the *Saratoga,* were converted from battle cruiser hulls, and they joined the fleet in late 1927. With their heavy cruiser-level gun battery, armor protection, and steel flight decks, the *Lexington* class was the only pre–World War II carrier considered capable of independent operations and served to remove all doubt about the effectiveness of the large aircraft carrier.

The *Lexington*'s entire complement of ninety aircraft could be parked on the aft end of the wood-sheathed flight deck. In fact, since the hangar bay could not accommodate all the aircraft, part of the flight deck remained a permanent deck park. Eight hydraulic arresting wires replaced the original weighted transverse wires in 1931. Two large elevators—one by the island, and the other aft of the huge starboard funnel—connected the flight and hangar decks. The storage of aviation fuel in integral bulk tanks, surrounded by spaces that could be filled with inert carbon dioxide gas, was

a fire control measure that became standard on U.S. carriers.

Both ships received gun refits in early 1942, but the *Lexington*'s close-range antiaircraft armament was substantially weaker than *Saratoga*'s. This was a flaw that was not corrected in time to avert her loss in the Battle of the Coral Sea. The *Saratoga* sustained severe damage from torpedoes and kamikaze attacks, but continued to be repaired, rearmed, and restored to service until her destruction as a target in the 1946 Bikini Atoll atomic bomb tests.[22]

Motivated by the desire for an improved carrier, capable of operating a larger air group composed of heavier aircraft, the *Essex* was commissioned in 1942 and became the mainstay of World War II and postwar fast carrier task forces. Of the thirty-two ships authorized in the *Essex* class, twenty-four were completed, making *Essex* the most numerous carrier class. It was also the most efficient in terms of aircraft operated per ton of displacement.

No longer limited by treaty weights, *Essex* was given a battery of sixteen 5-inch guns and a flight deck large enough to launch four squadrons per launch operation. The heavier planes were launched by hydraulic catapults in the CVS 9s and steam catapults in the later CVS 11s. The engine and boiler rooms were alternated for better damage control, and gasoline stowage was redesigned to avoid torpedo-induced explosion fires. Also, the decks were strengthened specifically to counter bombing, reflecting combat realities versus earlier carriers that were armored against shellfire.

Several *Essex* class features would have a lasting effect on carrier design, and with increased fuel capacity and range of over 17,000 miles, the *Essex* class proved ideal for operations in the Pacific. Along with the nine "war emergency" conversions from light cruiser to light carrier of the *Independence* class, they helped guarantee U.S. command of the Pacific and demonstrated America's immense industrial capacity. They also proved to have a long lifespan, with many being successfully converted to operate jet aircraft and serving in both Korea and Vietnam.[23]

While the United States was attempting to prepare its own defenses, other nations were looking to the United States for planes and armament to stop the sweep of Nazi Germany over all of Western Europe.

Lend Lease and the Arsenal of Democracy

In March 1941, Congress enacted a bill that would enable the United States to lend "defense articles" to those countries whose protection concerned U.S. safety. Thus the United States became the "Arsenal of Democracy." Many U.S. planes were flown to Alaska, where Russian pilots took over and flew them to battle on the eastern front. (In spite of his alliance with the Soviet Union, Hitler suddenly and unexpectedly turned on the country on 18 December 1940.) Great Britain used U.S. aircraft extensively against the German and Italian war machines in North Africa, and pilots from friendly countries were sent to schools in the United States, such as the Embry-Riddle Flight School, for training.[24]

The "Flying Tigers"

Somewhat like the Lafayette Escadrille in World War I, American volunteers got into the war in Asia ahead of U.S. military during World War II. The Flying Tigers (officially the American Volunteer Group) in China under the command of U.S. Gen. Claire Chennault shot down 286 Japanese planes during the six months of combat (18 December 1941 to 4 July 1942), and lost only twelve American pilots (see figs. 9.21–9.23). While flying their Curtiss P-40s, the Americans developed a technique and philosophy of aerial warfare that encouraged high discipline but at the same time invited initiative on the part of pilot.[25]

Pearl Harbor

Adm. Isoroku Yamamoto, following the samurai slogan "Win first, fight later," sought a strong preemptive strike against the American Pacific Fleet. On Sunday, 7 December 1941, at 6:00 A.M., the first Japanese airplane left its flight deck on a venture that would be marked by President Roosevelt as "a date which will live in infamy."

Since the first of that year, the U.S. military had been aware of the possibility of war between the United States and Japan. However, the U.S. military began to drop its guard when time passed and nothing happened, especially when Admiral Yamamoto publicly expressed his doubts as to the favorable outcome of a war for the Japanese. By September 1941, the U.S. military in the Pacific had returned to normal operations. So when two hundred Japanese planes began their two-wave attack, it

Fig. 9.21. Curtiss P-40 Warhawk of the Flying Tigers. Courtesy of the USAF Museum.

Fig. 9.22. Flying Tigers P-40s being maintained by Chinese technicians. Courtesy of the USAF Museum.

Fig. 9.23. The Flying Tigers' primitive airfield. Courtesy of the USAF Museum.

was a complete surprise to the U.S. Army and Navy at Pearl Harbor and the surrounding military bases.

The damage inflicted by Japan, which lost only twenty-nine planes, was catastrophic. Six U.S. battleships and twelve cruisers and destroyers were sunk, 164 planes were destroyed, 2,403 military and civilian men were killed, and 1,178 were wounded. So complete was the surprise that even the emperor's peace envoy in Washington, D.C., did not know of the impending attack. War had reached American soil precisely as Billy Mitchell had predicted.

The attack was costly to the United States, yet Admiral Nagumo did not inflict "maximum damage." He chose to withdraw his carrier strike force rather than risk a third strike against the dockyard, repair facilities, and oil tanks. And it eventually backfired on the Axis powers, for it jolted awake the "sleeping giant."[26]

In some ways, as we look back, it is obvious that the United States never would have been any better prepared militarily. With the violation of her own territory, all adversity to involvement vanished in a moment, and the American people became united behind a single cause: to rid the world of Axis tyranny.

With the U.S. battleship fleet effectively eliminated, the carriers, which had been at sea during the attack, would become the basis of U.S. naval strategy (see fig. 9.24). Although the attack allowed Japan time to consolidate its position in the East Indies and Central Pacific, it also accelerated the emergence of the carrier as the new capital ship. Its air group replaced the battleship's guns as the fleet's primary power.

War in the Pacific, 1942–1945

Following the attack on Pearl Harbor, Clark Field in Manila was thoroughly trounced by Japanese planes, completely destroying U.S. ability to protect the Philippines against invasion.

Hong Kong and Singapore were soon overrun because Japanese air attacks destroyed the British retaliatory capabilities. Three days after the attack on Pearl Harbor, 100 Japanese bombers attacked the impregnable

Fig. 9.24. Aircraft carrier USS *Yorktown* (CV-5) at Hamptons Roads, Virginia, 30 October 1937. By permission of the National Air and Space Museum, Smithsonian Institution, ©1999 Smithsonian Institution.

British battleships *Prince of Wales* and *Repulse.* Taking Billy Mitchell's word that it could be done, the Japanese sent both ships to the bottom of the sea with a loss of only three planes to antiaircraft fire. The battleship crews were confident they could cope with any air attack, and they failed to see the importance of maintaining air cover. The days of the mighty battleship were indeed at an end.

Java was taken and Darwin, Australia, was hit by a surprise air attack. The Japanese forces then took Wake Island and Guam from the U.S. forces and overran British Rabaul and New Britain in the Solomons.

By this time, the world was witnessing an American innovation. The aircraft carrier was proving its worth in the hands of our enemy. The carrier had now become the "Queen of the Seas."[27]

Raid over Tokyo

After Pearl Harbor, Japan seemed invincible, conquering Burma, Malaya, most of the East Indies, the Philippines, and several critical Pacific Islands. A retaliatory raid on Tokyo was planned by American forces, on 18 April 1942, with twenty-five B-25 Army bombers, flying from the carrier *Hornet,* to show that the Japanese homeland was indeed vulnerable to attack.

A Navy captain, Francis S. Low, came up with the idea: Why not launch Army bombers, which had a greater range than carrier planes, from a carrier deck? The idea sounded plausible, and a naval air officer, Capt. Donald B. Duncan, proved, on paper at least, that it could be done. He believed that the B-25 medium bomber, suitably modified, could be flown off a carrier deck and reach Japan while the carrier was far enough away from the islands to be reasonably safe from attack by Japanese land-based planes.

The war was brought home to the Japanese people when on 18 April 1942, sixteen North American B-25 "Mitchell" bombers took off from the carrier *Hornet* to bomb and strafe Tokyo, Yokohama, Kobi, Yokosuka, and Nagoya. This American counterattack on Japan, under the command of Lt. Col. Jimmy Doolittle, was officially known as the First Aviation Project. For weeks, the B-25 crews had practiced short-field takeoffs and low-level flying, and only on the morning of 1 April 1942, as they set out through the Golden Gate and into the Pacific on the flight deck of the carrier *Hornet,* did they learn from the announcement over the ship's speakers — "This force is bound for Tokyo!" Unfortunately, they were spotted by a Japanese trawler, and rather than take a chance that it had not reported the carrier's presence, they sank the trawler by gunfire, and the B-25s took off while further from Japan than intended. They were still 650 miles from Japan and 200 miles from the planned launch point, 450 miles east of Tokyo. Their plan was to fly low to avoid detection, bomb the Japanese mainland, and fly

Fig. 9.25. Launch of the Mitchell B-25s from the carrier dock. Courtesy of the USAF Museum.

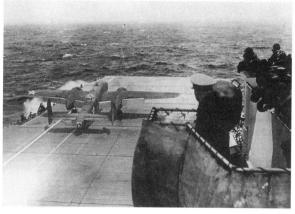

Fig. 9.26. Doolittle's B-25s en route for an attack on Japan. Courtesy of the USAF Museum.

into friendly China, where the planes would be turned over to the Chinese. None of the sixteen Mitchells suffered serious damage, but only one landed intact. This one made it to an airfield about 40 miles north of Vladivostok in the Soviet Union (see figs. 9.25 and 9.26). The crews of eleven other aircraft opted to bail out over China, and the other four planes crash-landed. These "30 seconds over Tokyo," however, provided more of a psychological than strategic victory. It provided a great boost to American morale, but the damage to Japan was minimal. Much of the Japanese public was not even aware of it. The raid also diverted two valuable carriers, *Hornet* and *Enterprise*, from the South Pacific, favoring the Japanese in the Battle of the Coral Sea.[28]

The Battle of the Coral Sea

Six months after Pearl Harbor, the Pacific Fleet engaged the Japanese invasion fleet, which was bent on moving into Port Moresby, New Guinea. The world's first carrier-versus-carrier battle, Coral Sea was a Japanese tactical victory, losing the small carrier *Shoho* in exchange for the large U.S. fleet carrier *Lexington*. Yet the Port Moresby invasion was called off, and the Japanese advance was stopped for the first time since Pearl Harbor. In addition, the *Shokaku* and *Zuikaku* would require significant repairs and new air crews, preventing them from participating at Midway. This naval battle is also significant in that it was the first fought entirely with airpower, the capital ships involved never coming within gunnery range of each other. During the battle in the Coral Sea, the United States lost the carrier *Lexington*, and the *Yorktown* received severe damage, but the Japanese also suffered heavy losses, and this caused the Japanese admiral to retire from his invasion attempt.[29]

The Battle of Midway

The Japanese surprised the United States at Pearl Harbor, but they had a big jolt awaiting them on 4 June 1942 at Midway, one month after the Coral Sea battle. Admiral Yamamoto divided his fleet to attack Midway and

Fig. 9.27. Douglas SBD-3 Dauntless, flown by the U.S. Marines, en route to a dive-bombing run. Note that the bomb is mounted on a "crutch" under the center section. Courtesy of the Fred Roos Collection.

Fig. 9.28. General Motors TBM-3 Avengers, flown by the U.S. Marines over southern Okinawa in mid-1945. Grumman designed and developed the Avenger (as the TBF), but the Eastern Aircraft Division of General Motors manufactured the majority of them. Courtesy of the Fred Roos Collection.

therefore presented to Admiral Nimitz a less formidable foe. Fortunately, the United States had broken the Japanese code, and so the defenders were better prepared than before, in that they could outguess the enemy.

Disregarding Japan's diversionary raid on the Aleutian Islands, the United States concentrated instead on meeting the main Japanese assault. Japan assumed only two U.S. carriers were active in the Pacific, but the *Yorktown*, damaged at Coral Sea, was battle worthy after three top-priority days at Pearl Harbor. The U.S. carriers were positioned 400 miles northeast of Midway long before a Japanese patrol line of fifteen submarines arrived to block their path. The Japanese had five carriers, seven battleships, thirteen cruisers, forty-five destroyers and

twelve transports loaded with 5,000 troops. The defending U.S. forces consisted of three carriers, no battleships, eight cruisers and twenty destroyers. Again, it was a naval battle of the air. When the smoke had cleared and the enemy had retreated beyond Wake Island, credit for the Japanese defeat could be given to the Navy Douglas SBD dive-bombers of the carriers *Enterprise*, *Hornet*, and *Yorktown* (see figs. 9.27 and 9.28).[30]

Twenty-six marine "Buffalo" fighters were destroyed by the 108 Japanese Zeros while defending Midway (see fig. 9.29). Boeing "Flying Fortresses" unsuccessfully bombed the Japanese ships. Thirty-five of the forty-one torpedo bombers were shot down on their first attack against the invaders. In spite of these U.S. losses, Midway was the

Fig. 9.29. Mitsubishi A6M-3 (Zero) in flight. Shown is a captured Mitsubishi A6M3 Zero (s/n EB-210). The print appears to be a copy of one retouched to show Japanese markings on the airplane, probably for use in recognition training. By permission of the National Air and Space Museum, Smithsonian Institution, ©1999 Smithsonian Institution.

decisive turning point in the war. Only six months after Pearl Harbor, the inferior U.S. forces twice had turned back the overwhelmingly superior Japanese armada. It had been a decisive victory because the heavy Japanese losses; four carriers, 250 aircraft, and nearly 45 percent of their most experienced airmen, brought the balance of power more closely together and, given time, the U.S. production capabilities could overtake and surpass the enemy.[31]

Leyte Gulf

By October 1944, the United States had begun closing in on Japanese-held territory in southern Asia. Over 700 ships, including 33 carriers, were assembled for the invasion of Leyte, the entry point for the recapture of the Philippines. The Japanese combined fleet, in three attack forces, was sent to meet the U.S. attack, with a decoy force stationed to the northwest. But with much land-based support already eliminated by American air raids on Formosa, the Philippines, and the Ryukyus, America's sheer numerical advantage in warships (3:1) heavily weighed the outcome in its favor. In four separate engagements over two days, the Japanese carrier fleet met its end, losing all four carriers committed to the operation. The Japanese ultimately relied on self-sacrifice as the first kamikazes hit American ships. Named for the legendary typhoon, or "Divine Wind," that repelled Kubla Khan's invasion of Japan in 1281, the kamikaze pilots were Japan's last, desperate hope in the final months of war. During the invasion of Okinawa, some 1,900 kamikaze sorties achieved the sinking of 36 U.S. ships and damage to over 350 more. Yet the sacrifice of these young, minimally trained kamikaze pilots began to have less impact as countermeasures such as "boxed" antiaircraft fire were developed. By the end of the battle for Okinawa, nearly 7,800 Japanese aircraft had been lost, compared with the American loss of only 763.

The treacherous island-hopping campaign by the U.S. troops in their climb up the various island chains to Tokyo was always preceded by softening-up processes by U.S. Navy and Marine airplanes. From newly won bases in New Guinea and the Solomon Islands, the recently developed fighters, the F6F Hellcat, F4U Corsair, and the revamped P-38 Lightning, began to turn the tide against the once superior Zero fighters (see figs. 9.30–9.32). It was now only a matter of time before the Pacific war would be won.[32]

European Theater of Operations, 1943–1944

In the meantime, the European phase of the global war was given a priority over the Pacific theater. Gen. Ira Eaker was ordered to England on 20 February 1942, by Gen. Hap Arnold with instructions to prepare the way for the arrival in Britain of the Eighth Air Force, which would become the largest of all the U.S. combat air forces sent overseas during the war. When he reached

Fig. 9.30. Lockheed P-38 Lightning. Courtesy of the USAF Museum.

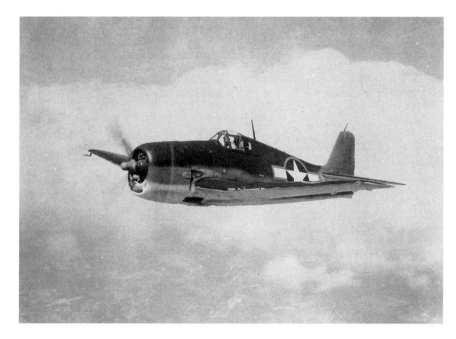

Fig. 9.31. Grumman F6F-3 Hellcat,
late summer 1943. Courtesy of the
Fred Roos Collection.

Fig. 9.32. A Vought F4U-1 Corsair of U.S. Marines, in flight over the Pacific in 1944, clearly shows characteristics of the inverted gull wing. Courtesy of the Fred Roos Collection.

England, he had no planes, no crews, no airfields, and no repair shops. And yet, by August he had twenty-four combat ready crews, and on the night of 16 August, eighteen of these crews were alerted for the mission that would be known as VIII Bomber Command, Mission No. 1.

Mission No. 1 was significant as the first U.S. Army Air Forces mission but also as a test of the theory of daylight precision attacks. Twelve B-17s were dispatched for a daytime bombing mission on Rouen, in northern France. The mission was executed perfectly. The B-17s had bombed from 23,000 feet—above the range of the Rouen flak—and only two had been slightly damaged (see fig. 9.33). All twelve returned safely to the 97th Group's main field near the East Anglian village of Grafton Underwood. It was an extraordinarily successful first mission, and it strengthened the argument in favor of daylight bombing.[33]

By late 1942, the U.S. Army Air Forces was established on bases in the southeastern corner of England, and its personnel were gaining operational experience in daylight offensive operations mainly with short-range and medium-range attacks on targets in the German-occupied regions of northwest Europe.

The U.S. Eighth Army Air Force was responsible for strategic bombing with the Boeing B-17 Flying Fortress and Consolidated B-24 Liberator heavy bombers, supported by the longer-range Lockheed P-38 Lightning and Supermarine Spitfire fighters.

The U.S. Twelfth Army Air Force had a tactical bombing role as its main responsibility with the Douglas A-20 attack bomber and the North American B-25 Mitchell and Martin B-26 Marauder medium bombers supported by the Bell P-39 Airacobra fighter, which doubled in a tactical reconnaissance role. There were also growing photo-reconnaissance and troop-carrier capabilities, the latter for the delivery of airborne forces in the planned invasion of northwest Europe.

As seen earlier, the German offensive effort was heavily dependent on tactical air support, but Allied bombers attacking targets in German-controlled Europe were inevitably engaged by German fighters. The destruction of the German aerial capability was clearly important to the success of the Allied war effort.

Fig. 9.33. Flight of B-17s en route to a target. Courtesy of the USAF Museum.

The German fighters could be engaged in the air as they maneuvered to attack Allied targets, or they could be engaged as they tried to prevent Allied attacks on German targets. The latter became increasingly important, as the growing strength of Allied bomber attacks served as a magnet for the German fighter force. The bombers drew large numbers of fighters into the air for destruction by the bombers' defensive guns or the growing numbers of long-range escorts. Most historians agree that the Germans were winning the air war until the Americans came up with the long-range fighters during the winter of 1943–44: the P-51 and long-range variants of the P-38 and P-47. Without fighter protection, formations of bombers were no match for German fighter aircraft.[34]

The German capability could also be destroyed at source by crushing Germany's airframe and aero engine manufacturing capabilities. It was in the course of such raids that Allied bomber forces encountered some of the most determined German fighter opposition, and in the process they inflicted decisive losses on the German fighter arm.[35]

North Africa

The British and American high commands had decided to invade Morocco and Algeria in northwestern Africa, both under control of the Vichy French, and then to capture Tunisia from the Germans and Italians stationed there. The purpose was to drive Axis forces from all of North Africa, securing bases from which to stage a cross-Mediterranean invasion of Sicily and, ultimately, Italy itself. Operation Torch, as the African invasion was code-named, would have priority. By the middle of 1942, the Royal Air Force was well established in North Africa and had been reinforced by South African and Australian units, as well as by detachments of French, Greek, and Yugoslav airmen from countries overrun by the Germans. This Allied force was now well experienced in the type of tactical air warfare required for operations over North Africa and was thus capable of providing the ground forces with accurate, speedy close air support.

The Middle East and Western Desert Commands had also received useful numbers of more advanced aircraft, although there were as yet too few Supermarine Spitfires to provide total air superiority. The primary fighter in the theater was still the Hawker Hurricane, but this usually operated in the ground-attack role, collaborating with Curtiss Tomahawk and Kittyhawk fighter bombers and Martin Baltimore attack bombers.

The commands were also provided with a useful offensive capability in the form of Bristol Blenheims and Vickers Wellingtons for the conventional bombing role, and Bristol Beaufighters and Beauforts for the vital task of intercepting and destroying the convoys on which the Axis forces were wholly dependent for the arrival of reinforcements, equipment, and supplies from Italy.

The German air strength consisted of a useful short-range and medium-range reconnaissance capability in the form of Messerschmitt MF-109F and Junkers JU-88 aircraft, respectively, and a small but relatively well-balanced offensive/defensive force of JU-87D attack warplanes and MF-109E fighter-bombers, both of them obsolescent but still effective types, with highly capable MF-109G fighters providing air cover.[36]

In March 1943, due to the assaults in the east by the British and in the west by the Americans, the Axis forces in North Africa were effectively penned into Tunisia, and they surrendered to the Allied forces.

Europe was invaded by Allied forces launched from North Africa. Italy was invaded at Anzio on 22 January 1944. On 4 June 1944, Rome fell and Italy was out of the war.[37]

Eastern Europe

The essence of Soviet thinking with regard to air operations was, first, the protection of "Mother Russia" by a potent air-defense organization and, second, the provision of overwhelming tactical air support for Soviet ground force operations. Long-established military philosophy regarded these as the Soviet Union's foremost weapon in strategic, operational, and tactical matters.

This thinking was reflected in the allocation of an air army to each front and ground forces organization that corresponded to a large army in western terms. Each of these air armies was an exceptionally mobile organization designed to operate from airfields (usually temporary) as close as possible to the front line for the provision of speedy defensive and offensive support when required. Each army therefore possessed at least one division of fighters that could undertake both de-

fensive and offensive work; one division of bombers for attacks on the area behind the Germans' front line for the interdiction of their supplies, equipment, and reinforcements; and one division of dedicated attack warplanes to provide heavy as well as virtually instant support for ground forces.

Soviet warplanes were accordingly optimized for great reliability under adverse operating conditions and for operations at altitudes that seldom exceeded 16,405 feet, as this was considered to be the maximum altitude for tactical air warfare.

By the middle of 1944, the Soviets had gained approximate technical parity with the Germans and were able to field much greater numbers of warplanes in their search for tactical air superiority at low and medium altitudes. The Germans' answer to Soviet overall air superiority was a constant effort to win local air superiority at decisive points, using their aircrews' superior skills to offset inferiority in numbers.

The Luftwaffe was stretched thinly along the eastern front. In both the Finnish front and the Baltic states on the northern end of the eastern front, a few high-quality defensive units were combined with a number of offensive bomber units, often flying obsolescent aircraft, and comparatively larger numbers of tactical reconnaissance and close-support aircraft. The latter were often conversions of training and other second-line aircraft, supplemented by a few specialized warplanes such as the ground-attack models of the Focke-Wulf FW-190 fighter.

This pattern was mirrored in the central sector of the eastern front, where there were large numbers of German aircraft as well as a higher proportion of more advanced fighters and bombers, but there were still sizable numbers of obsolete aircraft, such as the JU-87, adapted for the night attack role designed to keep the Soviets off balance.

The southern sector of the eastern front was the responsibility of a number of German, Hungarian, and Romanian air units tasked with the defense of Hungary and Romania. As on the northern and central sectors of the eastern front, operational and tactical reconnaissance was extremely important. So too was the ground-attack capability intended to inflict heavy losses on the Soviet armored forces operating in good "tank country." For this reason the southern sector had the only Henschel HS-129 units operating over the eastern front.

The German, Hungarian, and Romanian air units holding the extreme south of the Axis line on the eastern front flew a mixed assortment of aircraft with relatively smaller and greater proportions of attack aircraft and night-fighters, the latter mainly to provide protection for the all-important oil installations at Ploesti.[38]

Western Europe, 1943–1944

On the eve of the Allied invasion of northwest France in June 1944, the Luftwaffe in Western Europe was a mere shadow of its glory in the heady days of 1940, for most of its strength had been drawn away to meet more immediate threats on the eastern front and, to a lesser extent, the Italian front. Based in Paris, the Luftwaffe controlled only modest numbers of aircraft, and these were already affected by Allied domination of the air and fuel shortages.[39]

In the meantime, a great deal had to be learned about preparing northern Europe for invasion. The British remained committed to a policy of bombing Germany at night. Their losses, due to antiaircraft fire, were relatively low, but the damage inflicted against the Germans was not a great hindrance to the Nazi war effort.

Building on the success of Mission No. 1, the American B-17s and B-24s worked to perfect the technique of massive daylight bombing. While this increased the bombing accuracy, and thus the effectiveness, it also enabled German fighters, the ME-109s and FW-190s, to decimate the squadrons of American bombers (see figs. 9.34–9.36).

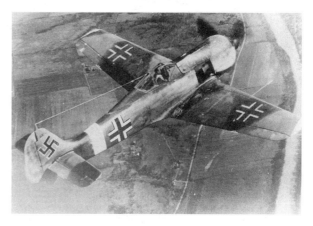

Fig. 9.35. FW-190. Courtesy of the USAF Museum.

Fig. 9.34. The consolidated B-24 Liberator bombing a target. Courtesy of the USAF Museum.

Fig. 9.36. A B-24 is fatally damaged over Germany. Courtesy of the USAF Museum.

By May 1943, the crucial battles for the skies over Europe were about to begin. For example, in October, sixty planes were lost in an American air attack against Schweinfurt and Regensburg, Germany. The U.S. fighters could accompany the bombers as far as the German border, and then because of limited range they were forced to turn back to England for refueling. From then on, the bombers were without fighter protection. An innovation that saved the day and virtually turned the balance in favor of the U.S. bombers was the addition of external, droppable belly and wing tanks for the fighters. Now the P-47, P-38, and P-51 fighters could escort the bombers into Germany, over the target, and provide protection throughout the flight and back to their home bases (see figs. 9.37–9.40).[40]

D-Day

During the last few days before the invasion (D-Day), Allied aircraft attacked every German installation on the French coast that was possible. Low-level attacks on trains, bridges, barges, airfields, and flak towers brought desired results, particularly in the area of the intended landing in Normandy. Axis installations from Holland to southern France were bombed, thereby keeping the Germans continually off-guard as to where the anticipated invasion would take place.

When D-Day finally came, on 6 June 1944, the fighters and light bombers made the invasion possible. Air superiority was now in the hands of the Allies. The Luftwaffe, once the hunter, was now the hunted. The Eighth's big bomber raids increasingly served two purposes. While the B-17s and B-24s bombed Hitler's industries, their escorting fighters were to bleed the Luftwaffe dry. The Ninth Air Force, which began operating from England during the late autumn of 1943, was organized for one vital purpose: to prepare the way for, and then support, Operation Overlord, the long-awaited invasion of Europe. The Ninth, equipped with nothing larger than twin-engined mediums, including the yet little used Martin B-26, was to give the American air effort a tactical second punch. The streamlined B-26 was a hot airplane, and it took a hot pilot to master it. The wings on the original version were so small that the plane was extremely difficult to land and soon became known as the widow-maker. The Ninth joined up with Brig. Gen. Elwood R. "Pete" Quesada, head of the Ninth Fighter Command, and began the job for which they had been activated: preparing the way for the Normandy invasion.

The preparation focused on a bridge-busting cam-

Fig. 9.37. Squadron of Republic P-47 Thunderbolts (Jugs). Courtesy of the USAF Museum.

Fig. 9.38. P-38s on escort duty. Courtesy of the USAF Museum.

Fig. 9.39. North America P-51 Mustangs escorting a flight of B-17s. Courtesy of the USAF Museum.

Fig. 9.40. P-51 with long-range tanks installed. Courtesy of the USAF Museum.

Fig. 9.41. C-47 "Gooney Birds" and their gliders, which they will tow, are lined up waiting for D-Day. Courtesy of the USAF Museum.

paign that was so effective that eventually every one of the nine spans crossing the Seine west of Paris was shattered. In all, according to some reports, thirty-five bridges were destroyed by the Ninth in the last three weeks before D-Day. This successful campaign, combined with unrelenting destruction of rail and road traffic, effectively sealed off the invasion area from the rest of France, from occupied Belgium, and from Germany itself. To make it possible, the Ninth flew 14,000 sorties (a sortie was one flight by one plane) between 20 May and the beginning of June.

As for the two-month campaign against the Luftwaffe's fields, it had been so effective that only 155 single-engined enemy fighters remained in northern France on D-Day and a mere handful showed up to contest the landings—three FW-190s flew over the invasion armada and after nightfall another twenty-two aircraft engaged

in a limited number of ineffective attacks on shipping.[41] On D-Day, air operations began shortly after midnight, and no fewer than 8,000 planes of the U.S. Army Air Forces and Royal Air Force took part in the assault. So vital was air support to the success of the landings that many aircraft made several sorties each as the day wore on and some squadrons, short of crews but not machines, sent out planes with partial crews. So omnipresent were the Allied planes that one German soldier confessed in a letter home, "the American fliers are chasing us like rabbits."

Although Allied beach landings at Normandy would begin in the early morning hours, the aerial invasion actually began in the dark hours just after midnight. Thousands of British and U.S. paratroopers dropped out of the night sky across the Cherbourg Peninsula, far behind enemy lines. Other airborne troops swooped down onto Normandy in wooden gliders, each carrying men, equipment, and even small vehicles. Theirs was one of the more dangerous tasks of the whole operation: leaping in darkness into enemy territory, each group with a specific task—a bridge to be blown up, a railroad line to be cut, an enemy defense post to be dynamited, or a landing field to be seized and held (see fig. 9.41). By achieving these objectives, the seaborne assault forces could have some assurance that a German counterattack would be weakened or delayed.

The Allies were new at the technique of airborne warfare. Before D-Day, only a few similar operations had been tried in Tunisia and Sicily. It was the Germans who pioneered the paratroop tactics in their Blitzkrieg conquests of the Netherlands and Crete. Gen. Erwin Rommel was expecting the Allies to use both paratroopers and gliders in an invasion force, and he had created some deadly defense measures. He had the plains and meadows around many Normandy rivers flooded, leaving treacherous water and very little open landing space for the paratroopers. For the gliders, Rommel had designed mine-tipped poles, nicknamed "Rommel asparagus," which he had planted across potential glider landing sites.

Rommel's defenses, as well as other factors, caused the airborne operation to teeter on the brink of disaster. Thick clouds and exploding clumps of flak (antiaircraft fire) caused most of the planes to veer off course. Fully three-fourths of the paratroopers were scattered far and wide. Many dropped into the sea. Others were dropped so far from their zones that it would be days before they rejoined their units. Some paratroopers were shot before they even landed, while others perished in the flooded plains, drowning before they could cut themselves free of their harnesses.

For those who landed without injury, the immediate problem was regrouping with their comrades. Training had taught them to look for their units by following the "drop pattern" left by the direction of the plane. The drop plane usually followed a straight line, leaving the paratroopers spread along a similar pattern. Upon landing, the men were to move along this line, gathering at its center. To avoid enemy flak, the actual flight path had been erratic; subsequently, there was no drop pattern to follow.

The U.S. 101st Airborne Division had planned to regroup in the dark by signaling each other with the click-ing of toy crickets. Unfortunately, a German patrol had captured a number of the early arrivals, discovered the clickers and their purpose, and used the toys to lure the Allied paratroopers into their gunfire. For U.S. paratroopers unable to tell friend from foe, it became a nightmare of confusion.

Despite these disasters, there were significant successes. Some glider groups made extremely accurate landings. One British team touched down fewer than twenty-five yards from their targeted bridge and overcame the enemy within minutes. Another glider landed directly on top of a building that housed a German sectional headquarters. The Germans inside were so surprised that they surrendered immediately, leading to the early capture of the entire village.

Amazingly, the paratroopers were far more successful than anyone could have expected. It was a remarkable tribute to the U.S. 82d and the 101st Divisions that while thousands of their men found themselves miles from their units and targets that night, they fought the Germans wherever they encountered them. The Germans did not know the landings were scattered and confused; they only knew that thousands of fierce paratroopers were all around them.

Apart from the destroyed bridges and captured roadways, the greatest achievement of the airborne forces on D-Day was to bring confusion and uncertainty to the Germans across the whole breadth of the Cherbourg Peninsula.

By 10 June, four days after the landings, the Ninth's advanced groups were doing two jobs, bombing and strafing German strongpoints at the request of the ground commanders while continuing their vigilant interdiction of rail lines and bridges to seal off the front.

After the invasion, the Army Air Force strategic planners had concluded that the destruction of the Axis oil industry held the key to the Luftwaffe's defeat and that of all Germany as well. The oil campaign had a swift and devastating effect on the Luftwaffe. Because of the lack of fuel, the training of new Luftwaffe pilots was radically curtailed, and they went into battle after only some 30 hours of flying time. The green pilots proved no match for the experienced Mustang, Lightning, and Thunderbolt pilots, who had more than 300 hours in the air before being assigned to operational units. Luftwaffe interceptions of the bomber streams from England and Italy became intermittent, since fuel had to be hoarded in order to assemble a large enough formation of fighters to effectively tackle the bombers. The Forts and Liberators increasingly seemed to roam the skies over Germany unchallenged, a majority of losses coming not from fighters but from flak. Heavy escorts were less and less necessary, which released yet more fighters to beat up enemy airfields. "We were almost reduced to immobility," Luftwaffe fighter chief Adolf Galland wrote, "by continuous raids on our airfields."[42]

Victory in Europe (V-E Day)

On 16 April, the long strategic air war officially came to an end; there were no more targets. By then the big bombers of the Eighth, the Fifteenth, and the RAF had destroyed all of Germany's coke and ferroalloy industries; 95 percent of its fuel, hard coal, and synthetic rubber capacity; 90 percent of its steel capacity; 75 percent of its truck manufacturing; 70 percent of its tire production; and 55 percent of its tank manufacturing. In the course of the air war, the Eighth's fighters alone had strafed into wreckage 4,250 Luftwaffe planes—to add to their score of about 5,222 shot from the air. Two senior fighter groups, the Fourth and Fifty-sixth, both ran their records to more than a thousand enemy aircraft destroyed.[43]

As crushing as the air victory was, it had been costly. In three years, the Eighth and Ninth Air Forces had lost 48,847 airmen, killed or missing in action and presumed dead, and the Eighth reported a staggering 3,908 planes destroyed. "Except for the infantry, always the hardest hit," General Arnold wrote, "no group in the Army, in the air or on the ground, including paratroops and armored divisions, suffered as high a casualty rate as did our heavy bomber crews over Germany."[44]

V-E Day (Victory in Europe) came at 2:41 A.M. on 7 May 1945, as surrender papers were signed at Gen. Dwight Eisenhower's headquarters at Rheims, France. Reich Marshal Hermann Goering, the man who had commanded the once-illustrious Luftwaffe, knew all too well the key reason behind Germany's crushing defeat. "The Allies owe the success of the invasion to the air forces," Goering confessed. "They prepared the invasion; they made it possible; they carried it through. Without the U.S. air force, the war would still be going on elsewhere, but certainly not on German soil."[45]

Victory in Japan (V-J Day)

The entire Pacific campaign was a process of trying to lever the enemy from its widespread outposts one by one. The strategy concocted by Gen. Douglas MacArthur, and the similar one used by Adm. Chester Nimitz, who was in charge of the Navy's island-hopping campaigns, depended on airpower. Aircraft were to pound the successive Japanese strongholds, softening them up for invasion by ground troops. Once an outpost was secured, airfields would be built from which bombers could go on to attack the next enemy enclave.

In the Pacific, as the island stepping stones came closer and closer to the Japanese homeland, U.S. bombers began their deliberate and devastating attack on Japan's cities. The policy adopted for the use of American strategic airpower, against the Japanese as well as the Germans, was a concentration of effort on attacks against targets whose survival was vital to the enemy's war effort.

Such attacks, first flown in daylight and at medium altitude but then switched to night at low altitude, drew the Japanese interceptor force into battle, and the concentrated bomber streams used their considerable defensive firepower to inflict major losses. This eased the task of the following bombers and inevitably reduced the number of skilled pilots available to the Japanese.

The major target groups for these attacks were the factories producing Japan's aero engines and the factories that produced their military aircraft. Without these, the Japanese air effort would be crippled, reducing their capability for both offensive and defensive air missions.

Preparation for the assault on the island of Okinawa itself became the primary goal with the invasion protected and supported by the carrier borne warplanes of the U.S. Navy and Marine Corps.[46]

This aircraft carrier effort was divided into two main parts. The task of the fleet and light carriers of the Fast Carrier Task Force (FCTF), cruising off the island, was to protect the invasion fleet from Japanese air and naval intervention. For this role the FCTF employed large numbers of the latest Grumman F6F Hellcat and Vought F4U Corsair fighters for air protection, and the Grumman TBF/TBM Avenger torpedo bomber and Curtiss SB2C/SBW dive-bomber for defense against naval attack.

The task of the escort carriers of the Amphibious Support Force and Special Escort Carrier Group, operating closer to the island, was to provide tactical support

Fig. 9.42. Boeing B-29 Superfortress. Courtesy of the Fred Roos Collection.

for land forces with modern Grumman TBM Avenger attack aircraft and a mix of modern F6F and obsolete Grumman Wildcat fighters, supported by the multi-role F4Us of the U.S. Marine Corps embarked on the escort carriers of the Special Escort Carrier Group.

The American assault on the island of Saipan had been met with Japanese resistance as fierce as any since fighting began. Just the week before, on the night of 6 July 1945, 3,000 Japanese had hurled themselves against the 27th Division in one mass banzai charge, all to be killed. No one, and least of all President Harry Truman, expected the final stages of the war to become anything but more and more costly.[47]

As the air and ground forces got closer to Japan itself,

General Arnold began to deploy a new plane in the Far East, the long-awaited Boeing B-29 Superfortress (see fig. 9.42).

The largest bomber manufactured during World War II, the B-29, weighed twice as much as its Boeing-built predecessor, the B-17, and could carry twice the bombload. Its four huge Wright engines provided 4,000 more horsepower than the Fort's engines. It could fly almost 70 miles per hour faster, and its maximum range was almost double that of the B-17—4,200 miles. From March 1945 to the war's end, B-29s laid waste to 180 square miles of sixty-nine major cities of Japan. When the two atomic bombs fell from the bomb bays of the Guam-based B-29s, invasion operations were being carried out that would eventually have brought Japan to its knees at the cost of hundreds of thousands of American casualties. As the end came, Japan had no navy and its defense system was being mobilized for the invasion they knew would come.[48]

As horrible and devastating as the Hiroshima-Nagasaki bombs were, the question remains, was the use of the atom bomb necessary? It should be noted that more people were killed in the fire raids on the Japanese cities than in the two cities that were A-bombed. At least these bombs put an end to the bloody conflict that was certain to demand more deaths if it had continued. The atomic age was upon us.[49]

Notes

1. Misenhimer, *Aeroscience*, 726–27.
2. Nevin, *The Epic of Flight: Architects of Air Power*, 18.
3. Nevin, 33.
4. Nevin, 71.
5. Misenhimer, 727.
6. Nevin, 150.
7. Nevin, 6.
8. *The Luftwaffe*, 17.
9. *The Luftwaffe*, 33–34.
10. *The Luftwaffe*, 18.
11. Barker, *The RAF at War*, 19.
12. *The Luftwaffe*, 44.
13. *The Luftwaffe*, 65–66.
14. *The Luftwaffe*, 78.
15. Barker, 52.
16. Barker, 73.
17. Barker, 103.
18. Jablonski, *The Epic of Flight: America in the Air War*, 18.
19. Misenhimer, 730.
20. Reynolds, *The Epic of Flight: The Carrier War.*
21. *Carrier: Fortress at Sea.*
22. *Carrier: Fortress at Sea.*
23. *Carrier: Fortress at Sea.*
24. Misenhimer, 730–31.
25. Misenhimer, 732.
26. Reynolds, 49.
27. Reynolds, 61.
28. Jablonski, 31–32.
29. Reynolds, 68–75.
30. *Wings: Midway to Hiroshima.*
31. Misenhimer, 733.
32. *Wings: Midway to Hiroshima.*
33. Jablonski, 53–59.
34. *Wings over Europe.*
35. Jablonski, 89–105.
36. *Wings over Europe.*
37. *The Luftwaffe*, 121.
38. *The Luftwaffe*, 136–38.
39. *Normandy: The Great Crusade.*
40. *Normandy: The Great Crusade.*
41. *Normandy: The Great Crusade.*
42. Jablonski, 129–42.
43. *Normandy: The Great Crusade.*
44. *Wings over Europe.*
45. Misenhimer, 735.
46. *Wings: Midway to Hiroshima.*
47. *Wings: Midway to Hiroshima.*
48. Reynolds, 170.
49. Misenhimer, 735.

References

Barker, Ralph, and the editors of Time-Life Books. *The RAF at War*. Alexandria, Va.: Time-Life Books, 1981.

Brown, Carl A. *A History of Aviation*. 2d ed. Daytona Beach: Embry-Riddle Aeronautical University, 1980.

Carrier: Fortress at Sea. Computer laser optical disk. Bethesda, Md.: Discovery Communications, 1996.

Franklund, Noble. *Bomber Offensive: The Devastation of Europe*. New York: Ballantine Books, 1970.

Jablonski, Edward, and the editors of Time-Life Books. *The Epic of Flight: America in the Air War*. Alexandria, Va.: Time-Life Books, 1982.

The Luftwaffe. Alexandria, Va.: Time-Life Books, 1982.

Misenhimer, Ted G. *Aeroscience*. Culver City, Calif.: Aero Products Research, 1970.

Nevin, David, and the editors of Time-Life Books. *The Epic of Flight: Architects of Air Power*. Alexandria, Va.: Time-Life Books, 1981.

Normandy: The Great Crusade. Computer laser optical disk. Bethesda, Md.: Discovery Communications, 1994.

Price, Alfred. *Luftwaffe*. New York: Ballantine Books, 1970.

Reynolds, Clark G., and the editors of Time-Life Books. *The Epic of Flight: The Carrier War*. Alexandria, Va.: Time-Life Books, 1982.

Sims, Charles Augustus. *The Royal Air Force*. London: Black, 1968.

Taylor, John W. Ransom. *History of Aviation*. New York: Crown, 1972.

Wings: Midway to Hiroshima. Computer laser optical disk. Bethesda, Md.: Discovery Communications, 1994.

Wings over Europe. Computer laser optical disk. Bethesda, Md.: Discovery Communications, 1994.

10

U.S. Air Carriers after World War II

Henry R. Lehrer

THE STORY OF THE U.S. air carrier industry since the end of World War II is one of volatility and stagnation, expansion and retrenchment, and perhaps as many good decisions as bad. This government-regulated service industry, oligopolistic in nature, has grown light-years beyond anything aviation pioneers could have envisioned. Some futurists predict that within a few years, few Americans will not have traveled by air.

Air Carrier Industry Overview

Post–World War II and the 1950s

The war's impact on the U.S. air transportation industry was significant—not only in the new awareness of the possibilities of air transportation but also in the presence of a great number of former military pilots and airplanes. The Douglas DC-3 became the C-47 during the war and was returned to the civilian version afterward (fig. 10.1). New variants of proven wartime airframes emerged as the DC-4 and the Lockheed Constellation (figs. 10.2 and 10.3). Boeing modeled its new B-377 Stratocruiser on the B-29 Superfortress.

There were also several technological and operational benefits from the war, including improved communications equipment and procedures, the development of radar, and the experience gained from the implementation of an air traffic environment.

With so many airplanes and pilots available, the air carrier industry expanded rapidly. Although the air carriers that had received certificates of public convenience and necessity (CPCN) from the Civil Aeronautics Board (CAB) before the war were still the industry's major players, several new feeder carriers emerged, including Allegheny, Mohawk, Piedmont, North Central, Frontier, Bonanza, and Pacific (see fig. 10.4).

The British and Germans developed the jet engine before World War II, but the use of this power plant was slow to come to the air carrier airplane. Undaunted by the crashes in the early 1950s of the ill-fated De Havilland Comet, Pratt and Whitney moved forward with the development of the J57, a 10,000-pound thrust engine that would ultimately power the Boeing 707. The British-built turboprop Vickers Viscount (shown in fig. 10.5) began to make inroads into the U.S. market, but the pure jet engine, despite its slow start, was soon to dominate (see fig. 10.6). The crown jewel in aviation history may well have been Pan American Airlines' B-707 turbojet service, introduced on 26 October 1958 (see fig. 10.7).

The 1960s

During the 1960s, the U.S. air carrier industry experienced much less turmoil. Having in many cases just added jets to their fleets, U.S. air carriers like United expanded service westward to Hawaii, Northwest became truly a U.S. to Asia force to be reckoned with, and Pan American continued to circle the globe. It seemed to be a decade of purposeful expansion when major U.S. airlines were focusing on expansion by adding cities and regions to their service network. However, the CAB kept things pretty much under control, and everyone seemed happy.

Fig. 10.1. TWA's amazing DC-3 at the boarding gate at Lambert Field in St. Louis, ca. 1950. Willard Thomas photo via Fred Roos Collection.

Fig. 10.2. American Airlines' Douglas DC-4 is actually a converted World War II C-54 Skymaster. Note the cargo door in the aft fuselage. Courtesy of the Fred Roos Collection.

Fig. 10.3. The Lockheed Constellation enters service with TWA. Courtesy of TWA.

Fig. 10.4. Mohawk Convair. By permission of the National Air and Space Museum, Smithsonian Institution, ©1999 Smithsonian Institution.

Fig. 10.5. A Vickers Viscount operated by Capital Airlines. Courtesy of United Airlines.

Fig. 10.6. A Firechild Hiller 227B operated by Ozark Air Lines. FH-227B was a development of the Dutch Fokker-designed F-27. Courtesy of the Fred Roos Collection.

Fig. 10.7. A Boeing 707-120 of TWA landing at Lambert Field in St. Louis in 1969. Courtesy of the Fred Roos Collection.

Airlines were making money (see table 10.1). Profits rose from an annual industry average of $61.1 million in the 1950s to $179.8 million in the 1960s.

The average load factor of the U.S. scheduled airlines is an important indicator of economic health. Load factor is the sum of revenue passenger miles (RPM)/available seat miles (ASM) multiplied by 100. An RPM is one revenue passenger transported one mile in revenue service, and ASMs are the aircraft miles flown in each flight stage multiplied by the number of seats available on that stage for revenue passenger use.

In the 1960s, average annual RPMs were up 350 percent domestically and up over 400 percent for international routes (table 10.2). The ASMs were on the upswing—due in part to the introduction of the larger, faster jets. Domestic, international, and system ASMs increased between 200 and 250 percent. Although load fac-

tors were low at 54–55 percent, Americans were beginning to enjoy air travel. The government was preparing for extensive growth in transportation as well. The interstate highway system was being built, and aviation was

Table 10.1 Average Yearly Net Profit of U.S. Scheduled Airlines

Years	Operating Profit ($000)
1950–59	61,142
1960–69	179,808
1970–79	336,576
1980–89	247,210
1990–94	−2,613,495

Source: Air Transport Association, Washington, D.C.

Table 10.2 Load Factor History for U.S. Airlines

Period	Total RPMs (000)	Total ASMs (000)	Average Load Factor
Domestic			
1950–59	185,086,995	297,781,545	62.16
1960–69	549,258,612	1,019,448,062	53.88
1970–79	1,409,942,068	2,555,343,216	55.18
1980–89	2,636,890,497	4,390,901,370	60.05
1990–94	1,753,751,322	2,820,896,077	62.17
International			
1950–59	43,949,424	71,178,407	61.75
1960–69	168,736,186	306,023,057	55.14
1970–79	358,529,391	640,885,330	55.94
1980–89	677,214,519	1,051,634,899	64.40
1990–94	639,493,144	935,930,779	68.33
System			
1950–59	229,036,419	368,959,952	62.08
1960–69	717,994,798	1,325,471,119	54.17
1970–79	1,768,471,459	3,196,228,546	55.33
1980–89	3,314,105,016	5,442,536,278	60.89
1990–94	2,393,244,466	3,756,826,856	63.70

Source: Air Transport Association, Washington, D.C.

becoming more important. With transportation burgeoning, the Department of Transportation (DOT) was created in 1965.

The 1970s

The route structure now had almost an overcapacity situation—once again, as in the 1960s, there were more seats available than there were passengers to fill them. Systemwide ASMs as well as the RPMs for the 1970s more than doubled; much of this increase was probably due to the introduction of the wide-body airplane and the increasing popularity of travel by air rather than by train (see table 10.2 and fig. 10.8).

The introduction of wide-body airplanes increased seating capacity from 250 to over 350 in some configurations. Pan Am was first with the wide-body when the B-747 entered commercial service on 22 January 1970. American added DC-10 service from Los Angeles to Chicago on 5 August 1971 and used the same airplane for the first time on the San Francisco to Washington route nine days later. Lockheed trailed the field with the L-1011; much of the delay was a result of Lockheed's selection of the Rolls-Royce engine as the airplane's power plant. Rolls-Royce was having serious financial problems at the time, and only a controversial $250 million loan

Fig. 10.8. A Boeing 747-400 (wide-body) belonging to Northwest Air Lines lands at Detroit Metropolitan Airport in 1990. Courtesy of the Fred Roos Collection.

Fig. 10.9. A Lockheed L-1011, known as the Whisperliner by Eastern Air Lines, landing at Lambert Field in 1976. Courtesy of the Fred Roos Collection.

guarantee by Congress saved the day; Trans World Airlines (TWA) and Eastern were flying the airplane by the mid-1970s (see fig. 10.9). Significantly, discussion in Europe among the early members of the Airbus Industrie had resulted in the A300 airplane being produced; in the mid-1970s, there was even a hint that the United States was approached to join this conglomerate, which was to become a significant force in air transportation.

The Airline Deregulation Act of 1978 was one of the most significant events in the history of the U.S. airline industry. Airlines had been heavily regulated since the passage of the Civil Aeronautics Act of 1938 and the establishment of the CAB with the amendment of that legislation in 1940. The CAB controlled entry and exit routes as well as fares. In 1978, U.S. carriers suddenly were free to compete. The CAB was phased out on 31 December 1984, and many of its certification responsibilities were transferred to the DOT. But for all practical purposes, the U.S. air carriers could decide where they wanted to go and what they would charge. The immediate result was a veritable traveler's smorgasbord, and load factors doubled.

The 1980s

Three themes seem to exemplify the air carrier industry adventure during the 1980s: new entrants, expanded operations, and corporate mergers. Several new airlines appeared, including People Express in 1981 and America West in 1983.

American Airlines may have been the catalyst in the rush to expand routes structures, gain market share, or both. American ordered lots of new airplanes, opened hubs in Nashville, Raleigh/Durham, San Jose, and San Juan, and purchased South American routes from a struggling Eastern Airlines in 1989. Under the strong leadership of Robert Crandall, American took over TWA's London operation as well and made an additional move to the "Southern Rim." Unfortunately, by the 1990s, many of these strategic market domination moves were earning American a considerable amount of red ink. United expanded to the West in 1985 when it took over the Pacific routes of a struggling Pan Am.

Mergers occurred frequently. Northwest and Hughes Air West merged in 1980; Piedmont acquired Empire in

1985 and then was acquired, along with Pacific Southwest (PSA), by USAir in 1987; Delta got the Pacific Northwest, a Salt Lake City hub, and a stronger West Coast persona when it bought Western in 1987. Some alliances made sense, but others did not; some were of a hostile nature, whereas others had the effect of propping up an otherwise struggling airline. When asked why his airline made steady profits in the 1990s while others floundered, Southwest CEO Herb Kelleher reportedly quipped, "We didn't merge."

The 1990s

Following the rapid expansion, the air carrier industry reeled from three assaults. One blow was a recession, the second was a dramatic increase in fuel prices as a result of the Gulf War, and the third was the fact that many of the true long-term costs associated with the expansion rampage of the 1980s were impacting the balance sheet.

American Airlines took over most of Eastern Airlines' South American and Latin American routes in 1990 and TWA's Heathrow routes in 1991, and arch rivals Delta and United divided the last of the Pan Am network.

The total losses in the U.S. air carrier industry by 1993 were greater than all the money earned by carriers since 1938. In addition, the upstart air carriers such as Kiwi, Reno Air, and Valuejet as well as the Southwest look-alikes like CALite and U2 were all tapping into the majors as well as rivals' bottom line. Bankruptcy became common, with TWA, America West, and Continental moving in and out of Chapter 11. However, by 1995 the turnaround had begun, and the industry, now keenly aware that costs must be trimmed, was in the black for the first time in the decade.

Air Carriers

Since the Airline Deregulation Act of 1978, U.S. carriers can be divided into four basic classes:

Basic Air Carrier Groups	Annual Operating Revenues
1. Majors	Over $1 billion
2. Nationals	$100 million to $1 billion
3. Large regionals	$10 million to $100 million
4. Medium regionals	Under $10 million

Within each of these classifications, there are also sub-groups based on the nature of each carrier's operations such as Combination Service (passengers and cargo), All-Cargo Service, and Charter Service.

U.S. air carriers, particularly the majors, are important in the global air transportation system. In 1994, U.S. airlines carried almost 44 percent of the world's passengers on 39.56 percent of the revenue passenger kilos (RPK), one revenue passenger carried one kilometer in revenue service (table 10.3). With respect to the carriage of freight, the U.S. carriers accounted for 29 percent of the world's freight ton kilos (FTK). The major carriers hauled over 80 percent of all the U.S. industry's passengers by way of 87.9 percent of the RPKs; the majors also carried the lion's share of the U.S. portion of

Table 10.3 Performance by U.S. Scheduled Airlines in 1994

	World Passengers	World RPKs	World FTKs
Majors	35.80%	34.78%	23.77%
Nationals	4.70%	3.83%	4.65%
Regionals	3.32%	.95%	.58%
Total	43.82%	39.56%	29.00%

Source: Air Transport World

the world's cargo tonnage with 81.9 percent of the traffic.

The following section will present an overview of the major airlines engaged in carrying passengers.

The Majors (* Cargo only)

American
American West
Continental
Delta
DHL *
Federal Express *
Northwest
Southwest
TWA
United
UPS *
US Airways

Individual Major Air Carriers

AMERICAN AIRLINES

Founded in 1931 as American AirWays

1997 Operating revenues: $14.3 billion

1997 Operating profit: $985 million

Significant mergers/acquisitions:

AirCal—1 July 1987

Trans Caribbean—2 March 1971

Fleet owned or leased in 1997

B-767 200/200ER/300ER	71
B-757 200	90
B-727 200	79
MD-11	13
DC-10 10/30	18
MD-80	260
A-300-600R	35
Fokker 100	75
Total	641

American Airlines traces its lineage to 1929, when the Aviation Corporation (AVCO) was formed from parts of five smaller airlines. Following a dismal financial performance in 1930, American Airways, Inc., was formed and the fledgling carrier soon won the southern portion of first transcontinental routes authorized at Postmaster General Walter Folger Brown's "spoils conference." American Airways quickly moved to expand into the northeastern and central portion of the nation and soon had acquired routes in that region from Transamerican and Martz.

In 1934, American Airways adopted that name as a result of the reallocation of the airmail routes under the Air Mail Act. C. R. Smith, who was to lead the carrier for over three decades, assumed the leadership of American. With the arrival of the DC-3, the plane that changed how the public viewed air travel, American expanded its route structure. What Smith had to sell was safety, customer service, new equipment, and reliability.

Following World War II, American launched international service over the North Atlantic to Europe, and it was flying jets from New York to Los Angeles by 1959. American was well on its way to building one of the nation's strongest routes, but in 1972 a possible merger

with Western Airlines was turned down by the CAB, and in the next year several key company officials were accused of taking kickbacks and making illegal political contributions. Employee morale hit a low point, work habits became sloppy, and the previously shining image of American as one of the great air carriers was tarnished. Severe steps were about to be taken. However, along the way, American acquired Trans Caribbean in March 1971.

C. R. Smith returned briefly to American from his post as commerce secretary under President Lyndon B. Johnson, and a young former treasurer from Bloomingdale's, Robert Crandall, orchestrated American's return to good fiscal health before Albert Casey took control in 1974. The mid-1970s saw a series of cost-cutting measures return the company to profitability as well as American's establishment of the SABRE computer reservation system in 1976. However, the genius behind the scenes may have been Crandall, who became president in 1980 and who set new directions for the industry with such innovative ideas as Super Saver fares, frequent flyer programs, and a two-tiered wage structure for pilots.

During the 1980s, American replaced B-747s with more suitable planes, opened new hubs, and began to dominate the domestic market and to create an international presence. Throughout the 1980s, American had the greatest number of airplanes, employees, and passengers. The acquisition of AirCal on July 1987 gave American a strong intrastate presence in the most populated corridor in the West.

In 1990 and 1991, American took over the South American and Latin American operations of Eastern Airlines and TWA's London-Heathrow operations. When the Gulf War began, most of the nation's carriers were forced into a period of retrenchment and refocusing, the war having had a longer impact than its short duration would seem to indicate. American was no different. At a 1993 meeting in Florida, Crandall announced, "American Airlines will no longer serve cities in which the carrier can no longer compete." Many communities where American went head-to-head with other airlines for market share suddenly lost service from American as well as many, if not most, other carriers. The notion of profitability was suddenly a distant memory, and many smaller communities paid the price.

AMERICA WEST AIRLINES

Founded in 1983

1997 Operating revenues: $1.68 billion

1997 Operating profit: $161.8 million

Fleet owned or leased in 1997

B-757 200	14
B-737 100/200/300	62
A-320-200	26
Total	102

Founded in 1983 in Phoenix, America West competed with Southwest Airlines and established itself as a key air carrier out of its Sky Harbor hub. Under the leadership of Ed Beauvais, American West quickly built a route structure in the West and focused on giving the customer quality service. Employees had some of the best fringe benefits in the industry, including profit sharing and day-care centers. One reason for the company's success was the extensive cross-utilization of a nonunion, low-cost, but highly motivated workforce. It seemed that America West would do nothing but succeed; however, profits were slow to come until the late 1980s.

Southwest Airlines was one of America West's chief competitors. Although America West had most of the regional traffic between Phoenix and Las Vegas, Southwest, already a successful air carrier in the same markets, was not about to let an upstart steal any significant number of passengers without a fight. Southwest was to find America West's Achilles heel via a time-proven device of fare matching and fare cutting. America West was soon in big financial trouble and in 1988 had to employ some severe cost-cutting measures such as reduction in the number of flights and employee layoffs. These drastic measures seemed to work, and the young company was soon back in the black.

The 1990s were just as tough on America West as on the rest of the industry. With an attempt at lengthening its route structure into the East and taking advantage of the demise of Eastern Airlines, America West soon provided service between New York and Washington and followed with service to the Southeast United States from a new hub in Columbus, Ohio. The dream of making the company a major player and a major airline was well on its way to realization, but the financial picture was bleak when, in 1992, America West filed for Chapter 11 protection and Ed Beauvais was out.

In 1995, the company emerged from bankruptcy and posted record earnings for the second year in a row. However, the message from president A. Maurice Myers is that the America West of tomorrow will be built on four tenets: keep cost low, know your customer, build staying power through financial stability and market muscle, and build a high-performance culture.

CONTINENTAL AIRLINES

Founded in 1926 as Varney Speed Lines

1997 Operating revenues: $716 million

Significant mergers/acquisitions/consolidations:
Merged with Pioneer in 1954
Purchased by Texas International in 1982
People Express and New York Air were purchased on 1 February 1987

Fleet owned or leased in 1997

B-757 200	25
B-747 200	4
B-737 100/200/300/500/700	142
B-727 200	33
DC-10 10/30	28
MD-80	69
DC-9 30	26
Total	327

Continental Airlines traces its roots back to the late 1920s, when Varney Air Transport served several locations in Colorado and New Mexico from its base in El Paso. However, when Robert Six, a flamboyant and dynamic leader, took the reins in 1936, he personally orchestrated the climb of the carrier. Moving to Denver in 1938, Six shed the Varney name and began transforming Continental into a force within the industry.

During World War II, the Continental fleet served as military transports. After the war, Six used the fleet, several interchange agreements, and a merger with Pioneer to build an extensive route structure in the West. Following that domestic expansion, Six looked further west, and by the mid-1960s, by using a long-range jet fleet, he was able to offer transpacific service. That route structure is still much in place today. The 1960s and early 1970s were good years for Continental, and although Six shut down the company in 1976 over labor disputes, he ultimately settled with the unions, and the strong sense of family prevailed. However, that sense of belonging was to be tested when Six relinquished leadership of Continental after more than forty years at the helm.

Following several failed merger talks between Continental and Western, Frank Lorenzo began acquiring stock in Continental and ultimately won control of the company via Texas International (TXI) in 1982. When Texas International acquired Continental, it took the unusual step of merging Texas International into Continental rather than lose the "brand familiarity" that Continental enjoyed. Things were not to go well. In August 1983, labor struck, and the company declared bankruptcy in September. Several related mergers then followed.

Three names seem to be most important in the Continental mid-1980s merger/acquisition scheme: Frontier, People Express, and New York Air. What is unique is that in several instances, the carrier was merely acquired and not merged, maintaining a product identity; however, all of these deals spelled the end for the carrier acquired.

Frontier Airlines was formed in 1946 as Monarch Airlines, and it concentrated its service in the West. Monarch merged with Challenger Airlines in 1949 and with Arizona Airways in 1950 and was renamed Frontier. In 1967, Frontier merged with Central Airlines, and in 1985 they were purchased by People Express but did not merge. Now a part of People Express, Frontier ceased operations in August 1986 after declaring bankruptcy.

Another important Continental-related carrier, New York Air, was formed in 1980 by Texas Air, then owner of Texas International. New York Air was ultimately merged into Continental in 1987, but this was not to last either.

It seemed that Lorenzo and Texas Air were on a collision course with destiny, and nothing seemed to be working. In short order, the company posted losses in 1987 and 1988, Eastern struck, and Texas Air went into bankruptcy. Lorenzo soon left the company with a $5 million debt.

The current company has been through several CEOs in recent years and has returned to profitability. Several major cost-cutting measures, such as drawing down activity at the Denver hub and replacing older airplanes, seem to be having a positive effect on the financial health of the company. Coupled with an attempt to renew customer confidence, Continental may be just about to return to a position of importance within the industry.

Delta Air Lines

Founded in 1929, out of business in 1930, resumed operations in 1934

1997 Operating revenues: $13.9 billion

1997 Operating profit: $1.6 billion

Significant mergers/acquisitions:
  Chicago and Southern acquired by Delta in 1953
  Northeast merged with Delta in 1972
  Western (formed in 1925) acquired Pacific
    Northern in 1967 and merged with Delta in 1987

Fleet owned or leased in 1997

B-767 200/300/300ER/	74
B-757 200	91
B-737 200/300	67
B-727	131
L-1011	46
MD-11	14
MD-88/90	136
Total	559

While most airlines that trace their heritage back to the time before World War II were primarily airmail carriers in their earliest days, Delta Air Lines first made a name in aviation through crop dusting. Formed in 1929 but out of business in 1930, Delta Air Service resumed operations in 1934 in Monroe, Louisiana. Delta was led for more than three decades by C. E. Woolman. It was under his leadership that the young company, relying primarily on east-west routes throughout the lower Southeast United States, moved to Atlanta in the early 1940s. Delta has had a strong presence throughout the region since that time.

Two key acquisitions lengthened and strengthened Delta's route structure. The first was the purchase of Chicago and Southern in 1953 and the securing of a New England presence with the purchase of Northeast in 1972. Led at this time by "Buster Tom" Beebe, the senior management had a tendency to be somewhat inbred and quite "southern." Ron Allen succeeded Beebe in 1983.

One of the unique things about the company was the sense of family that existed among the employees. Although only the pilots were unionized, employees assumed that there would always be a job with the company. Salaries ranked with the best in the industry. The result was productive and loyal workers who took pride in their work, and during the 1980s employees even bought a B-767, the *Spirit of Delta,* for the company. Delta became one of the Big Three, along with United and American. Interestingly, until the airline fiscal problems of the 1990s, workers believed that the company would always take care of everything.

From the customer's standpoint, Delta offered great service based on a fine blend of southern hospitality and reliable service. But what Delta gave had a high price, and that price was some of the highest operating costs in the business. Although Delta continues to carry almost as many passengers as United and American, labor costs drive the company's yield per passenger mile very low.

Delta built a large route structure throughout the United States but was a bit slow in developing international routes. A merger in 1987 with Western Airlines gave Delta a foothold in the Northwest and major bases in Salt Lake City and Los Angeles. Western was a dominate force in the Northwest, particularly after a merger with Pacific Northern Western in 1967.

In 1991, Delta acquired remaining operations of Pan Am, including its JFK and Frankfurt hubs. Then, within three years, Delta lost $1.6 billion, stockholders' equity dropped, long-term debt rose, and the airline lost its investment-grade rating. But a true test of the very fiber of this great company may reveal that an airline that for forty years was known to stand by its employees now found that its employees would stand by it. Delta tried to trim its operating budget by $2 billion as early as 1997. The plan was called Leadership 7.5, and it was intended to bring Delta's yield up and its costs down to 7.5 cents per ASM. Delta's employees and managers were optimistic that measures such as realignment of hubs, right-sizing the workforce, reduction of long-term debt, and cost-cutting measures would allow the airline to continue to provide top quality cabin service coupled with safe and efficient worldwide service. They were right.

Northwest Airlines

Founded in 1926 as Northwest Airways, renamed Northwest Orient, later dropping Orient

1997 Operating revenues: $10.2 billion

1997 Operating profit: $1.16 billion

Significant mergers/acquisitions:
Acquired Republic in 1987

Fleet owned or leased in 1997

B-757 200	48
B-747 100/200/F	33
B-727 200	40
DC-10 30/40	36
DC-9 10/30/40/50	179
MD-80	8
A-320	52
Total	396

Formed by Charles Dickinson in 1926 as a mail carrier serving the upper Midwest, Northwest Airlines began offering international service to Asia in 1947. Northwest was also one of the first U.S. carriers to use the B-747-400.

Until the 1980s, the airline quietly served the needs of transpacific customers. Then, in 1987, Northwest attempted to strengthen its domestic routes by merging with Republic. A stable company with hubs in Phoenix, Memphis, and Detroit, Republic was itself the result of many mergers. It began in 1979 when North Central and Southern merged. Hughes Air West then merged with Republic in 1980. Hughes Air West itself was formed in 1970 after a 1968 three-way merger of Bonanza, Pacific, and West Coast Airlines. But following these mergers, the new, expanded Northwest was plagued by labor unrest and an associated drop in customer service. The airline became known within the industry as "Northworst."

The attempt to blend the corporate cultures of Republic and Northwest caused internal employee problems that were to haunt the giant for many years. The core issue seemed to be seniority lists and the merging of employees. (Delta encountered the same issue when it acquired the last of Pan Am in the early 1990s.) The tensions extended to the flight deck, as pilots tried to determine whether Northwest or Republic procedures were better or most appropriate. But as the smoke cleared, what emerged was a major air carrier with a solid domestic route structure and a proven international presence.

In 1989, a leveraged buyout (LBO) of the company by Alfred Checchi caused financial problems. Saddled with debt as a result of a large aircraft order due for delivery in the 1990s and still feeling the burden of the LBO in the form of an increased debt-to-equity ratio, Northwest was to receive aid from an unexpected corner. The federal government made an unprecedented ruling, and KLM Royal Dutch Airlines gave Northwest a large amount of cash and a code-sharing agreement for North Atlantic service to the Netherlands. In return, Northwest gave up 49 percent ownership in the company, and the door was opened for a series of international alliances between major U.S. air carriers and foreign partners such as has never been seen within U.S. air transportation history.

The final chapter on the new Northwest has not been written, but it is clear that the airline may have scooped the competition in the development of both an Pacific and a North Atlantic service structure. With several hubs to choose from, all located in the northern part of the nation, Northwest has perhaps laid the foundation for the future. In 1994, the airline led world airlines in operating profits with $830.4 million and was fourth in the world in net profit with $292.5 million.

Southwest Airlines

Founded in 1931 as American Airways

1997 Operating revenues: $3.8 billion

1997 Operating profit: $524.2 million

Significant mergers/acquisitions:
  Morris acquired by Southwest 1994.
  Transtar (formerly Muse) purchased by Southwest in 1985 and dismantled by Southwest in 1987

Fleet owned or leased in 1997
  B-737 200/300/500/700   261

The history of Southwest Airlines is like that of no other air carrier. Southwest traces its roots to Texas and the late 1960s when the founder, Rollin W. King, set out to improve air service within the state. The carrier has always made a profit, and it has influenced the very fiber of a major transportation mode like no others before it.

In the late 1960s, intrastate air travel in Texas was dominated by Braniff International Airways and Texas International Airlines. However, service by these two carriers within the state was usually the beginning or end of a route segment that included interstate travel, and the service offered to the intrastate customer was sparse because many of the seats were occupied by full route customers. King thought that there was a niche for intra-Texas travel that was both lucrative and virtually untapped, and on 20 February 1968, a CPCN was issued to Southwest by the Texas Aeronautics Commission to operate a triangular route between Dallas, San Antonio, and Houston.

Lamarr Muse joined Southwest Airlines in the early 1970s, and the fledgling carrier quickly adopted the B-737 as its airplane, offered the lowest fares in their mar-

kets, and developed a corporate culture where everyone worked hard but had fun. Even in the earliest days, it was not uncommon to have the cabin staff dress as Easter bunnies or wear reindeer antlers. While the competition may have looked upon the "new kid at Love Field" as something that would not last, Southwest quickly moved into a position of preeminence in the region.

Perhaps the essence of this great carrier is captured in the Southwest mission statement:

> Dedication to the highest quality of customer service delivered with a sense of warmth, friendliness, individual pride, and company spirit. Creativity and innovation are encouraged and above all, employees will be provided the same concern, respect, and caring attitude within the organization that they are expected to share externally with every customer.

The formula used by Southwest is simple: low-cost, no-frills, frequent point-to-point service with market entry with at least ten flights a day. The company itself is strategically and financially conservative, relying on high employee productivity and airplane utilization, and when the airline expands, it "just takes out the cookie cutter and does the same old thing at another airport."

Southwest does not interline (provide connections from one airline to another). Considered by some the Wal-mart of air transportation, it uses only the B-737 and has very low employee turnover. More than 51 percent of the employees are women, and 82 percent of all employees are under forty years of age (1994 data). The company is union, and pilots as well as the newest employees make industry-competitive salaries.

The keys to the success of this company are the lowest operating costs in the industry, customer satisfaction, and high employee morale and work ethic. However, much of the success of Southwest must be attributed to the leadership of Herb Kelleher, who served the company first as chief counsel and then as president and CEO. Kelleher is a charismatic leader, respected by employees and fellow industry executives, who is known to visit maintenance areas late at night dressed as famous rock-and-roll entertainers. His success has been studied at major business schools and unsuccessfully copied by other air carriers. What was missing was that it takes more than a cheap seat a Southwest to make.

Southwest has confined most of its operation to the West with small excursions into the upper Midwest and the middle Atlantic seaboard. However, with the acquisition of Morris Air in Salt Lake City, a route structure in the upper great basin was secured.

The upstart United Shuttle gave Southwest some fits in the lucrative California corridor market in the early 1990s, but the airline once again made a profit. In fact, in 1994, Southwest was eighth among the world's air carriers in net profit, all by not straying from its time-proven formula of conservative growth, high productivity, and having fun.

TWA

Founded in 1930 as Transcontinental and Western
  Air, renamed Trans World Airlines in 1950

1997 Operating revenues: $3.3 billion

1997 Net operating (loss):($284.8) billion

Significant mergers/acquisitions:
  Ozark acquired by TWA in 1986

Fleet owned or leased in 1997

B-767 200	14
B-757 200	15
B-74	73
B-727 200	30
DC-9 10/30/40/50	58
MD-80/83	65
Total	255

Trans World Airlines (TWA) traces its lineage to the earliest of the contract airmail routes of the 1920s. One of the oldest of this nation's air carriers, TWA was formed in 1930 when Transcontinental Air Transport (TAT) and a portion of Western Air Express System (WAE) were renamed Transcontinental and Western Air. Utilizing a then state-of-the-art fleet of DC-3s and Boeing 307 Stratoliners, TWA quickly built a reputation for quality service, safety, and technical excellence.

Led by Jack Frye for twenty years, beginning in the 1930s, TWA was to develop a strong domestic as well as international route structure. Following CAB approval in 1944, TWA began to challenge Pan Am in the lucrative North Atlantic market.

TWA moved into jet airplanes in the late 1950s and offered an around-the-world service by 1968. However, merger talks with Pan Am failed in the 1970s, and a series of route swaps and temporary CAB route approvals took place. The result was an assumption of TWA's Pacific routes by Pan Am and a modification of several European segments.

The 1970s were difficult for TWA, and although the international routes were doing fine, there were problems in the domestic market. The lack of the "right sized airplane for the right sized market," a concept that is well known and embraced in the 1990s, was beginning to cause the carrier financial difficulties; a forty-five-day strike by flight attendants did not help either. Although the development of St. Louis and New York's JFK Airport as hubs took place and deregulation became a reality, TWA began to shrink. By the early 1980s, many of the diversified TWA corporate holdings such as Hilton Hotels, Century 21, Canteen Corporation, and Trans World Services were sold.

In the mid-1980s, Frank Lorenzo made a major play to take over the airline. TWA pilots surrendered wage concessions to Carl Icahn to avoid Lorenzo. Icahn quickly acquired Ozark in 1986. This move virtually assured TWA of domination of the St. Louis hub as well as providing TWA with a midwestern route structure that was mature and stable. However, TWA was saddled with one of the oldest fleets in the industry, and Icahn did not reinvest carrier profits in the company. Airplanes and physical facilities were wearing out and were not being replaced; Icahn was also not endearing himself to the TWA rank and file. In fact, it was reported that Icahn was "cannibalizing" portions of TWA so as to finance raids on other companies; this included the sale of TWA's highly valued Heathrow routes, a move considered by some as almost fatal to the company.

Icahn left TWA in 1993 when it was in the throes of Chapter 11 bankruptcy. His successor, Jeffrey Erickson, formerly of Reno Air and Midway, brought the airline back to profitability. TWA may never return to its former greatness as an envied world carrier, but it remains a contender in the aviation marketplace (see figs. 10.10 and 10.11).

UNITED AIRLINES

Founded in 1931

1997 Operating revenues: $17.4 billion

1997 Operating profit: $1.26 billion

Significant mergers/acquisitions:
  Acquired Capital Airlines in 1961

Fig. 10.10. Boeing 767. Courtesy of the Fred Roos Collection.

Fig. 10.11. Boeing 777. Courtesy of United Airlines.

Fleet owned or leased in 1997

B-777 200	30
B-767 200/300ER	42
B-757	94
B-747 100/200/400	49
B-737 200/300/500	210
B-727	75
DC-10 10/30	30
A-319/320	45
Total	575

United Airlines is one of the largest modern U.S. carriers. Formed in 1931 as Boeing Air Transport as a result of consolidation of several companies under the United Aircraft and Transport Corporation, the company relied on airmail subsidies rather than passenger revenues, as just about all of its rivals did at the times. However, Boeing Air Transport had one of the more lucrative routes, New York to San Francisco via Chicago. As a result of several earlier incorporations and the 1934 Air Mail Act, the fledgling company became United Air Lines, Inc., in 1934 and United Airlines in 1943.

W. A. Patterson, a hands-on manager, led the company from the mid-1930s until 1966. Patterson felt that he needed to know his employees as individuals who had an opinion that needed to be heard. He was instrumental in the development of United's Rule of Five—Honesty, Sincerity, Safety, Passenger Comfort, and Schedule Dependability.

United, always a major player in the east-west air routes through the heartland of the nation, began to build the earliest semblance of today's hub in Denver in the early 1950s. Relying heavily on the DC-6 and then the jet by the early 1960s, United built a major terminal building at New York (later JFK) International Airport at Idlewild.

The acquisition of Capital Airlines in 1961 was a move calculated to strengthen United's domestic routes. Capital, which was formed in 1938 as Pennsylvania Central Airlines, had a strong presence along the East Coast and in the Midwest. However, United really had its sights set elsewhere.

The CAB was interested in expanding service from the U.S. mainland to the Hawaii, and United wanted a piece of the action. Continuing their practice of granting route approvals to carriers that could provide the service already or to those struggling airlines that needed a bit of a financial boost, the CAB allowed United, Pan American, and Western to fly the route. United jumped into the market with both feet, dominated it, and further expanded into the Pacific. A major mistake was made in the late 1960s, though, when the airline added its new wide-body airplane to the route just like its competitors. Suddenly there was overcapacity, and United took a financial beating.

In the 1970s, all the major carriers were diversifying into hotels, catering services, and other related leisure markets; United did the same. United was looking forward to the planned deregulation of the industry. The airline felt that since the government would no longer award routes, approve fares, and control entry and exit by an airline, United could dominate weaker carriers that had thrived due to CAB protection under regulation. The carrier survived, virtually unscathed, the initial jockeying for position in the early 1980s. In fact, under the leadership of Richard Ferris, United launched the Apollo Computer System and maintained a strong route structure from strategically located hubs in Chicago, Denver, and San Francisco. But the early to mid-1980s were not so kind to the airline. American Airlines and Robert Crandall were seeking new routes and passengers, and United was not making a lot of money.

As a deregulation strategy, United gave up many domestic short-haul routes and began developing a long-haul route presence. In 1985, United took over Pan Am's Pacific operations, and in 1991, it took over Pan Am's London-Heathrow operations. In 1992, United received permission to operate Pan Am's Caribbean and South American routes.

United employees purchased the company in 1997, and CEO Stephen Wolfe was replaced by a new management team headed by Gerald Greenwald. Shuttle by United, a separate West Coast entity, is trying to reclaim lost passengers most recently claimed by Southwest.

US Airways

Founded in 1937 as All-American Airlines, later Allegheny Airlines, renamed USAir in 1979.
1997 Operating revenues: $8.5 billion
1997 Net profit: $1 billion
Significant mergers/acquisitions:
Lake Central acquired by Allegheny in 1968
Mohawk acquired by Allegheny in 1972.

Empire acquired by Piedmont in 1985
Pacific Southwest acquired by USAir in 1987
Piedmont acquired by USAir in 1989

Fleet owned or leased in 1997

B-767 200ER	12
B-757 200	34
B-737 200/300/400	195
DC-9 30	40
MD-80	31
Fokker 100	40
Total	352

Formed in 1937 as All-American Airlines, later Allegheny Airlines, and renamed USAir in 1979, this airline has always offered quality service on the East Coast and in the Midwest. To understand today's USAir, we must review the individual stories of Allegheny, Piedmont, and Pacific Southwest.

Allegheny was always a strong regional air carrier in the East and Midwest. Operating from a hub in Pittsburgh and a smaller facility at Washington National Airport, Allegheny began to dominate the upper Midwest when it acquired Lake Central in 1968 and Mohawk in 1972.

Piedmont began in 1940 as a charter carrier and offered scheduled service in 1948. It had a strong route structure throughout the Carolinas with service into the Midwest and eastern seaboard as well. Piedmont was known for good service, and it built hubs in Daytona, Charlotte, and Baltimore. The acquisition of Empire in 1985 strengthened Piedmont's presence on the eastern seaboard. USAir then acquired Piedmont in 1989. Surprisingly, this did not seem to fit the model for 1980s expansion of the other U.S. air carriers, who concentrated on route expansion. Piedmont and USAir served many of the same city-pairs, so the true reason for the merger may have been to eliminate head-to-head competition and to dominate the eastern United States.

Pacific Southwest, based in San Diego, was formed in 1949 and initially served as an intrastate carrier. One of the first U.S. carriers to offer Bae 146 four-engine jet service, Pacific Southwest was the darling of southern California and became quickly known for its fleet of Smileliners (Bae 146s with a smiling face painted on the lower portion of each airplane's nose). In a move to open east-west routes, USAir acquired Pacific Southwest in 1987. However, with all these acquisitions, USAir—

previously known for its conservative expansion—suddenly had hubs or mini-hubs in Pittsburgh, Dayton, Charlotte, Philadelphia, Buffalo, Baltimore, and Washington National, plus new West Coast facilities from the Pacific Southwest merger.

One of the most visible leaders of Allegheny was Edward Colodny, a Harvard lawyer and former CAB attorney who became president in 1975. Colodny opposed deregulation and continued to steer the air carrier toward an eastern niche centered on the fortress hub in Pittsburgh. The balance sheet was good for most of the 1980s, and the airline continued to grow slowly. However, even though the plan for implementing the mergers and acquisitions of the mid-1980s was to go slowly, there were to be some difficult days ahead. In 1989 and 1990, the difficulty of integrating Piedmont into the system and the high costs of maintaining long routes from eastern hub to southern California destinations (part of the old Pacific Southwest system) began to affect profits. The company, now under the leadership of Seth Schofield, began to lose money and quickly retrenched back east.

There were other problems. While the industry was losing more money every year in the early 1990s, USAir lost greater amounts, proportionally. The carrier had some of the highest operating costs in the industry; in addition, USAir took over management of the Trump Shuttle (formerly Eastern Shuttle) in 1991. Things were not looking good, but help came from an unusual source.

USAir had been unique among the major U.S. air carriers in that it had no significant international route structure. British Airways (BA), long courting a U.S. partner, and USAir, looking for cash, formed a somewhat shaky alliance in 1993. The resulting $400 million of financial support that British Airways gave for 25 percent of the USAir voting stock was a high price to pay, but it may have saved USAir. The airline pledged to maintain its "core strength" in Pittsburgh, Charlotte, Philadelphia, and Baltimore.

THE NATIONALS

Air Wisconsin
Alaska
American International
American Trans Air Arrow

Atlantic Southeast
Business Express
Carnival
Continental Express
Continental Micronesia
DHL Airways
Emery
Evergreen
Express One
Hawaiian
Horizon Air
Kiwi
Markair
Midwest Express
Reno
Simmons
Southern Air
Sun Country
Trans States
USAir Shuttle
World Tower

The national airlines are a diverse group. Many were regionals at one time, and many will be majors in the near future. Carriers in this classification also seem to have chosen to stay in a specific market niche either in a certain region or by serving a specific market.

Many nationals have very strong code-sharing (both the major, the national, and even a regional use the same flight number prefix) relationships with majors. Examples include Delta's partner, Atlantic Southeast, which offers service from Delta's Dallas–Fort Worth and Atlanta hubs, and Simmons, a code-sharing partner with American, which has service from American's hubs in Chicago to Dallas–Fort Worth. These relationships benefit both the major and the national because, with the hub-and-spoke system, one carrier can funnel passengers to the other. In recent years, there are even instances of the major partner giving up a particular route to the code-sharing partner so that the smaller carrier, usually flying airplanes with a smaller capacity and thus lower fixed operating costs, could more economically provide the service.

The nationals are important in the U.S. air transportation scheme. They carry almost 5 percent (see table 10.3) of the world's passengers and almost 11 percent of the U.S. scheduled air carriers passengers. With almost thirty carriers classified by the DOT as nationals, it is impossible to describe each. However, to best capture the flavor of the nationals, three nationals are portrayed below: Alaska, a well-established air carrier with a long history and a strong service niche; Reno Air, a new carrier trying to establish itself in the West; and Carnival, a charter service that now offers scheduled service.

Alaska

Alaska Airlines began in 1932 as McGee Airways with one single-engine airplane. It was renamed Alaska in 1944. After acquiring several smaller Alaskan airlines at about the same time, the modern company has established itself as a premier small airline. With service up and down the West Coast, the Seattle-based carrier serves points as far afield as Mexico and Russia. It has its own commuter affiliate in Horizon and a loyal customer corps. Operating in some very difficult weather locations within the state of Alaska, the airline was one of the first U.S. air carriers to add the Heads-up Display flight guidance system on the flight deck.

There have been several mergers and acquisitions. Alaska Coastal Airlines and Cordova Airlines were acquired in 1968, and Jet America, formed in 1981, merged with Alaska in 1986. Horizon Air Industries was acquired as a regional feeder for Alaska in 1986, so the carrier suddenly had an established short-stage length route structure in the Northwest.

The airline had a strong earnings record and a good balance sheet during the 1970s and 1980s. The airline felt it was well positioned to weather any storm, but after nineteen years of profitability, the bottom dropped out. One immediate solution was to implement a number of cost-cutting measures that included refinancing of loans, reduction or elimination of unprofitable routes and destinations, and general cost cutting throughout the company. Future orders for the MD-90 were reduced from twenty to ten as well.

In 1994, chairperson Raymond Vicci was ousted, but not before he orchestrated a dramatic financial turnaround for the company. After a net loss of $44.5 million in 1993, Alaska was in the black at $39.3 million and recovery was in sight. In the late 1990s, the Alaska fleet consisted of newer MD-80 and B-737 airplanes, approximately seventy, and boardings continued to rise.

Carnival Airlines

Carnival Airlines was originally started for the sole purpose of transporting tourists and gamblers between Fort Lauderdale and Carnival's Crystal Palace Resort and Casino in the Bahamas. It is now a full-fledged national airline with a fleet of twenty-five aircraft (six Airbus A-300s, six Boeing 727-200, eight Boeing 737-400, and five Boeing 737-200) and well over 1,300 employees. Unaudited revenues for the fiscal year ending 30 June 1995 exceeded $200 million. Carnival had impressive traffic increases in 1994.

Carnival Airlines was launched in 1988 when Ted Arison of Carnival Cruise Lines and Reuven Wertheim, an executive with twenty-three years of experience at El Al Intentional Airlines, acquired Pacific Interstate Airline's B-727-100 and about thirty employees; two more 727s followed. Although the Bahamas charter business was profitable, it was also very seasonal, so in 1991 Carnival began scheduled service to the Northeast, mainly concentrating on underserved airports. Its route structure covers the Northeast, Florida, California, the Caribbean, and the Bahamas. Nearly 30 percent of the airline's revenue comes from charter business, and there is codesharing. Carnival recently added service to Fort Myers, Florida, and Hartford, Connecticut.

Reno Air

Reno Air, formed in 1990, began scheduled service on 1 July 1992 with one McDonnell-Douglas MD-80 aircraft and 150 employees. By the late 1990s, this Reno-based national had about twenty MD-80 series airplanes, 1,500 employees, and its own regional, Reno Air Express, which flew six Jetstream 31s. Begun as a low-cost but full-service airlines, Reno now serves numerous West Coast cities from San Diego to Seattle, California, points in Arizona, New Mexico, British Columbia, Alaska, and even has nonstop service between its Reno hub and Chicago. Reno Air has set up a second hub in San Jose.

The airline offers customers assigned seating, an expanded first-class cabin, and a frequent flyer awards program in conjunction with American Airline's program. Reno also fully participates in all travel agency computer reservation systems. The young carrier is having a difficult time getting established financially; the West Coast market, although a well-traveled region and a lucrative market, is also very competitive. Losses in 1993 were about $7 million and double that in 1994; however, revenues rise each year and the carrier is developing a loyal group of customers.

THE REGIONALS

Air LA
Air Midwest
Air Molokai
Air Nevada
Air South
Air St. Thomas
Air Sunshine
AirTran
Air Transport International
Air Vegas
AirWays International
Alaska Island
Allegheny Airlines
Aloha Islanair
Alpha Air
Alpine
American Eagle
Arctic Circle
Arizona Airways
AV Atlantic
Bahamasair
Baker
Bellair
Bering
Big Sky
Braniff International
Buffalo
Camai
Cape Air/Nantucket
Capitol Air
Capitol Air Express
Casino Express
CCAir
Chautauqua
Chicago Express
Colgan Air
Comair
Commutair

Conquest
Dallas Express
Dolphin Express
Eagle
Empire
ERA
Executive
Express Airlines I
Express Airlines II
Flagship
Flamenco
Florida Gulf
40-Mile Air
Freedom
Frontier
Frontier (Alaska)
FS Air Service
GP Express
Grand Airways
Grant
Great American
Great Lakes
Gulfstream International
Hageland
Haines
Harbor
Iliamma
International Cargo Xpress
Jetstream Ketchikan
Larry's Las Vegas
Liberty Express
Loken
Lone Star
MarkAir Express
Mesa
Mesaba
MGM Grand Miami Air
Midway
Mountain West
North American
Northeast Express
Olson
Omni Air Express
Pacific Air
Paradise Island

Peninsula
Piedmont
Promech
Reeve
Rich
Ross Aviation
Ryan International
Scenic
Sierra Pacific
Skagway
Skyways
SkyWest
Spirit Air
Sportsflight
Sunaire Express
Sunbird
Sun Jet
Tacquan
Tanana Air
Trans American Charter
Trans World Express
UFS
UltrAir
ValueJet
Vanguard
Vieques Air Link
Viscount
Warbelow's
WestAir
Westates
Wings of Alaska
Wings West
Worldwide
Wright
Yute

The regional airlines are an interesting collection of large and small companies that operate with one airplane (Alpine or Empire Airlines) or as many as 190 (Mesa Air Group). The regionals carry 3.32 percent of the world's passengers and are becoming more important in the air transportation scheme as these smaller airlines absorb many routes previously served by larger air carriers. With respect to the DOT classification, large regionals are those airlines that have annual operating revenues of $100 million or less, and medium regionals have less than $10 million in operating revenues. Many of these carriers are well on their way to becoming nationals, and numerous code-sharing relationships exist between them and major airlines. However, ownership of regionals is a very mixed bag. Some regionals are owned solely by the majors, some are owned partly, while others are not owned in any part by the major.

In 1994, the regionals operated a fleet of over 2,100 airplanes, of which 72 percent were turboprops, 26 percent were pistons, and 2 percent were turbojets. FAR Part 135 (thirty seats or less) flight operations accounted for 73 percent of the aircraft used to carry 51 percent of the passengers. Approximately six hundred airplanes in the nineteen-seat configuration, such as the Beech 1900, the Jetstream J31, and the Fairchild Metro 23, are still used. In 1994, these airplanes flew 685,218, 563,683, and 292,973 of the block hours, respectively. This activity accounts for 29.7 percent of the 4,564,922 block hours logged by the fleet in 1994. However, the jets are coming, and Comair—a partner with Delta—has begun regional jet (RJ) service from Delta's Cincinnati and Orlando hubs; SkyWest, another Delta partner, has also begun using the RJ on longer routes out of Salt Lake City.

There is little doubt that the regional airlines are here to stay, and although the list of airlines shown above changes every year, the shaping of tomorrow's air service map relies heavily on these maturing carriers. One catalyst in the regional growth formula was essential air service.

Essential Air Service

Perhaps one of the most significant stories in the history of the regional airlines is the impact of essential air service. Government subsidy for contracted airline services is not a new idea. During the 1920s and 1930s, there was "mail pay," which may have been the only thing that kept several airlines in business. In 1938, there were even direct subsidies to those that would serve outlying cities. However, when deregulation became a reality in 1978 and airlines could select the cities that they served, there was a general fear among smaller, outlying communities that the air service they had come to expect might be curtailed or even discontinued. Thus an important part of the deregulation package was the establishment of Section 419, This was the guarantee for the essential air service (EAS) program which provided for a continuation of air transportation for ten years to all cities certifi-

cated on the date of the Airlines Deregulation Act's enactment, 24 October 1978.

The way it worked was that the U.S. government would pay a per passenger subsidy and guarantee a certain number of seats would be "funded" each day from designated EAS cities to a nearby large airport. The DOT determined need based on where service would be provided and to what hub, how many passengers were expected per day based on historic information, how many seats per day at 50 percent load factor, how many round-trips a day were required, and how many stops should be made. The groundwork for the regional airlines as we know it today was being laid.

The regional airlines, which in many cases now had the initial startup guarantee they needed and felt they could make money, began EAS with small airplanes that could be operated on the short, low-density routes. Suddenly, the regional airlines, in those days referred to as commuters, proliferated. Cities like Wolf Point, Montana, Moab, Utah, Manistee, Minnesota, Hastings, Nebraska, and Jamestown, North Dakota, were on the air transportation map for another decade.

The ten-year period for the 419 subsidy was extended in 1987 with the passage of the Airport and Airway Safety and Expansion Act, but things were slightly different. In 1988, taxpayers spent $379,000 to fly people to Atlanta from Moultrie (200 miles) and the average load factor was 1 person; this was viewed as quite excessive and not within the initial intent of the 419 subsidy. However, there were other areas of the country, particularly in Alaska, where air transportation was still considered fragile and marginal.

The compromise was that under the Airport and Airway Safety and Capacity Expansion Act of 1987 and other legislation that was to follow, more stringent rules were enacted. Specifically, these rules laid out new parameters with respect to the flying distance between the EAS city and the hub served, the insistence on service with at least nineteen passenger planes (the community could accept fewer seats), pressurized cabin over 8,000 feet above sea level, more round-trips per day for more days, flights at more "reasonable times," and a subsidy limit of no more than $300 per passenger.

The results have not been quite as expected. Many cities have fallen off the air map, and in several cases regionals don't want anything to do with EAS. This shift in viewing EAS as a sure source of revenue and now rejecting the 419 subsidy may be due to the fact that there is no guarantee for increased costs like fuel, DOT must approve route changes, EAS is only a small percent of revenues, the 419 subsidy awardee must fly a route that they receive a subsidy on until a replacement is found, EAS cities do not always line up together in a linear fashion, and in several airports where the regional code-shares with a major partner, valuable gate space is used for a small passenger load. In the 1990s, EAS 419 subsidies were about $33.4 million annually.

In 1994, Vice President Al Gore's National Performance Review recommended reduced EAS funding. In addition, the DOT did not include any EAS subsidies in the fiscal year 1996. Whatever the future of EAS is to be, it has left a significant mark on the air transportation map. Regionals, as we know them, might not have matured had it not been for EAS.

Tomorrow's Regionals

Tomorrow's regional airline may be more like today's national or major, at least with respect to the federal regulations that govern operations. Driven by the quest for safety and by what is viewed from some camps as a higher than acceptable accident/incident record, the regionals are under assault. The FAA specifically has called for numerous changes in the regulations under which the bulk of the regionals operate under, FAR Part 135. In 1995, the FAA proposed a Notice of Proposal Rule Making (NPRM) with the hope of moving this component of the industry closer to "One Level of Safety."

The intent of the one level of safety is to close the safety gap between ten to thirty seat FAR Part 135 operations and thirty-one to sixty seat FAR Part 121 operations, which are viewed as much more stringent. The key points of the NPRM are that flight operations conducted under FAR 135 operations need a dispatcher, crews need a reduction in flight duty time, crews need better training, and equipment must be updated. However, while FAA estimates that these modifications will cost eighty operators with 915 airplanes no more than $196 million, industry sources estimate the same changes will be in excess of $1 billion.

Gone Forever

The U.S. air carriers have a long history of merger and acquisition. Often such activity was undertaken so as to expand a route structure or eliminate competition. Thus in the last fifty years, many grand old airline names such as Capital, Piedmont, National, and Allegheny have disappeared. Recently, however, and particularly since deregulation and the demise of the CAB, bankruptcy has claimed several old as well as new U.S. carriers. Included in this group are established airlines such as Frontier, Midway, Eastern, and two airlines that were quite different from each other, People Express and Pan Am. People Express was a product of deregulation, and Pan Am was one of the oldest and most famous of all the U.S. airlines.

People Express

Founded in 1981 by Donald Burr with three 737 aircraft, People Express quickly defined what deregulation was meant to accomplish. Rising to be the fifth largest U.S. carrier in 1985, People Express became a business school study nationwide. People Express was unique in many ways. All employees were required to take stock in the company as part of their compensation, and everyone (including pilots and executives) was cross-utilized to keep costs down; every employee was also considered to be a manager.

People Express began in an abandoned maintenance hangar at Newark Airport, near New York City. Fares were cheap, and service into secondary markets was plentiful. Passengers paid to check bags and bought their tickets on-board as the plane was taxiing. Everyone seemed to be having a lot of fun. Service began to Buffalo, New York, Columbus, Ohio, and Norfolk, Virginia, in April 1981 using a fleet of B-737s acquired from Lufthansa. People Express continued to grow quickly for the next two years, and by 1983 it was offering transatlantic services to London Gatwick in a leased Boeing 747 and flying fifty Boeing 727-200s domestically to twenty-two cities. Service was begun to Los Angeles and Oakland, and the employee rolls had swollen from 250 to about 1,250. College students served internships with the carrier, many in reservations. As a result, People Express became not only the nation's fifth largest airline but perhaps also the best educated. Everything was looking great, but in 1985 the carrier began to lose money.

Many blame Don Burr for the unchecked journey of People Express from their unique industry niche carrier and the ultimate demise of the company. It seemed that Burr only knew how to acquire and expand. There were unsuccessful fare wars with established carriers and a new terminal at Newark. People Express acquired Frontier in 1985, Britt Airways (a Midwest regional) in 1986, and Provincetown-Boston Airways (a bankrupt regional carrier) in 1986. These acquisitions brought only debt and more problems, and by June 1986 People Express was up for sale. The two most interested parties were United Airlines and Frank Lorenzo of Texas Air.

Lorenzo acquired People Express in 1985 when United backed out of the negotiations and Frontier filed for Chapter 11. Lorenzo also acquired New York Air and other four commuter carriers. By early 1987, People Express ceased all operations.

Pan American World Airways

Pan American Airways formed in 1927 and ceased operations in December 1991. It was a magnificent airline, and it left its mark on the industry in many ways. Led by Juan Trippe, it was long known for dominating the overseas market and for Clipper service around the world. With the 1950 acquisition of American Overseas Airways (AOA), a division of American Airlines, Pan Am and rival TWA became the dominant U.S. flag carriers to Europe.

There are many theories as to why Pan Am ceased to exist. One theory is that the carrier never made the transition to modern air transportation in the 1970s and 1980s and that its executives made poor decisions. The Lockerbie bombing incident in 1988 may have been the last nail in Pan Am's coffin.

Pan Am was in poor financial health from the mid-1970s, and it never seemed to fully adapt to deregulation. The questionable acquisition of National Airlines in 1979 (a move calculated to give Pan Am a domestic route system but also saddled the airline with lots of older airplanes), may have forced Pan Am to make several desperate moves (sale of both the Pan Am building and the Intercontinental Hotel chain) to raise capital in the early 1980s. A machinists' strike soon followed, and the airline sold its Pacific routes to United in 1985 to raise part of the money required to launch its Northeast shuttle.

Soon to follow were the sale of airplane delivery positions, the sale of the London Heathrow operation to United in 1990, and finally the sale of the intra-German service Lufthansa. Pan Am declared bankruptcy in 1991 and sold its remaining assets to Delta.

However, Delta threw a lifeline to the struggling Pan Am and acquired a 45 percent interest. A "new" Pan Am served the Caribbean and South America. But the investment in Pan Am appeared to be financially flawed, and after providing almost $200 million cash to cover operating losses, Delta pulled the plug. On 4 December 1991, Pan Am ceased operations.

The Future

When considering the future of the U.S. air carrier industry, several factors must be considered. Among these are the very vast areas that must be covered on Atlantic to Pacific routes, the lack of mature public transportation in comparison to Europe and certain Asian countries, and a longtime love for the freedom of movement brought about by the automobile. These factors must be reconciled with a newer love for travel by air fed by a more affluent society that can well afford to continue to be strong leisure travel consumers. Many of these factors will be major catalysts in shaping the air transportation industry. So what will the "successful" U.S. air carrier look like in 2010?

Paul Stephen Dempsey and Andrew R. Goetz in *Airline Deregulation and Laissez-Faire Mythology* offer nine essentials for survival:

1. Multiple hubs, strategically located
2. Frequent flyer programs
3. Computer reservation systems
4. Sophisticated yield management
5. Fuel-efficient fleet of standardized aircraft
6. Low debt (conservative growth)
7. Low wages/flexible work rules
8. Superior service
9. International routes

Whether these nine items actually define the successful airline of tomorrow or not, they address many of the lessons that have been learned in the past fifty years.

However, if the course that this nation's airlines take in the next fifty years is anything like what has happened in the last fifty years, the ride will be full of surprises and quite an adventure.

Note

The major and perhaps the most current airline statistical data for the U.S. air carriers is available from the Air Transport Association (ATA) website. The address is www.airtransport.org and the sections on the site include general information on ATA and its members, industry statistical data (annual reports and historical data on load factors, traffic, earnings, yield, and history), a publications catalog, and an aviation calendar. Additional components of this site and statistical data can be downloaded in spreadsheet format.

Each year, a major portion of the July issue of *Air Transport World* is devoted to the World Airline Report. This contains information on world airlines traffic and financial statistics (by region), a profile of all world airlines, an overview of the U.S. carriers by category (major, national, and regional), and a complete listing of the world's airline fleet. Additional information is included on the current world code-sharing agreements.

Since this chapter was written, the U.S. air carriers have once again returned to profitability. Perhaps many of the lessons learned during the 1980s and early 1990s have resulted in the industry becoming more streamlined and fiscally sound. One can only hope that the agony and ecstasy, ups and downs, and boom or bust patina that have seemed an integral part of the industry will become a thing of the past. Time will tell.

References

Air Transport Association. *Data and Statistics.* (www.airtransport.org). Washington, D.C.: Air Transport Association, 1996.

Brenner, Melvin A., James O. Leet, and Elihu Schott. *Airline Deregulation.* Westport, Conn.: Eno Foundation for Transportation, 1985.

Carnival Airlines. *Carnival Airlines History.* (www.carnivalair.com/fact.htm). January 1996.

Dempsey, Paul S., and Andrew R. Goetz. *Airline Deregulation and Laissez-Faire Mythology.* Westport, Conn.: Quorum Books, 1992.

Doganis, Rigas. *Flying Off Course: The Economics of International Airlines.* 2d ed. London: HarperCollins Academic, 1991.

Gessell, Laurence E. *Airline Re-regulation.* Chandler, Ariz.: Coast Aire, 1990.

Jasper, Herbert N. *Winds of Change: Domestic Air Transport since Deregulation.* Special Report 230. Transportation Research Board. Washington, D.C.

Kane, Robert M. *Air Transportation.* 12th ed. Dubuque: Kendall/Hunt, 1996.

Kasper, Daniel M. *Deregulation and Globalization: Liberalizing International Trade in Air Services.* Cambridge, Mass.: Ballinger, 1988.

Meyer, John R., and Clinton V. Oster Jr. *Deregulation and the Future of Intercity Passenger Travel.* Cambridge: MIT Press, 1987.

O'Connor, William E. *An Introduction to Airline Economics.* 5th ed. Westport, Conn.: Praeger, 1995.

Oleson, Eric. *A Brief History of People Express Airlines.* (fohnix.metronet.com/ oleson/pehist.html). January 1996.

Peterson, Barbara Sturken, and James Glab. *Rapid Descent: Deregulation and the Shakeout in the Airlines.* New York: Simon and Schuster, 1994.

Reno Airlines. *About Reno Airlines.* (www.renoair.com/index.html). January 1996.

Shearman, Philip. *Air Transport: Strategic Issues in Planning and Development.* London: Pitman, 1994.

Truitt, Lawrence J., and Stanley E. Fawcett. "Emerging as a Major Carrier: A Case Study of America West Airlines." *Journal of Aviation/Aerospace Education and Research* 1, no. 2 (fall 1990): 8–23.

Wells, Alexander T. *Air Transportation: A Management Perspective.* 3d ed. Belmont, Calif.: Wadsworth, 1994.

Wolfe, Harry P., and David A. NewMyer. *Aviation Industry Regulation.* Carbondale: Southern Illinois University Press, 1985.

World Airline Report. *Air Transport World* 32, no. 6 (June 1995).

Wyckoff, Daryl D., and David H. Maister. *The Domestic Airline Industry.* Lexington, Mass.: Lexington Books, 1977.

General Aviation after World War II

William McCurry

THE HISTORY OF general aviation is considered by many to be tied to the city of Wichita, Kansas. In fact, the chamber of commerce in the city refers to Wichita as the "Air Capital of the World." It was not an easy task faced by the city and the aircraft manufacturers as World War II came to a close. Even though employment in Wichita aircraft plants was down to 38,000 in June 1945 from a peak of 60,000 in December 1943, more bad news was coming. When production of the B-29 was suspended in September 1945, Boeing Wichita had only 5,000 employees. This figure fell to 1,388 in 1946. The number of employees also fell for Beech, Cessna, and Culver from the following figures in June 1945: Beech, 10,200; Cessna, 2,467; and Culver, 612. Wichita built nearly 44 percent of the primary trainers and almost half of the B-29 bombers. The transition to a peacetime economy would be tough.

General Aviation Defined

General aviation refers to all civil aircraft and activity except those classified as air carrier or commuter. The types of aircraft include corporate multiengine jet aircraft piloted by professional crews to amateur-built single engine aircraft. All aircraft are included except those flown by scheduled airlines or the military. The impact of general aviation on the U.S. economy is significant. General aviation is a $15 billion industry that generates more than $45 billion annually in economic activity.

General aviation aircraft fly over 23 million hours (nearly twice the airline flight hours) and carry 130 million passengers. Approximately 70 percent of these hours are for business and commercial purposes. More than five thousand communities rely on general aviation for their air transportation needs (scheduled airlines serve about six hundred communities).

The Transition from War to Peace

Expectations

The expectations were high for "private" flying after the war. Aviation had played a significant part in the war effort. As a result, the large number of veterans with flight experience and the expanded manufacturing plants with highly skilled workers created a feeling that the airplane would replace the automobile as a means of transportation.

In 1945, a poll conducted by the *Saturday Evening Post* showed that 35 percent of Americans wanted to own an airplane and that 7 percent were actively planning a purchase. Light aircraft manufacturers predicted a significant increase in private flying. One Commerce Department official informed Congress that private plane sales represented the most logical area for postwar expansion of the aviation industry. He suggested that production would reach 200,000 aircraft a year. Other authors expected that as many as 500,000 light aircraft would be sold by 1950. Prices were forecast to be about $2,000 for a two-place aircraft and about $4,000 for a four-place aircraft.

The expectations were also influenced by predictions that many of the 12 million veterans would take advantage of the flight training program offered under the Servicemen's Readjustment Act (the GI Bill). The federal government also recognized the need to improve air navigation facilities and to increase the number of airports open to the public.

While the forecasts turned out to be overly optimistic, manufacturers were encouraged by record sales. In 1946, sale and production of light planes rose to approximately 35,000 aircraft. This was five times the high of approximately 7,700 in prewar 1941. In December 1946, an article in *Flying* magazine listed forty-six models manufactured by thirty-four companies.

Beech Aircraft Corporation

At the end of the war, the Twin Beech Model 18 was the company's only seriously marketable aircraft. This aircraft was produced until 1970 and was the forerunner of the AT-7 and AT-11 used extensively during the war. As an interim measure, while new aircraft designs were being developed, Beech engaged in the production of several new nonaviation products. These included pie pans, vending machines, and components for home refrigerators and dishwashers.

The Beech postwar general aviation classic, the Model 35 Beech Bonanza, was first flown in 1945 and was in production in 1947 (see fig. 11.1). The Model 35 had a variable-pitch propeller, a cantilever low wing, a range of 750 miles, fully retractable tricycle landing gear, and a distinctive V-tail. It became one of the most easily

Fig. 11.1. First flight of the first Beech Bonanza, 22 December 1945. Courtesy of Raytheon Aircraft Company.

recognized aircraft ever built. The initial price was just over $7,000; however, it was a four-place, all-metal construction, with full IFR navigation equipment, and a degree of comfort generally associated with fine automobiles to include a ventilation system, individual ashtrays, sunshades, carpeting, and woolen upholstery. Engine performance allowed a 180 mph cruise.

The basic Bonanza was a long-lasting, flexible, and very successful design. Its record for continuous production is still lengthening. The V-tail version was built into the 1980s. The basic airframe with the more traditional tail was being built in the 1990s, with a 300-horsepower piston-engine, twin-engine, and turboprop configurations.

Cessna Aircraft Company

To implement immediate aircraft production after the war, Cessna started a project to use as many components as possible from the T-50, which went into production as a light twin in early 1940. Production of the T-50 was halted shortly after Pearl Harbor; however, military versions were produced with minor changes until 1945. Another concept of the new project was to use the Air-master configuration (manufactured from 1939 to 1942), except to make the airplane larger and more comfortable, and to make the wings and tail surfaces all metal.

Based on these initial specifications, the Model 190 was developed. The first prototype made its first flight within six months. The aircraft was a four-place high-wing monoplane with all-metal wings and tail and a tubular steel fuselage with fabric covering. The engine, cowling, and propeller were the same as those on the Model T-50. The main landing gear was made of vanadium spring steel. This was Cessna's first use of the spring steel landing gear.

In the spring of 1945, Cessna canceled its "Family Car of the Air" project and also temporarily halted the Model 190 project in order to concentrate on developing a two-place aircraft. In June, the Model 140 prototype made its first flight (see fig. 11.2). The Model 140 was a two-place aircraft, powered by an 85-horsepower Continental engine. It was Cessna's first aircraft to have an all-metal fuselage, and its wings were fabric covered. Two versions were produced in March 1946. The Model 140 was a deluxe aircraft with wing flaps, deluxe upholstery, additional side windows, and an electrical system. The

Fig. 11.2. Cessna 140. Courtesy of Cessna.

Model 120 was an economy model for the training market without wing flaps or extra side windows. The electrical system was optional.

After the Models 140 and 120 were into production, further development resumed on the Model 190. The fuselage was converted from fabric to metal and became Cessna's first all-metal-covered aircraft. The first flight was made in October 1945.

Piper Aircraft Corporation

Piper opened a new plant in Ponca City, Oklahoma, in 1946 and transferred production of the J-3 Cub. This was followed by the PA-11 Cub and the PA-18 Super Cub. These aircraft had basically the same structural and aerodynamic characteristics as the E-2, first produced in 1932. The Cub formula provided business for Piper up to the 1950s. As a testament to the Piper Cub series, more than 80 percent of U.S. World War II pilots received their initial training in these aircraft.

General Aviation Aircraft Development and Sales

Industrial growth in 1946 led to great optimism about the long-term prospects of light aircraft manufacturing. Sales of light aircraft reached 35,000 from a prewar high of 7,700 in 1941. Piper led in production with nearly 7,800 aircraft; Beech was the leader in dollar value, manufacturing $18.7 million worth of aircraft. Backlogs were high, reaching nearly 21,000 two-place and 16,000 three- and four-place aircraft in October 1946.

At the same time, hundreds of civilian flight schools opened all over the country as many of the recently discharged veterans took advantage of flight training opportunities under the VA legislation. Airline service was also expanding, and conflicts began to develop between the airlines and the smaller aircraft operators over use of airspace and airports. The airlines demanded the government develop regulations to give the airlines "priority" over the small aircraft. The government chose not to intervene, so the good news continued.

Storms Ahead

A number of factors began to impacted the industry that would result in a downward trend and a change in the original optimism. There were not enough ground support facilities to support aircraft close to resort and vacation areas. The aircraft cost a lot more than originally thought when compared with the automobile. A high percentage of VA flight students dropped out of flight training programs. The small aircraft were noisy, cramped, drafty, and uncomfortable. Also, speeds were not comparable to the high performance military aircraft most pilots were accustomed to flying. Additionally, war surplus aircraft were available at bargain basement prices. The federally sponsored Reconstruction Finance Corporation sold more than 31,000 surplus military aircraft in 1946. Many of these aircraft were modified for corporate/business use and were direct competition for the civil aircraft market. To complicate this issue, additional aircraft manufacturers entered the market, which created a backlog of unsold aircraft.

Additional problems began to surface in early 1946; surplus supplies of fabric, plywood, and aluminum were disappearing. A shortage of steel tubing at the Piper plant in Lock Haven, Pennsylvania, due to a steel strike, resulted in a layoff of 1,900 workers. Marginal financial situations of most light aircraft manufacturers was cause for concern, particularly when the value of their stock severely declined in the second half of the year.

The predicted postwar boom collapsed in 1947 as production fell to 15,764. Cessna was only producing five aircraft per day. Surveys found that the two-place aircraft were being used for training, and the flight training requirements were filled. The expectation of every family taking to the air in a light aircraft had not taken place. While statistics showed that backlog orders were declining for two-place aircraft, orders fell only marginally for three- and four-place models. This was an indication that a new aircraft market was developing; business people were discovering the time and money that could be saved by using light aircraft. The four-place aircraft was preferred due to the larger load-carrying capability.

As a result, Cessna developed the Model 170. The first prototype flew in September 1947, and six months later production models were being delivered to customers. Beech and Cessna sold nearly $20 million worth of general aviation aircraft in 1947. Piper led the industry in production with more than 3,500 aircraft, with Beech selling a total of 1,209 Bonanzas.

Things were worse in 1948 with light aircraft sales dropping to less that 7,000 or 45 percent of the 1947 figure. Cessna was in first place in the depressed market with total sales of 1,600 aircraft.

The next year was worse. A recession in 1949 caused the gross national product to fall and unemployment to rise. Sales fell to fewer that 3,400 light aircraft, less that half of the number in 1948.

Cessna converted the Models 140 and 170 to all metal covering and created the Model 140A and Model 170A in 1949. By 1950, the Model 170A had taken most of the market, and by the end of 1950, the Model 140A was dropped from production.

Changing Expectations: The 1950s

A Different Aircraft

While sales in 1950 increased about one hundred aircraft over 1949, with Cessna leading Piper by a slight margin, it became apparent that mass producing aircraft for everyone at low prices was not the answer for growth. Dwane Wallace, CEO of Cessna (nephew of Clyde Cessna), wrote in 1950, "We have an outstanding forward step in transportation, and what we need to do most is simply demonstrate in the safest and most efficient manner how valuable this new tool is for those who travel and to demonstrate this is such a way that efficiently run companies cannot overlook the airplane as a money-making tool in this business."[1]

It was clear that a fleet of aircraft was needed that would provide solid, comfortable, reliable business transportation in instrument conditions with high speed and long range. Training aircraft would have to continue to be built to train new pilots, but a utility aircraft that the business person could afford was the target design for the future.

The Model 50 Twin Bonanza was designed to be marketed between the Model 35 Bonanza and the larger, heavier Beechcraft Model D18S. The Model 50 went from drawing board to first flight in 223 days, taking off in November 1949. Certification was granted in May 1951. The Model 50 was one of the first light twins after the war to gain acceptance by business people and helped pave the way for the later development of the Model 65 Queen Air.

The next step was airports, avionics, and simplified flying procedures for greater safety and convenience. Federal aid to airports through the Federal Airport Development Act was significant (though not quite up to the national defense subsidy that went to the interstate highway system during the 1950s). The installation of new very-high-frequency omnidirectional radio ranges (VOR) was making cross-country navigation simpler.

Pilots could now track a navigation needle on an instrument rather than using a flight computer and following a sectional chart for dead-reckoning or pilotage navigation. In 1950, a "unicom" frequency was assigned that allowed communication for general aviation aircraft for a variety of reasons to include air-to-air and air-to-ground communication. Also, during the same year, Bill Lear developed the first light aircraft three-axis autopilot, which made cross-country flight easier.

In 1951, production fell to 2,477 light aircraft. Cessna started design work on the Model 180 that was powered by a new 225-horsepower Continental six-cylinder, horizontally opposed engine. The Model 180 prototype flew in January 1952. In all, production was up a little in 1952 to 3,058. The Model 180 went into production, and first deliveries were made in March 1953. Over the next five years, this aircraft was to come one of Cessna's most famous products. Also during 1953, Beech was backlogged with orders for the Bonanza, the Twin Bonanza, and Super 18. Piper continued to produce the Tri-Pacer and the Super Cub. Production continued to increase with a total of 3,788 aircraft being produced.

Light Twins

In 1951, in response to the developing market for light twin-engine aircraft, Cessna initiated a preliminary design study for a new twin that would become the Model 310. The prototype made its first flight in January 1953. The Model 310, powered by two 240-horsepower engines, was certified in March 1954, and the first production units was delivered thirty days later. Piper introduced the Apache, also a four-place light twin, at about the same time.

Other Developments

During the early 1950s, customers were asking for tricycle landing gear because of the ease of ground handling and the resistance to ground loops, which was a real hazard with the conventional gear or "tail dragger" aircraft. To satisfy this demand, Cessna developed the Model 172 (shown in fig. 11.3) and placed it into production for the 1956 model year. The Model 172 was identical to the Model 170B except for the tricycle landing gear and a new square tail (instead of the rounded one). Because of the success of the Model 172, Cessna decided to offer a tricycle gear version of the Model 180, which was also a very successful aircraft.

Fig. 11.3. 1956 Cessna 172. Courtesy of the Kansas Aviation Museum, Wichita.

To satisfy the demand to replace older two-place training aircraft, Cessna developed the Model 150 and put it into production in the 1959 model year. The Model 150 had tricycle landing gear, square tail, 100-horsepower engine, and high lift wing flaps. The aircraft was very successful: 719 were delivered in 1959.

The Boom Years: The 1960s

Business Transportation

In the 1960s, general aviation became a major part of the nation's transportation system. Expansion and modernization were the key ingredients. Beech introduced the Baron B55, which was a larger version of the Travel Air twin (the Travel Air twin had been introduced earlier as a tribute to Walter Beech's association with the Travel Air Manufacturing Company in the 1920s). It was powered by a 260-horsepower Continental IO-470-L engine in a compact, low-drag, flat nacelle, and it featured a swept tail with long dorsal fairing. Maximum speed was 236 mph with a range of 1,200 statute miles and a 45-

minute fuel reserve for IFR flight; 190 Barons were produced in 1961.

Piper started production of the Cherokee, Comanche, and the Twin Comanche. The Cherokee, a new low-wing trainer, was the first aircraft produced in a new manufacturing plant in Vero Beach, Florida. Certified in 1961, it sold for around $10,000 depending on engine and other equipment. With few exceptions, this aircraft became the model for Piper piston-powered models for the next twenty years.

Beech continued to improve the Queen Air, first introduced in 1958 as the Model 65. By model year 1967, the Model A65 Queen Air was being produced. The Model A65 was powered by 340-horsepower Lycoming IGSO-480 engines, useful load of 2,740 pounds and a range of 1,265 statue miles with a 45-minute reserve.

In 1964, Beech introduced the Model 90, Beech King Air. It quickly became an industry standard in corporate turboprop aircraft. Between 1964 and 1966, 112 Model 90 King Airs were produced. The Model 90 was equipped with PT6A-20 power plants rated at 550 shp for climb and 495 shp for cruise. The improved pressurization system provided sea-level conditions at more than 10,000 feet AGL and an 8,000-foot cabin altitude above 21,000 feet.

General Aviation Jets

William P. Lear began to experiment with corporate transports in the 1950s after the Air Force gave him a Lockheed Lodestar as a test vehicle for work on his autopilot system. He converted the aircraft into an executive transport and sold it to Fairchild Corporation as a "Learstar." He realized that, to be attractive to business users, the cost must be controlled. Lockheed's JetStar and North American's Sabreliner were very costly. In order to meet the market demand that he thought was there, the aircraft had to be fast, efficient, and small. His goal was to sell the aircraft for less than $1 million. Controlling the size would keep the cost down and increase the speed necessary in the business world. After

all, time is money, and the business aircraft was a time-saving business machine.

While living in Switzerland, he started experimenting with an entirely new aircraft. By combining the existing wing design and other elements from a canceled Swiss fighter bomber, the P-16, and with off-the-shelf hardware and subcontracting components on a worldwide basis, Lear was able to control costs. Problems with parts suppliers were delaying production, so Lear decided to move his company back to the United States. Wichita won the competition for the plant location, so the SAAC (Swiss American Aviation Corporation) 23 became the Lear Jet 23. Lear did what many thought was impossible: he skipped the prototype stage and went directly into production. On 7 October 1963, the first Lear Jet flew. A later model, the Lear Jet 35A, is shown in figure 11.4.

By the spring of 1966, more than one hundred Lear Jets had been delivered; this represented sales of more

Fig. 11.4. Lear Jet 35A. Courtesy of the Kansas Aviation Museum, Wichita.

than $38 million. The Lear Jet Model 25 weighed 12,500 pounds and was powered by 2,850-pound-thrust General Electric CJ610-1 turbojet engines. Cruise was 561 mph as low as 25,000 feet, and the aircraft was approved for altitudes as high as 51,000 feet. It was also the first aircraft to have winglets on production models. In 1967, after some negotiations with Beech concerning a buyout, Lear sold his company to Gates Rubber.

Even though the Lear Jet was a success, Cessna studied the market for some time before announcing its plans to enter the market with the Fanjet 500. This aircraft became the Citation in 1967 and was designed to be quieter, simpler, and more capable of operating in and out of short fields (see fig. 11.5). The aircraft was powered by Pratt and Whitney JT5D-1 turbofan engines, which were more fuel-efficient and less expensive to operate than other business jets on the market. The only problem with the Citation was its slow speed; it did not exceed 400 mph and was thus about 100 mph slower than the competition.

A Decade of Change: The 1970s

Problems and Growth

Noise pollution became a concern for general aviation in the 1970s. The 1971 Noise Control Act forced the manufacturers to redesign engines and airframes to reduce noise to acceptable levels.

The country experienced two fuel crises, one in 1973 and another in 1978. An oil embargo resulted in shortages and forced avgas and jet fuel to record prices. This put pressure on manufacturers to develop more fuel-

Fig. 11.5. First two Cessna Citations. Courtesy of Kansas Aviation Museum, Wichita.

efficient engines and aircraft. One result of the high fuel costs was the sale of many fuel-inefficient aircraft by corporate flight departments.

General aviation continued to grow, even though the American economy went into a recession in the early 1970s. From a low of 7,292 General Aviation aircraft shipments in 1970, the market had expanded to reach a production high of over 17,800 aircraft in 1978.

Due to the total numbers of aircraft (general aviation, air carriers, and military), the airspace was becoming congested, particularly around large metropolitan areas. One governmental solution to the problem was to pass the Airport and Airways Development Act in 1970. This act was designed to provide revenue to expand and improve the airports and air traffic control systems. Federal regulations increased with the creation of terminal control areas (TCAs) around the larger, busier airports. To enter this airspace, aircraft were required to have two-way radio communication with air traffic control (ATC) and VOR navigation equipment with an altitude-readout transponder. These regulations placed an added burden and expense on the small aircraft operator.

Although the Airline Deregulation Act of 1978 did not have a direct effect on general aviation, it did impact the business traveler. Commercial airlines began to concentrate on the spoke-and-hub concept, and as a result there was a decrease in service to some locations and a longer travel time was necessary in many cases. One reaction to the reduced airline service and the development of new corporate aircraft was the growth of international corporate aviation. Many corporate pilots were flying better-equipped aircraft than the major air carriers.

The attention of the general aviation industry was also directed toward product liability issues. During the 1960s and 1970s, courts across the nation started to adopt the rule of strict liability, which shifted greater burden toward the manufacturers. Because aircraft must be designed and manufactured to strict standards, almost all aviation product liability cases involved claims of defective design. Annual liability premiums for the defense of an increasing number of liability cases quickly reached proportions of several million dollars each for the three large general aviation aircraft manufacturers. Insurance premiums increased from $51 per new aircraft in 1962 to $2,111 in 1972.

Response to Government Regulation

The impact of increased governmental regulation on general aviation led to the formation of organizations established for the purpose of lobbying and developing public relations efforts with the federal government in Washington. The General Aviation Manufacturers Association (GAMA) was formed in 1970 to represent those interested in national legislation and public information. The Aircraft Owners and Pilots Association (AOPA) had appeared as early as 1939 to promote recreational and business flying, and it took an increasing interest in state and federal legislation. The National Business Aircraft Association (NBAA), which was formed in 1947 to promote the interests of the corporate aviation community, also became an effective lobbying organization. On the government side, the Federal Aviation Administration (FAA) appointed a deputy administrator for general aviation.

New Aircraft

In development since 1967, Cessna delivered the first Citation in 1972. In 1976, the company increased its role in the market by announcing three new business jets: the Citations I, II, and III. The Citation II became the best-selling business jet in the world.

Piper wanted a training aircraft to compete with the Cessna 150. The identified requirements were to have an aircraft with low maintenance requirements that could use 100LL fuel, have good visibility, and demonstrate what a real stall would do. The answer was the PA-38, Piper Tomahawk. From initial introduction in 1978, Piper produced nearly 1,000 aircraft in nine months. Due to rapid production, quality problems developed that hurt production. Additionally, many instructors felt the stall characteristics of the aircraft were too severe for most beginning students.

The popular Beech King Air 200 series started in 1974. The military version, the C-12, was started in 1975 and is used by all four military services. The next step in the King Air progression for Beech was the Model C90. Sitting six, the C90 had a maximum cruising speed of 253 mph with an initial rate of climb of 2,000 feet per minute and a service ceiling of 25,600 feet. The King Air has continued to evolve and is one of the most recognizable business aircraft in the world (see fig. 11.6).

Fig. 11.6. Beech Super King Air 350. Courtesy of Raytheon Aircraft Company.

Due to the increased price of fuel, aircraft were needed that could provide low-cost twin-engine training. In response to the need, Piper developed the Seminole, Beech produced the Duchess, and Grumman-American introduced the Cougar.

More Problems: The 1980s

Major Changes

The 1980s brought soaring interest rates and a depressed economy. Aircraft sales dropped from nearly 12,000 in 1980 to a low of 1,085 in 1987. Foreign aircraft manufacturers began entering what had been an American-dominated market in large numbers in the 1980s. Major changes were in the making.

On 8 February 1980, Beech Aircraft Corporation became a subsidiary of Raytheon Company, a diversified electronics and technology company located in Lexington, Massachusetts. In 1984, Lear-Siegler took over Piper as part of a buyout of Bangor Punta, its former parent.

Learjet was purchased by Forstmann Little and Company, and in 1987 M. Stuart Millar purchased Piper. Late in 1983, General Dynamics Corporation began to buy large amounts of Cessna stock and would complete its acquisition in 1986.

Product Liability

Because of the product liability crisis, Cessna withdrew entirely from the single-engine aircraft market. Piper Aircraft Corporation sought Chapter 11 bankruptcy protection and is currently self-insured. In 1987, the largest general aviation manufacturers calculated that their annual costs for product liability ranged from $70,000 to $100,000 per aircraft built and shipped during the year.

More Government

The air traffic controllers went on strike in August 1981, and by October the General Aviation Reservation (GAR) system was started. The GAR lasted two years and put quotas on IFR general aviation flights in each of the ATC centers.

The IRS announced a proposal to eliminate the 10 percent investment tax credit in December 1985. The Tax Reform Act of 1986 eliminated a 10 percent investment tax credit given to owners of new business aircraft. The credit was extended for one year, as long as aircraft purchased by the end of 1986 were put into service before July 1987. This action had a noticeable effect on aircraft sales.

Aircraft of the 1980s

Beech introduced the Beech King Air 300 in 1984. This aircraft offered greater speed and performance in addition to more cabin amenities than earlier King Air models. Mitsubishi's successful Diamond-series executive product line was purchased by Beech Aircraft Corporation in 1986. Introduced as the Beechjet Model 400, it carried seven passengers with a crew of two. Powered by two Pratt and Whitney JT-15D-5 engines producing 2,900 pounds of thrust, the aircraft had a maximum speed of 530 mph. The Starship, manufactured by Beech (see fig. 11.7), first flew as an 85 percent proof-of-concept vehicle built by Rutan's Scaled Composites Company in 1983. Three full-scale prototypes were flying during type certification in 1987. While performance fell short of a business jet, it had a speed of 405 mph, a 41,000 foot cruising altitude, seating for as many as 10, and used 25 percent less fuel than a comparable jet.

Cessna replaced the Citation II with the improved Citation S/II in 1984. In September 1987, the Citation V was introduced as a larger, faster aircraft.

Fig. 11.7. Beech Starship. Courtesy of Raytheon Aircraft Company.

By the end of 1989, Piper was producing a full line of aircraft from the Cub to the Cheyenne 400 twin turboprop, with the Cheyenne IIIA being the trainer of choice for many foreign airlines. The six-seat Malibu was certified in 1983, and Piper claimed it was the first cabin-class, pressurized single-engine aircraft. It was powered by a 310-horsepower, turbocharged Continental engine, which was upgraded to a 350-horsepower Lycoming engine in 1988 to become the Malibu Mirage.

The 1990s

Production Turnaround

The number of general aviation aircraft shipments continued to drop from 1,144 in 1990 to a low of 928 in 1994; however, in 1996 the general aviation industry experienced the highest number of aircraft delivered since 1990 and the best dollar value ever. Total units delivered reached 1,132, up 5.1 percent from 1,077 delivered in 1995. Production of single-engine piston aircraft also dropped to a low of 444 in 1994. But in 1996, single-engine piston aircraft shipments increased 2.9 percent, from 515 units in 1995 to 530 units in 1996. In the area of turbine-engine aircraft, turboprop shipments were up in 1996 from 1,163 to 1,332 in 1995; turboprop transactions also increased 8.3 percent in 1996, from 1,111 in 1995 to 1,203. The downward trend in the number of hours flown in general aviation has also been reversed: dropping from 198,000 hours in 1990 to 184,400 in 1992. The hours flown showed further decline in 1993 and 1994; however, some of this decline can be attributed to the exclusion of commuters from the statistics in 1993. A positive turnaround was noted by an increase in hours flown from 170,660 in 1994 to 181,341 in 1995. According to GAMA, the flight hours flown in the business segment of general aviation increased significantly in the 1990s. Much of this growth appeared to be coming from international flights. Of great concern is the drop in the total number of pilots. According to GAMA, there were about 814,000 pilots at the end of the 1970s; these numbers fell to 702,000 in 1990 and continued to fall to 622,000 in 1996. Probably of greater impact is the more than 50 percent drop in student pilot certificates issued between 1979 (135,956) and 1996 (estimated 58,612).

The number of airports in the country also have an impact on general aviation. Overall, the total number of airports has fluctuated from 18,000 in 1972 to 17,021 in

1994 and up to 18,292 in 1996. Public use airports decreased from 6,512 in 1972 to 5,080 in 1994. On the positive side, this number showed a slight increase to 5,129 by 1996. Private use airports have shown almost a 13 percent increase during the same period. The number of public use airports must be maintained for general aviation access. It is critical for general aviation aircraft to have access to a large number of airports as many small towns no longer have scheduled air service. Also impacting general aviation is the decline in the number of fixed base operators providing service to general aviation aircraft at these airports.

The Fixed Base Operators and Their Role in General Aviation

It is difficult to define *fixed base operator* (FBO) because the term is elusive and can apply to almost any general aviation business existing on an airport. The term seems to imply a multiservice operation; however, not all FBOs offer a full range of services. Another area of confusion is the term *through-the-fence,* which means an aviation-related business situated on land not owned by the airport but with legal rights of access through an actual gateway or imaginary property line. Experts disagree as to whether a through-the-fence operation should be classified as an FBO.

As there continues to be some confusion concerning the term *FBO,* some in the industry think there should be an "official" name change. *Airport Services* magazine conducted a survey in 1988 and learned that 80 percent of readers preferred the term *general aviation center.*

The flying corporate executive (and the pilots) want many conveniences at an FBO. They want conference rooms, FAX machines, space and quiet conditions to work on a computer, and areas where the aircraft crew can relax. The expenses of these features, along with reduced income due to reduced fuel sales, have forced many small FBOs out of business. Consequently, the FBO franchises/chains have been expanding.

The Kit Aircraft Movement

Another result of the reduced production of the single-engine piston training aircraft is the lack of new training aircraft. This has led to an increased interest in amateur-built aircraft kits. Persons who have fabricated and assembled the major portion of an aircraft for their own education or recreation can request FAA certification of that aircraft as an experimental amateur-built aircraft. The Experimental Aircraft Association (EAA) was formed in 1953 by a group of aircraft enthusiasts interested in home-built aircraft. They have since expanded to become one of the major supporters of general aviation and are very concerned about promoting aviation education among young people and encouraging safe operating procedures.

The General Aviation Revitalization Act

The introduction of the General Aviation Revitalization Act by Sen. Nancy Kassebaum (Republican-Kansas) and a similar bill in the House of Representatives authored by Rep. Dan Glickman (Democrat-Kansas) made 1994 memorable. These identically worded bills were modified slightly before passing both houses of Congress. The act was signed into law by President Bill Clinton on 17 August 1994 and provides that no civil action for damages arising out of a general aviation accident may be brought against the manufacturer of the aircraft or the manufacturer of any component part, if the accident occurred more than eighteen years after the aircraft's delivery to its first purchaser. Exceptions include willful fraud, people injured on the ground, and medical evacuation.

Cessna Aircraft Company had indicated if the Statute of Repose passed they would reenter the single-engine piston market. Cessna announced in March 1996 that they would open a new single-engine piston plant in Independence, Kansas, on 3 July 1996. This production line would produce the first Cessna piston-engine singles since 1986. The first completed aircraft, a Model 172, was expected to be finished in late December. The first aircraft was displayed (without paint) in March 1996. The Model 172 prototype was upgraded to a 1996 production configuration for use in the FAA certification program that is in progress. The new aircraft will feature fuel-injected Lycoming power plants, which will turn the propeller at a lower rpm to reduce noise. Upgraded interiors, avionics, seats, and seat tracks, fuel systems, and standard corrosion proofing are expected changes.

The Challenge of the Future

The Major Issues

The first major issue facing general aviation is the need to build new student starts. GAMA and AOPA are involved in a program called Team 2000, which had a target of attracting 100,000 annual student starts by the year 2000. There were less than 60,000 student starts in 1996, an all-time low since the industry has been keeping statistics.[2]

The second issue is a new emphasis on industry research and development programs. NASA is involved in a program called the Advanced General Aviation Transport Experiment (AGATE). This project includes a whole range of advanced general aviation developments. Projects include development of advanced cockpits and displays, low-cost integrated design and manufacturing techniques such as making big primary structures in one piece, and advanced propulsion systems including new icing protection systems.

A third issue deals with FAA reform and the negative impact of user charges for general aviation. The industry, through GAMA, is urging Congress to continue the annual contribution of general revenue funds toward the FAA's operating costs and renew expired aviation excise taxes instead of establishing penalizing user fees and certification fees.

Other Issues

Continued growth of the general aviation industry is essential for the creation of new jobs, increased international activity, investments in research and development for new technology and products, and increased shipments, market shares, and backlog. Sales of U.S. aircraft abroad, particularly to China and the Pacific Rim, are also a critical element and may offer an opportunity to realize the happier production times of the 1960s and 1970s. Access to international airports must be improved to develop business entry to foreign markets. Safety programs must be developed to better educate and train pilots and maintenance technicians in an international market place.

Notes

1. Quoted in Rowe and Miner, *Borne on the Southwind*, which contains an excellent history of Wichita and the lives of many aviation pioneers.

2. This information is from a speech given by Keith Nadolski, vice president of sales and marketing, Raytheon Aircraft Company, to members of the University Aviation Association in Wichita, Kansas, on 20 April 1996.

References

Aerospace Facts and Figures, 1994–1995. Washington, D.C.: Aerospace Industries Association of America, 1994.

Bilstein, Roger E. *Flight in America: From the Wrights to the Astronauts.* Baltimore: Johns Hopkins University Press, 1994.

Deneau, Gerald. *An Eye to the Sky.* Wichita: Cessna Aircraft Company, 1963–64.

Emme, Eugene M., ed. *Two Hundred Years of Flight in America: A Bicentennial Survey.* Vol. 1, American Astronautical Society History Series. San Diego: Univelt, 1977.

Historical Overview of Raytheon Aircraft. Wichita: Corporate Affairs Department, Raytheon Aircraft Company, 1996.

Kovach, Kenneth J. *Corporate and Business Aviation.* Dubuque: Kendall/Hunt, 1994.

Phillips, Edward H. *Beechcraft, Pursuit of Perfection: A History of Beechcraft Airplanes.* Eagan, Minn.: Flying Books, 1992.

Rowe, Frank J., and C. Miner. *Borne on the Southwind: A Century of Kansas Aviation.* Wichita: Beacon, 1994.

Trimble, William F., ed. *From Airships to Airbus: The History of Civil and Commercial Aviation,* vol. 2, *Pioneers and Operations.* Washington, D.C.: Smithsonian Institution Press, 1995.

Wells, Alexander T. *Air Transportation: A Management Perspective.* Belmont, Calif.: Wadsworth, 1994.

Wells, Alexander T., and Bruce D. Chadbourne. *General Aviation Marketing and Management.* Malabar, Fla.: Krieger, 1994.

12

Military Airpower Developments after World War II

Paul A. Whelan

AVIATION developed rapidly following World War II. Thousands of propeller-driven military aircraft were converted to passenger and cargo carriers. The significant increase in the development of commercial aviation made it evident that the world was beginning to accept airplanes as the preferred mode of transportation. Military aviation development, no longer driven by the demands of an active war, was undergoing significant changes of its own. Though very important, Army and Marine aviation, both unique in their missions, are not included in this chapter.

In 1945, President Harry Truman began establishing the role the military forces would play after the war ended. The Army and Navy would face drastic budget cuts, yet it would be incumbent upon Americans to play a major role in maintaining world peace. By 1945, aviation had emerged as a major strength, and the dropping of the atomic bomb added a signature to the awesome airpower of the United States. The future of military aviation was ensured, but a heated debate evolved as to future roles and missions of various branches of the military. The debate was settled with enactment of the National Security Act of 1947. The president signed legislation that clarified these roles and created the Air Force as a separate organization, equal to the Army and Navy. All of the military branches were placed under the newly formed Defense Department.

Truman then issued an executive order assigning specific responsibilities. The Army was responsible for land operations and seaborne transportation. The Navy was charged with control of the seas in areas of United States' interest. The Air Force mission was tactical and strategic control of the skies as well as all airlift, with the exception of certain airlift services the Navy would provide for itself. Air Force responsibility included airlift, airborne operations, and air transport for the armed forces. The Navy also provided air cover for the fleet and had operational control of all Marine Air.[1] Arguments as to what this would entail were under discussion when events in Berlin reached crisis proportions.

At the end of World War II, the Allied powers agreed upon the joint occupation of Berlin, located deep within the Soviet zone of Germany, but it soon became evident that a fundamental political division existed between the French, English, and Americans on one side and the Russians on the other. This division became a major schism. Early in 1948, an assembly of the Four Power Allied Control Councils for Germany met to work out a policy for currency reform, but it ended when the Russians withdrew from the meetings.

The Russians refused to agree to the currency adopted by the other powers and attempted to force their own currency on beleaguered Berliners. They also made life increasingly difficult for their former allies. First, they demanded the right to inspect Western military trains passing through the Soviet zone on their way to Berlin. Second, the Russians stopped all railway and river traffic and blocked highways, thus limiting supplies to a dribble. Finally, they shut down all traffic, including food transports. Berlin was effectively cut off from the rest of Europe.

As a consequence, in June 1948, the Soviet Union acknowledged its motive was to force the Allied powers out of Berlin and incorporate the city into its sphere of influence. However, the Berliners refused their offer to feed them, and the English and Americans refused to leave.

Supply by air was now the only option, for air access to Berlin had been agreed to in the occupation accords, unlike access by land. It was up to the Allies to undertake the staggering responsibility of supplying the entire city with food, medicine, and coal entirely by air, while the Russians sat and waited for the effort to fail so they could take over the city.

On 26 June 1948, Gen. Curtis E. LeMay gave the Air Force its mandate to supply Berlin. Battered old "Gooney Birds," veterans of the Normandy Invasion and the Asian "Hump" airlift, took the first eighty tons into Berlin the same day (see figs. 12.1 and 12.2) With only 102 of these C-47s, along with a few British planes and two C-54s available in all of Europe, the maximum tonnage would be 700 per day; however, mere survival for the Berliners required 4,000 tons per day. The effort seemed doomed. In spite of strong pressures to abandon the project, Truman insisted they move ahead, saying, "The United States is going to stay. Period."

The call for planes and crews went out around the world, and on 29 June 1948 the Berlin Airlift Task Force was established. By late July 2,500 men had been recruited to form the Military Air Transport Service. On short notice they were able to deliver 1,500 tons per day to Berlin, and British planes accounted for another 750 tons.[2] As impressive as these figures were, it did not meet the city's minimal need of 4,000 tons a day to survive. That number would increase to 4,500 tons a day as winter approached.

More C-54s were gathered from around the world and were marshaled at several key bases in the Federal Republic of Germany. Then, in mid-October, the British and American forces were combined under the com-

Fig. 12.1. World War II C-47 "Gooney Birds," shown in the background, were used in the Berlin Airlift. Courtesy of the USAF Museum.

Fig. 12.2. A C-54 of the Air Transport Service is being loaded for a trip to Berlin. Courtesy of the USAF Museum.

mand of Gen. William H. Tunner as the Combined Air Lift Task Force.

An airlift expert, Tunner formed a professional force of air crews and support personnel that launched planes every three minutes from four airfields. This was a tough operation that demanded the absolute best of everyone involved. Airlift traffic moved in one direction up the two outside corridors into Berlin and back through the center corridor. Under radar guidance, landing approaches were made just once, and a missed approach meant returning home to base without the delivery of supplies. In spite of the difficulties, Operation Vittles, as the airlift was called, delivered enough food, coal, and other essentials for Berlin to survive.

Under constant demands for yet more, "Tons for Tunner" increased delivery to 5,000 tons a day by September. With the arrival of winter, the airlift faced fierce storms and dangerous icing conditions. Travel was hampered as snow and ice clogged runways and loading areas and planes were constantly turned back, unable to land and unload their cargoes. Food became scarce, and Berliners often had to resort to burning their furniture to heat their homes, yet they hung on. In addition to the threats posed by the weather, airlift crews had to contend with

hundreds of hostile acts by the Russians, as they continually tried to hamper delivery of supplies.

When the tonnage needed to increase to 5,600 per day, more aircraft were required. The airspace was becoming saturated. To alleviate the problem of introducing more aircraft into already crowded airspace, Tunner developed a conveyor-belt type system to streamline the flow of aircraft. Within the designated airspace, each aircraft would have its own "slot" from which it could not deviate. All flights were conducted under instrument flight rules at all times, and every landing was performed using a ground controlled approach under positive radar control. When the system was perfected, every Berlin air terminal within a 6-mile radius was able to support an aircraft movement every 31 seconds (see fig. 12.3).[3]

The European Command (EUCOM) Airlift Support Command and the British Army Air Transport Command worked together to perfect time-saving cargo handling procedures. Uniform cargo loads were developed. Aircrews returning empty from a Berlin delivery would call in and report their status. If no maintenance delay was needed, their next cargo would be positioned at their assigned parking area. While the plane was being reloaded, it would be refueled and, if necessary, a crew

Fig. 12.3. Constant stream of C-54 aircraft during Operation Vittles, as the airlift was called. Courtesy of the USAF Museum.

change would take place. The entire operation was completed in less than 30 minutes.

With spring came the return of dependable delivery of goods, and by Easter more than 1,235,000 tons had been delivered. The West had proved its ability to supply Berlin via air for indefinite periods, and airlift was accepted as routine (see fig. 12.4). On 12 May 1949, the Soviet Union called off the siege, but the airlift continued into September to stockpile emergency supplies.

Officially, the Berlin Airlift lasted from 26 June 1948 until 1 August 1949. All in all, 276,926 flights delivered two and a half million tons of food, coal, and medicine to Berlin, at a cost of $200 million and the loss of thirty-five U.S. aircraft and seventy-five lives.

The Berlin Airlift demonstrated the ability of airpower to move critical cargo and people anyplace where U.S. foreign policy was threatened. It also signaled the nation's resolve to contain any Soviet expansion of its influence and to maintain world peace.

General Tunner attributed the success to the spirit of cooperation of all the participants and the efficient and effective use of the large C-54 aircraft. He envisioned the need for still larger aircraft in the future because the transportation of people and cargo would be a vital factor in the success of any future military operation undertaken by the United States.[4]

The Berlin Airlift may have provided a firm argument for strategic airlift, but it did not resolve the need for tactical air transport support of airborne assault operations and routine airlift needs within a theater of operations. This would soon become the role of the C-82 and C-119 aircraft (shown in fig. 12.5).

The successful confrontation of Soviet heavy-handedness demonstrated by the Berlin Airlift was an important step in forming the North Atlantic Treaty Organization (NATO) and containing the Soviet threat. It helped provide the necessary stimulus to the German people to form the West German Republic. This was a period of uneasy tension in Europe. To shore up Allied resolve, F-84F fighter bombers were deployed throughout Germany. Strategic bases in North Africa and England provided forward locations for the Strategic Air Command to deploy nuclear bombers and their supporting tankers. Augmenting the airpower was newly developed nuclear ballistic missiles. This nuclear umbrella was intended to provide an implied threat rather than signal an impending offensive posture, and it acted as a deterrent to further Soviet expansion.

A theater airlift capacity was developed to augment the Military Airlift Command (MAC) strategic airlift to tie the network of European and North African bases together. The aging C-82s that had been used to carry

Fig. 12.4. Approximately 7,500 citizens of Berlin (principally women and children) who were sick or undernourished were airlifted out of Berlin to England or France for treatment. Courtesy of the USAF Museum.

Fig. 12.5. A C-119 being loaded for a flight to Berlin during the blockade. Courtesy of the USAF Museum.

oversized cargo during the airlift were due to be replaced by a troop-carrier wing assigned directly to Tunner in support of the NATO mission.

The 433d Troop Carrier Wing was activated at Donaldson Air Force just outside Greenville, South Carolina. The wing was equipped with the new C-119 "Flying Boxcar." The unit from northern Ohio was well below its authorized strength when it deployed to Donaldson. Its three squadrons, the Sixty-seventh, Sixty-eighth, and Sixty-ninth Troop Carrier Squadrons, and supporting units were brought up to strength with new second lieutenant graduates of the Aviation Cadet Program, pilots and crew members from other reserve units across the country.

Typical of such a crew was Capt. William O. Cooper, an FAA tower operator from Atlanta, Georgia. "Coop" was a gangly 6'2" sandy-haired, craggy-faced pilot, whose piercing eyes darted continually and missed nothing. He could teach anyone air discipline, but he had his hands full with his copilot, William R. McIver III. "Mac" was a newly minted second lieutenant, fresh out of Reese Air Force Base Texas Advanced Training School near Sherman, Texas. He was an ex-Navy seaman and a brilliant natural pilot. He was a redheaded, skinny fellow of Scottish descent about Coop's height, who smoked incessantly and learned quickly. All the units' aircrews were similarly mixed and matched.

The deployment of the unit overseas to Rhein-Main Air Force Base, Germany, and six months of barracks life together before families could join them, melded the divergent individuals into a highly capable organization. They could fly a single ship all over North Africa or Europe or operate in thirty-six ship formations dropping airborne troops with equal skill. The young pilots learned quickly from the old pros, and it was imperative they did so, as the recalled reservists began rotating home after twenty-one months, and the new pilots were quickly thrust into aircraft command positions.

The missions they flew were critical to NATO. They supported fighter unit deployments to Tripoli, supplied the far-flung bases around the Mediterranean, assisted the bombers and tankers stationed in England, flew relief missions, and even transported pilgrims to Mecca one year. Their service was also invaluable to the Army airborne mission.

At about this time the 433d was renamed the 317th Troop Carrier Wing, and its squadrons became the Thirty-ninth, Fortieth, and Forty-first Troop Carrier Squadrons. They were transferred to an air base near Munich, Germany, where they remained for two years, after which they were redeployed to Evereaux and Dreux, France. This was part of the plan to move the airlift forces to the rear of the fighter units. The repositioning also made the airlift mission more efficient.

The new C-130 replaced the C-119s, augmented by units from U.S. bases on a rotational basis. Some of the C-119s were transferred to the Italian Air Force, and the others were returned to the United States to be flown by reserve units in support of the Army airborne training and cargo requirements.

The closure of North African bases and consolidation of other forces reduced airlift forces to those at Rhein-Main and deployed units from the United States.

Strategic airlift units under MAC were soon equipped with C-141 "Starlifters" and later with the huge C-5 aircraft. In times of need these are augmented by the Civilian Reserve Aircraft Fleet (CRAF). CRAF aircraft are specially modified civilian aircraft that are used as needed to support major military force deployments. The CRAF program provides 260 wide-body aircraft and represents a third of the air cargo capability and 90 percent of passenger airlift capacity of MAC.[5]

The Korean War

Meanwhile, all of Asia was vulnerable to expansion by the Communist Chinese. In Korea, a situation was brewing that was far more volatile than Soviet containment in Europe. After World War II, the Allies agreed that Korea, a part of the Japanese Empire, should be independent. Pending formal arrangements, the United States took charge of Korea south of the 38th parallel and the Soviet Union occupied the north. In 1948, a Communist government was established in North Korea and a pro-Western government was formed in the south. The North Koreans decided to unite the country under their control and invaded South Korea.

The Korean conflict began on 25 June 1950 when the Communist forces of North Korea attacked the army of South Korea and rapidly overran them, forcing them south to the city of Pusan. The United States, acting on behalf of the United Nations, committed the bulk of the military forces to aid the South Koreans. The Soviet Union had withdrawn from the UN Security Council and was unable to veto the resolution to condemn the North Korean aggression. During the conflict, airpower played a major role, even though much of Korea's defense was provided by hardware left over from World War II.

In late August 1950, Maj. Gen. William H. Tunner arrived in the Far East to take command of airlift operations to Korea. His force of C-54s, C-46s, and C-47s was augmented with three squadrons of C-119s from Sewart Air Force Base in Smyrna, Tennessee. A combat cargo command was organized to mold the airlift effort into a tightly organized centralized effort. Cargo tonnage figures quickly improved. During the first months of the Korean War, the C-54-equipped 374th Troop Carrier Group achieved the highest utilization rate per aircraft in the history of airlift operation.[6]

The majority of fighters were the venerable F-51. Strategic airlift was carried out by MAC, and B-26 fighter bombers and T-6 observation planes rounded out the initial aviation force. The Army used light aircraft and helicopters to support ground operations, and the Navy patrolled offshore with its increasingly important aircraft carrier force.

During the first months of the war, inadequate targeting led to total failure for thousands of Air Force interdiction missions. Attempts to identify and bomb Communist troops resulted only in substantial casualties between friendly forces and endless refugee columns fleeing the destruction. Throughout the war, the UN air forces conducted bombing missions around the clock. They did create supply difficulties for the Communist

armies, but they never did succeed in blocking the continual movement of sufficient quantities of food, arms, and ammunition to their frontline forces. In an effort to strike a more effective blow against the Communist forces, the American air offensive, under Gen. O. P. Weyland, directed its attention to the destruction of Korean dams, hydroelectric plants, and oil refineries near the Soviet border.

The North Korean forces launched an offensive that drove the Eighth Army into a defensive posture called the Pusan perimeter where they held and were kept supplied by the ever-increasing airlift capability. The daily tonnage of ammunition, gasoline, and rations rose to impressive heights. The air evacuation of wounded to Japan proved a major factor in saving many lives among the combat veterans. The most unusual cargo airlifted by the C-119s was a complete pontoon bridge brought from Japan to Korea to span the Han River to aid the Eighth Army in breaking out of its defensive posture.

It became the primary role of the U.S. Air Force to launch a massive air superiority campaign against the 445 Chinese MiGs that enjoyed political sanctuary there and were now being flown by the North Korean Air Force.[7] This effort was concentrated in the northwest corner of Korea known as MiG Alley. This was to be the big test for American airpower.

The Russian-made MiG-15 made its combat debut 1 December 1950, quickly proving itself clearly superior to the F-51s and Navy Corsair fighters flown by the Americans (see fig. 12.6). The cry for a competitive jet fighter

Fig. 12.6. MiG-15. Courtesy of the USAF Museum.

Fig. 12.7. F-80 "Shooting Star." Courtesy of the USAF Museum.

Fig. 12.8. Flight of F-86 Sabres. Courtesy of the USAF Museum.

was answered by the F-80 "Shooting Star" (shown in fig. 12.7). This simple yet elegant machine had been produced by Lockheed under almost miraculous conditions just seven years earlier.

In 1943, the Air Force had challenged Kelly Johnson's "Skunk Works" at Lockheed to produce an aircraft that would match anything Germany had to offer. Johnson not only promised to produce it, but he also guaranteed to deliver the aircraft within 180 days. This legendary team worked aeronautical magic, building the aircraft around an imaginary engine, and 178 days after Lockheed had been given the go-ahead on the project, the F-80 made its first test flight.

The trial by fire for the jet fighter came with its introduction to the conflict in Korea. On 8 May 1950, 1st Lt. Russell J. Brown engaged his Shooting Star with a MiG-15 and made aviation history, scoring the world's first jet-to-jet aerial victory. Jet aircraft technology was rapidly advancing, and within a year the F-80 was replaced by the sleek, powerful F-86 "Sabre."[8]

The MiG-15 far outclassed anything the U.S. armed forces could offer, and it was now evident that they would have to bring in modern jet aircraft if they were to compete against the MiG, and they would have to do it fast!

The Fourth Fighter-Interceptor Wing was one of the first F-86 units assigned to Korea (see fig. 12.8). The three squadrons were flown from New Castle County Airport, Delaware, to Kimpo Airfield in Korea. The MiG-15 and the Sabre were evenly matched, but the American pilots had the edge in combat experience and skill over the Chinese pilots supporting the North Koreans.[9] Although there were never more than 150 Sabres deployed, they quickly gained air superiority for the United States.

Lt. Col. Bruce N. Hinton had the first Sabre victory over the MiG-15 on 17 December 1950. While he was leading a flight of four aircraft, he spotted an equal number of enemy aircraft 7,000 feet below. Ready to engage the Americans, the MiGs climbed toward his flight, and Hinton's flight dove to meet the challenge. They continued to close the range. Sensing their vulnerability to the American force, the MiG flight scattered and headed back across the Yalu River into Manchuria, considered a safe haven by the United Nations. Hinton hit one of the MiGs with three bursts from the F-86's six 50-caliber machine guns. The plane flipped on its back and spun to the earth in flames.

Flying the F-86, twenty-four pilots of the Fourth Wing achieved the status of ace during the course of the war, earning elite status for the unit (fig. 12.9). All in all,

Fig. 12.9. The harsh Korean winter is reflected in this photo of a maintenance technician working on an F-86. Courtesy of the USAF Museum.

Fig. 12.10. The Navy did its share with aircraft like the Grumman F9F-2 Panther.
Courtesy of the Fred Roos Collection.

the combination of aircraft, pilots, mechanics, and support personnel of the Fourth Fighter-Interceptor Wing accounted for 502 enemy aircraft (54 percent of total) destroyed during the conflict at a cost of just 57 Sabres.[10] The Navy acquitted itself well also with its fighting carrier-based Panthers (fig. 12.10).

Usually the U.S. Air Force planes were outnumbered by the Chinese MiGs, but the F-86 proved to be more than a match for the MiG-15, and this aircraft shifted air superiority back in the favor of the UN forces. Korean operations eventually were forced to close down during daylight hours, as the F-86 completely dominated the skies. Jim Low, exemplifying the hard-flying F-86 Sabre pilot, went home after ninety-five missions having shot down five MiGs. He went on to fly fighters again in Vietnam and spent five years as a POW in Hanoi. By the end

of the war, 792 MiGs had been confirmed destroyed at the cost of 78 F-86s.

After three years of conflict, the situation had become static. The Chinese had ceased their push at the 38th Parallel, and the American Joint Chiefs of Staff had decided that the war would not be pushed beyond the Korean peninsula. This resulted in a limited war, with airpower being used almost exclusively as a holding action and for close ground support. It was in this atmosphere that the peace process began, but little progress was made for several months.

In the spring of 1953, President Dwight D. Eisenhower directed that the use of atomic weapons be considered if there was no thaw at the peace conference table. Accordingly, Gen. Hoyt Vandenberg, USAF chief of staff, positioned some atomic weapons on Okinawa.

The stalemate continued, but when the threat of Korean escalation came to an end, an armistice was signed in July.

One of the key events leading to the diminished Korean threat involves one of the most daring but virtually unknown raids by the incomparable F-86. This is the story of 120 unauthorized sorties that stopped a million-man enemy offensive. During the resumption of peace talks, the Chinese launched a major ground offensive, hoping to gain an advantage at the talks. They managed to break through UN defensive lines and position themselves on the main road to Seoul. For the UN forces, defense seemed impossible. Ninety-two sorties by the F-86s of the Eighteenth Fighter-Bomber Wing on 15 July 1953 had uncovered few real targets. Then a late-reporting flight identified the location of a hundred enemy boxcars near the front that had exploded when attacked. Nearby was another yard with even more boxcars. Instant action was imperative!

Capt. Dee Harper, the group operations officer for the Eighteenth Fighter-Bomber Wing, relates the events that followed as almost unreal. He immediately contacted the duty officer at Fifth Air Force headquarters to secure the necessary authority to launch an attack; then he set in motion all the machinery necessary to destroy the huge amount of munitions suspected to be in the boxcars. From this point on, events moved so rapidly that the lack of authorization to fly the mission was ignored. It must be on its way! The mission went ahead—and wiped out every target. Harper had conducted a completely unauthorized major military offensive, and even though it had been a total success, he knew he would be in trouble if word got out. Initially, he decided to say nothing about his lack of authorization, but then two Sabres were lost in ground fire, and he knew the incident would be scrutinized.

The next day, Col. Maurice Martin, the Eighteenth Group commander, strode into Harper's office. To Harper's surprise, he was not subjected to an invitation to a court-martial; to the contrary, Martin praised him for making perhaps the best decision of his career. Martin had received hard information that the Chinese army had intended to launch a million-man offensive, but now it would never happen—because vital munitions required for the attack had been destroyed. Then this incident, which no doubt had significant impact on securing peace, was quietly buried.[11]

With the end of the Korean War, many shortcomings in American airpower became apparent. It was clear that the Air Force, like other military forces, was not ready to fight a protracted war. It was also clear that strategic bombing planning should be restricted to Europe and that theater airlift was appropriate for resupply missions but not for a large airborne invasion.[12] Budget cuts had prevented the development of a strong tactical force. (General Vandenburg had been forced to operate on a shoestring.) The effect of airpower in the Korean conflict was indefinite at best. Nevertheless, with all of this there was a positive side: the Air Force had begun to employ modern technology and had implemented the use of computers, and having recognized that an all-jet bomber and fighter force was necessary, it had already made the transition away from propeller-driven aircraft.[13]

The War in Vietnam

Within ten years of the end of World War II, France had lost its colonial possessions in Southeast Asia. The final defeat of its army was at Dien Bien Phu at the hands of the Communist Vietminh forces. This led to the Geneva Accords, which divided Vietnam at the 17th parallel. The north was under Communist domination, and South Vietnam was under a nationalist government supported by the UN led by the United States and its allies.

What was to follow was to be ironic indeed. The West continued to focus all of its containment efforts on the regions that had historically been under the threat of Communist expansion—Europe and Korea, while considering Southeast Asia unimportant. Yet it was in Vietnam, a heretofore inconsequential Southeast Asian nation, that the Communist threat exploded into a prolonged and bloody confrontation that divided the small nation and rocked the West. Beginning as a relatively local issue, the conflict escalated into a nightmare of nationalism, civil war, exploitation, and clashes pitching East against West and imperialism against UN policies. It was in Vietnam and its neighboring countries of Cambodia, Laos, and Thailand, that modern airpower met its first true test.

In 1961, the conflict in Vietnam first attracted American interest with low-grade conflict and counterinsurgency activities. Early Air Force response was called "Project Jungle Jim." Under this activity, a number of

American-manned helicopters and transports were sent to the country. These were augmented by a detachment of propeller-driven attack planes filling a training role. Their mission was to deploy to Bien Hoa Air Base to assist the South Vietnamese in the development of contingency tactics and equipment (see fig. 12.11).[14]

After the Gulf of Tonkin Resolution was passed on 7 August 1964, Congress authorized President Lyndon B. Johnson to send Marines ashore at Danang, South Vietnam, to thwart any attack from Communist forces in the north. Vietminh soldiers already in the south became guerrilla fighters and were called Viet Cong. They blended into the villages, ready to join invading forces from the north. UN forces, predominately from the United States, continued to increase in numbers and the battle lines were drawn.

Over the next few years, Air Force C-123 "Providers" and a variety of aircraft from all the other services developed a sizable aviation presence "in country" to support the South Vietnamese effort at nation building (fig. 12.12). They became heavily dependent on the air bridge to develop an aviation infrastructure to interconnect the many isolated villages, plantations, and hamlets scattered across the whole country.

Airstrips were constructed that would accommodate larger twin-engine transports under all conditions.

Slowly, a dependency on airlift developed. Civilians, government officials of all kinds, troops, equipment cargo, and livestock moved throughout the country this way (fig. 12.13).

Special Forces camps challenging Communist guerrilla forces manned by the Green Berets and indigenous forces and their families depended on airlift for everything. It was usual for C-123 "Provider" and C-7 "Caribou" aircraft to transport live poultry, eels, and cattle daily to these camps for the local troops and their families, along with the GI frozen and canned foods for the Americans. At night, aging C-47s converted to gunships (called Puff the Magic Dragon) prowled the night sky to provide air cover and illumination to ward off night attacks on the camps.

Bien Hoa Air Base was equipped with attack aircraft such as T-28s, B-26s, and A-1Es, which were effective in providing defense for the camps but were less successful in inflicting decisive harm on the enemy (see fig. 12.14). Their efficiency was improved by Forward Air Controllers (FACs) flying light single-engine aircraft to spot and fix enemy targets for the armed aircraft. Crews were resourceful, highly motivated, and creative in using their old equipment, but they were never able decisively to apply airpower to defeat the elusive Viet Cong guerrilla fighter.[15]

Fig. 12.11. A-1Es operated by the South Vietnamese Air Force at Bien Hoa Air Base. Courtesy of the USAF Museum.

Fig. 12.12. A C-123 Provider airlifts troops to a special forces camp. Courtesy of the USAF Museum.

Fig. 12.13. Typical day in the life of a C-123. Courtesy of the USAF Museum.

Fig. 12.14. U.S. A-1E being prepared for a mission at Nha Trang. Courtesy of the USAF Museum.

Probably the most disappointing aspect of these years was the noticeable interservice rivalry that at times seemed to overshadow defeating the Viet Cong. This coupled with the political instability in South Vietnam made this emerging nation weak and vulnerable. It was soon evident that the guerrilla forces were receiving increased assistance from North Vietnam and were becoming capable of defeating the South Vietnamese. In a 1965 landmark decision, American troops were sent to Vietnam and air units were increased sufficiently to provide them support. In June 1965, the B-52s dropped their first bombs on South Vietnam (see fig. 12.15).

From 1965 on airpower and artillery became partners. The ground forces would find and hold the enemy units while air forces and artillery fire power destroyed them.

B-52s carrying thirty tons of bombs added their punch to the battlefields. Combined with fighter bombers, gunships, and armed helicopters guided by FACs, they provided fast response to strike requests in what increasingly became a war of attrition.

Many hundreds of strikes attended the Army's major search and destroy operations and the 1967 battles at Dak To, Con Thien, Khe Sanh, and Loc Ninh. In the Khe Sanh campaign of 1968, in a situation resembling Dien Bien Phu fourteen years before, air power, in conjunction with air-supplied troops on the tactical defensive, won a clear victory.[16]

Meanwhile, Air Force and Navy strike forces over the Hanoi Delta came increasingly under attack by North Vietnamese (NVM) MiG-17s and the newer MiG-21 fighters (see figs. 12.16 and 12.17). More and more U.S. aircraft were forced to jettison their bombs to defend themselves against the coordinated NVM fighters, surface-to-air missiles (SAMs) and intense flak. The enemy had amassed the heaviest integrated ground

Fig. 12.15. The B-52 dropping conventional iron bombs was a devastating weapon. Courtesy of the USAF Museum.

Fig. 12.16. Profile of a MiG-17. Courtesy of the USAF Museum.

Fig. 12.17. Typical MiG-21 flown by the North Vietnamese. Courtesy of the USAF Museum.

defense in air combat history. U.S. losses increased dramatically. Gen. William Momyer, Seventh Air Force commander, summoned Col. Robin Olds, the Eighth Tactical Fighter Wing commander at Ubon, Thailand, to report to him with a plan to eliminate the MiG threat. Olds, a proven leader with the well-earned reputation as a maverick, was told only to "keep it simple."[17]

Olds met with Capt. J. B. Stone, Lt. Joe Hicks, and Maj. J. D. Covington to plan the operation. A week later Operation Bolo was ready to be put into action. The idea was to get the entire MiG force into the air by simulating a maximum-effort bombing mission. This would be accomplished by imitating the route, speed, and radio chatter of the F-105 fighter bombers that conducted most of the "Rolling Thunder" missions (nickname for air strikes flown against North Vietnamese target) near Hanoi. The ruse would be carried out by F-4 "Phantoms" armed only with air-to-air missiles.

The pilots were assigned their roles in the mission by Colonel Olds. They were to overwhelm any MiGs that accepted a day fight challenge and then prevent them from returning to a safe haven across the Vietnamese border when they chose to disengage. Meanwhile, eight more U.S. aircraft were lost. Olds briefed General Momyer on the plan and was told to set the mission for New Year's Day 1967.

A force of ninety-two fighter aircraft was gathered for the mission, with an additional forty support aircraft including twenty-four F-105F "Wild Weasels" to suppress the missile sites. All leaves were canceled, as was the New Year's Eve party. Crews grumbled, and a pessimistic weather forecast made matters worse, so the New Year's Eve party was reinstated. However, at 6:00 A.M. on 2 January, the mission was back on. Crews were briefed, and after another delay, 28 F-4 "Phantom" fighters were launched.

Code names for the flights that day were derived from popular automobiles (Olds, Ford, Rambler). Those blocking the escape to China were animals (Bear, Otter). The F-105s that attacked the missile sites were named for weapons (Shotgun). MiG bases were coded for simplicity of identification. A U.S. map was laid over the target area, and Phuc Yen in the northwest became Frisco. Gia Lam to the south of Hanoi was Los Angeles. Cat Bi Airfield on the East Coast was identified as Miami. When crew members heard a call sign or location over the radio, they would immediately know where the battle was taking place. Simple.

When Olds arrived in the Hanoi area, the weather had closed in, and there was a heavy overcast blanketing the target area. The airfields were protected by the cloud cover, but the SAMs could be fired at the American aircraft, and they would be lethal. Still Olds pressed on toward Hanoi. A faulty radar jammer on one of the aircraft in the formation necessitated a tighter than usual formation to avoid detection. Olds reversed courses with

Fig. 12.18. Col. Daniel "Chappie" James in the cockpit of his F-4. Together he and Col. Robin Olds were referred to affectionately as "Black Man and Robin." Courtesy of the USAF Museum.

his flight, and the MiGs scrambled, mounting a maximum effort against the deep-penetrating F-4s. Olds turned back toward Hanoi with his flight and was joined by Ford flight led by Col. Daniel "Chappie" James Jr. (shown in fig. 12.18).

Suddenly James warned Olds that he had a MiG-21 at his six o'clock (directly behind him). Three more MiGs joined the battle. Olds broke left toward a target. James was watching another MiG. There was total confusion now. Olds continued his turn and fired two missiles at a MiG while trying to keep tabs on another one that was slowly slipping to his rear. One of Olds's pilots got a clean shot, hitting a MiG near its stabilizer. Another MiG flew through the fireball of the destroyed aircraft. It snapped ends, lost its tail, flipped into a flat spin, and disappeared in flames through the clouds.

By now the sky was filled with dogfights, and the radio was wild with chatter. Aircraft were engaged in mortal conflict. In the heat of the battle it was hard to distinguish one plane from another. Olds saw another MiG start a barrel roll to pull into position for a shot and then lost the bird in the sun. He pulled the nose back to a 45 degree angle, rolled half upside down right on top of the MiG, and hung there while the MiG completed its turn. Olds continued his roll, slipping down and low behind him, and fired two Sidewinders. One missile blew the MiG's wing off. Just then, an SA-2 SAM flashed through the clouds. Olds picked up his wing, roared into afterburner, and left the area at supersonic speed, while the missile passed him harmlessly (see fig. 12.19).

In all, the fight lasted about nine minutes. Seven MiGs were destroyed before the NVM controllers ordered their aircraft to hide in the clouds. All U.S. aircraft made it safely back to base, and there was a big celebration that night at Ubon, Thailand. At that time, Operation Bolo was the largest air victory of the Vietnam War. Later it was learned that the enemy had sent up thirty-two fighters that day. If the weather had cooperated and the trap had been properly sprung, a truly decisive victory might have been gained.

Fig. 12.19. Col. Robin Olds adding another star to his F-4 Phantom after having shot down a MiG. Courtesy of the USAF Museum.

By mid-1967, the F-4C held a distinct lead in kills against the MiG-21, with a ratio of 21 MiGs destroyed for every F-4C (see fig. 12.20). However, this situation had changed dramatically by 1973 as the piecemeal attrition program used by the Americans taught the enemy how to even the score. It was to be a costly lesson of the Vietnam War.[18]

The KC-135 tanker aircraft played a major role in the conflict (see figs. 12.21 and 12.22). Both fighters and Guam-based bombers depended on the tankers to fulfill their missions. No fighter mission could make it successfully into the northern areas of Vietnam without refueling, and in-country fighter missions were greatly enhanced with the flexibility that refueling provided them.

Normally the tankers were positioned in regular tracks, or orbits, in northern and eastern Thailand, northern Laos, and over the Gulf of Tonkin. At times tanker crews went considerably further north to come to the aid of fuel-starved F-105s and F-4s (shown in fig.

Fig. 12.20. An F-4 Phantom, heavily damaged by a North Vietnamese surface-to-air missile (SAM), brings its crew home safely. Courtesy of the USAF Museum.

Fig. 12.21. F-100 being refueled by a KC-135 Tanker aircraft. Courtesy of the USAF Museum.

Fig. 12.22. B-52 being refueled by a KC-135. Courtesy of the Fred Roos Collection.

12.23). Many other aircraft also looked to the KC-135s for critical assistance. Most aircraft and crews survived because of the heroic efforts of the tanker crews, whose exploits are often overlooked. Although the KC-135s provided the bulk of the refueling, other aircraft also served in this role. HC 130 "Combat Shadows" refueled the HH-3E "Jolly Green" and HH-53 Air Sea Rescue helicopters, and Navy KA-3 "Skywarriors" and KA-6 "Intruders" refueled their aircraft on deep penetration missions. One mission flown by a KC-135 exemplifies the selfless dedication and heroism of these tanker crews.

A crew under the command of Maj. John H. Carsteel of the 4258th Strategic Wing was assigned a routine refu-

eling track over the Gulf of Tonkin. It was another normal day of boring holes in the sky waiting to hook up with fighter bombers with near-empty tanks.

Shortly after arriving on station, boom operator M.Sgt. Nathan C. Campbell fed gas to a pair of F-104s. Soon after a hookup had been established, there was a desperate call for fuel from two Navy KA-3s. They had plenty of gas to transfer but none they would use themselves. The F-104s took on a partial load and then backed off to fly cover for the tanker (see fig. 12.24). The first KA-3 took on a minimum load and disconnected to allow the other KA-3 to take on fuel. Almost immediately, two Navy F-8s were vectored to the tanker for an

Fig. 12.23. F-4 "Wild Weasel" used for seeking and destroying SAM sites. Courtesy of the USAF Museum.

Fig. 12.24. A flight of F-104s. Courtesy of the USAF Museum.

emergency refueling. One F-8 was so low on fuel that the pilot could not wait for the KA-3 to finish refueling, so he hooked onto that aircraft. This was probably the first three-ship hookup on record.

Then two Navy F-4s showed up with "bingo fuel" (emergency condition). Quickly the F-104s took another shot of fuel and got out of the way as the two F-4s approached to take on enough fuel to get back to their carrier.

After this series of ten refuels, the KC-135 did not have enough fuel to get back to its base. It changed course and headed to its alternate in South Vietnam. Meanwhile, the KC-135 continued to refuel the F-104s and give them enough fuel to get to their base. Eight crews and their aircraft were saved that day. It went on like this for eight years for these crews who served with little acclaim but upon whom so many missions were totally dependent.[19]

By 1967, the tide of battle in South Vietnam favored the allies, prompting the Communist forces to launch the ill-fated Tet Offensive. Airpower played a key role in preventing the Viet Cong from fulfilling its military objective in this battle.

Launched on 31 January 1968, the Tet Offensive was anticipated by the Seventh Air Force, which was ready and able to provide the ground forces with necessary support. Although the enemy seized all ten provincial capitals in their initial assault, they were quickly defeated and routed everywhere except at Hue. Airpower interdiction continued through the end of February, when the offensive sputtered to an end.

Over 16,000 strike missions were flown by 280 aircraft. C-130s, C-123s, and C-7s provided an airlift network that moved troops and equipment rapidly anywhere they were needed (see figs. 12.25–12.27).[20] The Communist forces were soundly defeated, and an intense pacification

Fig. 12.25. A C-130 delivering supplies by the Low-Attitude Parachute Extraction System (LAPES) at Khe Sanh. Courtesy of the USAF Museum.

Fig. 12.26. C-130 providing a lifeline of supplies. Courtesy of the USAF Museum.

Fig. 12.27. Takeoff of a C-130 at Camp Evans in the northern part of South Vietnam in 1968. Courtesy of the USAF Museum.

program was implemented throughout the whole of South Vietnam. The countryside was taken away from the Communist forces and security of the south seemed assured. After this the Viet Cong were no longer a major factor in the war, and the Communists changed strategy to rely hereafter on regular North Vietnamese forces.

When the Tet Offensive was launched, a simultaneous assault was undertaken against the Marine base at Khe Sanh. Gen. Vo Nguyen Giap intended to have his North Vietnamese forces gain another victory like the one he had achieved over the French at Dien Bien Phu in 1954. Although he invested three full infantry divisions in the venture and pounded the base for two and a half months, he did not succeed.

General Momyer ordered over 20,000 attack sorties against the Communist forces from December 1967 until the siege ended late in February 1968. Every day, 350 tactical fighters and sixty B-52s struck the enemy. Gunships provided night protection with gunfire and illumination. Airlift provided over 12,000 tons of supplies so that the fire base was never in danger of running low on equipment, ammunition, or food.[21]

This massive air effort was conducted under the command of General Momyer, who was designated as the single manager for air. Although he orchestrated the stunning defeat of General Giap's forces, in the end run it was American impatience with the war that signaled defeat for the South Vietnamese and withdrawal of American forces.

The United States Air Force continued to support military operations in South Vietnam as the policy of "Vietnamization" reduced the presence of American ground forces. Increasingly, airpower assumed the major American military presence in Vietnam. B-52 strikes prevented the enemy from massing an assault while South Vietnamese troops replaced American forces returning to the United States. In December 1969, B52s dropped over thirty million tons of bombs on enemy positions.[22]

American air forces began withdrawing from Southeast Asia during 1970. By the end of the year, the South Vietnamese Air Force was equipped with over 700 aircraft, and by the end of 1971, the U.S. Air Force had only 277 aircraft in the region that flew over 70 percent of the close air support missions.

The interdiction campaign achieved much and cost the North Vietnamese heavily. It inhibited their buildup in the south, providing time for the South Vietnamese to see to their own defense. In support of this initiative, the U.S. Air Force conducted Operation Command Hunt in Laos. Although it has been deemed an inefficient use of airpower, it did slow the enemy advance in South Vietnam and assisted the extraction of the U.S. forces.[23]

On 8 May, President Richard Nixon shifted the U.S. airpower emphasis to the north. The campaign, called Operation Linebacker, was conducted simultaneously with the fighting in the south and proved to be the most intensive air battle of the conflict because of the increased air defense capability of the North Vietnamese. Ninety-four targets were selected for this operation in a profound effort to support the peace negotiations in Paris. Beginning on 10 May 1972, the operation continued well into the fall as U.S. planes knocked out all major bridges, strangled railroads, crippled the petroleum industry, and mined channels into the nation's ports, effectively blocking the delivery of most supplies to North Vietnam.

Operation Linebacker II was ordered on 16 December 1972 by Adm. Thomas H. Moorer, chair of the Joint Chiefs of Staff, who directed the commander-in-chief of Pacific Command and the Strategic Air Command to launch a maximum effort against the Hanoi/Haiphong areas of North Vietnam.

Two days later, the first aircraft were launched on what was to be an eleven-day air campaign designed to strike at the heart of the North Vietnamese war-making capacity. The B-52 was the primary aircraft to spearhead the offensive. More than two hundred of the eight-engine strategic bombers, of which the Forty-third Strategic Wing was a major component, had been deployed to Thailand and Guam. Under the command of Col. James A. McCarthy, the Forty-third was deployed to Anderson Air Force Base in Guam. The wing was composed of fifty B-52Ds and divided into two squadrons, the Sixtieth, under Lt. Col. Charles R. Maynard, and the Sixty-third, commanded by Lt. Col. David D. Rines.

Guam, nicknamed "The Rock" by the B-52 crews, was over 2,650 miles from Hanoi, requiring long overwater flights and air-to-air refuelings. Because of tactical approach requirements, the flights could average 12–18 hours each. Although the D model was the oldest of the B-52s used, it could carry the heaviest conventional bomb load. The KC-135A tanker became the other essential part of the bomber force team, as the B-52Ds simply could not make it to the target and back without them. Most of the tankers were based in Okinawa, and from that position they could service all types of aircraft used in the conflict.

In addition to the B-52s, many other aircraft assisted in a Linebacker II, attacking surface-to-air missile (SAM) sites and antiaircraft positions, providing fighter cover, carrying out electronic countermeasures (ECMs), and conducting search and rescue when required. For example, in the 26 December attack, 120 B-52s were supported by 113 USAF, Navy, and Marine escort, attack, and electronic warfare aircraft.[24]

Thirty-four strategic targets were struck during the operation, all within a 60-mile radius of Hanoi, and most within 25 miles of the city, dubbed "Bullseye" by the aircrews. This area was very heavily defended, so the B-52s attacked at night to make defense as difficult as possible. A three-ship formation was used, and all bombings were carried out using all-weather radar and weapons-aiming computers. The system was extremely accurate.

The initial mission was flown on 18 December by 129 B-52s, of which 33 were from Colonel McCarthy's Forty-third Wing. The aircraft approached from the northwest in three waves 4–5 hours apart. Upon reaching the Initial Point (IP), they made a straight run at the target, taking no evasive action for four minutes until the bombs were away. Then they broke to the north and northwest. No aircraft were lost on this mission.

On 19 December, Colonel McCarthy, the Airborne Mission commander, led ninety-three bombers on a mission that destroyed the Kinh No railway yards and storage area.[25] The SAMs and antiaircraft shells exploded all around them, but again there were no losses. The following night, however, 220 SAM launches destroyed four B-52Gs and two B-52Ds and damaged a third. One aircraft was from the Forty-third Wing.

The following two nights, the attacks continued on the Lang Dang railway yards and three SAM sites. No missions were flown on Christmas Day. On 26 December, 120 bombers flew a concentrated attack lasting just 15 minutes. The ferocity of enemy ground fire was intense. In the thick of it, Colonel McCarthy saw his cockpit light up like day as a SAM came right up under the nose of his aircraft not more than 50 feet away. "At 'Bombs away' it looked like we were right in the middle of a fireworks factory that was in the process of blowing up. Despite the SAMs and 100 knot headwinds, the [aircraft] dropped their bombs on target at the exact second called for in the order."[26]

Two B-52s were lost on 26 December, and two more were lost the following night during a sixty-aircraft mission. However, this proved to be the last success for the North Vietnamese defense force. There were no losses on the missions flown on 28 and 29 December. Only a few SAMs were launched, and their guidance appeared erratic. It was believed that the North Vietnamese defense force failure came about because their command and control network had been made practically useless by the bombardment.

A cease-fire accord was agreed to at the end of Linebacker II, but B-52 missions continued into Cambodia and Laos until 15 August 1973. The eleven days of Linebacker II cost the United States fifteen B-52s and thirty-three crewmembers killed or missing in action. The North Vietnamese lost 80 percent of their electrical power and 25 percent of their petroleum stocks in the bombing.

With its spring offensive curtailed and facing destruction of its industrial base, Hanoi indicated interest in negotiations. In October, President Nixon stopped bombing the north. The North Vietnamese responded by stalling and actually withdrawing from the peace negotiations altogether.

British military analyst Sir Robert Thompson believed this mission forced the North Vietnamese back to the negotiating table.[27] Others believe the mission failed because it did not achieve its goal to destroy the enemy's will to continue fighting. The air war over North Vietnam lasted more than three thousand days, but in the end no decisive conclusion was achieved.[28]

The Vietnam conflict ended with no clear indication that airpower alone could bring about a decisive victory over an enemy force. It is not known whether it was misapplication of forces or their incapability to be decisive. What did become clear was that future wars would require joint operations with a single commander for air and that operational decisions would need to be made by field commanders to ensure timely response to enemy actions.

The Cold War

Simultaneous with the major confrontations in Asia, NATO continued to maintain its posture of containing Soviet expansion into Europe beyond the Iron Curtain that divided Germany. In support of the NATO mission, the United States backed its fighter and transport aircraft in Europe with its bomber force. The Strategic Air Command (SAC), under the command of Gen. Curtis E. LeMay, provided the nuclear deterrent. Armed initially with B-29s and K-B50 tankers, SAC provided the umbrella force necessary to maintain the uneasy peace of the cold war until the collapse of the Soviet Union in 1991.

The huge six-engine B-36 strategic bomber could reach targets in Europe from bases in the United States with a nuclear capability. Four jet engines were added to its wings to increase its speed. It was short-lived, however, because it was replaced by the B-47 (shown in fig. 12.28) and the B-58 Hustler. These, too, were rapidly replaced with the B-52. Supported by the KC-135 tanker, it gave the United States an all-jet worldwide nuclear deterrent air force.

SAC's fleet of bombers, tankers, and missiles were able to strike anywhere in the world at a moment's notice. General LeMay's strategy was to keep this force on a constant wartime alert with elements aloft 24 hours a day. Around the world, he conducted massive deployments and exercises. He also maintained nonstop flights to keep crews sharp and to show a clenched fist against any adversary, thus maintaining peace through a demonstration of strength.

The end of the cold war marked a change in the employment of strategic bombers when, on 27 September 1991, SAC officially ended their round-the-clock readiness for nuclear war. Bombers are now fully integrated into the conventional force as a part of the recently formed Air Combat Command.

The Single Integrated Operational Plan (SIOP, or nuclear war plan) capability still exists, though in highly modified form. Routine practice now includes the joint employment of F-15 and F-16 fighters and bombers.

The thirty-year-old B-52 is still the main platform for bomb delivery in the versatile conventional role. However, the B-1 and the B-2 are speedily supplanting it in the role of a deep penetration nuclear bomber. Soon

Fig. 12.28. B-47 of Strategic Air Command. Courtesy of the USAF Museum.

even the B-1 will switch to a conventional mission role.[29] The B-52 will more slowly move into an "iron bomb" role as its mission changes and the plane undergoes modification, even as it is being constructed.

Today's crewmembers are older and more experienced than in the past. In addition, Reserve and Air National Guard units are being trained to assume bombing mission roles, and the active force and reserves are integrating more of their missions, improving the flexibility of the strategic mission.

Big bombers will continue to be needed, as they are able to take a large payload a long way and drop it precisely on target. However, large payloads become less important as accuracy improves. One F-15E today can accomplish more than an entire squadron of B-17s in World War II.[30] Precision munitions for both bombers and fighters are the highest priority in Air Combat Command.

Throughout the cold war period, fighter bombers underwent many modifications. Some saw service in Vietnam, like the Navy's A-6A Intruder, and the Air Force's F-100 and the F-105 Thunderchief, or "Thud," which carried a bomb load equal to the B-17 (see figs. 12.29 and 12.30). Air defense duties were handled by such aircraft as the F-102 and F-106 (shown in fig. 12.31), delta wing fighters nicknamed "Daggers" and "Darts." The F-111 joined carrier-based F-14s to attack Libya and send a message that the United States would not tolerate that nation's support of terrorist training.

Evolving during these years were ultra-secret stealth aircraft, such as the high-flying SR-71. The first truly "stealth" combat aircraft, the F-117, was introduced on 10 November 1988, followed by the Northrup B-2 on 17 July 1989. The first of these aircraft to be used in a combat role was the F-117, which saw limited duty during the Panama mission to depose dictator Manuel Noriega.

Fig. 12.29. F-105 Thunderchief, or "Thud." Courtesy of the USAF Museum.

Fig. 12.30. The Navy's A-6A Intruder carries its load as well. Courtesy of the Fred Roos Collection.

Fig. 12.31. F-106 Interceptors. Courtesy of the USAF Museum.

Strategic airlift requirements were handled by the C-141 and C-5 aircraft, and tanker duties were enhanced by the tri-jet KC-10. These aircraft are still used extensively in this role. A special needs airplane was developed to support combat troop deployments and army cargo requirements. This aircraft, the McDonnell-Douglas C-17, "Globemaster III," underwent a difficult development process, but it was finally put into service during the Persian Gulf War.

As airpower applications changed, the employment of joint operations of military force evolved from lessons learned in Vietnam and the interventions in support of U.S. world policy that followed. Joint employment of military force can best be demonstrated by the Persian Gulf War.

The Persian Gulf War

In July 1990, it was clear that Saddam Hussein, the leader of Iraq, was one of the most powerful men in the world, and he had his eye on the rich oil fields in neighboring Kuwait. In one swift move, his army invaded and took control of the tiny nation. In spite of repeated warnings from the United States, it was obvious he had no intention of withdrawing his troops and returning the country to its own sovereignty. On the contrary, all intelligence data proved he intended to stay. Under the leadership of the United States, a United Nations coalition was formed to remove Saddam by force.

The primary task fell to airpower belonging to all four American services and a half dozen allied states.[31] The key to the successful application of airpower in this situation was to bring leadership, technology, planning, and people together to accomplish the mission.

Gen. Norman Schwartzkopf, the overall commander, assessed the cost of removing Saddam from Kuwait and determined that if he relied on the traditional Air-Land battle doctrine, expected casualties would be unacceptable. Accordingly, he asked the Air Force chief of staff for assistance. As joint air commander, Gen. Chuck Horner was assigned the responsibility of commanding all air assets and using them in such a way as to paralyze Iraq's command and control system at the outset. This would render their military force helpless and without guidance or sight. Within hours of the beginning of the war at 7:00 P.M. EST on 16 January 1991, destruction from the air was so complete that Iraq was deprived of any military flexibility or options.

For forty-two days and nights, the U.S. Air Force and the coalition allies dropped over 142,000 tons of bombs

Fig. 12.32. F-117 Stealth fighter bomber. Courtesy of the USAF Museum.

Fig. 12.33. FB-111 swing-wing fighter bomber. Courtesy of the USAF Museum.

on Iraq and occupied Kuwait with unprecedented accuracy. Fighter forces cleared the skies and performed interdiction tactics flawlessly, and airlift craft kept essential supplies and personnel flowing without interruption.

The air attack depended on precision targeting. B-52s from Barksdale Air Force base near Shreveport, Louisiana, flew nonstop to Iraq to launch their conventional cruise missiles. The launch of the missiles coincided with the dropping of laser-guided bombs by F-117s and FB-111s (shown in figs. 12.32 and 12.33). Along with the use of "Tomahawk" missiles, it was possible to impose a systemwide strategic shock on the Iraqis, crippling their command and control capacity and immobilizing it for the rest of the war.[32]

In addition to achieving more than 90 percent accuracy, the attack was accomplished without detection of

the aircraft. The stealthy F-117, which had never been tested in combat, approached its assigned targets undetected by enemy antiaircraft, delivered its bombs on target, and emerged untouched. Not one aircraft was lost.

On the third night of the war, Maj. Pete "Spaceman" Spacil and his weapons systems officer, Capt. Troy Campbell, departed Taif, Saudi Arabia, for their target. The first two nights they had used techniques that were pretty much standard for fighting with their F-111F "Vark." In essence this meant go in high, go low, hit, stay low, and then pop up high. Antiaircraft fire (AAA) was inaccurate but dangerous because there was so much of it. Spacil was to lead a two-ship element in a package of twenty-two aircraft. He would use Terrain Following Radar (TFR) all the way to target and while in enemy territory. At the initial point (IP), he would climb to get above the AAA, drop the bombs, ramp down and egress on TFR. The task was to precede the main force and suppress SAM sites and AAA on a field southeast of Baghdad so the following twenty aircraft could bomb the field into uselessness. That was the plan.[33]

Spacil's two ships took off and proceeded to the tanker track. A cell of five KC-135s waited for them there for a prestrike refueling. This was a bit tricky. Night, no moon, spotty radar, and tankers stacked 500 feet apart with four jets on each tanker made proper timing essential. All aircraft hooked up successfully, and they were the last to leave. The other twenty aircraft dropped to 22,000 feet and proceeded to a point northeast of the targeted field, hung a left, and then were cleared to target direct. They were supported by F-15Cs. F-4Cs and EF-111s were in the area sending confusing signals to confound ground acquisition radar.

Down low now, Spacil's two ships' initial target fix (TF) was 1,000 feet above the ground (AGL). They stepped down to 500 feet, then to 300 feet, maintaining 540 KGS (nautical miles per hour groundspeed). At this point, the main package was northeast of their position. Flying in a trail now 30 seconds apart, Spacil's two aircraft wove around suspected threat areas trying to be as invisible as possible. At the IP, they went through their checklist, banked toward the target field undetected, initiated a climb to 12,000 feet, and dropped four CBU-87s that would pepper the entire field with bomblets to keep everyone from shooting long enough for the main group to attack. Bombs gone, they made a left turn to the south. The sky below turned red. It seemed like daylight. The buffet was formidable. A quick glance confirmed to Spacil that his wingman had pickled his CBUs on target as well. Both aircraft turned on their TF and went to 1,000 feet to egress at a comfortable 1.1 mach back to Taif. At the debriefing, they heard that they had completed a successful mission. The main package attacked without a single one of their threat-warning receivers picking up any sign of opposition. The target airfield was now useless.[34]

On the same day at another location, Maj. Larry "Cherry" Pitts launched well before daylight in his F-15 "Eagle" on an air-to-air mission under the command of Lt. Col. J. B. Velk. The task was to provide escorts to a large strike package of over eighty F-16s, F-111s, and some SEAD (Suppression of Enemy Air Defenses) F-4G "Weasels."[35]

They had gassed at their assigned KC-10 tanker and waited for their push time when they got the word from the AWACS (Advance Warning and Control System) aircraft that the mission had been scrubbed, probably due to weather. Four aircraft, including Major Pitts's, were given another assignment. While they waited for the go signal, they watched a large Navy strike package ingress and begin their egress from their target near Baghdad. With so many aircraft in the air, it was vital to keep track of where everybody was to sort out the good guys from the bad guys. AWACS was very good at keeping things "sorted out and tidied up." This day the AWACS controllers were particularly outstanding. They started calling out "bandits" at 30 miles north of the Navy strikers that were apparently planning to attack the Navy aircraft. "These guys are ours," lead announced, and AWACS acknowledged.

The four F-15s pushed to the northwest in hot pursuit of the bad guys (see fig. 12.34). They were at 30,000 feet with good speed, with an apparently easy target solution, when the bad guys turned cold (reversed course) and headed back toward Baghdad.

During the chase, another group of bandits turned up 40 miles north streaking south. The four F-15s dropped the now retreating first group and focused on this new threat. They were low, down in the weeds, and fast. Radar was locked on the new target at 25 miles. It would be best to engage them head on and at long range while keeping an eye on the first group, for it seemed obvious the F-15s could be diving into a trap if the first group turned and attempted a pincer movement. Nevertheless, they stayed "cold."

Major Pitts locked on the low group, but they maneuvered and broke lock. Radars worked overtime trying to hold these guys. The original group finally did turn back toward the F-15s, but AWACS assured them that someone else would engage them. As the group reached 10,000 feet, a bandit appeared on Pitts's radar. He was at 500 feet five miles ahead crossing left to right doing 700 knots. Pitts called, "Engaged," and split-S down to jump the bandit, who was going so fast he went right off the radar. Still Pitts called a "Tally ho." Although he had over-"G"d the jet in the split-S, Pitts was able to use auto mode on the radar and lock on the bandit again. The bandit, a MiG-25, tried to break right, but this machine is not impressive in a high-speed turn. He managed a 270-degree turn to the south with Pitts now about 9,000

Fig. 12.34. Flight of two F-15s. Courtesy of the USAF Museum.

feet behind him. Pitts launched an AIM-9 missile, then an AIM-7, and another AIM-9. The MiG was doing a world class job on the defensive, but it was no use. A final AIM-7 went right up his tailpipe.

The pilot ejected and his emergency locator transmitter (ELT) began to transmit on the guard frequency. Pitts got out of there because he knew the downed pilot's wingman was out there somewhere and the signal would bring him on the run.

Before the sortie was over, another target was identified and shot down by one of the F-15s. By this time all were low on fuel, so they headed for the tanker and home with two victories to their credit.[36]

The air-to-air battle, which involved both F-15s and F-16s, wound down as the Iraqi aircraft disengaged and

sought sanctuary in neighboring countries (see fig. 12.35). From the beginning of the air attack, Iraq was in a state of semiparalysis, unable to conduct effective military counters, although it did attempt to do so at Khafji.

During about the third week of the war, a small force of Saudis and Americans were in close combat with a brigade of Iraqis in the border village of Khafji. Saddam had hoped to inflict unacceptably heavy casualties on the coalition forces, which would influence the American public to demand a quick withdrawal of their troops. It was not to be, however, because General Schwartzkopf would not allow his commanders to put their forces in harm's way. Saddam's forces had also suffered badly from the air attacks, and he needed to get the ground war started if he was going to generate the number of

Fig. 12.35. Air-to-air duties were also handled by the General Dynamics F-16 Fighting Falcon. Courtesy of the Fred Roos Collection.

casualties necessary to pressure the U.S. forces to return home. He planned an assault into Saudi Arabia intending to generate a ground counterattack from the UN coalition. The hamlet of Khafji was his marshaling point. The Iraqis clandestinely assembled an impressive force ready to move out after a probing attack on Khafji. The U.S. Command discovered the force.

General Horner brought the full weight of airpower against two assembled Iraqi divisions. Within 12 hours, both were destroyed, and the survivors retreated to Kuwait. This marked the first time airpower alone was used to destroy a powerful army ground force.[37]

The Gulf War ended on 26 February 1991, six weeks after it began. The partnership role of airpower in modern warfare was dramatically demonstrated. Air superiority was established before ground units moved to rout the enemy ground forces. Fighter bombers cleared the skies and dropped a whole gambit of accurate weapons. The A-10 Thunderbolt with the Gatling gun and heat-seeking or optically guided "Maverick" missiles provided support for ground units and destroyed Iraqi armor. All airpower assets operated as a single entity under the command of Gen. Chuck Horner in an effective application of this force. There is still much to be learned from this short war, but it was a clear victory and the beginning of the application of airpower as part of joint military planning.

Naval Aviation

Demobilization was rapid after World War II ended. Ships and planes were put in "mothballs," and thousands of aircraft were sold for scrap. Within just a few months, naval aviation forces were one-quarter that of the wartime peak. With the rapidly shrinking force came constant demands to cut it even more, and this time critics were attacking the mighty aircraft carrier, calling it obsolete and seeking its withdrawal from the fleet. When construction of a new carrier was halted, the secretary of the Navy resigned in disgust.

In spite of the cutbacks and the constant struggle for funding, there were several dramatic developments in naval aviation during this period, including the qualification of the first carrier jet squadron, Fighter Squadron 17A, flying the FH-1 "Phantom," and the nonstop world distance record of 11,235 miles, set by a Navy P2V "Neptune."

Then, in June 1950, the Korean War sparked a brief, albeit temporary, reprieve for naval aviation and the mighty aircraft carriers. Just eight days after President Truman ordered U.S. forces to support the Republic of Korea, the U.S. and British carriers *Valley Forge* and *Triumph* launched attacks on Pyongyang.

The aircraft carrier came to provide the air superiority that ultimately gave the United States and its allies the margin of power that led to a truce in Korea. Relatively few naval fighters were launched from carrier decks to face air-to-air combat. Instead, they flew deep support missions against critical enemy targets and assisted ground troops slugging it out in the brutal weather of the Korean peninsula. The advent of the steam catapult as the standard means of launching aircraft from carrier decks caused the replacement of propeller-driven planes with jets (see fig. 12.36).

Following the Korean War, naval aviation enjoyed a period of spectacular technological growth. Now super-

Fig. 12.36. The McDonnell F2H-2 Banshee, one of the Navy's early carrier-based jets. Courtesy of the Fred Roos Collection.

sonic aircraft such as the F-8J "Crusader" (shown in fig. 12.37) could deliver nuclear weapons to almost any target, and aircraft guns were replaced by air-to-air missiles and rockets. Submarines could now be tracked by P-3 "Orions" using magnetic anomaly detection (MAD) equipment, and helicopters were fitted with dipping sonar detection devices (see fig. 12.38). This explosion in technology provided the impetus to develop bigger, faster, more adaptable aircraft carriers, and the age of the supercarrier began with the commissioning of the USS *Forrestal* in 1955. It was not long before the first nuclear-powered supercarrier, the USS *Enterprise,* was launched. The USS *Enterprise* sailed 30,000 miles in 65 days without refueling, proving the awesome potential for nuclear-powered vessels.

The 1984 Grenada operation demonstrated the first use of the modern carrier battle group, a virtually self-contained force of surface, subsurface, and aviation assets. At the heart of the battle group is the aircraft carrier. With a crew of approximately five thousand and a complement of about ninety aircraft, it gives the battle group a balanced air offensive capability and a complete defense against air, surface, or subsurface attack. In the Grenada operation, naval aviation units flew strike missions against Cuban and Grenadan resistance, and marine helicopters provided assault force transportation and close air support, contributing a vital element of this highly successful operation.

Yet again the role of the aircraft carrier in modern warfare came under intense criticism. Many critics cited

Fig. 12.37. Ling-Temco-Vought F-8J Crusader. Courtesy of the Fred Roos Collection.

Fig. 12.38. The Lockheed P-3 Orion tracking a submarine. Courtesy of the Fred Roos Collection.

the carrier's huge size as providing a very tempting target for enemy forces. This vulnerability, coupled with the staggering cost of a modern carrier prompted some to propose that the supercarriers be replaced with smaller, less expensive craft. Navy officials pointed out that not only are the huge ships the only craft capable of providing tremendous airpower from virtually anywhere in the world, but they are also, in fact, not very vulnerable at all. A 1969 fire aboard the USS *Enterprise* ignited nine 500-pound bombs, the equivalent of six cruise missiles—on the flight deck, unlocking enough devastation to sink a lesser vessel. The ship survived the

explosions and was launching aircraft within a few hours.

When Iraq invaded Kuwait in the summer of 1990, it unleashed a chain of events that would prove the value of the aircraft carrier. However, the defeat of the Iraqis reinstated America's faith and trust in all the armed forces.

Within five days, two U.S. carriers, the *Independence* and the *Dwight D. Eisenhower,* were on-station to check the advance of Iraqi forces and protect the arrival of land-based forces. During the seven-month UN-imposed Maritime Interdiction Force (MIF) operations that followed, four U.S. carriers provided the backbone of the operation that prevented Iraq from garnering support or supplies.

The real value of the carriers and the aircraft they carry was proved in the Persian Gulf War. This action was notable not only for what it accomplished but for how it was done.

From the beginning, Navy strike planners participated in the plan that was to become the air portion of the Persian Gulf War, and Navy representatives ensured that Navy forces were integrated into all aviation planning. Throughout Desert Shield and Desert Storm, six U.S. carriers brought the weight of their awesome striking power to bear against the Iraqi aggressors. Navy E-2s worked closely with their USAF AWACS counterparts to keep an eagle eye on all operations and to coordinate airborne command and control. Navy and Marine Corps aircraft strikes were integrated with those of the UN coalition. Enemy air defenses were crippled by EA-6B jamming and antiradiation missiles during USAF and Coalition strikes, and photography from Navy F-14s was extremely valuable for planning and assessing battle damage.

Carrier aviation supported the ground campaign by attacking Saddam's army before and after the ground action and by providing solid credence to the possibility of amphibious assault, a diversion that succeeded in tying up Iraqi army divisions so they could not be used in the ground war. The destruction of the Iraqi navy was largely accomplished by carrier aviation. By the end of the war, more than a hundred Iraqi vessels had been sunk and the Iraqi navy had ceased to exist.

Never did the carriers become vulnerable to attack. They had the protection of overwhelming coalition forces, and they could remain far out of enemy range and still provide attack power. Long-range strikes could be provided from all the carriers because of the tanking support provided by Navy KA-6s and S-3 "Vikings" as well as USAF and RAF tankers.

In the Persian Gulf War, UN policy goals were achieved quickly, decisively, and at reasonable cost, due to the integrated efforts of all members of the UN coalition, of which naval aviation proved to be a highly effective and versatile component.

The Future of Military Airpower

Changes in technology, communications, and global conditions have been so rapid that it would be folly to even try to guess what structure will emerge in the war-making capacity of the United States. However, a posture of deterrence in order to avoid total war dictates certain requirements for airpower. For example, the threat of force must be believable, and the ability to apply that force in selective target terms must be so overpowering as to demand complete disarmament of an enemy almost immediately. To allow any time for buildup invites one's own total destruction.[38]

The unknowns and uncertainties surrounding the limited war application of airpower are just as obscure as those involving total war. Still, it seems the United States must maintain a military establishment to prevent others from destroying it. Airpower selectively applied seems to offer the best choice of decisive delivery of sufficient force to signal to any aggressor the fruitlessness of their effort. Hopefully, peace is the only prevailing choice, and U.S. airpower is the instrument that makes this choice a reality.[39]

Airpower has evolved into a uniquely successful instrument of warfare but one that is limited in its effectiveness by the level of conflict in which it is applied. At times it is indecisive. Some of its awesome selectivity can always transmit clear messages to an aggressor. Airlift provides a special strength essential in peace and war. Air-to-air refueling gives the United States global presence quickly.

At this point in its evolution, U.S. airpower application is in need of rethinking. It is becoming a weapon system that offers the nation's leadership a spectrum of options to confront an adversary and defeat it.

Midway through the 1990s, the Air Force began thinking about the capabilities it will need thirty years from now. "Don't wait for the 'coming' Revolution in military affairs because it's already happened, and the Air Force led it," Air Force Secretary Sheila E. Widnall told attendees at the Air Force Association's symposium in Los Angeles in October 1995.

The new way of war will be one of stealth, global mobility, long-range precision strike, information warfare, and the effective use of space (see figs. 12.39 and

Fig. 12.39. The U.S. Air Force's most modern bomber, the stealth B-2. Courtesy of the U.S. Air Force.

Fig. 12.40. The Lockheed C-5A Galaxy is the largest airlifter operated by the Air Mobility Command. Courtesy of the Fred Roos Collection.

12.40). The focus will be on the war competencies of air superiority, space superiority, precision weapons employment, global mobility, and information dominance.[40]

The Air Force restructuring after the Persian Gulf War has been completed. The cuts made since 1990 have been significant—half the fighters, two-thirds of the bomber force, and one-third of the bases have been cut. Airlift requirements are estimated at 49.4 million to 51.8 million ton-miles a day, below that of Air Mobility Command's (48 million ton-miles a day at maximum effort.)[41]

The Navy and Army have undertaken similar modifications in their plans. As Widnall told the USAF Scientific Advisory Board, "There has never been a period in our country's history when swift adaptation to new developments was more important."[42]

Perhaps it is time to look back to the English translation of the motto of the Air Corps Tactical School of pre–World War II times for guidance: "We proceed unhampered by tradition."

Notes

1. Miller, *Airlift Doctrine*, 173.
2. Miller, 177.
3. Miller, 180.
4. Miller, 181.
5. Tirpak, "Heavyweights for the New Strategy," 26.
6. Thompson, *The Greatest Airlift*, 10.
7. Stewart, *Airpower: The Decisive Force in Korea*, 258.
8. Davisson, "Shooting Star," 50.
9. Nalty, "MiG Alley," 149.
10. Nalty, 152.

11. Harper, "My Favorite Fighter-Bomber Sabre Story," 3–5.
12. Stewart, 268.
13. Stewart, 289.
14. Bowers, *Tactical Airlift,* 314.
15. Bowers, 314.
16. Bowers, 315.
17. Wetterman, Ralph, "Operation Bolo," 40.
18. Wetterman, 39–43.
19. Frisbee, "Tribute to the Tankers," 49.
20. Gropman, "The Air War in Vietnam, 1961–73," 43.
21. Gropman, 45.
22. Gropman, 46.
23. Bowers, 320.
24. Robinson, "Bombs on Target," 80.
25. Robinson, 82.
26. Robinson, 83.
27. Robinson, 85.
28. Ethell and Price, *One Day in a Long War,* 178.
29. Tirpak, "Heavyweights for the New Strategy," 29.
30. Tirpak, "Heavyweights for the New Strategy," 32.
31. Warden, "Airpower in the Gulf," 12.
32. Warden, 15.
33. Spacil, "Third Night," 18.
34. Spacil, 19.
35. Pitts, "Kill More MiGs," 20.
36. Pitts, 21.
37. Warden, 17.
38. Brodie, *Strategy in the Missile Age,* 404.
39. Brodie, 408.
40. Tirpak, "The Air Force Today and Tomorrow," 20.
41. Tirpak, "Heavyweights for the New Strategy," 25.
42. Grier, "New World Vistas," 22.

References

Bowers, Ray. *Tactical Airlift: The United States Air Force in Southeast Asia.* Washington, D.C.: Office of Air Force History, 1983.

Bowman, John, et al. *The Vietnam War: An Almanac.* New York: Pharos Books, 1985.

Bowman, Martin. "Hell over Vietnam." *Air Combat* 23 (December 1995): 32–33, 46–56.

Brodie, Bernard. *Strategy in the Missile Age.* Princeton: Princeton University Press, 1959.

Brown, Ashley, and Jonathan Brown, eds. *The Elite: The World's Crack Fighting Men Series.* Harrisburg, Pa.: National Historical Society, 1986.

Cunningham, Randy, with Jeff Ethell. *Fox Two.* Mesa, Ariz.: Champlin Fighter Museum, 1984.

Davis, Larry. *Wild Weasel: The SAM Suppression Story.* Warren, Mich.: Squadron/Signal, 1986.

Davisson, Budd. "Shooting Star." *Popular Mechanics,* October 1990, 48–50, 126–27.

Dorr, Robert. *McDonnell Douglas F-4 Phantom II.* London: Osprey, 1984.

Drendel, Lou. *And Kill MiGS.* Warren, Mich.: Squadron/Signal, 1974.

Drew, Dennis, M. "Rolling Thunder: Anatomy of a Failure." *Airpower Research Institute, Cadre Paper Report No. Av-AR1-CP-86-3.* Maxwell Air Force Base, Ala.: Air University Press, 1986.

Ethell, Jeffrey, and Alfred Price. *One Day in a Long War.* New York: Random House, 1989.

Frisbee, John L. "Tribute to the Tankers." *Air Force Magazine* 79 (January 1992): 49.

Futrell, Robert Frank. *Ideas Concepts Doctrine: Basic Thinking in the United States Air Force.* Vol. 1, 1907–1960, vol. 2, 1961–1984. Maxwell Air Force Base, Ala.: Air University Press, 1989.

Futrell, Robert Frank, et al. *Aces and Aerial Victories.* Washington, D.C.: Government Printing Office, 1976.

Giap, Vo Nguyen. *People's War Against U.S. Aero Naval War.* Hanoi, Vietnam: Foreign Languages Publishing House, 1975.

Gilster, Herman L. *The Air War in Southeast Asia: Case Studies of Selected Campaigns.* Maxwell Air Force Base, Ala.: Air University Press, 1993.

Grier, Peter. "New World Vistas." *Air Force Magazine* 79 (March 1996): 20–25.

Gropman, Al. "The Air War in Vietnam, 1961–73." *The American War in Vietnam: Lessons, Legacies, and Implications for Future Conflicts,* ed. Lawrence E. Grinter and Peter M. Dunn. Contributions in Military Studies, no. 67. New York: Greenwood Press, 1987. 43–46.

Harper, Flamm D. "My Favorite Fighter-Bomber Sabre Story: The Graybeards." *Korean War Veterans Association* 10 (September–October 1995).

Hastings, Max. *The Korean War.* New York: Simon and Schuster, 1987.

Hersh, Seymour. *The Price of Power.* New York: Summit Books, 1983.

Hurley, Alfred F., and Robert C. Ehrhart, eds. *Air Power and Warfare: The Proceedings of the 8th Military History Symposium.* U.S. Air Force Academy, 18–20 October 1978. Washington, D.C.: Government Printing Office, 1979.

Karnow, Stanley. *Vietnam: A History.* New York: Viking Press, 1983.

Kennett, Lee. *A History of Strategic Bombing.* New York: Scribner's Sons, 1982.

Kropf, Roger F. "The U.S. Air Force in Korea." *Air Power Journal* 4 (spring 1990): 30–46.

Lavalle, Major A., et al. *Air Power and the 1972 Spring Invasion.* Washington, D.C.: Government Printing Office, 1976.

Lohide, Curtis D. "Desert Storm's Siren Song." *Air Power Journal* 9 (winter 1995): 101–10.

Marolda, Edward, et al. *A Short History of the United States Navy and the Southeast Asian Conflict, 1950–1975.* Washington, D.C.: Naval Historical Center, 1984.

Meilinger, Phillip S. "Hoyt S. Vandenberg and the Independent Air Force." *Air Power History* (fall 1990): 27–36.

Mersky, Peter, and Norman Polmar. *The Naval Air War in Vietnam.* Annapolis, Md.: Nautical and Aviation Publishing Company of America, 1981.

Mets, David R. *Master of Air Power, General Carl A. Spratz.* Novato, Calif.: Presidio, 1988.

Miller, Charles E. *Airlift Doctrine.* Maxwell Air Force Base, Ala.: Air University Press, 1988.

Momyer, William. *Air Power in Three Wars.* Washington, D.C.: Department of the Air Force, 1978.

Nalty, Bernard C. "MiG Alley." *The Air Fighters,* ed. Ashley Brown and Jonathan Brown. Harrisburg, Pa.: National Historical Society, 1986. 146–52.

Osgood, Robert Endicott. *Limited War Revisited.* Boulder, Colo.: Westview Press, 1979.

Pitts, Larry. "Kill More MiGs." *Daedalus Flyer* 34 (spring 1996): 20–21.

Richardson, Doug, and Mike Spick. *F-4 Phantom II.* London: Salamander Books, 1984.

Robinson, Anthony. "Bombs on Target." *The Bombers,* ed. Ashley Brown and Jonathan Brown. Harrisburg, Pa.: National Historical Society, 1986. 78–85.

Spacil, Pete. "Third Night." *Daedalus Flyer* 34 (spring 1996): 18–19.

Stewart, James T. *Airpower: The Decisive Force in Korea.* New York: D. Van Nostrand, 1957.

The Tale of Two Bridges and the Battle for the Skies over North Vietnam. Washington, D.C.: Government Printing Office, 1976.

Thompson, Annis G. *The Greatest Airlift: The Story of Combat Cargo.* Tokyo: Kai-Nippon, 1954.

Tirpak, John A. "The Air Force Today and Tomorrow." *Air Force Magazine* 79 (January 1996): 20–26.

———. "Heavyweights for the New Strategy." *Air Force Magazine* 78 (October 1995): 24–32.

Uhlig, Frank, Jr., ed. *Vietnam: The Naval Story.* Annapolis, Md.: Naval Institute Press, 1986.

Warden, John A. III. "Air Power in the Gulf." *Daedalus Flyer* 34 (spring 1996): 12–17.

Wetterman, Ralph. "Operations Bolo." *Retired Officer Magazine* 1 (November 1995): 39–43.

13

Government and Aviation

David A. NewMyer

Since the inception of manned aircraft flight in this country in 1903, the development of commercial aviation has had a strong connection with government and military endeavors.

—Robert C. Lieb, *Transportation: The Domestic System*

ALTHOUGH THE FIRST powered flight in America occurred without federal government support, aviation developed after that point with considerable government investment and legislative guidance. Many times the investment or legislation was not necessarily the result of a direct interest in aviation policy. Rather, government involvement occurred because of what aviation could do in some other policy area, such as in the nation's defense, in carrying the mail, or in responding to the Great Depression of the 1930s. Of course, legislation was also written to respond to specific safety, economic, or other concerns about the aviation industry itself. Of interest is that, within limits, the states and local government also have been involved in aviation investment and/or regulation over time.

The purpose of this chapter is to present the wide range of government involvement in the aviation industry in the United States. The chapter will begin with an overview of government involvement in aviation at the federal, state, and local levels. Types of agencies and examples of their involvement will be provided. Next, the chapter will describe government involvement in the development of aviation, particularly aircraft, airports, and the national airspace system. Finally, the chapter will present an anthology of key aviation-related legislation at the federal level.

Federal Agencies

Historically, the U.S. Signal Corps was one of the first federal agencies to be involved in aviation. They indicated their interest in powered flight by investing in the efforts of Samuel Langley to fly his powered Aerodrome using a pilot. The Aerodrome had flown in May 1896 without a pilot aboard, and Langley was then funded to attempt powered flight with a pilot. As Langley made two unsuccessful attempts to fly in October and December 1903, the Wright brothers made their successful flight without government funds on 17 December 1903. However, the Wrights did not quickly capitalize on their success, and in 1908 Glenn Curtiss made a successful flight and began to challenge the Wrights in terms of both public attention and advances in the air.[1] As noted in chapter 4, the Wrights were finally recognized with a U.S. Army contract after successful aircraft trials in July 1909. The work of the Signal Corps was the beginning of a long list of military projects that focused on developing aircraft that could meet specific military objectives. The government role in military aircraft development continues today on a very large scale: for example, $2.2 billion on the F-22 Advanced Tactical Fighter in the years 1994–96 alone through the Department of Defense.

The National Advisory Committee for Aeronautics (NACA) was established in 1914 and was, prior to the involvement of the Unit Office in aviation, "the sole federal instrumentality outside of the armed services with a clear mission in airmail."[2] A key aspect of the NACA's involvement in aviation was its unwavering endorsement of the concept of a civil aviation regulatory body at the federal level. While this idea did not come to fruition until 1926, the NACA performed a crucial role when no other federal agency outside the military had the ability to provide policy recommendations for civil aviation.

The Morrow Board, appointed by President Calvin Coolidge in 1925, carried on the NACA's views in its report released in December of that year. With the weight of public opinion in favor of doing *something* about aviation in the United States due to a number of aviation accidents, the Morrow Board was one of several entities that weighed in with various solutions to the problem of regulating aviation. Central to its report was the thesis that the "peace time activities of the United States have never been governed by military considerations." Therefore, the Morrow Board recommended a "Bureau of Air Navigation" within the Commerce Department for the regulation of civil aeronautics only. This meant that the idea of a department of aviation overseeing both military and civil aviation was rejected by the Morrow Board.[3] This was the psychology that Congress eventually followed in forming the Air Commerce Act of 1926.

The U.S. Postal Service began its role in aviation on 15 May 1918, with its first official airmail flight in the northeast corridor (Washington, D.C., to New York).[4]

While this role eventually ceased after the passage of the Contract Airmail Act of 1925, the post office played an important role in mapping out an early U.S. airline route system. This system was then contracted out to private carriers under the 1925 act. Today the post office is itself a contractor of airline space and of aircraft. It uses space daily on the U.S. scheduled airlines and operates, under contract, a small fleet of transport aircraft to serve its special needs.

With the departure of the post office as an operator of the airmail system, the economic regulation role of the airline industry at the federal level began. The post office was identified as the likely federal agency to select the private contractors, to monitor their performance, and to award authority to carry the mail. The postmaster general of the United States was, for a time, the most im-

portant person in the aviation regulatory structure, since much of the power related to the above functions was vested in this position. When President Herbert Hoover came to office in 1929, he appointed Walter Brown as postmaster general. Brown soon launched a program to restructure the airmail routes of the United States and, with it, the airline industry. Eventually what Brown had done was unraveled, as the result of Senate hearings, into what was believed to be a scandal in the airmail contracting process of the post office. Eventually all contracts were rescinded, and the U.S. Army was given the job of flying the mail in 1934. The result was the tragic loss of Army pilots, aircraft, and mail as the ill-prepared Army pilots attempted to do what the airmail pilots had done every day.

This lack of success in replacing the airlines led to the involvement of a triumvirate of government agencies to do what the post office had once done. The post office, the Commerce Department, and the Interstate Commerce Commission were all involved in economic regulation of airlines while Congress debated what to do next. What they came up with in 1938 was a new system of economic regulation of airlines overseen by a new agency initially called the Civil Aeronautics Authority. Within a year this was changed to the Civil Aeronautics Board. The Civil Aeronautics Board regulated airline economics until 1985, when the aviation economic regulatory functions that remained were assigned to the secretary of transportation.

Another key federal agency is the Federal Aviation Administration. Beginning with the Air Commerce Act of 1926, the role of the federal government in the area of aviation safety and other areas was identified. The FAA's predecessor agencies began with the Bureau of Air Commerce of the Commerce Department and evolved through such titles as the Civil Aeronautics Authority, the Civil Aeronautics Administration, and the Federal Aviation Agency (FAA). The FAA's role goes beyond just a regulatory one. Key tasks of the agency include the operation of the National Airspace system, aviation safety regulation, some aircraft accident investigation (in conjunction with the National Transportation Safety Board), aviation industry promotion, and the operation of a small fleet of aircraft to support various parts of the mission of the FAA.

Juxtaposed with the FAA in the civil aviation safety arena is the National Transportation Safety Board

(NTSB), which is responsible for investigating all fatal aviation accidents in the United States. The NTSB grew out of the Air Safety Board of the Civil Aeronautics Board, which was created in the late 1930s. The NTSB itself was created by the Department of Transportation Act of 1966 reporting to the Department of Transportation (USDOT). It became completely independent of the USDOT in 1974. A key function of the NTSB is to determine the "probable cause" of aviation accidents and to make safety recommendations to the FAA regarding issues stemming from these investigations.

A number of other federal agencies are involved in aviation from an operational or regulatory point of view. These include the Environmental Protection Agency (regulatory), the Coast Guard (air/sea rescue), the Atmospheric and Oceanic Administration (air navigation chart standards), and the Forestry Service/Agriculture Department (aerial forest fire fighting contracting). So the reach of the federal government in the aviation industry is a wide one.

In addition, it should be noted that many federal agencies are significant users of aircraft for a variety of air transportation and agency-specific reasons. For example, the Coast Guard, the Border Patrol, Department of Immigration and Naturalization, Customs, and the Drug Enforcement Agency all use a variety of aircraft to monitor, identify, and interdict illegal aliens, drugs, and illegal goods being smuggled into the United states. Also, the Agriculture Department/Forestry Service contracts with a number of private operators to fight forest fires. Finally, the Federal Bureau of Investigation, the Treasury-Alcohol/Tobacco/Firearms unit, the Federal Bureau of Prisons, and other law enforcement agencies must make extensive use of aviation to conduct their daily functions.

State and Local Agencies

With the fairly recent addition of Colorado and Nevada, all fifty states have some form of aviation regulatory body in place. In fact, the State of Connecticut had state regulatory laws related to aviation in place by 1911,[5] well before the first federal legislation of its type. Since aviation is not just a federal government domain, there are some boundaries among the levels of government involvement in aviation in an attempt to keep confusion and duplication of effort to a minimum. For example,

the federal government largely preempts state and local government involvement in any form of aviation safety regulation. In addition, the Airline Deregulation Act of 1978 prohibits the replacement of any discontinued federal aviation regulation in the area of aviation economic regulation at the state and local levels. Furthermore, any regulatory action at the state of local levels related to aviation cannot interfere with interstate commerce. This, for example, has been one of the primary preemptive barriers to the establishment of noise-related airport operations curfews by local airport authorities. Another similar barrier is FAR Part 161, which was created to prevent the airports from enacting a more stringent timetable for reducing aircraft noise faster than the federal deadlines for reducing noise at the source contained in 1990 legislation.

The states are involved in a number of activities in the aviation field, including the operation of over one thousand public airports in the United States. Also, the states are heavily involved in airport financing and construction, airport establishment, airport authority creation, and aircraft operation in support of state functions.

At the local level, cities, counties, port authorities and/or districts, park districts, airport authorities, and other forms of local governments are involved in the ownership and/or operation of airports. These functions include the creation of airport use regulations and, in some cases, minimum standards for operation of a business at local airports.

Aircraft

John Wise, one of the great nineteenth-century balloonists, saw clearly the immense potential of aerial warfare. In 1846, with the United States at war with Mexico, he proposed that a captive balloon on a long cable be positioned over the Mexican fortress of Vera Cruz, where it could drop bombs and torpedoes on the garrison while soaring out of range of any counter fire. The War Department looked strangely at his proposal, but it was not so far-fetched as it seemed. Three years later, the idea was used in battle.

Where there are heroes, there are usually legends, but most individuals consider the Wright brothers the inventors of powered flight. Of all the early trailblazers, one of the most controversial and one of the unluckiest was Samuel Pierpont Langley. While the Wrights traced their interest in aeronautics to a toy helicopter that their father had brought home in 1878, Langley was well into his fifties when the lure of the air gripped him. Langley was a distinguished astronomer, the director of the Smithsonian Institution, and he began his quest for powered flight by making elastic-band-propelled models based on Alphonse Pénaud's little aircraft. As noted in chapter 2, this work served as an inspiration for others, including the Wright brothers. Langley constructed the first of his model "aerodromes" in 1891. In 1898, the United States went to war with Spain, and suddenly the War Department showed considerable interest in a controllable, power-driven airplane. As a result, Congress granted Langley $50,000 and asked him to go ahead and build such a machine.

After they were convinced that a gasoline engine offered more promise of powered flight than steam, Charles M. Manly and Stephen Balzer of New York developed a radically new type, with the cylinders arranged around a crankshaft. Most of the parts, even the spark plugs, had to be made by hand. Manly hoped that this radial gasoline engine might produce 2 horsepower, but when finally tested, the 5 cylinders of the little power plant (it weighed only 125 pounds) produced 53 horsepower.[6]

Everyone in aviation knows about 17 December 1903, at Kitty Hawk, on the day two brothers from Dayton, Ohio, flew for 120 feet. The final flight of four that day was an extraordinary effort lasting 59 seconds and covering 582 feet over land. In January 1905, the brothers had offered their invention and scientific knowledge to the War Department, which flatly rejected the idea.

In January 1905, 13 months after Kitty Hawk, the Wright brothers did what they had more or less always planned to do: they offered the airplane to the U.S. government for use by the Army for scouting and carrying messages in time of war. They proposed either to provide machines of agreed specifications, or to turn over all scientific and practical information, together with a license to use their patents, thereby placing the government in a position to operate a monopoly. The airplane was to be an exclusive military secret of the United States, both as to the machines themselves and the know-how. To the Wrights' utter astonishment, the War Department's reply was a flat turndown, the idea being so stupid as to be insulting. It said, in short, that it de-clined to lend financial support to the experimental development of devices for mechanical flight and would give consideration only to devices that had been brought to the stage of practical operation.[7]

In February 1908, the U.S. Army finally accepted the Wrights' bid to build an airplane for military use. The Army purchased the flying machine from the Wrights on 2 August 1909. The brothers trained the first Army pilots until the airplane crashed on 5 November 1909.

For three years after the Army had accepted its first Wright machine in 1908, that lone airplane had been the United States' air arm. Each year the Signal Corps had tried in vain to get additional aviation funds. Until March 1911, when Congress appropriated $125,000 for the Signal Corps air branch to purchase five more planes, just one military training plane existed in the United States. By the end of 1913, of the twenty-eight aircraft purchased by the Army, nine had crashed. Of some forty Signal Corps officers trained as pilots, eleven had been killed.

When tension arose along the Mexican border in 1914 and 1915, detachments of the First Aero Squadron were sent to Texas. In March 1916, after the revolutionary leader Pancho Villa crossed the Rio Grande and killed seventeen Americans, eight planes were assigned to Gen. John J. Pershing to aid in his pursuit of the Mexican.

At the outbreak of World War I in 1914, the airplane was still a toy, though potentially a deadly one. The first American airman to die in a war was Victor Chapman, one of the original members of the Lafayette Escadrille, a volunteer unit of American flyers fighting for France. While revolutionary advances were being made in Europe, aviation in the United States was lagging badly. Almost no progress had been achieved in the development of military aircraft.

By April 1916, only two Army airplanes were left, and these were declared unfit for service. The fiasco prodded Congress to appropriate $13 million for the expansion of military aviation, but the lawmakers were soon to learn that dollars could not be converted into aircraft overnight.[8] Of the 336 machines ordered in 1916, only 64 were delivered, and most of the manufacturers who were under contract simply could not build the planes, and they asked to be relieved of the assignment.

When the United States entered the war on 6 April 1917, the Aviation Section of the Signal Corps had 131 officers, most of them pilots; about 1,000 enlisted men; and fewer than 250 aircraft. There was only one airplane plant, Curtiss, that could be called a factory. It was not until April 1918 that American flyers were in combat, and even then they had to fly French planes. At the Armistice, American frontline air strength consisted of 740 combat airplanes, almost 800 pilots, and 500 observers. Losses in 7 months of increasing violent fighting had been 289 planes and 48 balloons, as against confirmed claims of 781 enemy aircraft and 73 balloons destroyed by American air fighters.[9]

Billy Mitchell, the American commander, a son of a Wisconsin senator, enlisted as a private in the Spanish-American War and later served as a Signal Corps officer in the Philippines and Alaska. In 1915, when he was thirty-six years old, he took up flying and was in Europe as an observer when the United States declared war on Germany. He was the first pilot wearing an American uniform to fly over the enemy lines.

Gen. Billy Mitchell came home raging that as a combat commander he had received exactly 196 American warplanes, and none had ever been flown in combat. Where had all the money gone? Was the DH-4 obsolete even when American production of it had been ordered? Why had the United States tried to fit American engines to European airframes instead of building its own planes from scratch? A series of investigations captured a few headlines but proved essentially nothing. Americans quickly forgot the questions of the past in their glorious enjoyment of the Roaring Twenties.

In 1919, Gen. Billy Mitchell was now assistant chief of the Army Air Service in Washington, D.C., and he continued to be a driving force behind Army air activity. In the face of official indifference, Mitchell continually argued that the bomber and torpedo plane had rendered surface warships obsolete. Mitchell produced embarrassing magazine articles and gave out uninhibited newspaper interviews calling for a stronger air force. Privately he expressed his conviction that behind the resistance to his views lurked sinister big business groups interested primarily in the profits to be made from building battleships. His statement to the press made it sound as if the struggle were basically between a decaying Navy and an eager young Air Service. This was not so; many top Navy experts agreed with him. Adm. William S. Sims, who had commanded American naval

forces in European waters during the war, came out flatly for aircraft carriers as opposed to battleships. One of the Navy's most brilliant strategists, Adm. W. F. Fullam, prophesied that "sea power," or fighting power, in the future would be largely dependent on control of the air.[10] Mitchell continued to plot aerial feats that would capture public attention and help build his arguments for an independent air force. In 1924, Billy Mitchell toured Europe and was convinced that German militarism was very much alive and that the Germans were already planning to exploit air power in a war of the future. Additionally, a visit to the Far East had also left him highly critical of American defense, especially at Pearl Harbor. "If our warships there," he wrote, "were to be found bottled up in a surprise attack from the air and our airplanes destroyed on the ground, nothing but a miracle would enable us to hold our Far East possessions. It would break our backs. The same prediction applied to the Philippines."[11]

In November 1925, Mitchell endured a court-martial for insubordination and conduct unbecoming to an officer. While the Mitchell controversy dominated the headlines, men in the background were working on proposals that would set the pattern of development for military aviation in this country for the next two decades. As noted earlier, President Coolidge in September 1925 appointed the Morrow Board to study the "best means of developing and applying aircraft in national defense." He named Dwight Morrow, a partner in the banking firm of J. P. Morgan, as board chairperson. The Morrow Board submitted its report, which rejected some of Mitchell's arguments. Airpower, the report noted, was not sufficiently developed to justify creation of an independent air arm; building up a strong air force at the expense of naval armaments, limited by international treaty, would be a disservice to the cause of world disarmament. "The next war may start in the air," the Morrow Board predicted, "but in all probability it will wind up, as the last one did, in the mud."[12]

To pacify the less violent military critics of America's defense establishment, the Morrow Board suggested that the Air Service be renamed the Air Corps to give it more prestige, but it failed to recommend that its status within the War Department be changed. The essential provisions of the report were incorporated in the Air Corps Act, passed by Congress on 1 July 1926. This law changed the name of the Air Service to Army Air Corps, and created the post of assistant secretary of war for aeronautics. It also authorized the War and Navy Departments to begin a five-year expansion plan. Although lack of funds delayed the start of this program until 1927, the new orders for military planes, in time, ensured the development of a domestic aircraft industry.

On 19 May 1927, Charles Lindbergh, a captain in the Missouri National Guard with over 2,000 flight hours, impacted American aviation and captured imaginations everywhere. In a single year after Lindbergh's solo flight across the Atlantic Ocean, applications for pilot licenses in the United States jumped from 1,800 to 5,500. In 1928, the nation's airline operators doubled their mileage, tripled their mail load, and quadrupled the number of passengers they had carried since 1927. Airlines stocks boomed. In 1929, before the stock market crash, the public bought aircraft manufacturing securities to the tune of $400 million.

Growth in civilian aircraft development was further encouraged by the provisions of the 1930 Airmail Act, which "provided extra remuneration for contractors flying multiengine aircraft."[13] This, in turn, fueled the aircraft manufacturing industry to build larger airplanes. The eventual result was the construction of two important twin-engine aircraft, the Boeing 247 (which was the industry's first streamlined, twin-engine monoplane) and, after some evolution, its rival, the Douglas DC-3. The DC-3 was larger and faster and it flew further than the 247. The DC-3 eventually became a transport workhorse during World War II and in the postwar airline industry. In all, more than 10,000 were made in various versions in only eleven years of production.[14]

World War II provided a huge impetus for the development of aircraft. When the German Blitzkrieg in Europe began on 10 May 1940, American leaders began a wholesale strategic review of defense preparations. On 16 May, President Franklin D. Roosevelt presented the new defense program in an address to a joint session of Congress. He attempted to define the altered geographical position of the United States with the advent of the new weapons of the air and in view of the obvious intentions of Nazi Germany and Japan. The president called for what was then an enormous military budget to include $546 million for ordinance, flying fields, and aircraft for the Army; $250 million for naval armaments;

and $286 million for miscellaneous items including aircraft and antiaircraft guns. He called for an annual production of 50,000 airplanes.[15]

During the nineteen years of peace between the two world wars, only seven thousand pilots had been trained by the Army Air Corps. Also, only 2,200 aircraft were produced in the United States in 1939. Two years after Pearl Harbor, the Army Air Force boasted over one hundred thousand pilots and a half million aircraft technicians. Also annual aircraft production had reached one hundred thousand by 1944.[16] World War II brought air power to the foreground as a dominant military force in war.

In all, the U.S. government spent an estimated $45 billion for aircraft in World War II, eventually producing basic fighter and bomber models. An example was the North American P-51 Mustang, which still flies in air shows and air races today. A reason for its availability today is that 14,490 of this aircraft were built. Its purpose was to be long-range escort aircraft for Allied bombers flying from Britain to cities in Germany, providing total bomber mission coverage that previous aircraft could not provide.

Aircraft continued to be developed for both civilian and government purposes after World War II. A key example where the two interests came together was with Boeing 707. In this instance, the airlines in the United States were looking for a jet-powered aircraft to compete with the British De Havilland Comet, which had entered service on a limited basis in 1952. At the same time the airlines were looking for a jet transport, the U.S. Air Force was trying to solve the problem of finding an air refueling tanker aircraft that could keep up with its jet bomber fleet. The result of the merger of the two interests was an initial Air Force order for twenty-nine jet tankers (the KC-135) in October 1954. This order for a parallel military version of the 707 helped Boeing achieve the financing needed to reduce the risk of building the civilian 707. Airline orders for the 707 followed in mid-1955, and the aircraft first flew in scheduled service in late 1957. The Boeing effort prodded longtime rival Douglas Aircraft into action to develop what became the DC-8, which competed with the 707 for orders. The resulting competition for jet aircraft orders continues today, although Boeing is the acknowledged leader in commercial aircraft sales.

The government has continued its involvement in the development of a variety of military aircraft since World War II. In fact, an interesting comparison of average fighter cost between the World War II era and today is:[17]

Average Fighter Aircraft Costs
World War II — $50,000 each
Today — $30 million each

While the government is no longer directly or indirectly subsidizing commercial aircraft development on a large scale (the so-called Orient Express suborbital craft may be an exception), they are still doing so in the military arena. For example, the 1994 Defense Department budget for contracts with outside vendors totaled over $118 billion. Some of the key aircraft projects included in this amount are:

McDonnell Douglas C-17	$1,901 billion
McDonnell Douglas F/A E & F 18	$1,806 billion
Boeing AH-64 helicopter (Army)	$ 475 billion
Bell/Boeing V-22 Osprey	$ 472 billion
Lockheed/Martin F-16 C/D	$ 436 billion

Future projects such as the F-22A advanced tactical fighter or the completion of the B-2A and C-17 production runs will mean an investment from the government of tens of billions of dollars over the next ten years.[18]

Airports

Federal government involvement in airport development was limited by a policy statement in the 1926 Air Commerce Act that prohibited the secretary of commerce from establishing, operating, or maintaining an airport. This policy was an outgrowth of earlier NACA reports that likened airports to seaports. Since seaports were the responsibility of municipalities, they reasoned, so should airports. Congress obviously agreed.[19] This policy has not changed since that time insofar as direct ownership of airports in the United States is concerned. However, in only seven years the economic circumstance of the nation encouraged President Franklin Roosevelt to consider federal funding of airports as a way to put people to work and to encourage economic development. In Roosevelt's first one hundred days in office, he proposed and was able to get Congress to pass a large number of pieces of legislation designed to put people back to work as countermeasures to the Depression. In

the end, about $500 million was spent on airport-related construction through such agencies as the Works Progress Administration, the Federal Emergency Relief Administration, and the Civilian Conservation Corps.[20]

Another key event in history, World War II, further shaped government airport investment policy. The war effort encouraged significant investment in aircraft technology, which in turn triggered a need for more stateside airfields to handle all of the new aircraft being built. Over $750 million was invested in U.S.-based airfields during World War II through War Department funds. One airfield that benefited from their funds was Orchard Field, Illinois, or ORD (as it was known by its three-letter designation), which would become Chicago-O'Hare International Airport. The base for C-54 transport production, ORD later became the world's busiest airport when the city of Chicago's airline operations were transferred to ORD from Chicago-Midway Airport in 1962. All of this came to the city of Chicago for a mere one dollar investment in war surplus property payments to the U.S. government. This transfer process was repeated in many places around the United States in the late 1940s.

At the end of World War II, it became obvious to Congress that the "no federal investment in airports" policy from the 1926 act was no longer pertinent. This was especially true in the fact of over $1.25 billion in investments in airports between 1933 and 1945! The result of reconsideration of this old policy was the passage of the Federal Airport Act of 1946. This act provided for $500 million in airport investment from general revenue over the next seven years. The investment was required to be based on a national airport plan to be submitted annually to Congress by the Civil Aeronautics Administration (CAA).

The Federal Airport Act was renewed periodically over the twenty-four years when there was exposure growth in U.S. aviation due to population growth, the jet age, and other related factors. Also, there were times when Congress and President Dwight D. Eisenhower did not see eye-to-eye on airport issues. The result was a lack of federal airport funds during part of the 1950s. A result was that airport development did not keep up with growth in U.S. aviation in the 1950s and 1960s.

Congressional response was finally organized behind the Airport and Airways Development Act of 1970. This law was quite different than the 1946 act in three key ways: (1) More money ($250 million in the first year for airports—much more than the annual amounts in the 1946 act); (2) Airways were included in the act as a partner in federal policy for aviation infrastructure investment; and (3) The funding for airports and airways was provided through an airport and airways "trust fund" financed by user taxes on airline tickets, jet fuel, aviation gasoline, and so on.

In spite of short periods of interruption in funding, the airport and airways trust fund, and authorized expenditures from it have continued to the present day. Key changes have been made in the amounts spent on airports. They generally increased to about $2.0 billion for airports by 1992, declining to about $1.4 billion in 1996 parallel with federal cutbacks in most budget areas.

An important supplement to federal airport funding via the trust fund came in 1990 with congressional approval of passenger facility charges (PFCs) at airline-served airports. Until 1990, "head taxes" were expressly prohibited by federal law. Now there is a national policy implemented by 14 CFR 158 (FAR Part 158) which allows the collection of passenger facility charges via airline passenger tickets at a rate up to three dollars per departing trip in most instances. All such PFCs must be approved through the process identified in FAR Part 158, and the first PFCs were granted in 1992.

Airways

A first impetus to provide a nationwide airway system was the birth of the airmail system in 1915. As airmail grew in popularity, the ability to fly at night over vast expanses of unpopulated countryside became increasingly important. After a 1921 coast-to-coast demonstration of around-the-clock airmail flying, which cut the day-airmail/night-airmail time from 108 hours to 33 hours for all airmail, steps were taken to light the airways. By July 1924, a system of 289 lighted beacons lighted the route from Chicago to Cheyenne, Wyoming, via Rock Springs, Wyoming. This stretch was selected for night flying because it was relatively flat and either end could be reached in daylight operations.[21] This completion of an initial segment of lighted airway was followed by a transfer of responsibility and personnel from the post office to the Commerce Department as a result of the Contract Airmail Act. Finally, with the completion of a beacon at Miriam, Nevada, on 29 January 1929, the entire transcontinental airway was lighted. In 1933, the total miles of lighted airways in the United States reached 18,000.[22]

With the completion of lighted airways, and with an accompanying growth of air traffic by the mid-1930s, an airway and terminal (airport) traffic control became an issue. Because airports at the time were still largely municipal investments, municipalities led the way with airport air traffic control investments. The first air traffic control tower with two-way radio communication capability was built at Cleveland, Ohio, in 1930. However, the mere provision of facilities did not provide safety. As traffic grew, and standard procedures for the use of airports and airways by increasing volumes of traffic became necessary, it was clear that some uniform air traffic control system was needed. Finally, conflicts between different types of traffic on the airways-airline, airmail, and private operators promoted high level meetings during 1935. These meetings resulted in a proposal that the airlines initiate airway traffic control immediately, with the idea that the Bureau of Air Commerce take over the airway system within a few months. The takeover did not happen until mid-1937. But when it did, the Bureau of Air Commerce also took over the Cleveland, Chicago, and Newark air traffic control facilities, designating them as "airway traffic control stations." As one author put it, "The federal government had undertaken a responsibility that would ultimately become, in terms of manpower and facilities employed, its most demanding civil aviation function."[23]

This "federalization" of the airway functions of the United States was not parallel with the way in which federal policy toward airports was handled. Airports were designated a state or local government or private function in the 1926 Air Commerce Act and have remained as such to this day.

The airway system today consists of about 400 federally owned air traffic control towers and approximately 45,000 employees in the Federal Aviation Administration. The FAA currently receives over $4.5 billion per year for airways from the Airport and Airways Trust Fund. As in the 1930s, modernization is still an issue, since antiquated equipment acquisition rules have not allowed the FAA to move quickly in acquiring high-speed digital equipment to process the large quantities of data it receives and transmits each day.

An Anthology of Key Aviation Legislation

Legislation pertaining to aviation began to be considered at the federal level in response to several issues: the need to refine the role of the government in air transportation operations via the post office, the poor financial status of privately owned airlines, and the lack of an extensive lighted airway system. The first major U.S. law pertaining to aviation was the Contract Airmail Act of 1925, also called the Kelly Act. Its key provision was the authorization given to the postmaster general to contract with private companies to carry the mail on behalf of the post office. This provision is considered the starting point for the privately owned airline companies that are flying today. This act, as well as amendments to it, established airmail rates. This act is also considered the beginning of economic regulation of the airline industry.[24]

The Air Commerce Act of 1926, or the Bingham-Parker Act, initiated the federal government's role in aviation safety regulation. The Commerce Department, Aeronautics Branch, was established as the first federal regulator of aviation safety. It was charged with the maintenance and operation of the airway system and the enforcement of aviation safety regulations (e.g., aircraft and pilot registration). This was the law that limited federal involvement in airports, specifying airports as a municipal and/or private responsibility.[25]

The Airmail Act of 1930, or the McNary-Watres Act, gave the postmaster general nearly unlimited powers over the airmail system of the United States. The act eliminated competitive bidding in favor of negotiation, began the computation of airmail, encouraged aircraft manufacturers to build larger aircraft, and encouraged the airlines to fly them. The new aircraft no longer forced as many tradeoffs between carrying mail and passengers. Now both could be carried in larger airplanes. Also, financially strong airlines began to emerge from the capacity-based airmail rates and from some airline consolidations forced by the tighter allocation of airmail routes.[26]

The Airmail Act of 1934 was passed after the new postmaster general appointed by President Roosevelt rescinded all airmail contracts that were awarded under the prior administration via the 1930 Airmail Act. As noted earlier, the Army flew the mail in the intervening months with mixed results—less total flying was done than when the airlines did it, and the Army had more safety problems. A key feature of the 1934 Airmail Act is that it went back to the competitive bidding process of airmail routes with a three-way oversight of aviation economic regulation. The three agencies involved were the post office, the Interstate Commerce Commission, and the Bureau of Air Commerce of the Commerce Department. The act also created a Federal Aviation Commission to study aviation regulatory policy. A key outcome was the commission's report, which led to the key provisions of the Civil Aeronautics Act of 1938. Another feature of the 1934 Airmail Act was that it required the separation of aircraft manufacturers and airlines. For example, this requirement led to the divestiture of United Airlines (Boeing Air Transport was one of the original carriers making up the United Airlines) by Boeing Aircraft.[27]

The Civil Aeronautics Act of 1938 was really the first federal law that covered both aviation safety and aviation economics. This act, after an interim step, created two agencies to handle aviation: the Civil Aeronautics Board (CAB) to deal with aviation economics and the Civil Aeronautics Administration (CAA) to deal with aviation safety. The CAB was created as an independent regulatory body, and the CAA, true to its roots to the old Bureau of Air Commerce, was administratively housed in the Commerce Department. The CAB, however, was given the safety rule–making authority, and the CAA was given the power to enforce the rules. This was considered to be a balance of power.

The two-pronged approach to aviation regulation remained unchanged for twenty years until a series of aviation accidents led to congressional hearings and new legislation to strengthen the aviation safety side of the 1938 act. The resulting legislation was the landmark 1958 Federal Aviation Act. This act allowed the federal government to deal with aviation safety with one voice as it never had before. The Federal Aviation Agency was created out of the old Civil Aeronautics Administration, and most important, it was made independent of the Commerce Department. The safety rule making authority of the CAB was transferred to the new FAA, and the administrator of the FAA was named as the key person responsible for the rule-making process. In the area of airspace, the FAA was given the power to allocate airspace all over the United States and its territories.[28] Previously, there were at least three agencies with airspace controls: the military, the CAA, and the Airways Modernization Board. The designation of the FAA truly clarified the situation.

The next major piece of aviation-related legislation was the Department of Transportation Act of 1966. This act created a cabinet-level post, the secretary of transportation, and a Department of Transportation to go with it. The FAA was renamed the Federal Aviation Administration and placed in this new department as one of the "modal agencies." In another aviation-related move, the Air Safety Board function of the CAB was moved to a newly created National Transportation Safety Board. Housed in the USDOT, this board was charged with investigating all interstate transportation accidents on air, rail, marine, highway, and pipeline modes. While this act did recognize aviation on a more or less equal footing with the other modes of travel, the aviation industry was not totally pleased with the loss of the independent regulator status of the FAA.

Another key piece of legislation that has been passed at the federal level so far in the regulatory arena is the Airline Deregulation Act of 1978. This act was thoroughly debated for several years leading up to its passage and signing into law by President Jimmy Carter on 24 October 1978. Some of the concerns expressed were negative impacts on labor, small impacts on community air service, and the need for gradual rather than rapid deregulation. These points were ultimately addressed in the final law. For example, the deregulation provisions were to phase in over a period of several years, and the CAB was to remain in existence to oversee the transition. Small community air service was protected by a provision that said all communities that currently had air service, or had been served in the past ten years prior to the act being passed but had lost service, would be eligible for small community air service. Market entry was immediately loosened up by allowing any airline to ask CAB permission to serve routes currently on another airline's certificate if these routes were not being served. Airline executives gathered outside CAB headquarters on the morning after the bill was signed to take advantage of this provision. Market entry and exit were also made easier, and incumbent airlines were allowed to protect one monopoly route for up to three years after the passage of the act. There was also a 180-day rule that if the CAB was asked to do something, it had to respond within 180 days with an answer. Prior to the passage of the Deregulation Act, the CAB had taken years to decide some questions before them. Airline rates were also deregulated in that airlines could raise fares 5 percent or drop them 55 percent without asking permission of the CAB.

In deregulating the airline industry from an economic perspective, Congress was attempting to respond to the tide of opinion of that era, which was that the airline industry no longer needed the protection from itself that it needed when it was a fledgling industry. The market entry and fare controls that helped to start and strengthen the industry were, in the views of many, no longer needed. However, in the deregulation era, the airlines now had to respond to a more businesslike environment in which fares were to be raised and lowered to respond to business conditions and not to the whims or desires of the CAB. Some airlines and their executives were not prepared for this new world in the airline industry and business failures occurred. The first was Braniff International Airways in 1982. Eastern, Midway (a so-called new entrant airline created after deregulation), and Pan Am went out of business in 1991. Between the two dates, several well-known airlines were merged out of existence in a flurry of merger activity that took advantage of cash-rich airlines and the last couple of years of merger activity without the veto power of the Justice Department. Some of the airlines lost in the heat of the mergers in the period after 1978 were Air California, Pacific Southwest Airlines (PSA), Piedmont Airlines, Ozark Airlines, North Central, Southern, Republic, Hughes Airwest, Flying Tigers, and Western.[29] A final landmark piece of legislation that both corrected a negative market factor in aviation and provided an important legal relief to the general aviation industry is the General Aviation Revitalization Act of 1994 (see chap. 11). This piece of legislation has already led to the opening of a new Cessna piston engine aircraft manufacturing plant in Independence, Kansas.

There is no doubt that government has had a key role in the development of the U.S. aviation industry and is, in fact, still involved. However, the U.S. aviation industry is no longer an emerging industry. It has matured on the domestic front but is looking outward to the global environment to expand and to survive. In the global market, the U.S. aviation industry has several strengths. It has about 40 percent of the world market in airline passengers, it has about 62 percent of the world market in large commercial airline production (over 100 seats), and it has the finest and largest general aviation industry segment in the world. To a significant degree, the U.S. aviation industry has a largely benevolent U.S. government to thank for helping to put it in this enviable position. The question for the future is that, as the aviation industry works with Congress to define future issues such as the privatization of some or all of the FAA, the wisdom of user fees for FAA services, the future status of the Airport and Airways Trust Fund, what to do about subsidized air service to small communities, and other issues yet defined, will Congress continue to be benevolent and helpful? Much will depend on the budget situation that the federal government faces. After all, the amount of federal financial involvement in the development, operation, and regulation of the U.S. aviation industry has had a lot to do with the formal policies of the federal government related to investing federal funds in such items.

The status of federal funding policies related to aviation matters will also have an impact on how much more involved the states and local governments will get in such matters. However, it is expected that the state role in airport development will continue to be important, especially in those states with "Block Grant" authority from the FAA. The expansion of such authority would increase state involvement in the investment of federal funds. State and local government regulatory involvement in aviation is expected to be strong within the relatively narrow areas that are presently regulated.

Notes

1. Lopez, *Aviation: A Smithsonian Guide*, 32.
2. Komons, *Bonfires to Beacons*, 36.
3. Komons, 78.
4. Wells, *Air Transportation: A Management Perspective*, 39.
5. Wolfe and NewMyer, *Aviation Industry Regulation*, 68.
6. Josephy, *American Heritage History of Flight*, 84.
7. Josephy, 119.
8. Josephy, 164.
9. Josephy, 167.
10. Josephy, 200.
11. Josephy, 201.
12. Josephy, 202.
13. Wells, 46–49.
14. Mosteller, "The Big 10," 47.
15. Josephy, 244.
16. Lopez, 126.
17. Lopez, 186.
18. *World Aviation Directory*, summer 1998, 997.
19. Komons, 173.
20. Horonjeff and McKelvey, *Planning and Design of Airports*, 15–19.
21. Komons, 131.
22. Komons, 144.
23. Komons, 308.
24. Wolfe and NewMyer, 21.
25. Wells, 64–65.
26. Wolfe and NewMyer, 23.
27. Kane and Vose, *Air Transportation*, 20–23.
28. Wolfe and NewMyer, 27.
29. Wells, 200–202.

References

Emme, Eugene M. *The Impact of Air Power: National Security and World Politics.* Princeton, N.J.: D. Van Nostrand, 1959.

Federal Aviation Administration. "Thunder from the Canyon." *Federal Aviation Administration World,* 8 August 1993.

Hardaway, Robert M., et al. *Airport Regulation, Law, and Public Policy.* New York: Quorum Books, 1991.

Horonjeff, Robert, and Francis X. McKelvey. *Planning and Design of Airports.* 3d ed. New York: McGraw-Hill, 1983.

Josephy, Alvin M., Jr., ed. *The American Heritage History of Flight.* New York: American Heritage, 1962.

Kane, Robert M., and Allan D. Vose. *Air Transportation.* 8th ed. Dubuque: Kendall/Hunt, 1982.

Komons, Nick A. *Bonfires to Beacons.* Washington, D.C.: Smithsonian Institution Press, 1989.

Lieb, Robert C. *Transportation: The Domestic System.* Reston, Va.: Reston, 1978.

Locklin, D. Philip. *Economics of Transportation.* 7th ed. Homewood, Ill.: Richard D. Irwin, 1972.

Lopez, Donald S. *Aviation: A Smithsonian Guide.* New York: Macmillan, 1995.

McFarland, Marvin W., ed. *The Papers of Wilbur and Orville Wright.* 2 vols. New York: McGraw-Hill, 1953.

Mosteller, D. "The Big 10: Counting Down the Winners." *Air and Space Magazine,* February/March 1996.

Rollo, Vera A. Foster. *Aviation Law: An Introduction.* 3d ed. Lanham: Maryland Historical Press, 1985.

Sherry, Michael S. *The Rise of American Air Power: The Creation of Armageddon.* New Haven: Yale University Press, 1987.

Wells, Alexander T. *Air Transportation: A Management Perspective.* 3d ed. Belmont, Calif.: Wadsworth, 1994.

Wolfe, Harry P., and David A. NewMyer. *Aviation Industry Regulation.* Carbondale: Southern Illinois University Press, 1985.

World Aviation Directory. Summer. New York: McGraw-Hill, 1998.

14

Balloons and Dirigibles

Robeson S. Moise

Throughout the centuries, humans have watched the drifting clouds and the soaring birds and dreamed of flight in the vast ocean of air that surrounds them. For the most part, the dreams and experiments designed to realize these dreams have involved winged flight in heavier-than-air vehicles or winged flight demanding that extraordinary physical activity previously described by such proponents as Leonardo da Vinci. Ironically, the first commonly recorded flight by a human involved neither wings nor unusual physical activity. However, flight was accomplished using the principle of buoyancy, known since the time of Archimedes, and a lighter-than-air vehicle, the balloon. The early balloons utilized either hot air or hydrogen to obtain sufficient lift, and balloon flight became common by the beginning of the nineteenth century.

Although balloons allowed flight, they did not provide the critical control of direction and velocity necessary to escape their capture by the wind. Thus, balloons were limited in their practical application. Attempts to provide dirigibility, or steerability, began early in the evolution of the balloon. However, successful efforts had to await the development of a lightweight propulsion system. Such a propulsion system was available by the end of the nineteenth century, and soon large dirigibles, or airships, capable of carrying a number of passengers were being developed. By the mid-1930s, giant airships capable of long overwater passenger flights were operat-

ing. These airships were fast for their time and quite comfortable, even luxurious in many cases.

An unfortunate series of disasters involving American, British, and German airships, combined with the development of the modern airliner, led to the demise of these large airships. Balloons and dirigibles were used in military operations throughout World War II. But the technological advances in heavier-than-air flight limited the contributions to aviation of lighter-than-air craft. Balloons are still used today in sport aviation and in scientific observation and exploration, while nonrigid dirigibles, called blimps, are used in television broadcasting and aerial advertisement. For a century and a half, lighter-than-air vehicles made a major contribution to the advancement of aviation. Any serious discussion of the history of aviation should at least include the major events and leading characters of this exciting and colorful era of the balloon.

Early Balloons

The first mention of a balloon is in Ministere's history of the city of Lyon, France, where a balloon allegedly descended in about A.D. 800, during the reign of Charlemagne. The people in the balloon were denounced as sorcerers and condemned to death.[1] Lack of any other mention of this curious flight leaves it open to speculation, and such vehicles were not mentioned again until the seventeenth century. Experiments conducted by Evangelista Torricelli and Blaise Pascal determined that the atmosphere had weight and that the weight decreased with height. These findings coupled with the creation of a vacuum by Otto von Guericke led an Italian Jesuit priest, Francesco de Lana-Terzi, to speculate that lighter-than-air flight was possible. He designed, in theory, a boatlike vehicle that would be lifted and supported aloft by four large copper balls from which the air had been removed. Fortunately for de Lana, his design was never constructed, as hindsight suggests the surrounding atmospheric pressure would have crushed the copper balls.

By the early eighteenth century, further experiments with small balloons seem to have been conducted by another Jesuit priest, Laurenco de Gusmao, who evidently kept the balloons aloft attached to troughs filled with "burning spirits." In a demonstration before King John V of Portugal, a balloon rose to a height of about 12 feet. It was quickly extinguished, though, when it strayed too close to some curtains. It was not until sixty years later that further experiments were conducted. The experiments were prompted by Henry Cavendish's discovery of phlogiston (inflammable gas), or hydrogen as it would later be known, in 1766. By 1770, Dr. Joseph Black of Scotland lectured on the floating properties of animal bladders filled with phlogiston and predicted that soon such balloons would be successful.

Many tried in vain to capture the new gas in some sort of container. Tiberius Cavallo, whom most acknowledge as the first aviation historian, tried to capture the gas. Experimenting with Black's theories, Cavallo found that the gas passed readily through paper and cloth bags. Joseph Michel Montgolfier observed the same results. However, as he watched bits of ash and paper rise in a chimney—or, as some claim, watched a shirt hung over a fire to dry rise in the air—he conducted new experiments with smoke. He watched as a silken bag, filled with smoke, rose to the ceiling and remained there for over a minute. Excited by this event, he hastened to contact his brother, Jacques Etienne.

The brothers were the sons of Pierre Montgolfier, who controlled a prosperous paper manufactory that provided stationery for the kings of France. This allowed Joseph and Etienne both the time and the financial resources to conduct their many scientific ventures. Early in 1783, they built a large, paper-lined cloth balloon with a fixed frame at the bottom. Etienne estimated the nearly spherical balloon to be 110 feet in circumference. On 5 June, with hundreds in attendance at the Market Square in Annonay, France, the brothers had eight men hold the balloon over a fire. When the men released the ropes, the balloon rose to nearly 6,000 feet, drifted slowly in the wind, and finally landed more than a mile and a half away. Speculation on why the balloon descended was focused on the new gas, which the brothers believed was contained in smoke and which quickly escaped through the balloon material.

When news of this remarkable feat reached Paris, the Academy of Sciences invited the Montgolfier brothers to demonstrate their balloon. One of their members, Jacques A. C. Charles, was also petitioned to do further experiments in this new science. Charles knew of phlogiston and decided to use this gas for his smaller balloon (13 foot diameter). On 23 August, he began the arduous task of filling the balloon with gas. The only known method of producing such gas at that time was to pour sulphuric acid over iron filings and transport the gas into the bag through pipes. To hold the gas, Charles used a special cloth that had been impregnated with a rubber coating developed by the Robert brothers.

The task of filling the bag was complicated by many factors, and the balloon was not deemed ready for flight until late in the evening of 26 August. A crowd gathered to watch, and Charles decided to move the partially filled balloon to the launching area at the Champs-de-Mars to avoid the crowd. This tactic did not work: the crowd followed the bag in a torchlight parade. It seemed a miracle that a torch did not ignite the highly flammable gas. The following day, Charles struggled to fill the bag. Finally, at about 5 P.M., he released the bag, and it rose gently into the cloudy sky, remaining aloft for 45 minutes. Unfortunately, the new creation landed in the small village of Gonesse, 15 miles from Paris. The villagers, thinking the bag to be some sort of monster, promptly dispatched it with pitchforks, observing the "beast" to hiss and belch a terrible cloud of "poisonous gas."[2]

In mid-September, the Montgolfier brothers arrived in Paris and demonstrated a new balloon 43 feet in diameter to the Royal Academy. This prompted a request for a demonstration before King Louis XVI and Marie Antoinette at Versailles, scheduled for 19 September. Since the demonstration balloon had been damaged on ascent at the Academy, the brothers built a new balloon of similar dimensions from cotton cloth lined with paper. The balloon was built in only four days and arrived in Versailles at the appointed time. Rumor abounded that a man might be on this flight; however, Joseph had decided to send three animals aloft with the express purpose of checking the effects of the upper air on life. At 1 P.M., after lunching with the monarch, the brothers released the balloon from a special fire platform, and the cage containing a rooster, a sheep, and a duck lifted off to the cheers from the huge crowd that had gathered. The balloon rose 1,700 feet and remained aloft for over 8 minutes before coming to rest over 2 miles away. The first to reach the cage was a young scientist, Pilatre de Rozier, who found the animals in amazingly good shape. The rooster had suffered some mishap, but that probably occurred before the actual flight. An interested spectator, Benjamin Franklin, envoy

to France from the United States, when asked of what use the balloon would be, made the famous reply, "Of what use, sir, is a newborn baby?"[3]

The success of this flight again raised speculation that the next flight would carry a human, and this time the king agreed only if criminals were used. Pilatre de Rozier, a daring young scientist and Academy member, was aware of the significance of this event. He engaged the Marquis d'Arlandes to intercede with the king to allow him to make the flight. The plot worked; however, Rozier was chagrined to learn that d'Arlandes insisted on making the flight, too. The Montgolfier brothers constructed a special lemon-shaped balloon, 75 feet high and 48 feet in diameter, with a circular wicker gallery around the base (see fig. 14.1). A fire basket was attached about 5 feet below the gallery by chains. The balloon was painted blue and gold and ornamented with gold fleurs-de-lis, the monogram of Louis XVI.

Fig. 14.1. Montgolfier balloon. By permission of the National Air and Space Museum, Smithsonian Institution, ©1999 Smithsonian Institution.

After several tethered flights by Rozier, which eventually reached a height of 350 feet, the gaily decorated balloon was moved to the Bois de Boulogne on 20 November. The next day, more captive flights were conducted, and the balloon was damaged. The huge crowd, estimated at half a million, began to get restless. However, volunteers were able to repair the balloon, and at 2 P.M. it lifted off, carrying Rozier and d'Arlandes. At 300 feet, the two doffed their hats; however, the crowd was too astonished to reply. As d'Arlandes candidly recalled, "I was surprised at the silence and the absence of movement which our departure caused among the spectators and believed them to be astonished and perhaps awed at the strange spectacle."[4]

The balloon did rise, however, to an estimated 3,000 feet, and it floated silently over the city. After the fuel ran out, in 25 minutes, the scorched balloon set down nearly 5 miles away. The success of this first flight left Charles's supporters discouraged, but he insisted on continuing with his new hydrogen balloon, 26 feet in diameter. Although drab, compared with the colorful Montgolfier creation, the new balloon contained several improvements and, more importantly, provided more lift for a longer period. The balloon had an open neck, from which hydrogen could escape when expanding, as well as an alternate escape valve on top, and it carried sufficient ballast to regain lift lost when using the valve.

On 1 December, Charles was ready to try the balloon, and he graciously handed a small wind test balloon to Joseph Montgolfier to release. Observing that conditions were right, Charles climbed aboard with Noel Robert and, after releasing some sand ballast, they slowly rose. Benjamin Franklin observed the two to wave a white handkerchief, signaling that they were proceeding as planned.[5]

After an hour they left Paris, and during the second hour they drifted near the small town of Nesle, 27 miles from Paris, where the balloon softly landed. The excited Robert jumped from the balloon, and it promptly shot back into the air with Charles aboard. The balloon ascended to an altitude of nearly 10,000 feet, where Charles became the first airborne witness to two sunsets on the same day. He also experienced cold, combined with pain in his ear and jaw, so he quickly descended again. This was to be Charles's first and last flight. In the short span of ten days, four men had flown in two lighter-than-air balloons, now to be known as Mont-

golfiers or Charlieres, depending on the type of lifting agent used. Not to be outdone, Joseph Montgolfier planned a second manned flight in January 1784, with himself and Rozier aboard. Just at liftoff, however, four noblemen jumped aboard with swords drawn and demanded to go. In the confusion, a spectator also boarded, so the balloon lifted off with the seven aboard. All received a hero's welcome on return; however, this was to be Joseph's last flight.

After these flights, balloons, now known as aerostats, and their flyers, now known as aeronauts, practicing the science of aerostation, became a national obsession in France. Even Benjamin Franklin had to confide that aerostation took all the attention in France and small balloons were observed in all shop windows. Competition mounted between the two types of balloons and continued into the next century. Charlieres eventually became more popular, because they were reusable and did not need to be as large. However, they remained dangerous because of the inflammable gas.

First flights were made in many countries, but perhaps the two most famous flights should be mentioned. By September 1784, the first flight had been made in England by Vincent Lunardi, an employee of the Neapolitan embassy. He was accompanied by a cat—apparently unwillingly, because he descended halfway through the flight to release his passenger. Since England was now familiar with the new science, Jean-Pierre Francois Blanchard came from France to plan a spectacular flight across the English Channel, taking advantage of the predominant west-to-east winds.

Blanchard had earlier experimented with a parachute and "flying chariot" designs, but after Charles's successful flight, he turned his attention to aerostation. His first flight in March 1784 reached an altitude of 9,500 feet and lasted over an hour. This was followed by at least twelve other ascents. His theories and attempts to steer by using oars and wings brought ridicule from fellow French aeronauts and prompted him to go to England to seek his fame.

In London, Blanchard soon became sponsored by Dr. John Jeffries, an American-born Tory who fled the colonies during the Revolution. Word that English aeronaut James Sandler was planning a channel flight and knowledge that Rozier had been commissioned by the king of France to fly the channel against the wind hastened Blanchard's preparations. Finally, the weather cleared on 7 January 1785, and the flight was set. Blanchard attempted to keep Jeffries from making the flight in order to gain greater fame, but his ruse was discovered, and the two climbed into the gondola underneath the balloon. The gondola was well stocked with food, brandy, cork jackets, oars, and even a small propeller.

The two men lifted off at 1 P.M. and drifted out over the channel, displaying the colors of both France and England. As the cooler air of the channel caused the aerostat to lose altitude, ballast was quickly jettisoned to no avail. All of the items in the boat including the oars and even Blanchard's trousers were thrown overboard.[6] As they approached the coast, the warmer air lifted the aerostat into France around 3 P.M., and half an hour later, the gondola landed in a forest near Calais. Both aeronauts were immediately proclaimed heroes, and Blanchard was even given a cash award and a small pension from the king of France.

The publicity and acclaim afforded these two aeronauts undoubtedly heightened the efforts of Rozier, who probably also felt the pressure of the king's commission. Although flight against the wind was a true challenge, Rozier felt he could do it in a hybrid balloon designed by Pierre Romain. The balloon was a cylindrical Montgolfier mounted underneath a spherical Charliere with a fire grate attached under the two. Rozier felt that he could control the lift by controlling the fire, but he was uncertain about the dangers of open fire near the hydrogen. He had doubts and confided to friends that he felt he would die. However, like many aeronauts after his time, Rozier persisted anyway.[7]

After bad weather forced three delays, favorable winds finally arrived. Rozier and Romain left Boulogne into a gentle breeze toward England. The balloon rose quickly to 5,000 feet, then seemed to hang suspended before slowly drifting back to shore. Frantic activity by the aeronauts was observed shortly before the balloon burst into flames and crashed to earth 300 feet from shore. Rozier was killed instantly, and Romain lived only for a few moments. Evidently, Rozier's young English fiancée, Susan Dyer, witnessed the tragedy and became the third victim after she collapsed and died not long afterward. Ironically, the flame that consumed the aerostat began at the top escape valve and in all probability was caused by static electricity, not by the open fire.

Less than two years had passed between the first and last flight of Pilatre de Rozier. In this short time, the world had been introduced to flight. To the casual observer, balloon flights seem relatively tame. However, put in proper perspective, the flights of these early aeronauts were equivalent to the space flights of the astronauts less than two centuries later. Both ventured bravely into unknown and hostile environments to open new frontiers of science. Some gave their lives in these explorations and challenges of manned flight.

A Century of Show Aeronauts

For nearly a century after the early aeronauts had introduced balloon flight, a group of professional men and women thrilled thousands with their aerial antics. The Charliere had become the balloon of choice of these nineteenth-century "barnstormers" due to its ability to be reused and the increasing ability to produce hydrogen and coal gas within a reasonable time. By 1850, nearly every large fair or other spectator event worth attending featured a balloon show, and most featured balloon rides for the public. As the novelty of flight wore off, the spectators began to demand more spectacular shows, and soon night ascensions, complete with dangerous fireworks, were common. Women aeronauts were popular, and flights soon featured trapeze acts, flights on horseback, and parachute jumps. The first recorded wedding in an airborne balloon was performed near the end of the century.[8]

One of the earliest of the aerial showmen was Vincenzo Lunardi, who had been the first to fly in England. Lunardi conducted a series of flights from Liverpool, Glasgow, Edinburgh, and London. His skill at promoting, combined with handsome features and wit, soon gained him a large following. Although roundly ridiculed by the press, Lunardi became the first of the ballooning show idols. His popularity soured when a young man was killed after being caught in the anchor rope of a rising balloon in 1786, and Lunardi was soon forced to leave England. He continued to seek fame on the Continent for another twenty years. However, Lunardi was forced to give up ballooning due to ill health and died in a convent near Lisbon in 1806.

Another of the early showmen was Jean-Pierre Blanchard, who had gained fame by his flight across the English Channel. Blanchard was a traveling showman, who is credited with inaugural flights in several countries including Germany, Belgium, and Switzerland. When the

French Revolution hampered his ability to perform on the Continent, Blanchard sailed to the United States to seek further fame and financial reward. He arrived in Philadelphia in 1792 and began to promote the first untethered balloon flight in the New World. The flight was scheduled for 9 January 1793 at the Walnut Street Prison in Philadelphia. President George Washington and future presidents Adams, Jefferson, Madison, and Monroe were in attendance. Washington provided Blanchard with a letter of identity, since he did not speak much English. Blanchard lifted off shortly after 10 A.M. accompanied by a small dog and flew for approximately 45 minutes, landing in Deptford Township, New Jersey. The flight was about 15 miles in distance (see fig. 14.2).

When met by a local farmer, Blanchard produced Washington's letter; however, the farmer could not read. Then Blanchard produced a bottle of wine, which he proceeded to share with the farmer in a gesture of friendship. Finally, someone who could read appeared, scanned the letter, and promptly had Blanchard escorted back to Philadelphia. Blanchard himself recalled, "I could not, nor did I know how to answer all the friendly questions which they asked me; my passport served me as an interpreter. In the midst of a profound silence it was read with a loud and audible voice. How dear the name of Washington is to this people."[9] That evening, Blanchard presented a flag that he had carried to President Washington; it had the French tricolor on one side and the Stars and Stripes on the other.

If the flight in America was a political success, it was not a financial success. The gate receipts totaled slightly more than $400, far short of the $2,000 for which Blanchard had hoped. Shortly thereafter, he returned to Europe where he felt there were more rewarding oppor-

Fig. 14.2. Photo of a watercolor by Joseph Jackson showing the ascension of Jean-Pierre Blanchard on the first air voyage in America, 1793. By permission of the National Air and Space Museum, Smithsonian Institution, ©1999 Smithsonian Institution.

tunities. Financial success in Europe was more elusive than he had anticipated; however, he continued his career until he suffered a heart attack in midair in 1808. He gradually declined in physical and mental health and died in early 1809. During his remarkable career, he made over sixty ascents in at least nine countries.

During the first half of the nineteenth century, the premier balloonist was probably Charles Green of England. He began ballooning in 1821 at the age of thirty-six and continued his flights for over thirty years. He often used the cheaper and more readily available coal gas to inflate his balloons, and he was a master at promoting his flights. He was innovative, offering lucky lottery winners a ride, even ascended on a pony, and was often accompanied by musicians or singers who charmed the audiences below. Green never flew on Sunday, but by 1835 he had logged over two hundred flights covering all of the British Isles. Green wanted to build the perfect aerostat. With the backing of the Vauxhall Gardens in London, he built a 60-foot-high Italian silk balloon, which he named the *Royal Vauxhall.*

On the balloon's maiden flight, it quickly soared to 13,000 feet with nine persons aboard. Green felt the time was right for a distance flight, so he enlisted two others, Robert Holland and Thomas (Monck) Mason, and departed on 7 November 1836. The aeronauts drifted over the English Channel, dined over Calais, and as darkness approached found themselves over Belgium. After spending the night aloft, the crew arrived over Germany at sunrise. Eighteen hours after departure, they landed, rather roughly, in a swamp over 380 miles from their departure point. Based on the success of this flight, Green planned a flight from North America to England across the Atlantic in the balloon, which he renamed *The Great Balloon of Nassau.* Green found no backers and was finally forced to abandon the project. During his remarkable career, he logged over five hundred flights before retiring in 1852.

In the United States, Charles Ferson Durant was thrilling audiences with his flights from New York's Battery Park, which would usually end in nearby New Jersey. In 1834, Durant landed on a steamer in Boston Harbor. Although he soon retired, he inspired others to ballooning. One of those he inspired was John Wise, who was to become one of America's best-known aeronauts. Wise was very popular and often amazed audiences with his quick descents. He learned that a partially collapsed balloon acted like a parachute, and he often used this technique. He is also credited with the invention of the "rip panel," which allowed the aeronaut to quickly release the gas, once on the ground, to prevent being dragged some distance by the wind.

Wise had the same dream as Charles Green: a flight made across the Atlantic. It was well known by the middle of the nineteenth century that there was a current of high-speed air from west to east above 12,000 feet. By 1859, Wise had secured a backer, O. A. Gager, to build a balloon capable of achieving his goal. This 120 by 60 foot balloon, named *Atlantic,* needed to be tested, and Wise proposed a flight from St. Louis to the east coast. He attached a lifeboat-sized gondola to the balloon and carried 1,000 pounds of ballast and a store of food. Gager, John LaMountain, the builder of the balloon, and journalist William Hyde accompanied him on the flight.

The balloon left Washington Square in St. Louis at dusk on 1 July 1859 and reached Lake Erie by dawn. The crew reached the eastern shore around 11 A.M., but strong ground winds prevented a landing, and the balloon was blown over Lake Ontario. The crew had jettisoned much of the ballast throughout the flight and were then forced to throw everything overboard to avoid the windswept waves. After a harrowing time, the balloon finally reached the far shore, where Wise threw out the heavy grapnel hook. The hook merely tore off limbs, and the balloon continued through the forest, leaking gas and bouncing about. The crew hung on, and finally the balloon was impaled in a tree about 20 feet high. The battered crew scrambled to safety to learn they had come to rest near Henderson, New York, 809 miles from St. Louis. The crew had been aloft nearly twenty hours and had set a distance record that would last until the end of the century.

Although Wise was forced to abandon his dream, two others planned to tackle the Atlantic Ocean. LaMountain recuperated and bought the remains of the now famous balloon; however, on a test flight he drifted into Canada, where he was stranded for four days. A young Thaddeus Lowe, who would gain fame in the Civil War, set out on a test flight from Cincinnati, but the expected westerly winds blew him instead to South Carolina.

Although he landed seven days after Fort Sumter had been fired upon, he was released after a local resident identified him as a balloonist. The ensuing Civil War halted exhibition ballooning in the United States, but in Europe, larger and larger balloons were being flown.

The first of the giant balloons was a 163-foot vehicle called *Le Geant* (the giant) built by a Frenchman known as Nadar. The balloon made only two ascents, both in 1863. The first flight was for only 15 miles and the second, a 400-mile flight, ended in a wild, bounding landing that burst the balloon. The second giant, *Le Captif* (the captive), built by Henri Giffard, was flown tethered on a steel cable. By the end of the Paris World Fair in 1878, it had carried over 35,000 people aloft.[10]

When the Civil War ended in the United States, ballooning resumed with the dream of an Atlantic crossing still alive. An acrobatic balloonist, Washington Donaldson, proposed to join Wise in an attempt. However, Wise soon withdrew from the project, and the subsequent flight in 1873 traveled only from Brooklyn to Connecticut. Donaldson was soon recruited by P. T. Barnum for his circus, but he was later presumed drowned on a flight over Lake Michigan in 1875 as his body was never recovered. The ballooning world suffered a second loss when Wise was killed on a flight over the same lake.

Throughout the nineteenth century, several female aeronauts became famous for their daring flights. Elisabeth Thible was the first female aloft in 1784. However, Jean Labrousse, who later became the wife of Jacques Garnerin, a noted balloonist and parachutist, was the first to fly solo in 1798. By 1805, Madeleine Blanchard, wife of Jean-Pierre, had soloed and begun regular flights. The petite Mrs. Blanchard was fond of staging all-night flights over Paris, and she made a flight to celebrate the wedding of Napoleon in 1810. Her evening flights often featured fireworks, which finally resulted in ignition of her balloon on a flight in 1819. The balloon crashed onto the nearby rooftops, and the unfortunate aeronaut was thrown to her death on the pavement below.

Another popular female balloonist was Margaret Graham, who always seemed to experience some unexpected problem over the rooftops of London, only to return safe and sound shortly afterwards. She performed with her husband, George, before Queen Victoria in 1838 and remained popular for another fifteen years. Elisa, a niece of the Garnerins, became well known for her flights and her parachuting accuracy. Others, such as

Caroline Durof and Wilhelmine Reichardt, gained popularity as members of husband-and-wife teams with the latter making several solo flights over Austria.

The last of the female performing balloonists was an American, Mary Hawley Myers, who performed under the name "Aerial Princess Carlotta." She made her first flight in 1880 and soon became a master of her profession. She was extremely popular throughout the eastern United States, where she continued to perform until 1891. After her retirement, exhibition ballooning soon lost popularity, and by the beginning of the twentieth century, the public had found a new "star," the heavier-than-air vehicle.

Military Uses of Balloons

Although balloons were often limited in other uses, they proved to be useful in a military role. Since the first flight, many had recognized this potential, including Joseph Montgolfier himself, who had predicted that the mighty Gibralter could be captured by balloons, but he was ridiculed by the British. Benjamin Franklin envisioned an airborne invasion by 5,000 balloons, each with two men, which would be impossible for any country to defend against. Henry Walpole, the English writer, even issued a written plea that these new machines not be converted to engines of destruction for the human race.[11] Balloons were mostly used in a reconnaissance role, and manned balloons were not used for this after World War I.

Balloons were first used after the French Revolution, when France was at war with Austria, Prussia, and Holland. By 1794, the French had formed a balloon unit, the Compagnie d'Aerostatiers, under the leadership of Capt. Jean-Marie Coutelle. The unit's captive balloons were used to observe the enemy and drop propaganda leaflets. Although the balloons proved hard to transport and took a long time to inflate, they were used in battles at Mauberge and Fleurus. Although the Austrians were dismayed at this new form of warfare, they soon learned to elevate their guns in a rudimentary form of antiaircraft fire. By 1795, the French had formed a balloon school, but this was disbanded by Napoleon in 1805 after a bad experience with balloons during his campaign in Egypt.

It was not until 1849 that balloons were used again, this time by the Austrians. During a siege of Venice, they tried launching balloons fitted with timed-fuse bombs.

Although the winds were favorable at launch, they soon changed, and many of the balloons fell among the Austrian troops. This first strategic use of balloons caused little damage on either side, and it would be another twenty-one years before balloons were used again in Europe. The use of military balloons now shifted to the United States, where the Civil War erupted in 1861.

Although the use of balloons had been advocated for military purposes in the United States as early as 1840, in the campaign against the Seminoles, and again in 1846, on a Mexican War campaign against Vera Cruz, they had not been accepted by the military. Shortly after the Civil War broke out, balloonists, particularly in the north, volunteered their services. Among the volunteers were well-known aeronauts such as James Allen, John Wise, John LaMountain, and Thaddeus Lowe. Unfortunately, the balloons of Wise and Allen were both destroyed in accidents en route to the front lines. LaMountain's balloon was used successfully at Ft. Monroe; however, he soon ran short of hydrogen, and by the time he returned to action he was assigned under Lowe's command and subsequently resigned.

Lowe was able to consolidate his position by October 1861, and the First Balloon Corps was formed under his command. Lowe's balloons performed valuable services for the Union armies under General McClellan, and one of his balloons even made captive flights from a converted coal barge in the Potomac River (see fig. 14.3). His highly ornamented balloons, aptly named *Constitution, Washington,* and *United States,* served at numerous battles in 1861 and 1862. By 1863, however, McClellan's drive to Richmond had failed, and he was replaced. Although Lowe made final flights for Gen. Joseph Hooker at Chancellorsville, his unit had been placed under the command of a ground officer, and the disheartened Lowe resigned in May 1863. His resignation ended the balloon efforts of the Union army.

Although the Confederate army flew at least three balloons, under the leadership of Capt. John Bryan, the troops and commanders were not inspired by the venture. Bryan admitted, "The Confederate troops, almost to a man, had never seen a balloon and each time that I went up, they crowded around the balloon squad to watch this novel performance and amused themselves by making many and varied remarks."[12]

One of the most successful uses of balloons occurred during the Franco-Prussian War in 1870. The city of Paris had been surrounded and was under siege. A circus balloon, flown by Jules Durof, ascended quickly to fly over the Prussian lines and carry the news of the siege outside Paris. The city was able to build and fly sixty-six balloons between September 1870 and late January 1871. They were used to carry passengers and mail out of the city, but not back. In order to get messages back into Paris, the French used carrier pigeons and microfilm letters. In addition to Durof, several of France's premier aeronauts, such as Nadar, Gaston Tissandier, and Louis Goddard, were in Paris and quickly trained others. During the siege, the sixty-six balloons carried 102 passengers, including Leon Gambetta, head of the provisional government, more than two million letters, and four hundred pigeons out of Paris.[13]

This unique use of free balloons proved to be the exception, as captive balloons were used by the French in Indochina in 1884. In the same year, portable cylinders for transporting and storing hydrogen were introduced. By 1893, the kite balloon, which was streamlined to provide stability into the wind, was introduced. By 1896, the German Parseval Sigsfeld Drachen (dragon) balloons, later known as "sausages" in World War I, were used. During the Spanish-American War of 1898, one tethered balloon was used by the American forces, but as American Lt. C. de W. Wilcox observed: "As the Spaniards saw it rise from the ground, they got its range at once and destroyed it before it could be of any material use. Indeed, it is charged that it caused serious loss to the advancing infantry by revealing their position and attracting the enemy's fire."[14]

Captive balloons were used by the British in the Boer War of 1899, the Japanese during the Russo-Japanese War of 1904, and the French in Morocco. However, the greatest use of manned captive kite balloons for reconnaissance and communications was during World War I. All of the major armies—German, French, British, and American—employed balloon groups on the western front. These balloons were often employed as high as 6,000 feet to avoid ground fire. The balloons proved vulnerable to antiaircraft artillery and were often helpless prey for the now well-armed airplane.

Since balloons counted as "kills" for airplane pilots, balloon "busters" soon became common. Observers in the balloons soon began to wear and use parachutes. During one 15-day period in 1918, American balloonists made thirty parachute escapes, while losing thirty bal-

Fig. 14.3. View of Union soldiers on the ground holding tether lines while Thaddeus Lowe ventures aloft in the balloon *Intrepid* during the Battle of Fair Oaks, 31 May–1 June 1862. A Union camp can be seen in the background. Balloons were used for aerial reconnaissance during the Civil War. By permission of the National Air and Space Museum, Smithsonian Institution, ©1999 Smithsonian Institution.

loons to enemy antiaircraft fire and aircraft. American ace, Frank Luke, was credited with the destruction of three Drachen shortly before his aircraft was forced to land and he was killed by German soldiers.[15]

Balloons also proved dangerous on the ground, in many cases, because the hydrogen was highly flammable. The Germans alone lost 655 balloons to enemy fire, accidents, and weather. This experience, coupled with the flexibility and sophistication of the airplane, resulted in the termination of manned captive balloons for military reconnaissance.

Although manned balloons were no longer used, unmanned captive and free balloons were used during World War II. The British used captive barrage balloons against raiding German aircraft. They were generally successful in protecting against airplanes, since the cables attached to the balloons could easily slice through an aircraft wing. Barrage balloons were credited with sixty-six confirmed crashes or forced landings and were also responsible for over 8 percent of the German V-1 "flying bombs" destroyed over Britain. One female ground crew member in London even remarked that if the balloons were cut loose, England might just well sink.[16] Barrage balloons were also used by the Allies during invasion landings in North Africa and Italy and during the D-Day invasion of France in 1944 to protect troops and ships against low-flying aircraft.

One of the unique uses of free balloons occurred between November 1944 and April 1945, when the Japanese launched smaller hydrogen-filled balloons against the United States. The balloons were equipped with ballast, barometers, and bombs and were designed to fly in the jetstream from west to east between 30,000 and 35,000 feet. The barometer released ballast when the balloons began to sink at night and released gas when the balloons ascended too high. The balloons released their bombs after approximately 40 hours in the air. Although many balloons fell short and some detonated in midair, experts estimated that as many as 1,000 may have reached the North American continent between Alaska and Mexico.

The United States put a complete blackout on news about the balloons, but the dangers were spread by word of mouth to farmers, hunters, and police. The only known casualties were five children and a woman on a school picnic in Oregon when they found a balloon and tugged on the strings, detonating the bombs. General Kusaba, the Japanese commander of the balloon project, credited the news blackout with cancellation of the project in 1945 because the Japanese had not read any reports of landings in the American press.[17]

Balloons for Science and Sport

Many early aeronauts used balloons for scientific experimentation, particularly in research about the ocean of air that surrounded them. The balloon proved especially adaptable to this task, since it could rise to great heights, even when carrying scientists and instruments. One of the first experimenters was John Jeffries, whose first flight to 9,000 feet in 1794 revealed that the temperature and pressure both dropped with increase in altitude.

Unfortunately, Jeffries had to jettison his scientific equipment during the flight with Blanchard across the English Channel, and this seems to have been the last of his experimentation. By July 1803, Etienne Robertson had discovered that the boiling point of water was much lower at higher altitudes. The following year, Joseph Gay-Lussac ascended to 23,000 feet where he found that magnetism remained the same as on earth as did the composition of the atmosphere. After Gay-Lussac's flight, there was a lull in experimentation that lasted until 1850.

Two Frenchmen, Jean Barral and Jacques Bixio, studied temperature and humidity at altitudes slightly above 20,000 feet in 1850 and are credited with discovering that cirrus clouds contain ice crystals. By 1862, two Englishmen, Henry Coxwell and James Glaisher, captured the scientific spotlight. Glaisher, a noted meteorologist, convinced veteran aeronaut Coxwell to build a new 90,000-cubic-foot balloon especially for experimentation in the atmosphere. After two practice ascents, the pair lifted off from a field in the British Midlands on 5 September 1862. They rose rapidly to over 21,000 feet, where the thin oxygen content of the air and the low temperature took its toll on the pair. Glaisher lapsed in and out of consciousness while Coxwell tried desperately to release some of the gas with frostbitten hands. At nearly 30,000 feet, Coxwell finally grasped the line in his mouth, yanked, and heard the reassuring hiss of escaping gas. The two soon returned to earth to become heroes. Glaisher made several other flights during which he learned that temperature does not decrease at a constant rate with altitude and that humidity seems to disappear above 25,000 feet. He also discovered a high altitude flow of warm wind from the Southwest over England similar to the Gulf stream.

The adventures of Coxwell and Glaisher led to the invention of an oxygen breathing device by two Frenchmen, Joseph Spinelli and Theodore Sivil. The device was simply a mouthpiece connected to a small balloon containing air and pure oxygen. After testing the device in a vacuum chamber, Spinelli and Sivil enlisted the assistance of veteran aeronaut Gaston Tissandier, a pilot during the siege of Paris in 1870. The three, with an array of instruments and the vital oxygen devices, ascended from Paris in April 1975. They rose to 14,000 feet, where the oxygen system proved positive, then quickly to 25,000 feet, where intermittent pulls on the oxygen did not suffice.

Tissandier became unconscious for over 30 minutes, and when he revived he found the other two also unconscious, but the balloon was descending. He fainted again and awakened just as Spinelli jettisoned ballast and the balloon quickly rose. Again Tissandier lost consciousness, and this time when he revived he found the other two dead as the estimated height the balloon reached was over 30,000 feet.

The death of Sivil and Spinelli led to a temporary halt to high altitude research until 1894 when a German, Arthur Berson, reached an altitude of 30,000 feet, followed by an ascent to 35,000 feet in 1901. By then, the French had developed devices to automatically record atmospheric conditions and then be parachuted back to earth, which temporarily replaced the balloonist. Similar devices are used today to measure temperature, winds, and other information at altitude.

The scientific frontier moved to arctic exploration with the proposal of Swedish adventurer Salomon Andrée for a polar expedition. Backed by the king of Sweden and a wealthy industrialist, Andrée constructed his special balloon, the *Ornen* (eagle), with gas valves on the lower portion of the balloon to prevent icing and with three drag ropes to control altitude. Andrée and two crewmen set out from Spitsbergen, 700 miles south of the North Pole, in July 1897 and drifted into the unknown.

Although a brief message by carrier pigeon was received, which indicated all was well on the second day, no further word was heard from the expedition for over thirty-three years. In 1930, walrus hunters found the remains of the three on White Island, only 280 miles from the liftoff point. Diaries, papers, and even preserved photographs told the story of the downing of the balloon by ice and the desperate trek for survival. Further Arctic attempts by balloon were not made, since airplanes had reached the pole by then.

By the time Andrée's remains were discovered, aeronauts again had explored by balloon, this time in the stratosphere, the area between 7 and 12 miles above the earth. The first of these new scientific aeronauts was U.S. Army Capt. Hawthorne Gray, a veteran balloonist. After an abortive attempt in early 1927, Gray ascended to over 42,000 feet in May 1927, but on return he had to bail out when the balloon dropped abruptly. Gray went aloft again in December 1927 and reached an altitude of over 40,000 feet; however, he died from oxygen starvation, and his body was discovered later on a farm in Tennessee.

Gray's death led to the development of a sealed and pressurized gondola, to protect the aeronauts in the stratosphere, by Swiss physicist Auguste Piccard. On the first flight in 1931, Piccard and his assistant reached an altitude over 51,000 feet, finally landing at night on a glacier in the Austrian Alps. His second flight set a new altitude record at 53,152 feet and helped him gather important information on cosmic rays. After this accomplishment, Piccard turned to ocean exploration in a pressurized gondola, named a bathyscape. Piccard's twin brother, Jean, with his wife, Jeanette, bettered the record with a 1934 ascent to 57,000 feet, making her the first female in the stratosphere.

Piccard's success with the pressurized gondola soon led to an altitude race between the United States and the Soviet Union. Although the efforts of the Soviets, sponsored by the government, and the Americans, sponsored jointly by the Army Air Corps and the National Geographic Society, were scientific, they also involved the prestige of these two powerful countries. The Soviets broke the altitude record in 1933 with an ascent to 58,700 feet, only to see this mark fall two months later when Americans Chester Fordney and Thomas Settle reached a height of 61,221 feet. A subsequent Soviet attempt ended in disaster when the gondola broke free and the three aeronauts plunged to their deaths in early 1934, after reaching a height of 70,000 feet. An American attempt in a balloon named *Explorer* ended at 60,000 feet when the bag ripped, forcing the three balloonists to parachute to safety.

The final flight in this competition was made by two of the *Explorer* survivors, Capt. Albert Stevens and Capt. Orvil Anderson, who went aloft in November 1935 in their balloon, *Explorer II*. The pair set a new altitude record of 72,395 feet and brought back valuable information about cosmic rays, ozone, and the ability of humans to survive at such high altitudes. Further scientific attempts were ended as World War II dominated events for the next twelve years.

Shortly after World War II ended, scientist Otto Winzen designed balloons of a new material, polyethylene, which could carry aeronauts and instruments to the edge of space. The U.S. Navy began unmanned testing on the new balloons in 1947 under the code name "Project Skyhook." By the mid-1950s, both the U.S. Navy with "Project Strato-Lab" and the U.S. Air Force with "Project Manhigh" began a series of manned flights designed to test humans' ability to survive in space. Comdr. Malcolm Ross and Comdr. Morton Lewis reached a height of 76,000 feet in 1956, followed by Capt. Joseph Kittinger Jr.'s flight to 96,000 feet in 1957. The second Air Force flight, with Maj. David Simons aboard, reached the edge of space at 101,516 feet.

With the dawning of manned space flight in the 1960s, manned balloon flights were numbered; however, the final two U.S. flights were exciting. In 1960, Kittinger, wearing a test pressure suit, bailed out of a balloon at 102,800 feet above New Mexico. His parachute opened at approximately 17,500 feet and he drifted down unharmed. In 1961, Comdr. Malcolm Ross and Comdr. Victor Prather ascended to a record height of 113,740 feet, testing space suits developed for the U.S. Mercury astronauts. Unfortunately, their capsule fell into the Gulf of Mexico, and Prather drowned during the rescue attempt.[18]

Just as balloons had served the scientific community well, they appealed to affluent sports people by the early twentieth century. An aero club had been established in France in 1898, and soon other countries, including the United States and Great Britain, had similar sport groups. Competition was fostered at club meets, and one of the most famous of the competitions, held by the French aero club, featured long-distance flights from Paris. In 1900, Count Henri de La Vaulx set a distance record of 1192 miles in a balloon called *Centauri*. He landed in Russia, where he was jailed for the first 24 hours. Soon such distance flights were common, with several flights in Germany and France estimated to be over 1,000 miles.

Competition between countries was not common until after 1906, when the French formed the Federation Aeronautique Internationale (FAI) to maintain records and establish standards. American publisher James Gordon Bennett decided to create a trophy for flight similar to one he established in 1902 for automobiles. However, the FAI insisted on restricting the competition to lighter-than-air, and Bennett was forced to create a sepa-

rate trophy competition for heavier-than-air in 1909. The first Bennett Cup balloon race was won by American Frank Lahm with a distance of 402 miles from Paris.

Bennett Cup competition was conducted in different countries every year until 1914, when a German crew set a distance record of 1897 miles but, like Count Vaulx, were jailed in Siberia. Boundary crossing flights were suspended during World War I, and the Cup races were not resumed until 1920. In 1923, the race survived its most disastrous events. Storms and poor weather resulted in the deaths of five balloonists and the rescue from the North Sea of others. In spite of the risks, the competition continued each year until 1931, when the race was canceled due to lack of travel money by nearly all teams. Resumed in 1932, the races continued again until the outbreak of World War II in 1939.

After World War II, ballooning reached its lowest ebb, as interest was now firmly directed at the airplane, particularly the jet airplane. Balloons were expensive to operate and still dangerous. A survey in 1959 revealed only fourteen balloons in the United States in airworthy shape. Although newer materials had been discovered, it was not until 1960 that navy worker Ed Yost designed a propane burner that could be turned on and off in flight. Now interest in hot air balloons began to increase, and by 1961 the Balloon Federation of America (BFA) was formed. By 1964, the British Balloon and Airship Club was formed, and hot air ballooning made a remarkable comeback in other countries as well. By 1979, there were over 1,700 balloonists in the United States with similar growth in other countries. Today, there are annual meets in Albuquerque, New Mexico, and at other sites selected by the BFA. The BFA has an estimated membership of over 6,000 balloonists with corresponding meets held in many other parts of the world.

Gas ballooning also made a comeback in 1979 with the resumption of the Bennett Cup races in Long Beach, California. Although hot air ballooning is cheaper due to the cost of propane versus helium, hot air balloons generally are not routinely capable of long-distance flight. Gas balloon teams from many countries compete annually with most of the teams from Europe and other areas still using hydrogen for its superior lifting ability.

Another area of sport ballooning interest was flight over the world's natural boundaries. In particular, flight across the Atlantic was a challenge that attracted many aeronauts, including Washington, Wise, and millionaire Malcolm Forbes. At least five aeronauts, including one woman, were killed in failed attempts. In spite of new, lighter, and stronger materials, the availability of helium, and the knowledge of the strong west to east winds at altitude, it was not until the late 1970s that the Atlantic was finally conquered.

Aeronauts Max Anderson and Ben Abruzzo tried a crossing in 1977, but they were forced down in Iceland. The following year they added a new crewman, Larry Newman, and were finally successful in a balloon named *Double Eagle II*. The trio landed in Misery, France, after jettisoning most of their food, water, and rafts nearly 84 hours after leaving the United States. Their record-setting flight of 3,120 miles held the interest of thousands of enthusiastic fans, a remarkable event in a world accustomed to space flight and moon landings.

Abruzzo followed this record flight with an even more impressive one in 1981, when he crossed the Pacific Ocean from Japan to the United States, a record distance of 5,768 miles. He was accompanied by Newman, Ron Clark, and Rocky Aoki. Not to be outdone, aeronauts Per Lindstrand and Richard Branson crossed the Atlantic in a hot air balloon in 1987, then followed with a Pacific crossing record of 4,600 miles in 1991. On this final flight, the balloon carried over five tons of propane tanks.[19]

There was one great flight that had eluded all efforts, the nonstop circumnavigation of the earth by balloon, a lighter-than-air feat to match the remarkable flight of the heavier-than-air craft *Voyageur*. Although there were over twenty publicized attempts to accomplish this feat, all failed due to weather, equipment failure, or restriction of overflight rights by unfriendly countries. Finally, on 1 March 1999, the team of Brian Jones and Bertrand Piccard lifted off from the Swiss Alps in a 180-foot-tall, high-tech, combination gas and hot air balloon named *Breitling Orbiter 3*. Twenty days later, the team passed the circumnavigation point in Mauritania and continued to a safe landing in Egypt. This world-spanning flight was a fitting climax to the third century of manned balloon flight, especially since Piccard is the grandson of Auguste Piccard, the first man to reach the stratosphere in a balloon.

Early Dirigible Development

While the early aeronauts, show persons, and military balloonists operated in the limited environment of free ballooning, a small group of dedicated aeronauts heeded Samuel Johnson's advice in 1794: "The vehicles can serve no use till we can guide them."[20] As early as 1783, Jean-Marie Meusnier, a French army engineer, had drawn a streamlined, elliptical vehicle capable of flight against the wind. Meusnier had also designed the *ballonet,* or air bag, to help maintain the shape of the balloon as the lifting gas expanded and contracted. In 1814, John Pauly and Durs Egg designed a movable weight that could be attached to an elliptical balloon to trim the craft for level ascending or descending flight. By the middle of the nineteenth century, the balloon's envelope, *ballonet,* rudder, propeller, trim, and even semikeel had been designed. However, an engine capable of pushing such a vehicle against the wind was not yet available.

In 1852, Henri Giffard, a noted designer of steam engines, took a step toward powered flight in a 144-foot-long balloon driven by a 3-horsepower steam engine. The craft flew at 6 miles per hour for 17 minutes, and although noted as the first powered flight, it was not capable of controlled flight against only the lightest of breezes. By 1883, the Tissandier brothers, Gaston and Albert, made two flights in an electrically powered balloon, which proved incapable of flight against the wind. In 1884, Frenchmen Charles Renard and Arthur Krebs designed a battery-powered craft, *La France,* which was able to take off and return just barely to the departure point. This proved that navigation was possible but not yet very practical.

Steam and electric engines had limited success due to their weight versus horsepower ratio. It was not until 1888 that a lightweight version of the internal combustion engine of Paul Hanlein, improved on by his countryman Gottlieb Daimler, proved a practical solution to the propulsion problem. The first flights made by Karl Woelfert that year with a 2-horsepower, single-cylinder engine were successful. However, the craft was obviously underpowered, and Woelfert resolved to build a bigger craft with a larger engine. Although it took nearly nine years to complete the new ship, the *Deutschland,* was ready by the 1896 Berlin Trade Fair, where it was displayed. Kaiser Wilhelm took an interest in the craft and ordered test flights in Berlin. In May 1897, Woelfert and his mechanic Robert Knabe departed in the 2-cylinder, 8-horsepower engine dirigibles. Unfortunately, the car containing the engine, with its open flame ignition, was too close to the gas bag, and at an altitude of 2500 feet the balloon burst into flames and the two aeronauts plunged to their deaths.

During the previous year, David Schwarz, an Austrian, constructed an aluminum dirigible with the skin attached to tubing and filled with several small fabric balloons, which were then inflated with hydrogen. Schwarz's first design in 1894 failed to fly, and he died in 1896 before the second flight. His widow arranged a test flight in November 1897. With an inexperienced pilot at the controls, the slippage of a leather belt used to drive the three propellers from the 12-horsepower Daimler engine caused the craft to descend rapidly and crash in an open field.

Undoubtedly, the most famous of the early dirigible aeronauts was a dapper young Brazilian named Alberto Santos-Dumont. Santos-Dumont, the son of a wealthy planter, read stories by Jules Verne and others about the fantastic flying machines. When he was sent to Paris by his father in 1892, he expected to see such machines, but he did not find any. With his fortune, estimated at a half million dollars, Santos-Dumont began to fly balloons owned by Henri Lachambre, builder of Andrée's balloon *Ornen,* and he ordered a specially developed small balloon for his personal use. He soon became a familiar sight around Paris, even flying at night and in most weather conditions.

Santos-Dumont also joined the Paris Automobile Club and delighted in driving a 3.5-horsepower three-wheeled vehicle in races. He reasoned that this engine could be used in a small dirigible and had an 82-foot silk balloon built, which he called *Number 1.* Using movable sandbags as elevators, Santos-Dumont made his first trial ascent on 18 September 1898. Heeding the advice of local aeronauts, he took off with the wind, as in a normal balloon. He promptly sailed into the trees, but with a lesson learned. Two days later, Santos-Dumont ascended into the wind and cleared all obstacles. The craft proved very maneuverable even into a light breeze, but Santos-Dumont flew to a height of over 1,300 feet, where the gas contracted and the balloon folded in the middle. Undaunted, Santos-Dumont built Number 2, which also

folded, and Number 3, which he flew in 1899 at a speed of nearly 12 miles per hour.

Dirigibles of the Early Twentieth Century

As the twentieth century dawned, there was still no practical, dependable dirigible, although internal combustion engine technology was advancing rapidly. The first fourteen years of the century saw an unparalleled growth in dirigible development culminating in the operation of a dirigible commercial airline.

The early, nonrigid dirigibles with *ballonets,* control car, and engine suspended below by netting was soon replaced by the semirigid vehicles, with a lightweight keel along the bottom to provide support and structure. This permitted the construction of larger dirigibles. However, the development of the rigid dirigible, with an internal metal or wood framework covered with fabric and filled with a number of gas bags, provided for the ultimate size.

Santos-Dumont's flights were becoming well known. In order to spur competition, Henri Deutsch de la Meurthe, a petroleum millionaire, offered a prize of 100,000 francs for a craft that could fly a designated course of nearly 7 miles in under 30 minutes.[21] Santos-Dumont's *Number 3* was not fast enough, so he built *Number 4* with a 7-horsepower engine and *Number 5* with a 12-horsepower engine. After several trial flights, he tried for the prize on 13 July 1901. Bucking a headwind with a faltering engine at the end, Santos-Dumont reached the finish line in 40 minutes. Another try on 8 August resulted in a crash landing atop a Paris hotel, and Santos-Dumont decided to build *Number 6.* Finally, on 19 September 1901, he flew the course in a time only 40 seconds over the limit. While the contest committee balked at awarding him the prize, the Paris crowds, who had watched the flight, demanded that the prize go to "Le petit Santos," and after two weeks the committee agreed. The prize was donated to the poor of Paris and to Santos-Dumont's assistant and crew; however, he was awarded a similar amount by the Brazilian government, which he kept.[22]

After visiting Britain and the United States as a celebrity, Santos-Dumont returned to Paris and built *Number 7,* a racing ship, but could find no competition. Skipping a number, since he did not like the number 8, he built a 36-foot runabout, *Number 9,* which he flew around the city, stopping at sidewalk cafés to the delight of the citizens of Paris. He finally built *Number 10,* a large craft designed to carry ten people, and several other dirigibles. However, he did not pursue these projects because he had become interested in heavier-than-air flight by this time.[23]

The flights of Santos-Dumont led to a flurry of dirigible activity, not all of which was as successful. In 1902, fellow Brazilian Augusto Severo and his mechanic were killed when their airship, *Pax,* burst from unrelieved gas pressure at 2,000 feet. Later in the same year, Baron Bradsky Laboun and his mechanic Paul Morin were killed when the car in which they were riding separated from the balloon. Two French brothers, Paul and Pierre Lebaudy, were successful in designing a new type of dirigible, the semirigid. Using a steel tube keel, running the length of the airship, they flew their larger dirigible, *Le Jaune* (yellow), powered by a 40-horsepower Daimler engine, on several impressive flights in 1902–3. After these flights, the ship was donated to the French government and became the basis of a contract for the brothers to build other ships for military use of the government.

The semirigid dirigibles had become popular in France, and two other companies were formed: the Astra Company, financed by Henri Deutsch, and the Zodiac Company. An entirely different and larger dirigible was being developed in Germany. Through the persistence and determination of Count Ferdinand von Zeppelin, the rigid dirigible, consisting of a metal or wooden framework with a number of individual gas bags and much greater lifting capability, became a practical reality.

As a young man, Zeppelin had entered the military service of the state of Württemberg. In 1863, he visited the United States as a military observer to the Civil War. While in this capacity, he took a balloon flight. In 1870, he fought for Prussia in the Franco-Prussian War and observed the balloon flights from Paris. In 1874, he wrote a description of a large dirigible containing separate gas cells and large engines in a section of his diary entitled "Thoughts about an Airship."[24] After several military commands and service as ambassador from Württemberg to Prussia, he was promoted to general. Zeppelin was retired by Chancellor Bismark, who was consolidating Prussian control over Germany.

The count returned to his family estate near Lake Constance and began to bring his ideas to reality. Reading of French successes, he urged the German military to investigate the use of dirigibles. In 1895, a board of Prussian experts rejected his ideas, and Zeppelin attempted to secure funds through an unsuccessful bond issue. However, he was rescued by the Union of German Engineers, who urged several industrialists to invest. This support, along with the count's personal funds, helped found the Society for the Encouragement of Aerial Navigation, and work was started on the first Zeppelin rigid airship, the LZ-1.

The first flight of the LZ-1 was on 2 July 1900. The huge 416-foot-long gas bag, powered by two 16-horsepower Daimler gasoline engines, was a spectacular sight as it emerged from the work shed. The flight lasted only 18 minutes because the sliding weight cable, used to control the craft, broke and the ship settled on the lake. The LZ-1 flew twice more in October 1900, but it was finally broken up and sold when the firm was not offered any government or private contract for further development. The count managed to keep his chief engineer, Ludwig Durr, on a meager payroll.

Undaunted, Count Zeppelin attempted another fundraising effort in 1903 and was allowed by the king of Württemberg to conduct an all-kingdom lottery. The money raised, combined with money from mortgaging his wife's estate, allowed him to build LZ-2, which was subsequently wrecked on a test flight in 1906. This time the kaiser authorized a nationwide lottery, and LZ-3 was built with horizontal fins added for stability. The LZ-3 restored the count's faith with a 2 hour and 17 minute test flight and a speed of 25 miles per hour. The German military took notice and provided additional funds for development of a military machine capable of a flight of 24 hours duration.

The LZ-3 design was modified to the LZ-4. After a promising start, the test flight was grounded at Echterdingen by engine trouble. While on the ground, the dirigible was blown about by a sudden storm, and it exploded. Although there was no loss of life, the old count was devastated; however, to his great surprise, the German people themselves came to his aid, and contributions began to pour in. The remarkable total of this "miracle at Echterdingen" was over 6.5 million marks.[25]

In 1908, the government bought LZ-3, and the count

formed the Zeppelin Airship Construction Company, hoping to furnish airships for the military. When the army refused to buy LZ-5 and LZ-6, the count decided to start a commercial airline, later known as DELAG, to buy his airships.

DELAG began operations in 1910 with LZ-7, *Deutschland,* which was soon wrecked but with no loss of life. LZ-8, *Deutschland II,* was subsequently damaged by high winds. This prompted Dr. Hugo Eckener, now flight director, to institute a rigorous training program and establish a weather forecasting network. He also urged the use of Maybach 145-horsepower engines. The new Maybach-equipped LZ-10, *Schwaben,* was an instant success. DELAG was soon bolstered by the addition of three new ships, *Hansa, Sachsen,* and *Viktoria Luise.* Between 1910 and 1914, the ships carried over 10,197 passengers on 1,585 flights without injury.[26] The success of DELAG drew the interest of the military, and ships were built for the army and navy, while DELAG trained military crews.

Two other German dirigible manufacturers deserve mention. The Schutte-Lanz SL-1 was finished in 1911 and was distinctive due to the wooden framework. It was more streamlined than the Zeppelins and was powered by two 240-horsepower Mercedes-Daimler engines that gave a speed of 44 mph. Twenty-one ships were built before the war, and the company eventually became part of the Zeppelin enterprise. The other builder of note was Maj. August Parseval, whose dirigibles were powered descendants of the kite balloon. He built twenty-seven of the small, nonrigid ships, some of which other countries, such as Russia, England, and Japan, bought.

Although Germany and France were in the lead in dirigible development, some activity was conducted in England, Italy, and the United States. The British purchased a Lebaudy from France and a Parseval from Germany but did attempt to build some craft. Five small nonrigid Willows ships were built, and Willows Number 3 was the first to cross the English Channel. The Willow also introduced a swivel engine, which could be used to advantage on liftoff.

In 1907, American Samuel Cody was involved in the design of the first ship for the British army. Built at Farnborough, the *Nulli Secundus* was redesigned in 1908 as a semirigid and was flown for another year, providing valuable training. The Farnborough Balloon Factory built several other semirigid ships for the army; Beta, in 1910, which contained the first British-built engines, Gamma, in 1912, Delta, in 1912, and Eta, in 1913. Vickers Company built a large rigid dirigible, *Mayfly,* which was destined for the Royal Navy, but it was destroyed by an accident before the first flight.

The first successful dirigible built in the United States was the *California Arrow,* built by Thomas Baldwin. He was a circus acrobat and balloonist who first flew his 54-foot ship, powered by a Glenn Curtiss 10-horsepower engine, in July 1904. The ship was a hit at the 1904 World's Fair in St. Louis, and Baldwin soon contracted to build a ship for the U.S. Army. The SC-1, delivered in 1908, was 96 feet long and powered by a Curtiss 20-horsepower engine. This ship was later flown by notables such as Frank Lamm, Benjamin Foulois, and Thomas Selfridge. However, it was scrapped after three years (see fig. 14.4).

Other unsuccessful efforts were made by John Morrell, whose huge dirigible crashed on its first and only flight at Berkeley, California, in 1908. Walter Wellman attempted to fly to the North Pole in a large dirigible, the *America,* but failed in two attempts in 1907 and 1909. His next venture was an attempt to fly the Atlantic in 1910. However, the ship landed in the water. The crew was rescued and watched the ship disappear into the Atlantic mists. Wellman's engineer, Melvin Vaniman, built his own ship, the *Akron,* which burned and killed the crew in 1912. Forlanani built other semirigid dirigibles for the Italian army before the war.

Dirigibles in World War I

When the war broke out in 1914, the generals expected a quick war, so they saw no immediate need for the dirigible. As the war continued, however, dirigibles took on two roles, reconnaissance and strategic bombing. The Allies were not well equipped with dirigibles. France had about twenty-five nonrigid Astra-Torres ships and several produced by Clement-Bayard. These would be used mostly for submarine patrol in the Mediterranean. The Italians had the three Forlanani semirigids plus a number of smaller nonrigids, which were also used for naval duties.

The British had only a few dirigibles at the beginning of the war, used by the Royal Navy, but soon saw the

Fig. 14.4. Baldwin SC-1 airship. By permission of the National Air and Space Museum, Smithsonian Institution, ©1999 Smithsonian Institution.

need for a fleet of smaller semirigids for submarine patrol. The first craft, a Willows envelope that was shortened and a fuselage from a BE-2-C aircraft proved successful. From this developed three classes of nonrigid ships, soon nicknamed "blimps."[27] S.S. (Sea Scout), C (Coastal), and N.S. (North Sea) blimps were used throughout the war for submarine spotting and other reconnaissance duties. The 262-foot N.S. ships carried a crew of ten and achieved speeds of 58 knots from two 250-horsepower engines. The blimps were used not to attack submarines but to spot and track them, relaying their location to surface ships.

The United States entered the war late, and the navy had only a few craft in operation. A nonrigid, the DN-1, was built but failed testing in 1917. The navy did begin production of the more successful B type blimps in late 1917. These blimps, built by the Goodyear Corporation, were used in training. A navy dirigible group was formed in 1917, and graduates flew B type blimps on convoy escort and submarine patrol from U.S. and overseas bases. By 1918, ten of the newer C class blimps had been built. These blimps performed an important role in convoy patrol.

The most predominant use of the dirigible during the war was by Germany, which was well equipped with a variety of rigid and other ships. They also had a number of DELAG trained crews. While the German army used some nonrigid and semirigid balloons on both fronts, these were not very successful and resulted in the loss of several ships.

The German Naval Airship service was commanded by Peter Strasser, who had been trained by Eckener. Strasser began to build a fleet of the rigid dirigibles, now called Zeppelins, and urged the use of these ships for strategic bombing against England. The potential for such a mission was clear. The Zeppelins were capable of carrying three tons of bombs at an altitude of nearly 10,000 feet. The kaiser held back on this controversial use of the Zeppelins until 1915, possibly due to the fact that his cousin was the king of England, George V.

Winston Churchill understood the threat posed and ordered aircraft raids against the Zeppelin base at Düsseldorf and the factory at Friedrichshafen. This resulted in the destruction of the LZ-25 and one under construction. The kaiser authorized bombing against military targets in England (but not London) in January 1915. The first raid that month resulted in four casualties at Yarmouth. Thus strategic bombing, which would blur the distinction between soldier and civilian, was added to the arsenal of warfare. The British reacted with cries of inhumanity and brutality, calling the Germans beasts and "Huns."

Although England suffered the brunt of the bombing campaign, Zeppelin raids were also made against France, Belgium, Poland, and Russia. Most of the raids were made on moonless nights during good weather when the ships were hard to spot. Since intercepting aircraft were limited at night and usually limited to lower altitudes, antiaircraft artillery was used against the earlier raiders with little success.

In May 1915, the kaiser lifted the restrictions on bombing London, but he restricted bombing historical sites such as St. Paul's Cathedral. The brightly lit city was an easy target to find, and the city was first bombed by a German army ship that month, resulting in seven deaths and considerable damage. The most damaging raid was made by Heinrich Mathy on 15 September 1915. Mathy had visited London and was able to pinpoint his position, even though his bomb run was made from 7,000 feet. The raid resulted in the deaths of thirty-two people and destruction in excess of $2.5 million. W. E. Shepherd, an American journalist in London, remarked,

"Suddenly you realize the biggest city in the world has become the night battlefield on which seven million men, women, and children live."[28]

Raids continued throughout 1915 and early 1916; however, German losses began to mount. The first casualty was LZ-37, destroyed over Belgium by a British aircraft that bombed the huge ship from above. Antiaircraft fire and aircraft became more effective. LZ-33 and LZ-32 were downed in September 1916, then a week later, Mathy was downed in LZ-31. Artillery and the aircraft had finally caught up with the Zeppelin. Strasser persisted and had new lightweight "height climbers" built, capable of operations around 20,000 feet. By March 1917, the army had ceased Zeppelin operations and begun to concentrate on large bomber aircraft.

Strasser continued the navy raids, but weather, the effects of high altitudes on people and engines, and the effectiveness of defensive forces was becoming prohibitive. British aircraft began to attack Zeppelins on the ground and on reconnaissance and mine clearing operations in the North Sea. Finally, on 5 August 1918, Strasser himself was shot down in LZ-70. Three months later, the war ended.

The effectiveness of the Zeppelin bombing operations was debatable; however, the craft were successfully used by the navy in other roles. In fifty-one raids, the Germans had inflicted 557 deaths and over 1,300 injuries plus millions in property damage. They had kept countless British airmen on the island for defensive purposes and had disrupted life in London, but this was not an overwhelming loss for the British. The Germans, however, lost over 40 percent of their crewmen, fifty-three of the seventy-three airships used by the navy and twenty-six of the fifty used by the army.

One of the Zeppelins performed a most spectacular mission during the war. In November 1917, LZ-59 left Jamboli, Bulgaria, with supplies for the German army fighting in German East Africa. After flying 2,800 miles, the ship was recalled to Jamboli and landed after covering 4,225 miles in 95 hours. This feat demonstrated the long-range capability of the Zeppelin and led to the design of LZ-72, a ship capable of bombing New York. Count Zeppelin became involved in the production of large bomber airplanes, but he died in 1917.

Shortly after the war, most German airship bases had been looted. In June 1919, German crews destroyed seven of the remaining Zeppelins as a final act of defiance. This ended the military use of the large rigid airship. Interestingly, nonrigid blimps used by the Allies were much more successful. However, the potential of the Zeppelin for peacetime use was noted by all.

Postwar Development

After the war, the Allies put a stop to German aircraft production and tried to take advantage of German expertise in the dirigible field. One of the Zeppelins, shot down over England, had landed relatively intact, and soon copies of the airship plans were available. By 1919, Britain used the plans to build R-33 and R-34. Attention was now focused on crossing the Atlantic. Although a west to east crossing was made by aircraft, the British decided to attempt an east to west flight by airship. The R-34, commanded by Maj. George Scott, left England on 2 July 1919 with airship enthusiast General Maitland on board. Fighting fog, cold, and gale force winds at times, the R-34 crossed Newfoundland on 4 July and finally landed in Mineola, New York, on 6 July. The craft had made the nonstop crossing in just over 108 hours. The return trip took only 75 hours.[29]

Although the British were to build other airships, some countries depended on German ships received as reparations to begin their fleet. The destruction of the Zeppelins by the crewmen left only seven rigids to be taken by the Allies with two smaller ships used by DELAG for three months after the war. The ships were divided between Britain, France, and Italy, with the United States to receive no ships.

The United States had become air-minded. In 1919, Congress authorized funds to build an airship base and two rigid airships, one in the United States, and the R-38, being constructed in England. The R-38 was built from Zeppelin plans with an extra section added. In August 1921, while American and British crews were making an acceptance test flight, the R-38 broke apart over the Humber River near Hull. Only five persons, one American, survived the accident.

Although British airship development stopped temporarily, the United States pushed ahead with the ZR-1, to be constructed at the Philadelphia Naval Yard. In 1922, the Allies approved a plan to let the Zeppelin Company build an airship to replace the R-38. Soon a new airship base was completed at Lakehurst, New Jersey. The ZR-1

was completed in 1923 and christened *Shenandoah* (see fig. 14.5)

Meanwhile, the French were cautiously testing their war reparations LZ-72 Zeppelin, renamed the *Dixmude,* for use on long-range flights to French Africa. In December 1923, the ship left France with forty crewmembers and ten observers. The ship vanished. On 29 December, fishermen pulled up wreckage and then the body of the airship commander from the Mediterranean. This brought airship development in France to an end.

The United States continued to feel that rigid airships were needed, particularly in the Pacific. Adm. William Moffett, an outspoken proponent of the large rigids, pushed ahead, in spite of the deadly crash of the *Roma,* an Italian ship purchased by the U.S. Army. The ship was filled with hydrogen, yet helium, a safer but heavier gas, was available, although it was costly. The public insisted that future ships be filled with helium, and the *Shenandoah* was subsequently filled with the new gas.

A number of test flights were made by the *Shenandoah* under her new captain, Zachary Lansdowne, in 1924. After its last flight, the *Shenandoah* was joined by the new Zeppelin built in Germany for the United States. The ship was flown to the United States by Hugo Eckener, who had replaced Count Zeppelin as head of the Zeppelin Company. The ZR-3 (LZ-126) ship was named the *Los Angeles* and was a passenger-capable airship, rather than a luxurious airship, owned by the U.S. Navy. For the first flight in 1925, helium was transferred from the *Shenandoah,* in for repairs, to the ship, and it made several routine flights that year.

In June 1925, the helium was placed back in the *Shenandoah,* which then set off for a goodwill tour around the United States. Departing at sunset on 2 September 1925, the ship was caught in a vicious squall line near Ava, Ohio, and it crashed early in the morning of 3 September (see fig. 14.6). The ship broke apart, and all in the control car were killed, including Lansdowne. However, there were survivors in the bow and stern sections, which continued to be airborne for some time after the breakup. The loss of the ship and fourteen members of the crew caused Army Air Corps Gen. Billy Mitchell to write a seventeen-page press statement of criticism that ultimately contributed to his court-martial.[30]

The years from 1919 to 1925 had been costly ones for rigid airships and experienced aircrew. The *Los Angeles*

Fig. 14.5. U.S. Navy Airship ZR-1 *Shenandoah* flies over the Capitol in 1924. By permission of the National Air and Space Museum, Smithsonian Institution, ©1999 Smithsonian Institution.

Fig. 14.6. The wreck of the *Shenandoah* in September 1925. By permission of the National Air and Space Museum, Smithsonian Institution, ©1999 Smithsonian Institution.

was a worthy ship; however, it was often used moored to a surface ship, the fleet tender *Patoka*. Only this rigid ship remained, as the Zeppelin Company was not yet allowed to produce airships. Meanwhile, the airplane was making great strides, and the future looked bleak for the large airship.

One final achievement should be noted. Dreams of a polar flight by airship persisted, and Norwegian explorer Roald Amundsen, who had failed to reach the North Pole by aircraft, teamed with American Lincoln Ellsworth to purchase an Italian semirigid, the *Norge.* The ship was flown by the designer, Umberto Nobile, and it left Rome in April 1926. After leaving Spitsbergen Island in May, they flew over the pole on 12 May and landed on the ice 60 miles north of Point Barrow, Alaska. Nobile attempted a return trip in 1928 in the *Italia,* but the trip ended in disaster and eventual disgrace for Nobile in Mussolini's Italy. Unfortunately, Amundsen was lost when his aircraft disappeared on a search mission for the Italian crew.[31]

The Great Airships

Between 1927 and 1937, seven large rigid airships were constructed and flown. Three of the airships were built in Germany, which had been allowed by the Allies to resume aircraft production in 1926, two in England, and two in the United States. By 1937, four of the airships had suffered disastrous accidents with losses of experienced aircrew and influential airship proponents. England voluntarily destroyed her last rigid airship, and Germany destroyed the last two remaining airships in 1940. Although this was the last of the large airships, to date, these giants of the sky proved that international passenger flight was feasible, even flight around the world. By 1939, the airplane had begun to assume this role, which today they dominate.

The first of the large airships was begun in Germany by the Zeppelin Company as LZ-127, later named *Graf Zeppelin* in honor of the old count. Eckener and a number of volunteers toured Germany raising funds for construction of the ship, which was completed in 1928. The airship was the largest dirigible at that time, over 775 feet long and filled with 3.5 million cubic feet of gas. Powered by five Maybach engines, which ran on both fuel and a propane gas called "blaugas," the ship could cruise

at 75 miles per hour. The gondola featured a lounge/dining area and accommodations for twenty passengers in ten sleeping rooms.[32]

After only five trial flights, Eckener made the first of the airship's transatlantic voyages in October 1928. The flight was across the southern portion of the North Atlantic from Friedrichshafen to the U.S. Navy base at Lakehurst, New Jersey. The flight was successful, in spite of stormy conditions that caused minor damage. Although convinced of the structural integrity of the airship, Eckener felt it was not well suited for the North Atlantic run. The interest generated by the flight caused him to consider several publicity flights.

One of the most publicized tours was made when American William Randolph Hearst provided $100,000 for an around-the-world attempt. Hearst stipulated that the flight should begin in the United States. In August 1929, Eckener headed west in *Graf* to Lakenhurst, then flew to Germany with twenty-two passengers aboard. After five days in Germany, Eckener headed east with twenty passengers across the vast stretches of Russia and Siberia to Japan. The flight took 101 hours, and the crew and passengers were received with great fanfare in Japan.

After a five-day layover in Japan, *Graf* headed across the Pacific to Los Angeles, then across the United States to Lakehurst. The total flight time for the remarkable voyage had been 12 days, 11 minutes, which caused a sensation around the world. Plans were even started for American participation in a transoceanic airship airline, but the stock market crash two months later sank these plans.

Eckener then turned to other flights and found South America, a promising area due to the large number of German emigres there. *Graf* made the first trip to Brazil in May 1930, flying over southern France, the eastern coast of Spain, southwest through the Canary Islands, then to Recife. The last of the publicity flights came in July 1931, when the airship flew from Leningrad to the Arctic on a scientific exploration and charting mission. After 1931, the airship began regular flights to South America.

The early success of the *Graf* was closely watched in England, where the thought of rigid airship travel had been revived in 1924. Although many envisioned airship flights to the far-flung areas of the British Empire, the government cautiously approved construction of only two large rigid ships. One ship, the R-100, was to be constructed with private funds, and the other, the R-101, with government funds. The 709-foot R-100 was finished first and made the first flight in December 1929. After several trial flights, the R-100 made a highly successful demonstration flight across the North Atlantic to Canada in July 1930. The ship proved airworthy and made the trip to Montreal in only 79 hours with a return time of only 57 hours.

Meanwhile, the R-101 was having problems. Overweight, leaky, and well behind schedule, the airship's problems might have been cured with time, but the secretary of state for air, Lord Thomson, pushed hard for a scheduled flight to India. Finally, with an extra gas section added amidship and with questionable airworthiness certification, the airship left England on the evening of 4 October 1930. The overloaded airship struggled at a low altitude through adverse weather and strong headwinds over the coast of France. Early in the morning, 5 October, the airship could remain aloft no longer and came to earth near Beauvais, France.

Although the ship landed at slow speed, the gas bags ruptured and the ship exploded in flames. Of the fifty-four persons aboard, only six survived. Lost were Lord Thomson and the airship's commander, George Scott, who had flown R-34 across the Atlantic. The crash, which was the worst in British aviation history at that time, caused public mourning and an outcry to "ban the gas bags."[33] The airship program was soon abandoned, and the R-100 was dismantled and sold as scrap.

In the United States, the navy continued to press for construction of rigid airships for long-range patrol, particularly in the Pacific. Spearheaded by Admiral Moffett, the campaign was successful. In 1926, Congress authorized $8 million for construction of two rigid airships and an airship base in California. In 1928, the Navy contracted with the Goodyear-Zeppelin Corporation for the airships. The corporation had been formed in 1923 as the U.S. arm of the Zeppelin Company, and engineers had come from Germany to assist in the production.

A large, streamlined hangar was built at Akron, Ohio, and work was begun on the first airship, ZRS-4, in 1929. As launch time neared in 1931, the airship was christened the USS *Akron*. The 785-foot-long ship powered by eight inboard engines reached speeds of nearly 80 miles per hour. One unique feature of the new airship was a 70-by-58 foot hangar inside the hull. A retractable trapeze was used to launch and recover the three scout airplanes carried aboard.[34]

Initial flight of the *Akron* was in September 1931, and the airship flew throughout the United States for nearly two years, suffering several minor and two major mishaps (see fig. 14.7). The first serious mishap occurred when a fin was crushed on landing, and the second

Fig. 14.7. Navy Airship ZRS-4 *Akron*. By permission of the National Air and Space Museum, Smithsonian Institution, ©1999 Smithsonian Institution.

occurred when two ground handlers fell to their deaths after suddenly being lifted aloft. On the evening of 3 April 1933, the *Akron* departed on a training mission with Admiral Moffett aboard as an observer. The airship flew into a fierce storm near the coast of New Jersey and attempted to escape by heading east over the water. The *Akron* was soon caught in a violent downdraft, and it struck the water under full power and maximum up elevator. The airship broke apart and became a floating coffin for seventy-three of the seventy-six aboard, including Moffett.[35]

With the loss of the *Akron* and Admiral Moffett, public sentiment turned against further rigid airship development. However, the second airship, ZRS-5, later named the *Macon* (shown in fig. 14.8), had been completed only two weeks earlier. The new airship was assigned as a long-range patrol ship to operate out of the new facility in California, later named Moffett Field. The *Macon* continued training flights in 1933 and 1934. How-

ever, the airship was not judged highly effective, particularly since the navy now had aircraft carriers in service.

On 12 February 1935, the *Macon* was returning from training exercises and was near the coast at Point Sur, California. As the airship passed through rain, a sudden gust of wind struck. The upper vertical fin, which had been damaged on a previous flight and not completely repaired, separated from the ship and *Macon* was forced to ditch near the shore. Fortunately, the ditching had been observed from shore, and all but two of the crew were rescued. The loss of the *Macon* meant the end of the large airship program in the United States.[36]

Meanwhile, the *Graf*'s scheduled flights to South America had become almost routine in spite of several minor incidents. The success of the airship encouraged Eckener to build a larger dirigible, designed for the North Atlantic flight between Europe and the United States. The new airship, the LZ-129, later named the *Hindenburg*, was over 803 feet in length and held over seven

Fig. 14.8. Navy Airship ZRS-5 *Macon*. By permission of the National Air and Space Museum, Smithsonian Institution, ©1999 Smithsonian Institution.

million cubic feet of gas. With four new Daimler-Benz lightweight diesel engines, the airship could cruise at over 80 miles per hour for a range of 11,000 miles. Passengers would be carried inside the hull in luxurious accommodations that included a smoking lounge.[37]

The *Hindenburg* was begun in 1931; however, when the Nazi government came into power in 1933, completion seemed questionable. Dr. Joseph Goebbels, minister for propaganda in the new government, saw the value of the airship for public relations and provided funds to complete the project. Hugo Eckener was an outspoken critic of the Nazis, so the government formed a new corporation, Deutsche Zeppelin Reederi (German Zeppelin Airship Company), with Lufthansa as a majority partner. The corporation chose Ernst Lehmann, Eckener's assistant and a former Zeppelin captain in World War I, to be superintendent of flight and appointed Eckener to the limited position of chairperson of the board.

The new airship was completed in March 1936. Shortly after the maiden flight, Captain Lehmann took the ship on a publicity tour with *Graf* in support of Adolf Hitler's remilitarization plan. Eckener's strong protests led Goebbels to ban the use of his name or photograph in the German press. The airship had originally been designed to carry helium. However, the United States was reluctant to sell the scarce gas to a foreign power, so Eckener was forced to use hydrogen. He insisted on thorough training for the crew in safety precautions and understanding of the hazards of this lighter gas.

The first passenger flight of *Hindenburg* was to South America in March 1936. During the year, the airship made five additional trips to South America and ten trips across the North Atlantic to the United States. Eckener had secured landing rights at the navy base at Lakehurst from President Franklin Roosevelt. On all flights across the North Atlantic, the *Hindenburg* carried the maximum fifty passengers. The luxury and relative speed of the airship made it very popular on both sides of the Atlantic.

On all scheduled routes, the airships had begun to make a profit. The future of the corporation and commercial travel by dirigible looked very promising. Eckener had begun construction of two new airships, LZ-130 and LZ-131, designed to carry 100 and 150 passengers, respectively. At the beginning of 1937, *Graf* was

scheduled for twenty flights to South America, *Hindenburg* for eighteen trips to North America, and the new LZ-130 for a maiden run to South America.

Hindenburg's first flight to North America in 1937 was scheduled to leave the new Rhein-Main World Airport on 3 May. Veteran captain Max Pruss was in command as the giant airship gently lifted off with thirty-six passengers and a crew of sixty-one, including Ernst Lehmann. The flight was uneventful, almost dull, but the airship was delayed by weather and arrived at Lakehurst on the afternoon of 5 May, nearly 24 hours behind schedule. Pruss encountered unfavorable landing conditions and held for another 3 hours.

Finally, at about 7:20 P.M., *Hindenburg* began a landing approach. While the airship was still about 75 feet from the ground mooring mast, the stern suddenly lit up and burst into flame. The airship settled to the ground, completely ablaze. The shocking disaster, emotionally described as it happened by Chicago radio newscaster Herb Morrison, remained vivid in the minds of most people for years (see fig. 14.9).

Although sixty-three people escaped, thirty-six, including thirteen passengers and Ernst Lehmann, were killed. Eckener was later to write: "It appeared to me the hopeless end of a great dream, a kind of end of the world."[38]

Although sabotage was suspected as the cause of the disaster, the official inquiry concluded that St. Elmo's Fire, a type of static electricity, had somehow ignited leaking hydrogen. This conclusion has remained controversial, and many still believe the sabotage theory. Eckener vowed never to carry passengers again in a hydrogen-filled airship, and he appealed to the United States to release helium, which had become more plentiful. He was nearly successful, since the vision of *Hindenburg* was still fresh in the minds of Americans, but Hitler's invasion of Austria convinced President Roosevelt to deny the request in the interests of security.

The president may have been right in suspecting the German government's plans as the new airship, *Graf Zeppelin II*, was soon taken over by the Luftwaffe. The airship was used on electronic espionage flights over Czechoslovakia, Poland, the Netherlands, and near the coast of Great Britain. Fortunately, they did not detect the British RADAR, which proved decisive a short time later during the Battle of Britain.[39]

Fig. 14.9. Destruction of the *Hindenburg*. By permission of the National Air and Space Museum, Smithsonian Institution, ©1999 Smithsonian Institution.

In early 1940, Luftwaffe commander Hermann Goering ordered the destruction of the remaining two airships, *Graf I* and *Graf II*, and the metal frameworks used for aircraft construction. The airship hangar at Frankfurt was also removed as a hazard to aircraft operations. Although large dirigibles were not used after 1940, smaller manned blimps were successfully used by the U.S. Navy in World War II for Anti-Submarine Warfare operations. In all, over 50,000 flights were made, both in the Atlantic and Pacific Oceans. Blimps escorted nearly 90,000 surface vessels, and the record indicates that, with one possible exception, no vessels under escort were lost to submarine attack. The Navy continued to use blimps for Anti-Submarine and Airborne Early Warning operations until 1961. This ended the remarkable dream of Count Zeppelin, brought to reality only forty years earlier. Although many have dreamed of large airships utilizing modern technology, to date no large airship has been successfully flown. Lighter-than-air flight now consists of the increasingly popular hot air ballooning, with limited competitive flight in gas balloons and in nonrigid blimps, which are used for advertising and television broadcasting.

Notes

1. *Hot Air Balloons,* 1.

2. Payne, *Lighter than Air,* 3.

3. Jackson, *The Aeronauts,* 14.

4. Payne, 6, quoting from a letter written by d'Arlandes to a friend and published in *Harper's Monthly* in 1854.

5. Rolt, *The Aeronauts,* 45.

6. Aymar, *Men in the Air,* 88–95, contains the story of Dr. Jeffries's flights.

7. Rolt, 91. Evidently, Dyer and her friends tried to talk Rozier out of making the flight.

8. Jackson, 68. Donaldson piloted the balloon while the minister prayed that the couple would be "lifted above the adversities of life." The balloon was named *P. T. Barnum.*

9. Glines, *Lighter-than-Air Flight,* 34. Also referenced in Payne.

10. Rolt, 152. Also referenced in Jackson.

11. Jackson, 76. He referred to them as "mechanical meteors" and remarked, "Men often used their talents for the destruction of fellow creatures."

12. Glines, 113. A Confederate balloon even ascended from the deck of the CSS *Teaser,* making it the first and only Confederate naval aviation.

13. Jackson, 92, and Glines, 122. Only eight balloons were lost; six fell into German hands, and two were lost at sea.

14. Glines, 128, and Payne, 18. Glines indicates that the balloon did direct artillery fire against the enemy.

15. Aymar, 262–68, contains an article on Luke's "balloon busting" published in the *Air Force Digest* in 1955.

16. Gurney, *The War in the Air,* 187. The winged flying bombs were vulnerable on their glide into the target area, and many were lost to aircraft and antiaircraft as well.

17. "Japan Bombed Oregon 50 Years Ago"; "300 Bombs May Still Be in U.S."

18. Payne, 268. Evidently Prather was wearing a space suit designed for the Mercury program that failed and filled with water.

19. Payne, 277.

20. Botting, *The Giant Airships,* 20. Johnson was referring to free balloons.

21. Rolt, 226. The course was from the St. Cloud Aero Club grounds around the Eiffel Tower and return.

22. Payne, 35. Payne quotes several passages from Santos-Dumont's book *From My Airships,* published in 1904.

23. Payne, 35. Santos-Dumont's first heavier-than-air flight was on 23 October 1906.

24. Payne, 57. Count Zeppelin originally envisioned wings to be used for takeoff and landing.

25. Clarke, *The History of Airships,* 51, and numerous other references. The count wrote a thank-you letter to the German people that was widely published.

26. Botting, 20. Payne, 57, puts the total number of passengers carried at 37,500, and Clarke at 35,000.

27. Pratt, *Commercial Airships,* 15, 16. The name evidently was taken from the sound the vehicle made when "thumped" to check for proper gas fill.

28. Botting, *The Giant Airships,* 58. He described reactions while observing the bombing from Fleet Street.

29. Pratt, 218.

30. Aymar, 131–40, is an account of the accident by C. E. Rosendahl, a survivor. Toland, *The Great Dirigibles,* has a chapter entitled "Daughter of the Stars" explaining the accident. Althoff, *Sky Ships,* also has a chapter on the *Shenandoah.*

31. Toland devotes two chapters to the *Italia* and the fate of its crew. The loss of Amundsen is mentioned on 210.

32. Dick and Robinson, *Graf Zeppelin and Hindenburg,* 170. Dick was a Goodyear-Zeppelin employee who was sent to Germany as a liaison with Zeppelin Airship Company. He was a friend of Hugo Eckener and helped with design engineering on the *Hindenburg.* He also flew on both ships, and his book contains numerous details on airship procedures, flight routines, engineering specifications, and the like.

33. Botting, *The Giant Airships,* 140.

34. Althoff, 88. Actually, the *Akron* could store five aircraft. Initial experiments with the trapeze were conducted on the *Los Angeles.* The aircraft finally used was the F-9C *Sparrowhawk.*

35. Glines, 200.

36. Vaeth, "USS *Macon,*" 117. The last pilot to "hook on" to the *Macon* was Lt. Comdr. Harold Miller, who was aboard at the time of the crash.

37. Botting, 150. The smoking lounge was sealed off from the rest of the ship, and the only lighter allowed was chained to the wall.

38. Payne, 231. Quotations are from a translation of Hugo Eckener's book, *My Zeppelins.*

39. Dick and Robinson, 170.

References

Althoff, William F. *Sky Ships: A History of the Airship in the U.S. Navy.* Pacifica, Calif.: Pacifica Press, 1994.

Aymar, Brandt, ed. *Men in the Air.* New York: Crown, 1990.

Botting, Douglas. *The Giant Airships.* Alexandria, Va.: Time-Life Books, 1980.

Boyne, Walter J. *The Smithsonian Book of Flight.* Washington, D.C.: Smithsonian Books, 1987.

Clarke, Basil. *The History of Airships.* New York: St. Martin's Press, 1964.

Collier, Basil. *The Airship.* New York: G. P. Putnam, 1974.

Dick, Harold G., and Douglas H. Robinson. *Graf Zeppelin and Hindenburg.* Washington, D.C.: Smithsonian Institution Press, 1985.

Dollfus, Charles. *Orion Book of Balloons.* New York: Orion Press, 1961.

Eckener, Hugo. *My Zeppelins.* Trans. Douglas Robinson. 1958. New York: Arno Press, 1980.

Glines, Carroll V., ed. *Lighter-than-Air Flight.* New York: Franklin Watts, 1965.

Gurney, Gene. *The War in the Air.* New York: Crown, 1962.

Hot Air Balloons. Kansas City, Mo.: Terrell, 1988.

Howard, Frank, and Bill Gunston. *The Conquest of the Air.* New York: Random House, 1972.

Jackson, Donald Dale. *The Aeronauts.* Alexandria, Va.: Time-Life Books, 1980.

"Japan Bombed Oregon 50 Years Ago." *Kansas City Star,* 6 September 1992.

Josephy, Alvin M., Jr., ed. *The American Heritage Book of Flight.* New York: American Heritage, 1962.

Kincaid, Tim. "Airships to Spaceships." *Air and Space/ Smithsonian* 10 (February–March 1996): 100.

Loening, Grover. *Takeoff into Greatness.* New York: G. P. Putnam, 1968.

Mondey, David, ed. *International Encyclopedia of Aviation.* New York: Crown, 1977.

Moolman, Valerie. *Women Aloft.* Alexandria, Va.: Time-Life Books, 1981.

Mooney, Michael M. *The Hindenburg.* New York: Dodd, Mead, 1972.

Nowarra, Heinz J. *German Airships.* West Chester, Pa.: Schiffer, 1990.

Payne, Lee. *Lighter than Air.* Rev. ed. New York: Orion Books, 1991.

Pratt, H. B. *Commercial Airships.* London: Thomas Nelson, 1920.

Rolt, L. T. C. *The Aeronauts.* New York: Walker, 1966.

Scamehorn, H. Lee. *Balloons to Jets.* Chicago: Henry Regnery, 1957; reprint, Carbondale: Southern Illinois University Press, 2000.

Schuessler, Raymond. "Attack on America by Balloon." *Modern Maturity,* February–March 1985.

Shiner, Linda. "Fierce to Win." *Air and Space/Smithsonian* 8 (February–March 1994): 52–63.

Taylor, Michael J. H., and David Mondey. *Milestones of Flight.* London: Jane's, 1983.

"300 Bombs May Still Be in U.S." *Kansas City Star,* 26 November 1984.

Toland, John. *The Great Dirigibles.* New York: Dover, 1972.

Vaeth, J. Gordon. "USS *Macon:* Lost and Found." *National Geographic,* January 1992, 114–27.

15

African American Pioneers in Aviation

Isaac Richmond Nettey

Early Developments in Africa

Ancient Archaeological Discoveries

Renowned archaeologists and anthropologists have traced the origins of humanity to the continent of Africa.[1] After several decades of work in Kenya, the British-born archaeologist and anthropologist Louis Seymour Bazatt Leakey and his son, Richard Leakey, an anthropologist and paleontologist, traced the first human beings to eastern Africa.[2] Other scientists also credit Africa with the first machine, a rudimentary water pump invented along the banks of the Nile.

Another staggering discovery was made in the nineteenth century at Sakkarah (also spelled Saqqarah) and officially registered at a museum in Cairo in 1898.[3] The said discovery was a 2,300-year-old model of a flying machine that had been invented by a man named Pa-di-Imen, which literally means "Gift of Amon."[4] Amon was the name of an ancient African deity from southern Egypt.

Pa-di-Imen's model was a monoplane fashioned out of sycamore wood with a wing span of exactly 18 cm and a length of exactly 14 cm.[5] The model weighed 39.120 grams and boasted tapered leading edge wings with dihedral. The dihedral is uneven in both wings. One wing tip dips 15 mm below the upper surface of its wing root, and the other dips 10 mm. The 5 mm difference in dihedral may be the result of a slight distortion in the wood caused by the passage of centuries. The fuselage displays a beautifully carved and smooth airfoil shape with a 3 cm wide rectangular groove to serve as a point of attach-

ment for the wing. The fuselage also supports an upright tail or a vertical fin 3 cm in height.[6] The aerodynamic features of Pa-di-Imen's model are quite revolutionary and sophisticated (see figs. 15.1 and 15.2). Some of those features took several decades of serious research and dramatic discoveries to become inculcated into modern aircraft design. Discovery of the same aerodynamic features may have been the result of considerable research and several experimental trials by Pa-di-Imen.[7] The realization that such advanced concepts of aeronautical technology were available in ancient Egypt some four thousand years ago is stupendous.

Pa-di-Imen's model was clearly the discovery of an ancient invention dating back to the fourth or third century B.C.[8] Unfortunately, there were no airplanes in 1898, the year of its discovery. Neither *airplane* nor *aeroplane* was part of English vocabulary in 1898. No European language, including French, had a comparable word or concept in 1898. As stated in the early chapters of this book, knowledge about gliders and aeronautics in gen-

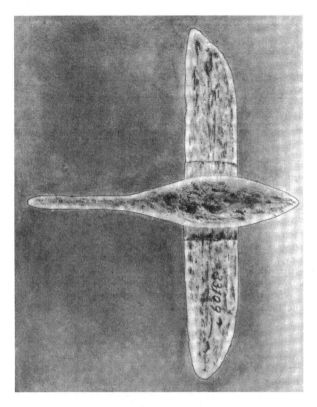

Fig. 15.1. An ancient model flying machine discovered in Africa in 1898. Dated back to fourth or third century B.C., it is the earliest known model of an airplane. Courtesy of NASA.

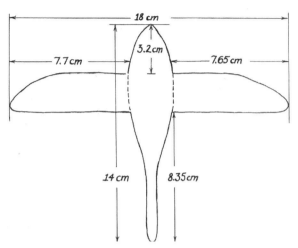

Fig. 15.2. Sketch of an ancient airplane model discovered in Africa. Courtesy of NASA.

eral was scarce and rudimentary at best. In 1898, such knowledge was rather limited to a few maverick experimenters. Naturally, the discoverers of this ancient model of a flying machine in 1898 could not have known what they had found. They did the logical thing, however. The flying machine model was cataloged as number 6347 and stored in room 22 of the museum with models of birds in a glass box.[9] As a result of limited knowledge, this ancient model of a flying machine was classified with models of birds.

Pa-di-Imen's flying machine model remained with the birds until 1969, when it was rediscovered by Dr. Khalil Messiha.[10] The anomaly of a vertical fin on the model of a bird was fascinating yet incredulous. Birds have horizontal tails, not vertical fins. The presence of a vertical fin led to further examination and subsequent classification of the model as an airplane model. Dr. Khalil Messiha is convinced that this model is a scaled-down version of a much larger airplane model. Egyptian engi-

neers living in the period during which the model was built had a tendency to build small models of larger contraptions.[11] The discovery of the full-size replica of this airplane model may still lie in the future. Discovery of the full-size glider will give aviators a major opportunity to conduct detailed studies into the science and history of these ancient African aviators.

Ancient African Myths about Flight

Centuries after construction of Pa-di-Imen's airplane model, flight-related activity on the African continent took on a more metaphysical quality. Unfortunately, much of the flight activity in this later era was neither documented nor scientifically preserved. Very little was preserved outside of well-built structures or sheltered works of art and artifacts. Natural calamities, wars, and migration made survival paramount in the daily lives of most people. Much of what could be classified as flight activity in Africa during this era was shrouded in mystery and metaphysical intrigue. Mystery and metaphysical intrigue do not lend themselves well to scientific analyses or scrutiny. At present there may be no scientific evidence that bears useful testimony to flight activity on the African continent in the post Pa-di-Imen era.

In the absence of documentary evidence or other artifacts, flight activity since the third century B.C. has been handed down through another paradigm, namely, myths and legends. Oral history plays a significant role in the transmission of history and culture across generations in traditional cultures. It is therefore to oral history that we turn for information, albeit unscientific, about flight activity in Africa during this period. The most notable story is that of Kibaga,[12] the legendary African chieftain whose feats of invincible flight have been documented in chapter 1.

Early Airline Service in Africa

Aviation appears to have quietly entered into another phase of its development after Orville Wright's historic flight on 17 December 1903 at Kitty Hawk; the airplane started a definitive march, albeit in ignominy, to launch aviation as a viable means of transportation. Today, the airplane clearly dominates air transportation. Airplanes have also demonstrated the potential of becoming the dominant mode of transportation for long-distance travel. In the United States, the airplane has already replaced trains and buses as the leading mode of transportation for long-distance travel over 200 miles.

Airlines were established in Africa for similar reasons that rail had been established in the preceding century, specifically, to provide local service. Initial airline service in colonial Africa was started on 1 July 1920 by LARA (Ligne Aerienne du Roi Albert), the Congo network of what ultimately became Belgium's national airline, SABENA. LARA's original service was provided with three-seater Levy Lepen hydroplanes between Kinshasa and N'Gombe, a distance of over 350 miles in the former Belgian Congo, now Zaire.[13] In colonial Africa, Great Britain sponsored most of the early airline development effort, which focused primarily on local service. Trunk service over long-haul routes were provided by Imperial Airways Ltd., which had been established by the merger of four other airlines on 31 March 1924.[14] Most of the early airline services used aircraft made of wood and fabric built by the De Havilland Company in Britain.

Credit for the earliest documented efforts by indigenous Africans to provide organized air transportation services is given to Ethiopia, which started an airline as early as 1929.[15] This accomplishment is unique for an African nation because in 1929 airline service was still embryonic even in the United States. It is also remarkable to note that with the exception of a six-year occupation by Italy between 1935 and 1941, Ethiopia remained free of European colonization.[16] Ethiopia was thus able to successfully establish and operate an airline in Africa

free of European control long before colonization officially waned on the African continent. Ethiopia's success in establishing and operating an indigenous national airline was an isolated accomplishment in Africa.

Developments in the United States

Early Black Aviators

Among persons of the African Diaspora, African Americans have made the most laudable accomplishments in aviation. Most were made despite a hostile environment created and fostered by racial hatred and prejudice. This general sentiment was summed up by the experienced aviator Kenneth Brown Collings when he erroneously asserted that "Negroes cannot fly—even the bureau of Air Commerce admits that."[17] The racially jaundiced atmosphere was not helped much when Charles Lindbergh weighed in that aviation was "specially shaped for Western hands, a scientific art which others only copy in a mediocre fashion . . . one of those priceless possessions which permit the White race to live at all in a pressing sea of Yellow, Black and Brown."[18] Incredibly, Lindbergh cast further aspersions on the intellectual capability of African Americans in aviation by condescendingly recounting his alleged encounter with an elderly lady in rural Mississippi during his barnstorming days in the early 1920s. He claimed that the lady asked, "Boss! How much you all charge foah take me up to Heaben and leave me deah?"[19] In a paradoxical irony quite typical of racial prejudice, Lindbergh sometimes relied on an African American aviator, Frank Hammond, to pack his parachute at a time when most pilots seldom entrusted that sacred task to anyone but themselves. Hammond, a 1905 native of Carrol County, Maryland, reportedly entered the history books himself in 1931 when he successfully completed thirteen parachute jumps in one day.[20]

In spite of the indignities and obstacles, which are too numerous to mention, several African Americans still managed to excel in aviation, albeit in anonymity from mainstream society. "Their accomplishments were principally heralded in black newspapers and magazines."[21] The epochal accomplishments of African Americans in aviation actually preceded the Wright brothers and transcended gender, which was atypical in aviation, and encompassed various facets of aviation. The areas of endeavor included aerostats, parachuting, aircraft design, aerobatics, cross-country flying, and military aviation.

As early as 1899, John J. Pickering, of Gonaives, Haiti, applied for a patent from the U.S. Patent Office for his design of a motorized, steerable balloon.[22] In 1900, Mary Doughtry was reported to have performed as a parachutist before a crowd in New Orleans by jumping from an aerostat, perhaps a balloon.[23] Aerostats had enjoyed a special place in French culture dating back to the Montgolfiers in 1782. Flight demonstrations by aviators in balloons had also enjoyed some popularity in France over two centuries. New Orleans, being the premier French city in the United States, was an ideal venue for Doughtry's aerobatic feats.

Six years later, an obscure laborer simply known as Jackson performed exhilarating stunts with parachute jumps from a balloon during Fourth of July festivities in Pittsburgh.[24] To properly complement his daredevil image, Jackson eventually took on the pseudonym Ajax Montmorency. Paul Lawrence Dunbar worked as an assistant for the Wright brothers in their bicycle shop in Dayton, Ohio. It is believed that Dunbar played an important role in the Wrights' experimental work in aviation.[25] Unfortunately, his accomplishments remained unknown for decades until he was praised by Thomas C. Allen, one of the "Flying Hobos," during a preview of the exhibition "Black Wings" at the Smithsonian in 1982.

Charles Wesley Peters

In 1889, Charles Wesley Peters of Pittsburgh was born. By age fourteen, he had built several kites and gliders, one of which he managed to fly in 1906.[26] To his credit, he also built a monoplane with a 40-foot wingspan that was powered by an air-cooled engine. He completed ten flights in his airplane before it was destroyed in a fire.[27] Peters's aeronautical successes resulted in an invitation to participate in the Georgia State Colored Fair at Macon in 1911 under special billing that read "For the First Time in the History of Fairs a Colored Man Goes Up in a Air Ship—Everybody Should See It." Enthusiasm over Peters's performance ran so high that 9 November 1911 was proclaimed "Airship Day. Colored Aviator."[28] Regrettably, misunderstandings over monetary matters between the fair's organizers and Peters precluded his participation, and a white aviator performed in his stead.[29]

Pioneering Inventors

At age twenty-one, Walter Swagerty of Los Angeles claimed to have invented a heavier-than-air machine in 1911.[30] His feat was followed by James Marshall of New York City, Walter G. Madison of Ames, Iowa, and James Smith of Oakland, California, who received patents for flying machines in 1912.[31] In 1914, they were followed by John E. McWhorter of St. Louis, who was reported in the alphabetical list of inventions as the inventor of an aeroplane.[32] There are no records of successful flights accomplished in any of these patented aircraft. Invention and development of these aircraft are, however, an eloquent testimony to the technological advancement of African Americans and their level of interest in aviation in the early 1900s.

It is even more impressive to consider the accomplishments of Lucian Arthur Hayden of North Carolina, who performed aerial demonstrations during tours throughout the South in 1912 and acquired a French pilot's license in 1913.[33] As an inventor he developed an aeronautical "equalizer" or "stabilizer," which he marketed overseas after the U.S. government declined an offer to adopt it. The British, however, adopted Hayden's "equalizer" or "stabilizer" and used it during World War I.[34] Hayden, who is sometimes referred to as Lucian Headin, was reportedly commissioned as a second lieutenant in the Royal Flying Corps by the British.[35]

Eugene Jacques Bullard

Another African American pioneer who served in a European military flying corps was Eugene Jacques Bullard (see fig. 15.3), dubbed the "Black Swallow of Death" by the French. Bullard was born of a father from the French island of Martinique into a poor family in Columbus, Georgia, in 1894. Buoyed by his father's elegant stories of a France free of crippling racial prejudice, Bullard stowed away on a ship to Scotland and ultimately made it to France, where he earned a living as a prize fighter before joining the French foreign legion during World War I. Bullard initially fought as an infantryman on the western front and was severely wounded at Verdun.[36] For his efforts, he won the croix de guerre.[37] He transferred either to the Lafayette Flying Corps or perhaps the French Aviation Service (the record is not specific) on 30 November 1916.[38]

Fig. 15.3. Eugene Jacques Bullard, World War I pilot with the French Aviation Service. Courtesy of the U.S. Air Force.

In August 1917, Bullard completed training as a chase pilot, the precursor of today's fighter pilot and resumed active duty as a pilot on the front. Within a week, Bullard shot down two German aircraft, becoming the first African American military aviator with recorded combat kills.[39] Bullard's heroics in air combat earned him the French appellation Black Swallow of Death. But his application to join the U.S. Army Air Service was rejected when the United States entered World War I.[40] After the war, Bullard remained in Paris and married Marcelle Straumann on 17 July 1923 at the mayoralty of the tenth arrondissement.[41] Bullard operated two nightclubs and a gym and managed to prevail through a series of slanderous controversies, altercations, and lawsuits. In addition to his services in combat, Bullard served as a French spy during World War II.

In recognition of his services, Bullard received fifteen medals from the French, but he received no recognition from the U.S. government during his lifetime. On 9 Oc-

tober 1959, he became a Chevalier of the Legion of Honor of France at what Eleanor Roosevelt called "a very interesting little ceremony" at the Consulate General of France in New York.[42] The New York Times ran Bullard's obituary on 21 October 1961. Unlike other African American aviators of his time, Bullard's accomplishments and competence as an aviation pioneer are well documented. In April 1989, Bullard became one of seven aviators to be honored in the Georgia Aviation Hall of Fame at the Museum of Aviation, Robins Air Force Base.[43] Bullard's photographs and the fifteen medals he earned from France were prominently exhibited at the Air Force Museum near Dayton.[44] In a private ceremony on 14 October 1992, the National Air and Space Museum added to Bullard's posthumous honors in the United States by unveiling a portrait bust of him during a ceremony attended by Gen. Benjamin O. Davis.[45]

Bessie Coleman

The successes and accomplishments of Bessie Coleman (see fig. 15.4) are presented in greater detail in chapter 16 with other distinguished female aviators, or aviatrixes. Coleman, the twelfth child in a poor family of thirteen children,[46] was born on 26 January 1892 in Atlanta, Texas, from where her family moved to Waxahachie. After completing eighth grade and a short stint as a laundress, she saved enough money to see herself through one semester at the Colored Agricultural and Normal University in Langston, Oklahoma. Coleman's determination to escape poverty and constant terror from the Klan in rural Waxahachie propelled her to join her two brothers in Chicago in 1915.[47]

In Chicago Coleman worked as a manicurist and operated a chili parlor while securing help from such leaders in the African American community as John Abbott,[48] publisher of the *Black Defender,* and Jessie Binga, proprietor of Binga State Bank, to pursue her dream of becoming a pilot. At Abbott's suggestion, Coleman studied French and sailed for France where she learned how to fly at the Caudron School of Aviation at Le Crotoy. On 15 June 1921, she obtained pilot license number 18.310 from the Federation Aeronautique Internationale (FAI) —five years before the U.S. government started licensing pilots.[49] Coleman returned triumphantly to New York in September 1921 but could secure no employment in aviation.[50] She therefore returned to France in 1922 to learn aerobatics in preparation for a career as a barnstormer in the United States. Her debut performance as the "Black Joan of Arc" was held on Labor Day in 1922 at Curtiss Field in Long Island.[51] After her debut, she returned to perform at Checkerboard Field in Chicago. Coleman also performed throughout the South, including Houston, where she successfully insisted on common access for both blacks and whites attending her air show.

Bessie Coleman was successful in gaining a movie contract due to the growing popularity of aviation in the movie industry. But she refused to play demeaning stereotypical roles. Leaving Hollywood with a newly purchased Jenny, she crashed outside Santa Monica when her motor failed. Her leg and ribs were fractured.[52] After recovering, she returned to the barnstorming and lecture circuit in an effort to ultimately raise money to establish a flight school for African Americans. However, tragedy struck Coleman during flight rehearsals on 30 April 1926 in Jacksonville, Florida. Her plane overturned and plunged her 2,000 feet to her death at age thirty-three. The same accident killed her mechanic, Willie

Wills. The wrecked airplane was set ablaze by the lit cigarette of a bystander. Irregularities about the flight caused suspicions about the cause of Coleman's accident.[53] Coleman was laid to rest in Lincoln Cemetery in Chicago where admiring aviators commemorate her legacy by dropping flowers onto her grave.[54]

Bessie Coleman's dream of establishing a school was realized in 1926 when Lt. William J. Powell founded the Bessie Coleman Aero Clubs in Los Angeles.[55] Coleman has since been honored by both female aviation groups and African American aviators. Her energetic commitment to promoting aviation, coupled with her flamboyance and charm, greatly endeared her to the African American community.

Cross-Country Flights and "The Flying Hobos"

As the age of the barnstormer gradually waned halfway through the Roaring Twenties, the urge to set distance records increased significantly. *Opportunity,* a monthly magazine published by the National Urban League, reported that Samuel V. B. Sauzereseteo had flown from Moscow to Berlin, from Belgium to the Congo, and from Paris to London.[56] Sauzereseteo, also known as Sargusetsio, claimed to have made his flight from Moscow to Berlin on 25 June 1925.[57]

In February 1927, Joel "Ace" Foreman and Artis Ward, his mechanic, set off from Los Angeles for New York in an attempt to become the first African Americans to complete a transcontinental flight. They were sponsored by the *California Eagle* and the Los Angeles chapter of NAACP. Unfortunately, their slightly dilapidated Curtiss JN-4 "Jenny" suffered an engine malfunction that kept them in Salt Lake City for several weeks. Another valiant attempt brought them only as far as Chicago.[58]

To bridge international borders and foster the growth of aviation among the African American and Afro Caribbean communities, the International Colored Aeronautical Association sponsored a flight by Leon Paris from New York City to his native Haiti in 1932.[59] Accompanying Paris was John W. Greene, who received his private pilot's license in June 1929 and earned the commercial pilot's license as well as certification as an airframe and power plant mechanic by 1937.[60] Records of the result or accomplishments of this flight are scanty at best. As an international effort, it appeared to be a precursor to the Pan American Goodwill Flights by Dr. Albert E. Forsythe and C. Alfred "Chief" Anderson.

Fig. 15.4. Bessie Coleman. Courtesy of the Ninety-Nines, Inc.

The title for the first transcontinental flight by African Americans belongs to J. Herman Banning and his mechanic, Thomas C. Allen, dubbed the "Flying Hobos" (see fig. 15.5).[61] Banning, born in 1900, grew up in Oklahoma but attended an aviation school in Chicago after studying engineering for two years at Iowa State University in Ames. No aviation school in Chicago would admit him in the early 1920s because of his race. Banning persevered and moved to Des Moines, where he received flight training from Army Lt. Raymond Fischer. Banning moved to California and became one of the first to receive a pilot's certificate in 1927[62] from the newly established Bureau of Air Commerce. Allen, who was born in 1907, had his first exposure to aviation at age nine when he was sent to protect a crashed airplane from the ravenous cows on his family's farm in Texas.[63]

With a used aircraft and less than a hundred dollars for expenses,[64] Allen and Banning set off on 21 September 1932 from Dyer Airport in California for Valley Stream Airport in New York.[65] After several stops for repairs on the open cockpit biplane, they completed their transcontinental flight on 9 October 1932 with a flight time of 41 hours, 27 minutes over 18 days.[66] Banning and Allen received a rousing welcome from the African American community in New York.[67] Their celebration was short-lived, however. Banning died in a plane crash on 5 February 1933.[68] Allen continued his work in aviation until he passed away on 12 September 1989.[69] After Bessie Coleman's death in 1926, Banning and Allen's transcontinental flight in 1932 greatly boosted interest in aviation among African Americans.

Other transcontinental efforts with laudable accomplishments were made by the team of Dr. Albert E. Forsythe and C. Alfred "Chief" Anderson. Forsythe was

Fig. 15.5. Publicity poster for J. Herman Banning and Thomas C. Allen's transcontinental flight, the first by African Americans. Courtesy of the USAF Museum.

born in 1898 in the Bahamas and raised in Jamaica.[70] He migrated to the United States, where he paired up with Anderson, who was born on 9 February 1907 in Bridgeport, Pennsylvania.[71] To acquire flight training, Chief Anderson had to purchase his own aircraft, since he was refused flight instruction in aircraft owned by whites. With his own airplane, Anderson became the first African American to be qualified as an air transport pilot.[72] Together, Anderson and Forsythe flew the first round-trip transcontinental flight by African Americans from Bader Field in Atlantic City on 17 July 1933 to Los Angeles with a successful return trip in September.[73] Upon their return from Los Angeles, there was a welcoming throng of 1,000 well-wishers. A few months later, Anderson and Forsythe completed another flight to Montreal (see fig. 15.6).[74]

To mark the centennial anniversary of the emancipation of the West Indies, Anderson and Forsythe embarked on a Pan American Goodwill Flight in their newly christened aircraft, *Booker T. Washington*.[75] Unfortunately, the Pan American Goodwill Flight, which had initially enjoyed considerable success hopping islands in the Caribbean, ended with a crash in Port-au-Spain, Trinidad. Upon returning to the United States, Chief Anderson utilized his experience as an aviator before becoming the chief flight instructor at Tuskegee. Chief Anderson passed away on 13 April 1996 at Tuskegee after a long bout with cancer. Dr. Forsythe practiced medicine until 1977. He died in Newark, New Jersey, on 6 May 1986.[76]

Of the early aviators, few if any were more colorful than Hubert Fauntleroy Julian. Born in 1897 in Trinidad,[77] Julian was undeterred by the death of the pilot at his first air show at age twelve. Julian immigrated to the United States around 1921 by way of Canada, where his patented air safety devices had reportedly fetched an offer of $300,000 from the Curtiss Company and $150,000 from the Gerni Aeroplane Company of Montreal while he was a student at McGill University.[78] He settled in New York City as a parachutist and pilot. Known as the "Black Eagle" of Harlem, he became a close associate of his Afro Caribbean compatriot, Jah Jah

Fig. 15.6. Tuskegee Institute president R. R. Moton (*far left*) and his wife pose with C. Alfred Anderson (*holding bouquet*) and Albert E. Forsythe in front of the airplane Mrs. Moton christened the *Booker T. Washington*, 14 September 1934. Courtesy of the Tuskegee University Archives.

Marcus Garvey. Marcus Garvey came to the United States in 1916 and became a champion of black pride and a "back to Africa" movement that operated under the umbrella of the Universal Negro Improvement Association (UNIA).[79] In August 1922, Julian was named head of the "Black Eagle Flying Club," the aeronautical arm of UNIA.[80]

On Independence Day 1924, Julian set off from Long Island on a publicly funded transatlantic flight from New York to Liberia.[81] Unfortunately, he crashed before the throng of well-wishers and spectators who had funded and come to witness this historic flight.[82] Julian's subsequent attempts at transatlantic flights in 1926 and 1928 proved unsuccessful. Julian performed in several air shows as a parachutist with Clarence Chamberlain. In response to derogatory remarks about Negroes made by Hermann Goering, head of Nazi Germany's Luftwaffe, Julian boldly challenged him to aerial combat over the English Channel.[83] Goering did not respond to the Black Eagle's challenge.

After serving in the Italo-Ethiopian War of 1935, Julian returned to the United States with the rank of colonel in the Ethiopian air force. Julian's service in Ethiopia is reported to have ended on a sour note after he damaged the airplane reserved for the coronation festivities of Emperor Ras Tafari.[84] When Sir Offori Atta, a paramount chief of Ghana, was knighted by King George, Julian visited him and gave him some pointers on aviation, primarily for publicity purposes.[85] The Black Eagle traveled extensively to several troubled parts of the world for sundry purposes, including sale of arms. Throughout his colorful career, Julian received a mixed bag of press coverage in several news publications before his death at Veterans Hospital in the Bronx.[86]

Unlike Hubert F. Julian, John C. Robinson gained considerable fame for his service in the Ethiopian air force. Robinson, from Gulfport, Mississippi, arrived in Addis Ababa, the capital of Ethiopia, on 29 May 1935 to serve as a commissioned officer in the Ethiopian air force.[87] Four years before his journey to Ethiopia, Robinson became the first African American to graduate from the Curtiss-Wright School in Chicago after attending Tuskegee Institute in Alabama. In June 1935, Joe Louis, who became known as the "Brown Bomber," had knocked out Italian boxer Primo Carnera in the sixth round to win the world heavyweight title. Hoping for a similar feat in military aviation, black correspondents dubbed John C. Robinson the "Brown Condor." John C. Robinson was not Joe Louis, Carnera was not Mussolini, and Ethiopia's small air force was no match for the Italian air force. In spite of Robinson's success in destroying two Italian fighter planes,[88] there was not much of a contest.

The Brown Condor primarily flew courier missions and served as the personal pilot of Haile Selassie.[89] On 5 May 1936, Italian forces captured Addis Ababa, and Ethiopia fell.[90] Robinson attributed Ethiopia's rapid fall to tribal insurrection instigated by Ras Hailu.[91] Benito Mussolini thus managed to partially avenge Italy's ignominious defeat by Ethiopia under Emperor Menelik II in 1896 at Adowa.

Notwithstanding Ethiopia's fall, Robinson received a rousing hero's welcome from the African American community, especially in New York and Chicago where he was feted by thousands of admirers.[92]

Much of the publicity on his return was carefully orchestrated by his alma mater, Tuskegee Institute, with the anticipation that he would establish an aviation program there to train African Americans.[93] Unfortunately, Robinson declined to go to Tuskegee, citing misunderstandings about financial matters, control over funds raised in his name to purchase airplanes for Tuskegee, and terms of his contract. After his anticlimactic refusal to go to Tuskegee, he established the John C. Robinson National Air College and School of Automotive Engineering in Chicago on 28 September 1936.[94] Subsequent attempts by Robinson to transfer his school and equipment from Chicago to Tuskegee Institute failed.[95] He died after a plane crash and was buried with high military honors in Addis Ababa.[96]

Early Flying Clubs

To foster the growth of aviation among African Americans, considerable efforts were made to establish flying clubs. Records indicate the existence of an African American aviation club in Los Angeles as early as 1921.[97] After an initial attempt by Hubert Julian to establish an aviation arm of Marcus Garvey's UNIA in 1922, the Black Eagle of Harlem announced the formation of the National Association for the Advancement of Aviation Among the Colored Races in 1929.[98] In the fall of 1929, the Universal Aviation Association organized the first air show for African American aviators at Yackey Checkerboard Field in Maywood, near Chicago. Participating

Fig. 15.7. Heavyweight boxing champion Joe Louis *(second from left)* and his wife visiting William Powell at the Bessie Coleman Aero Club Workshop in Los Angeles. Courtesy of the USAF Museum.

were Louis Melgoza, Ira V. Evans, Eugene White, Robert Miller, Charles Watkins, and W. C. Mareno of Chicago and Dr. A. Porter Davis, who flew his own airplane from Kansas City, Missouri.[99]

Bessie Coleman Aero Clubs

Few in the African American community did more to promote the growth of aviation than William J. Powell, who moved from Chicago to Los Angeles where he established the Bessie Coleman Aero Clubs. To encourage "airmindedness" in the African American community, the Bessie Coleman Aero Clubs sponsored an air show by African American aviators on Labor Day 1931 that was attended by 15,000 spectators.[100] Powell also established a school in Los Angeles to train mechanics and pilots through the government's emergency education program.[101] In 1934, Powell published *Black Wings,* in which he expressed considerable optimism about professional opportunities in aviation for African Americans and issued the challenge "to fill the air with black wings." It is of considerable historical importance that soon after Powell issued this challenge, the Air Line Pilots Association officially restricted its membership to whites only.[102] As part of his efforts to promote aviation in the African American community, Powell hosted visits by Joe Louis and Oscar De Priest, the first African American congressman after reconstruction (see fig. 15.7).

To create jobs for African Americans in aviation, Powell organized Craftsmen of Black Wings in New York and Los Angeles. In addition to the *Bessie Coleman Aero News,* Powell also published the *Craftsmen Aero News,* which he claimed to be the first African American trade journal. Powell, like Dr. Forsythe and Chief Anderson, believed that the sight of African Americans flying airplanes would eliminate racial prejudice. In 1929, Powell and J. Herman Banning were forced down after running out of fuel during a flight in southern California.[103] They wandered for four days without food and little water before being held in custody by Mexican officials at Calexico. They were released when American officials interceded on their behalf.

Organizational Activity in Chicago

Originally founded by Jean Baptiste Pointe du Sable, an African American born of a Haitian mother and a French father, Chicago turned out to be a fitting nexus of early aviation activity among African Americans. At the forefront of this pioneering trend was Robert J. Abbot, publisher of the *Chicago Defender,* who had helped Bessie Coleman launch her illustrious aviation career at Checkerboard Field. John C. Robinson, a 1931 graduate of the local Curtiss-Wright School, organized the Brown Eagle Aero Club, which flew over Chicago on Memorial Day and scattered flowers in memory of Bessie Coleman. The Brown Eagle Aero Club was subsequently reorganized as the Challenger Air Pilots' Association,[104] which built its first airstrip in the black township of Robbins, Illinois, in 1933. Shortly after the hangar was built, a sudden windstorm damaged it. The Challenger Air Pilots' Association then moved its flight operations to Harlem Airport near Chicago. Its first airplane was bought by Janet Waterford Bragg, a registered nurse.

In 1931, Robinson met Cornelius Coffey in Chicago and converted him from an auto mechanic to an airplane mechanic. Born in 1903, Coffey became the first African American to be certified as an airplane mechanic in 1932.[105] Together, Robinson and Coffey trained several African American pilots, mechanics, navigators, and parachutists who formed the core of a Chicago-based national association of African American aviators. After Robinson left for Ethiopia in 1935, the mantle of leadership for this group fell on Coffey.

In 1936, Willa Brown, an aviation enthusiast with a flair for showmanship and publicity, joined Coffey in leading this group of African American aviators in Chicago. She solicited help from Enoch Waters, city editor of the *Chicago Defender,* to publicize the group's aeronautical activities. With the blessing of Robert Abbott, Waters worked together with Brown, Coffey, and nine other local aviators to establish the National Airmen's Association of America (NAAA) in 1937.[106] NAAA was chartered in Illinois and maintained its headquarters at the *Chicago Defender.*

After Coffey's tenure, Brown served as president of NAAA. Over a long and distinguished career as an aviation educator, she worked tirelessly to promote aviation among African American youth. During World War II, she also trained for military service. On 18 July 1992, Willa Brown Chappell died of a stroke at age eighty-six.[107]

Among the charter members of NAAA was Chauncey E. Spencer, a pilot and parachutist who played a pivotal role in securing the inclusion of African Americans in the Civilian Pilot Training Program.[108] In May 1939, Spencer flew with Dale L. White on a ten-stop promotional flight from Chicago to Washington, D.C., under the sponsorship of NAAA.[109] Unfortunately, they were

grounded near Sherwood, Ohio, by a broken crankshaft. They were rescued by Coffey, president of NAAA. On this flight, Spencer met Sen. Harry Truman, which led to the establishment of a civilian pilot training program for African Americans.[110]

The early organizational efforts of African American aviators paid off in significantly modest increases in the number of African American pilots. In June 1936, the *Crises* reported the results of a survey by the Division of Negro Affairs in the Commerce Department which indicated that 55 blacks held Bureau of Air Commerce licenses. By 1939, 125 blacks held pilot's licenses, an increase of 250 percent since 1935, when the Department of Commerce first began compiling statistics on African American aviators.[111]

Negro Airmen International

The Negro Airmen International (NAI) was formed in 1967 by Edward A. Gibbs and other aviators including Chief Anderson, William Broadwater, Ulysses Gooch, Horace Noble, and Leslie Norris. NAI was established to promote aviation among African Americans through a special emphasis on exposing youth to careers and opportunities in aviation.[112] After its formation, NAI evolved into an umbrella group for several aviation clubs and associations established to support African American involvement in aviation. As an umbrella group, NAI organizes an annual Memorial Day fly-in at Tuskegee, which is attended by several groups including the Tuskegee Airmen, Bronze Eagles, and the Organization of Black Airline Pilots (OBAP).[113] NAI works with OBAP to foster interest in aviation among African American youth.[114]

Military Aviation

Colonial America to the Civil War

Military service by African Americans has a long and torturous history punctuated by distinction and triumph against considerable odds. Two decades after the first Africans arrived in colonial America, the Virginia General Assembly passed legislation that required all residents of the colony, except African Americans, to arm themselves.[115] Exclusion from the requirement to bear arms constituted de facto exclusion from true citizenship as embodied in the right to defend society through the militia. If free African Americans did not have the right to defend the community, they were not entitled to the rights of citizenship. Legislative entities in the other English colonies followed Virginia's precedent and passed similar legislation barring African Americans from bearing arms or serving in the militia.[116] The de facto exclusion of African Americans from military service was reinforced by the Militia Act of 1792, which mandated service in the militias by able-bodied white males.[117] In 1820, the Army issued an order stating that "no Negro or Mulatto will be received as a recruit of the Army" and reserved military service for "free white male persons."[118]

Against this background of exclusion from military service, African Americans still served the nation against aggressors in many theaters of war and conflict. Crispus Attucks was one of the first patriots to die during the Boston Massacre of 1770. Gen. George Washington fought with a battalion of African Americans from Rhode Island until they were disbanded in 1783. When combat valor was rewarded with manumission, African Americans fought gallantly for personal freedom. In November 1775, Lord Dunmore, royal governor of Virginia, established an Ethiopian Regiment that fought primarily for the *promise* of freedom.[119] During the War of 1812, when British troops burned the White House, six hundred African Americans fought against British regulars in the Battle of New Orleans.[120] In spite of these accomplishments in defense of the United States, Chief Justice Roger Taney employed exclusion from militia service to rule in the Dred Scott case of 1857 that African Americans "form no part of the sovereignty of the State, and are therefore not called upon to defend it."[121]

President Abraham Lincoln's Emancipation Proclamation on 1 January 1863 changed the legal status of African Americans in American society. It also marked a major turning point in the prospects of African American aspirations for military service. Lincoln requested the formation of four African American regiments who ultimately became known as the United States Colored Troops.[122] On the brink of its catastrophic loss, the Confederate Congress ironically approved the recruitment of 300,000 African Americans to defend the Confederacy in exchange for manumission.[123] That desperate move could not forestall the utter defeat of the Confederacy in the Civil War.

In an effort to reorganize the U.S. Army after the Civil War, Congress reserved 10 percent of the regular Army for African American enlistees in 1866. These enlistees formed two cavalry regiments (the Ninth and Tenth) and four infantry regiments (the Thirty-eighth, Thirty-Ninth, Fortieth, and Forty-first). The four infantry regiments were subsequently consolidated into the Twenty-fourth and Twenty-fifth Infantry Regiments in 1869.[124] The two infantry and two cavalry regiments survived until the Armed Forces was desegregated by President Truman after World War II. In their frontier posts west of the Mississippi, the African American regiments served with distinction under harsh conditions to provide protective services and to fight in skirmishes with Native Americans, who called them Buffalo Soldiers in recognition of their valor and buffalo skin overcoats. In this effort, they earned seventeen Medals of Honor.[125] Because of climactic conditions and the ravages of yellow fever in Cuba, the African American regiments were among the first to be deployed to Cuba in 1898, and they rode with the Rough Riders in the famous charge up San Juan Hill.

The Struggle for Military Aviation Training

Reflecting on the importance of military service to the African American struggle for citizenship, Frederick Douglass stated, "Let the black man get upon his person the brass letters U.S.; let him get an eagle on his buttons and musket on his shoulder, and bullets in his pocket, and there is no power on Earth which can deny that he has earned the right to citizenship."[126] About 400,000 African Americans served in the U.S. Army during World War I. Unfortunately, none saw action as aviators, but most worked as labor and service troops throughout World War I.[127]

A racial uprising by African American soldiers stationed on the outskirts of Houston during World War I resulted in the death of eighteen whites and four African Americans in August 1917. The uprising, which involved discharge of firearms over a two-hour period in Houston, was triggered by the severe beating of two African American soldiers by Houston police officers.[128] In December 1917, before the results of the investigation were released, twelve of the African American soldiers were secretly hanged after an investigation and court-martial. In September 1918, six more African American soldiers were convicted and executed.[129] The effect of the Houston riot and a 1925 study by the Army War College on "The Use of Negro Manpower in War"[130] had a very deleterious effect on military service by African Americans.[131]

African Americans and the Civilian Pilot Training Program

When World War II broke out in Europe, the U.S. Army was not particularly enamored of African American soldiers. The original bill authorizing the creation of Civilian Pilot Training (CPT) programs under the supervision of the Civil Aeronautics Authority (CAA) did not provide for the training of African American pilots.[132] During an NAAA-sponsored flight to ensure the inclusion of African Americans in the Air Corps and CPT Program, Dale White and Chauncey Spencer met with Senator Truman, who was surprised to learn that African Americans were excluded from the Air Corps. Upon seeing Spencer and White's airplane at the airport, Truman said, "If you had guts enough to fly this thing to Washington, . . . I've got guts enough to see that you get what you are asking for."[133] Truman worked with Rep. Everett M. Dirksen of Illinois to ensure the inclusion of African Americans in the final version of the Civilian Pilot Training Act when it was approved on 27 June 1939 after a very stormy debate in Congress.[134]

Six Historically Black Colleges and Universities (HBCUs) were selected to participate in the CPT program: Delaware State College, Dover, Delaware; Hampton Institute, Hampton, Virginia; Howard University in Washington, D.C.; North Carolina Agriculture and Technical State University, Greensboro, North Carolina; Tuskegee Institute, Tuskegee, Alabama; and West Virginia State College, Institute, West Virginia. There were also two noncollege units in Chicago, one of which was the Coffee School of Aeronautics. Of the six institutions, West Virginia State College was the first to win approval to offer the CPT program. In addition to being the only CPT program at an HBCU with a seaplane unit, the West Virginia State College CPT program boasted a racially integrated class in the summer of 1940. This was an oddity in West Virginia in 1940. The CPT program at Howard University was perhaps one of the first to fold.[135]

Tuskegee Institute and the War Training Service

Of the HBCUs approved to participate in the CPT program, Tuskegee Institute was clearly the standard-bearer. It had both primary pilot training through the CPT program and advanced pilot training through the Air Corps flight training program. Chartered by an act of the Alabama legislature in 1881, Tuskegee opened for enrollment on Independence Day in 1881 under the remarkable leadership of Booker T. Washington, an alumnus of Hampton University. Tuskegee originally functioned as a vocational school that provided practical training for teachers, farmers, and tradesmen, while offering academic courses at the high school level. As Washington informed a group of students in 1896, "We are not a college and if there are any of you here who expect to get a college training you will be disappointed."[136] In 1927, Tuskegee organized a collegiate division with degrees in agriculture, home economics, and education.[137] Tuskegee's involvement in aviation may be traced to John C. Robinson, who flew an airplane to Tuskegee on 22 May 1934 for his tenth-year class reunion.[138] The sight of a Tuskegee alumnus flying an airplane to his class reunion as early as 1934 must have profoundly impacted perceptions of the opportunities offered by the airplane.

After the Japanese invasion of Pearl Harbor, the CPT program was changed to the War Training Service (WTS). Unfortunately, African Americans who completed the CPT program were denied acceptance into the Air Corps. When President Roosevelt signed the Burke-Wadsworth Bill, or the Selective Training and Service Act (and the Wagner amendment), into law on 16 September 1940, this was supposed to end the exclusion of African Americans from the Air Corps, but it did not. On the same day the Selective Training and Service Act was signed, the White House announced, "The Civil Aeronautics Authority, in cooperation with the Army, is making a start in the development of colored personnel for aviation service."[139] Intransigence by War Secretary Henry L. Stimson, Army Chief of Staff Gen. George C. Marshall, and Maj. Gen. H. H. Arnold, chief of the Air Corps, deferred the implementation of this law.

Pressure was brought to bear on the Roosevelt administration to end the de facto exclusion of African Americans from the Air Corps. With the assistance of Eleanor Roosevelt, Walter White, executive secretary of the NAACP, A. Philip Randolph, president of the Brotherhood of Sleeping Car Porters, and Arnold Hill, acting head of the National Urban League, met with President Roosevelt on 27 September 1940 to discuss the issue of African Americans in the military.[140] Secretary Stimson cited prior commitments and declined the invitation to attend the meeting. Even though Roosevelt gave assurances of his commitment to open up the Air Corps to African Americans during the meeting, the War Department subsequently issued a policy statement asserting that "the policy of the War Department is not to intermingle colored and white enlisted personnel in the same regimental organization. . . . To make changes would produce situations destructive to morale and detrimental to the preparation for national defense."[141] Since the policy was issued soon after what they reported as a positive meeting with the president, Hill, Randolph, and White felt betrayed and co-opted. The NAACP led a propaganda assault by the African American media and a consortium of civic-minded advocates against the government's discriminatory policies.

James L. Peck, a well-published African American author and aviator who had reportedly flown with Loyalist forces in the Spanish civil war, wrote several articles in which he exposed the government's mendacious claims of opening up the Air Corps to African Americans.[142] It gradually became clear that the government's commitment stopped at civilian, not military, pilot training for African Americans and continued segregation of the military. African Americans were allowed to participate in the civilian CPT program under the guise preparing for military service in the Air Corps. This charade infuriated the African American community and increased the pressure on Secretary Stimson's War Department.

The War Department rejected applications for a cadet's position in the Air Corps by Yancey Williams, a licensed private pilot and an engineering student at Howard University. The NAACP sued the War Department on behalf of Williams.[143] The War Department ultimately relented and announced the acceptance of African Americans into the Air Corps and training for aerial combat at Tuskegee Institute on 16 January 1941.[144] This announcement was followed by official activation of the Ninety-ninth Pursuit Squadron, a segregated air unit for African American aviators, on 19 March 1941.[145] The Ninety-ninth Pursuit Squadron was part of the fourth corps, which had some 43,900 African American troops who were mostly stationed in segregated facilities in the South. On 22 January 1942, Secretary Stimson announced that four outfits in the Army, scattered among the nine corps in the United States, were under the command of African American officers.[146]

Establishment of a segregated flight training program and a segregated fighter squadron for African Americans generated considerable protest from persons who were fundamentally opposed to the creation of a segregated African American unit in the Air Corps' training program. Others protested because they preferred Chicago as a training site over Tuskegee, which was in the racially segregated South. The protest gradually waned, and the African American community threw its support behind Tuskegee.

Frederick Douglass Patterson, the third president of Tuskegee, and George L. Washington, head of the mechanical industries department, were primarily responsible for the selection of Tuskegee as the site for aerial combat training over other HBCUs and the Coffey School of Aeronautics in Chicago. Washington successfully recruited Chief Anderson from Howard University as one of five Tuskegee flight instructors. After initial flight training at an airport in Montgomery, Tuskegee moved its flight training activities closer to Auburn before building its own airports much closer to campus. The first airport, Kennedy, was also known as the mother field. The second airport, which was named after Russa Moton, Tuskegee's second president, was built with funds from the Julius Rosenwald Fund through the help of Eleanor Roosevelt, a member of Tuskegee's board of trustees. A third airport served as a military airport, known as Tuskegee Army Air Field.[147] During a trustees' meeting in March 1941, Roosevelt elected to go up for a ride in an airplane with Chief Anderson at the controls. Roosevelt's favorable account of her ride with Chief Anderson in her newspaper column "My Day," contributed toward dispelling the myth that African Americans could not fly.[148]

The first class of African American Air Corps cadets, class 42-C, began training at Tuskegee on 19 July 1941.[149] The class comprised twelve aviation cadets and Benjamin Oliver Davis Jr., a 1936 graduate of West Point who served as commandant.[150] Eleven of the cadets were college graduates.[151] Davis was the son of Brig. Gen. Benjamin Oliver Davis Sr., the first African American to reach the rank of general in the U.S. Army. As the fourth African American to graduate from West Point, and the first in the twentieth century, Davis Jr. was "silenced" (never spoken to except in the line of duty) by his fellow cadets at West Point (see fig. 15.8).[152]

The original quota of students allowed entry into pri-

Fig. 15.8. A flight instructor with students at Tuskegee Institute preparing for a cross-country flight. Courtesy of the U.S. Air Force.

mary training at Tuskegee was ten every five weeks. As a result of this low quota, the waiting list for African American applicants who had cleared the cadet examining board exceeded two hundred by fall 1941.[153] Denial of entry to qualified African Americans into cadet training continued to cause an increase in the waiting list. The increasing size of the waiting list generated concern about the Army's commitment to open up the Air Corps to African Americans. This caused the African American press to mount a campaign to open up the Air Corps. On 8 December 1941, General Arnold privately recommended to General Marshall that he activate an additional pursuit squadron for African Americans.

In making his recommendation, General Arnold noted, "There has been some criticism with reference to the long delay in ordering aviation cadets (Colored) for flying training. . . . If the training of negro pilots is to continue, it will be necessary to organize additional Air Corps units (Colored) . . . to provide units to which Aviation Cadets (Colored) may be assigned upon graduation from the flying school and to increase the number of flying cadets per class."[154] On 17 January 1942, approval of General Arnold's recommendation was finally made public, and in February 1942, the quota of students entering primary training at Tuskegee was doubled to twenty per class. Approval of General Arnold's recommendation also resulted in the activation of the 332d Fighter Group for African Americans at Tuskegee on 13 October 1942.[155] To accommodate the logistical needs of the expanded African American unit, the hub of training activity was moved from Tuskegee to Selfridge Field, Michigan. The 332d comprised the 300th, 301st, and 302d Pursuit Squadrons.

Of the original class of thirteen African American

cadets, five successfully completed advanced training to become military pilots on March 7, 1942 (see fig. 15.9).[156] The commandant, Benjamin O. Davis Jr., was promoted to captain and transferred from the infantry into the Air Corps. The other four graduates, Lemuel R. Curtis, Charles H. DeBow, George S. Roberts, and Mac Ross, were commissioned as second lieutenants in the Air Corps Reserve.[157] As reservists, the newly commissioned officers and other African Americans who subsequently received their commissions as military pilots remained in the United States, away from combat zones overseas. An intense media campaign was mounted by African Americans and civic-minded citizens to ensure that African American military pilots were deployed to the front and given the opportunity to gain combat experience.

Service in World War II

Two years after its activation, the Ninety-ninth Pursuit Squadron finally left the United States on 2 April 1943[158] for combat duty overseas with thirty-three officer pilots, a ground force of four hundred officers and enlisted men, and thirty-three aircraft.[159] They were originally stationed in North Africa, where they received P-40L aircraft in which they practiced dogfighting with the Twenty-seventh Fighter Group. In North Africa, the Ninety-ninth was entertained by Josephine Baker, a famous entertainer who had emigrated to France before World War II to overcome racial barriers in the United States. As part of the French resistance, Baker was able to introduce the Ninety-ninth Squadron to French and colonial soldiers in North Africa. During her performances for American troops stationed overseas, Baker in-

Fig. 15.9. The first five African American cadets to earn their wings at Tuskegee Army Air Field, standing next to a Vultee BT-13. Courtesy of the U.S. Air Force.

sisted on integrated seating for her audience. The African American aviators also enjoyed visits from Ella Fitzgerald and Joe Louis.

The Ninety-ninth Squadron flew its first combat mission on 2 June 1943.[160] Their early missions primarily consisted of harbor protection duties, convoy escorts, and strafing missions over Pantelleria in an attempt to gain control of shipping lanes to Italy and Sicily. Their first encounter with enemy aircraft occurred on 9 June 1943 while they were escorting twelve A-20s on a bombing run.[161] They drove off the enemy planes. On 21 July 1943, Charles B. Hall of Brazil, Indiana, became the first member of the Ninety-ninth Pursuit Squadron to shoot down an enemy fighter, a German Fw 190, during an escort mission of B-25s over Italy.[162] Hall received the Distinguished Flying Cross for this feat, which occurred on his eighth mission. During a congratulatory visit by Generals Eisenhower and Spatz, as well as Major General Doolittle and Air Marshall Cunningham of the Royal Air Force, Eisenhower reportedly said, "I would like to meet the pilot who shot down the Jerry."[163] Hall managed to shoot down three enemy aircraft before the end of his combat tour. Tragically, 21 July 1943 was marred by the death of two pilots from the Ninety-ninth, Sherman White and James McCullin, during takeoff on a mission.[164]

On 3 September 1943, Lieutenant Colonel Davis was suddenly ordered to return to the States to take command and prepare the 332d Fighter Group for combat. Upon his arrival, Davis discovered that senior military personnel had received a critical letter from Colonel Momyer of the Thirty-third Fighter Group that requested the transfer of the Ninety-ninth to coastal patrol because "the Negro type had not the proper reflexes to make a first-class fighter pilot."[165] General Arnold subsequently recommended to General Marshall that the Ninety-ninth "be removed from tactical operations; that the 332d Fighter Group, when ready for deployment, be sent to a non combat area," and "that the planned African American bombardment group, the 477th, be scrapped."[166]

In effect, the Ninety-ninth had "successfully" proved the inability of African Americans to serve as military pilots. General Marshall ordered an investigation before taking action. *Time* magazine reported that the Army was having difficulties finding combat areas to send African American pilots since no commanders wanted

large numbers of African Americans. In addition, political pressure from the African American media and public opinion had also made it impossible to exploit African American soldiers in menial labor.[167]

The *Time* article provoked a firestorm of protest from several persons including Agatha Scott Davis, wife of Lt. Gen. Benjamin O. Davis Sr., who wrote a letter to *Time*, decrying the gross injustice of the defamation campaign formally launched by Momyer's letter.[168] Six months later, *Time* wrote a complimentary article about the Ninety-ninth Squadron entitled "Sweet Victories." *Time* chronicled the award of an official commendation to the Ninety-ninth Squadron from Army Chief of Staff Arnold for shooting down eight German aircraft in one day, four in another, with twelve kills, two probables, and four damaged aircraft over three days of providing escort under Maj. George "Spanky" Roberts during the Allies' invasion of the Nettuno beachhead.[169] After brilliantly leading the Ninety-ninth Squadron throughout the critical winter months of 1943 and 1944, which included joint missions with the Seventy-ninth Fighter Squadron at Anzio during the Allied landings, Major Roberts returned to the United States, having completed seventy-eight missions.[170]

To avoid racially motivated civil strife, which could be detrimental to the war effort, *Time* reported that the Army relented and Benjamin O. Davis Jr. returned to the Mediterranean with the 332d Fighter Group. The 332d was issued P-47 "Thunderbolt" and P-51 "Mustang" fighter aircraft as replacements for its older P-39 "Airacobra" and P-40L aircraft. The 332d moved to Ramitelli, Italy, in February 1944 and was joined by the Ninety-ninth in April to become a four-squadron fighter group under the leadership of Colonel Davis.

As a fighter group, the 332d painted the tails of their aircraft red and became known as the "Red Tails" to their colleagues and the British Eighth Army under Gen. Bernard Montgomery for whom they briefly flew air support. The Germans referred to the 332d as "Schwarze Vogelmenschen," the "Black Birdmen."[171] The 332d attacked enemy installations and engaged in air combat while escorting B-17s and B-24s on bombing missions to central and eastern Europe as part of the Fifteenth Air Corps. During an escort mission for B-17s en route to an airfield in southern Germany on 18 July 1944, Lt. C. D. "Lucky" Lester shot three German Messerschmitt Bf 109s in a short, intense aerial battle near the Po Valley in northern Italy.[172] Lester received the Distinguished Flying Cross for this feat (see figs. 15.10 and 15.11).

Capt. Wendell O. Pruitt of St. Louis led a formation of the 332d that made history by sinking a German destroyer with only 50 caliber cannon fire. Pruitt shot down three airplanes and destroyed eight on the ground during seventy missions in World War II.[173] He died in a training accident while serving as an instructor at Tuskegee. Maj. Joseph D. Elsberry of Langston, Oklahoma, is believed to have been the first 332d pilot to shoot down three enemy aircraft in a day.[174] Among the pilots of the 332d, Lt. Lee A. Archer of New York City had the distinction of scoring ten kills, four in the air and six on the ground (see fig. 15.12).[175] Capt. Roscoe C. Brown Jr. of the 100th Fighter Squadron became the first pilot in the entire Fifteenth Air Corps to shoot down the much faster and more powerful ME 262 German jet fighter.[176]

A historical moment occurred on 11 September 1944, when Brigadier General Davis Sr., the highest ranking African American in the military, pinned the Distinguished Flying Cross on his namesake for valor in a strafing attack in southern Germany (see fig. 15.13).[177] The 332d Fighter Group also received the Distinguished Unit Citation[178] for "outstanding performance and extraordinary heroism" for flying the longest mission in the history of the Fifteenth Air Corps—a 1,600-mile round-trip escort mission to Berlin on 24 March 1945 during which they successfully fought off ferocious attacks from German aircraft and ground installations without losing any bomber under their escort.[179]

The 332d returned to the United States and was deactivated in October 1945. African American aviators in the Army Air Corps flew 1,578 missions and 15,533 sorties with the Twelfth and Fifteenth Air Corps and destroyed or damaged 409 enemy aircraft in World War II.[180] They flew escort missions for bombers that struck strategic targets including oil refineries, factories, airfields, and marshaling yards in Austria, Bulgaria, Czechoslovakia, France, Germany, Greece, Hungary, Italy, Poland, Roma-

Fig. 15.10. Lt. C. D. "Lucky" Lester in his P-51 Mustang showing three swastikas that signify three kills of German airplanes in World War II. Courtesy of the U.S. Air Force.

Fig. 15.11. P-51 Mustang 7 joins fighters from the Fifteenth Air Corps in a flight over Yugoslavia. Courtesy of the U.S. Air Force.

Fig. 15.12. Lt. Lee A. Archer of New York City. Courtesy of the U.S. Air Force.

Fig. 15.13. Gen. Benjamin O. Davis Sr. pins the Distinguished Flying Cross on his son, Col. Benjamin O. Davis Jr., in Italy, 29 May 1944. Courtesy of the U.S. Air Force.

nia, and Yugoslavia.[181] On all their missions, the 332d never lost a bomber aircraft under their escort.[182] They won 150 Distinguished Flying Crosses, 14 Bronze Stars, and a Silver Star.[183]

Col. Benjamin O. Davis Jr. won a Silver Star, a DFC, an Air Medal with four oak leaf clusters, and the Legion of Merit with one oak leaf cluster.[184] In 1965, Davis also became the first African American three-star general before his retirement on 1 February 1970. Nine hundred African American aviators were trained at Tuskegee, half of whom fought overseas with sixty-six fatalities and thirty-two wounded or captured.[185] Through distinguished service and valor, African American aviators of the Ninety-ninth and 332d triumphed against considerable odds and managed to completely refute both the appalling conclusions of the 1925 War College study and Momyer's letter in 1943. Unfortunately, not a single African American aviator in World War II secured employment as a pilot with the major airlines after the war.

African American military aviators initially flew only fighter aircraft in pursuit squadrons that provided escort services for larger and more expensive bomber aircraft. Training of African Americans as bomber pilots eventually became reality at Selfridge Field in Michigan with the activation of the 477th Bombardment Group in 1943. The 477th comprised the 616th, 617th, 618th, and 619th Bombardment Squadrons.[186] From Selfridge Field, the 477th was moved to Godman Field in Kentucky and Freeman Field in Indiana before being moved back to Godman Field. Air crewmen of the 477th were trained at Hondo and Midland Fields in Texas and Mather Field in California, while the aircraft technicians received their training with technicians from the Ninety-ninth Squadron at Chanute Field in Illinois.

At Mather Field in California, there was no formal racial segregation among the officers of the 477th until Maj. Gen. Ralph P. Cousins ordered segregated use of the mess hall after an inspection visit in 1944.[187] After Cousins's order, African American officers stopped using the mess hall at Mather Field. The 477th was subsequently moved to air fields where segregated use of facilities was the norm. Constant relocation from bases and stiff headwinds of racial opposition took a major toll on the 477th. Thus, the 477th was plagued with low morale and racial strife that erupted in several racial altercations and incidents. Among the racial altercations was the Freeman Field mutiny of April 1945 over the right of African American officers to use the segregated officers' club. Lt. Roger Terry was accused of instigating the Freeman Field mutiny, the "granddaddy of all riots," which ultimately ruined his military career.[188]

In response to the Freeman Field mutiny, General Arnold reorganized the command structure of the 477th and replaced its officers with African American officers under the leadership of Colonel Davis. The 477th neither left the country nor saw combat before World War II ended in 1945. The 477th bombardment group was subsequently reorganized into the 477th composite group, which absorbed parts of the returning 332d to become the 332d fighter wing under Colonel Davis in an independent U.S. Air Force that was established in 1947.[189]

In addition to the pioneering African American pilots who fought in World War II were African American paratroopers known as the Triple Nickels. The effort to train African Americans as paratroopers in World War II took shape in 1944 with the arrival of sixteen African Americans at Fort Bennington, Georgia.[190] In spite of bitterly provocative taunts and a lack of faith in their prospects for success, they persevered to become the core of the 555th Parachute Company. The 555th was the first African American paratroop unit in the world. It also had the distinction of being the first Army unit to be integrated into the Army Strategic Reserve.[191]

Post–World War II Heroes

Shortly after World War II ended, President Truman signed Executive Order 9981 on 26 July 1948 to officially end segregationist policies in the U.S. military. Executive Order 9981 also endorsed equality of treatment and opportunity for all persons in the military. To implement Executive Order 9981, Truman established the Fahy Commission, which significantly contributed toward the integration of African Americans into various military roles and positions (see fig. 15.14). The newly created independent Air Force was the first military service to integrate its personnel.

After official integration of the armed forces, career opportunities for African American aviators became less restricted. Several served with distinction in integrated units during the Korean conflict and the Vietnam War after President Truman officially banned segregation in

Fig. 15.14. Members of the Fahy Commission with President Harry Truman.
Courtesy of the U.S. Air Force.

the military. Among this group of outstanding military aviators was Daniel "Chappie" James (shown in fig. 15.15), who rose through the ranks of the Air Force to become the first African American four-star general in the armed forces.

Born in Pensacola, Florida, in 1920, Chappie James started his military aviation career at Tuskegee, where he received his early flight training under the CPT program and later served as a flight instructor before his commissioning as a second lieutenant in July 1943.[192] In 1945, James was among a group of young officers who were charged with mutiny for their attempts to integrate an officer's club in Kentucky. James was defended at the mutiny trial by Thurgood Marshall (who became the first African American Supreme Court justice) and

William T. Coleman, a former Tuskegee Airman who later became the secretary of transportation.[193] In May 1953, James took command of the 437th Fighter Squadron, a four-hundred-man unit at Otis Air Force Base in Massachusetts responsible for the defense of New York, Boston, and Washington, D.C.[194] As squadron leader of the 437th, Major James became the first African American aviator to command a non–African American aviation unit.

Chappie James completed more than a hundred combat missions in Korea and seventy-eight combat missions over Vietnam. After the Vietnam War, Chappie James was promoted to the office of deputy assistant secretary of defense for public affairs for the Air Force and then head of the North American Air Defense

Fig. 15.15. Gen. Daniel "Chappie" James, the first African American to reach the rank of a four-star general in the U.S. armed forces. Courtesy of the U.S. Air Force.

Fig. 15.16. Lt. Gen. William Earl Brown. Courtesy of the U.S. Air Force.

Command (NORAD) in 1975. As commander of NORAD, the joint U.S.-Canadian defense system, General James was responsible for a $1.6 billion budget and 58,000 employees around the world. He was "the only U.S. military officer with authority to deploy nuclear weapons without presidential approval."[195] On 25 February 1978, he died of an apparent heart attack at age fifty-eight and was buried at Arlington National Cemetery.[196] On 10 May 1987, President Ronald Reagan dedicated the $9 million Gen. Daniel "Chappie" James Center for Aerospace Science and Health Education at Tuskegee University.[197]

Another outstanding aviator in the newly integrated Air Force was William Earl Brown, who rose to the rank of a lieutenant general before his retirement from active duty (see fig. 15.16).[198] As a combat pilot in the Air Force, Brown flew 125 combat missions in Korea and 100 missions in Southeast Asia during the Vietnam War.

Unlike the Air Force, the Navy was very slow to accept African Americans into its officer corps, especially in naval aviation. It was not until 1948 that the Navy hired Jesse LeRoy Brown, its first African American aviator.[199] As a naval aviator, Ensign Brown flew several tactical aircraft including the Grumman F8F Bearcat. Brown was the first African American aviator in the Navy to lose his life in any war when he was shot down behind enemy lines in 1950 during combat in Korea.[200] Valiant attempts by his fellow naval aviators to rescue him were unsuccessful. He was posthumously awarded the Distinguished Flying Cross, Air Medal, and Purple Heart. On 17 February 1973, the destroyer escort USS *Jesse L. Brown* was launched in Boston during commissioning ceremonies involving his widow, Rear Adm. Samuel L. Gravely, and his comrades from Korea.[201] USS *Jesse L. Brown* was the first naval vessel named in honor of an African American.

On 22 October 1952, Frank E. Petersen Jr. of Topeka, Kansas, became the first African American to receive his wings and commission as a pilot in the Marine Corps (see fig. 15.17).[202] He served with distinction in both Korea and Vietnam. In 1968, Petersen became the first African American aviator to command a squadron in either the Navy or the Marines. In 1972, he became the first African American Marine to enter the National War College at a time when only 1.3 percent of the African Americans in the Marine Corps were officers, even though they constituted 12 percent of the Marine Corps.[203] In 1979, Petersen became the first African American to reach star rank in the Marine Corps after twenty-nine years of service as a pilot. After serving as chief of staff of the Ninth Marine Amphibian Brigade at Okinawa and commanding general of the Marines Development and Education Command at Quantico Bay, Virginia, he retired as a brigadier general.[204]

Born 10 July 1933 in New Orleans, Bernard P. Randolph enlisted in the Air Force in 1955. After completing aviation cadet training at Ellington Air Force Base in Houston and Mather Air Force Base, he served in several positions with the Air Force before serving at Chu Lai and Tan Son Nhut Air Base during the Vietnam War. In 1974, he became a distinguished graduate of the Air War College. On 1 August 1987, Randolph became the second African American to be promoted to the rank of a four-star general in the Air Force.[205]

In 1974, the Air Force finally opened the doors of its elite demonstration squadron, the Thunderbirds, to the first African American, Capt. Lloyd "Fig" Newton. He served as a narrator in his first season with the Thunderbirds before becoming one of the five demonstration pilots. Newton was privileged to serve two three-year terms with the Thunderbirds, even though a single three-year term is the norm.[206] Before joining the Thunderbirds, Newton had served in Vietnam. The last bastion of elitism in military aviation to open its doors to African American aviators was the Navy's precision demonstration team, the Blue Angels.

In 1986, Comdr. Donnie Cochran from Pelham, Georgia, became the first African American to join the Blue Angels. Cochran was commissioned an ensign through Navy ROTC in June 1976, and he earned his wings in June 1978. After his commission, he served an extended deployment aboard the aircraft carrier USS *Nimitz*. He served three tours with Fighter Squadron 124 and one

Fig. 15.17. Col. Frank E. Petersen Jr., first African American pilot in the Marine Corps. Courtesy of the U.S. Marine Corps.

tour as an instructor pilot in the F-14A Tomcat.[207] A graduate of the Air War College, Cochran was deployed as a carrier-based pilot on the aircraft carriers USS *Enterprise* and USS *Ranger*. After his selection in 1986, Cochran first flew the A-4F Skyhawk as left wing (#3) and two years in the F/A-18 Hornet, as left wing and as slot pilot.[208] In 1995, he returned to the Blue Angels for a two-year tour of service as the commanding officer of the Blue Angels. In introducing Cochran at a lecture on 21 October 1995 during the Wings over Houston Airshow Festival in Houston, I. Richmond Nettey, director of Airway Science at Texas Southern University, remarked that Cochran's rise to lead the Blue Angels is an eloquent testimony of the accomplishments of African American aviators in the military.

Postwar Civil Aviation

Even though wartime military flight training programs produced a large number of highly qualified African American aviators, racial discrimination and high costs severely limited their role in civil aviation since the war. In spite of the restrictive climate, several African Americans were propelled by their love of aviation to play meaningful roles in civil aviation. Among this band of postwar African American civil aviators was August Harvey Martin, who was born in Los Angeles in 1919 and tutored by his mother until the age of thirteen.

August Martin paid for his flight training by fueling and washing airplanes at Oakland Flying Service and managed to solo in a Fleet Model 2 on 8 January 1940. After completing flight training through the CPT program at University of California, Martin worked as a civilian flight inspector in the Navy V-12 program at Cornell University. He joined the Army Air Corps and received flight training at Tuskegee before becoming a bomber pilot. He did not serve in combat before his discharge from the Army Air Corps during the postwar drawdown in January 1946.

After World War II, Martin worked as an aircraft mechanic at Willis Air Services in Teterboro, New Jersey, and as a stevedore on the New York city docks to support his family. Between 1946 and 1955, he flew as a part-time pilot for Buffalo Skylines, El Al Airlines, and World Airways. In 1955, Martin became the first African American captain of a scheduled airline when he was hired by Seaboard World Airlines. At Seaboard World Airlines, Martin flew DC-3, DC-4, Lockheed Constellation, and Canadair CL-44 aircraft. On 1 July 1968, Martin lost his life while trying to land on a highway in a rainstorm during a mission to Biafra, Nigeria.[209]

Neal V. Loving, a glider pilot and builder of several experimental aircraft, flew an all-wood, single-seat, midget-class aircraft he built, the WR-1 Love, from his home in Detroit to his native Jamaica and Cuba, a distance of over 2,200 miles in 1954. Neal Loving's WR-3 was designed with folding wings, which made it capable of being driven on vehicular roads.[210]

Another African American who built airplanes in the postwar years was Lewis A. Jackson, who purchased his first airplane in 1932 and worked his way through college by barnstorming throughout the Midwest. Jackson served as chief instructor at the Coffey School of Aeronautics and as director of training over the Division of Aeronautics at Tuskegee during World War II.[211] From the early 1960s through the 1980s, Jackson built several airplanes with removable and retractable wings that could be driven on roads.

James O. Plinton, an instructor at Tuskegee, co-founded a shuttle air service, Quisqueya Ltd., between Haiti, the Grand Turks, and Caicos Islands with Maurice DeYoung after World War II.[212] Plinton also made his mark as a pioneering airline executive at TWA and Eastern Airlines, where he rose to the rank of vice president for marketing development before his retirement in 1979.[213]

Commercial airlines generally refused to hire African American pilots until Marlon D. Green won a court battle against Continental Airlines that started in June 1957 and ended with a unanimous decision by the Supreme Court in February 1965. In the course of his long trial, Green, who had served as a captain in the Air Force for nine years, sent out some six hundred applications.[214] After the Supreme Court ruled in favor of Marlon Green, American Airlines hired David E. Harris and Jack A. Noel, and United Airlines hired William R. Norwood. These hirings marked the beginning of a very slow process to increase the number of African American pilots at the major airlines, which still has a long way to go.

Space

Manned space exploration has been accomplished by only the United States and Russia, or the former Soviet Union. Space exploration in the United States has been primarily carried out by the National Aeronautics and Space Administration (NASA) with a team of scientists, technicians, and astronauts. Formal involvement in the space program by African Americans could be traced to Dr. Vance H. Marchbanks, who joined the Army Air Corps at Tuskegee in 1941 and won a Bronze Star in Italy while serving with the 332d. Marchbanks joined the Air Force after World War II and became the first African American flight surgeon. His research work on sickle cell anemia was instrumental in the removal of all restrictions on persons with the sickle cell trait by the Air Force on 26 May 1981.[215]

In February 1962, Marchbanks worked on Project Mercury by monitoring John Glenn's medical conditions from a tracking station in Kano, Nigeria. In addition to Marchbanks, several African Americans including Katherine Johnson, Ted Scopinsky, James Langston, Leonard Beale, Harold Thames, Joseph Swafford, Nathaniel Crump, Clinton Rayford, Tom Gentry, and William Pynter assisted in different phases of Project Mercury in 1962.[216] Another African American who held an important administrative position at NASA was Isaac T. Gilliam IV, who served as the special assistant for space transportation systems at NASA after serving as the director of shuttle operations at Edwards Air Force Base in California.[217]

In manned space exploration, astronauts are obviously the most visible actors. In 1962, Edward J. Dwight, an Air Force pilot, became the first African American to be selected for astronaut training by NASA with the support of President John F. Kennedy. After Kennedy's assassination, Dwight was somehow passed over in the final selection phase. He ultimately resigned from the astronaut corps in 1966 amid deplorable accounts of racial discrimination. After his subsequent retirement from the Air Force, Dwight became a full-time sculptor in Denver.[218] A year later, the second African American selected for astronaut training, Air Force Maj. Robert H. Lawrence, died in an aircraft accident during landing at Edwards Air Force Base in California. Major Lawrence, a highly educated thirty-one-year-old scientist and pilot with a doctorate degree in nuclear chemistry, had been selected for the Defense Department's 30-day Manned Orbiting Laboratory program when he died in December 1967.[219]

After the setbacks for the first two African Americans to enter the astronaut training program in the 1960s, the mantle fell on Arnaldo Tamayo Mendez, an Afro Cuban from Guantanamo, to become the first person of African ancestry to fly in space. Mendez successfully flew with Yuri Romanenko aboard a Soviet space capsule that linked up with the manned Salyut-6 space laboratory in 1980.[220]

After Lawrence's death in 1967, the next African American selected for astronaut training in the United States was Guion Stewart Bluford Jr., an Air Force pilot. Prior to his selection as an astronaut in August 1979, Bluford had earned a doctorate degree in aerospace engineering from the Air Force Institute of Technology and completed 144 combat missions in Vietnam. Bluford became the first African American in space on 31 August 1983, twenty-two years after America's first manned space flight. Bluford's second mission into space occurred on 30 October 1985 aboard STS-8. On 28 April 1991, he went back to space as a mission specialist on an eight-day military mission.[221] He went up on his fourth and final mission (STS 53) on 2 December 1992 before leaving NASA in 1993 to work with an engineering and computer firm in Greenbelt, Maryland.

Ronald McNair, a physicist with a doctorate degree from MIT, became the first African American astronaut to die on a space mission in the Challenger disaster of 28 January 1986.[222] Frederick Drew Gregory, a 1964 graduate of the Air Force Academy from Washington, D.C., became the first African American to pilot a space mission (STS-51-B) on 29 April 1985. He accomplished another first when he commanded a classified mission, STS-33, on 29 November 1989.[223] On 24 November 1991, he commanded another classified military mission on the shuttle, Atlantis, which launched a military satellite.

Charles Bolden, a Marine Corps pilot who applied to test pilot school five times before he was accepted, was selected as an astronaut candidate in May 1980.[224] On 12 January 1986, he piloted STS-61 into space. He subsequently piloted STS-31 on 24 April 1990 and commanded two missions on 24 March 1992 and 3 February 1994.[225] Bernard Harris became the first African American astronaut to complete a space walk when he flew on STS-63, which was launched on 2 February 1995.

In June 1987, Mae Carol Jemison, a physician and engineer who had served in Sierra Leone as a Peace Corps volunteer, became the first African American woman to be selected as an astronaut candidate. On 12 September 1992, Jemison went into space on board Endeavor (STS-47) on a historic joint mission with Japan that marked the fiftieth flight in the space program. As a mission specialist on her epochal flight, which also included the first married couple on a space flight, Jemison conducted fertilization studies on South African clawed frogs and the use of biofeedback techniques to control space-induced motion sickness. After her mission, Jemison retired from NASA to teach at Dartmouth College. Reflecting on space exploration, Jemison advocated the need to "get every group of people involved because it is something that eventually we in the world community are going to have to share."[226]

The development of aviation and aerospace involves technologies and technological paradigms that transcend any single group of people. As the world evolves further into a global village, the impacts and benefits from aviation and aerospace affect all humanity. The future development and growth of both aviation and aerospace must be a collaborative effort that includes all persons, because no one is certain of the challenges that will face aviation or the sources of solutions to those challenges.

African Americans have made impressive strides in aviation and aerospace against considerable odds. Regrettably, there are still considerable barriers. Also, the number of African Americans holding senior-level operational and executive positions in aviation and aerospace is disproportionately low. It is obvious that African Americans have demonstrated a strong commitment to earning a place in aviation and aerospace. The future holds much promise. It would be in the better interest of our global village to include everyone in that future.

Notes

1. *New Encyclopedia Britannica,* 1994, 20:576:1b.

2. *Britannica,* 7:222:2a and 7:222:3b.

3. Gamal Mokhtar, "Official Statement on the Messiha Discovery," in *Blacks in Science: Ancient and Modern,* ed. I. Van Sertima (New Brunswick, N.J.: Transaction Books, 1983), 97.

4. Khalil Messiha and Guirguis Messiha, "An Ancient Egyptian Aeroplane Model," in *Blacks in Science: Ancient and Modern,* ed. I. Van Sertima (New Brunswick, N.J.: Transaction Books, 1983), 92.

5. Messiha and Messiha, 97.

6. Messiha and Messiha, 94.

7. Michael Frenchman, "A 2,000 Year Old Model Glider," in *Blacks in Science: Ancient and Modern,* ed. I. Van Sertima (New Brunswick, N.J.: Transaction Books, 1983), 99.

8. Frenchman, 98.

9. Messiha and Messiha, 92.

10. Frenchman, 98.

11. Frenchman, 99.

12. Carl Brown, *A History of Aviation* (Daytona Beach, Fla.: Embry-Riddle Aeronautical University, 1980), 1.

13. R. E. G. Davies, *A History of the World's Airlines* (London: Oxford University Press, 1967), 72.

14. Davies, 34. Imperial Airways was formed through the merger of Daimler Airway, Handley-Page Transport, the Instone Airline, and British Marine Air Navigation (BMAN).

15. *From Mules to Jets: A Short History of Aviation in Ethiopia* (Switzerland: Ethiopian Airlines, 1981).

16. Dominick A. Pisano and Cathleen S. Lewis, eds., *Air and Space History: An Annotated Bibliography* (New York: Garland, 1988), 184 n. 619.

17. Kenneth Brown Collins, "America Will Never Fly." *American Mercury,* July 1936, 292.

18. Charles A. Lindbergh, "Aviation Geography and Race," *Reader's Digest,* November 1939, 64.

19. Charles A. Lindbergh, *"We": The Famous Flier's Own Story of His Life and Transcontinental Flight, Together with His Views on the Future of Aviation* (New York: Grosset and Dunlop, 1927), 54–60.

20. Raymond Eugene Peters and Clinton M. Arnold. *Black Americans in Aviation* (San Diego: Neyenesch Printers, 1975), 6, 42.

21. Robert J. Jakeman, *Divided Skies: Establishing Flight Training at Tuskegee, Alabama, 1934–1942* (Tuscaloosa: University of Alabama Press, 1992), 54.

22. Henry E. Baker, "The Negro in the Field of Invention," *Journal of Negro History,* 2 January 1917, 34.; Carter G. Woodson, and Charles H. Wesley, *The Negro in Our History,* 12th ed., rev. and enl. (Washington, D.C.: Associated Publishers, 1972), 464; U.S. Patent Office, *Official Gazette* 90 (20 February 1900): 1506.

23. Joel Rogers, "Your History," *Pittsburgh Courier,* 6 May 1944, 7.

24. George Edward Barbour, "Early Black Flyers of Western Pennsylvania, 1906–1945," *Western Pennsylvania Historical Magazine,* April 1986, 95–97.

25. Tom Zito, "Blacks in Aviation," *Washington Post,* 23 September 1982, D9.

26. Barbour, 97.

27. Barbour, 98.

28. *Atlanta Independent,* 28 October 1911, 11.

29. Elizabeth Ross Haynes, *The Black Boy of Atlanta: A Biography of Richard Robert Wright, Sr.* (Boston: House of Edinboro, 1952), 81.

30. *Christian Recorder,* 21 January 1911, in *Tuskegee Clippings File* 242:671.

31. Jakeman, 54.

32. U.S. Patent Office, *Official Gazette* 208 (3 November 1914): 84.

33. *New York Age,* 18 January 1912, in *Tuskegee Clippings File* 242:672–73.

34. *Iowa State Bystander,* 16 February 1912, 2, and 28 February 1913, 3.

35. *Iowa State Bystander,* 16 February 1912, 2, and 28 February 1913, 3.

36. Curtis Albert, "Bullard, French Ace, Wins 'Truth' Fight," *Chicago Defender,* 16 June 1923, 1; Betty Kaplan Gubert, *Invisible Wings: An Annotated Bibliography on Blacks in Aviation, 1916–1993* (Westport, Conn.: Greenwood Press, 1994), xii.

37. Jakeman, 56.

38. Edmond Charles Clinton Genet, *An American for Lafayette: The Diaries of E. C. C. Genet Lafayette Escadrille* (Charlottesville: University Press of Virginia, 1981).

39. Jakeman, 56.

40. "Bullard, Former U.S.A. Subject, Weds Paris Girl," *Chicago Defender*, 1 September 1923, 1.

41. P. J. Carisella and James W. Ryan, *The Black Swallow of Death: The Incredible Story of Eugene Jacques Bullard, the World's First Black Combat Aviator* (Boston: Marlborough House, 1972).

42. Eleanor Roosevelt, "My Day," newspaper column, 1 November 1959, bound copies, Eleanor Roosevelt Papers, Franklin Delano Roosevelt Library, Hyde Park, N.Y.

43. Pat Burson, "State Inducting Seven into Aviation Hall of Fame," *Atlanta Journal and Constitution*, 27 August 1989, B5.

44. Nick Apple, "Flying High in AF Museum," *Columbus Ledger-Enquirer*, 13 February 1990, C-1.

45. "National Air and Space Museum Unveils Bust of First Black Combat Pilot," *New York Voice*, 15–21 October 1921, 11.

46. Gubert, xii.

47. Audrey Fischer, "Bessie Coleman: Flying in the Face of All Odds," *Woman Pilot* 3 (March/April 1995): 9, 10.

48. Gubert, xiii.

49. Fischer, 8, 10.

50. *New York Age*, 1 October 1921, 1.

51. "Negress in Flying Show," *New York Times*, 27 August 1922, 2.

52. Ralph Eliot, "Bessie Coleman Says Good Will Come From Hurt" *Chicago Defender*, 10 March 1923.

53. "Bessie Coleman and White Pilot in 2,000 Ft. Crash," *New York Amsterdam News*, 6 May 1926.

54. "The 1st Black Woman Flyer," *Chicago Tribune*, 8 May 1980.

55. Fischer, 11.

56. *Opportunity* 5 (July 1927): 216.

57. "Colored Birdman Tells Interesting Story of His Air Exploits," *New York Amsterdam News*, 18 June 1927.

58. *Pittsburgh Courier*, 12 March 1927, 1; 17 September 1927, 5.

59. *Newsweek*, 29 September 1934, 36.

60. Von Hardesty and Dominick Pisano report that by 1930 John W. Greene was one of only three African Americans to hold an air transport pilot rating as a pilot. Hardesty and Pisano, *Black Wings: The American Black in Aviation* (Washington, D.C.: National Air and Space Museum, 1983), 70.

61. Hardesty and Pisano, 9.

62. Gubert, xii.

63. Hardesty and Pisano, 8.

64. Bessye J. Bearden, "Two Fly from Coast to Coast in an Old Plane," *Chicago Defender*, 15 October 1932, 2. Robert J. Jakeman in *The Divided Skies* (65) reports that Banning and Allen's transcontinental flight originated in Los Angeles and terminated at Roosevelt Field on Long Island as contrasted with Bearden's claim that the said flight ended at Valley Stream Airport in New York.

65. Hardesty and Pisano, 8.

66. "Harlem Honors Coast-to-Coast Negro Flyers," *New York Herald Tribune*, 7 October 1932 (or shortly thereafter). Claude A. Barnett Papers, Chicago Historical Society.

67. "Died," *Crises* 40 (April 1933): 92.

68. Sharon Carter, "Aviation Pioneer Thomas Allen Dies," *General Aviation News*, 6 November 1989, 7, 19.

69. Alecia McKenzie and Karen Turner, "The Father of Black Aviation," *Everybody's*, January/February 1985, 22–24.

70. Rufus Hunt, "Among the First Black Aviation Pioneers," *Chicago Defender*, 18 August 1981, 6.

71. Hardesty and Pisano, 27. A picture of Anderson's CAA issued airman's certificate shows a birthdate of 2/9/07 whereas a newspaper article entitled "Transport License Given Negro Pilot," *Washington Post*, 28 February 1932, places the date of birth on 2/7/09.

72. "Negroes End Flight," *New York Times*, 29 July 1933.

73. Mary J. Washington, "A Race Soars Upward," *Opportunity*, 12 October 1934, 300.

74. Cleveland G. Allen, "Hop-Off Near for Good Will S. Amer. Flight," 9 August 1934, Gumby Collection, Columbia University, scrapbook no. 1.

75. Jakeman, 18.

76. "Dr. Albert Forsythe, 88, Dies; Among First Black Aviators," *New York Times*, 9 May 1986, D22.

77. Gubert, xi.

78. U.S. Patent Office, *Official Gazette* 286 (24 May 1921) confirms the award of a patent to Julian for his safety device on p. 732. There is, however, no confirmation of the purported offers from the Curtiss and Gerni companies for rights to the safety device.

79. John Hope Franklin, *From Slavery to Freedom: A History of Black Americans*, 5th ed. (New York: Alfred A. Knopf, 1980), 354–56.

80. Theodore Draper, *The Rediscovery of Black Nationalism* (New York: Viking Press, 1970), 51.

81. Morris Markey, "The Black Eagle," *New Yorker*, 11 July 1931, 22–25.

82. John Peer Nugent, *The Black Eagle* (New York: Stein and Day, 1971), 40–47.

83. Allen H. Smith, *Low Man on a Totem Pole* (Garden City, N.Y.: Doubleday, Doran, 1941), 72–81.

84. "RAS Sends Flyer Back To Harlem," *New York Sun*, 31 October 1930.

85. "Julian Meets Chief," *New York Amsterdam News*, 22 September 1934, 3.

86. Loose Jaws, "The Tatler," *New York Amsterdam News*, 1 October 1983, 16.

87. William Randolph Scott, "Colonel John C. Robinson: The Condor of Ethiopia," *Pan African Journal* 5 (spring 1972): 61–62.

88. "American Negro Pilot Bests Two Italian Planes," *New York Times*, 5 October 1935.

89. W. R. Scott, 64.

90. Jakeman, 23.

91. David W. Kellum, "Defender Scribe Greets Robinson," *Chicago Defender,* 23 May 1936, 1, 2.

92. *New York Times,* 24 May 1936, 3.

93. "Selassie's Air Aide Back from Africa," *New York Times,* 19 May 1936.

94. "Col. Robinson Starts Own Aviation College," *New York Amsterdam News,* 3 October 1936, 24.

95. *Baltimore Afro-American,* 29 August 1936.

96. "Ethiopia Honors Dead U.S. Flyer," *New York Amsterdam News,* 3 April 1954, 1–2.

97. James de T. Abajian, *Blacks in Selected Newspapers, Censuses, and Other Sources: An Index to Names and Subjects* (Boston: G. K. Hall, 1977), 1:82, citing the *Los Angeles News Age,* 24 June 1921, 1.

98. Nugent, 51–52.

99. "Aviation," *Opportunity* 7 (November 1929): 353.

100. Hardesty and Pisano, 7.

101. "Aviation," *Opportunity* 15 (May 1937): 156.

102. George E. Hopkins, *The Airline Pilots: A Study in Elite Unionization* (Cambridge, Mass.: Harvard University Press, 1971), 71.

103. "Two Negro Pilots Forced Down in Lower California," *Los Angeles Times,* 2 November 1929, pt. 2, p. 10.

104. *Chicago Defender,* 30 May 1936, 5.

105. Art Golab, "Black Aviator Still Flies High," *Chicago Sun-Times,* 14 July 1993, 24.

106. "Negroes Organize: National Airmen's Association of America Holds First Meeting in Chicago," *American Aviation,* 1 October 1939, 14.

107. "Willa Brown Chappell, 86, Trained WW II Pilots," *Chicago Sun Times,* 20 July 1992, 41.

108. Chauncey E. Spencer, *Who is Chauncey Spencer?* (Detroit: Broadside Press, 1971).

109. "Flyers Are Grounded by Motor Fault," *Chicago Defender,* 13 May 1939, 1, 4.

110. Diane Kirsh, "Aviators Recall Struggle to Fly," *News and Advance,* 29 August 1991. B1, 7.

111. U.S. Department of Commerce, Bureau of the Census, *Negro Aviators,* Negro Statistical Bulletin no. 3, September 1940, containing retrospective data for the years 1935, 1936, 1937, and 1939.

112. Peters and Arnold, 19.

113. Robertson Blair, "Black Pilots Honor Aviation Pioneer," *Birmingham Post Herald,* 24 May 1992, 1B–2B.

114. Seth Schiesel, "Black Airmen Gather to Pay Tribute," *Boston Sunday Globe,* 16 August 1992, 26.

115. Morris J. MacGregor and Bernard C. Nalty, eds., *Blacks in the Military: Basic Documents* (Wilmington, Del.: Scholarly Resource, 1977), 3.

116. Jack D. Foner, *Blacks and the Military in American History: A New Perspective* (New York: Praeger, 1974), 3.

117. Bernard C. Nalty, *Strength for the Fight: A History of Black Americans in the Military* (New York: Free Press, 1986), 19–20.

118. Foner, 27.

119. Nalty, 10–18.

120. Foner, 23–25.

121. *Dred Scott v. Sandford,* 19 Howard (U.S.), 414–17, 15 L. Ed. 705 (1884).

122. Benjamin Quarles, *The Negro in the Civil War* (Boston: Little, Brown, 1953); Taylor Dudley Cornish, *The Sable Arm: Negro Troops in the Union Army, 1861–1865* (New York: Longmans, Green, 1956).

123. Barbara C. Ruby, "General Patrick Cleburne's Proposal to Arm Southern Slaves," *Arkansas Historical Quarterly* 30 (autumn 1971): 193–212.

124. Nalty, 51–52.

125. William H. Leckie, *The Buffalo Soldiers: A Narrative of the Negro Cavalry in the West* (Norman: University of Oklahoma Press, 1967), 26.

126. Arthur E. Barbeau and Florette Henri, *The Unknown Soldiers: Black Army Troops in World War I* (Philadelphia: Temple University Press, 1974), xii.

127. Ulysses Lee, *United States Army in World War II. Special Studies: The Employment of Negro Troops* (Washington, D.C.: Office of the Chief of Military History, U.S. Army, 1966), 5.

128. Robert V. Haynes, *A Night of Violence: The Houston Riot of 1917* (Baton Rouge: Louisiana State University Press, 1976).

129. Robert V. Haynes, "The Houston Mutiny and Riot of 1917," *Southwestern Historical Review* 76 (April 1973): 418–39.

130. The 1925 War College study concluded that "blacks were inferior to whites in every way. They lacked intelligence and courage, were morally weak and of such low character that they should never be mixed with whites, that it was a foregone conclusion that they would never be skillful enough to fly aircraft of any type." C. V. Glines, "The Red-Tailed Fighter" *Retired Officer,* September 1992, 28.

131. Alan M. Osur, *Blacks in the Army Air Forces During World War II* (Washington, D.C.: Office of Air Force History, 1977), 5.

132. Jakeman, 90.

133. Peters and Arnold, 7.

134. Civilian Pilot Training Act, *Statutes at Large,* 53:856 (1939).

135. Patricia Strickland, *The Putt-Putt Air Force: The Story of the Civilian Pilot Training Program and the War Training Service (1939–1944)* (Washington, D.C.: Department of Transportation, Federal Aviation Administration, Education Staff, [1971]), 39–44. Since authorship and publishing dates are uncertain, additional references shall be made under *Putt Putt Air Force.*

136. Jakeman, 4.

137. Louis Harlan, *Booker T. Washington: The Making of a Black Leader, 1856–1901* (New York: Oxford University Press, 1972).

138. *Tuskegee Messenger,* June 1934, 11.

139. White House press release, 16 September 1940, 1940 Folder, OF 93, FDR Library.

140. Morris J. MacGregor Jr., *Integration of the Armed Forces, 1945–1965,* Defense Studies Series (Washington, D.C.: Center of Military History, U.S. Army, 1981), 15.

141. MacGregor and Nalty, 5:29–31.

142. *Current Biography,* 3 August 1942, 40–42. The record of Peck's military service as a pursuit pilot with Loyalist forces in Spain is disputed by Allen Herr in "American Pilots in the Spanish Civil War," *American Aviation Historical Society Journal* 23 (fall 1978): 235.

143. Roy Wilkins and Tom Matthews, *Standing Fast: The Autobiography of Roy Wilkins* (New York: Viking Press, 1982), 181.

144. Jakeman, 228.

145. *Putt Putt Air Force,* 45.

146. "The American Negro in the U.S. Army," *Crises,* February 1942, 48.

147. Charles E. Francis, *The Tuskegee Airmen: The Story of the Negro in the U.S. Air Force* (Boston: Bruce Humphries, 1955).

148. Eleanor Roosevelt, "My Day," newspaper column, 1 April 1941, bound copies, Eleanor Roosevelt Papers, Franklin Delano Roosevelt Library, Hyde Park, N.Y.

149. George L. Washington, *The History of Military and Civilian Pilot Training of Negroes at Tuskegee, Alabama, 1939–1945* (Washington, D.C.: Author, 1972), 195.

150. Jakeman, 256.

151. Valora H. Spencer, *Reaching for the Skies: The Overseas Experiment of the Tuskegee Airmen in World War II* (London: Academy Editions, 1995), 2.

152. Jakeman, 256.

153. Jakeman, 300.

154. Memorandum, Lt. Col. C. E. Duncan, Secretary of the Air Staff, to the Chief of Staff, 8 December 1941, Xerox 732, Marshall Foundation.

155. Hardesty and Pisano, 40.

156. V. Spencer, 1.

157. Jakeman, 304.

158. Contrary to the 2 April 1943 departure date, Hardesty and Pisano state, "The 99th Fighter Squadron boarded a troopship for North Africa on April 15, 1943 and arrived at Casablanca on the morning of April 24" (*Black Wings,* 36). Both Strickland in *Putt Putt Air Force* and V. Spencer in *Reaching for the Skies* place the departure date on 2 April 1943.

159. *Putt Putt Air Force,* 45, and V. Spencer, 4.

160. Francis, 30.

161. Benjamin O. Davis Jr., *Benjamin O. Davis, Jr. American.* (Washington: Smithsonian Institution Press, 1991), 93–94, 179.

162. Hardesty and Pisano, 39.

163. Davis, 40–41.

164. Hardesty and Pisano, 39.

165. Davis, 103.

166. V. Spencer, 4.

167. *Time,* 20 September 1943, 68.

168. *Time,* 18 October 1943, 8, 11.

169. *Time,* 14 February 1944, 68.

170. Hardesty and Pisano, 40.

171. Glines, "Red-Tailed Fighter," 30.

172. Hardesty and Pisano, 49.

173. *St. Louis Post Dispatch,* 28 November 1944.

174. "World War II Air Force Hero Joseph Elsberry Dies," *Jet,* 29 April 1985, 29.

175. "Archer Leads All U.S. Negro Airmen," *New York Sun,* 29 January 1945.

176. Robert Rose, *Lonely Eagles: The Story of America's Black Air Force in WWII* (Los Angeles: Tuskegee Airmen, Western Region, 1976), 73; John Holway, *Red Tails, Black Wings: The Men of America's Black Air Force* (Las Cruces, N.M.: Yucca Tree Press, 1997).

177. V. Spencer, 5.

178. V. Spencer, 6, and Glines, 30, state the 332d received the Presidential Unit Citation.

179. Hardesty and Pisano, 55, and V. Spencer, 5.

180. Gubert, xv.

181. *Putt Putt Air Force,* 45.

182. Glines, 30.

183. Gubert, xv.

184. Henry E. Dabbs, *Black Brass: Black Generals and Admirals in the Armed Forces of the United States* (Freehold, N.J.: Afro-American Heritage House, 1984), 52.

185. *Birmingham Post Herald,* 1 March 1995, F-1.

186. Hardesty and Pisano, 31.

187. Bombadier, "The Story of the 477th Bombardment Group," June 1944, 141–42. Reprinted from the *Pittsburgh Courier,* 11 March 1944.

188. James C. Warren, *The Freeman Field Mutiny* (Vacaville, Calif.: Conyers, 1996).

189. The United States Air Force was established as an independent military branch of the United States Armed Forces in 1947. The Signal Corps was originally responsible for Army Aviation until World War I when the Air Service was established. After World War I, the Air Service was reorganized as the Air Corps in 1926. After major changes were made to the Air Corps on the eve of World War II, the War Department established three military branches by March 1942. The three branches were the Army Air Forces, Army Ground Forces and Army Service Forces. Under this troika, the Army Air Corps was nominally a part of the Army but remained an administratively independent branch of the War Department. Charles A. Ravenstein, *Organization of the Air Force* (Maxwell Air Force Base, Ala.: Albert F. Simpson Historical Research Center, 1982).

190. "The Baggy Pants of Black Paratroopers," *Eagle and Swan* 1 (March 1978).

191. Bradley Biggs, *The Triple Nickels: Americas First All Black Paratroop Unit* (Hamden, Conn.: Archon Books Shoe String Press, 1986).

192. *Putt Putt Air Force,* 46.

193. Jacqueline Trescott, "The Law and Gen. James," *Washington Post,* 11 May 1976, B1, 3.

194. William Ulman, "Chappie James Has Twenty Minutes," *Argosy,* December 1954, 33, and Ulman, "Squadron Commander," *Look,* 19 October 1954, 129–35.

195. John Huey, "Guarding the Skies: Black 4 Star General Is a Man Accustomed to Tough Assignments," *Wall Street Journal,* 23 November 1976, 1, 34.

196. Joseph B. Treater, "Gen. Daniel James Jr. Dies at 58; Black Led American Air Defense," *New York Times,* 26 February 1978.

197. "Four-Star Black Pioneer," *New York Times,* 11 May 1987.

198. William Earl Brown, *A Fighter Pilot's Story,* National Air and Space Museum Occasional Paper Series no. 4 (Washington, D.C.: Smithsonian Institution, 1992).

199. T. J. Christmann, "'We All Shared a Common Bond,'" *Navy Times,* 16 December 1985, 71.

200. "Ens. Brown, Navy Pilot, Dies a Hero," *Journal and Guide,* Norfolk, Va., 12 December 1950, 1, 2.

201. Yvonne Price, "Navy Honors Black Hero," *Crises* 80 (8 October 1973): 277–78.

202. N. Laluntas, "Col. Frank E. Petersen Becomes the First Black Marine Corps General," *Eagle and Swan* 2 (May 1979): 44.

203. "Marine Corps," *Tuesday* 8 (4 December 1972): 9.

204. Tom Huntington, "An Eagle's Wings," *Air and Space/Smithsonian,* June/July 1988, 102–5.

205. Gen. Bernard P. Randolph biography, U.S. Air Force, Washington, D.C., Secretary of the Air Force, Office of Public Affairs.

206. "Major 'Fig' Newton a Thunderbird in the Sky," *Eagle and Swan* 1 (June 1978): 28–29.

207. Comdr. Donnie Cochran biography, U.S. Navy, Pensacola, Fla.

208. Aldore Collier, "The First Black Blue Angel," *Ebony,* June 1986, 27–30, 33–34.

209. August Martin, *Biographical Activities Book* (Washington, D.C.: Federal Aviation Administration, August 1980), GA-300–143A.

210. Neal V. Loving, *Loving's Love: A Black American's Experience in Aviation* (Washington, D.C.: Smithsonian Institution Press, 1994).

211. "Willa Brown Praised by CAA Chief Visiting Air School," *Nashville Defender,* 22 June 1940.

212. Roy Garvin, "Negro Aviator First to Land Aircraft on Turks Island in Bahama Group," *Negro History Bulletin,* October 1952, 19.

213. "T.W.A. Chooses Negro to Fill Executive Job in Office Here," *New York Times,* 28 August 1957.

214. "Bias Fight Won in Court, Negro Pilot Waits a Job," *Detroit News,* 23 April 1963, 1, 8.

215. Roland B. Scott, "U.S. Air Force Revises Policy for Flying Personnel with Sickle-Cell Trait," *Journal of the National Medical Association* 74 (September 1982): 835–36.

216. Larry Still, "Many Negroes Helped in Glenn's Epic 'Team Effort,'" *Jet,* 8 March 1962, 20–23.

217. "Gilliam Elected Fellow to American Astronautical Society," *Eagle and Swan* 2 (May 1979): 9.

218. Susan Heller Anderson, "Chronicle," *New York Times,* 22 September 1990, 27.

219. Scott Minerbrook, "No Room in Space for Earlier Black," *Newsday,* 4 September 1983.

220. "Careers Behind the Launchpad," *Black Enterprise,* February 1983, 59–60, 64.

221. William J. Broad, "First U.S. Black in Space: Guion Stewart Bluford Jr.," *New York Times,* 29 April 1991, B6.

222. Margaret L. Knox, "Ron McNair Was Always a Dreamer," *Atlanta Journal and Constitution,* 1 February 1986, A1.

223. William J. Broad, "Shuttle Atlantis Is Launched with Military Satellite," *New York Times,* 25 November 1991, A7.

224. "Maj. Bolden Joins NASA Space Shuttle Project," *Eagle and Swan* 3 (September 1980): 42.

225. John Noble Wilford, "Shuttle Lifts Off to Study Atmosphere," *New York Times,* 25 March 1992, A20.

226. Warren E. Leary, "U.S.–Japan Mission Is a Shuttle First," *New York Times,* 13 September 1992, 42.

References

Barbour, George Edward. "Early Black Flyers of Western Pennsylvania, 1906–1945." *Western Pennsylvania Historical Magazine,* April 1986, 95–97.

Davies, R. E. G. *A History of the World's Airlines.* London: Oxford University Press, 1967.

Davis, Benjamin O., Jr. *Benjamin O. Davis, Jr., American.* Washington: Smithsonian Institution Press, 1991.

Fischer, Audrey. "Bessie Coleman: Flying in the Face of All Odds." *Woman Pilot* 3 (March/April 1995): 8–11.

Foner, Jack D. *Blacks and the Military in American History: A New Perspective.* New York: Praeger, 1974.

Francis, Charles E. *The Tuskegee Airmen: The Story of the Negro in the U.S. Air Force.* Boston: Bruce Humphries, 1955.

Frenchman, Michael. "A 2,000-Year-Old Model Glider." In *Blacks in Science: Ancient and Modern,* ed. I. Van Sertima. New Brunswick, N.J.: Transaction Books, 1983.

Glines, Carroll V. "The Red-Tailed Fighter" *Retired Officer,* September 1992, 28.

Gubert, Betty Kaplan. *Invisible Wings: An Annotated Bibliography on Blacks in Aviation, 1916–1993.* Westport, Conn.: Greenwood Press, 1994.

Hardesty, Von, and Dominick Pisano. *Black Wings: The American Black in Aviation.* Washington, D.C.: National Air and Space Museum, 1983.

Jakeman, Robert J. *Divided Skies: Establishing Flight Training at Tuskegee, Alabama, 1934–1942.* Tuscaloosa: University of Alabama Press, 1992.

MacGregor, Morris J., and Bernard C. Nalty, eds. *Blacks in the Military: Basic Documents.* Wilmington, Del.: Scholarly Resource, 1977.

Messiha, Khalil, and Guirguis Messiha. "An Ancient Egyptian Aeroplane Model." In *Blacks in Science: Ancient and Modern,* ed. I. Van Sertima. New Brunswick, N.J.: Transaction Books, 1983.

Nalty, Bernard C. *Strength for the Fight: A History of Black Americans in the Military.* New York: Free Press, 1986.

Nugent, John Peer. *The Black Eagle.* New York: Stein and Day, 1971.

Peters, Raymond Eugene, and Clinton M. Arnold. *Black Americans in Aviation.* San Diego: Neyenesch Printers, 1975.

Spencer, Valora H. *Reaching for the Skies: The Overseas Experiment of the Tuskegee Airmen in World War II.* London: Academy Editions, 1995.

Strickland, Patricia. *The Putt-Putt Air Force: The Story of the Civilian Pilot Training Program and the War Training Service, 1939–1944.* Washington, D.C.: Department of Transportation, Federal Aviation Administration, Education Staff, [1971].

16

Women in Aviation

Hope Bouvette Thornberg

The Early Days, 1784–1900

Ballooning

IN A FLURRY OF PETTICOATS, women followed ducks, chickens, sheep, and men into the air in 1784—one year after the Montgolfier brothers' first balloon flights. Like the Montgolfier brothers, the first women's balloon ascents were made in France. Elisabeth Thible of Lyons, France, became the first woman passenger to fly in an untethered balloon, followed a few months later by Letitia Ann Sage in England. Sage was not only the first English woman to fly in a balloon, but she also had the distinction of being the heaviest person to take to the air![1]

Madeleine Sophie Blanchard was forced to earn her own living following her husband's death. Blanchard used her skill as a balloon pilot to produce magnificent fireworks displays, often accompanied by orchestra music on the ground. Her reputation throughout France resulted in Napoleon naming her "Official Aeronaut of the Empire." Blanchard made her first solo balloon ascent in 1805. She sought the peace and quiet of her balloon in flight to escape the noise of the city. She died in 1817 during a daring fireworks display.[2]

By the end of the 1800s, American women as well as European and British women had piloted their own balloons. In 1886, Mary H. Myers soared four miles above Franklin, Pennsylvania, establishing a world altitude record. This milestone flight was made without oxygen. As the century closed, interest grew in using balloons for scientific research with women working alongside men in their fragile gondolas.[3]

Parachutes

Ballooning displays provided colorful entertainment. However, while balloon flight offered grace and beauty, it did not appear to offer much risk and daring. Parachuting from balloons was introduced to thrill audiences. André Garnerin demonstrated the first successful parachute in France in 1797. His wife made her first and only jump in 1815, thus becoming the first woman to parachute. Eliza Garnerin, their niece, earned recognition as the first female professional parachutist, making thirty-nine jumps between 1816 and 1836.[4]

Dolly Shepherd, a young worker at the Ostrich Feather Emporium in England, talked her way into her first parachute jump during a balloon and parachute show at Alexandra Palace in 1903. Her jump was so successful that August Gaudron, the French balloonist and parachutist providing the entertainment, invited her to join his troupe of jumpers. Surprisingly, Dolly's parents did not forbid this activity. She received the mandatory thirty minutes of instruction, consisting primarily of the landing lesson, and went on to parachute for eight years. She retired a celebrity, the "Parachute Queen," at age twenty-five in 1912. The question of why Dolly Shepherd's parents allowed her to parachute was answered many years later. It was revealed that Madame Papillon, a parachutist in exhibitions near London, was her mother! Shepherd died at age ninety-six in 1983, after a life that included paramilitary service during both world wars.[5]

In spite of female involvement in flight almost from its inception, women's role in aviation and the question of the appropriateness of women flying as passengers—

let alone as pilots—was debated, primarily by men. Is it any wonder that, as recently as 1900, women arrived at a ballooning site well disguised? Flying, even as a passenger, was a highly suspect activity for the socially respectable woman.

Women and Their Flying Machines, 1910–1918

The airplane was a product of American ingenuity and perseverance, but it was in France that the first woman earned her wings. Raymonde de Laroche soloed in the single-place, kitelike Voisin aircraft after taxiing the length of the airfield. She earned her pilot's license from the Aero Club of France in March 1910. Helene Dutrieu, Belgium's first woman pilot, made her first flight in 1910 and a few months later astonished the world with a 28-mile nonstop cross-country flight. She went on to establish women's altitude, endurance, and cross-country records, and she won at least one race against an all-male field of contestants.[6]

De Laroche and Dutrieu, like their aviation-minded counterparts in other countries, were not typical early twentieth-century women content with lives dedicated primarily to husband, children, and homemaking. Those women who either chose or were forced to earn their own way generally elected such "female" occupations as teaching, nursing, secretarial work, or dressmaking. Before flying, de Laroche drove race cars, went ballooning, and performed on the stage besides sculpting and painting portraits. Dutrieu was a trick bicycle rider.[7]

Blanche Stuart Scott

Blanche Stuart Scott (fig. 16.1) learned to fly in 1910 from an American pioneer aviator, Glenn Curtiss. Scott attracted Curtiss's attention following her solo cross-country drive from New York to San Francisco. Scott was his first and last female student. It is not known whether Scott's first solo flight was intentional or accidental due to a wind gust—or assisted by a mechanic who removed the throttle block installed by Curtiss. After a few weeks of instruction, Scott joined the Curtiss flying team. She suddenly retired in 1916, voicing her discouragement over the lack of opportunities for women in the aviation field.[8]

Bessica Medlar Raiche

Bessica Medlar Raiche was named "First Woman Aviator of America" by the Aeronautical Society following her 1910 solo flight in the bamboo, piano wire, and silk airplane constructed by Medlar and her French husband. Although this event occurred after Blanche Stuart Scott first became airborne, the question about the intent of Scott's first takeoff remained. Born in the small community of Beloit, Wisconsin, Bessica Medlar was far from the typical midwestern small-town young woman. She wore bloomers, excelled in sports, and drove a car! Her parents allowed her to study music in France, where she met her husband. The Raiches formed the French-American Aeroplane Company and built two additional aircraft before Medlar became ill. Although she left aviation upon recovery, she did not abandon her nontraditional choice of careers. She became a physician, thus

Fig. 16.1. Blanche Stuart Scott. Courtesy of the Ninety-Nines, Inc.

entering another occupation in which women were not welcome in the early 1900s.[9]

Harriet Quimby

Harriet Quimby (fig. 16.2), a newspaper and magazine writer, was America's first licensed female pilot. Quimby was a beautiful woman who maintained an aura of mystery around her childhood and education. In 1903, she moved from California to New York City, where she began writing for *Leslie's Illustrated Weekly.* After describing for readers her ride around a race track at 60 mph in "A Woman's Exciting Ride in a Motor Car," Quimby earned her driver's license and began driving herself around the city. Clearly, this was a woman of action. After seeing her first air show at Belmont Park, Long Island, she asked John Moisant, brother of her friend Matilde, to teach her to fly. The lessons in the open cockpit of the Moisant monoplane had to wait until spring, and by then John Moisant had died in an airplane crash. The 35-year-old Quimby, along with Matilde Moisant, began flying lessons with Alfred, John's brother. Quimby disguised herself in men's clothing for lessons that were scheduled at sunrise. She wrote about her lessons for *Leslie's Weekly* in "How a Woman Learns to Fly."

In August 1911, after thirty-three lessons that included less than two hours in the air, her instructor invited officials from the Aero Club of America to witness from the ground her execution of the prescribed flight maneuvers. They agreed to her test only because there was also a male student ready for testing. Quimby performed the maneuvers correctly but failed the landing test. Nevertheless, two days later she not only became the first American woman to earn her pilot's license but also set a new precision landing record. Quimby noted in *Leslie's Illustrated Weekly:* "Flying seemed much easier than voting!" Women's suffrage did not occur until nine years later. She was the thirty-seventh pilot in the world to be licensed and the first American woman. Twelve days later, Matilde Moisant became America's second licensed woman pilot. Moisant abandoned aviation after less than a year, saying, "My flying career didn't last awfully long because in those days that was man's work and they didn't think a nice girl should be in it."[10]

Harriet Quimby's mother was a strong, determined woman who instilled in her younger daughter values and beliefs that supported women's rights and independence. While Quimby did not call herself a feminist, her writing often reflected these values. She wrote, "In my opinion, there is no reason why the aeroplane should not open up a fruitful occupation for women. I see no reason why they cannot realize handsome incomes by carrying passengers between adjacent towns, why they cannot derive incomes from parcel delivery, from taking photographs from above or from conducting schools for flying." Somewhat of a visionary, she added, "It is entirely feasible that airlines could be established to regularly fly distances of 50 to 60 miles."[11]

After earning her license, Quimby flew exhibitions in the United States and Mexico with the Moisant International Aviators. She competed in air shows and was the first woman to fly at night. On 16 April 1912, nine years after the Wright brothers' first flight, Quimby became the first woman to fly across the English Channel. She flew the 22 miles from England to France in one hour and nine minutes. Quimby returned to the United States by ship to find that her accomplishment was almost unnoticed due to the sinking of the *Titanic.* It was, nevertheless, an accomplishment. Quimby had navigated with only a compass over an unfamiliar route in an unfamiliar, reportedly tricky airplane with the unreliable engine of the time.[12]

Airplane accidents were common in the early days of flight with few pilots managing to avoid this misadventure. Harriet Quimby was among those few and was known as a cautious, skillful pilot. In an article for *Leslie's Illustrated Weekly,* she wrote, "There is nothing to fear if one is careful. Only a cautious person should fly. I never mount my machine until I check every wire and screw. I have never had an accident in the air. It may be luck but it is also due to the care of a good mechanic." Quimby's luck ran out at the 1912 Boston Air Show. Before the show, she was to fly the course with air show manager William Willard as her passenger. They took off in the new 70-horsepower Bleriot monoplane, a French two-place airplane with high performance (for that time) but challenging control characteristics. They had flown out to the Boston Light and turned inbound at

Fig. 16.2. Harriet Quimby in an open-cockpit Moisant monoplane. Courtesy of the Ninety-Nines, Inc.

2,000 feet when the airplane's tail abruptly rose and Willard was thrown from the plane. The airplane's balance was disturbed by the loss of Willard and the tail rose even further into the air, throwing out Quimby. Both pilot and passenger died. The airplane eventually leveled itself and glided to a watery landing.[13]

Seatbelts were not standard equipment in the airplanes of the day, and even when an aircraft had a restraining strap to restrict forward movement, pilots and passengers were not required to use them. On 27 April 1991, the U.S. Postal Service issued a commemorative stamp in honor of Quimby.

Julia Clark

Julia Clark, the third American woman to earn a pilot's license, was born in London but became a U.S. citizen. She received her license on 19 May 1912 and was killed in the crash of her airplane less than a month later, two weeks before Harriet Quimby's death.[14]

Ruth Law

Ruth Law (fig. 16.3), who had taken her first flying lesson earlier in the day, was among the crowd of people who witnessed Quimby's tragic death. In spite of this, Law soloed her airplane a few weeks later and went on to become the sixth woman to earn her pilot's license in 1912. She began a successful aviation career that was encouraged and supported by both her husband, Charles Oliver, and her brother, a trick parachutist and movie stunt man. Law was a skillful pilot but also daring and competitive. Her goal was to set flight records that would stand against both men and women. In November 1916, Law set out to beat Victor Carlstrom's American nonstop cross-country record of 452 miles. She took off from Chicago bound for New York City in a cold wind, flying her old 100-horsepower Curtiss Pusher. She had modified the airplane with auxiliary fuel tanks, a rubber fuel line, and a low aluminum windshield placed across the Pusher's open cockpit. Law had cut strips from the large Geodetic Survey maps along her route of flight, pasted them to cloth and rolled the cloth into a loop, providing a manageable method of tracking her route in the open windy cockpit. Law had flown for almost six hours and 590 miles when a sputtering engine forced her to land at Hornell, New York. While a bit short of New York City, she had established a new American nonstop cross-country record for both men and women. Law also set a new world's nonstop cross-country record for women. After a change of spark plugs and fueling, she continued to New York City where her accomplishment was acclaimed by the American public, including President and Mrs. Woodrow Wilson.[15]

With the entry of the United States into World War I in 1917, Ruth Law volunteered her flying skill to the Army. Newton Diehl Baker, secretary of war, responded: "We don't want women in the Army!" Law's contribution to the war effort was confined to fund-raising and recruiting flights. She later wrote an article for *Air Travel Magazine,* "Let Women Fly!" in which she commented, "There is the world-old controversy that crops up again whenever women attempt to enter a new field—is a woman fitted for this or that work?"[16]

Following the war, Ruth Law's Flying Circus toured Asia and the Philippines giving exhibitions of stunt flying. Her husband, serving as business manager, traveled with her. She appeared at state fairs, including a week at the 1920 Minnesota State Fair where she flew day shows featuring races against an automobile and night shows with fireworks displays. Her fee was $9,000! Law was among the first women to loop-the-loop, an aerobatic stunt that frightened her husband. In spite of her success, Law's penchant for taking risks was becoming a source of increasing concern to Oliver. In 1922, without consulting her, he announced her retirement to the press. Ruth Law retired, saying, "Things are so proper now . . . so many rules and regulations . . . the good old crazy days of flying are gone."[17] Law died in 1970 at the age of seventy-nine.

The Stinson Sisters

Following Harriet Quimby, Matilde Moisant, and Julia Clark, Katherine Stinson became the fourth American woman to earn a pilot's license and, at age sixteen, the youngest. Katherine (fig. 16.4), her sister, Marjorie (fig. 16.5), and their two brothers were encouraged by their mother, Emma, to learn to fly. Katherine earned her license in 1912 and embarked on a successful aviation career that encompassed aerobatic exhibitions both at home and abroad as well as endurance and distance record setting. In 1917, she broke the American nonstop cross-country record set by Ruth Law the year before by

Fig. 16.3. Ruth Law. Courtesy of James Goke.

flying from San Diego to San Francisco, a distance of 610 miles. Marjorie followed her into the air and earned her license in 1914. She, too, had a successful—if brief—aviation career, becoming the first woman to fly for the U.S. experimental airmail service at age seventeen. With the advent of World War I, the service was discontinued and did not restart until peacetime. Katherine and Marjorie gave flight instruction to American and Canadian men during World War I. Katherine joined Ruth Law in making flights for Liberty Loan Drives. The Stinson sisters were rejected when they attempted to enlist in the Army as pilots. Eventually Katherine drove an ambulance in France and Marjorie became an aeronautical draftsman for the U.S. Navy.[18]

The public clamored for news about aviation and aviators. News articles describing the feats of both men and women pilots were read eagerly. Stories about women aviators invariably included a description of their attire. Finding something suitable to wear flying was almost as challenging as flying itself. At a time when socially acceptable women's dress consisted of long skirts and large hats, women pilots were forced to stuff their petticoats into heavy bloomers to free their legs for flight. It was noted with appropriate shock that Belgium's Helene Dutrieu flew without wearing corsets. Knickers worn with high boots, a sweater, and a fabric helmet with goggles were the choice of most women aviators. An exception was Harriet Quimby's designer purple satin hooded flying suit worn with high laced black kid boots and elbow-length driving gloves. The full satin knickers could be converted to a walking skirt. A matching full-length cape for cold weather completed the ensemble.[19]

Fig. 16.4. Katherine Stinson. Courtesy of the Ninety-Nines, Inc.

Fig. 16.5. Marjorie Stinson. Courtesy of the Ninety-Nines, Inc.

In 1917, the Aero Club of America listed eleven licensed women pilots. The license was not required, and many women, who flew only occasionally for recreation, chose not to take the qualifying test. The air remained a male domain where only the most independent of women dared to trespass. Social pressures of the time dictated that the occupation of choice for the majority of women was homemaking. Flying was not among the "accepted" occupations for the woman who must earn an income. Men, anxious to preserve the air and flight for themselves, were not eager to encourage women in this new pursuit. Also, flying was expensive, and few women had the necessary resources at their disposal. The physical strength required to control early airplanes restricted many women from flying and further supported the notion that flying could not be undertaken by the "weaker sex." As airplane design improved, this barrier was removed. However, social pressure and economic barriers were not so easily removed. While women pilots are accepted today, they may not always be welcomed. Economics continues to deny females full access to careers as professional pilots.

Fig. 16.6. Bessie Coleman. Courtesy of the Ninety-Nines, Inc.

Peacetime and Flight, 1918–1930s

After the wartime ban on civilian flying, female and male aviators were eager to once again take to the sky. Many of the male pilots released from the military bought surplus airplanes and became barnstormers. They would fly from town to town throughout the country, bringing the excitement of flight to small-town America. Women, too, became barnstormers. If they could not afford to purchase an airplane, they began as wingwalkers or parachutists. Barnstorming enabled both men and women to maintain their flying skills (and, hopefully, earn a few dollars) until a real aviation job became available.

Bessie Coleman

The war provided the indirect impetus for at least one American woman to learn to fly. Bessie Coleman, an African American living in Chicago, had been searching for a way to "amount to something" ever since leaving her home in Texas in 1915. Coleman's brother John had served in France during the war. His stories of French

women pilots opened a new world to Bessie, one where she believed she finally could realize her ambitions. When Coleman was unable to find a flight instructor willing to help her achieve her goal, she went to France, where she earned her pilot's license from the Federation Aeronautique Internationale in 1921. She returned to the United States with her dream of opening a flight school that would teach African Americans to fly. But first she had to raise the money. So, wearing the French pilot's attire of leather helmet, long leather coat, and leather leggings, she barnstormed her way across the country in war-surplus Jenny trainers. In 1926, while Coleman was practicing for an exhibition flight in Florida, the airplane stalled and flipped over. Coleman was not wearing a seat belt, and she fell to her death.[20] In 1990, Chicago honored Bessie Coleman by naming a road on O'Hare Airport Field after her. The post office issued a Bessie Coleman stamp in April 1995 as part of the Black Heritage series (fig. 16.6).[21]

Military airplanes were technologically superior to earlier aircraft and could fly long distances. The Atlantic Ocean represented the greatest challenge to aviators of the day, particularly to those former military pilots who had flown in Europe. Few women were prepared to accept the challenge of long-distance flight. Military flying was prohibited to women, thus excluding them from the kind of training that prepared male pilots for transcontinental and transoceanic flight. The economic barrier remained with jobs available to women generally paying far less than those open to men. Few aviation jobs were open to women. Women pilots found it difficult to obtain financial backing for long-distance flights. Most did not have access to investors who frequently sponsored such flights made by male pilots. Finally, women pilots of the time lacked the confidence in their own piloting skills that would have allowed them to pursue long-distance flying, had the resources been available to them.

The practice of using women to promote goods and services related to aviation began in the early 1920s and continued into the 1960s. Women were still a minority in aviation, and each time one piloted an airplane, flew as a passenger, parachuted from an airplane, or walked upon its wing, it was, in today's terms, a "media event." The aviation industry saw no reason why it should not use the publicity value of women to promote aviation. Well-known women pilots were used in visual advertising to attract and hold consumer attention and imagination long enough for a message about a product or service to be noted.

Women pilots endorsed products ranging from engine oil, aviation fuel, and goggles to cigarettes. The most desirable endorsement opportunities were those for airplanes. Such endorsements sometimes led to flying jobs with the manufacturer as demonstration pilots or sales people. While the industry capitalized on the press value of women, the women were given the opportunity to earn money, remain more or less in aviation, and, in the case of airplane endorsements, often fly at company expense. In the latter, the message was "If a woman can do it, anyone can!" This was a trade-off, but one that women pilots were willing to accept as a means to the coveted end—flight!

Ruth Elder

Male and female pilots on both sides of the Atlantic wanted to replicate Charles Lindbergh's successful transoceanic flight of 1927. Nineteen pilots lost their lives trying during that year alone. Ruth Elder (fig. 16.7), an inexperienced American pilot, was one of the more for-

Fig. 16.7. Ruth Elder. Courtesy of the Ninety-Nines, Inc.

tunate ones. She and George Haldeman, her flight instructor, were well along in their late 1927 transatlantic flight when an overheated engine forced them to ditch. The two were flying the *American Girl,* a Stinson Detroiter, which Elder had optimistically boarded carrying a picnic basket full of provisions for the long flight. They were picked up by a Dutch tanker, and Elder went on to place fifth in the first Women's Air Derby in 1929. She later became a Hollywood screen actress.[22]

Amelia Earhart

Amelia Earhart, probably the best-known woman in aviation, began her aviation career in the competition to be the first woman to fly across the Atlantic. Mrs. Frederick Guest, an American living in England, had purchased a Fokker Trimotor, which she planned to use for such a flight. After her wealthy family objected to her plan, she agreed to remain on the ground—but only if an "American girl of the right image" could be found to fly in her place. Publisher George Palmer Putnam served on the committee to find such a woman, and it was his associate who suggested Amelia Earhart as a candidate (fig. 16.8).

After earning her private pilot's license in 1922 in California, Earhart flew in a few small air shows and established a new women's altitude record of 14,000 feet. However, the most famous of all women pilots professed to "not like public flying." Flying remained an avocation while Earhart pursued college, taught, and worked with immigrants at the Denison Settlement House in Boston. The thirty-year-old Earhart was engaged in this latter

occupation when she was invited to fly across the Atlantic in the place of Mrs. Guest, who remained the flight's sponsor. The pontoon-equipped Fokker Trimotor was named the *Friendship* and was flown by two experienced male pilots, Wilmer Stultz and Louis "Slim" Gordon. Earhart lacked the requisite instrument and multiengine skills essential for transoceanic flight. From the time she agreed to make the trip in April 1928, she knew she would be flying only as a passenger.

Secrecy surrounded the planned flight to avoid publicity and prevent competition for the first woman's transatlantic flight. While the flight crew waited for favorable weather, Earhart continued her work at Denison House and wrote letters of farewell to her family to be

Fig. 16.8. Amelia Earhart's pilot's license. Courtesy of the Ninety-Nines, Inc.

opened if she died. The *Friendship* departed on 3 June 1928, with Earhart wearing a borrowed fur-lined flying outfit and sharing space with the extra fuel tanks. The first leg of the flight was from Boston Harbor to Trepassey, Newfoundland, where the airplane was fueled and then sat on the ground for two weeks waiting for improved weather. On 17 June, the *Friendship* took off on its final leg. After 20 hours and 40 minutes of flying in largely overcast conditions and fog, pilot Stultz landed at Burry Port, Wales. Amelia Earhart became an instant celebrity! While Stultz and navigator Gordon were all but ignored, Earhart found herself elevated to "star" status by an adoring public, a role that she believed was undeserved. In responding to a congratulatory cable from President Calvin Coolidge, she wired, "Success entirely due great skill of Mr. Stultz."[23]

The *Friendship*'s successful transatlantic flight abruptly thrust Earhart into the mainstream of aviation where she remained until the end of her life. Her style as well as her flight captivated the public. The attire of women pilots was always scrutinized, often earning them criticism for dressing in "men's clothing." However, Earhart was a style-setter in tailored slacks and shirts, simple dresses, and a short, casual haircut (fig. 16.9). The press capitalized on her physical resemblance to Charles Lindbergh by calling her "Lady Lindy." This dismayed Earhart, who clearly was her own person—an intelligent, attractive woman who downplayed her role in the *Friendship*'s flight. She was quick to agree with editorial comments in the *London Evening Standard* suggesting that her presence on the flight had added little to its success. She did not realize at the time that her passenger role had created a rallying point—a new goal—for women pilots. The next time a woman crossed the Atlantic by air, it must be alone as the pilot!

George Palmer Putnam had continued his involvement during preparations for the *Friendship*'s flight. When Amelia Earhart ("AE" was the nickname she adopted during the flight) returned to the United States from Great Britain, it was Putnam who took over the management of her aviation career. Putnam decided which speaking engagements Earhart should accept, which products she should endorse, and which promotional tours she should undertake. Earhart recognized that celebrity status often lends an aura of authority to one's words and actions, and she used this to become a spokesperson for women's role in aviation. She was an outspoken proponent of the achievements and contributions that could be made by women aviators, while she criticized the aerobatic and stunt flying associated with flying circuses. Earhart wanted women pilots to be accepted on the basis of their aviation skills and accomplishments. Her job as aviation editor of *Cosmopolitan* magazine offered a forum for her opinions on women's role in aviation as well as more general topics such as aviation safety. Later, she became an advocate for women's rights in general. Earhart's philosophy and spirit of independence were reflected in the letter given to Putnam before their marriage ceremony, which stated her reservations about marriage along with certain conditions for the marital relationship with him.[24]

In May 1932, Amelia Earhart became the first woman to pilot an airplane across the Atlantic Ocean. She flew a fast Lockheed Vega and, after 15 hours and 18 minutes, landed in a farmer's field near Londonderry, Ireland. In spite of mechanical and weather problems, Earhart set a

Fig. 16.9. Amelia Earhart. Courtesy of the Ninety-Nines, Inc.

new record for a transatlantic flight. Upon her return to the United States, President Herbert Hoover awarded her the gold medal of the National Geographic Society. Perhaps more important than this distinction was the knowledge that she had proven her skill as a pilot and vindicated her earlier Atlantic crossing as a passenger. Three years later Earhart, again flying the Vega, became the first pilot to fly solo between Hawaii and California. Her flying skills honed by these record-setting flights, Earhart was determined to fly around the world at the equator. She would become the first woman to circle the globe and the first pilot of either gender to tackle this longest, most difficult route.[25]

In 1935, Earhart accepted a position at Purdue University counseling women students on their role in aviation. Purdue established the Amelia Earhart Research Foundation, which would purchase and equip an aircraft for Earhart to use as a flying laboratory. Contributions mounted, and soon there was sufficient money to purchase the airplane she wanted—a twin-engine Lockheed Electra. The Electra had a top speed of 200 miles per hour and a spacious cabin that would accommodate the extra equipment and fuel tanks needed for a globe-circling flight. Earhart believed that such a flight would provide an appropriate environment for research addressing such questions as gender differences in flight and physiological effects of altitude.

Earhart acquainted herself with the Electra by flying cross-country trips followed by the 1936 Bendix race from New York to Los Angeles. Meanwhile, Putnam arranged for fuel and oil supplies and spare parts to be stored along the planned equatorial route and obtained the necessary government permissions from the countries where Earhart would either overfly or land. After studying aviation charts and global weather patterns and locating emergency landing sites, Earhart decided that a navigator would be necessary for the long legs over the Pacific. Harry Manning, a sea captain on leave, agreed to serve as chief navigator with aerial navigator Fred Noonan assisting him on the most difficult Honolulu to Howland Island leg. Earhart would fly on alone after the Pacific part of the route. On 17 March 1937, the crew of four—Earhart, Manning, Noonan, and technical adviser Paul Mantz—departed from Oakland, California. Mantz was flying only as far as Hawaii. Unfortunately, the Electra ground-looped during takeoff from Honolulu and

had to be shipped back to the Lockheed factory in California for extensive repairs requiring two months. This delay brought a change of seasons and worldwide weather patterns, making it preferable to reverse the route of flight. The new route would take the Electra east over the Atlantic, leaving the Pacific legs for last. Noonan, sole navigator when Manning returned to his shipboard duties, and Earhart had to acquaint themselves with different weather patterns and emergency landing fields. Putnam had to make new arrangements for fuel, oil, and spare parts and obtain new government permissions. There was concern about the crew's ability to locate tiny Howland Island. Mantz had installed the best available radio equipment, including a 250-foot trailing antenna wire, which allowed signals to be sent from the Electra to a receiver aboard the USS *Itasca* stationed off Howland Island. While Earhart and Noonan were using the airplane's direction finder to locate the island, the Coast Guard would be using its equipment to locate the Electra.[26]

On 1 June 1937, Amelia Earhart and Fred Noonan departed east from Miami, Florida. The initial legs of the globe-circling flight were uneventful. The Electra landed in Lae, New Guinea, the last stop before Howland Island, on 30 June. While the aircraft had performed well on the long flight, Noonan had problems with the precision timepieces that were needed for dead reckoning navigation over water. On 1 July, the Electra, carrying maximum fuel, departed Lae for the 18-hour flight to Howland. Several U.S. Navy ships with the latest radio equipment as well as the *Itasca* received Earhart's voice radio transmissions only erratically and the Electra was not sighted. Earhart's airplane never arrived at Howland.

President Franklin Roosevelt authorized an unprecedented air-sea search costing millions of dollars. On 18 July 1937, Amelia Earhart and Fred Noonan were officially declared lost at sea. Investigation of the tragedy indicated that they had left behind emergency flares and the trailing radio antenna had either been left behind or broken off during the trip. In addition, neither Earhart or her navigator had expertise in radio operation. The disappearance of the Electra and its crew has inspired books, television documentaries, and privately funded searches of Pacific islands. The where and why of the Electra probably will never be discovered. Nevertheless,

Amelia Earhart, her achievements, and her contributions will not be forgotten! The Amelia Earhart stamp issued by the U.S. Postal Service on 24 July 1963 was the first to honor a woman pilot.

Ruth Nichols

Eleven months before Amelia Earhart's successful transatlantic flight, Ruth Nichols had attempted to fly the Atlantic. On 22 June 1931, Nichols took off from New York in the *Akita,* a Lockheed Vega equipped with extra fuel tanks and the most sophisticated navigation instruments. Her flight was to take her to St. John, New Brunswick, for refueling and then on to Harbour Grace, Newfoundland, and finally to Paris. Nichols overshot the runway at St. John, crashing into a hill and severely injuring herself as well as damaging the airplane. Bad weather forced postponement of her second attempt in September 1931. Nichols then decided to try to better the world distance record of 1,849 miles established by French pilot Maryse Bastie. Her plan was to fly nonstop from California to New York, but poor weather interfered and she was forced to land in Louisville, Kentucky. Nichols had flown 1,977 miles and established a new nonstop cross-country record. It was the last flight the Vega would make. On takeoff the next day, the fuselage burst into flames when a leaking fuel valve caught fire. Nichols managed to escape from the aircraft only moments before the fuel tank exploded. The fire not only destroyed the Vega but also Ruth Nichols's dreams of a transatlantic flight.[27]

Nichols grew up in an affluent family in New York, where she attended private schools. While vacationing in Florida, she made her first flight with a barnstorming pilot who allowed her to handle the seaplane's controls. After graduating from Wellesley College, Nichols earned her private pilot's license. Since her career choices of medicine or aviation were unacceptable to her family, she began working in a bank and continued to fly. In 1928, her former flight instructor Harry Rogers asked her to serve as his copilot on a record-setting flight of 12 hours from New York to Miami. Ruth Nichols instantly became famous and, at the age of twenty-seven, began her aviation career as a sales representative for the Fairchild Company.

Ruth Nichols's preparation to fly solo across the Atlantic Ocean included challenging speed and altitude records in a borrowed Vega. By 1931, she had established a new woman's speed record of 210.6 miles per hour and a new woman's altitude record of 28,743 feet.[28]

Following her attempted transatlantic flight, Ruth Nichols became an outspoken proponent of aviation, emphasizing the role of women within this emerging career field. She founded Relief Wings, a humanitarian organization that was merged into the Civil Air Patrol during World War II. In 1949, Nichols became the first woman to complete a globe-circling flight when she flew as a crew member in a DC-4 on a relief flight.[29]

Women's Air Derby and the Ninety-Nines

The first Women's Air Derby was held as a part of the 1929 National Air Races (fig. 16.10). Although women pilots had been making and breaking records in speed, distance, altitude, and endurance for several years, few had entered air races. The 1929 Women's Air Derby would give pilots such as Ruth Nichols, Amelia Earhart, Louise Thaden, Evelyn "Bobbi" Trout, Blanche Noyes, Phoebe Omlie, and Florence "Pancho" Barnes the opportunity to compete as well as overcome the unwillingness of men to accept women in the air. Entry requirements were a private pilot's license and at least 100 hours of solo flying time. It was estimated that only thirty women pilots in the country met these requirements. The Women's Air Derby consisted of nine days of challenging flying—2,800 miles—over mountains, desert, and flat lands between Santa Monica, California, and Cleveland, Ohio. Prior to the start of the race, one contestant received a threatening telegram, and oil was found in the fuel tanks of two of the race airplanes. Negative male reaction appeared in the press, which dubbed the women "Flying Flappers," "Petticoat Pilots," and "Ladybirds." The name that humorist Will Rogers gave the race, "Powder Puff Derby," persisted for many future women's air races. Twenty women pilots entered the race and fifteen finished. Marvel Crossen, a commercial pilot from Alaska, died when her parachute failed to open after she bailed out of her damaged aircraft. The press seized upon Crossen's death as further proof of female incompetence, and demands were made to cancel the race. The race committee refused. Louise Thaden, current holder of women's speed, altitude, and endurance records, placed first. Gladys O'Donnel placed second and Amelia Earhart third.[30]

Fig. 16.10. First Women's Air Derby, 1929. Courtesy of the Ninety-Nines, Inc.

The nine-day Women's Air Derby had proven that women pilots were competent and determined as well as mentally and physically strong. A bond had been forged among the contestants, and the women were unwilling to let it go. Four of the contestants along with twenty-two other women met at Curtiss Field, Long Island, on 2 November 1929 to form an organization of women pilots. Invitations to join the new organization were sent to the 126 licensed women pilots in the United States. Ninety-nine accepted and, at Amelia Earhart's suggestion, the name "Ninety-Nines" was selected for the group. Earhart was elected its first president. The goal of the Ninety-Nines was—and is—to encourage and support women in aviation and to enhance opportuni-

ties for women seeking careers in this male-dominated field. The Ninety-Nines has been international almost from its beginning, and today it has more than 6,000 members.

The Middle Days, Mid-1930s

In 1935, there were between 700 and 800 licensed women pilots in the United States—a substantial increase over the 200 in 1930. A 1935 *National Aeronautics* magazine survey of 142 women pilots revealed that twenty-one were employed professionally in aviation, thirty-five were homemakers, and thirty-three had independent incomes. Aviation occupations included flight instructor, ferry pilot, flight school operator, aerial crop surveyors, executives, and transport pilots. Other occupations represented by women pilots were physician, teacher, social worker, journalist, artist, nurse, and college student.

Among the women employed in aviation was Inez Gibson, owner of Gibson's Union Air Services in Burbank, California. Union Air Services was a charter service catering to businessmen and wealthy travelers who wanted to fly to destinations not served by the few scheduled airlines. Although a pilot herself, Gibson did not fly her own charters—nor did she hire female pilots. The flying public preferred to see a male pilot in the cockpit, and Gibson believed it only good business to please her customers.

Penn School of Aviation in Pittsburgh, Pennsylvania, was convinced that women learned to fly differently than men and therefore required different methods of instruction. A "woman's division" was created in 1930, and Louise Thaden, an experienced pilot and aviation record setter, was appointed director. The same instructors and equipment were utilized for the women as for the male students. Thaden kept careful records of her women students' progress. At the end of the first year of operation, she reported that women were quicker than men to learn takeoffs and air maneuvers but slower in acquiring landing skill.

In 1934, the first woman pilot was hired by a regularly scheduled airline. Central Airlines hired an accomplished racing and aerobatic pilot from Pittsburgh, Helen Richey (fig. 16.11). While growing up, Richey, a tomboy, preferred boys' toys to the traditional dolls, and when she was twelve, she ran away with a circus. Her father brought her home. After high school, she enrolled in college to become a teacher. Richey lived near an airport but had not flown until she and a friend took an impromptu flight from Pennsylvania to Cleveland, Ohio. Ruth Nichols landed at Cleveland that same day and impressed Richey so much that she decided to learn to fly. She earned her private pilot's license in 1930 at the age of twenty. Her father gave her an airplane as a reward.

While Richey's goal was to fly commercially, she recognized that no airline in the United States had hired a woman pilot. So she learned aerobatic flying and began air racing. Soon after being hired by Central Airlines,

Richey realized that her gender and aviation reputation were the basis for her employment. During the ten months with Central, she was scheduled to make only a dozen flights. Richey found herself behind a speaker's lectern more than in the cockpit of a Ford Trimotor aircraft. The Federal Bureau of Air Commerce had forbidden Richey to fly in bad weather, setting her apart from Central's male pilots. Further, the all-male pilots' union denied her membership. Helen Richey resigned in disappointment. It was not until 1973 that a U.S. airline would hire a second woman pilot. In 1936, Richey joined the U.S. Bureau of Air Commerce's national air marking program. When the program ended, she became the first woman to train flight cadets for the U.S. Army Air Corps. In the early 1940s, Richey served as a ferry pilot with the British Air Transport Auxiliary, but in 1943 she returned to the United States to join the Women's Airforce Service Pilots (WASP). After World War II, Helen

Fig. 16.11. Helen Richey. Courtesy of the Ninety-Nines, Inc.

Richey became despondent in her belief that the doors to an aviation career were closed to her. She died alone, apparently of suicide, in 1947.[31]

Meanwhile, Phoebe Omlie (fig. 16.12), who had been appointed special assistant for Air Intelligence of the National Advisory Committee for Aeronautics in 1933, convinced the chief of the Airport Marking and Mapping Section of the U.S. Bureau of Air Commerce to start a national air marking program. At 15-mile intervals, the name of the nearest town or city would be painted on the roof of the tallest building. If there were no buildings, white painted rocks would be used. The purpose of this program was to make navigation easier for private pilots who were reluctant to fly the established airways. In 1934, Omlie was named director of the air marking program and promptly named five prominent women pilots to serve with her—Helen Richey, Louise Thaden, Nancy Harkness, Helen McCloskey, and Blanche Noyes, who later became chief of the air marking staff. These five women worked

Fig. 16.12. Phoebe Omlie. Courtesy of the Ninety-Nines, Inc.

throughout the country, and by 1936 thirty states were involved in the program with more than 16,000 signs approved. As the western world moved toward World War II, the air marking program was ended. Many markers were removed or painted over to prevent invading enemy aircraft from receiving navigational assistance or building identification. Air marking is now a national project of the Ninety-Nines, Inc., with local chapters painting the city name on the airport surface.

Phoebe Fairgrave Omlie began her aviation career as a parachutist and wingwalker. Vern Omlie, a World War I flyer, taught her to fly, and later they married. She was the first woman pilot to earn the most advanced of pilot certificates, the Transport license. She served as Franklin D. Roosevelt's pilot during his 1932 presidential campaign and again in 1936. Many years later, Phoebe Omlie became an outspoken opponent of the federal government's regulation of aviation. Poverty-stricken following business failures, she died of lung cancer and alcoholism in 1975 at seventy-two.[32]

Blanche Noyes was a corporate pilot for Standard Oil of Ohio when Phoebe Omlie asked her to become a member of the air marking team. Noyes had learned to fly from her husband, Dewey Noyes, and she was the first licensed female pilot in Ohio. She flew in air races, worked as a demonstration pilot, and promoted aviation through lecture tours. Noyes learned instrument flying from her husband, and the couple was planning to circle the globe when he was killed during a flight of his Beechcraft Staggerwing. She later was named chief of the air marking staff, and for many years was the only woman the federal government allowed to fly its airplanes. Blanche Noyes was a lifelong advocate of aviation, women pilots, and flight safety.

Anne Morrow Lindbergh contributed to aviation both through her flying and through her writing. She was the first American woman to earn a glider pilot's license; a year later, she earned her private pilot's license. Anne grew up in an affluent family and led a traditional life until meeting and marrying famed transatlantic pilot Charles A. Lindbergh (fig. 16.13). After she earned her private pilot's license, the couple began flying, studying and mapping commercial air routes over the Atlantic together. Anne Lindbergh served as navigator, copilot, and radio operator on these flights. The most famous

Fig. 16.13. Anne Morrow Lindbergh and Charles A. Lindbergh pose in front of their Lockheed Sirius, *Tingmissartoq*. By permission of the National Air and Space Museum, Smithsonian Institution, ©1999 Smithsonian Institution.

flight was later described in her book *North to the Orient*. She was the first woman to be awarded the National Geographic Society's Hubbard Medal.[33]

Jeanette Piccard and husband, Jean, also flew together, but their aircraft was a balloon. The balloon had been featured at the 1933 Chicago World's Fair. Afterwards, the balloon was turned over to the Piccards because of Jean's interest in studying cosmic rays in the stratosphere. Neither Jean nor Jeanette had a balloon pilot's license. The couple decided that Jeanette would earn a license and fly the balloon while Jean served as the scientific observer. Jeanette completed her flight training in May 1934. On 23 October of that year, the Piccards made their historic

flight. There was considerable opposition to a woman serving as pilot for the flight. The National Geographic Society, a frequent backer of such expeditions, stated that it wanted nothing to do with sending a woman—a mother!—up in a balloon. The flight was successful, and at 57,579 feet Jeanette Piccard became the undisputed holder of the women's altitude record. After raising three sons and being widowed, her independence and determination led her to achieve her lifelong goal of ordination as a priest in the Episcopal Church.[34]

Women were employed in aircraft manufacturing in the early 1930s, the majority in the wing and fuselage fabric covering departments. Seventeen of the Boeing

Company's 852 employees were women. Although women performed the same work as men, they were not paid the same. Women earned only 40–45 cents per hour while men earned 60–65 cents.

Few women sought careers as aeronautical engineers in the 1930s, and those who did found few engineering schools that would accept them. Aero engineer Isabel Ebel worked with Amelia Earhart to lay out the course for Earhart's record transcontinental flight in 1932. Later, Ebel persuaded the New York Board of Education to offer aeronautics classes in high schools to both girls and boys.

The most conventional aviation career for women is that of flight attendant or, as it was called in the 1930s, stewardess. Ellen Church, a pilot and registered nurse, tried to talk Boeing Air Transport into hiring her as an airline pilot. When she was clearly making no headway, Church adroitly maneuvered the discussion to focus on the advantages of adding a stewardess to the flight crew. She managed to convince Boeing that hiring female registered nurses as stewardesses would free the male copilot for flying duties. This would demonstrate to the flying public the company's concern for their safety and welfare. The stewardess had to be single, no older than twenty-five, weigh no more than 115 pounds, and be no taller than 5'4". At first, all stewardesses were required to be registered nurses, and they wore the white nurse's uniform and cap. The women were paid $125 per month for 100 hours of flying. Stewardesses were expected to clean the aircraft, assist in its refueling, wind the aircraft's clock, and serve passengers. An important duty was to watch passengers on their way to the rest room to make certain they opened the rest room door rather than the emergency exit! Boeing hired eight women as stewardesses with other airlines following so that by the mid-1930s there were 200–300 in airline service in the United States.

Women in Wartime, 1939–1944

The world was heading toward war, and women were eager to contribute to their country's role. Government and military leaders in the United States as well as in other countries considered how women might best serve the war effort. Women pilots were given special attention because they already knew how to fly—a skill scarce at the beginning of World War II. From the beginning,

German and Russian women pilots were allowed to use their flying skills. However, only in Russia were women pilots recruited, militarized, and allowed to fly fighter and bomber combat missions. Women pilots in most other countries had to content themselves with replacing men in ground jobs, working in aircraft manufacturing, or joining a military auxiliary organization that would allow them to serve as parachute riggers, air traffic controllers, or instructors.

The British Air Ministry formed the Air Transport Auxiliary (ATA) to ferry aircraft during the war. Pauline Gower was able to convince the Air Ministry to allow women pilots in this organization. Gower was able to do this because of her service as a commissioner of the prewar Civil Air Guard and because her father was a member of British Parliament. She was given permission to recruit eight women pilots for a women's section of the ATA that would ferry small training aircraft. These highly experienced women pilots were paid 20 percent less than the ATA's male members and, unlike the men, had to pay for their own lodging. Soon there were more than 100 women flying almost every type of aircraft that the Royal Air Force flew. Long-distance British flyer Amy Johnson was the most famous ATA female pilot. She was one of the fifteen women who were killed on duty.[35]

Record-breaking American pilot Jacqueline Cochran had tried to convince the U.S. government and its military leaders that an organization of women pilots should be formed to provide services similar to those of the ATA should this country enter the war. Her suggestion was viewed with skepticism by the military, who doubted the flying competence of women. Cochran convinced Gen. Henry "Hap" Arnold to allow her to ferry a Lockheed Hudson bomber to England in 1941 as a demonstration of the role women might play. She trained for the flight in Montreal, Quebec, making sixty takeoffs and landings and was pronounced qualified and assigned the ferry flight. Male ferry pilots believed that ferrying aircraft was "men's work" and threatened to strike if Cochran were allowed to make the flight. The resulting compromise placed a male copilot in the cockpit who would take off and land.[36]

Jackie Cochran returned to the United States with additional knowledge about women's role in the ATA. She contacted by mail almost 3,000 women pilots to determine their interest in becoming members of a women's flying organization that would support the war effort in the event the country became involved. In the late 1930s, the government-sponsored Civilian Pilot Training program (CPT) had enabled men and a limited number of women to receive pilot training provided by selected colleges and flight schools. This program had quickly increased the number of both men and women pilots. Response to Cochran's letter was overwhelmingly positive. She again approached General Arnold with evidence of the women pilots' interest. Cochran was turned down with the suggestion that she recruit these women for service with the ATA. In late summer 1941, twenty-five experienced women pilots were selected, and along with Cochran they left for England. These women joined women pilots from throughout the world who wanted to contribute their flying skills to the global war. All the American women completed their 18-month contracts

with the ATA, and some remained for the rest of the war. One American died, and several were injured.[37]

Women's Auxiliary Ferrying Squadron (WAFS)

When Jackie Cochran returned to the United States, she found that the Women's Auxiliary Ferrying Squadron (WAFS) had been formed under the Army Air Forces' Air Transport Command (ATC). Nancy Harkness Love, wife of Maj. Robert Love who was deputy chief of staff of the ATC's ferrying division, was director of the WAFS. Nancy Love was twenty-seven with over 1,200 hours of flight time acquired since earning her private pilot's license in 1930 at age sixteen. She earned a limited commercial pilot's license while attending Vassar College, and she was hired to sell new airplanes by Inter-City Air Service, a company started by Robert Love.

Fig. 16.14. Nancy Harkness Love. Courtesy of the Ninety-Nines, Inc.

Fig. 16.15. Women's Auxiliary Ferrying Squadron (WAFS) at the Fairchild plant in Hagerstown, Maryland, assembled in 1942 to pick up PT-19s, a primary trainer, to ferry to Air Force bases. Dressed in their winter flight suits, they are briefed by the control officer, Captain Frank. *(Left to right):* Squadron Cmdr. Betty Gillies, Nancy Batson Crews, Esther Nelson, Mary Helen Clark, Teresa James, Evelyn Sharp, and Captain Frank. Courtesy of the Ninety-Nines, Inc.

In 1935, Phoebe Omlie named Nancy Harkness (fig. 16.14) as one of five women pilots to serve as field representatives for the national air marking program. Nancy married Robert Love in 1936, and in 1937 she became a test pilot for the Gwinn Aircar Company in Buffalo, New York. When war became imminent in Europe, Love moved to Boston and earned her instrument rating. She once helped ferry an airplane from the United States to Canada and then to France. Nancy Love and Jackie Cochran both believed that women pilots should be allowed to contribute their flying skills to their country. However, Love wanted to bring women into the ATC's male ferrying unit while Cochran wanted a separate women's military organization. Love's original proposal,

like Cochran's, had been turned down. In 1940, the United States was not yet at war. Government and military leaders were not ready to recognize women pilots' flying competence or to agree that they might play a role in wartime flying.

Nancy Harkness Love's proposal was given a second look following the United States' entry into World War II in December 1941. The WAFS were born, and as Cochran had found with her earlier letters of inquiry to women pilots, the women were eager to support their country's war effort (fig. 16.15). By fall 1942, twenty-three women pilots having the required 500 hours of flight time were accepted into the WAFS at New Castle Army Air Base, Wilmington, Delaware. These women brought to the organization thousands of hours of flight time acquired through instructing, barnstorming, and demonstrating new aircraft.

The WAFS were to ferry aircraft for the military, and Love and her pilots believed that they would be treated like male ferry pilots. Men were commissioned in the Army Air Forces after a 90-day trial period and given flight pay. However, it was not to be. The military had no provision for flight pay for women, and rather than postpone the WAFS program, the WAFS were brought into the ATC as Civil Service employees without military privileges. At first, the WAFS ferried small training aircraft from manufacturing plant to airbases and from one airbase to another. Soon they were ferrying almost every type of airplane the Army Air Forces had (fig. 16.16). By 1943, the WAFS had expanded into four squadrons stationed at Romulus, Michigan; Long Beach, California; Dallas, Texas; and New Castle. The women pilots purchased gray slacks and jackets at their own expense. Since military air bases had no accommodations for women other than for nursing staff, the WAFS had to secure their own lodging in towns adjacent to the bases. The small per diem allowance they were paid barely covered a room and meals. If a WAFS member had the misfortune of becoming ill, she was free to visit the base physician; however, if he advised hospitalization, she would have to enter a civilian hospital. The WAFS soon earned the respect of the Army Air Forces for their dedication, enthusiasm, and excellent safety record.[38]

The Women's Flying Training Detachment

By 1941, Jackie Cochran had established herself in aviation as the holder of seventeen aviation records and the first and only woman to fly a bomber across the Atlantic Ocean. She was confident and occasionally arrogant, assertive (some said aggressive), flamboyant, demanding, outspoken, and used to getting her own way. She was very different from the quiet, competent Nancy Harkness Love. But, unlike so many women pilots of the time, Cochran was said to be feminine and comfortable with herself as a woman in the male-dominated field of aviation. She believed that women had special talents and abilities that made them excellent pilots. Upon her return to the United States from England in 1942, Cochran found that Love's proposal for the formation of the WAFS had been accepted. Cochran protested to Gen.

Fig. 16.16. Teresa James *(left)* and Betty Gillies pose for an Air Force photographer after delivering a couple of P-47s to the modification center at Evansville, Indiana. Courtesy of the Ninety-Nines, Inc.

Hap Arnold and other military leaders, questioning why Love's proposal had been implemented while her own had been ignored. Cochran prevailed. There would be two women's flight programs: Nancy Love's highly experienced WAFS would ferry aircraft for the ATC, and Cochran would recruit and organize the Women's Flying Training Detachment, which would prepare inexperienced women pilots to move into the WAFS.[39]

Jackie Cochran

Victory was not new to Jackie Cochran (fig. 16.17). She managed to succeed at almost every thing she tried. Unlike Nancy Love, Cochran grew up without parental support and affection, without affluence, without sufficient food, without adequate education—even without shoes. She was raised by foster parents and took the name Cochran from a telephone book. Cochran learned early that if she was to lift herself out of poverty it must be through her own efforts. She learned midwifery before she was old enough to bear children, and she earned a bit of money assisting women to give birth. By the time she was ten, Cochran was supervising other children working in the sawmill where her foster parents worked. Her next job was in a beauty salon, and by the time she was fifteen, she had acquired the skills needed to work as a beautician. Cochran had little formal education and learned how to read by studying the lettering on passing railroad boxcars. After saving enough money to buy her first car and complete a three-year nursing program, she worked for a country doctor in Florida. However, she found the work depressing and poorly paid. She again worked as a beautician and soon was able to purchase a half interest in a Florida beauty shop.

Jackie Cochran's ambition took her to New York City, where she found work at Antoine's on Fifth Avenue. After returning to Florida to manage Antoine's Miami salon, she met Floyd Odlum, a prosperous businessman and attorney. He recognized Cochran's strong desire to succeed in creating her own cosmetics business but told her she would "need wings" to keep up with the competition. And that began her flying career.

In 1932, Cochran soloed after only three days of flight instruction and earned her private pilot's license in only two weeks. She established her cosmetics firm, but her first love became flying. Fortunately, Jacqueline Cochran Cosmetics succeeded, and the earnings enabled Cochran

Fig. 16.17. Jackie Cochran. Courtesy of the Ninety-Nines, Inc.

to purchase airplanes and begin her aviation career of distance flying and record breaking. She married Floyd Odlum, and they enjoyed a happy marriage on the Odlum Ranch near Palm Springs, California. Amelia Earhart was a frequent visitor. Cochran believed she had psychic powers, and when Earhart disappeared while attempting to fly around the world, George Putnam asked Cochran to use her powers to help locate his wife.[40]

Jackie Cochran received more than 25,000 applications from women pilots interested in joining the Women's Flying Training Detachment. Twenty-eight were selected. All were between twenty-one and thirty-five years of age and had at least 200 hours of flight time. They reported at their own expense to Houston's Rice Hotel, where Cochran greeted them. Early each morning they were picked up by an Army truck and driven to Howard Hughes Field for training. The training was conducted by the Army Air Forces and not always done by officers supportive of the women's detachment.

The day was divided between ground school studies and flight training given in old civilian aircraft. At the end of each day, the women would perform calisthenics for an hour, eat dinner, and then be trucked back to town. Avenger Field near Sweetwater, Texas, became the home of the Training Detachment and in 1943 the Women's Airforce Service Pilots (WASP). There the trainees lived in barracks and trained like male cadets. However, the women already knew how to fly, so fundamentals of flight was omitted, as was gunnery training and formation flying. Cochran insisted upon the military training and discipline, for she was confident that the women trainees would eventually be militarized just as would the WAFS. The women were not issued uniforms, but they did adopt a practical outfit of khaki slacks, white shirt, and khaki overseas cap. A uniform of Santiago blue slacks, battle jacket, and beret was adopted in 1943. The women pilots were civil servants and thus did not have military medical benefits, insurance, veterans' benefits, or death benefits.

Congress considered its first bill to militarize women pilots in spring 1944 and defeated it on 21 June. This action was due largely to lobbying by civilian male flight instructors who feared they would be eligible for the draft with the closing of the Army Air Forces wartime pilot training program. They believed they were qualified to ferry aircraft and that, if the women pilots were militarized, all ferrying of military aircraft would be assigned to these women.[41]

Women's Airforce Service Pilots (WASP)

The WAFS and the women pilots of the training detachment were merged into one organization in August 1943. Cochran had convinced the Army Air Forces that the two organizations should be combined with one person in charge—herself. Thus, the Women's Airforce Service Pilots were born (fig. 16.18). Cochran became director of women pilots, and Nancy Love became the WASP representative to the ATC's ferrying division. The WASP continued to provide prompt, efficient, safe ferrying of aircraft within the United States, and they were often preferred over male ferry pilots. The women pilots' competence was still viewed with skepticism by some and resented by others, but they performed any assignment they were given.

While ferrying military aircraft remained the primary task of the WASP, the towing of targets for student anti-aircraft gunnery practice was added in 1943. The women pilots flew old, beat-up aircraft towing targets for inexperienced, inaccurate gunnery students. At least one WASP died when her aircraft caught fire and crashed. WASP were also responsible for smoke laying during exercises, simulating gas attacks, and engineering test flights. After it was decided that the women could fly at night, missions to train radar and searchlight trackers were added. However, the women were not allowed to fly ferry flights at night, and they had to land and guard their airplanes, which often contained secret equipment. The 1,074 women of the WASP flew over 60 million miles and delivered 12,650 planes of seventy-seven types. Thirty-eight women died, and because they received no military death benefits, fellow WASP had to take up a collection to pay for transporting the body back to the woman's hometown for burial. Often another WASP, at her own expense, would accompany the casket.

The WASP program was ended on 20 December 1944. A second militarization bill had failed to pass in the Senate. The loss of Army Air Forces pilots during the war was lower than expected. As the military pilots returned home, they were assigned tasks formerly performed by the WASP. The WASP had done its job well, and General Arnold favored retaining the organization, but he could not do so without militarization. Just before Christmas, the women of the WASP were sent home.[42]

Enabling legislation authorizing the secretary of defense to make a determination regarding the military status of the WASP finally was passed by Congress in 1977. On 8 March 1979, the secretary of the Air Force granted military recognition and veteran status to the WASP (Public Law 95-202). This action officially recognized the contributions of the WASP and awarded the women well-deserved—albeit belated—veterans' benefits. Recognition required thirty-five years of waiting. Was it all worth it? According to Elizabeth Strohfus, former WASP living in Faribault, Minnesota, "You bet it was!"[43]

Women's Auxiliary Organizations

The Air WAACs were a part of the Women's Army Auxiliary Corps created by passage of a bill introduced by Rep. Edith Nourse Rogers in May 1942. The WAACs began with 25,000 women, but by the end of that year

Fig. 16.18. View of Boeing B-17 Flying Fortress on the ground with four pilots of the Women's Airforce Service Pilots (WASP) walking away from the plane holding their parachutes. They have been trained to ferry the B-17s across the Atlantic. The B-17 nose art is "Pistol Packin' Mama." By permission of the National Air and Space Museum, Smithsonian Institution, ©1999 Smithsonian Institution.

they numbered 150,000. From the beginning, the Army Air Forces was very interested in using WAACs for nonflying jobs. Forty-three percent, or 65,000 women, were assigned to the AAF. Here the WAACs were used as Link trainer instructors, gunnery instructors, airframe and power plant mechanics, teletype and radio operators, and air traffic controllers. It is interesting to note that, while black women comprised approximately 10 percent of WAACs' strength, relatively few served as Air WAACs because of the policy of segregation in the AAF. In 1943, the WAACs were integrated into the Army as the Women's Army Corps (WAC).

In the summer of 1942, Congress passed the law that created the Women Accepted for Volunteer Emergency Service (WAVES). The Navy Bureau of Aeronautics was eager to utilize this new source of help and immediately requested 20,000 WAVES, who were put to work in many of the same capacities as Air WAACs. While WAVES were prohibited from flying Naval aircraft as pilots, they were allowed to serve as noncombat crew members. Navigation instructor training included 50 hours of flight time. The few women pilots who joined the WAVES found ways to unofficially use their aviation skills. WAVES also served as parachute riggers, electronic technicians, machinists, gunnery instructors, and air traffic controllers. At first, there was concern among Navy pilots regarding the women's ability to serve as air traffic controllers—doubts that women could master the complexities of the control tower. The only problem the women encountered was climbing up the ladder to the tower wearing skirts. Pants became regulation wear, and the first female air traffic controllers performed so well that women were recruited for the job.

The Marine Corps did not begin its women's reserves program until early 1943. At the start, 50 percent of the women were assigned to aviation units where they served as control tower operators, parachute riggers, Link trainer and gunnery instructors, and aerographers. In late 1942, the Coast Guard women's program began. The number of SPARs assigned to aviation was limited, and those worked primarily as instructors.[44]

The laws that created the women's military groups included mandates for demobilization following the war. The majority of the women returned to civilian life, leaving behind irrefutable proof that women could serve successfully in the military in many of the same roles as men.

Women in the Civilian War Effort

In 1941, before the entry of the United States into World War II, the Civil Aeronautics Administration (CAA) suggested that women flight instructors be used to teach military pilot trainees. The Tennessee Bureau of Aeronautics began training women flight instructors in a special school directed by Phoebe Omlie. Graduates were qualified as CAA ground instructors. By December 1941, there were forty-three women teaching in schools that the CAA had "qualified." The school closed when federal funding ended.

The Civil Air Patrol (CAP) was formed just before the country's entry into the war. From its start, the CAP welcomed women and young adults as well as men. While women were not allowed to fly CAP aircraft to patrol the coasts, those who were qualified flight instructors frequently trained the men who did.

Following the entry of the United States into World War II, the aviation manufacturing industry, trying to gear up for wartime production, found a severe shortage of qualified workers. The male aeronautical engineers, technicians, and assembly-line workers had gone off to war. At that time, few engineering schools welcomed

women; thus, there were few women engineers. In 1942 alone, the industry faced a shortage of 6,000 new engineers if its demand for 18,000 was to be met. The need was so acute that manufacturers decided that women with mathematics or physical science backgrounds could be given intensive engineering preparation and used as engineering technicians or associate engineers. Qualified women who were finishing their junior year of college were offered scholarships to complete the engineering program. In return, they had to sign with the sponsoring company for one year of employment. The manufacturing industry not only got the skilled workers it needed but it got them at a bargain. Engineering technicians were paid less than engineers, and with these available, companies needed to hire fewer engineers.

During the war years, thousands of women abandoned their traditional female roles and became assembly-line workers in the aircraft manufacturing industry. Homemakers, teachers, and secretaries traded skirts for slacks and homes, schools, and offices for factories. In 1943, 500,000 women were working in the production of airframes, engines, and propellers. They comprised 40 percent of the workforce in airframe plants and 30 percent in engine and propeller manufacturing. To the surprise of skeptics who believed that women could not function effectively in factory jobs, production curves rose. If female workers wanted to acquire higher skills, they were permitted to participate on an equal basis with male workers in plant training programs. Upgrading led to the promotion to foremen and supervisors. Government-financed college-level courses in technical areas were offered in the plants, and some women went on to earn aeronautical engineering degrees. When the war ended, most women returned to their former occupations. However, the percentage of female workers in the aircraft manufacturing industry did not return to the prewar level of 5 percent. Wartime had expanded job opportunities available to women, and women were unwilling to give up what they had gained.[45]

In the spring of 1942, the CAA advertised for workers to fill air traffic control jobs and indicated that these jobs were open to women. Requirements were a pilot's license or a college degree. When initially hired, the women were trained as "aircraft communicators" on the "B Board." Aircraft communicators were similar to today's flight service station specialists, and they accepted flight plans from pilots over the telephone. Seventy-five percent of trainees for this position were female in 1942. Next was training on the "A Board," which allowed the women to control airway traffic under supervision. The next promotion was to assistant air traffic controller in the control tower. Few women were promoted beyond this level. Women were assigned to control towers throughout the country but only if there was no objection from the male chief controller. Air traffic controller jobs were exciting and well paid. Many women who became air traffic controllers during the war remained on the job after the war ended.[46]

The Postwar Years, 1945–1950

The war had given thousands of women their first taste of financial and personal independence. The CPT and the WASP programs had given women an opportunity to fly. Women who had flown during the war wanted to continue flying. However, airlines hired women to fly as stewardesses—not as pilots! A few women pilots could earn a living in aviation, but the vast majority returned to homemaking and motherhood. Many of these women joined the Ninety-Nines to continue a level of involvement in aviation. The Ninety-Nines requires a pilot's license for membership. Until the postwar years, most members were recreational pilots rather than professionals who primarily flew for, as Amelia Earhart said in 1929, "the fun of it."

The infusion of more serious pilots rejuvenated the organization. The Ninety-Nines took on air marking as a national project and sponsored women's air races. The All Woman Transcontinental Air Race was instituted in 1949. The Amelia Earhart scholarship was established in 1947 and continues to this day. Each year the Earhart scholarship is awarded to several deserving Ninety-Nines who wish to acquire advanced flight ratings. The Earhart research scholarship may be awarded to a member who submits a worthy proposal. Individual chapters of the Ninety-Nines sponsor various philanthropic projects that involve aviation.

Women pilots serious about a flying career tried to find jobs as flight instructors, aerial photographers, and, occasionally, cargo and charter pilots. There were a limited number of positions, and postwar demobilization returned many experienced male pilots to the national pilot pool.

In spite of women successfully filling engineering roles during the war, the field remained dominated by men with few engineering schools willing to admit women. Historically, aeronautical engineering has attracted more women than any other engineering specialty field. In 1942, Elsa Gardner was the only woman to serve as a aeronautical engineer in the Navy. Another aero engineer, Isabel Ebel, after graduating in 1932, found a job with Grumman Aircraft Corporation in 1939. In 1942, she became a research engineer with United Airlines.

Olive Ann Beech

Olive Ann Mellor Beech (fig. 16.19) began her aviation career in 1924 with the Travel Air Manufacturing Company. A native of Kansas, she completed secretarial school in Wichita and was hired by Travel Air as secretary and bookkeeper. She was the only woman on the

Fig. 16.19. Olive Ann Beech. Courtesy of Raytheon Aircraft Company.

twelve-member staff and the only nonpilot. Her job encompassed the company's financial business as well as usual secretarial tasks. The company merged with Curtiss-Wright in New York City in 1929, and in 1930 Olive Ann Mellor married her boss, Walter H. Beech. During the two years they lived in New York, Olive Ann was inactive in business. However, Walter missed involvement with the design and manufacture of aircraft, and in 1932 the couple returned to Wichita, where they founded the Beech Aircraft Company. He was president and she was secretary-treasurer. During World War II, the Beech Aircraft Company employed 14,000 people and produced 7,400 military Beechcraft plus subcontracting for other aircraft manufacturing firms. Walter Beech died suddenly in 1950, and a month later his widow was elected president and chairperson of the board. Under her leadership, Beech Aircraft expanded, diversified, and prospered. The company was an early entry into the nation's space program. Although she gave up the presidency in 1969, Olive Ann continued as chair until retiring in 1982. When Beech Aircraft became a subsidiary of the Raytheon Aircraft Company in 1980, she was elected to Raytheon's board of directors. Olive Ann Beech has been honored by many organizations, but perhaps the most significant was her induction into the Aviation Hall of Fame in 1981. Her husband was inducted in 1977. The Beeches were the second couple to be enshrined. Charles and Anne Lindbergh were the first.[47]

Changing Times, 1951–1980

Times were changing but not fast enough for women pilots. In the 1950s and 1960s, a limited number of women found employment at small airports and flight schools. They worked as instructors, aerial photographers, cargo pilots, and occasionally charter pilots. A few women were employed as corporate pilots by companies owning their own aircraft. Women continued to find employment as demonstration pilots with light airplane manufacturers and dealers for the same reason they always had: If a woman can fly the airplane, then it cannot be terribly difficult. While bias against women pilots continued to exist, the late 1960s heralded an increasing awareness of the flawed thinking associated with stereotyping certain career fields.

The Airline Industry: Pilots

Increasing numbers of women pilots were finding work in general aviation, but until 1973, the high pay, large transport aircraft, and glamour of the airlines eluded them. By the early 1970s, foreign airlines had hired a few women pilots, but in the United States, the image of the airline pilot continued to be the "gray beard" or father figure. Until 1978, federal airline regulations prohibited route or fare competition; thus, the airlines had to sell themselves on the basis of service, safety, and convenience. Would placing women pilots in the cockpit detract from these selling points? Airlines found out in the 1970s when they were forced to become "Equal Opportunity Employers" if they wished to continue receiving federal funds. The all-male cockpit did not die without a struggle! Meeting the hiring requirements was difficult for women, particularly that of minimum height. And few women had the financial resources necessary to build the required flight experience.

Emily Howell Warner

Emily Warner was hired by Frontier Airlines in January 1973, thus becoming the second female pilot to be hired by a scheduled U.S. airline (fig. 16.20). Thirty-nine years had passed since Central Airlines hired Helen Richey. Warner was thirty-three and had 7,000 hours of flight time. She began flying at seventeen and had been a flight instructor before becoming manager of a flight school and an FAA pilot examiner. Warner first applied to Frontier, a regional airline, in 1967. She regularly submitted updated applications to the airline for six years. In spite of her impeccable credentials, she was not always welcome in the previously all-male cockpit. Contrary to the air transport industry's expectation, she did not leave Frontier for husband, home, and children. Warner flew almost fifteen years for Frontier. She became the first female member of the Air Line Pilots Association. In 1990, Warner retired as a Boeing 727 captain with United Parcel Service. She now lives in Colorado, where she is an FAA examiner. Her Frontier pilot's uniform is on exhibit in the Smithsonian Institution.[48]

Fig. 16.20. Emily Howell Warner. Courtesy of the Ninety-Nines, Inc.

Bonnie Tiburzi

Bonnie Tiburzi (fig. 16.21) was the second woman hired by a U.S. air carrier and the first to be hired by a major airline. In March 1973, Tiburzi was hired by American Airlines. Now a captain with American, she again disproves the expectation that female pilots will retire early for a more traditional role. Tiburzi followed her father and brother in learning to fly. At age twenty, she was a copilot for a European charter service. Tiburzi was the first woman to earn a Flight Engineer's rating. In 1993, 1,413 women held this rating, 11.4 percent of the total.[49]

By 1978, there were approximately 50 women pilots out of 38,000 pilots flying for U.S. airlines. The majority of these were flight engineers or second officers in a three-person flight crew. On smaller regional airlines flying aircraft requiring a two-person crew, a woman crew member generally would fill the copilot or first officer slot. In the 1970s, women pilots did not have the experience (flight time) or seniority to be upgraded to captain. In 1978, only 270 women had earned the Air Transport Pilot certificate, the top pilot certificate issued by the Federal Aviation Administration. In 1993, 2,738 women held this certificate, 6.9 percent of the total certificate holders.[50]

The Airline Industry: Flight Attendants

Jet aircraft with the capacity for transporting large numbers of passengers across great distances in a fraction of the time required by propeller-driven aircraft significantly changed the role of the flight attendant. While passenger service and amenities were major marketing tools used by the airlines, these became more difficult to provide as passenger loads increased and

Fig. 16.21. Bonnie Tiburzi. Courtesy of the Ninety-Nines, Inc.

flight times decreased. Further, in-flight service had become secondary to safety. The flight attendant's job was growing more difficult. In spite of this, the airlines and the public continued to view the job as a short-term adventure for young, single, attractive women. Three developments caused this perception to change over time: the new emphasis on safety in both training and job performance; the increase in educational requirements and de-emphasis of physical attractiveness; and the union organization of flight attendants with subsequent strikes. By the late 1970s, airline management began to realize that flight attendants were an important resource and should be given the respect, pay, and job benefits commensurate with the career professionals they were.[51]

Records

The tragic end to Amelia Earhart's 1937 attempt to circle the globe discouraged other women pilots from accepting the challenge of an around-the-world flight. However, in 1964, two American women tried and succeeded.

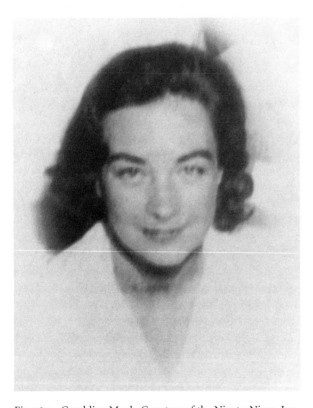

Fig. 16.22. Geraldine Mock. Courtesy of the Ninety-Nines, Inc.

Geraldine "Jerrie" Mock (fig. 16.22), thirty-eight and a mother of three, had been flying for less than eight years when she decided to make her historic flight in the family's single-engine Cessna 180. She had 750 hours of flight time and an instrument rating. Mock's route was slightly different from Earhart's in that it involved more miles over water. This was especially hazardous given that her aircraft was not equipped with floats for water operation. Mock and her husband were successful in finding sponsors for the proposed flight, and her airplane was well-equipped with modern avionics. Mock's solo attempt to set an around-the-world flight record was sanctioned by the prestigious Federation Aeronautique Internationale (FAI). She took off from Columbus, Ohio, on 17 March 1964. In spite of bad weather and mechanical problems, Mock completed her flight, landing in Columbus on 11 April 1964. The first woman to complete an around-the-world flight had flown over 22,858 miles in 158 hours and set seven records.[52]

Joan Merriam Smith, twenty-seven years old, married, and a professional pilot, sought to duplicate Amelia Earhart's 1937 route of flight. She took off in her twin-engine Piper Apache two days before Jerrie Mock. However, because Mock had filed her flight earlier with the FAI, Smith's flight was not sanctioned by the organization. Smith's aircraft was plagued by mechanical problems, but she successfully completed her flight around the world.[53]

The Military

From the mid-1950s to the 1960s, the remaining women in the military were gradually being replaced by men. However, women were preferred for roles in defense combat control centers, air intelligence, and passenger air transport operations. By the time the Vietnam War began, there were only about 30,000 women on active duty.

Many Americans held the opinion that the Vietnam War was unjust, and their unwillingness to serve in it created a personnel shortage for the military. The military began rethinking its attitude toward women. Again, women were needed to serve in noncombat roles to release men for combat duty. It is interesting to note that, while female nurses traditionally have served near combat zones, this proximity was considered unacceptable for other military women. All restrictions on the promotion of female officers were removed as well as limitations on the number of women who could serve in the military. Women could not fly in combat, but they could train the men who did. The Air Force had begun to study the possible use of women as pilots and made public these considerations in the late 1960s.

In 1973, Congress created an all-volunteer military, causing much anxiety among those responsible for maintaining military personnel levels. Again, the role and functions of women in the military were discussed. In January 1973, it was announced that eight women had been selected to enter Navy flight training at Pensacola, Florida. The training program was to be separate but identical to that provided to male trainees. The Navy was eager to determine whether women pilots could be trained to perform in noncombat flying positions. The answer was clear in 1974 when Barbara Ann Rainey became the first woman to earn Navy wings, followed by the other seven. While male Navy pilots could enter propeller, helicopter, or jet areas of specialization, females were not allowed to enter the jet area because jets were fighter aircraft. Women were not allowed to land on aircraft carriers because these were combat ships. In 1975, the first woman was allowed to become carrier qualified in propeller aircraft.

The Army opened its helicopter flight training to women about the same time as the Navy but with one significant difference—female and male Army pilot trainees were trained together. Sally Murphy was the first woman to complete Army flight training, and she was given a battalion command in Japan in 1991. The Army also trained women in helicopter maintenance. Women were permitted to train as Air Force pilots and navigators in 1976 but were restricted to noncombat roles. Eight years later, women finally were allowed to earn tanker pilot qualification. In 1977, the Coast Guard became the last to open flight training to women.

The nation's military academies were opened to women by congressional mandate in September 1976, thus enabling women to earn the military leadership roles that traditionally are awarded to academy graduates. The Air Force appeared to be the most willing to accept the decision forced upon it by Congress. It is interesting to note that Jacqueline Cochran, head of the WASP program during World War II, believed that women had no place in a peacetime military and urged Congress to bar women from military academies.

The Federal Aviation Administration

The Federal Aviation Administration (FAA) experienced a shortage of air traffic controllers in the late 1950s. While some wartime women controllers continued in that role after the war, in 1959 only sixty females were certified air traffic controllers out of 12,000. Many women who responded to the FAA's active recruiting efforts had been involved in aviation during the war. By the late 1960s, 5 percent of controllers were female. In 1971, two women were promoted into positions never before held by women: Ruth Dennis became chief of a FAA flight service station, and Gene Sims became an airport tower chief. In the late 1970s, the FAA revised its Career Services information to include only gender-neutral terms, thus making FAA careers appear more accessible to young women.

In 1964, President Lyndon Johnson created the Women's Advisory Committee on Aviation within the FAA. The committee had little money or influence over policy making, and its recommendations were hardly new or innovative. However, it did serve to remind the Washington policymakers that women were interested and involved in aviation on many levels. President Jimmie Carter dissolved the committee in 1977.

The Aerospace Industry

The number of women employed in the aerospace industry grew in both number and percentage during the 1970s. During the 1950s, women comprised between 14 and 17 percent of the aerospace workforce. Both the number and percentage of women workers increased during the 1970s, and in 1979 21.3 percent of the workforce—234,500 individuals—were women. These numbers had increased to 23.4 percent and 280,600 by 1983. Women, generally with smaller hands than men, appeared to be ideally suited for microelectronics assembly, the fastest growing segment of the industry.

Women also worked as public relations specialists for aerospace industries and as aeronautical engineers. In 1953, Nancy Fitzroy joined General Electric as a heat transfer engineer. In the 1960s, she worked for GE's jet engine division, often commuting between various work sites in her own airplane. Fitzroy wrote a pamphlet about her job as a female aeronautical engineer and noted difficulties she had encountered on the job. General Electric, like the airlines, believed that a female engineer would remain on the job only until she embraced the more traditional role of marriage and homemaking. This stereotype had resulted in the company passing over Fitzroy for promotions and paying her less than her male counterparts.

Dr. Dora Dougherty Strother had served as a WASP during World War II, and Bell Aircraft hired her in the 1950s as a human factors engineer to design helicopter cockpits. While Strother was a skilled fixed wing pilot, she had never flown a helicopter. After only 34 hours of helicopter flight time, Strother set records for distance and altitude.[54]

The 1950s brought a period of rapid change for the aerospace industry as it geared up to meet the challenges of the space age. From 1954 to 1957, the number of scientists and engineers increased 75 percent. Still, few of these were women. In 1955, Boeing Aircraft employed only forty-seven female engineers—less than 1 percent of the engineering staff. By the 1970s, federal equal opportunity legislation helped to change the attitude of engineering schools toward women students. Women were actively recruited, and the number of women receiving four-year engineering degrees tripled. While the number of female aeronautical engineers remained small, they were successful in attaining responsible positions in the aerospace industry and they were recognized for their professional contributions.

Moya Lear stepped into the role of chairperson of the board of LearAvia Corporation when her husband died in 1978. Bill Lear, inventor of the Learjet airplane, was working on the Lear Fan, a composite aircraft designed for business and corporate aviation. During his final illness, he asked Moya to finish his work and make certain his last airplane flew. The Lear Fan made its inaugural flight in December 1980. The project was completed in 1985 with flight testing. Moya Lear, well educated but neither as an engineer nor as a businesswoman, has received many honorary degrees and titles as well as several awards from aviation organizations. In 1992, she was inducted into the aviation "Pioneers Hall of Fame."[55]

The "Would-Be" Women Astronauts: The Mercury 13

In the late 1950s, Dr. W. Randolph Lovelace of the Lovelace Foundation in Albuquerque, New Mexico, learned of the Russian plan to send a woman into space. Lovelace had worked with the National Aeronautics and Space Administration (NASA) in the physical examination of male astronauts and was convinced that American women were physically capable of going into space. Air Force Brig. Gen. Donald D. Flickinger, also a physician skilled in the emerging field of aerospace medicine, shared this opinion. In 1959, Geraldine "Jerrie" Cobb (fig. 16.23), a twenty-nine-year-old professional pilot, was selected to undergo physical and psychological testing to determine whether women were capable of going into space. Cobb began flying at age twelve, was licensed at sixteen, and flew professionally at eighteen. She had logged thousands of flight hours and held four world's flight records. In early 1960, Cobb underwent strenuous physical testing that she passed with flying colors. During that summer she passed the psychological tests. In April 1961, she successfully completed the stress tests, the third and last phase of testing used to select the first seven Mercury astronauts. Like her male counterparts in the Mercury program, Cobb was judged fit for space

Fig. 16.23. Geraldine Cobb. Courtesy of the Ninety-Nines, Inc.

flight. However, while Alan Shepard entered space in May 1961, Cobb remained on the ground and was appointed a consultant to NASA administrator James Webb. She was never consulted.

Although Cobb's test results were outstanding, NASA was unwilling to believe that these could be replicated by other American women. Twenty-five women pilots were selected to undergo the same tests. These women were between the ages of twenty-one and thirty-nine, held bachelor's degrees, and had logged 1,000 hours of flight time. They received physical examinations in Albuquerque, and thirteen passed. These thirteen were to go to Pensacola, Florida, for psychiatric and centrifuge testing . However, the day before they were to leave, NASA canceled the testing program. The women had moved through the first phase of testing—the physical exams—alone or by twos and had been told not to discuss the program with anyone. NASA conducted the testing program of women in secret, apparently never intending to allow women on space flights. Most of the thirteen women who passed the first phase of testing did not have an opportunity to meet until 1994 (see fig. 16.24).

Jane Hart, wife of Michigan senator Philip Hart, was among these thirteen women. She and Jerrie Cobb decided to go public with the women astronaut testing program. They had passed the first phase of testing, were ready for subsequent testing, and wanted to participate in the space program. The two women testified at a two-day hearing held by the House of Representatives. While they set forth an excellent rationale for the inclusion of

Fig. 16.24. The Mercury 13. Courtesy of the Ninety-Nines, Inc.

women in the space program, in 1961 Congress was having none of it. After all, women did not fly large airplanes, nor did they fly for the airlines. Women were not allowed to fly for the military, so they could not meet the astronaut requirement of military test pilot experience. Finally, the male astronauts had worked hard to replace monkeys on space flights, and they did not want women infringing on their rights. There was little support for women's rights in the early 1960s, and despite NASA's encouragement of women scientists' applications for mission specialists in 1964, not one was selected.

With the program terminated, Jerrie Cobb left for South America, where she still lives and works as a pilot, flying missionaries along the Amazon. Most of the thirteen resumed careers in aviation. Mary Wallach "Wally" Funk became the first woman appointed to the National Transportation Safety Board (NTSB). She is now retired. Gene Nora Stumbaugh Jessen and her husband own a fixed base operation (FBO) in Boise, Idaho. Jane Hart left flying for sailing and, now in her seventies, is an active long-distance sailor.[56]

Today's Women in Aviation, 1981–Present

Seventy years after Harriet Quimby expressed her opinion in *Leslie's Illustrated Weekly* that "there is no reason why the aeroplane should not open up a fruitful occupation for women," her vision became reality. Women finally were accepted into the U.S. aviation industry on the same set of occupation-related criteria as were men. These criteria depend upon the occupation and may include such factors as flight experience, education, test scores, performance evaluation, and physical condition. Even pregnancy no longer automatically disqualifies a woman from flying as a member of the flight or cabin crew.

The Airline Industry: Pilots

While U.S. airlines are reluctant to provide data on diversity within their workforces, available information indicates that the number of female airline pilots is increasing. In 1994, the Air Line Pilots Association (ALPA) reported that 2.95 percent of its members were female.[57] ALPA represents over 43,000 pilots at thirty-seven U.S. airlines. If this percentage is valid for the total U.S. airline pilot workforce of about 72,000, the number of female pilots would be approximately 2,100. This figure may appear low, but it compares favorably with the number of qualified female pilots in the nation's pool of pilots meeting U.S. airline hiring criteria. FAA data indicate that women held only 4.3 percent of commercial certificates and 2.5 percent of Airline Transport Pilot certificates in 1994. It is reasonable to assume that less than half of the female pilots holding commercial certificates meet additional airline hiring criteria. United Airlines was mandated under a 1976 consent decree to increase hiring of women and minorities. In 1994, United employed over 500 female pilots and thus had the highest percentage (6.24 percent) in the U.S. airline industry. United Parcel Service was second with eighty-two female pilots for 5.46 percent. In 1994, major airlines employing the lowest percentages of female pilots were Delta with thirty-five (0.37 percent) and TWA with forty-four (1.40 percent). The mixed gender flight crew is becoming more common on flights of both major and regional airlines. In December 1986, Capt. Beverly Bass, American Airlines' first female captain, headed a Boeing 727 flight crew of three female pilots. This all-female crew was a first for American and among the first in airline history. Female pilots continue to serve most often as first officers (copilot) in aircraft requiring a two-member flight crew or flight engineer in aircraft requiring a three-member crew. While less than 300 women are flying as captain for U.S. airlines, this number will increase as female pilots acquire the necessary seniority and experience for upgrade to captain. ALPA recently removed from its application form the question regarding gender—over sixty years after denying membership to Helen Richey, the first female U.S. airline pilot.

The nation's airlines have long looked to the military as a primary source of experienced pilots. Today's military pilot—male or female—frequently remains in the military, thus limiting the number of former military pilots available to the airlines. Airlines are hiring increasing numbers of pilots with four-year college degrees who have learned to fly at a local airport and then built experience through flight instructing, night cargo flying, aerial photography, and charter flying. Female pilots have greater access to airline pilot positions than ever before. However, the number of women holding pilot certificates in the United States remains at 6 percent of the total—the same as a decade ago.[58]

The International Society of Women Airline Pilots

ISA + 21 was founded in 1978 by twenty-one female airline pilots. Frontier Airlines pilot Emily Warner served as its first president. Members must fly for an airline that operates under FAA Regulations Part 121 and operates at least one aircraft weighing 90,000 pounds or more. The organization has about 500 members who fly for more than sixty airlines in almost thirty countries. In 1994, ISA + 21 awarded $45,000 in scholarships to aspiring female airline pilots. At its annual convention, the members share information and concerns that arise from being female in a field dominated by males. ISA + 21 estimates that about 2,500 female pilots are flying for airlines worldwide with more than 400 of them captains.

Sandra L. Anderson

Capt. Sandra L. Anderson (fig. 16.25) began her flying career when she decided to learn to fly an airplane rather than jump from it with her parachuting husband. In 1995—her sixteenth year with Northwest Airlines—Anderson was named assistant chief pilot/flight manager at the airline's Minneapolis–St. Paul crew base. She is the first woman to hold this position at NWA—or at any other major U.S. passenger-carrying airline.

Captain Anderson's career at Northwest Airlines began in 1979 when she was the second female pilot to be hired. Ten years later, she became a Boeing 727 captain, the second woman to achieve this status at NWA. In 1992, she became the only female captain instructor/ check pilot at the airline. In 1994, Anderson was selected as a fleet check captain, the first woman named to this post at any major U.S. airline. Anderson has accumulated over 14,000 hours of flight time, both in the B727 and the B747, and has flown both domestically and internationally.

Flying was not Sandy Anderson's first vocation. She taught for two years before marrying, and then she began working as a graphic artist and earning her private pilot's certificate. Following the accidental death of her husband in 1975, Anderson decided to "use her loss to move her life in a different direction." With the advice and encouragement of her flight instructor, she quit her job and set about earning the necessary ratings and certificates to equip her for her new goal—flying for the airlines. She taught and flew night cargo to gain experience before joining Northwest Airlines.

Captain Anderson has incorporated her previous school teaching and her artistic skills with her love of flying. She has developed resource materials for pilots to use in presentations about their careers. Among her many honors is recognition by the National Aviation Club for her "tireless dedication to promoting aviation as a career." Anderson's philosophy may be summed up in this statement: "When a career has been good to you, I believe it's important to contribute something back to that occupation by means of school and community involvement."

In 1995, Anderson received her master's degree in human resources and organization development. She

Fig. 16.25. Sandra L. Anderson. Courtesy of Sandra L. Anderson.

plans to earn a doctoral degree and, upon retirement from Northwest Airlines, to return to the classroom as a professor in a university aviation program.[59]

Christine Jones

In 1983, Christine Jones was completing her sophomore year at the University of Minnesota when, on her birthday, she was given a gift certificate for her first flight lesson. Seventeen years later, Jones is a Northwest Airlines Airbus 320 first officer (copilot). Jones completed her bachelor of science degree in aerospace engineering/flight training and then taught at the University of Minnesota Flight Facility. Jones also served as a pilot for the University's air ambulance and staff transportation service.

Jones's engineering degree provided her entry into the airline industry in 1988 when she was the first female to be hired in performance engineering at Northwest Airlines. During the next six years she moved on to become manager of flight procedures for the Airbus 320 and later the Boeing 727. She earned a flight engineer rating and flew with Northwest's flight test and ferry operation. In November 1994, her big break came. Northwest opened its line pilot hiring to qualified pilots already employed by the airline in non–line pilot positions. Jones was one of twenty-five pilots selected from within and one of five women. She credits affirmative action for the increase in female pilot hiring at Northwest Airlines. Currently, Northwest employs more than 6,000 pilots, including about 100 women.[60]

The Airline Industry: Flight Attendants

Flight attendants and their labor unions have continued to struggle over pay, scheduling, vacation, and retirement benefits. However, in the mid-1990s, issues left over from the days when physical attractiveness was a primary hiring criteria were finally put to rest. Delta Airlines ended its policy of mandatory, monthly weigh-ins for female flight attendants and the subsequent grounding of those whose weight exceeded prescribed limits. Female flight attendants at Delta objected to the practice because it was demeaning and not required for male flight attendants or for pilots of either gender. American Airlines also abandoned its weight criteria in favor of flight attendants' ability to perform duties related to in-flight service and safety procedures.

The changes in the role of flight attendants were brought about by changes in the airline industry since the advent of jet aircraft. In 1978, federal airline deregulation made the occupation more attractive to both women and men. While the majority of attendants are female, the number of males is growing. Flight attendants range in age from nineteen to over seventy, over half are married, and many are parents and even grandparents. Many flight attendants who were forced to resign upon marriage and/or parenthood at an earlier time have reentered their chosen career field. Virtually all flight attendants have some postsecondary education and many have bachelor's degrees. Speaking fluency in a foreign language is often required for service on international flights. While flight attendants must be in good health, many physical restrictions have been removed, including wearing glasses and flying during pregnancy. Flight attendants—particularly women—tend to be very supportive of female airline pilots. A significant number are pursuing flight education with the goal of trading membership in the cabin crew for membership in the flight crew.

Records

JoAnn Osterud. JoAnn Osterud was a college student when she took her first flying lesson at Hillsboro Airport near Portland, Oregon. Twenty years and more than 12,000 flight hours later, she is a Boeing 767 first officer with United Airlines based in Los Angeles and a record-setting aerobatic pilot performing throughout the United States. At the 1989 North Bend, Oregon, air show, Osterud's 208 outside loops broke Dorothy Stenzel's record, which had stood for fifty-eight years. In 1991, she broke records for inverted distance and inverted endurance flying. Osterud flew upside down from Vancouver, Washington, to Vanderhoof, British Columbia, covering 658 miles in 4 hours, 38 minutes, and 10 seconds.

In addition to her aerobatic records, she has acquired some "firsts" during her career: in 1975, she was the first female pilot hired by Alaska Airlines, and in 1987, the first female to compete in the unlimited division of the Reno Air Races. Osterud sums up her opinion of women in aviation this way: "It seems in aviation if you do your job right, eventually people don't really care what you are."[61]

Jeana Yeager. The 1986 round-the-world flight of co-pilots Jeana Yeager (fig. 16.26) and Dick Rutan in the Voyager aircraft established a new milestone in aviation history. Yeager and Rutan lived for nine days in a cockpit 3.5 feet wide by 7 feet long while they circled the globe nonstop without refueling. Their flight covered 26,358 miles and used most of the 1,200 gallons of fuel on board. The physical and psychological challenges induced by fatigue, limited diet, lack of privacy, violent wind, turbulence, weather concerns, and the aircraft's mechanical problems were overcome in their effort to realize a dream.

Yeager learned early that she could "do anything I set my mind to if I was willing to work hard enough." Her winning attitude served her well when, in junior high school, she joined the track team. Running brought freedom, and when track was replaced by a love of horses, the lessons learned in competition about trying and succeeding remained. Yeager later moved to California where she found a job drafting and surveying. At age twenty-six, her early fascination with flight led to a fixed wing private pilot's certificate. While drafting for Capt. Robert Truax, USN, ret., a pioneer in rocket design, she visited an air show where she first saw Rutan-designed aircraft. Yeager began working for Burt Rutan and the Rutan Aircraft Company as chief test pilot and production manager. She and Burt's brother, Dick, began competing in setting records. At the time of their Voyager flight, Yeager held five world records in speed and distance. In 1987, Jeana Yeager became the first woman to win one of aviation's most prestigious awards, the Collier Trophy.[62]

Fig. 16.26. Jeana Yeager. Courtesy of the Ninety-Nines, Inc.

Patty Wagstaff. In 1991, Patty Wagstaff (fig. 16.27) achieved her goal of winning the U.S. National Aerobatic Championship. This was the first time a woman had captured the title since separate competitions for women and men ended in 1972. Wagstaff entered her first competition in 1984 and was named to the U.S. Aerobatic Team the following year. By 1987, Wagstaff was ranked at the top of women aerobatic pilots in the United States and it became apparent that she was a major contender for the U.S. National Aerobatic Championship.

Wagstaff's father was a Boeing 747 captain for Japan Air Lines. She was educated in Europe and Australia. She then moved to Alaska, where she met her husband. Her sister is a Boeing 727 pilot for Continental Airlines. Wagstaff still lives in Anchorage, but she trains with her German-built aerobatic aircraft over the desert near Tucson, Arizona. When she is not flying in air shows all over the United States or competing in aerobatic competition, Wagstaff designs maneuver sequences for aerobatic competition and judges flying events.[63]

The Military

The final barrier to women in the military came tumbling down on 28 April 1993, when Secretary of Defense Les Aspin removed restrictions preventing women from flying combat roles. Soon after the announcement, the military made plans to give female pilots the same fighter and bomber flying opportunities afforded their

Fig. 16.27. Patty Wagstaff. Courtesy of the Ninety-Nines, Inc.

male counterparts. The Air Force immediately instituted gender-neutral pilot training and aircraft assignment systems. The ten top performing female pilots were selected as combat candidates. The Navy and Marines also gave women the opportunity to fly fighter aircraft. In 1995, Lt. Kara Hultgreen, one of the nation's first female combat pilots, was killed when her Navy F-14 crashed into the ocean off the southern California coast during a training exercise.

Capt. Pam Melroy. During Operation Desert Storm and Just Cause in 1990, Air Force Capt. Pam Melroy flew more than 200 combat and combat support hours in the KC-10. While flying over Iraqi airspace, she was shot at but could not shoot back. In response to the policy change allowing female pilots to fly combat aircraft, Melroy said, "Now we get to shoot back!" While based at Edwards Air Force Base, California, Melroy was a C-17 developmental test pilot and one of few women to log flying time in fighter aircraft. In an interview published in *Airman* magazine in late 1993, she pointed out that women have been subjected to G's (gravity units) while flying the T-38 and thus have been meeting the physical requirements for flying fighter aircraft. Melroy noted that fighter aircraft are very responsive and do not demand great physical strength. Giving female pilots the opportunity to fly fighters will ensure that the best qualified pilots, male or female, will be selected. And because promotion rates are higher for fighter pilots and they are often appointed to command-level positions, flying fighters may offer these professional benefits to women. Melroy's test pilot role allows her to test aircraft flown in combat. Pam Melroy has been selected as an astronaut candidate.[64]

Maj. Jackie Parker. Air Force Maj. Jackie Parker was the first female pilot in the United States to be assigned to a F-16 fighter squadron.

Parker graduated from college with a bachelor's degree in computer science and spent two years as a space flight controller with NASA. She then joined the Air Force and went through pilot training at Reese Air Force Base, Texas, where she later became Reese's first female T-38 instructor pilot. Reese, being one of the last bases to have women in this role, was not quite ready for diversity—there were no women's rest rooms in the buildings.

Parker's next assignment was to Charleston, South Carolina, where she flew the C-141 and became the Air Force's youngest instructor pilot for this aircraft. Parker went on to test pilot school and served as a test pilot at Wright-Patterson Air Force Base, Ohio, in a squadron that had several female pilots and navigators. In 1989, she met Gen. Mike Hall, then commander of the 174th Fighter Wing of the New York Air National Guard. Following the announcement that women were going to be allowed in combat, Hall contacted her. Parker was sworn into the New York Guard on 1 May 1993.

Parker believes that the basis for military standards should be dependent upon the needs of the job or mission. Height standards and strength standards should not disqualify women when the job for which they are being evaluated does not require a certain height or body strength. Female pilots try to plan pregnancy around their flying tours of duty. While pregnant women are permitted to fly cargo aircraft in their second trimester, ejection seat forces prohibit flying fighters while pregnant. When female pilots cannot fly, they are assigned ground duties.

Parker has achieved many "firsts" in her military career. Being the first female fighter pilot probably was the most challenging. The military population has long been predominantly male, and with the change in that population, accommodations will be made. These will range from the design of aircraft to uniforms to the installation of women's rest rooms. According to Parker, strong leadership on the part of commanding officers will minimize problems that may occur when women are integrated into previously all-male units. In the aftermath of discrimination incidents, Parker requested and was granted relief from flight duties in June 1995. She was reassigned as a logistics and plans officer at New York Air Guard headquarters in Albany.[65]

Maj. Cathy Clothier. Cathy Clothier is the commander of the 22d Operations Support Squadron, Wichita, Kansas, assigned to McConnell Air Force Base. Her command provides operational support to active duty members as well as Kansas Air National Guard and Air Force Reserve personnel. Clothier began her Air Force career in 1978 when she was in the third class at the Air Force Academy to admit women. At fourteen, she had written to a congressman protesting the "men only" policy of the academy. That same congressman appointed her to the academy two years after it opened its doors to women. She earned a bachelor's degree in general engineering in 1982 and married Brian Clothier, an academy classmate. Both earned their wings at Vance Air Force Base in Oklahoma. Clothier was assigned to KC-135 (inflight refueling tanker) school at Castle Air Force Base, California. She graduated first in her class and reported to the 384th Air Refueling Squadron at McConnell Air Force Base. As the cold war was drawing to a close, Clothier and her KC-135 crew were on alert every third week. She describes the KC-135 missions as "forming air bridges." The job of the tanker and its crew is to fuel other aircraft in flight so that they can continue their missions. Clothier has over 2,100 hours of flight time and is now a KC-135 captain. She has built air bridges over England, Germany, Iceland, Saudi Arabia, and Spain.

Clothier earned a master of arts degree in human resource development from Webster University, and she attended the University of Texas in Austin for further graduate education, culminating in a degree in social psychology. She returned to the Air Force Academy in 1991 to teach in the Department of Behavioral Science and Leadership. Clothier's first daughter was born while she was teaching at the academy. To create a more stable family life, Brian resigned from the military to concentrate on his home-based career as an inventor.

The 22d Operations Support Squadron commanded by Clothier includes airfield operations, weather, intelligence, plans and tactics, and current operations. Clothier's life has taken her from a small town with a dirt landing strip at the airport to the Air Force Academy to the KC-135 and now to a squadron command. She is the mother and role model to two daughters.[66]

In June 1997, 1st Lt. Kelly Flinn became the center of a controversy focusing on adultery, deception, and disobedience in the military. Flinn, a graduate of the U.S. Air Force Academy and the first and only female B-52 bomber pilot, faced allegations of fraternization and adultery. In late 1996, she was ordered by her commanding officer to have no further contact with the civilian husband of a female airman. Although Flinn signed a statement indicating her understanding of the order, she did not immediately end the affair. She was later accused of twice lying under oath to Air Force investigators. Flinn's Air Force superiors chose a court-martial rather than administrative or "nonjudicial" punishment based largely on the premise that officers do not lie. According to Air Force chief of staff Gen. Ronald R. Fogleman, "This is an issue about an officer, entrusted to fly nuclear weapons, who lied." Sheila Widnall, secretary of the Air Force, was urged to allow Flinn's case to move forward to trial and probable dishonorable discharge. Military women appeared to support this position in the belief that making an exception for Flinn would undermine women's status in the military. In mid-1997, Flinn was allowed to resign from the Air Force and receive a general discharge.

The Air Force maintains that the Kelly Flinn case was about disobedience and deception rather than adultery. However, the issue has caused the military to examine its policies regarding inappropriate and unacceptable sexual behavior. Barbara Spyridon Pope, first female assistant secretary of the Navy (1989–1993), wrote in *Newsweek* that "human nature cannot be changed by orders from military superiors." The military must avoid the appearance or fact of a double standard by applying policy and discipline appropriately and consistently to everyone, regardless of rank or gender. She further notes that "ethics are hard to regulate." The military

needs to review its policies and rules regarding sexual behavior and clarify which behaviors may affect military readiness.[67]

General Aviation

Capt. Jan Orr. Jan Orr had a role model in her mother, Rita Ann Orr, who was among those female pilots accepted into the last class of the WASP in 1942. Later, Rita Orr was instrumental in founding the Minnesota Chapter of the Ninety-Nines, Inc. In 1976, Jan Orr (fig. 16.28) had graduated from college, found a job, and saved enough money to earn her private pilot's certificate. Her commitment to aviation came with her decision to pursue advanced pilot training. Orr began her career as a line person at the flight operation where she was working on her instrument rating and commercial certificate. She gave up her journalism job, and when not working at the airport, she was flying. Orr was the flight operation's first female student to earn the certificated flight instructor rating and its first female instructor. She completed the FAA ground and flight instructor ratings and, finally, the airline transport pilot (ATP) certificate. Orr, an active member of the Ninety-Nines, received an Amelia Earhart scholarship from the organization in 1979. She was awarded a Gold Seal Flight Instructor certificate by the FAA and, in 1984, was named FAA Accident Prevention Counselor of the Year for the Great Lakes Region.

Orr continued as a full-time flight instructor for ten years. She also taught pilot ground schools at two colleges and served as corporate pilot for Carl Bolander and Sons. In 1989, she became a copilot with Life Link III, an air ambulance service based at the St. Paul, Minnesota, airport. Orr was Life Link's second female pilot, and after two and a half years she was upgraded to captain—the first woman to hold the position with the company.

In 1991, Orr was appointed an FAA designated flight examiner. Her twenty-year career in general aviation took another turn in 1996 when she joined the FAA Flight Standards District Office in Minneapolis. She served as an aviation safety inspector, and she is now a principal operations inspector.

In the mid-1930s, Blanche Noyes (fig. 16.29) was a corporate pilot with Standard Oil of Ohio. Female pilots had been employed as sales people and demonstration

Fig. 16.28. Janice Orr standing in front of a Life Link plane. Courtesy of Janice Orr.

pilots for aircraft manufacturer since the 1920s. Occasionally, they were hired as corporate pilots to provide transportation service in the company-owned aircraft. Smaller companies generally have been more willing to hire female pilots than larger firms, perhaps because smaller companies often fly smaller aircraft. Larger companies frequently fly jet aircraft, and few women pilots have had access to jet experience. The 3M Corporation with its worldwide manufacturing facilities only recently hired its first female pilot for its jet fleet.

Government Aviation

For many years, Blanche Noyes was the only female pilot allowed to fly U.S. government aircraft. Women now fly for many governmental agencies, including various branches of law enforcement. Laura Goldsberry became the first female pilot for U.S. Customs in 1986, flying the Cessna Citation jet airplane and the UH-60-Blackhawk helicopter. Goldsberry flies both domestically and internationally, and as a federal officer she frequently works undercover. In spite of a less than warm welcome from her male colleagues, she is happy with her career.[68]

Fig. 16.29. Blanche Noyes. Courtesy of the Ninety-Nines, Inc.

Government Flying

Individual states also own aircraft and employ women to fly them. Many state law enforcement agencies use small airplanes and helicopters for actions ranging from criminal apprehension to traffic surveillance to saving people from flooded rivers. State governments and universities often provide transportation service for elected officials and high-ranking administrators. Capt. Linda Davis flew the University of Minnesota Beech King Air for several years before her death in 1990 at the age of forty. Davis, a librarian, traded library stacks for the sky when she took her first flying lesson in the early 1970s. After earning her flight instructor certificates, she gave flight and ground instruction at the University of Minnesota Flight School. Davis flew air ambulance flights for the university hospitals and transported university, legislative, and hospital personnel. Davis recounted with amusement her reception at smaller airports when, after she had taxied the airplane to a stop, the line person invariably would go to the right or copilot side of the aircraft if a male pilot were in that place and inquire whether fuel or other services were needed.[69]

The Federal Aviation Administration

The Professional Women Controllers organization was founded in 1979 by Jacqueline Smith and Sue Mostert to provide communication and support for female air traffic controllers. This was formed as a professional association rather than a labor union, and when the Professional Air Traffic Control Association (PATCO) was disbanded following its 1981 strike, the PWC survived. By 1983, approximately 8 percent of all air traffic controllers were female. In that same year Elizabeth Dole was appointed U.S. secretary of transportation. The position has responsibility for federal aviation programs and, during peacetime, those in the U.S. Coast Guard. Dole was the first woman to occupy this position, the most powerful in U.S. aviation.

Barbara McConnell Barrett was appointed to the Civil Aeronautics Board (CAB) in the early 1980s and was vice chairperson when the board was dissolved in 1984. In 1988, she was appointed deputy administrator of the FAA, the first woman to serve in the post. During her nine months in office, Barrett focused her attention on the capacity of the nation's airports.

In 1993, Linda Hall Daschle was appointed deputy FAA administrator, and two of six assistant administrators are women. Daschle is an outspoken advocate of recruiting qualified women and minority people for FAA positions. Unfortunately, the reduction in total FAA employment during the mid-1990s slowed her goals for workforce diversity. However, women within the FAA were promoted far more often than in previous years. Women serve not only as air traffic controllers but also as supervisors and air traffic managers at airport control towers and en route control centers. Women have been promoted to management positions at FAA Flight Standards district offices and other large FAA facilities throughout the country.[70]

The FAA's New England region was the first to have a female administrator. Aviation attorney and pilot Arlene Feldman was named to the post after serving as deputy director of the Western Pacific region. Unlike the posts occupied by Dole, Barrett, and Daschle, regional administration jobs are not political appointments. Feldman is the highest-ranking woman in FAA history who was not politically appointed to her position. She is an outspoken advocate for the FAA and for women in aviation.[71]

Feldman was the first woman to be named New Jersey's director of aeronautics. She sponsored the 1983 Airport Safety Act in New Jersey and initiated an aviation education program in the public schools. Feldman's career has taken her to the FAA Technical Center in Atlantic City and to Los Angeles in the Western Pacific region.[72]

Jane F. Garvey was sworn in 4 August 1997 as the first female administrator of the Federal Aviation Administration. In an unprecedented move, she was confirmed by the Senate to a five-year term. Garvey previously was acting administrator of the Federal Highway Administration and had served as director of Boston's Logan International Airport and commissioner of the Massachusetts Department of Public Works. Garvey's focus as FAA administrator will be to enhance flying safety.[73]

The Aviation Industry

In the 1990s, no Olive Ann Beeches or Moya Lears are heading aircraft corporations. There are no women serving as presidents or CEOs of major U.S. airlines. However, women do sit on the boards of airlines and aviation-related companies. Colleen Barrett, executive vice president for customers at Southwest Airlines, is the highest-ranking woman at a major U.S. airline. Barrett has been with Southwest since its beginning, and believes that the 1990s brought about a "huge acceptance" of women in management.

June Morris founded Morris Air, a regional airline in the western United States. Ill health forced her to sell to Southwest Airlines, and she is now a member of Southwest's board of directors. Regional airlines American Eagle Wings West and Keys Air have women presidents, as does FedEx contractor Corporate Air. Kathleen Iskra serves as president of Horizon, a national airline.

Mary Rose Loney is the assistant director of aviation for the San Jose, California, airport. She began her career in aviation as a clerk at Grand Canyon Airlines. Three years later, she moved from the flight side of aviation to the ground side. In 1984, she was the third woman in the United States to earn the status of accredited airport executive. In 1995, the American Association of Airport Executives reported that 41 of its 377 accredited members were women. Loretta Scott became the first female president of AAAE in 1998–99.

The 1993 directory of the National Association of State Aviation Officials listed two women serving as directors of a publicly funded state aviation agency and one serving as deputy director. Altogether, there were thirty-three women employed in nonclerical, professional positions in the fifty agencies, including the three in top positions. This represented 8 percent of the total and has not changed appreciably.

A U.S. General Accounting Office study of women and minority aerospace managers and professionals reported that the number of female aerospace managers grew from 3.9 to 7.3 percent between 1979 and 1986. The number of female professionals, primarily engineers, doubled—from 8.2 to 16.3 percent during the same period. From the mid-1970s to the mid-1980s, the number of female engineering graduates increased significantly. This trend appeared to peak in 1987. The number of FAA Aircraft Mechanic certificates held by women has remained nearly stable over the past several years, around 1 percent of the total. While female aircraft mechanics (airframe and power plant mechanics) appear to be highly employable, few women are attracted to the occupation.[74]

Women in Space

In 1963, the Soviet Union accomplished the feat that the United States was unwilling to undertake—sending a women into space. Valentina Tereshkova, a Russian textile worker and recreational skydiver, orbited the Earth forty-eight times in the Vostok IV. This broke the women's altitude record set by Jeanette Piccard in 1934. In the 1960s, the Soviet Union, like the United States, did not recruit women as astronaut candidates. Tereshkova's space flight would not be repeated by another Russian woman for twenty years.

Between 1964 and 1978, studies were undertaken to determine whether women were physically and psychologically capable of participating in missions into space. The performance data obtained did not differ significantly from that obtained from the study of the thirteen "would-be" women astronauts in 1960–61. Once again, it was demonstrated that women were, in all aspects, equal to the challenge of space flight. In fact, women possessed some characteristics that might make them superior to men in certain situations.

Sally Ride

In 1978, Sally Ride (fig. 16.30) was looking for a job in research physics when she read an article about NASA's need for young scientists to serve as "mission specialists" on future space shuttle and space station missions. NASA received 8,000 applications, including 1,000 from women. Ride was among six women chosen to be part of the group of twenty mission specialists and fifteen pilots who would participate in the program. She was a highly educated scientist with a doctorate in physics along with baccalaureate degrees in physics and English literature. This Encino, California, native also had excellent health and natural athletic ability, which earlier had led to her national ranking as a junior tennis player.

Sally Ride received her mission specialist/astronaut training at Johnson Space Center. While there, she learned to fly a jet and later earned her private pilot's license. The astronauts, who were a part of the space shuttle/space station program, helped design and develop parts of the shuttle. Ride helped design the remote mechanical manipulator arm that would be used to deploy and retrieve satellites and other space "payloads." In 1982, Navy Capt. Robert Crippen was assigned to the

Fig. 16.30. Sally Ride. Courtesy of the Ninety-Nines, Inc.

shuttle mission on which the arm would be tested. He selected Ride as the crew member who would work with the arm. While Ride was chosen on the basis of her qualifications and experience, public attention focused on her gender. There was intense interest in her space apparel, her cosmetics, and the shuttle's sanitary facilities. One recurring question concerned her need for a bra in zero gravity. On 18 June 1983, the United States launched its first female astronaut into space. In 1984, Ride returned to space aboard the Challenger. During that mission, Kathryn Sullivan, a geologist, became the first woman to walk in space. Ride left NASA in 1987 to become a Science Fellow at Stanford University.[75]

Judith Resnick and Christa McAuliffe

Astronaut Judith Resnick (fig. 16.31) and civilian school teacher Christa McAuliffe were the first women to perish in the U.S. space program. They were part of the seven-member crew who died when the shuttle Challenger exploded following launch on 28 February 1986. Resnick, an electrical engineer, was serving as a mission specialist. McAuliffe had been selected through a competition of over 10,000 teachers to represent all Americans.

Lt. Col. Eileen Collins

On 3 February 1995, USAF Lt. Col. Eileen Collins (fig. 16.32) became the first American woman to serve as pilot of a space shuttle. While female engineers, physicians, and scientists had served as mission specialists since 1983, the pilot's seat had been occupied by male military test pilots. A very special cheering section was present at this launch. Seven of the surviving eleven women of the Mercury 13 were crowded into the bleachers. These "would-be" astronauts had been invited to the launch by Eileen Collins and NASA headquarters. Collins had met the women the previous summer when they had traveled to Oklahoma City for their first reunion at the Ninety-Nines headquarters. After over thirty years,

Fig. 16.31. Judith Resnick. Courtesy of the Ninety-Nines, Inc.

Fig. 16.32. Lt. Col. Eileen Collins. Courtesy of the Ninety-Nines, Inc.

NASA gave the Mercury 13 the official welcome they so richly deserved.[76]

Eileen Collins was attending the Air Force Test Pilot School at Edwards Air Force Base, California, when she was selected by NASA for the astronaut program. She graduated in 1990 and became an astronaut in 1991. Collins, a native of Elmira, New York, has a bachelor's degree in mathematics and master's degrees in operations research and space systems management. She has served as an instructor pilot at Vance Air Force Base, Oklahoma, at Travis Air Force Base, California, and at the U.S. Air Force Academy, Colorado. She has logged over 4,000 hours in thirty types of aircraft. Her first shuttle mission in 1995 traveled 2.9 million miles in 198 hours and orbited the Earth 129 times. Collins later gave birth to her first child, and in 1999 she returned to space as commander of STS-93 Columbia.[77]

In 1784, when Elisabeth Thible climbed aboard a tethered balloon in France, she had no idea that this act would begin women's involvement in the world of aviation. Through more than two centuries, determined women have overcome societal and economic barriers to expand the boundaries of aviation. In 1911, just eight years after the Wright brothers made their historic flight, Harriet Quimby became the first American woman to earn her pilot's license. As the twentieth century drew to a close, Eileen Collins became the first woman to command a space shuttle flight. Woman have earned the right to be full participants in the world of aviation, both on the air side and on the land side, and they will continue to share the challenges, the pleasure, the risks, and the glory of aviation.

Notes

1. Lomax, *Women of the Air,* 3–5.
2. Lomax, 3–5.
3. Moolman, *Women Aloft,* 14.
4. Lomax, 6–15.
5. Lomax, 6–15.
6. Moolman, 15, 17.
7. Moolman, 15, 17.
8. Moolman, 18.
9. Moolman, 22.
10. Holden, *Her Mentor Was an Albatross,* 28–29.
11. Holden, 28–29.
12. Holden, 28–29.
13. Holden, 28–29.
14. Holden, 28–29.
15. Moolman, 31–37; Lomax, 33–34.
16. Moolman, 31–33.
17. Lomax, 33, 34.
18. Moolman, 29–30; Lomax, 35–40.
19. Moolman, 29–30; Lomax, 35–40.
20. Fischer, "Bessie Coleman: Flying in the Face of All Odds"; Rich, *Queen Bess, Daredevil Aviator.*
21. Braden, "Black Aviator 'Queen Bess' Is Honored with Stamp"; Moolman, 29–30; Lomax, 35–40.
22. Moolman, 45–47; Lomax, 76–78.
23. Moolman, 46–54; Lomax, 80–98, 109–33.
24. Moolman, 46–54; Lomax, 80–98, 109–33.
25. Oakes, *United States Women in Aviation, 1930–1939;* Moolman, 46–54.
26. Moolman, 46–54; Lomax, 80–98, 109–33.
27. Moolman, 57–59.
28. Lomax, 74–76.
29. Nichols Collection.
30. Moolman, 55–57.
31. Richey Collection; Holden, 255–56.
32. Omlie Papers.
33. Lomax, 115–27.
34. Piccard, personal interview, 1980.
35. Moolman, 136–41.
36. Moolman, 141.
37. Moolman, 142–43.
38. Scharr, *Sisters in the Sky: WAFS;* Moolman, 143–47.
39. Moolman, 147–50.
40. Cochran, *Jackie Cochran: An Autobiography;* Lomax, 198–211.
41. Moolman, 147–51.
42. Keil, *Those Wonderful Women in Their Flying Machines;* Verges, *On Silver Wings;* Moolman, 151–53.
43. Strohfus, personal interview, 1992.
44. Bradley, "Women in Uniform."
45. Horton, "The Women's Angle," 10, 55.
46. Scyos, "Aviation Career of a Pioneer Female Air Traffic Controller."
47. Cooper, "Olive Ann Beech: A Legend in Her Time"; "Mrs. O. A. Beech Dies at Age 89"; Raytheon Aircraft Company, Olive Ann Beech biographical information.
48. Holden and Griffith, *Ladybirds,* 195; Stanley, "Taking Flight."
49. Tiburzi, *Takeoff! America's First Women Pilots;* FAA, *Administrator's Fact Book.*
50. FAA, *Administrator's Fact Book.*
51. McLaughlin, *Footsteps in the Sky.*
52. Holden and Griffith, 195.
53. Holden and Griffith, 195.
54. Holden and Griffith, 89.
55. Holden and Griffith, 188–90; Lear, *Bill and Moya Lear: An Unforgettable Flight.*

56. Jessen, telephone interview, 1994; Cross, "Return of the 'Mercury 13'"; Holden and Griffith, 200–203, 228–30.

57. *Airline Transport World,* 40–43.

58. Henderson, "The Drive for Diversity."

59. Anderson, personal interview, 1996.

60. Jones, personal interview, 1997.

61. Kjos, "A Look at Attitudes Toward Women in Aviation"; Potter, "Stunt Pilot Sees the World from Totally Different Angle"; Holden and Griffith, 130–32; United Airlines, personal communication.

62. Yeager and Rutan, *Voyager.*

63. Holden and Griffith, 125–29.

64. Barela, "Now We Get to Shoot Back"; Muradian, "Embattled New York Fliers Face New Era."

65. Hehs, "Major Jackie Parker Fighter Pilot"; Muradian.

66. Rowley, "Cathy Clothier."

67. Pope, "Fighting the Next War."

68. Holden and Griffith, 223.

69. Davis, personal interview, 1988.

70. Henderson.

71. Holden and Griffith, 34.

72. Holden and Griffith, 220–22.

73. Jane F. Garvey, http://www.faa.gov/apa/bios/ garvey.htm, 1998.

74. FAA, *Administrator's Fact Book.*

75. Fox, *Women Astronauts Aboard the Shuttle;* Golden, "Sally's Joy Ride into the Sky"; speech by Dr. Sally Ride, Anchorage, Alaska, 1984.

76. Jessen, personal interview, 1994.

77. NASA, 2000.

References

Ailand, Noel E., and Gerald N. Sandvick. *Minnesota Aviation History, 1857–1945.* Chaska, Minn.: MAHB, 1993.

Airline Transport World, September 1995, 40–43.

Barela, Timothy P. "Now We Get to Shoot Back." *Airman,* December 1993, 34–35.

Bilstein, Roger. *Amelia Earhart: The Final Story.* New York: Random House, 1967.

Boase, Wendy. *The Sky's the Limit: Women Pioneers in Aviation.* New York: Macmillan, 1979.

Braden, William. "Black Aviator 'Queen Bess' Is Honored with Stamp." *Chicago Sun Times,* 18 November 1994, 4.

Bradley, LaVerne. "Women in Uniform." *National Geographic Magazine,* October 1943, 445–48.

Brooks-Pazmany, Kathleen. *U.S. Women in Aviation, 1919–1929.* Washington, D.C.: Smithsonian Institution Press, 1985.

Cochran, Jackie. *Jackie Cochran: An Autobiography.* New York: Bantam Books, 1987.

Cole, Jean Hascall. *Women Pilots of World War II.* Salt Lake City: University of Utah Press, 1992.

Cooper, Ann. "Olive Ann Beech: A Legend in Her Time." *Ninety-Nine News,* May 1992, 5–6.

Cross, James M. "Return of the 'Mercury 13.'" *Ninety-Nine News/International Women Pilots,* March/April 1995, 5–7.

Federal Aviation Administration. *Administrator's Fact Book.* Washington, D.C.: Government Printing Office, 1995, 1996.

Fischer, Audrey. "Bessie Coleman: Flying in the Face of All Odds." *Woman Pilot* 3 (March/April 1995): 8–11.

Flowers, Sandra. *Women in Aviation and Space.* Ozark: Alabama Aviation and Technical College, 1989.

Fox, Mary Virginia. *Women Astronauts Aboard the Shuttle.* New York: Julian Messner, 1987.

Franche, Linda Bird. "In the Company of Wolves." *Time,* 2 June 1997, 38.

Gibbs, Nancy. "Wings of Desire." *Time,* 2 June 1997, 28–34.

Golden, Frederic. "Sally's Joy Ride into the Sky." *Time,* 13 June 1983, 56–58.

Gruber, Douglas. "Sally's Ride." *Smithsonian,* September 1983, 22–24.

Hehs, Eric. "Major Jackie Parker Fighter Pilot." *Code One,* April 1995, 13–18.

Henderson, Donna K. "The Drive for Diversity." *Air Transportation World,* September 1995, 33–43.

Holden, Henry. *Her Mentor Was an Albatross.* Mt. Freedom: Black Hawk, 1993.

Holden, Henry, and Lori Griffith. *Ladybirds.* Mt. Freedom: Black Hawk, 1991.

———. *Ladybirds II.* Mt. Freedom: Black Hawk, 1993.

Hollander, Lu. "Thrill of a Lifetime: Blink and You'll Miss It." *Ninety-Nine News,* March/April 1993, 15.

Horton, "The Women's Angle," *Air Trails,* March 1951, 10, 55.

Keil, Sally. *Those Wonderful Women in Their Flying Machines.* New York: Four Directions Press, 1990.

Kjos, Kristine. "A Look at Attitudes Toward Women in Aviation." *FAA Aviation News,* April 1993, 21–24.

Lear, Moya Olsen. *Bill and Moya Lear: An Unforgettable Flight.* Reno: Jack Bacon, 1996.

Lomax, Judy. *Women of the Air.* New York: Random House, 1986.

Lospaluto, Dawn. "Women and Minorities in Aerospace." *Aviation Week and Space Technology* (advertiser sponsored supplement), 28 May 1990.

Lovell, Mary. *The Sound of Wings: Amelia Earhart.* New York: St. Martin's Press, 1987.

Luce, Clare Boothe. "But Some People Simply Never Get the Message." *Life,* 28 June 1963, 30–31.

Mazzio, Skip, and Donna Veca. *Just Plane Crazy: Biography of Bobbi Trout.* Santa Clara, Calif.: Osborne, 1987.

McLaughlin, Helen E. *Footsteps in the Sky.* Denver: State of the Rt, 1994.

Moolman, Valerie. *Women Aloft.* Virginia: Time-Life Books, 1981.

"Mrs. O. A. Beech Dies at Age 89." *AIAA Region V Newsletter,* extracted from the *Beech Crafts,* 6 July 1993.

Muradian, Vago. "Embattled New York Fliers Face New Era." *Air Force Times,* 15 January 1996, 21.

Myles, Bruce. *Night Witches: The Untold Story of Soviet Women in Combat.* Novato, Calif.: Presidio, 1981.

National Aeronautics and Space Administration (NASA), Lyndon B. Johnson Space Center, http://www.jsc.nasa.gov/bios/htmlbios/collins.html, 2000.

Newman, Richard J. "Tell Us Your Name, Rank, and Sex Life." *U.S. News,* 16 June 1997, 34.

Nichols, Ruth. Collection. International Women's Aviation and Space Museum, Dayton, Ohio.

Oakes, Claudia M. *U.S. Women in Aviation, 1930–1939.* Washington: Smithsonian Institution Press, 1991.

———. *U.S. Women in Aviation Through WWI.* Washington: Smithsonian Institution Press, 1985.

Omlie, Phoebe. Papers. National Air and Space Museum Archives, Smithsonian Institution, Washington, D.C.

Pope, Barbara Spyridon. "Fighting the Next War." *Newsweek,* 2 June 1997, 31.

Potter, Connie. "Stunt Pilot Sees the World from Totally Different Angle." *Oregonian,* 11 June 1992.

Raytheon Aircraft Company. Olive Ann Beech undated biographical information, received August 1992.

Rich, Doris. *Queen Bess, Daredevil Aviator.* Washington: Smithsonian Institute Press, 1993.

Richey, Helen. Collection. National Air and Space Museum Archives, Smithsonian Institution, Washington, D.C.

Rowley, Patric. "Cathy Clothier." *International Women Pilots Magazine,* November/December 1995, 6–7, 18.

Scharr, Adela Riek. *Sisters in the Sky: WAFS.* St. Louis: Patrice Press, 1986.

———. *Sisters in the Sky: WASPs.* St. Louis: Patrice Press, 1986.

Scyos, Mary Chance. "Aviation Career of a Pioneer Female Air Traffic Controller." *Journal of ATC,* April/June 1994, 24–33.

Smith, Elizabeth Simpson. *Coming Out Right.* New York: Walker, 1991.

Stanley, Don. "Captains Courageous." *Sacramento Bee,* 18 March 1990.

———. "Taking Flight." *Sacramento Bee,* 2 December 1992.

Tiburzi, Bonnie. *Takeoff! America's First Women Pilots.* New York: Crown, 1984.

Van Biema, David. "The Rules of Engagement." *Time,* 2 June 1997, 36.

Verges, Marianne. *On Silver Wings: The Women Air Force Service Pilots.* New York: Ballantine Books, 1991.

Vistica, Gregory L., and Evan Thomas. "Military: Sex and Lies." *Newsweek,* 2 June 1997, 26.

Whyte, Edna Gardner. *Rising Above It.* New York: Orion Books, 1991.

Yeager, Jeana, and Dick Rutan. *Voyager.* New York: Alfred A. Knopf, 1987.

17

Space History

Lance Erickson

THE SAME CURIOSITY that has motivated us to explore the world's frontiers has inspired us to explore space. The earliest stories of mythical travel through the heavens by the Babylonians, Egyptians, and Greeks are evidence of a universal interest in other worlds. Those stories have also served as an inspiration to many of those responsible for developing the theory and design of our space flight hardware and some of today's aircraft. Tales of space flight by scientists such as Galileo and Kepler were not just imaginary travels but important thoughts that led to the scientific and mathematical foundations of space flight. The concept of space travel has continued through the centuries and appears in more recent fiction by authors such as Jules Verne *(From the Earth to the Moon)* well before the first space flights. Some of the works were surprisingly insightful in predicting some of the forms, conveyances, and even hazards of space flight.

Rocketry

Records from the third century B.C. describe how the Chinese dropped gunpowder charges into their ceremonial fires. Some of these made a dazzling escape from the fire with a trail of smoke and fire, creating the first primitive rockets.[1] Almost ten centuries later, the Chinese filled bamboo tubes with gunpowder and launched them over the Great Wall in a defensive barrage against Mongol attackers. Although these Chinese "fire arrows" lacked the stability and control of today's offensive weapons, the launches marked the beginning of military rocketry.

Success against the Mongol invaders was short-lived. The Mongols quickly learned to produce their own rockets, and by the thirteenth century, they were using rockets throughout Europe and Arabia as an offensive weapon. By the sixteenth century, the rocket had become an integral part of warfare in Europe. In 1812, the British army formed a complete rocket brigade.[2]

Improvements in the solid rocket design through the years were limited mostly to stability and size before the advent of the more efficient liquid fuel rocket. Before 1900, the solid rocket could launch payloads over several miles. However, it was not sufficiently advanced to leave the atmosphere or travel across continents. The technology and theory required for those goals would be slow to evolve and require an entirely new approach.

Important work on the mathematical background for this new propulsion design was first published in 1903 by Konstantine Tsiolkovsky.[3] Although lacking in design detail, the concepts he explored led to the development of liquid fueled launch vehicles, orbital techniques, and satellites.

While the groundwork had been laid for the next step in the development of rockets by Tsiolkovsky and others, the technology to build them did not exist. In addition, the advances required for long-range or high-altitude flight would have to wait for a launch vehicle capable of greater thrust and more stability and control. The breakthrough in the critical design—that of the liquid fuel engines developing more thrust than solid fuel motors—was made by Robert Goddard, an American scientist (fig. 17.1).

Although successful, the first liquid fuel rocket flights were not an improvement over the range of the solid rockets. Goddard's 1926 rocket traveled only 41 feet in altitude and 184 feet down range. The significance of Goddard's first flight was in the increased propulsion performance and efficiency that would allow flight into space. A chemical rocket improves in efficiency as the exhaust gas becomes lighter and as fuel flow increases—both of these favoring liquid fuel propulsion over solid.

Soon after Goddard's first liquid fuel rocket flights, a

Fig. 17.1. Robert Goddard with the first successful rocket fueled by liquid oxygen and gasoline. Courtesy of NASA.

German civil group began improvements on his design to reach higher altitudes than the solid rockets could achieve. This group was called the Verein für Raumschiffart (VfR), or the Society for Space Travel. In the early 1930s, these exploration rockets would carry scientific instruments into the atmosphere for upper-level meteorological studies. The German army became interested in the group's efforts because it applied to their aerial weapons development during the World War II. The United States had some interest in Goddard's rockets; however, there was little communication between Goddard and the interested groups because of adverse press coverage of his work. Germany, therefore, progressed quickly in advanced rocket design while the United States fell behind.

After the Germany army reviewed the work being done by the VfR, they established a formal testing ground in the town of Kummersdorf, in contravention of the Treaty of Versailles. Germany's rocket program quickly outgrew the small base, and a new rocket research center was constructed at Peenemünde, Germany. From this center came the German military rockets — the A series, which evolved into the more advanced V-2.

The V-2 became the ultimate weapon of terror that soared throughout France and England in the closing stages of the World War II. Although this effort came too

Fig. 17.2. German V-2 rocket with Bumper second stage attached. First launch at Cape Canaveral. Courtesy of NASA.

late in the war to have a serious impact on the outcome, the U.S. Army was fully aware of the near-orbital capabilities of the next generation of the V-2 rocket (fig. 17.2). As Germany was preparing for defeat, the U.S. Army organized Operation Paperclip to capture and transport the German rocket hardware and personnel to the United States.

The Germans did not want other countries to gain control of the Peenemünde rocket program. Hitler therefore ordered the SS to capture and kill everyone associated with the project. Scientists and engineers immediately surrendered to the Allies in hopes of being transported to America. In 1945, 118 German rocket engineers escaped to the United States and joined American rocket teams. Wernher von Braun, the most widely recognized of the German scientists, and dozens of captured V-2 rockets were placed under military command for weapons development. This was the beginning of a program that produced increasingly larger rockets capable of delivering weapons over thousands of miles and lifting payloads above Earth's atmosphere.[4]

Early Space Programs

The flight performance of the new military rockets created interest for many scientists in the United States because of the capability of flight above Earth's atmosphere. The conversion of the weapon's payload to a scientific platform was relatively simple on these missiles. Plans were soon made to utilize these early high altitude rockets for scientific missions. The Redstone, a direct derivative of the German V-2 rocket, is an example of an early ICBM utilized for scientific payload launches in the late 1950s and early 1960s. More recently, ICBM missile conversions have evolved into today's expendable launch vehicles, including the Delta, Atlas, and Titan.[5]

During the late 1950s, many advisory groups were formed to establish a U.S. policy for developing the technology, the facilities, and the direction for a space program. Scientific debate on manned versus unmanned exploration, Earth versus lunar research, and the need for deep-space exploration was interrupted dramatically on 4 October 1957. This date marked the launch of the first satellite into space, the Soviet Sputnik (fellow traveler), on a converted Soviet ICBM.

The small beeping satellite stunned the United States. The Soviet ICBM launch capabilities caused the greatest concern. The scientific impact of the probe was minimal, since the satellite only carried a few instruments and a transmitter as its payload. The United States promptly began exploring the quickest route to launch a satellite into orbit. While the Navy put the final touches on the Vanguard satellite project, the Soviet Union launched Sputnik II in November 1957. Unlike its sister craft, the Sputnik II carried with it a living payload: Laika, a dog.

The American answer to the initial Sputnik launches was anything but masterful. Leery of using captured German technology, President Dwight D. Eisenhower ordered the Navy Vanguard team to develop and launch a payload immediately. He felt that Americans should be responsible for launching the first American satellite. Vanguard exploded on the launch pad in December 1957, marking the end of the Navy's rocket program. Following this embarrassing failure, von Braun's rocket team was given the go-ahead to complete the launch vehicle.

The German crew did not fail. A scientific payload was carried into orbit by a converted Redstone missile on 31 January 1958—the Explorer 1 (fig. 17.3). The instrument package was advanced for its time, containing transducers for measuring temperatures inside and outside the vehicle during flight. It also contained a microphone to detect micrometeoroid impacts, a Geiger-Müller tube to measure ionized particle density, and two transmitters.

Explorer 1 was designed to measure the properties of space above the atmosphere. The small spacecraft found ionized particles concentrated in a belt surrounding Earth in approximately the same geometry as Earth's magnetic field. These are the van Allen radiation belts, named after Dr. James van Allen of the University of Iowa, who designed the experiment around a Geiger-Müller tube. Later Explorer flights (73 total) and several of the early Pioneer series spacecraft were used to measure and model Earth's space environment.[6]

In 1957, Sputnik, Explorer, and the International Geophysical Year (IGY) forced the United States to develop an agency that could direct civilian space programs. President Eisenhower had convened a science advisory

Fig. 17.3. The Explorer 1 spacecraft on top of the Jupiter-C rocket, a converted Redstone missile. Courtesy of NASA.

committee in the wake of the Sputnik launch, leading to the establishment of the National Aeronautics and Space Act of 1958. The Space Act created the National Aeronautics and Space Administration (NASA) on 1 October 1958. T. Keith Glennan served as its first director. The first NASA headquarters was housed in the Dolly Madison House in Washington, D.C. NASA was directed to develop and administer the nation's manned and unmanned civil space policy and oversee the already existing Jet Propulsion Lab.[7]

The first of NASA's exploration projects was to explore the Moon with the early Pioneer spacecraft, beginning in 1958. Pioneer 1, 2, and 3 were not successful. However, the lunar flyby by Pioneer 4 was a distant encounter and was considered a partial success. At the same time, the Soviet lunar program, Luna, began with the Luna 1 flyby mission on 2 January 1959, but it failed to achieve a flyby trajectory. Luna 2 was a lunar flight that impacted the Moon, returning the first closeup images. Luna 3, launched on 4 October 1959, provided the first images of the Moon's far side. The Luna 3 flyby trajectory ended in a permanent Earth-Moon orbit that can still be tracked today.

The U.S. Ranger spacecraft was also designed for impact missions on the lunar surface. Ranger was to provide detailed images of the surface, similar to Luna; however, the series was not successful until the seventh Ranger flight. In 1961, the first planetary probe was launched, starting a successful Soviet program of Venus exploration, Venera. Soon the U.S. Mariner series of planetary exploration spacecraft was launched for a Venus flyby with the Mariner 2 craft. Mariner 3 followed in 1964 for a Mars flyby. By 1964, the lunar programs of both the United States and the Soviet Union were developing soft landing exploration vehicles.

The Apollo Legacy

On 25 May 1961, President John F. Kennedy announced the beginning of NASA's Apollo project and predicted that the United States would land a man on the Moon within a decade. His prediction had social, political, and scientific significance well beyond the spectacular manned flights that followed. The international impact of the program was a tremendous boost to the United States' image and stature. It would also prove to be a sig-

Fig. 17.4. The Mercury 7 astronauts shown in front of a Convair 106-B. *Left to right:* Scott Carpenter, Gordon Cooper, John Glenn, Virgil "Gus" Grissom, Walter Schirra, Alan Shepard, and Donald "Deke" Slayton. Courtesy of NASA.

nificant advancement for the nation's science programs, education, technology base, and industry.

Even before Apollo, manned exploration projects were being planned. Seven U.S. astronauts were selected in 1959, chosen for their pilot skills and personality traits. Scott Carpenter, Gordon Cooper, John Glenn, Virgil "Gus" Grissom, Walter Schirra, Alan Shepard, and Donald "Deke" Slayton were almost instant American heroes (fig. 17.4). Over the years, each contributed to space flight history and to the foundation of our current manned space programs, including the space shuttle and soon-to-be international space station. The second NASA astronaut group was announced as the "New 9" on 17 September 1962. The little-known Mercury 13 astronauts, all women, were selected in 1961, but they never flew on a space mission.[8]

The Apollo manned lunar program rapidly increased in scale and complexity after Kennedy's 1961 proclamation. The project scientists and engineers quickly integrated the Ranger lunar imaging program, the Surveyor program, and the Mercury projects into the manned lunar program to keep Apollo flights within the decade, as promised by Kennedy.

Throughout the 1960s, NASA's management of the enormous manned lunar landing program proved to be successful but difficult. Congressional support and funding were often larger problems for NASA than the enormous technical hurdles.[9] One of the greatest problems that NASA faced at the beginning of the Apollo program was the shortage of engineers and scientists. The vast areas of new technology and engineering necessary for the lunar missions had to be developed from a much smaller collection of manned and unmanned programs. Because of the limited number of qualified personnel in the early 1960s, the thousands of scientists and engineers needed for the Apollo project had to be recruited from outside NASA and trained in the various disciplines. Grants to enlarge university science and engineering programs were required. Such grants also expanded the nation's schools and helped develop the succeeding industrial technologies.

The first of the U.S. manned flights began in the Mercury-Redstone (MR) program with Alan Shepard in a suborbital flight on 5 May 1961 (MR-3). The first U.S. orbital flight was the Mercury-Atlas (MA) flight of John Glenn (MA-6), which followed Yuri Gargarin's first

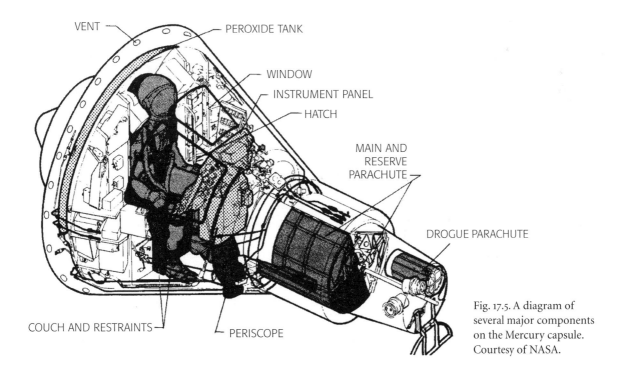

VENT — PEROXIDE TANK

WINDOW
INSTRUMENT PANEL
HATCH

MAIN AND RESERVE PARACHUTE

DROGUE PARACHUTE

COUCH AND RESTRAINTS — PERISCOPE

Fig. 17.5. A diagram of several major components on the Mercury capsule. Courtesy of NASA.

Fig. 17.6. The Gemini 10 spacecraft docking with the Agena target vehicle. Courtesy of NASA.

orbital flight by ten months (fig. 17.5). It was soon recognized that a significant increase in the launch vehicle lift capacity was required to lift the Mercury spacecraft into orbit for longer flights. This capacity problem was not limited to the early manned program, but it represented an almost continual demand for greater and greater lift capacity to get man and equipment to the Moon and back.

In order to develop rendezvous docking techniques in orbit, dual-pilot operation skills, and experience in manned flight, the Gemini follow-on program was established. The two-man capsule allowed extra vehicular activity (EVA) and docking capability, as well as extended duration operations in anticipation of the next stage of the mission to the Moon. The fourteen-day operational capacity of the Gemini capsule provided a research and development platform for the later Apollo spacecraft (fig. 17.6). The capsule also provided the opportunity to measure the effects of weightlessness and isolation on the astronauts. Gemini 3 was launched on 23 March 1965 (Grissom and Young), after two

unmanned development flights. The last Gemini was launched on 11 November 1966 (Lovell and Aldrin).

Development of the Apollo spacecraft and the launch vehicle was far more complex than the Mercury and Gemini projects. The new Apollo systems demanded new technologies in propulsion, structures, electrical power, thermal systems, navigation, and more. As expected, Wernher von Braun was involved in the planning, design, fabrication, and operations of the Mercury, Gemini, and Apollo projects (fig. 17.7). With his expertise in launch vehicles expanding to almost all areas of spacecraft flight and design, and his overwhelming interest in the U.S. space program, von Braun molded much of the NASA agenda. His efforts in the Apollo program were perhaps most pronounced in the Saturn launch vehicle. The smaller Saturn Ib was used in the earliest Apollo development flights and in the Apollo-Soyuz flights and the Skylab program. The Saturn 5 vehicle with a lift capacity of 7.5 million pounds was required to get the Apollo assembly into Earth orbit for its flight to the Moon and back.

Fig. 17.7. The Saturn 5 vehicle lifting off at Cape Canaveral with the Apollo 11 payload. Courtesy of NASA.

The first flight to the Moon was made by Apollo 8, launched on 21 December 1968, which had the notable lunar flyby and return trajectory. Apollo 10 was a dress rehearsal with the lunar module separating from the command module in lunar orbit and descending to within 50,000 feet of the lunar surface.[10] The first landing on the Moon was the Apollo 11 flight, along with the first walk on the Moon, made by Neil Armstrong, and a lunar surface sample return. This flight was not without a few problems. One problem related to the continuing overflow of data in the flight computer as the lunar lander approached the Moon's surface. A greater concern was with the Soviet Luna 15 spacecraft, which was launched and placed into lunar orbit just before the arrival of Apollo 11. The Luna 15's mission was to soft-land and return lunar soil samples before the Apollo 11 return. The potential for collision between the two spacecraft was serious. The Soviets delayed the landing attempt until July 21, after the Apollo 11 departure. Regrettably, Luna 15 was destroyed on landing from too high a descent speed.

The Apollo flights were a tremendous boost for the U.S. space program and a significant step ahead of the Soviet Union in manned space flight. The political gains and the surge of nationalism were obvious benefits of the lunar flights. What was not so obvious, however, was the importance of the scientific objectives of the Apollo program. The Apollo project was to cost approximately $20 billion, some $150 billion in 1994 dollars.[11] The cost to NASA was significant, since much of the Apollo funding came at the expense of other exploration programs. To make the lunar exploration flights as scientifically productive as possible, many experiments were placed on the spacecraft and included in the lunar studies. These experiments were planned by NASA and collaborating scientists to try to answer many questions related to the Moon, Earth, and the solar system.

From the several hundred pounds of particle and rock samples returned from the Moon by the Apollo astronauts, we know the age of the oldest lunar rock, the approximate age of both the Moon and the Earth, and the approximate age of the solar system. We also know much about the origin of the surface material of the Moon and the likelihood that the Moon came from the Earth, based on the similar oxygen isotopes found in the rocks. We have uncovered the differences between the rock and particle materials making up the lunar surface and those

of Earth, showing that the Moon has a much smaller core in relation to Earth. This conclusion favors the formation theory that the Moon resulted from a small planet-sized object impacting Earth. Many questions of volcanic activity, remelting, and original materials on the Moon have been answered by experiments conducted on the Moon's surface and by studying the samples brought back to Earth (fig. 17.8).

The Soviet lunar project initially included a manned lunar program, but it was halted when the technology and hardware failed those efforts. A heavy launch vehicle designed for the project, the N-1, never had a successful launch and was abandoned soon after the final Apollo flights in 1974. Soviet lunar exploration programs were still competitive as seen in the highly successful Soviet Luna program. Later flights included Luna 16 (the successful lunar sample return flight launched on 12 September 1970), Luna 20 (February 1972), and Luna 24 (August 1976). The lunar rover robotic vehicles were successful in surveying and sampling the lunar surface (Luna 17 and Luna 21, launched on 10 November 1970 and 8 January 1973, respectively).

In addition to the near-Earth and lunar exploration projects that began in the 1960s, Jovian planet projects were being planned in the same decade by NASA scientists using the Mariner-class spacecraft. The first of these, the Pioneer 10 and Pioneer 11 craft, were launched in 1972 as part of the "grand tour." The outer planet exploration program also included the highly successful Voyager 1 and Voyager 2 spacecraft launched in 1977.

Mariner 10 was the first Mercury explorer and the last of the Mariner series. The Mercury mission also included a flyby Venus and an exploration of the inner solar system, including the Sun. To date, the Mariner 10 is the only spacecraft to rendezvous with Mercury, providing the only close-up images of the planet that show features strikingly similar to those on the Moon.

The planetary exploration endeavors were not without problems, either for the United States or for the Soviet Union. The complexity of the space-qualified hardware required for operations in the severe conditions of space make reliability and durability an absolute necessity. Even with the increasing reliability of the launch vehicles and improved spacecraft components that evolved with flight experience, errors and failures did occur, as they do today. The Soviet Mars exploration program, as an example, had only one success in seven launches. More

Fig. 17.8. The Apollo 16 lunar module Orion and the lunar rover vehicle on the EVA. John Young is shown in the background at the Descartes landing site. Courtesy of NASA.

recently, the U.S. Mars Observer mission ended in the loss of the spacecraft in 1994 from a communications system failure or attitude control loss. Earlier Mars projects flown by the Soviet Union suffered from an incorrect instruction sequence being sent from a ground controller (Phobos 1) and a loss of communications (Phobos 2) after orbit insertion.

The Pioneer exploration spacecraft series represented one of the most diverse spacecraft in NASA's history. These included Earth and lunar exploration series (Pioneer 1–4), the solar exploration Pioneer 5, the Jovian planetary exploration, and beyond, with Pioneer 10 and

Pioneer 11 and the missions to Venus by Pioneer 12 and Pioneer 13. Pioneer 10 and Pioneer 11 were the first spacecraft to leave the solar system. Pioneer 10 is still transmitting data to Earth on the conditions in interstellar space.

The success of Pioneer 10 and Pioneer 11 in discovering exciting features on Jupiter and Saturn and their numerous moons allowed the Voyager mission to be modified to take advantage of new data. The Pioneer preview allowed complete observations of the more interesting and the more puzzling features. The most active body in the solar system, other than the Sun, was found to be Io, one of the Galilean satellites of Jupiter. Its volcanic activity is changing its surface so rapidly that measurements between the Voyager I and II flights show distinctly different features. There were significant surface changes in only a matter of months. Saturn's moon, Titan, was found to have a significant nitrogen and methane atmosphere, unknown on any other moon including our own. This notable discovery influenced the mission for the future Saturn exploration project, Cassini, which was launched in 1997 and will reach Saturn in 2004. Cassini also carries an atmospheric probe that will separate during the arrival phase to explore the clouds, atmosphere, and surface of Titan.

Since Apollo, there have been only two U.S. lunar mis-sions: Clementine and the Lunar Prospector. Clementine was a joint Department of Defense/NASA project that completed an orbital survey of the surface, then left lunar orbit to rendezvous with the asteroid Geographos. The objectives for the Clementine project were to produce a small, inexpensive exploration spacecraft from the technology developed for the Space Defense Initiative (SDI).[12] The $80 million budget was, in reality, extremely small, and the eighteen-month development time was considered extraordinarily short. The success of the project was due to the new generation of lightweight instruments. Clementine detected water vapor on the Moon, as well as new rock and soil types (fig. 17.9).

Fig. 17.9. Clementine spacecraft drawing. Courtesy of the Lawrence Livermore National Lab.

An unfortunate mishandling of flight instruction data uplinked to the spacecraft sent Clementine into uncontrolled flight that resulted in its being unable to respond to commands from Earth. Although contact was reestablished in 1995, little attitude control fuel remained, and the spacecraft performed some experiments on a limited basis.[13]

The Lunar Prospector, launched on 7 January 1998, provided a detailed map and surface composition of the Moon. The nine-month polar orbit mission also verified the presence of water ice on the moon first suggested by the Clementine data. A final experiment for the Prospector was for water vapor detection as it crashed to the surface on 31 July 1999. No evidence of water vapor was found.

Space Stations

The long flight times to other planets and even the extended flight periods for experiments in Earth orbit and flights to the moon require extensive research on humans in the space environment. Experiments on the effects of microgravity began on the earliest manned flights and continue today on the space shuttle (Space Transportation System, or STS) and Russian Mir space station.

The first space station was the Soviet Salyut 1. Its crew was killed upon reentry when the cabin depressurized early. Of the seven Salyut space stations, only the Salyut 2 was not available for manned flight. The Salyut 6, launched in 1977, was the first extended-duration space station. With the exception of only a few months, the Salyut 6 and the Mir stations have been in almost continuous habitation. All of the space flight endurance records have been set by the Russians aboard Mir. However, the United States has the record for the number of manned space launches (STS), primarily from the space shuttle.

The Salyut has been redesigned to serve many functions since its first flight in 1971. Its configurations include propulsion and logistics modules and research and habitation laboratories. The Mir space station core, a Salyut derivative, was launched in 1984.

The United States' first space station was Skylab, which was derived from the Apollo project hardware. Its purpose was to prove that humans could live and work in space. Research would expand in solar astronomy and physics experiments.[14] The main laboratory was a converted Saturn Ib booster stage, with the launch vehicle a Saturn 5 rocket. The four flights of Skylab included the launch of the orbital workshop on 14 May 1973 (fig. 17.10). The three manned flights to Skylab began on 25 May 1973, with the first Skylab astronauts—Conrad, Weitz, and Kerwin—using the Apollo command module for rendezvous and return. This first manned mission began with the repair of the solar heat shield on the workshop damaged during launch. The 28-day mission included 6.3 hours of EVA and was the longest U.S. manned mission at that time. Two other missions followed, with the last flight holding the U.S. record of eighty-four days, until the Mir mission flown with the U.S. astronaut Shannon Lucid in 1996. The Skylab workshop was deactivated in 1974. It remained in stable orbit until increased solar activity expanded Earth's upper atmosphere. This led to a rapid decay in Skylab's orbit. Reentry (burnup) occurred on 11 July 1979.

The cooperation between the United States and Russia began with the exchange of data on space operations after the dissolution of the Soviet Union. This cooperation continues with the international space station (ISS) (fig. 17.11). Component design and utilization, launch operations, and rendezvous and docking flights of the space shuttle and the Mir space station are continuing. Construction and assembly flights for the ISS will include approximately forty launches involving the U.S. space shuttle and the Russian Proton/Vostok/Zenit launch vehicles. One provisional launch by the European Ariane vehicle is also planned. The fully operational ISS is expected to be completed in 2005, which began with the first module, the Russian Faria, on 20 November 1998. Included in the international effort are Japan, which is to provide an experiment module (JEM), Canada, with the Remote Manipulator System, and the European Space Agency's laboratory module.

Crew and supply flights for the ISS will be provided by the STS, the Salyut, and Soyuz spacecraft. The emergency crew return vehicles will consist of attached Soyuz and U.S. vehicles. The U.S. vehicle is based on the current X-38 composite prototype that can be flown in the shuttle's payload bay.

Fig. 17.10. The Skylab orbital workshop in inverted view. Courtesy of NASA.

Fig. 17.11. A rendering of the completed international space station docked with the space shuttle. Courtesy of NASA.

The U.S. Space Transportation System

During the Apollo program, the need for a launch vehicle with manned capability as well as inexpensive space access capability led to the design of a versatile space launch system. Those first designs were intended to solve the increasingly expensive costs of space flight and the flagging public and congressional interest in space. These first designs included a return-to-Earth orbiter that could land on a conventional runway. The other reusable hardware would dramatically reduce the cost of placing equipment in space. The fifty-five flights per year envisioned and the $50 per pound of payload were never approached, either on the first flights or on today's mis-

sions.[15] The original fully reusable systems were replaced by partially reusable boosters to lower costs, making turn-around time longer and launch-to-orbit costs significantly greater.

The authorization for the STS program, the space shuttle, was signed by President Nixon in 1972 and announced while the first space shuttle pilot-commander, John Young, was on the Moon during the Apollo 16 mission. Authorization for the enormous project also meant that much of the NASA funds for other exploration and space science projects would be reduced dramatically.

The first space shuttle, STS-1, would fly on 16 October 1981, with John Young as the commander and Robert Crippen as the pilot on the Columbia orbiter. Three of

Fig. 17.12. STS-76, Mir view of the Atlantis Orbiter. Courtesy of NASA.

the orbiters, the Challenger, Discovery, and Atlantis, were built for the shuttle fleet by Rockwell. The Enterprise, the first of the orbiters, was developed specifically for aerodynamic and structural tests (fig. 17.12).

Successful and spectacular STS missions were complicated by various problems in the main engine and booster motor reliability. This caused flight delays at times, eventually leading to the explosion of the Challenger (STS 51-L) in 1986. A complete review of the shuttle procedures and hardware followed the Challenger accident, concluding with greater safety margins in the solid rocket motor design and the elimination of liquid fuel booster engines from the payloads carried in the orbiters. The Centaur booster, a liquid oxygen and hydrogen dual-engine rocket, could no longer be used for interplanetary probes, delaying some flights and extending the flight times of others (Galileo, for example).

The success of the space shuttle cannot be overlooked, since one hundred flights in twenty years have provided manned and unmanned space operations that were not available by any other means. The shuttle fleet is scheduled to fly through 2010 and likely beyond, providing versatile manned access to space and the U.S. international space station. The STS, with the assistance of newer expendable launch vehicles and the possibility of a single-stage-to-orbit vehicle (SSTO or the X-33), should satisfy the scientific, exploration, commercial, and defense needs of the future.

The Future

Besides budgetary concerns, the accidents and failures on high-profile projects, especially the manned missions, had far-reaching effects on NASA's exploration and science projects. On earlier missions, NASA personnel had decided to reduce the potential for failures on space exploration missions by using dual spacecraft to increase reliability. The concept was promoted by JPL in order to improve mission success for expensive, deep-space operations. The costs were obviously greater, and justification for dual spacecraft flights became more difficult with time.

The success of the Pioneer, the Voyager, and the Viking missions and decreasing funding made the next generation of spacecraft more attractive as larger single-flight spacecraft. It was thought that, with the success

rate experienced for the NASA missions in the 1970s, the follow-on spacecraft could be reduced to single spacecraft missions with expanded objectives and increased complexity while saving money.

However, some of these projects were too large to have reasonable success ensured with the NASA management and operating techniques, especially with the limited budgets available for testing. The resulting failures of the Mars Observer, the Hubble space telescope's primary mirror focus, and the Galileo high-gain antenna have shown that the larger missions, although well planned, were not tested sufficiently to ensure complete operational success. In response to these problems, the demands made by Congress, and the need for sustaining the scientific research level of the past with fewer dollars, NASA managers have been forced toward smaller and more efficient spacecraft.

Examples of the newer technology and smaller scale projects include the Pluto-Kuiper Express exploration dual spacecraft, a small, lightweight, inexpensive craft that will have improved reliability with lower costs. Another example, the Mars Pathfinder exploration project, has been renamed and rescaled to reflect the lower budgets available for spacecraft development, operation, and expanded mission objectives. NEAR (Near-Earth Asteroid Rendezvous), launched in 1996 for a flyby encounter with Eros in 1999, was an example of the current, smaller spacecraft missions. Similarly, the Mercury Polar Flyby and Wind spacecraft are part of the Discovery spacecraft missions that emphasize simplicity, reliability, and low cost. Not all of the more recent spacecraft have had the success hoped for in the smaller, cheaper mission concept. Mars Observer (1992), Mars Climate Observer (1998), and Mars Polar Lander (1999) were missions that, for various reasons, failed. And although these were setbacks to several programs, they have not altered the newer strategy of providing a greater number of diverse missions with smaller, less expensive spacecraft.

Notes

1. Internet, http://www.ksc.nasa.gov/history/rocket-history.txt.

2. Internet, http://www.ksc.nasa.gov/history/rocket-history.txt.

3. Tsiolkovsky, "Investigation of Space by Means of Reactive Devices."

4. Internet, http://history.msrfc.nasa.gov/history/mm/sect001.html#The V-2.

5. Burrows, *Exploring Space.*

6. Internet, http://titania.osf.hq.nasa.gov/history/explorer.html.

7. Durant, *Between Sputnik and the Shuttle.*

8. Internet, http://www.ninety-nines.org/mercury.html.

9. Launius, *NASA.*

10. Osman, *Space History.*

11. Launius.

12. Internet, http://www.nrl.navy.mil/clementine.

13. Internet, http://nssdc.gsfc.nasa.gov/planetary/clementine.html.

14. Launius.

15. Burrows.

References

Bergaust, Erik. *Wernher von Braun.* Washington, D.C.: National Space Institute, 1976.

Burrows, William E. *Exploring Space: Voyages in the Solar System and Beyond.* New York: Random House, 1990.

Durant, Fredrick III, ed. *Between Sputnik and the Shuttle.* AAS History Series, vol. 3. Washington, D.C.: American Astronautical Society, 1981.

Launius, Roger. *NASA: A History of the U.S. Civil Space Program.* Malabar, Fla.: Krieger, 1994.

Newkirk, Dennis. *Almanac of Soviet Manned Spaceflight.* Houston: Gulf, 1990.

Osman, Tony. *Space History.* New York: St. Martin's Press, 1983.

Tsiolkovsky, Konstantine. "Investigation of Space by Means of Reactive Devices." In *Konstantine Tsiolkovsky: Collected Works.* Moscow: Akademii Nauk, 1954.

Appendix

Contributors

Index

Appendix

Leonardo da Vinci and the Science of Flight

IN THE SPRING of the year 1334, the Republic of Florence passed a decree for the building of a Campanile "so magnificent as to surpass in height and excellence of workmanship whatever of that kind had been made by the Greeks and Romans in the time of their utmost greatness." The result stands four-square to the winds of heaven. How far the intention was fulfilled may be gauged by Ruskin's tribute "of living Christian art none so perfect as the tower of Giotto." The breadth and suavity of ordered purpose which characterize Giotto's work in art are nowhere more apparent than in the series of bas-reliefs round the base of the tower, which formed an epitome of human progress from the time of the Creation, in mastery over the elements, and in growth to fulness of intellectual and spiritual life.

Designed by Giotto, executed in part by Andrea Pisano, and uniting Giotto's naturalism and humanity with the dignity and repose of the Pisanesque tradition, the reliefs were an important influence in the development of Florentine sculpture.

Giotto is one of the very few artists to whose work Leonardo da Vinci makes specific reference in his writings, and these reliefs must have been observed by him times without number during the period of his apprenticeship in Verrocchio's studio. The figure of Jabal in one, representing pastoral life, seated at the door of his tent with his sheep and watch-dog around him, has just that fidelity and naivete in the interpretation of nature for the possession of which Leonardo characterizes Giotto's work in painting. From another of the series Leonardo may have derived his first conception of a mechanism for flight. The relief, which is one of those executed by Andrea Pisano, represents Daedalus in the act of trying his wings, thus symbolizing man's conquest of the air. A note by Ruskin may serve to convey an impression of its artistic quality:

> The head superb, founded on Greek models; feathers of wings wrought with extreme care, but with no precision of arrangement or feeling. How far intentional in awkwardness I cannot say; but note the good mechanism of the whole plan, with strong standing-board for the feet.

It may not be entirely fantastic to suppose that the study of this relief is perceptible in the treatment of the angel's wings in the small panel of the Annunciation in the Louvre, which is now accepted on internal evidence as one of Leonardo's earliest works. Certainly the description, "feathers of wings wrought with extreme care, but with no precision of arrangement or feeling," would apply equally to the picture. This shows the artist's study of the structure of a bird's wing in the rows of feathers and tufted plumage, the big feathers which end the wings, the lesser ones above them, the tufts of down that nestle beneath the shoulders. Yet the resultant impression is neither of precision nor decoration, as is often the case in the treatment of wings by the earlier Italian and Byzantine artists, but simply one of strength. The wings seem almost to quiver with life and vigor of movement. Their use has been considered in the mind of the artist.

Edward McCurdy, "Leonardo da Vinci and the Science of Flight," *19th Century* 68 (July 1910): 126–42.

In contrast with the somewhat similar version of the same subject in the Uffizi (No. 1288) they are of dimensions sufficient to support the figure of the angel.

But Leonardo's interest in the bas-relief of the Campanile was not primarily artistic. The myth of Daedalus is the earliest expression of man's belief in his ultimate inheritance of the air, and he looked beyond the problem of its plastic representation to the thought itself, from the art of Giotto and Andrea Pisano to that of Daedalus, the maker of wings. Something of the extent of that intellectual activity for which he was celebrated above almost all his contemporaries, and the workings of which time has made more fully manifest, is suggested by the words which conclude his earliest biography, "his spirit was never at rest, his mind was ever devising new things." More than of any other character of the Renaissance this is true of him. He was occupied with the study of the exact workings of the forces of nature and of their application to human purposes. When in course of time things old in promise are established and the long-fought battle has been won, it first becomes possible to estimate with some degree of exactitude the *role* of each precursor and to discern how far he traveled along the road of the final advance. In the case of Leonardo, considered as the pioneer of the modern science of aviation, the evidence is of a concrete character. It is possible to define very narrowly the character of his researches and the nature of his conclusions. A sentence of Otto Lilienthal's, one of the greater names in the history of the recent advance, who paid for his devotion with his life, expresses succinctly that measure of contempt which the practical inventor is apt to affect for the mere theorist, however much he may be indebted to his researches: "To conceive of a flying machine is nothing, to construct one is something, but to make trial of it is everything." That Leonardo put his knowledge of theory to the proof is to be inferred from the only reference to these researches which is found in contemporary record. It occurs in the *De Subtilitate* of that somewhat empirical physician and philosopher, Jerome Cardan, who visited England and cast a horoscope for Edward the Sixth, in which he foretold long life for that monarch. As a chronicler Cardan is on more stable ground than in the *role* of astrologer, and after including the invention of flight in a list of "the excellent arts which are hidden," he continues: "It has turned out badly for the two who have recently made a trial of it: Leonardo da Vinci, of whom I have spoken,

has attempted today, but he was not successful; he was a great painter." The laconic antithesis suggests—it almost summarizes—the attitude of contemporary criticism with regard to Leonardo's scientific and mechanical pursuits. The standpoint is the same as that of Vasari, who regarded them as deviations from those purposes which Leonardo alone could accomplish. The criticism has been justified by the march of events. One by one the mechanical and scientific problems to which a great part of Leonardo's creative power was devoted have been solved. He stands revealed as "the forerunner." But the debt of later investigators has been primarily as was that of Leonardo to nature herself. His researches were not links in a chain. He foretold what others afterwards accomplished, and it happened not infrequently that he foretold what proved to be the right method of performance. But in art what Leonardo left tentative and fragmentary must ever be incomplete. Others may partake of his influence but there is no renewal of the spirit; none can add to the substance or use the crucible of his thought. Therefore his achievement in art is something more intimate and more unique, and as such it outweighs the sum of his researches and discoveries although these traversed the whole domain of nature. In the one he is a creator, in the other a student, and the records of his work as such are to be found only in the thousands of pages of his manuscripts. The researches which these contain in the science of flight are of themselves sufficient to reveal the unflagging zeal with which he devoted himself to the study of primary causes. The subject has given its name to one of the two of his treatises which exist in a more or less complete form (*Il Codice Sul Volo degli Uccelli*—Code on the Flight of Birds); but this would seem to be only an early draft of the results of his observations. It is also treated in the *Codice Atlantico,* and in seven of the twelve of Leonardo's manuscripts which are now in Paris in the Library of the Institut de France. Three of these manuscripts, B, E, and K, together with some of the pages in the *Codice Atlantico,* contain his ultimate conclusions as to the nature of the flight of winged creatures and the application of these principles to a mechanism for human flight. The subject is treated of on a hundred and ninety-four pages of the manuscripts, apart from those which treat of the laws of motion and force and the underlying problems of animal mechanics. Some of these references consist of a few lines, or a diagram with a brief note in explanation, but many consist of pages or half pages of closely written matter, the contents of which are far more voluminous than the writings of any other student of the subject down to Leonardo's time. The material falls naturally into two groups, the first being a series of investigations of the laws which govern the power of flight as manifested in nature by birds and other winged creatures, the second consisting of deductions from these principles in the construction of a mechanism which would be capable of sustaining and being worked by man. The interdependence of the two parts of the inquiry is stated with great succinctness in a passage in the *Codice Atlantico* (161 r.a.):

A bird is an instrument working according to mathematical law, which instrument it is within the capacity of man to reproduce with all its movements, but not with a corresponding degree of strength, though it is deficient only in the power of maintaining equilibrium. We may therefore say that such an instrument constructed by man is lacking in nothing except the life of the bird, and this life must needs be supplied from that of man.

The life which resides in the bird's members will without doubt better conform to their needs than will that of man which is separated from them, and especially in the almost imperceptible movements which preserve equilibrium. But since we see that the bird is equipped for many obvious varieties of movements, we are able from this experience to deduce that the most rudimentary of these movements will be capable of being comprehended by man's understanding and that we will to a great extent be able to provide against the destruction of that instrument of which he has himself become the living principle and the propeller.

In the analogy thus drawn from nature to the problem before him Leonardo has anticipated the attitude of modern research. With his words may be paralleled those of Captain Ferber: "Il nous faut apprendre le mètier d'oiseau, comme l'enfant apprend à marcher, et même, ce qui paraîtra à beaucoup extraordinaire, comme le jeune oiseau apprend à voler." (We need to learn the job of a bird, just like a child learns how to walk, just as it may seem to a lot of people extraordinary that a young bird learns how to fly.)

The famous discovery by the brothers Montgolfier has tended to retard almost as much as to advance the progress of aeronautical discovery, through the resultant difference of opinion as to whether the apparatus necessary for flight should be lighter or heavier than air. With Ferber the solution has been arrived at, and he restates the problem on the same lines as Leonardo.

Flight is a natural phenomenon, and consequently its laws are to be deduced by observation of nature. In acting on this principle Leonardo followed the course marked out by Aristotle in the chapters on the flight of birds in the treatise "on the method of progression of animals," with which treatise it is reasonable to suppose him to have been acquainted. The references to Aristotle in his manuscripts are more numerous than to any other classical writer, and a note in the *Codice Atlantico* allows us to infer that he either possessed or had access to translations in manuscript of works which had not then been printed. It may also be noted that the list of books in the *Codice Atlantico* which are believed to have formed Leonardo's library includes the names of Pliny and Albertus Magnus, both of whom, the one in his *Natural History,* the other in *De Animalibus,* have investigated the causes of birds' flight. But both added little, if anything, to the sum of Aristotle's researches, and Albertus Magnus is in a special sense his follower and is the translator of various of his treatises. In relation to Leonardo the three may be looked upon as a single influence, and this proceeds from "il maestro di color che sanno" (The Teacher of Those Who Know).

By contrast, however, with Aristotle's inquiry, which is limited to considering the rudimentary principles of structure and movement of wings and tail in birds, insects, and fishes, the scope of Leonardo's investigations is almost encyclopedic. As a means to determine the exact conditions of flight, which is the movement of one substance within another, he will consider also such operations of nature as offer parallel principles.

In order [he says] to give the true science of the movement of birds in the air, it is necessary to give first the science of the winds, which we shall prove by means of the movements of the water; this science is in itself obvious to the senses, it will serve as a ladder to arrive at the knowledge of winged creatures in the air and the wind. (E 54 v.)

And again:

Of the bird's movement—in order to speak of this subject it is necessary that in the first book you treat of the nature of the resistance of the air; in the second the anatomy of the bird and of its feathers; in the third the action of these feathers in various of its movements; in the fourth the strength of the wings and tail without beating of wings, with the help of the wind to serve as guide in various movements. (F 41 v.)

And again:

Before writing about winged creatures, make a book about how inanimate things descend through the air without wind, and another about their descent with the wind. (F 53 v.)

Accordingly we find him considering the descent of a board of uniform thickness placed first horizontally and then slanting in the air; and he shows how of bodies of equal gravity that will show itself less heavy which extends in greater breadth, and how the heaviest part of a moving object will serve as a guide of its movement, and how the variation of shape of the front or rear portions will deflect its course.

In treating of the science of the winds he shows how the wind varies in power according to its altitude, as is proved by the fact that birds always fly low when the course of the wind is contrary. The movement of the wind is similar in all respects to that of the water. The rudder behind the ship is imitated from the tail of birds; and swimming upon the water teaches men how birds do upon the air. The hand of the swimmer strikes and rests itself upon the water and causes his body to glide away in an opposite movement; and so the wing of the bird does upon the air, for when two forces strike against each other that which is the more rapid always springs back.

He also defines the resistance of the air, and shows how there is as much pressure exerted by a substance against the air as by the air against the substance; and he shows how the fact of a bird remaining motionless on its wings in the air is due to an equilibrium of forces; and how the air beneath the movable substance which descends in it is condensed, and the air above it is rarefied.

After establishing these principles, with others of movement and weight fundamental to his purpose, he addresses himself to the theme more narrowly. Another introductory passage serves to show the order of the work:

I have divided the *Treatise on Birds* into four books, of which the first treats of their flight by beating their

wings; the second of flight without beating the wings and with the help of the wind; the third of flight in general, such as that of birds, bats, fishes, animals, and insects; the last of the mechanism of this movement. (K 3 r.)

The material which corresponds to these divisions is sufficient to render it comparatively simple to construct the treatise from the manuscripts. Each part is based upon many detailed observations as to the distinctive features of the flight of various birds and other winged creatures. There are notes of this kind about the thrush, the swallow, the lark, the eagle, the kite, the magpie, the dove, and the rook, as well as about butterflies, flies, and bats. That these observations were at first hand is shown conclusively by such a passage as this:

I have seen the sparrow and the lark fly upwards in a straight line, being in a level position, and this comes about because when the wing is raised with swift motion it remains pierced through (by the air). (C.A. 160 r.b.)

or the note, with diagram:

See tomorrow morning whether the bird which wheels round coming against the wind *n* stays in the line *a b*, keeping the head in *b* or whether it is in the line *c d*. (C.A. 220 r.a.)

So "of the commencement of the flight of birds" it must be in one of two ways.

The one begins by their lowering themselves with their bodies to the ground, and then producing a leap into the air by extending very rapidly the legs which are folded up; at the end of this leap the wings have finished their expansion, and the birds immediately lower them rapidly towards the ground and rise to the second stage, which is slanting like the first; and so continuing repeatedly they rise to whatever height they please.

The second method is when they drop down from a height:

They then merely throw themselves forward, and at the same time open their wings above and in front, and in the course of their leap they drop the wings down and backwards, and by this rowing they continue their slanting descent.

Others throw themselves with their wings closed, and as they descend they open their wings, and when they have opened them they are checked, and then they close them and fall. (G 64 r.)

So also the successive stages of the flight, either with or against the wind, soaring, tacking, flying in loops, curving, gliding, falling, alighting, are all described with a like closeness of observation and precision of detail.

The manuscripts contain many drawings of birds and other winged creatures. These are of the nature of diagrams subsidiary to and explanatory of the text; but the hand of the artist will not be denied, and some are of great beauty. Certain maze-like delineations of the curves of a bird's flight may serve to recall various *intrecciamenti* (interlaces) which he made as studies for the design on the ceiling of the Camera delle Asse in the Castle of the Sforza at Milan, and the design itself perhaps owes something to his studies of birds' movements.

Flight is the movement through the air of a body which conquers the resistance of the air by means of wings, which are worked by the tendons or muscles of the chest and shoulders somewhat after the manner of levels. The line of this movement is regulated according to Leonardo by the position of the centre of gravity, by the position of the tail, and by the angle at which the planes of the different parts of the body stand to each other. He thus defines the nature of straight and curved movement:

> All bodies which have length, and which in moving through the air have their lateral extremities equally distant from the line of their centre of gravity, will make straight movements. . . . If the lateral extremities of the bodies which have length are at an unequal distance from the line of their centre of gravity, then the movement of the body will describe a curve in the air, and this curve will have its concave part on the side where the extremity of the body is more remote from the line of the centre of gravity. (E 35 v.)

The same result is also brought about by lowering one of the sides of the tail. The line of movement will then describe a curve, and the curve so formed

> will have its concave side towards the side of the tail that is lowered, and the wing of that same side will be slower than the opposite wing in proportion as the bird's movement is more curved. (E 36 r.)
> The bird which takes longer strokes with one wing than with the other will proceed by a circular movement. (C.A. 220 v.c.)

Or one wing may be held at rest and then the curve will be of the sharpest, because "the bird beats its wing repeatedly on one side only when it wishes to turn round, while one wing is held stationary" (K 7 r.). If the movement of the wings is equal above and below the bird's centre of gravity, but the downward beat of the wings is more rapid than the upward beat, the line of the bird's movement will slant upwards; and conversely the slant will be downwards if the wings move more rapidly in rising than in falling.

The exact action of the wing when the bird is in flight without the help of the wind is thus defined:

> The bird drops half the wing downwards, and thrusts the other part towards the tip backwards; and the part which is moved down prevents the descent of the bird, and that which goes backwards drives the bird forward. (K 12 v.)

The bird's power to increase the speed of its movement when descending is by pressing itself closer together in the wings and tail, because by the fourth law of gravity "that heavy substance makes the most rapid descent which takes up a less space of air" (E 37 v.). Its speed is checked by the opening and lowering of the tail and the spreading out of the wings at the same time to their full extent.

The helms or projections on the shoulders of the wings are formed of very small hard feathers, and are "provided by resourceful nature" to enable the bird when in rapid descent to turn from one direction to another, without the slackening of its movement which would be caused by the bending of the whole wing.

The tail when lowered equally will cause the bird to descend by a direct slanting movement; if it is more lowered on the right side the direct descent becomes curved, and the bird moves towards the right side with a greater or less curve according to the extent to which the right point of the tail is lowered, and similarly with the left side; if the tail is raised equally a little above the level of the backbone of the bird, the bird will rise up by a direct slanting movement, and if it raises the right point of the tail more than the left, the movement will curve towards the right side, and if the left point of the tail is more raised it will curve towards the left side.

The structure of the wing, convex on its upper surface and concave on the lower, is adapted to help the bird to sustain itself upon the air, because the air flies more readily from the stroke to the wing as it rises than as it falls, for then the fact that the air is enclosed within the concavity of the wing produces its condensation more speedily than its flight. The extremities of the wings are of necessity flexible because

> when the bird is in position to receive the percussion of the wind slantwise, the extreme part of the lower wing is considerably bent, and makes itself in the form of a foot upon which the weight of the bird is supported somewhat. (E 53 v.)

In thus treating of the structure of the bird's members and the natural law of their movements the scope of Leonardo's investigation is the same as that pursued by Aristotle. But whereas in the one case this forms the limit of the inquiry, in the other conclusions are modified by the consideration of natural causes, such as the action of the wind and the operation of the laws of gravity.

The atmosphere, either still or in motion, is the substance within which the body in flight has to make its movements, and the instinct of the bird enables it to make use of the movement of the wind to serve its own purposes.

In descending the workings of this instinct Leonardo shows how the wind serves as a wedge below or above the bird, for

> birds which rise on the wind in circles hold their wings very high, so that the wind may serve as a wedge to raise them up; similarly in their descent they lower their wings so that less air sustains them, and the wind may act as a wedge above them and drive them down. (K 58 v.)

He describes these circles in which birds rise by the help of the wind as being of two kinds, simple and complex:

> The simple comprise those in which, in their advancing movement, they travel above the flight of the wind, and at the end of it turn and face the direction of the wind, receiving its buffeting from beneath, and so finish the reverse movement against the wind.
> The complex movement by which birds rise is also circular, and consists of an advancing and reverse movement against the direction of the wind in a course which takes the form of a half-circle, and of an advancing and reverse movement which follows the course of the wind. (C.A. 308 r.b.)

These are only notes for a projected treatise, fragmentary as such, and in selection seeming still more so. To multiply quotations would not, however, of necessity intensify the impression which these are intended to serve. So far he is a student of natural science, and as such his presentation of the connection between the phenomena of flight as seen in nature and the operation of natural laws is of direct and primary value. "Nature," he says, "is full of infinite causes which were never set forth in experience." But in the mind of their author these facts are considered in relation to an ultimate problem.

From the fact of the bird acquiring lightness by extending itself and spreading out its wings and tail, he deduces the principle that heavy substance shows itself lightest which extends over the greatest space—and so to the problem:

> From this conclusion it may be inferred that the weight of a man can be supported in the air by means of a great circumference of wings. (E 39 r.)

The objections are put into the mouth of an imaginary opponent, who urges that the sinews and muscles of a bird are incomparably more powerful than those of a man

> because all the girth of so many muscles and of the fleshy parts of the breast goes to aid and increase the movement of the wings, while the bone in the breast is all in one piece, and consequently affords the bird very great power, the wings also being all covered with a network of thick sinews and other very strong ligaments of gristle, and the skin being very thick with various muscles. (*Sul Volo d. Uccelli* 17 r.)

But Leonardo shows that this great strength gives the bird a reserve of power beyond what it generally makes use of in order to support itself on its wings, which enables it to fly very fast or high or to bear in its talons a weight corresponding to its own weight. Man has not any such great reserve of power, but he possesses nevertheless an amount of strength which Leonardo estimates to be more than double that which is required by his own weight.

The first model took the form of a pair of large wings worked by means of the arms, or arms and legs, and attached to the body by a band which passes beneath the armpits. It was in such a fashion that the sculptor of the bas-relief on the Campanile had represented the art of Daedalus.

The type in nature which Leonardo selected to serve as a model was the bat, "because its membranes serve as an armour, or rather as a means of binding together the pieces of its armour, that is the framework of the wings" (*Sul Volo d. Uccelli* 16 r.). He admits that the wings of feathered creatures are more powerful in structure of bone and sinew, but attributes this to the fact that they are penetrable; that is, that the feathers are separated so that the air passes through them, whereas the bat is aided by its membrane, which is not penetrated by the air.

He has also shown that birds like the lark which fly high with the rising of their wings, because these are then pierced through with air, have their feathers spread out more widely than birds of prey which can only rise by a spiral or circular movement. He attempted, therefore, to combine both types by making the wing of the instrument like that of the lark as it rises and like that of the bat as it descends—or, as he calls it, "a method by which the wing is full of holes as it rises and closed up when it falls" (B 73 v.). This he did by attaching various shutters (*sportelli*) to the surface of the wing. The drawings of these, together with the notes in MS. B of the Institut, render possible an exact description. A net connected the framework of the wing, to the canes of which the shutters were fastened along their length on the one side, and on the other side were attached to them by cords at either end. The shutters had rims of cane and were covered over with taffeta, which had been either well soaped or rubbed with starch to render it airtight. As the wing rose the air would pass through the net, and force open the shutter to the extent allowed by the cords. As the wing descended the air below it would drive the shutter up against the net, and so close up the holes, and this would cause the wing to present a solid surface to the air beneath it. He considered that in proportion as the shutters were smaller so they were more useful.

There is a certain natural sequence in the various drawings in the *Codice Atlantico* and MS. B of the Institut, in which the instrument, or a part of it, is reproduced, and this enables us to trace the general progress of the design. The first intention, apparently, was to construct wings which should be attached immediately to the body—in the classification of instruments by M

Berget this is the type known as *ornithopters.* Then the necessity of bringing all the muscles of the different parts of the body into play caused the machinery to become more complex, and as a greater amount of force was made available to move the wings it became possible for these to be constructed with a larger surface.

In the second type the instrument has something of the appearance of the body of a huge dragon-fly, tapering slightly towards the tail, and the framework of the wings arched above the head resembles antennae. Within the body the aeronaut lies at full length, face downwards. His feet are in stirrups, which work the wings by means of cords, one of these causing them to fall and the other to rise. Round the neck is a leather band to which a cord is attached, described as "a rudder which is fixed with a band to the head at the place of the neck" (B 75 v.). The position of the instrument he states to be such that the wings in descending drop partly downwards and partly backwards, that is, towards the feet of the man. The necessity of increasing the power of control led him so to change the mechanism that the wings were lowered by the force of both feet at one and the same time. By this means the downward pressure becomes twice as great and

> you are able to delay and to maintain yourself in equilibrium by lowering one wing more rapidly than the other according to necessity, as you see done by the kite and the other birds. (B 74 v.)

The raising of the wings will then, he says, either be by the force of a spring, or by the hand, or by drawing the feet towards you, the last being the best method, because then the hands are left free.

In a passage in the *Sul Volo degli Uccelli* (On the Flight of Birds—fol. 6) he says that a man in a flying machine should be free from the waist downwards to be able to balance as in a boat, so that his centre of gravity may balance that of the machine.

With the various drawings of the instruments are notes as to the materials of which the parts are to be constructed. Sometimes a word or more is written in the particular part itself, such as "staff of green pine," "fustian," "taffeta," "try first with leaves of chancery," which latter may be interpreted to mean a form of parchment. Two parts of the covering of a wing are described, one as of "fustian stuck over with feathers," the other of "starched taffeta," "and for the experiment," he continues, "you will use fine pasteboard" (B 74 v.).

The joints are to be of stout tanned leather bound with strong raw silk, and no iron clasps are to be used, because either these are soon broken at the joints or else they become worn out. The joints of the canes are to be padded with leather. The springs may be made of ox-horn, and, for the purpose of a model, quill pens may be used. As an alternative, the springs may be of steel wires of equal thickness, number, and length. The staff is to be of stout canes, and it may be made as long as is necessary because it is made up of pieces. The cord is to be a strip of ox-hide, well greased, as also should be the bindings where it plays, or these may be smeared with soft soap. In order to lessen the risk of accident the cord should be double. "For the wings you should make one cord to bear the strain and another more slack in the same place, so that if the one is strained and breaks, the other remains for the same purpose" (H 29 v.).

The same forethought prompts a note that the machine should be tried over a lake, and that a long leather bottle should be carried in the girdle as a safeguard against drowning in case of a fall; and again, in writing of another type of machine, he says, "Try the actual instrument in the water so that if you fall you will not do yourself any harm" (B 89 r.).

The various notes and drawings which relate to what was probably the latest type of the machine are among the most difficult to interpret. The machinery, although more compact, has become more complicated, and an attempt to define the practical value of the parts of it is only possible to the practiced student of mechanics. A drawing of a man (B 79 r.) suspended by the waist, in an attitude as though swimming immediately below the drum around which the cord is turned, is apparently a preliminary to this latest type; the note below it describes how it may be worked either with one pair of wings or with two, and refers to a ladder or ladders of light thin pine at the base. These ladders are found only in the latest type of the instrument, and he defines their use as serving the purpose of legs when it is desired to rise above a plain, and so rendering it possible to beat the wings. He mentions the instance of the martin, which cannot raise itself by flying when settled on the ground, because it has short legs. A drawing shows how, after the ascent had been commenced, the ladders are to be drawn up so that they lie flat against the bottom of the instrument. They are made with curved ends in order apparently to lessen the risk of their becoming fixed in the ground. Finally, the position of the man is changed.

I conclude [he says] that standing upright is more useful than flat on one's face, because the machine can never turn upside down, and moreover the habit created by long use requires it thus. And the rising and falling of the movement will proceed from the lowering and raising of the two legs, and this is of great force, and the hands remain free, and if one had to be flat on one's face the legs in the fastening of the thighs would have great difficulty in supporting themselves; and the feet have the first shock when it alights. (C.A. 276 v.b.)

A drawing in MS. B of the Institut (80 r.) is the most complete representation of this type of the instrument. In it the figure of the man is seen standing on his feet, but bowed like Atlas under his burden. Above him are two pairs of wings, which are worked by cords and pulleys controlled by his head and limbs. He is placed between two posts, which support at the top a wheel. Cords passed round it raise and lower the wings as the wheel moves. The posts descend to the base of a low basket-shaped car, where are pedals on which the man stands. These pedals are connected by cords with the wings. The car is resting on short ladders. Above the drawing is a note:

The man exerts with his head a force equal to 200 pounds, and with his hands he exerts a force equal to 200 pounds, and this is then man's actual weight. The movement of the wings will be crosswise, like the gait of a horse. So for this reason I maintain that this is better than any other.

Another note below states the dimensions:

Ladder to mount and descend; let it be 12 braccia (6 yards) high, and let the span of the wings be 40 braccia, and their elevation 8 braccia, and let the body from poop to prow be 20 braccia and 5 braccia in height, and let all the outer framework be canes and linen.

In its general outline the instrument has some resemblance to certain examples of the type known as *helicop-*

ters. But both in this and in the earlier model, of which the general structure has somewhat more resemblance to certain types of the modern aeroplane, the only motive power to be discerned is derived directly from the strength of the human agent. The capacity of the instrument to overcome the resistance of the air is the capacity of his muscles to lift weights and to endure pressure, transferred to this particular purpose by the use of suitable implements. Numerous passages in the manuscripts show that Leonardo doubted the adequacy of this power to accomplish more than at most short experimental flights. He contrasted it with that reserve of power possessed by the larger birds, and he sought for a fresh source of motive power to supplement or take the place of that exerted by man.

It was in this that his researches were most in advance of his time.

On a page of MS. B of the Institut (83 v.) is a drawing of a large screw constructed to revolve round a vertical axis. The notes at the side and below the drawing tell of the materials and dimensions, and reveal also the purpose which it was intended to serve:

Let the outer extremity of the screw be of steel wire as thick as a cord, and from the circumference of the centre let it be 8 braccia.

I find that if this instrument made with a screw is well made, that is to say made of linen of which the pores are stopped up with starch and is turned swiftly, the said screw will make its spiral in the air, and it will rise high.

Take the example of a wide and thin ruler whirled very rapidly in the air, you will see that your arm will be guided by the line of the edge of the flat surface. The framework of the above-mentioned linen should be of long stout cane.

You may make a small model of pasteboard, of which the axis is formed of fine steel wire, bent by force, and as it is released it will turn the screw.

M. Govi, who first called attention to the significance of these passages in a paper presented to the French Academic des Sciences (*Comptes Rendus de l'Academic des Sciences,* 29 Août 1881), speaks of them as proving not only that Leonardo invented the screw-propeller, but that he had considered its application to aerial navigation, and that he had constructed small paper models for

this purpose which were set in motion by fine bent steel wires.

The function of these springs in the machinery of the instrument is shown in two drawings of a flying machine on page 314 r.a. of the *Codice Atlantico.* The one is a machine of the vertical type, the other a planimetric sketch of the base, within which is written *fondamento del moto* (Foundation of Motion). These, together with an elaborate study of the mechanism of the right wing (308 r.a.), represent the ultimate stage of the conception as found in the manuscripts—which stage is separated from those which preceded it by the addition of a motive power. To this instrument the architect, Luca Beltrami, does not hesitate to apply the word *aeroplane.* I am indebted to his detailed description of this drawing in his study (*L'Aeroplano di Leonardo*), issued on the occasion of the aviation meeting at Brescia in the autumn of 1909. Signor Beltrami's wide technical knowledge, combined with his enthusiasm and interest in all that concerns Leonardo, have caused his description of what is a technical drawing to be eloquent in exposition. Would that some measure of its clearness might survive in my abbreviated rendering of it!

The apparatus consists of a rectangular horizontal plane, from the middle of the longer sides of which rise two vertical shafts made firm by two supports crossed diagonally. The vertical plane so formed is made rigid by two pairs of supports which connect the upper extremities of the shafts with the angles of the plane of the base. Two strong springs, each fastened at one end to the centre of one of the lesser sides of the horizontal plane, are bent round its sides by means of ropes, which by the interposition of pulleys are made to turn around a horizontal axle placed at the base of the two shafts; a cog-wheel situated in the centre of this axle allows the force stored up in the springs in tension to be able gradually to relax the rope, so causing the revolution of a second axle parallel to the first, and at the extremities of this are cranks for the purpose of moving the wings. These wings are poised at the upper extremities of the shafts, the right wing being fixed upon the left shaft and *vice versa,* so that the space between the two shafts, along which the motive power is exerted, forms the arm of a level of which this power may avail itself. Each wing is moved by a vertical rod which is looped to the shaft by two rings, and gliding through these it is able to be raised and lowered accordingly as the fastening to one of the above-mentioned cranks is loose or tight. The lowering of the rod not only moves the arm of the lever, of which the wing is a continuation, but displaces a pulley which turns the cords that correspond to the various loose sinews, which together make up the subsidiary structure of the wing; consequently, as the wing is raised and lowered, these sinews and the surface of the wing are expanded and contracted.

All this relates to the construction of the parts of the instrument.

Signor Beltrami, in a few sure words, shows how these parts would be controlled by the human agent:

> The man who guided the machine had his place in the part of horizontal plane enclosed within the two springs where the words *fondamento del moto* occur in the sketch. He had the cog-wheel in front of him, and could by a simple turn so adjust its revolution as to allow gradually and at his pleasure the ropes pressed by the springs to relax, and so cause the revolution of the axle where are the two cranks which communicate with the wings; as the slackening of the rope is quicker to slower, so the beating of the wings is more or less rapid, and so the flight is controlled.

If Leonardo did not enter the Promised Land, here, surely, he had a Pisgah-sight of it! In arriving at this stage he was separated from that of ultimate attainment only by the lack of knowledge of a light motor with power sufficient to move the mechanism, such as has only been rendered possible by the use of petrol.

In the history of discovery, in the words of Lilienthal, "the trial is everything." It remains to consider the evidence of actual construction and experiment. Except for the sentence in the *De Subtilitate* of Jerome Cardan, already quoted, this evidence consists of passages in the manuscripts; these are the more difficult to interpret because they exhibit that tendency to mystification which is not infrequently in evidence there; which, for example, led him to invert the order of the letters in the names of places in a note about the arrangements for a proposed journey to Rome and Naples, and which has caused some of the place-references to be a perpetual stone of stumbling to the commentator. But for the letters patent of his appointment to the office of military engineer to Caesar Borgia, such records of his visit to the fortresses of the Romagna as are to be found in the manuscripts might be thought to be merely the notes of an autumn holiday of a mind eclectic in its interests in art and nature: so likewise by contrast with the precision of the inquiry as to principles, the records of experiment in the flight have something of the inconsequence of a dream.

An enigmatic sentence on the cover of *Sul Volo degli Uccelli,* which was written in 1505, refers apparently to an attempt which was then shortly to take place:

> The great bird will take its first upon the back of the great swan, filling the whole world with amazement, and filling all records with its frame; and it will bring eternal glory to the nest where it was born.

In 1505 Leonardo was at Fiesole, and "the back of the great swan" was probably a reference to Monte Ceceri, the mountain to the south-west of Fiesole. The word for swan in Italian is *cecero,* and Leonardo is playing upon the double significance of the word. The flight referred to is believed to have been a trial of the machine from one of the peaks of Monte Ceceri. Apparently the trial was made under circumstances of some publicity, and it may conceivably have been that of which Carden chronicled the ill success. A dated note in the *Codice Atlantico* (318 v.a.) — "to-morrow morning, on the 2nd of January 1496, I will make the leather for the straps and the trial" — when read in conjunction with the notes as to materials to be used in construction, may be interpreted as possibly a reference to an attempt to use a machine for flight, and if this is the case the date of this attempt is more than nine years previous to that made during Leonardo's visit to Fiesole.

On another page of the same manuscript (C.A. 214 r.d.) various notes reveal the scene and something of the method of another trial, and afford a glimpse of the precautions which he took in order to prevent the secrets of his discoveries from becoming known. The reference is apparently to small models such as those referred to in the passage in which the screw is mentioned.

> Make a small one over the water [he says], and try with the wind in a small space of water over some part of the Arno, with the wind natural, and then as you please, and twist the sail and the rudder.
>
> See to-morrow to all these changes and the copies, and then deface the originals and leave them at Florence, so that if you lose those which you carry with you you will not lose the invention.

To these records of actual experiment may be added that of yet another page of the *Codice Atlantico* (311 v.d.). It contains three studies of artificial wings. Of these the most elaborate has a very strong frame, which would make it heavy to work. Its main support is curved like a collar-bone, and the lower part where it divides crosses the wing to a point about one-third distant from the shoulder to the tip. There is a considerable amount of detail, and the wire cords which cause the wing to open and shut are clearly indicated. Above it are the words "for Gian Antonia de Mariolo," and below "not to make it with shutters (*sportelli*) but united."

The only reasonable inference to be drawn from these notes is that they refer to the construction of a machine for flight as a commission for a patron whose name was Gian Antonio de Mariolo, who had moreover given Leonardo instructions "that the wings should not be made the self-adjusting shutters (*sportelli*)" which occur in some of Leonardo's studies, "but should be united" — that is, not such as to be penetrated by the wind. This commission, of which nothing more is known, is surely the earliest of any in which the subject is a machine for artificial flight! After a lapse of four hundred years it has had successors.

Contributors

Tim Brady, Ph.D. Dean of the School of Aviation, Embry-Riddle Aeronautical University, Daytona Beach, Florida. When this book was in the beginning stages, Brady was a professor and the chair of the Department of Power and Transportation (Aviation) at Central Missouri State University. He is a past president of the University Aviation Association, an airline transport pilot, a former USAF pilot, and the former editor of an aviation safety magazine. He has published more than twenty-five articles, and he serves on the editorial board of the *Journal of Aviation/Aerospace Education Research.*

Thomas J. Connolly, Ed.D. Chancellor of Embry-Riddle Aeronautical University, Daytona Beach, Florida. He is an airline transport pilot, a former naval aviator (commander, ret.), and a past president of the University Aviation Association. He has received both the Brewer Trophy and the Wheatley Award.

James E. Crehan, M.S. Dean, College of Aviation, Western Michigan University and former chair of the Division of Aviation Technology, University of Alaska at Anchorage. He is a past president of the University Aviation Association and a former USAF pilot with more than 5,000 flying hours (lieutenant colonel, ret.). He teaches in the areas of airport management and aviation systems.

Lance Erickson, Ph.D. Professor in the Applied Aviation Sciences Department at Embry-Riddle Aeronautical University, Daytona Beach, Florida. Erickson developed the space studies curriculum at Embry-Riddle University. He is also involved in radio astronomy research and curriculum development for NASA. He is an avid pilot and flight instructor.

Henry R. Lehrer, Ph.D. Professor at the University of Nebraska at Omaha and formerly a professor at Embry-Riddle Aeronautical University, Daytona Beach, Florida. Lehrer is an airline transport pilot and holds the certified flight instructor instrument and multiengine ratings with gold seal. He is a past president of the University Aviation Association and is widely published. He is the founding editor of the *Journal of Aviation/Aerospace Education and Research.*

William McCurry, Ph.D. Chair of the Aeronautical Management Technology Department at Arizona State University (East Campus) since 1995. Before that, he chaired the Department of Aerospace Technology at Indiana State University. He has extensive aviation safety, maintenance, and operational flight experience, having left military service as a master army aviator. McCurry holds commercial SEL, MEL, rotorcraft, instrument, advanced ground, and CFI certificates. He has served as secretary and treasurer of the University Aviation Association.

Robeson S. Moise, Ed.S. Professor at Central Missouri State University. He is a commercial pilot, a former USAF pilot (lieutenant colonel, ret.), and a former airline training analyst. He teaches aviation history, airport planning and design, cockpit resource management, and FAA private pilot and instrument pilot ground schools.

Isaac Richmond Nettey, M.B.A. Professor and director of airway science at Texas Southern University. He has also worked in airport operations at Houston Intercontinental Airport. Nettey is a past president and treasurer of the University Aviation Association, a Dwight David Eisenhower Transportation Fellow, and past chair of the Airway Science Curriculum Committee of the UAA. His research project on intermodal transportation was published by the Texas Transportation Institute at Texas A&M University. He served on a National Academy of Science committee that published a study on aviation education and training. He serves on the FAA's Aviation Rulemaking Advisory Committee for Airport Certification.

David A. NewMyer, Ph.D. Professor and chair of the Department of Aviation Management and Flight at Southern Illinois University Carbondale, where he has been since 1977. NewMyer has been an airport planner in Chicago and Los Angeles. He is widely published in aviation and is a coauthor of *Aviation Industry Regulation.*

Charles Rodriguez, Ph.D. Assistant Professor in the Department of Aviation Technologies at Southern Illinois University Carbondale. He is a private pilot and an FAA-licensed airframe and power plant mechanic with an inspection authorization certificate. He has commuter airline and industry experience as an airline mechanic, and he has published widely in aviation history and aircraft maintenance. He has also given many presentations on the development of early aviation and conducts aviation science workshops for teachers and school children.

Hope Bouvette Thornberg, Ph.D. Professor in the Aviation Department at St. Cloud University, St. Cloud, Minnesota. Thornberg holds the FAA commercial, instrument, and certified flight instructor certificates and ratings and is a past president of the University Aviation Association. She is a member of the Ninety-Nines, Inc., and she has received the Wheatley Award in recognition of her contributions to aviation education. She chaired the UAA Airway Science Committee and received the FAA Administrator's Award in recognition of airway science curriculum design.

Paul A. Whelan, Ph.D. Vice president emeritus for Parks College of Saint Louis University and former president of Lewis University. Whelan is a past president of the University of Aviation Association and a former USAF pilot (colonel, ret.). He serves on numerous state and national aviation committees and consults regularly on aviation administration and other aviation areas relating to leadership, management, organization, and development.

Index

Law, Ruth, 370–71
Lawrence, Charles, 139, 165
Lawrence, Robert, 360
Leakey, Louis, 335
Leakey, Richard, 335
Lear, Bill, 245, 247, 396
Lear, Moya, 396, 406
LearAvia Corporation, 396
Lear Jet, 247, 396
Lear-Siegler Company, 250
Learstar aircraft, 247
Lebaudy, Paul, 322
Lebaudy, Pierre, 322
Le Captif balloon, 314
Lee, 130
Le Geant balloon, 314
Lehmann, Ernest, 331
Le Jaune dirigible, 322
Le Mans, France, 77
LeMay, Curtis, 256, 279
Leonhardt, E. J., 132
Les Baraques, France, 79
Lester, C. D., 351
Levavasseur, Leon, 76, 79
Levy Lepen hydroplane, 337
Lewis, Fulton, 177
Lewis, Morton, 319
Lewis, William, 132
Lewis machine gun, 99
Liberty Aero Oil, 107, 109, 126
Liberty engine, 130, 132, 139–42, 173
Life Link III, 404
Lilienthal, Otto, 26–28, 52–53
Lincoln, Abraham, 346
Lindbergh, Anne Morrow, 381
Lindbergh, Charles Jr., 144, 300, 337, 374; transatlantic flight, 153–57
Lindbergh, Charles Sr., 153
Lindstrand, Per, 320
Lipsner, Benjamin, 125–29
Little Looper, 93
Lockheed Aircraft Company, 163, 263; Constellation, 218; Electra, 377; Hudson bomber, 283; P-38 Lightning, 204, 206; Vega, 163, 376, 378
London, England, 7
London-Heathrow operations, 224; American Airlines, 225; TWA, 230
Lorenzo, Frank, 227, 230
Los Angeles (ZR-3), 326

Loughhead, Allen, 163
Loughhead, Malcolm, 163
Louis, Joe, 343, 344, 350
Louis XVI, King, 308
Love, Nancy Harkness, 384, 385, 386
Love, Robert, 384, 385
Lovelace, W. Randolph, 396
Lovell, Jim, 420
Loving, Neal, 359
Low, Francis, 201
Low, Jim, 264
Luddington Line, 177
Luftwaffe, 202; D Day, 210; operations against Poland, 189; in Western Europe, 209; in WWII, 192–95
Luke, Frank, 104, 316
Luna projects, 417, 422, 424
Lunardi, Vincent, 310, 311
Lusitania, 105
Lycoming engine, 252

MacArthur, Douglas, 178
Macon (ZR-5), 330
Macready, John, 162
Madison, James, 312
Madison, Walter G., 338
Maginot Line, 192
Malibu aircraft, 252
Malmsbury Abbey, 7
Man carrier, 7
Manly, Charles, 48, 298
Manned balloons: in the military, 314; Montgolfier, 310; in WWII, 316
Manning, Harry, 377
Mannock, 105
Mantz, Paul, 377
Manufacturers of Aircraft Association, 106
Marchbanks, Vance, 359
Marie Antoinette, 308
Marine "Buffalo" fighters, 203
Marine Corps, 390, 402; Women's Reserve, 390
Mariner series (U.S. spacecraft), 418, 422
Marshall, George, 347, 349
Marshall, James, 338
Marshall, Thurgood, 356
Mars Observer, 423, 429
Mars Pathfinder, 429
Martin, August, 359
Martin, Glenn, 135
Martin, Maurice, 265

Martin Aircraft Company, 188; B-10, 179, 192; B-26, 210; MB-2, 188; seaplane, 135, 141

Mason, Thomas (Monck), 313

Mathy, Heinrich, 325

Mauberge battle, balloons used in, 314

Maxim, Hiram, 29, 31–33

May, O. J., 126

Maybach engine, 323

Mayfly airship, 323

Maynard, Charles, 277

McAuliffe, Christa, 408

McCarthy, James, 277

McClellan (Union Army general), 315

McCloskey, Helen, 381

McConnell Air Force Base, 403

McCullin, James, 351

McDonnell-Douglas MD-80, 234, 235

McGee Airways, 234

McIver, William III, 260

McNary-Watres Act, 174

McWhorter, John, 338

Melroy, Pam, 402

Mercator projection chart, 155

Mercedes-Daimler engine, 323

Mercury (god), 5

Mercury projects, 319, 419, 422; the Mercury 13, 396–98; Mercury-Atlas flight, 419; Mercury-Redstone flight, 419

Messerschmitt: BF 109, 351; ME-109B, 208

Messiha, Khalil, 336

Metal Airplane Company, 161

Meurthe, Henri, 321

Mexican War, 325

Michelin trophy, 68

Midway Airlines, 236

MiG force, 261, 263, 264

Military Airlift Command (MAC), 258

Military Air Transport Service (MATS), 256

Militia Act of 1792, 346

Minerva, 2

Ministere (French historian), 307

Minos, King, 2–4

Mir space station, 425

Mitchell, Billy: on the potential use of airplanes in war, 185–88; in WWII, 191, 200, 201, 299, 326

Mixner, George, 106

Models, early, of aircraft, 14–46

Moffett, William, 326, 329, 330

Mohawk Airlines, 218, 233

Moisant, John, 369

Moisant, Matilde, 369

Moisant International Aviators, 369

Momyer, William, 270

Mona Lisa. See da Vinci, Leonardo

Monarch Airlines, 277

Monk of Malmsbury. *See* Elmer (a.k.a. Oliver the Monk of Malmsbury)

Monroe, James, 312

Montgolfier, Jacques Etienne, 308

Montgolfier, Joseph, 308, 310, 314

Montgolfier, Pierre, 308

Montgolfiers' balloon, 310

Montgomery, Bernard, 351

Montgomery, R. L., 106

Moorer, Thomas, 277

Morane-Saulnier: Bullet aircraft, 102–3; sea plane, 86, 87; single-wing, 101, 102

Morin, Paul, 323

Morrell, John, 323

Morris, June, 407

Morris Air, 230, 407

Morrison, Herb, 331

Morrow, Dwight, 299

Morrow Board, 296

Mostert, Sue, 406

Mouillard, Louis, 42

Mozhaiski, Alexander, 21–22

Murphy, Sally, 395

Murray, Jimmy, 132

Muse, Lamarr, 229

Myers, A. Maurice, 226

Myers, Mary Hawley, 314, 367

Napoleon, 314

NASA. *See* National Aeronautics and Space Administration (NASA)

Nassau Aviation Corporation, 124

National Advisory Committee for Aeronautics (NACA), 105

National Aerobatic Championship, U.S., 401

National Aeronautics and Space Administration (NASA), 359, 396, 407, 417, 419, 422, 427

National Airmen's Association of America (NAAA), 345, 347

National Airspace System, 296

National Air Transport, 136, 139, 143, 174, 177

National Aviation Club, 399

National Business Aircraft Association (NBAA), 249

National Geographic Society, 377, 382

Rogers, Harry, 378
Rogers, Will, 142, 378
Rolling Thunder mission, 270
Rolls, C. S. *See* Rolls-Royce Company
Rolls-Royce Company, 118; engine, 222
Roma ship, 326
Romain, Pierre, 311
Romans, ancient, 5
Rome, ancient, 5
Roosevelt, Eleanor, 339, 347
Roosevelt, Franklin: administration, 177; African American pilots, 166; Burke-Wadsworth Bill, 347; Japanese attack on Pearl Harbor, 198; New Deal, 177; Phoebe Omlie, 381; policies toward aviation, 177–79; preparation for WWII, 196; WWII, 300–303
Ross, Malcolm, 319
Rotary engine, 113–14
Royal Academy, 308
Royal Air Force (RAF), 194–95
Royal Dutch airlines, 228
Royal Navy, 323
Royal Vauxhall balloon, 313
Royce, Henry. *See* Rolls-Royce Company
Rozier, Pilatre, 309–11
Russia, 383
Russo-Japanese War of 1904, 315
Rutan Scaled Composites Company, 251
Ryan, Claude, 141
Ryan, John, 108
Ryan Company, 155; Brougham, 142; M-1 monoplane, 140, 163

SABENA (Belgian airline), 337
SABRE computer reservation system, 225
Safety bicycles, 48, 49
Sage, Letitia, 367
Salyut-6 space laboratory, 360, 425
SAM (surface-to-air missiles): in the Gulf War, 284; in the Vietnam War, 268, 270–71, 278
Sandler, James, 310
San Francisco harbor, 89, 93
Santos-Dumont: dirigibles, 26, 43, 321–22; early dirigible aeronauts, 321; semirigid dirigibles, 322
Santos-Dumont, Alberto, 26, 43
Saracen, 7
Sardinia. *See* Daedalus
Saturn exploration project, 424
Saturn launch vehicle, 420
Saulnier, Raymond, 11
Sauzereseteo, Samuel V. B., 340

Saxe (English poet), 1
Schirra, Walter, 419
Schofield, Seth, 233
Schoonmaker, J. M., 110
Schutte-Lanz SL-1, 323
Schwartzkopf, Gen. Norman, 282
Schwarz, David, 321
Scientific American trophy, 73, 74
Scott, Blanche, 368
Scott, George, 325, 329
Seaboard World Airlines, 359
Seguin, Laurent, 94
Seguin, Lewis, 94
Selassie, Haile, 343
Selfridge, Thomas E., 70, 72, 73, 94, 323
Servicemen's Readjustment Act (GI Bill). *See* GI Bill (Servicemen's Readjustment Act)
Settle, Thomas, 318
Severo, Augusto, 32
Shakespeare, William, 7
Shenandoah (ZR-1), 326
Shepard, Alan, 419
Shepherd, Dolly, 367
Shepherd, W. E., 325
Shepler, Harry, 106
Sheppard, Morris, 125
Sicily. *See* Daedalus
Silver disc, 14
Simons, David, 319
Simon the Magician, 6
Simplex Auto Company, 105
Sims, William, 299
Single Integrated Operational Plan (SIOP), 279
Single-stage-to-orbit (SSTO) vehicle, 429
Sivil, Theodore, 317
Six, Robert, 226
Skylab program, 420, 425
SL-1 Schutte-Lanz. *See* Schutte-Lanz SL-1
Slayton, Donald "Deke," 419
Smith, C. R., 225
Smith, Dean, 130
Smith, Jacqueline, 406
Smith, James, 338
Smith, Joan Merriam, 394
Smith, Wesley L., 132
Smithsonian Institution, 392
Sopwith Camel, 111
Sopwith Triplane, 112
Southern route, 175